RELIGION, LAW, AND POWER

RELIGION, LAW, AND POWER

The Making of
Protestant Ireland
1660–1760

S. J. CONNOLLY

CLARENDON PRESS · OXFORD
1992

Oxford University Press, Walton Street, Oxford OX2 6DP

Oxford New York Toronto
Delhi Bombay Calcutta Madras Karachi
Petaling Jaya Singapore Hong Kong Tokyo
Nairobi Dar es Salaam Cape Town
Melbourne Auckland

and associated companies in
Berlin Ibadan

Oxford is a trade mark of Oxford University Press

Published in the United States
by Oxford University Press, New York

British Library Cataloguing in Publication Data
Data available

Library of Congress Cataloging in Publication Data
Connolly, S. J. (Sean J.)
Religion, law, and power: the making of Protestant Ireland,
1660–1760/S. J. Connolly.
p.   cm.
Includes bibliographical references and index.
1. Ireland—History—18th century.   2. Ireland—History—17th
century.   3. Protestants—Ireland—History—18th century.
4. Protestants—Ireland—History—17th century.   I. Title.
DA947.C66   1992   941.06—dc20   91–39688
ISBN 0–19–820118–4

Typeset by Best-set Typesetter Ltd., Hong Kong
Printed and bound in
Great Britain by Biddles Ltd.,
Guildford and King's Lynn

Acknowledgements

The research on which this book is based was facilitated by grants towards the cost of travel, subsistence, and microfilming from the British Academy and from the Faculty of Humanities of the University of Ulster. The University of Ulster also granted me two terms of study leave, one in 1985, when the work for this book was begun, the second in 1989, when the first draft was completed.

For permission to consult manuscript sources I am grateful to: His Grace the Archbishop of Armagh; Mr H. F. Blackett; the Bodleian Library, Oxford; the British Library; the Syndics of Cambridge University Library; the Governing Body of Christ Church, Oxford; Mrs E. Cooke; the Earl of Dartmouth; Dublin Corporation Public Libraries; the Right Honourable the Earl of Harrowby; Lincolnshire Archives Office; Kevin McMahon, Esq.; the Viscount Massereene and Ferrard D. L.; Viscount Midleton; the Director, National Archives of Ireland; the National Library of Ireland; the National Trust; the Keeper of Manuscripts, Nottingham University Library; Northumberland Record Office; Dermot O'Hara, Esq.; the Public Record Office, London; the Deputy Keeper of the Records, Public Record Office of Northern Ireland; Ms Mary-Lou Legg; the Representative Church Body; the Right Honourable the Earl of Shannon; Staffordshire County Record Office; Surrey County Record Office and the borough of Reigate and Banstead; and the Board of Trinity College, Dublin.

Among the individuals who have helped me in the course of research and writing, I must make particular mention of Dr D. W. Hayton, who generously agreed to read the entire text. His detailed commentary has helped me to clarify many points, and saved me from numerous errors. I have also benefited at different times from discussions with Dr David Dickson and Dr A. P. W. Malcomson. My debt to the published work of all three of these historians, as well as to that of Professor L. M. Cullen, will be evident from the footnotes. I have further benefited from discussions over a long period with Mr Graeme Kirkham, who in addition provided a number of valuable references to newspaper and other sources. My wife, Mavis Bracegirdle, maintained a tolerant interest in the project throughout, and on occasion brought a healthy Protestant scepticism to bear on some of my more ambitious attempts to rethink the contours of eighteenth-century Irish history.

Contents

List of Figures

List of Tables

References and Conventions

Primary and secondary sources are referred to in the footnotes by abbreviated titles, full details being given in the bibliography. The following abbreviations are used throughout:

Arch. Hib.	*Archivium Hibernicum*
Coll. Hib.	*Collectanea Hibernica*
CSPD	*Calendar of State Papers, Domestic Series*
CSPI	*Calendar of State Papers Relating to Ireland*
HMC	Historical Manuscripts Commission
IHS	*Irish Historical Studies*
Nat. Arch. Ire.	National Archives of Ireland, Dublin
NLI	National Library of Ireland, Dublin
NHI	*A New History of Ireland*, ed. T. W. Moody *et al.* (Oxford 1976–)
PRONI	Public Record Office of Northern Ireland, Belfast
RCB	Representative Church Body Library, Dublin
SP63	State Papers (Ireland), Public Record Office, London
TCD	Trinity College, Dublin

Spelling, punctuation, and so forth have been modernized in all quotations. Dates are given in old style, as used by contemporaries, except that the year is taken as beginning on 1 January. Where more than one variant of a proper name exists—the earl of Midleton, for example, spelt his own name indiscriminately with one or two *d*'s, and his family name was regularly written as both 'Brodrick' and 'Broderick'—I have used the shortest version.

With regard to place-names I have followed contemporary usage in referring to the modern counties of Laois and Offaly as, respectively, Queen's County and King's County, and what seems to me a sensible compromise in referring to the city of Derry and the county of Londonderry. Where religious denominations are concerned, I have used 'Catholic' where Protestant contemporaries would have used 'Papist', 'Romanist', or—when they wished to be more polite than usual—'Roman Catholic'. 'Protestant', which contemporary members of the Church of Ireland used exclusively for themselves, here means both adherents of the established church and Dissenters. 'Anglican', used here to refer to the Church of Ireland and its members, is not a contemporary term; it was coined (by an Irishman, Edmund Burke) in 1797. On the other hand, adherents of the established church in the early and mid-eighteenth century regularly referred to themselves as belonging to the Church of England. The anachronism is thus verbal rather than conceptual, and as such seems preferable to the uniformly cumbersome alternatives.

Introduction

George, elector of Hanover, succeeded to the crowns of Great Britain and Ireland on 1 August 1714. Nine days later the proclamation of his accession reached Macroom in County Cork. The local magistrate, Captain Richard Hedges, proceeded to organize the appropriate ceremonies.

I immediately sent to all the Protestants in the neighbourhood to appear in arms here, and likewise the townsmen. Major Gibson drew out his company and we proclaimed his Majesty on horseback in a great congregation, after which the soldiers fired three volleys, another at the drinking his Majesty's health, another at the Prince's health, another at the Royal family's. The town and countrymen also fired several volleys by themselves pretty well, being most of them old soldiers. I sent a hogshead of beer out of my cellar and claret, at a large bonfire, and Major Gibson provided a large bowl of punch. Every window illuminated and the bells ringing and innumerable huzzas. We did not go to bed that night.

Despite these exertions, Hedges was on the road next morning, to Kilmeedy, 'where we proclaimed his Majesty with all the solemnity we could', to Millstreet, where 'I treated the company with claret and what other liquor was to be had, and left the soldiers money to close the evening at their barracks', and then to Killarney in County Kerry, where the king was proclaimed on the evening of the 11th to the sound of cannon fired by the local garrison.

The next day Hedges and a group of other magistrates got down to more serious business. They fixed the date for a series of court sittings, where males between the ages of 16 and 60 were to be summoned to come and take the oath of allegiance. The first signs were promising. Florence O'Donoghue, head of the notoriously troublesome clan based in a ruined castle in the rugged valley of Glenflesk, had already 'found it his only safety' to take the oath and offer £500 security for his good behaviour. Other persons considered suspect were to be called on to do the same, 'for we thought 'twas better to bring them to, between threats and fair means, than by rigorous practices to throw them into rebellion at such a juncture as this'.[1]

The events that Captain Hedges describes are not, at first sight, of any great significance. The accession of a new king was proclaimed, without fuss, in a remote and unimportant corner of his dominions. It had not always been so, of course. In the 1640s the religious and political conflicts of Ireland had helped to precipitate a civil war that had torn the British state apart, one in which Ireland itself had been the bloodiest theatre. During 1688–91 Irish affairs had again been central to the downfall of one English king and the

[1] Hedges to Dawson, 23 Aug. 1714 (Hedges Letters).

triumph of another. But thereafter, for two generations or more, the religious, political, and ethnic conflicts that had made Ireland a battleground for so long seem somehow to fade from view. The verdict of textbook history, leaping as it does from the 1690s to the 1760s, seems to confirm that the world in which the fires lit at Macroom and elsewhere were kindled, blazed up, and died was one of the backwaters of history.

And yet, for anyone interested in the long-term development of Irish society, it is precisely this sudden calm that arrests attention. For conflict did not disappear. It was only the Protestant inhabitants, after all, who were even invited to celebrate the accession of the new king; once the festivities were over, Hedges and his colleagues had to meet to concert measures to contain the threat posed by the O'Donoghues and others. Later, in the last two decades of the century, political and religious violence was to reappear in new and ferocious forms. What, then, permitted so long an interval of superficial peace? How, during that interval, did Catholic and Protestant, settler and native, perceive and behave towards one another? What combination of coercion and mutual accommodation—'threats and fair promises'—maintained the social order in a divided society?

The central argument to be developed in the chapters that follow may be briefly summarized. Essentially it is that Ireland in the century or so following the Restoration is best seen as first and foremost a part of the European *ancien régime*. It was a pre-industrialized society, ruled over by a mainly landed élite, in which vertical ties of patronage and clientship were more important than horizontal bonds of shared economic or social position, and in which even popular protest was conducted within the assumptions that underlay the existing social order. It was also, like the rest of Europe, a confessional state, in which religion remained a central aspect of personal and political motivation, and in which differences in religious allegiance were a cause of fundamental conflict.[2] Such a perspective, it is suggested, does more to make sense of the central characteristics of post-Restoration Ireland than the alternative label of a colonial society, so casually yet so persistently applied.[3]

This is not to deny that Irish society had built into it conflicts of a kind not found, by the eighteenth century at least, in most other parts of Europe. The upheavals of the sixteenth and seventeenth centuries had left a dangerous

---

[2] This is to use the term *ancien régime* in its wider sense, to mean the whole political and social order of pre-revolutionary Europe, rather than in the narrower sense of those parts of the French state that the reformers of the 1780s wished to abolish. See Doyle, *The Ancien Régime*, 1, 43–51. The extension of the term to cover England also, as advocated by Clark (*English Society*), would fit neatly with the argument being advanced here: that much of what is said about the supposedly unusual features of post-Restoration Ireland is based on unrealistic standards of comparison. But Clark's arguments on this point have been effectively criticized by Innes, 'Jonathan Clark', 194–200.

[3] Below, ch. 4, sect. 1.

legacy: a dispossessed élite, shrinking in size, but still potentially a threat to the established order, and a population most of whom continued to reject the religion of the state. Indeed, it is argued here that the threat posed by a disaffected and potentially rebellious Catholic population was in fact more real, particularly in the period from 1691 to around 1720, than a tradition of historical writing still unduly influenced by the apologetics of nineteenth-century Catholicism has generally allowed. What are questioned are some of the conclusions that have been drawn from this fact. The supposed colonial origins and uneasy tenure of power of the Protestant élite have been invoked to explain characteristics as diverse as theological conservatism and a taste in drinking and duelling.[4] Yet this image of a ruling class tortured by a constant sense of its own insecurity belongs essentially to a later period, to the era of the French Revolution and the struggle for Catholic emancipation. Irish Protestants in the early and mid-eighteenth century did not ignore the threat from an unreconciled Catholic population and its continental allies. But their most characteristic outlook was that reflected in Captain Hedges' report: a wary confidence in the face of a real, but containable, threat.

This is not to suggest that attitudes were either simple or uniform. It is important to stress the qualification. The world of early eighteenth-century Irish Protestantism has all too often been approached through the study of a handful of outstanding thinkers on the one hand and a misleadingly systematic-looking body of statute law, the so-called penal code, on the other. The result has been an unduly schematic approach: a tendency to think in terms of an 'Anglo-Irish intellect', or even a 'Protestant mind'.[5] In fact, as will become clear, there were, throughout this period, fundamental differences of opinion within the Protestant establishment. The nature of the threat posed by the Catholic majority and the steps that should be taken to contain it, the treatment of Protestant Dissenters, the relationship between Ireland and England: all these were subjects of disagreement and debate. With the benefit of hindsight, some of these debates—the question of whether the main threat to church and state came from Catholics or Dissenters, for example, or the possibility of converting the Catholic Irish to Protestantism—can be seen to have been blind alleys. The task of the historian, however, is to strike a balance between teleology and antiquarianism: to keep in sight those lines of development that were in the long run to prove of greatest significance, but at the same time not to abstract them from a context in which other possibilities, other courses of action, could seem to be equally compelling. The High Church divines of Queen Anne's reign, agitating for a return to the days when the church courts could exercise a coercive moral discipline, or a figure like Lord Chancellor Porter, arguing as late as 1695 that it might at some time be necessary to arm Irish Catholics in order to subdue the Scots of Ulster, may

---

[4] Below, pp. 66, 175.   [5] e.g. Deane, 'Swift and the Anglo-Irish Intellect'.

have misread the drift of history. But they remain as much a part of the society in which they lived as those whose concerns happened to coincide more closely with the preoccupations of a later age.

The Protestant élite of the late seventeenth and early eighteenth centuries can hardly be seen as victims of social deprivation. Yet they have had their share, along with less favoured groups, of posterity's condescension. At best they have been defined in negative terms: through the fears imputed to them or—as in the contrasts drawn between their patriotism and 'true' Irish nationalism—in terms of what they were not. More commonly they have been simply 'the ascendancy': a muddled, anachronistic label that has somehow become a substitute for serious analysis. Nor has the older image of a rootless, predatory group, whose religion and politics alike can be reduced to a desire to retain and extend their ill-gotten gains, entirely disappeared.[6] This study attempts to look at the Protestant élite primarily in its own terms: to reconstruct the way in which its members saw the society in which they lived and the issues that seemed to them to matter most. It also suggests that some of the central institutions of that élite, most notably its parliament and its church, should be taken more seriously, as forums for rational and even principled behaviour, than has generally been assumed. None of this means that what follows should be read as an apology or a defence. The point is rather that beliefs and attitudes that were shared by all or most of the members of a particular society cannot, by definition, have been either stupid or immoral. This being so, it is surely better to reconstruct the context in which they once made sense that to pillory the past for not having been more like the present.

---

[6] Since chapter 4 below was written, the vocabulary of analysis has been enriched by a new coinage: 'the Anglo-Irish kleptocracy'. See Kevin O'Neill, *Irish Literary Supplement*, 8/2 (1989), 39. See also Mokyr, *Why Ireland Starved*, in which Ireland's economic underdevelopment is attributed to 'the creation of the landlord class from British and Scottish adventurers and mercenaries, a class of parvenus and foreigners' (p. 212).

I

A New Ireland

1. December 1659: 'A Nation Born in a Day'

At five o'clock on the evening of Tuesday, 13 December 1659, three soldiers from a company quartered in an outbuilding of the castle of Dublin approached the main gate of the fortress. The guard, who knew the three men, let them in. As soon as he had done so, he was overpowered, and the rest of the company, led by Colonel William Warden, rushed in to surprise the garrison. Inside the castle they took prisoner Colonel John Jones, the acting commander-in-chief of the Irish army. Soon after, in another part of the city, soldiers under Major Edward Warren apprehended the two commissioners who, with Jones, controlled the country's civil and military administration. Meanwhile, parties of horsemen rode through the streets, breaking up any groups that attempted to come together. In less than two hours the operation was complete, and the government of Ireland had been bloodlessly overthrown.[1]

This action was only one of a series of military intrusions into the politics of what had formerly been the three kingdoms of the British crown. That crown had ceased to exist in 1649, when King Charles I had been executed and the monarchy abolished. Since then the effective rulers of England had been the army that had defeated the king in the civil wars of 1642–6 and 1647–8. In 1653 the principal army leader, Oliver Cromwell, had forcibly dissolved the parliament, and the following year he had commenced a personal rule under the title Lord Protector. When Cromwell died in September 1658, his son Richard succeeded to the title of Lord Protector, but proved unable to control the army, which deposed him in April 1659. In his place the military leaders brought back the parliament his father had suppressed six years before, only to dismiss it again in September. This time, however, the revival of naked military rule found opponents within the army itself. George Monck, commander in Scotland, condemned the dissolution of parliament, while in December the garrison at Portsmouth offered a base to the leaders of the expelled MPs. It was in support of the same cause, the restoration of the dis-

---

[1] There is no detailed modern account of these events. That given here relies on the conspirators' own version (Bridges *et al.*, *A Perfect Narrative*) and, for the mechanics of the operation, Ludlow, *Memoirs*, ii. 185–7. See also the first-hand account in *Montgomery Manuscripts*, 219–21. For more general accounts of the Restoration in Ireland, see Davies, *Restoration of Charles II*, ch. 13; McGuire, 'The Dublin Convention'.

solved parliament, that the Irish officers acted on 13 December. The commissioners they overthrew were those installed by the English army leaders, and one of their first actions following the success of their operation was to send messages to Monck in Scotland and to the parliamentary leaders in Portsmouth.[2]

The initial seizure of Dublin Castle was the work of a small group of middle-ranking officers: three colonels, a lieutenant-colonel, a major, four captains, and a lieutenant. Major General Sir Hardress Waller, who had been passed over for the supreme command in favour of Jones and was in fact the senior army officer in Ireland, had not been party to the details of the plan. Nevertheless, he had been 'some weeks before prepared by some general discourse concerning it', and he now assumed command. More important, however, were the demonstrations of support from outside military circles. In Dublin the officers' declaration in support of a restoration of parliament was met 'with general acclamations from the highest to the lowest', and the city militia were mobilized to provide support.[3] In the provinces of Connacht in the west and Munster in the south the two leading magnates, Sir Charles Coote and Roger Boyle, Lord Broghill, secured places of strength, and displaced suspected opponents, before making their way to Dublin to add their weight to the provisional administration established there by the officers. Elsewhere, too, there were indications of general support from the nobility and the gentry. In the flowery language of Sir Hardress Waller, writing to the newly restored Speaker of the English House of Commons, 'in a few days the army, ministry, churches and the whole country save a very few owned the undertaking of a few poor little ones, so that I may say a nation was born in a day'.[4] It was this response that made the events of December 1659 more than one in a series of military *coups*. After several years in the background, the natural leaders of Irish society had begun to assert themselves.

Who were these natural leaders? The first half of the seventeenth century had seen a complex struggle for power between religiously and culturally defined groups within Irish society. For reasons that remain controversial, but which clearly had much to do with the incomplete control that government then exercised over the country, the Reformation had made little headway in sixteenth-century Ireland. The great majority both of the Gaelic Irish and of the descendants of pre-Reformation settlers, the so-called Old English, remained Catholic. Initially, the Old English did not pay too high a price for their recusancy. In the absence of any alternative group through whom Ireland could be governed, their English culture and loyalty to the crown counted for more than their Catholicism. In the early seventeenth century, however, their position was progressively undermined. One reason was that

---

[2] Bridges, *et al.*, *Perfect Narrative*, 11.
[3] Ibid. 9.
[4] Waller to Lenthall, 6 Jan. 1660 (HMC, *Portland Manuscripts*, i. 693).

the Old English were no longer the only group through whom the day-to-day running of the country could be managed. There was now a growing 'New English' population of more recent settlers and administrators: equally loyal to the crown and also sharing its religion. These New English had an obvious interest in making religion the sole test of political loyalty. But their hostility to the Old English had a wider basis than mere self-aggrandizement. Europe as a whole was, by the early seventeenth century, divided along religious lines. In England the persecution of Protestants under the Catholic Queen Mary and a succession of Catholic plots against her Protestant successor, Elizabeth, had confirmed the image of Catholicism as an international conspiracy aimed at the eradication of Protestantism. A series of revolts in Ireland, culminating in the Nine Years' War of 1595–1603, had seemed to confirm that Catholic Ireland represented Protestant England's weakest flank.

Traditionally the Old English had held themselves aloof from the conspiracies and rebellions of the Gaelic Irish. But during the first four decades of the seventeenth century their loyalty was placed under increasing strain. They were excluded from local as well as central government; heavy fines were imposed on prominent citizens refusing to attend Protestant services; even their titles to land, like those of the Gaelic Irish, began to be questioned in courts that inevitably found for the crown. The turning-point came in 1640–1, when it seemed that the king, with whom the Old English had been able to hope for some sort of accommodation, trading toleration for political and financial support, was about to lose power to a parliament that reflected much more closely the strong anti-Catholicism of ordinary Englishmen. Charles I himself blurred the question of loyalty by encouraging the arming of the Gaelic Irish of Ulster, as a reserve force to be used against his English and Scottish enemies. In October 1641 these Ulster Irish rose in arms, claiming to be defending the prerogatives of the crown against its enemies in parliament and elsewhere. The Old English, after several weeks of hesitation, agreed to join them.

The Irish rising of October 1641 also brought to a head the political crisis in England. The first engagements of the civil war were fought in July and August 1642. Ireland's part in the conflict that followed took the form of a vicious, three-cornered struggle. On one side there were the Old English and Gaelic Irish, now organized as 'the confederate Catholics of Ireland'. These continued to insist on their loyalty to the crown, while at the same time demanding guarantees of the free exercise of their religion and of a share in political power in Ireland.[5] Irish Protestants, meanwhile, were divided. Some supported the king, while others accepted the authority of the English parliament. Initially, royalists and parliamentarians were at war both with each other

---

[5] Clarke, 'Genesis of the Ulster Rising'; Beckett, 'The Confederation of Kilkenny Reviewed', in *Confrontations*, 47–66.

and with the Confederates. By 1649, however, the royalists, facing total defeat in England, had concluded an alliance with the Catholics. It was this alliance which Oliver Cromwell came to Ireland to defeat, and a number of his victories—including the notorious capture of Drogheda, with the subsequent massacre of the garrison and some of the civilian inhabitants—were in fact achieved against royalist (and partly English) forces.

Cromwell's ruthless campaign of conquest in 1649–50 earned him a prominent place in subsequent Catholic demonology. However, it by no means guaranteed him the support of Irish Protestants. If the majority of these had eventually come to attach themselves to the cause of parliament rather than that of the king, this was in many cases only because they recognized that parliament was the force best able to defeat the Catholics. Even then some had resisted this conclusion until Charles I's dealings with the Confederates had left them no alternative. Lack of enthusiasm for the republican regime established after the king's execution was reinforced by a distaste for the religious radicalism of many of its representatives. As a result, Cromwellian Ireland was at first ruled by an externally imposed stratum of army officers and their civilian associates. After 1655, Oliver Cromwell's son Henry managed to institute a regime more acceptable to established Protestant interests in Ireland, transferring local power back to the Protestant landed class and withdrawing official support from religious radicals.[6] In June 1659, however, Henry Cromwell followed his brother into political obscurity. Power in Ireland now passed to five commissioners appointed by the restored parliament in England and to the veteran English republican Edmund Ludlow, appointed commander-in-chief of the Irish army. This administration immediately began to reverse the conciliatory policy of recent years, removing former associates of Henry Cromwell from the commission of the peace and other positions of power and replacing them with political and religious radicals. The officers who seized Dublin Castle in December 1659 complained in particular of Ludlow's purge of the Irish army, in which 200 officers were allegedly dismissed without a hearing.[7] But behind their particular grievances and reflected in the support for their action of men like Coote and Broghill was the insistence of the Irish Protestant establishment as a whole that it should retain the influence it had reacquired under Henry Cromwell.

This determination on the part of the Irish Protestants to retain control of their own destinies was even more apparent in the months that followed. Edmund Ludlow had opposed the dissolution of parliament in October 1659, and had successfully blocked efforts to have the Irish army endorse it. Yet, when he attempted to return from England on hearing of the Dublin *coup*, he was prevented from landing. Meanwhile, the Council of Officers and their

---

[6] Barnard, 'Planters and Policies'; idem, *Cromwellian Ireland*.
[7] *A Letter Sent from Ireland*.

civilian advisers arranged for the summoning of a convention elected on the basis of the parliamentary constituencies. The Convention of 137 members sat between March and May 1660. Its initial purpose was to raise money, particularly for the pay of the army; but it went on to take up wider issues, declaring that the sole right of Ireland to tax itself and legislate for itself had been encroached on by the Commonwealth regime and hearing arguments that acts of the English parliament were not binding on Ireland. The whole project of a convention caused considerable alarm in England. But when the restored parliament called on the Irish assembly to disperse, its instruction was simply ignored.[8]

Of more immediate concern than Anglo-Irish relations, however, was the nature of the political and religious settlement that should follow the collapse of army rule. In December 1659 hostility to the existing regime had united men of very different political outlooks. There followed a period of complex and often devious manoeuvring, in which the affairs of three separate kingdoms were inextricably linked. Initially the contest was between those who upheld the rule of the English MPs restored by Monck's intervention at the end of 1659, and those who argued either that these should be joined by the members expelled ten years earlier in the purge that had prepared the way for the execution of Charles I, or else that there should be a wholly new parliament. In Ireland the decisive confrontation came in February 1660, when Coote and Colonel Theophilus Jones began to organize an army declaration in favour of the excluded members. They were opposed by Sir Hardress Waller, who had himself assisted in the expulsions of 1649 and remained a supporter of what critics of the purged parliament now derisively called the Rump. On 15 February Waller attempted to seize the initiative by arresting Coote and others, but was prevented by Jones's soldiers. He took refuge in Dublin Castle, but the city authorities, in sharp contrast to their action of December, called out the militia against him, and he was eventually handed over to Coote by his own men. Waller's defeat cleared the way for a further purge of the army, to remove irreconcilable republicans. By this time Coote had already made contact with the exiled court, and had received Charles II's commission to act on his behalf.[9] Like Monck in England, however, he chose not to risk open conflict by any sudden initiative. Instead, he held back, while support for a return to monarchy became steadily more apparent.

Charles II was proclaimed king in London on 8 May. The news reached

---

[8] Although the Convention has been accorded steadily increasing importance in the work of recent historians, there is no detailed study of its composition or proceedings. See, however, Barnard, 'Planters and Policies', 65–6; O'Donoghue, 'Parliament in Ireland under Charles II', 10–26; McGuire, 'Dublin Convention'.

[9] According to Ormond, writing three years later, Coote's emissary, Sir Arthur Forbes, approached the court 'in the month of January, some months before your Majesty had any address out of England, or was well assured that your restitution was intended in any of the changes then happening there' (*CSPI 1663–5*, 310).

Dublin four days later. The Convention was immediately recalled, and on 14 May it issued a proclamation declaring Charles king of Ireland, Scotland, and England. That afternoon a procession of Convention members, office-holders, members of Dublin Corporation, gentlemen, and nobles made their way round the city, repeating the proclamation at strategic points. Bells rang, volleys were fired, and bonfires and fireworks blazed. Hogsheads of wine were distributed to the crowd. Later on came an elaborate piece of street theatre, 'the solemnization of the funeral of a certain monster they called the commonwealth, represented by an ugly misshapen body without an head, but with a huge insatiable belly and a prodigious rump'. The effigy, stuffed with straw, was paraded about to the sound of trumpets, 'one while dolefully in form, another while confusedly as they use to sound when some devil is conjured up in a play', before being partly burned and partly torn to pieces by the crowd.[10]

The religious settlement followed a similar pattern, with former allies pulling away from one another once the common enemy had been defeated. Dislike of the religious radicalism associated with the military regime had been a major motive behind the latter's overthrow. A participant in the December *coup* recalled how he and others had been detailed to patrol the streets on horseback, 'hindering the anabaptists to get to a body'; a Dublin merchant, observing the king's proclamation, rejoiced that 'the heretics and sectaries are deservedly laid aside'.[11] The general preference, among men of property and influence at least, was clearly for a disciplined national church. There was no agreement, however, on the form that church should take. The committee of religion appointed by the Convention in March 1660 included advocates both of a revival of episcopacy and of a presbyterian form of church government. By the end of April, however, the Convention had begun to extend recognition to the bishops who survived from the pre-civil war regime. Further powerful support for the revival of episcopacy came from what was by now the court-in-waiting, in particular from the duke of Ormond, leader of the Irish royalists during the civil war and still the king's chief adviser on Irish affairs. Already by June 1660 the government had chosen the men who would fill the vacant sees and other offices of the Anglican hierarchy in Ireland. In January 1661 the return of episcopacy was given dramatic formal expression in the simultaneous consecration in St Patrick's cathedral, Dublin, of two archbishops and ten bishops.

It is impossible, in a period when most men made it their priority to be on the winning side, to say how closely this religious and political settlement reflected the real wishes of those who had brought it about. Where religion is

---

[10] *Parliamentary Intelligencer*, no. 22 (21–8 May 1660); Toby Bonnell to Revd John Johnson, 16 May 1660 (Strype Correspondence, I, fo. 2).

[11] *Montgomery Manuscripts*, 219; Bonnell to Johnson, 16 May 1660 (Strype Correspondence, I, fo. 2). For the religious settlement, see McGuire, 'Dublin Convention'.

concerned, the restoration of episcopacy was probably unavoidable once the return of monarchy was agreed on. At the same time, it appears that it was the strength of support in Ireland for the restoration of the traditional hierarchy that led the government to act so much more quickly there than it did in England.[12] Attitudes to the return of monarchy are more difficult to ascertain. Support for a restoration certainly became increasingly apparent in the early months of 1660, but it is difficult to know how much of this represented a genuine aspiration and how much an acceptance of the inevitable. Historians of mid-seventeenth-century Ireland have in general emphasized the pragmatism of Irish Protestant political attitudes, based as they were on a recognition that stability and strong government in England were essential if their own position in Ireland was to be secure. Thus, even Irish Protestants who sympathized with the demands of the English parliament continued in the early 1640s to support Charles I against his critics.[13] Once civil war had broken out irretrievably, on the other hand, and once it had become clear that parliament was both the stronger and the more reliable ally, even former royalists were prepared to give it their support. Thus in the 1650s Irish Protestants were among the firmest supporters of the Cromwellian regime. By 1660 conditions had changed again. Now it was the reinstatement of Charles II that seemed to offer the best hope of stable government in both islands.

Pragmatism is certainly evident in the careers of the individuals most closely identified with the restoration of monarchy in Ireland. Coote and Broghill were both former royalist military commanders who had transferred their allegiance to parliament. Coote had served the Cromwellian regime as president of Connacht. Broghill had become the Cromwell family's most prominent Irish supporter and had taken a leading part in 1657 in the framing of the Humble Petition and Advice, which had called on Oliver Cromwell to assume the crown himself. After the Restoration he was to produce, during periods when gout kept him away from public affairs, a series of historical plays on the subject of usurpation. In these a recurring figure is the general who for the good of the state gives his services to the usurper, before turning in the end to the legitimate ruler.[14] Even Broghill might have faltered, however, at the prospect of producing a retrospective justification for the career of Henry Jones, who served as dean of Kilmore and later bishop of Clogher in the old Anglican dispensation, went on to become scoutmaster-general to the Irish army under Cromwell, yet in 1661 was promoted to the bishopric of Meath in recognition of his services—along with those of his brother, Colonel Theophilus Jones—during the crucial months preceding the Restoration.

All three of these men were members of the 'old' Protestant population,

[12] This is the case argued in McGuire, 'Dublin Convention'.
[13] See in particular Canny, *Upstart Earl*, 33–7.   [14] Lynch, *Roger Boyle*, 146–59.

from families established in Ireland before 1641. During the 1650s there had been further settlers, soldiers and financial backers of the parliamentary army who had been rewarded with land confiscated from royalists and Catholics. Later events were to show that some of these remained loyal to their republican principles. Most, however, proved as capable as their longer-established neighbours of adjusting to political reality. Indeed, it was a Cromwellian grantee, Henry Whaley, who had been allocated 6,000 acres in County Down, who proposed in the Irish Convention the formal motion for the recall of Charles II.[15]

It is this united and effective action by a propertied, mainly landed élite that gives the events of late 1659 and early 1660 their significance. In the first half of the seventeenth century, Irish political life had largely revolved around the relationships between three rival, if by no means equal, élites: the Protestants, mainly descended from sixteenth- and seventeenth-century settlers; the Old English, mainly the Catholic descendants of pre-Reformation settlers; and the Gaelic Irish.[16] The wars of the 1640s had united Old English and Irish Catholics in the Confederacy, and had ended in their defeat at the hands of the English Commonwealth and its Irish Protestant allies. What remained was a single élite, combining Protestant families established before 1641 with the minority of more recent settlers. Already in the 1650s Henry Cromwell, representing the Commonwealth ruled by his father, had discovered that Ireland could be ruled effectively only with the co-operation of this élite, regardless of its origins or past political loyalties. With the collapse of the Commonwealth, the same Protestant land-owning class confirmed its dominance by delivering Ireland safely into the hands it had decided now best served its interest. In doing so, of course, its members accepted the constraints both of the monarchical constitution they were restoring and of the inherently unequal relationship between Ireland and Great Britain. Thus the chief governors of Restoration Ireland were not to be men like Coote and Orrery, but rather the returned royalist Ormond, and after him a succession of English politicians appointed as one outcome of factional competition at the English court. The demands for greater legislative independence voiced at the Irish Convention were to be wholly ignored. Within these limits imposed by a wider political reality, however, the Protestant land-owning class, combining old and new elements, had established a hegemony that was to be the central fact of Irish history for the next two hundred years.

2. Settlement and Explanation

By the end of 1660 the restoration of the monarchy was complete. Charles II had been proclaimed king in all three of his kingdoms, and the men respon-

---

[15] O'Donoghue, 'Parliament', 19.   [16] For these distinctions, see below, ch. 4, sect. 2.

sible for his reinstatement had been duly rewarded. Monck was now duke of Albemarle, while Coote and Broghill had become earls, of Mountrath and Orrery, respectively. There had also been limited retribution. Ten persons directly involved in the execution of Charles I were hanged, drawn, and quartered in October 1660. Others, including Sir Hardress Waller, had their sentences of death commuted to life imprisonment. With the sacrifice of these token victims, the quarrel between monarch and people was in theory buried. The annulment of all legislation that had not received the royal assent swept away the reforms on which the English republic had been built, restoring—in theory at least—the constitution that had existed in the summer of 1641.[17]

In Ireland, by contrast, there was never any question of simply turning back the clock. There the years 1641–60 had seen not just the suspension of monarchical government, but a revolution in land ownership. The Commonwealth regime of the 1650s had shared the general belief that Irish Catholics were as a body guilty of the massacre of tens of thousands of Protestants in the autumn of 1641. In addition, the war against the king had been financed by allocations of land to be confiscated in Ireland. Moral outrage and financial exigency combined to produce a punitive settlement, in which virtually all Catholic landowners lost their estates. Many were dispossessed outright. Others, held to be guilty of lesser offences, received new grants of smaller amounts of land, in a group of western counties specifically set aside for this purpose. In 1641 Catholics had owned 59 per cent of the profitable land of Ireland. By 1660 this had been reduced to 8 or 9 per cent, almost all of it in County Clare and parts of Connacht. The confiscated land was used to pay for the wars of 1641–53. Adventurers who had subscribed towards the cost of reconquering Ireland were to be repaid in land, allocated by the drawing of lots, while 35,000 soldiers were to receive their arrears of pay in the same form.[18] With the fall of the Commonwealth, this enormous redistribution scheme, still only partially implemented, was suddenly thrown into question. Catholics, citing the consistent loyalty of the Confederation to Charles I and his son, spoke openly of their hopes of seeing the whole settlement reversed. Some former proprietors attempted to take immediate possession of their estates by force.[19]

The first official response to these claims was a royal declaration in November 1660 announcing that Catholics who had not been guilty of rebellion in 1641 or the years that followed and those who had served the crown in exile were to have their estates restored. The same declaration, however, confirmed the adventurers and soldiers in all lands granted to them. Any of their number displaced by the restoration of innocent Catholics were

---

[17] Assessments of the real political power of the restored monarchy vary. The view that its powers were curtailed by the precedent set in 1649 is questioned in much recent writing: see e.g. McInnes, 'When was the English Revolution?'; Miller, *James II*, 30–6. For a more traditional view, see Hutton, *The Restoration*, 181–4.

[18] Bottigheimer, *English Money and Irish Land*, 141–2.   [19] *CSPI 1660–2*, 130.

to be compensated by equivalent grants of land elsewhere. For good measure, royalist officers with arrears of pay outstanding from before 1649 were to receive what was due to them out of land not otherwise disposed of. It was this bland undertaking to meet all claims while disadvantaging no one that provoked Ormond's famous remark that if the declaration was to be implemented, 'there must be discoveries made of a new Ireland, for the old will not serve to satisfy these engagements'.[20] Nevertheless, the plan was given legal force in the Act of Settlement passed through the Irish parliament in the summer of 1662. A court of claims, set up to hear the cases of those claiming restoration under the act, commenced work in January 1663. By August it had granted decrees of innocence to the great majority of the claimants who had come before it. At this point the government, either because of alarm at the violent hostility that the court's proceedings had aroused among Protestants or because it was itself put out by the large number of decrees of innocence granted to Catholic claimants, suspended the work of the court, even though it had given judgement to less than one-seventh of those seeking a hearing.[21] There remained the problem of finding land for Cromwellian proprietors displaced by those Catholics who had had their land restored, as well as meeting the claims of royalist officers. This was done by an Act of Explanation, which required adventurers and soldiers to surrender one-third of the land granted to them. With this concession, steered through a hostile Irish parliament in December 1665, the Restoration land settlement was completed.

'Settlement' is, of course, too dignified a term for the crude lottery that had taken place. The earl of Essex, lord lieutenant in the 1670s, compared the whole process to 'flinging the reward upon the death of a deer among a pack of hounds, where every one pulls and tears what he can for himself'.[22] The declaration of November 1660 included a querulous reply to its expected critics: 'The laying of the foundations is not now before us, when we might design the model of the structure answerable to our own thoughts.' Yet the procedures adopted—the initial wild promise to meet all claims with losses to no one, the arbitrary winding up of the court of claims, and the multitude of provisions made for favoured individuals—all helped to maximize the inevitable anomalies. Catholics and Protestants alike alleged that bribery had played a part in determining which cases were heard and which succeeded before the court of claims.[23] Certainly it is clear that many of those who

---

[20] Text of the Act of Settlement, incorporating the declaration of November 1660, in Curtis and McDowell, *Irish Historical Documents*, 158–69; Ormond, quoted in Bagwell, *Ireland under the Stuarts*, iii. 22–3.

[21] Arnold, 'The Irish Court of Claims'. For the traditional view, that Charles II and his ministers retreated from their intention of restoring to their land significant numbers of Catholics in the face of Protestant outrage, see Bottigheimer, 'The Restoration Land Settlement'. For the view that there was no such intention, see Hutton, *Charles II*, 196–7, 200–1, 207–10, 236–40.

[22] Quoted in Lynch, *Roger Boyle*, 213.

[23] 'Declaration of the Irish Rebels' (*CSPI 1666–9*, 62–3); Anglesey to Ormond, 5 Apr. 1664 (HMC, *Ormonde Manuscripts*, NS iii. 160).

succeeded in recovering their lands did so through influence or personal connections. The duke of Ormond, for example, ensured that various Catholic
relatives in County Tipperary and elsewhere received decrees of innocence.
William Sarsfield, heir to the family estate at Lucan, initially found his decree
of innocence of little value, for these lands were held by Sir Theophilus Jones,
whose services at the Restoration had ensured that he was confirmed in his
life interest in the property. Yet, when William married the sister of Charles
II's natural son, the duke of Monmouth, other lands were found to induce Sir
Theophilus to give up possession.[24]

Lower down the scale of influence, William Montgomery of County
Down procured a decree of innocence for a Catholic family from whom he
had purchased land, in order to secure his own title. At the same time
he complained bitterly when the Allens of County Kildare, whose lands
had been provisionally granted to his patron and brother-in-law Viscount
Mountalexander, obtained a decree of innocence through the intervention of
Richard Talbot, a close friend of the king's brother, the duke of York.[25] The
most potent influence of all of course was that of the king. In County Louth,
for example, three Catholic proprietors, who between them received three-
quarters of all the land restored to Catholics in that county, all owed their
success to direct personal claims on the gratitude of Charles II.[26]

The overall effect of the Acts of Settlement and Explanation was to increase the Catholic share of profitable land to around 20 per cent, more than
twice what it had been at the end of the Cromwellian regime, but only a little
over one-third of what it had been before 1641. What the Catholics had lost
was divided between Old Protestants and Cromwellian settlers. Catholic
propagandists lamented the triumph of the 'Cromwellian scum of England', 'a
generation of mechanic bagmen' who had come to power by conquest.[27] This
theme was to be endlessly repeated by the Gaelic poets of the century that
followed. But this was the propaganda of a dispossessed and traditionally
minded élite. Just over a thousand adventurers and 33,000 soldiers were
allocated land in Ireland by the governments of the Commonwealth. Many of
these sold their allocation without ever attempting to settle. This was particularly true of the lower ranks of the army who had been given only
smallholdings; even before the Restoration it was claimed that the private
soldiers had almost all sold out to their officers, so that not one in fifty owned
a foot of land in Ireland.[28] Some presumably failed in their attempts to
establish themselves profitably on their new property, and others may well
have lost out in the rough justice offered by the various instruments of the
Restoration land settlement. In the end, some 500 adventurers and 7,500

[24] 'Memorandum on the Sarsfield-Vesey Papers', 344–5.
[25] *Montgomery Manuscripts*, 229–35.
[26] Quinn, 'Religion and Landownership in County Louth', 13–21.
[27] Quoted in Bagwell, *Ireland under the Stuarts*, iii. 53–4.
[28] *CSPI 1660–2*, 166.

soldiers had their lands confirmed to them under Charles II.[29] The relative importance of this new element in the Protestant propertied class may be assessed from the composition of the parliament elected in 1661. Of 254 members, only 16 were adventurers and less than 50 were soldiers who had come to Ireland with the parliamentary armies.[30] Some new fortunes had undoubtedly been made. But the ruling class that emerged from the crisis of the mid-seventeenth century had deeper roots in Ireland than its enemies cared to admit.

If Catholics were the undoubted losers by the Restoration land settlement, Protestants were also left feeling angry and resentful. The five years following the Restoration were a time of deep insecurity and uncertainty. The final settlement, when it came, was deeply unpopular. When the Act of Explanation was debated in December 1665, MPs faced each other with swords half drawn, 'some being heard to say that the lands they had gotten with the hazard of their lives should not now be lost with ayes and nos'. Later, when supporters of the bill brought in candles to allow the debate to continue, opponents put them out, and the two sides 'wanted very little of going to cuffs in the dark'.[31]

Behind such protests lay, not just concern for property at risk, but a conviction that Catholics guilty of murder and rebellion were being restored to lands they had justly forfeited and whose recovery would enable them to do further mischief. Modern writing on the Ulster rising of autumn 1641 tends to emphasize the extent to which contemporaries exaggerated the scale and ferocity of the assault on the settler population and the role of such exaggerated accounts in legitimizing the subsequent seizure of Catholic property. Such an emphasis tends to obscure two things. The first is the extent to which, by the 1660s, Irish Protestants had come to believe their own propaganda. The second is that tales of massacre, however exaggerated, were not invented. One estimate is that 4,000 Ulster Protestants were killed in the early weeks of the rising, and perhaps twice that number subsequently died of hunger, fever, or exposure.[32] When Catholics who had taken part either in the Ulster rising or in the conflict that had followed began to receive decrees of innocence from the court of claims, most Protestants reacted with outrage and

---

[29] *NHI* iii. 370–3; Bottigheimer, *English Money and Irish Land*, 140–1.

[30] Bottigheimer, 'Restoration Land Settlement', 7; Barnard, 'Planters and Policies', 67. McCracken's calculations for the reign of George II are unfortunately not directly comparable. Of the MPs who sat in the Irish parliament between 1727 and 1760, 57% were of Cromwellian or early Stuart origin, compared with 21% descended from Tudor settlers and 10% of Norman origin: 'Central and Local Administration', 110. Of 63 peers active in the House of Lords during 1692–1727, 58 represented families established in Ireland before the 1640s, 15 of them before the Reformation: James, 'Active Irish Peers', 59–60.

[31] *CSPI 1663–5*, 687, 699.

[32] Corish, in *NHI* iii. 291–2, citing figures first put forward by Lecky. Corish does not consider this a 'massacre', though the retaliatory killing of Catholics by Protestant forces in the period that followed apparently qualifies for the term.

incomprehension. The earl of Mountalexander saw the former owner of his lands restored, despite evidence that the earl considered so clear that he had offered odds of 100 to 1 against the claim succeeding. He quoted with approval the words of his counsel: 'Sirs, if you judge this man innocent, we must believe the English cut one another's throats and that there was no Irish rebellion or rebels.'[33] Nor did resentment fade with time. Almost thirty years later, a leading member of the Church of Ireland reacted with alarm to suggestions that a forthcoming bill of attainder against the defeated supporters of James II might include provision for a court of claims to hear the cases of those claiming innocence, 'which is so odious a thing and had such mischievous effects on the last settlement that nothing could be more dreadful to Protestants'.[34]

3. A Foreign Jurisdiction

The fears and hopes aroused by the prospect of a revision of the land settlement dominated the years following the Restoration. But there was also a second, and in some ways related, issue to be resolved. This concerned the legal status of the Catholic church and its clergy. In the 1650s a determined attempt wholly to suppress Catholic religious practice had produced significant numbers of conformists—enough to raise the question of just how well Catholicism, normally seen as one of the givens of Irish history, would in fact have survived a sustained period of real repression.[35] As it was, the offensive had already slackened before the fall of the Commonwealth, and Charles II inherited a kingdom in which the great majority of the population, perhaps three-quarters, were Catholics. With his return, secular and regular clergy[36] still in the kingdom once again came out into the open, while numbers of priests began to enter Ireland from continental Europe.

This presented problems, not only of policy, but also of law. In England, under legislation dating back to the reign of Elizabeth, Catholic religious practice was illegal, and priests found in the kingdom could be executed. In Ireland, Catholics, right up to the 1640s, had retained sufficient political influence to block proposals for similar legislation. The repression of the early and mid-1650s had been carried out on the basis that English law also applied in Ireland. With the Restoration, the parliamentary union of the two countries was at an end, and there was once again no clear-cut law forbidding Catholic worship or religious organization. In December 1660 the lords justices installed by the restored monarchy reported that they were continuing to

---

[33] *CSPI 1663–5*, 19.
[34] King to Robert Southwell, 3 Feb. 1691 (TCD MSS 1995–2008/113).
[35] Barnard, *Cromwellian Ireland*, 180, 297–8.
[36] Regular clergy were those who lived, according to a rule, as members of religious orders.

arrest priests found officiating, even though their activities were not penal as in England, on the grounds that 'these men have always been incendiaries here'. In January the Privy Council issued a proclamation prohibiting all religious assemblies by Catholics or Nonconformists. Yet policy remained unclear. In late 1661 reports of a planned Catholic rising led to a general round-up of priests and friars; but those taken were released three months later, even though the lords justices felt, 'such is our previous experience of them', that they could well have been kept in custody. In November 1662 the government reiterated the ban on religious assemblies, citing as justification the unacceptable challenge to royal authority presented by the introduction of a papal jurisdiction and the levying of money on the king's subjects. In practice, however, priests who did not make themselves unduly conspicuous seem to have been left largely undisturbed.[37]

Uncertainty also attached to the position of the Catholic laity. Under the Commonwealth, Catholics had been wholly excluded from central and local government. When the Restoration parliament was elected at the end of 1660, Catholics were given little say in the process. However, this was achieved by *ad hoc* methods, and with some difficulty. In Cashel, where the Catholic inhabitants announced their intention of putting up two candidates, they were prevented by the hurried creation of 100 Protestant freeholders. In Tuam a Catholic was in fact returned, but the election was disallowed.[38] A royal order in May 1661 to the effect that no one was to be excluded from living and trading in a town on the grounds of religion or nationality was initially interpreted as readmitting Catholics to full participation in urban life. But in August, following representations from Ireland, the English Privy Council announced that the instruction had not been intended to cover readmission to civic office. The Acts of Settlement and Explanation further whittled down the original concession, by forbidding those who had not taken the oath of supremacy from leasing or purchasing urban property and by requiring that innocent Catholics claiming restoration of property in corporate towns be compensated instead with equivalent lands outside their boundaries.[39] All this, however, continued to fall short of formal exclusion. In both central and local government the Protestant monopoly depended in the last resort not on explicit laws, but on the self-perpetuating power of existing local oligarchies.

The reign of Charles II saw no attempt to clarify the legal standing of Catholicism. The king's personal religious preferences remain obscure. The conventional wisdom suggests a secret sympathy with Catholicism. The most recent biography, on the other hand, presents a man of little religious feeling,

---

[37] *CSPI 1660–2*, 129, 191, 520–1, 615. The importance of the absence of specific legislation was first noted by W. P. Burke, *Irish Priests in the Penal Times*, 1–2.

[38] *CSPI 1660–2*, 113–14; O'Donoghue, 'Parliament', 42.

[39] *CSPI 1660–2*, 338–9; *CSPI 1663–5*, 195–7; proclamation, 27 July 1663 (ibid. 188); Gale, *Enquiry into the Ancient Corporate System of Ireland*, 55–62, cxxx–clvi.

whose apparent tolerance came down in reality to a wish to reward specific individuals and groups to whom he felt a personal obligation, combined with a determination to retain for himself the maximum freedom of action.[40] Whatever the reason, Ormond, acting on the king's instructions, took care to block an attempt by the Irish House of Commons in 1663 to pass a bill extending to Ireland the English laws against Catholic religious organization.[41] Meanwhile individual Catholics, both in England and in Ireland, continued to enjoy the king's open favour and protection. The result was a world of bizarre double standards, in which the earl of Orrery, the leading Irish advocate of tough anti-Catholic measures, rubbed shoulders on familiar, even friendly, terms with 'Dick Talbot', the chief spokesman for the Irish Catholic interest; in which the queen's Catholic chaplain, Patrick Maginn, could visit County Down in 1665 to arrange for the farming of the county's inland excise by his relatives and friends and be feted by pillars of the Protestant establishment; in which Oliver Plunkett, the newly appointed Catholic archbishop of Armagh, could stop off at the court for two audiences with the queen before going on his way to Ireland, disguised with wig, sword, and pistols and travelling under the pseudonym of 'Captain Browne'.[42] At a more mundane level, Ormond's general policy as lord lieutenant, again clearly approved in London, was to discourage interference with Catholic worship, as long as this was conducted discreetly, but to deal severely with anything smacking of 'presumption' or 'insolence' that might give offence to 'sober Protestants'.[43]

The one attempt to arrive at a clearer definition of the relationship between Irish Catholics and the state was initiated by the Catholics themselves. In December 1661 a group of prominent laymen, alarmed by recent allegations of a Catholic conspiracy and with an eye to the forthcoming land settlement, drew up a comprehensive declaration of political principles. The central issue that had dogged Irish Catholics ever since the Reformation was that of jurisdiction: how to reconcile allegiance to a Protestant monarch with the obedience claimed by the Pope. The Remonstrance of 1661 offered an unqualified acceptance of Charles II as lawful king, to be obeyed in all civil and temporal affairs, any papal claims to the contrary notwithstanding. The declaration was signed by 121 of the leading Catholic nobility and gentry and by some of the clergy, including one bishop. The great majority of priests and bishops, however, refused to accept so uncompromising a rejection of papal authority. The document was also condemned both by the Pope himself and

---

[40] Hutton, *Charles II*, 455–7.   [41] *CSPI 1663–5*, 65, 91–2.

[42] For Talbot, see Orrery's letters in *CSPI 1663–5*, 291; *CSPI 1666–9*, 182. In Aug. 1666 Talbot stayed for a period at Orrery's house in Charleville, County Cork (*CSPI 1666–9*, 195). Talbot's brother, the Catholic archbishop of Dublin, was regarded by some as a client of Orrery's: see *CSPD 1671–2*, 34; Plunkett, *Letters*, 110, 120. For Maginn, see *CSPI 1663–5*, 134, 142, 637; *CSPI 1666–9*, 437; *CSPI 1669–70*, 91. For Plunkett, see his *Letters*, 50, 54–5, 59.

[43] For characteristic statements of Ormond's views, see *CSPI 1663–5*, 324; *CSPI 1666–9*, 108; Burke, *Irish Priests*, 21.

by the theological faculty of the University of Louvain. At this point the attempt to strengthen the political position of Irish Catholics became a largely self-inflicted disaster. The court and the Irish administration, having been offered the Remonstrance, insisted on taking it as a test of political loyalty. Over the next five years, supporters of the declaration were tolerated and even favoured by the government, while its opponents were imprisoned and harassed. Matters came to a head in June 1666, when Ormond was persuaded to permit leading Catholic ecclesiastics to meet in Dublin as a national congregation. When the assembled clergy refused to endorse the Remonstrance, Ormond reacted strongly. Archbishop O'Reilly of Armagh, who had returned from France under safe conduct to attend the congregation, was imprisoned, threatened for a time with prosecution for high treason, and eventually deported, while throughout the country anti-Remonstrant clergy were arrested or forced into hiding.[44]

The precise significance of the Remonstrance controversy is difficult to assess. Catholic historians have tended to argue that the government, represented in particular by Ormond, had no real interest in seeing a formula worked out by which Irish Catholics could testify to their political loyalty. Instead, they were concerned simply to divide and embarrass the Catholic clergy. A more accurate interpretation might be that Ormond approached the whole issue with a mind conditioned by his experiences during the 1640s, when he had found the Confederate Catholics divided between those who were prepared to pledge their support to the king and those who instead took their lead from the papal nuncio, Archbishop Rinuccini. The leading clerical defender of the Remonstrance, the Franciscan Peter Walsh, had been an opponent of Rinuccini, while O'Reilly had been a supporter. Thus Ormond had every reason to see what was taking place as another conflict between those Catholics willing to act as loyal subjects and those whose commitment to papal authority made it impossible for them to do so. In these circumstances the precise content of the Remonstrance did indeed become largely irrelevant. At the same time the episode had its importance. The leading participants in the congregation of 1666 found themselves under attack not only from Ormond for having rejected the Remonstrance, but also from Rome on account of the alternative declaration they had offered in its place. This formula, based on propositions drawn up by the Sorbonne, had accepted the absolute authority of monarchs in temporal matters and rejected the claim that the Pope could dispense subjects from this allegiance. Its condemnation reminds us that the issue of foreign jurisdiction was not a mere slogan coined to legitimize anti-Catholic measures. There was a genuine difficulty, given the parameters of seventeenth-century theological and political thinking, in devis-

---

[44] For general accounts of the Remonstrance controversy, see Bagwell, *Ireland under the Stuarts*, ch. 43; Millett, *The Irish Franciscans*, ch. 6; Ryan, 'Religion and State', 129–31.

ing a formula which would allow Catholic subjects to offer a watertight declaration of their loyalty to a Protestant prince.

With the failure of the Remonstrance, religious policy continued largely as before: a succession of improvisations and sudden reversals determined primarily by the exigencies of English domestic politics. In 1669 Ormond was replaced as lord lieutenant, first by Baron Robartes of Truro and then, in April 1670, by Baron Berkeley of Stratton. With Berkeley's arrival, selective connivance at the activities of Catholic clergymen gave way to something close to open toleration. The new lord lieutenant, in private meetings with Catholic bishops, promised to leave them unmolested so long as they avoided interfering in political matters. In Ulster and Dublin the local authorities, civil and religious, fell into line with the new policy. When the governor of Dungannon tried to prevent Plunkett from holding confirmations, he was rebuked by the earl of Charlemont, who invited the archbishop to make use in future of the courtyard of his own house. The Anglican archbishop also received Plunkett courteously, and gave him permission to set up Catholic grammar schools in the diocese. In Munster the earl of Orrery initially tried to uphold traditional restrictions. But in summer 1672, after the earl had ignored stiffly worded warnings to moderate his zeal, the crown abolished the provincial presidency, which had given him his power to thwart official policy.[45]

By this time Berkeley had also been ordered to admit some Catholics to the commission of the peace and to other minor offices and to use his powers under the Act of Explanation to issue a general licence to all subjects to hold property, trade, and be admitted as freemen in the corporate towns. In addition, and potentially of much greater importance, Richard Talbot had been permitted to present a petition on behalf of Irish Catholics setting out the injustices they had suffered under the Restoration land settlement, and a royal commission was set up to examine the whole question. In the early months of Berkeley's administration, his secretary, Sir Ellis Leighton, himself a Catholic, combined optimism with discretion: 'Many Catholics are in, more may be if they will be prudent. But they must not cry "Roast Meat" or sing "Victoria".'[46] By 1672, however, prudence no longer seemed necessary. Agents raising funds to finance the assault on the land settlement operated openly throughout the country, going so far as to distrain the property of Catholics who would not pay. In County Kerry Catholics resisted the collection of quit rent on the grounds that 'they are now, by secret intelligence, possessed of having their estates suddenly restored to them'.[47]

All this took place against a background of wider diplomatic and political upheaval. In May 1670 the king had concluded his notorious secret treaty with Louis XIV, in which he had agreed to join in a war against Holland and

[45] Plunkett, *Letters*, 93–258 *passim*; Irwin, 'The Suppression of the Irish Presidency System'.
[46] Leighton to Joseph Williamson, 8 Oct. 1670 (SP63/329/106ᵛ).
[47] *CSPD 1672*, 565; cf. Plunkett, *Letters*, 430.

in addition, in return for financial and military aid, to declare himself a Catholic. In March 1672, just before the war began, he issued a Declaration of Indulgence, suspending all penal laws against Catholics and Dissenters. The precise purpose behind these moves continues to be debated. But the more liberal religious policy introduced in Ireland was clearly part of the same general programme. One recent account, it is true, argues that Berkeley, in showing such open favour to Catholics, was going beyond, or even contravening, his instructions.[48] But in fact Berkeley's departure from Ireland in August 1672 brought no marked change in policy. Three months later, Archbishop Plunkett reported that Berkeley's replacement, the earl of Essex, was 'a wise, prudent and moderate man . . . in no way inferior to his predecessor in his affection for me'.[49] Instead, what eventually forced a reversal in official attitudes were quite clearly developments in England. By early 1673 the king, fatally weakened by failure to win the expected easy victories against the Dutch, was in retreat before a ferocious backlash of anti-Catholic feeling. Catholics who had been admitted to the magistracy and other offices were turned out. The Protestant monopoly of urban government was restored. The enquiry into the land settlement was wound up, and Richard Talbot, its main champion, sent abroad. In addition, in what was to be an important precedent, a proclamation issued on 27 October ordered all bishops, vicars-general, and others exercising ecclesiastical jurisdiction, as well as all regular clergy, to leave the kingdom by 31 December.

The resulting campaign of repression, initiated to appease English opinion, went no further than was necessary for that purpose. A number of bishops and regulars left the country or were arrested and deported, while others went into hiding. Yet Plunkett admitted in June 1674 that soldiers and constables had not been very active in enforcing the order against bishops and regulars. In August of the following year he noted that Essex had 'behaved very moderately in the application of the edicts published against us'. His real fear was that renewed difficulties in the English parliament, or even more a meeting of parliament in Ireland itself, would force the authorities to adopt really effective methods of repression.[50] In fact, the policy of official discountenance enforced without excessive zeal continued until 1678, when the sensational revelations of Titus Oates regarding a Catholic plot to assassinate the king once more dragged Ireland into what was essentially an English crisis of political and religious passions.

Perceptions of the Irish dimension of the Popish Plot have been unduly coloured by one dramatic episode: the execution for treason of Oliver Plunkett, subsequently canonized to provide Ireland with its only recognizably Catholic saint. In fact, Plunkett's downfall was organized wholly in England.

[48] Hutton, 'The Making of the Secret Treaty of Dover'.
[49] Plunkett, *Letters*, 351.   [50] Ibid. 450, 414.

He was brought to the notice of the opposition leader, Shaftesbury, by William Hetherington, a disreputable former bounty-hunter who had broken gaol in Dublin and was anxious to avoid rearrest. Shaftesbury took up Hetherington's fabricated story of an Irish plot because his campaign to expose Popery in high places, and in particular to have the king's brother, James, duke of York, excluded from the succession on account of his Catholicism, had begun to run out of momentum.[51] In Ireland itself Ormond, who had returned as lord lieutenant in 1677, certainly responded to news of the plot with the measures needed to allay public anxiety and safeguard his own position. A fresh proclamation on 16 October ordered all bishops and regular clergy to leave the kingdom; Catholics were forbidden to keep weapons, and mass houses in the cities and towns were ordered to be closed. On the other hand, Ormond expressed nothing but contempt ('They find it more honourable and safe to be the king's evidence than a cowstealer') for the witnesses against Plunkett, and no comparable judicial murders took place within his jurisdiction.[52] A substantial number of regular clergy and some bishops were imprisoned or deported. Peter Talbot, archbishop of Dublin and formerly the queen's chaplain, was kept in strict confinement, despite his poor health, until his death in November 1680. The secular clergy, on the other hand, were left largely in peace, although at the height of the crisis some were harassed by over-zealous local authorities, and a few were arrested on treason charges.[53] Towards the end of the crisis, in 1681, the Catholic archbishop of Cashel reported to Rome that 'the government here is far more moderate and—not having given credence to the calumnies—has not oppressed us at all so much as in England'.[54]

The passing of the political crisis in England, with the reassertion of royal authority and the destruction of the Whig opposition during 1681–3, brought some relaxation of pressure, although Catholic ecclesiastics continued for some time to move with caution. In the late summer and autumn of 1683 there was another clamp-down. Some friars who had set up a community at Burrishoole in County Mayo were prosecuted and heavily fined. Ormond ordered the authorities in Kilkenny city to prevent the erection of several proposed friaries and to suppress all public mass houses in the town. To some extent, as in Kilkenny, Catholic ecclesiastics may have been moving too fast in anticipation of more liberal policies. But the main reason for this new round of prohibitions was the discovery, in June 1683, of the Rye House Plot, a

[51] Brady, 'The Arrest of Oliver Plunkett'; idem, 'Oliver Plunkett and the Popish Plot'. Hetherington later claimed to have led the party that arrested Plunkett in December 1679, but Brady regards this as unlikely ('Oliver Plunkett and the Popish Plot', 350).

[52] Ormond to Arran, 17 Nov. 1681 (HMC, *Ormonde Manuscripts*, NS vi. 231).

[53] Plunkett, *Letters*, 530, 532; Burke, *Irish Priests*, 66–71. See also the cases of priests released once it had been established that they exercised no ecclesiastical jurisdiction: Burke, *Irish Priests*, 58, 60, 61.

[54] Power, *Bishop of the Penal Times*, 70–1.

radical conspiracy to assassinate the king and his brother. The government had responded by closing Nonconformist places of worship, and was anxious not to seem to make invidious distinctions by leaving Catholic churches open.[55] In terms of religious policy, the reign of Charles II thus ended much as it had begun, with a succession of expedients, some genuine and others largely cosmetic, but all adopted in response to immediate pressures.

4. Papists and Fanatics

The Restoration monarchy lived with the constant threat of rebellion. The danger to be feared from religious and political dissent may have been exaggerated by some, but the problem was nevertheless real. In England in the years immediately following the Restoration there were risings of republicans and religious radicals, in London in January 1661 and in the north in October 1663, as well as a number of other conspiracies abandoned or broken up before they could develop. Later in the reign, radical disaffection reappeared in the Rye House Plot of 1683 and in Monmouth's rebellion in 1685. In Scotland, Covenanters unwilling to accept the return of episcopacy staged insurrections in 1666 and again in 1679, while the duke of Argyll led a rising in support of Monmouth in 1685. In Ireland the problem was twofold: there was the possibility, as elsewhere, of action by the unreconciled opponents of monarchy and episcopacy; and there was also the threat perceived to come from the Catholics and their allies in continental Europe.

The threat from religious and political radicals was at its most intense in the early years. The Irish Restoration had itself been achieved only by means of a power struggle, dramatized in the *coup* and attempted counter *coup* of December 1659 and February 1660, respectively. Both confrontations had been followed by purges of the army. Sporadic reports of secret meetings of known opponents of monarchy, seditious publications, and the stockpiling of arms continued over the next two years. Then, in 1663, came evidence of a conspiracy to seize Dublin Castle and at the same time stage risings in Munster and Ulster. What was alarming was that the plot involved more than just the usual nondescript cliques of displaced junior officers and religious extremists. With the court of claims threatening to reverse the Cromwellian land settlement, men of status and political influence had also been drawn into the scheme for a *coup* in defence of the Protestant interest. Among them were no less than ten members of the Irish parliament, of whom one, Colonel Alexander Jephson, MP for Trim, was later hanged, and another seven expelled from the Commons. It is true that the exact dimensions of the plot

[55] Burke, *Irish Priests*, 68–70; HMC, *Ormonde Manuscripts*, NS vii. 115–16, 121, 124, 139, 314–16.

remain unclear. Ormond and his colleagues manipulated the crisis both to incriminate as many radical extremists as possible and to head off a threatened revolt by the Irish Commons against the proceedings of the court of claims. Part, at least, of the official version of what was allegedly planned is highly dubious.[56] Unless the charges against Jephson and others were wholly fabricated, however, it seems clear that the conspiracy of 1663 represented by far the most formidable threat that the Restoration monarchy was to face from any group within Ireland.

The vulnerability of the government in the first years after 1660 was enhanced by its continued dependence on an army inherited from the Cromwellian regime. By 1663 Ormond had already reduced the existing force from around 15,000 men to less than 6,000, while at the same time creating a new regiment of 1,200 foot guards recruited entirely in England and so more reliable politically. Despite these changes, however, he still believed that the army, 'dangerously composed as to the inferior officers and common soldiers', could not have been counted on if the plot to seize the castle had succeeded. In the months that followed, there were further reductions in every Irish foot company, those discharged being once again replaced by men freshly recruited from England.[57] A few years later the same doubts regarding the political reliability of any force raised from among Irish Protestants led Ormond to oppose calls for the creation of an Irish militia. And indeed, even Orrery, the main advocate of a militia force, believed that only 'old Protestants' should be allowed to serve in it.[58]

Repeated purges of the Irish army, along with the termination of the crisis created by the activities of the court of claims, meant that the government was never again to be as vulnerable as it had been in the early 1660s. It continued to keep a careful eye on the activities of known republicans and other dissidents. The outbreak of war with Holland and France in 1665–6 encouraged some revival of activity. Orrery, in December 1665, was assured by one of his informants that 'that party was never so high as now they are in their hopes. They say to their friends that the French and Dutch will do so much work abroad that they will have a fair game to play at home.' The previous month he had submitted a detailed account, derived from 'a phanatick intelligencer', concerning a meeting of radicals in Liverpool and the subsequent despatch of agents to Ulster and Munster.[59] In 1672 Captain Thomas Walcott of Limerick city was arrested and questioned closely about allegations that he was planning a rising. Walcott was to be executed eleven

---

[56] The government's version, in *The Horrid Conspiracy of Such Impenitent Traitors*, seems in fact to borrow heavily from a plan drawn up as part of the *coup* of 1659. See *CSPI 1669–70*, 454–6. The most recent and detailed account of the plot is Greaves, *Deliver us from Evil*, 140–50, but this tends to take the government version of events very much on trust.

[57] *CSPI 1663–5*, 141. See Beckett, 'Irish Armed Forces', 41–5.

[58] *CSPI 1666–9*, 157.   [59] *CSPI 1663–5*, 679, 663.

years later for his part in the Rye House Plot. What he was accused of in 1672, however, was a somewhat improbable plan to seize the city of Limerick and hold it while the wool stored there was shipped off to Holland and exchanged for arms to supply a more general rising.[60] Nor did the other alarms of the period turn up anything remotely comparable to the 1663 conspiracy. The absence of any response in Munster or Dublin to the Scottish and English risings of 1685 would seem to confirm that Protestant republicanism and religious radicalism had ceased to be significant threats.

In assessing the danger it faced from dissident Protestants, the government had also to take into account the Presbyterians of Ulster. Prior to the 1640s the Scottish population of the north had been somewhat uneasily contained within the Church of Ireland. By 1660, however, they had established their own distinct ecclesiastical organization. As such, they made up the largest religious denomination in Ulster. Like their counterparts in Scotland, they had opposed the abolition of the monarchy, thus coming into conflict with the Cromwellian government of the 1650s. At the same time, their allegiance was to a monarch who would uphold the principles of the Scottish National Covenant of 1638. Those principles could not easily be reconciled with the revival of episcopacy in 1660 or with the apparent favour shown to Catholics in the years that followed. There was also the dangerous geographical proximity of the Ulster Presbyterians to their discontented co-religionists in Scotland.

Relations between the Ulster Presbyterians and the Restoration government were initially tense. There was no attempt to make conformity to the new regime easy. Ministers who had been installed during the interregnum were required to accept episcopal ordination. Those who refused, sixty-one out of a total of sixty-nine, were deprived of their livings. The newly restored bishops, backed up by the civil authorities, sought to prevent Presbyterian assemblies, and in some cases excommunicated and imprisoned ministers.[61] Even though only a handful of individuals were involved in the 1663 conspiracy, the authorities launched a general campaign of harassment against Presbyterian congregations in Ulster. In 1666 parliament passed an Act of Uniformity, forbidding any person not episcopally ordained from celebrating the sacrament of communion and requiring all schoolmasters to be licensed by the Anglican bishop. Already by this time, however, it was becoming clear that Presbyterianism was too well established to be suppressed. Greater tolerance was also encouraged by the government's growing sense of its own security, as well as by the political passivity of the Presbyterians themselves. Irish Nonconformists, an Anglican merchant conceded in 1666, 'are not troublesome nor quarrelsome as those of Scotland lately were, which also makes our

---

[60] *CSPD 1672–3*, 120–1, 151–2, 336–8; HMC, *Ormonde Manuscripts*, NS iii. 321.
[61] Neville, 'Irish Presbyterians under the Restored Stuart Monarchy'.

bishops connive the more'. Moreover, it 'stomached' the constables to be required to harass Protestant Dissenters unduly, 'when they say they may not disturb the Papists at their meeting'.[62] Dissenters, as well as Catholics, benefited from the more tolerant policy introduced, for whatever reason, after Ormond's recall in 1669. From 1672 Presbyterian ministers in Ulster began to receive the *regium donum*, a contribution to their maintenance payable, by royal order, out of the customs revenue of the port of Belfast. Unlike the concessions made to Catholics, this was not rescinded after Charles II was forced to cancel his Declaration of Indulgence, although its actual payment, like most official subventions in Restoration Ireland, was never wholly to be counted on.

A measure of distrust remained, nevertheless. Repeatedly during the 1670s—in 1674, 1676, 1677–8, and 1679—the Dublin government responded to the prospect of disturbances in Scotland by sending troops into Ulster, and there was constant concern about contacts between disaffected Presbyterians on the two sides of the North Channel.[63] In 1680 it was reported that money had been collected from among the Ulster Presbyterians to assist one of the fugitive killers of Archbishop Sharp of St Andrew's, assassinated by Covenanters the previous year. Two years later there were reports that collections for charitable purposes were in fact to be used for the purchase of arms. The information, from a disreputable former minister, had in the end to be discounted. But Bishop Hopkins of Derry remained convinced 'that some great mischief is now brewing among the faction'.[64] The unveiling of the Rye House Plot in 1683 brought new security measures: extra troops once again sent into Ulster, lists drawn up of justices of the peace and militia officers who attended Dissenting meetings, and the closure of Nonconformist places of worship. The governor of Derry reported in August 1683 that not a single meeting-house in the county had been open the previous Sunday. In Tyrone by early 1684 the local authorities had gone so far as to begin levying fines of a shilling a time, as provided for by the Act of Uniformity, on those who failed to attend Anglican worship.[65]

In addition to radical Protestant disaffection, the government had to consider the danger of another Catholic rising. The two threats, of course, came from opposite poles of the political spectrum, and some took comfort in the thought that they cancelled one another out.[66] Others were not so sure, however. In 1663 there were persistent reports that Edmund O'Reilly, archbishop

---

[62] Toby Bonnell to Revd John Johnson, 25 Dec. 1666 (Strype Correspondence, I, fo. 1).

[63] Beckett, 'Irish-Scottish Relations in the Seventeenth Century', in *Confrontations*, 36–40.

[64] W. Ellis to Sir Cyril Wyche, 17 July 1680 (Wyche Papers, 1/1/34); Hopkins to Archbishop Michael Boyle, 16 Jan. 1683 (HMC, *Ormonde Manuscripts*, NS vi. 513).

[65] HMC, *Ormonde Manuscripts*, NS vi. 96; vii. 181.

[66] Col. Edward Vernon to Bennet, 14 June 1663 (*CSPI 1663–5*, 136); Ormond to Arlington, 17 Jan. 1666 (*CSPI 1666–9*, 8).

of Armagh and the Catholic clergyman most loathed by Irish Protestants, was working with the exiled regicide Edmund Ludlow 'in order to a conjunction between the Nuncio-Popish party and the fanatics'.[67] In 1666 Orrery warned that there was 'a crew of desperate English' ready to take advantage of any rising by the Catholics. 'Though it may be objected that they will not stir if the Irish do, I have found their malice to be stronger than their judgement.'[68] This is easily dismissed as the wildest paranoia, and there is no reason to believe that any such contacts between Catholics and radicals ever took place. Yet the wars of the 1640s and 1650s had produced some strange alliances. In 1648–9 O'Reilly, then vicar-general of Dublin, had acted as intermediary in negotiations between the Catholics opposed to a truce with Ormond's royalists and the Irish parliamentarians. It was even believed that he had been responsible for Ormond's defeat at Rathmines in August 1649, by betraying the royalist position to the parliamentary forces.[69] Against such a background, few could place all their faith in the possibility of playing off the two groups of religious and political dissidents against one another.

Reports of projected rebellion among the Catholic Irish, with or without the co-operation of Protestant radicals, recur throughout the reign of Charles II. In August 1661, for example, the lords justices and Privy Council reported that a number of Irish officers in the Spanish army and a great many priests and friars had recently entered the country 'to disquiet the Irish and urge them to rebellion'.[70] The coming of war with Holland in 1665 and France the following year brought new alarms. From Ulster there were accounts of clandestine activity among 'the Irish clergy and such as have been officers abroad and live here in want'. Agents were said to be traversing the country under cover of attending the various county assizes, and emissaries had been sent to Rome and Spain. In Munster, Orrery reported that the French were attempting 'to prepare many of the Irish who are apt for mischief to be ready to run into it'. The Catholics 'do much talk, in their private meetings, of the French, and rely on them'. In 1671 Protestants already alarmed by the government's religious policies were again disturbed by reports of Irish soldiers returning from Spain and other foreign parts.[71]

Catholic historians, emphasizing the function of reports such as these in legitimizing despoliation and religious repression, have perhaps been too quick to assume that they could not possibly have contained any truth. After all, we now know that not only Charles II and his court, but also the leaders of the Whig opposition, were engaged around this time in highly dubious dealings with a supposedly hostile France. There is no reason in principle why Catholics should not have maintained similar contacts. On at least one

---

[67] HMC, *Ormonde Manuscripts*, NS iii. 128; Burke, *Irish Priests*, 2–5.
[68] *CSPI 1666–9*, 92–3.
[69] Ó Fiaich, 'Edmund O'Reilly', 180–1.
[70] *CSPI 1660–2*, 405–9; Burke, *Irish Priests*, 2–5.
[71] *CSPI 1663–5*, 551, 565–6, 622, 644; *CSPD 1671*, 116.

occasion, in 1680, a leading Catholic layman, Colonel John Fitzpatrick, seems to have told the papal nuncio in Brussels that the Catholics would rise in support of the duke of York or any other Catholic prince who would give them weapons.[72] But this was during the crisis of the Popish Plot and the Exclusion campaign. In more normal times such projects were less likely to appeal. As well as risking what property they retained, Catholics would be violating the loyalty to the crown that had been central to their political self-image since the 1640s. There were of course others—the dispossessed or discontented waging a private war as tories against the new order and the exiled army officers who figure so prominently in informers' reports—whom neither consideration was likely to restrain. But there is no evidence, for the moment at least, that any foreign power ever offered significant assistance to these potentially explosive but marginal groups.

The spectre of another Catholic rising, however ill-founded, was a cause of recurrent alarm among the Protestant population. The agent for the Conway estate in County Antrim reported in January 1665 that fear of 'a general reinsurrection against the English' was so general that tenants were unable to sell any part of their produce. In June 1666 Ormond confirmed that the report of a Catholic conspiracy 'is so much believed by the English that they forbear to buy and sell, and are on their guard to the neglect of their affairs'.[73] Just over six months later, reports of a massing of the Irish in County Cavan created new alarm. From Charlemont in County Tyrone to Lisburn in County Antrim, 'about Lurgan, Magheralin and all the way the English inhabitants were drawn together by 40 or 50 in a company, with pitchforks and such arms as they had, for their own defence'.[74] The religious policy of open tolerance adopted from 1670 deeply disturbed those who saw it as a fatal dropping of the Protestant guard. Captain Thomas Walcott, interrogated in 1672, left a vivid account of his state of mind: his anxiety at

the condition of the times . . . had so stupefied him, that he had, the day before, ridden four miles out of his way in a country he well knew, not considering what he was about. . . . The cause of his fear and trouble [was] that remembering how the Irish Papists had in 1641 murdered his father, and turned all his children a-begging, whereof he being one and a spectator, he believed their principles were the same now as then . . . and therefore he wished himself out of the kingdom.[75]

Major Joseph Stroud, visiting Lord Hillsborough's house in the summer of 1671, was horrified to find Oliver Plunkett being entertained as a guest of honour: 'You may see how we are courting the Irish to cut our throats, that have cut so many thousand before, and are as ready now to do it as ever.'[76] News of the Popish Plot in the autumn of 1678 led to a mass flight of

[72] Brady, 'The Arrest of Oliver Plunkett', 87.
[73] *CSPI 1663–5*, 530; *CSPI 1666–9*, 133.
[74] Rawdon to Conway, 11 Jan. 1667 (SP63/322/32).
[75] Examination of Capt. Walcott, 11 Nov. 1672 (*CSPD 1672–3*, 152–3).
[76] *CSPD 1671*, 340.

Protestants from rural areas of Cork and Kerry into the comparative safety of the towns. In Dublin a harassed official complained that, despite a nightly guard of 500 men, 'the English are so afraid that they never let me rest, but every now and then inform me of great store of concealed arms, and private meetings of regular priests, and when I send parties out in search we never find either'.[77]

Comment of this kind makes clear that many Irish Protestants were disposed to see themselves as a threatened minority, in constant danger of attack from a powerful and potentially treacherous Catholic majority. The same self-image was reflected in the continued popularity of works like Sir John Temple's lurid history of the events of 1641, as well as by the celebrations each 23 October of the anniversary of the rising.[78] At the same time it would be a mistake to see this sense of constant vulnerability, formalized as it was in a highly visible literary and ecclesiastical tradition, as reflecting the sum total of Protestant attitudes. The extent of the threat posed by Catholic discontent was in fact a central issue of debate throughout the period. Some of those who sought to stress the enormity of the danger were motivated by genuine alarm; for others the cry that the security of the kingdom was being neglected was a political tactic. Supporters of the existing administration, not surprisingly, tended to take a different line. Ormond, for example, was quite prepared to believe that 'all the old Nuncio party with those that have no estates, or no hope to recover their estates' could easily be led into rebellion by the French. But he also insisted that any such rising, though causing much devastation and expense, 'will infallibly end in their own ruin'. Sir Robert Southwell, similarly, argued that those few Irish who had kept their estates were for the most part 'well disposed to quietness', while the common people were actually better off under their new landlords than they had ever been under the old Gaelic order. The only real threat came from the Catholic clergy and from those dispossessed gentry for whom 'nothing but change and confusion can amend their case'.[79] It is also important not to generalize too widely from the views expressed at times of particular alarm. Sir Richard Cox, for example, took the Popish Plot very seriously, devoting a long charge to the quarter sessions of County Cork to an attack on those who denied the existence of a conspiracy. Yet, in the calmer atmosphere of the mid-1680s, he assured readers of his account of County Cork that there was not 'any part of the world more free from fear and disturbance than this kingdom'.[80]

The confidence of those who played down the threat of a Catholic rebellion

[77] Orrery to Ormond, 22 Nov. 1678 (Wyche Papers, 1/1/25); A. Warr to Wyche, 30 Nov. 1678 (ibid. 1/1/26).

[78] Barnard, 'Crises of Identity among Irish Protestants', 50–8.

[79] Ormond to Arlington, 5 May 1666 (SP63/321/8–9); Southwell to Sir John Perceval, 16 May 1682 (HMC, *Egmont Papers*, ii. 111–15).

[80] Cox, *Autobiography*, 11; Account of County Cork, 1685 (Molyneux Papers, 883/1, 256).

rested less on a denial that such a move might be contemplated than on a conviction that any conflict would end in a decisive Protestant victory. Sir William Petty, writing in 1672, argued that the Protestants, though out-numbered, controlled the towns and places of strength, that a far higher proportion were men of military experience, and that they would always be reinforced from England. For all these reasons he considered the danger of another rising remote. Southwell, too, thought it plain, 'as things stand, that the Protestants, having the authority of the government, the garrisons and arms in their hands, could drive the Irish into the sea, if that were fit and thought convenient in such sort to unpeople the land'.[81] And indeed, even the deeply alarmed Captain Thomas Walcott, in 1672, believed that if there were to be another show-down, Protestants would undoubtedly win. What had worried him, he made clear, was the apparently pro-Catholic policy of the court. 'If the king would stand neuter, he doubted not but we were able to beat them into the sea.'[82]

Even if we accept that many Irish Protestants were haunted by a fear of Catholics wholly out of proportion to the actual threat they presented, we must recognize that they were not alone. Late seventeenth-century England, after all, was plagued by similar nightmares. The Great Fire of London in September 1666 was widely believed to have been the work of Popish agents. Later, in December 1688, wild reports that Irish soldiers brought to England by James II had turned to massacre and pillage touched off a spectacular popular panic, 'the Irish fright', that spread through nineteen counties.[83] In some respects, indeed, English Protestants seem to have been more prone to irrational panic than their Irish counterparts. During the period of the Popish Plot a total of eighteen priests were executed, along with several Catholic laymen, on the basis of wholly groundless, and in many cases fantastic, allegations. In Ireland there were no executions. That this was so can to some extent be attributed to the attitude of the Irish government, which in turn was able to adopt this stance because the Irish parliament had not met since 1666 and there was no immediate prospect of its being recalled. At the same time there are also indications that Irish Protestant opinion in general was more sceptical than English. In Waterford and Limerick grand juries threw out indictments against the crypto-Catholic Lord Tyrone and others.[84] 'As to the Irish plot,' a Limerick gentleman wrote in April 1680, 'we believe more is spoken of it there [in England] than we hear of it here.'[85] Oliver Plunkett,

[81] Petty, *Political Anatomy*, 26–9; HMC, *Egmont Papers*, ii. 112.

[82] *CSPD 1672–3*, 153.

[83] Kenyon, *The Popish Plot*, 2; Miller, *Popery and Politics in England*, 103–5; G. H. Jones, 'The Irish Fright of 1688'.

[84] Bagwell, *Ireland under the Stuarts*, iii. 132–3. For the poem of praise in Irish addressed to Lord Chief Justice Keating, who presided over these acquittals, by the Munster poet David Ó Bruadair, see below, p. 117.

[85] Daniel Hignett to Perceval, 23 Apr. 1680 (HMC, *Egmont Papers*, ii. 94).

facing his first trial in Ireland, did not object even when his accusers peti-
tioned for a wholly Protestant jury. In his speech from the scaffold he reiterated his conviction that the charges against him would have been rejected
out of hand by any Protestant jury in Ireland.[86] All in all, it is an important
pointer to the psychological dynamics of a panic like that set off by the Popish
Plot that the spectre of a Catholic conspiracy received more credence in
England, where Catholics were an insignificant minority, than in Ireland,
where they made up three-quarters of the population and where memories of
a real Catholic uprising were less than thirty years old.

   There remains one further respect in which the events of 1678–81 offer an
insight into the changing character of Restoration Ireland. At the height of the
crisis, Orrery, seizing the opportunity once again to condemn the inadequacy
of his rival Ormond's management, called for a range of emergency measures,
including the immediate expulsion of Catholics from all cities and towns. His
proposals were promptly rejected both by Ormond and by the lord chancellor,
Archbishop Michael Boyle of Armagh. The Catholics, Boyle pointed out, had
been removed from the towns before. If they were there now, it was because
'the English themselves received them in again for their own advantage, they
knew not well how to live without them, they wanted servants, they wanted
tenants, and they wanted tradesmen'. Ormond wrote angrily of Protestant
landlords who 'pretend they cannot sleep for fear of having their throats cut
by the Papists, and asperse the government because there are so many of
them, though they themselves are the men that brought them to inhabit their
houses in towns and to plant and labour their lands'.[87] Here again, of course,
security policy was an issue in an essentially factional struggle. Yet the refusal
to offer even a token gesture towards the sort of expulsions called for by
Orrery is significant. Only thirty years before, government had seriously
proposed the transportation of the entire Catholic population to the counties
west of the Shannon. That scheme had been abandoned within two or three
years once it became clear that the economic consequences of any such
wholesale clearance would be disastrous. Now the Irish executive rejected as
impractical the expulsion of Catholics even from the towns. Economic inter-
dependence, if nothing else, had finally rendered obsolete all schemes that
would have achieved the security of Ireland by treating the Catholic population like the native peoples of some overseas colony, to be cleared or corralled
so as to make the land safe for settlers. For better or for worse, the Protestant
élite, in town and country alike, would from now on have to live with the
Catholic lower classes, as they were or as they might be made to be.

[86] Plunkett, *Letters*, 556, 574, 586.
[87] Boyle to Orrery, 18 Mar. 1679 (Wyche Papers, 1/1/30); Ormond to Wyche, 7 Mar. 1679
(HMC, *Leyborne–Popham Manuscripts*, 244). For the Cromwellian precedents to this proposal, see
Barnard, 'Planters and Policies', 39–44.

5. Counter-Revolution Defeated

'If the king would stand neuter', Captain Thomas Walcott reported himself as saying in 1672, 'he doubted not but we were able to beat them into the sea.' For twenty-five years after the Restoration, the deepest anxieties of Protestants in Ireland arose from the uncertain religious allegiance of the monarch. After February 1685 there was no further uncertainty. Charles II died, and was succeeded by his brother James. The three kingdoms of the British crown were now ruled by a Catholic who was determined to restore to his co-religionists at least a share of power and privilege. The crisis that followed is revealing in two respects. First, the response of Irish Protestants to the accession of James II provides important clues to their political outlook on the eve of the Glorious Revolution. Secondly, the events of James's reign make it possible to define with a new clarity the mechanisms of power operating in late seventeenth-century Ireland.

The full implications of the change of monarch only gradually became clear. James II's main concern was consistently with England, where his aim was to put the small Catholic minority in a sufficiently strong position to ensure its survival after his death. Too many concessions to Irish Catholics could only make that task more difficult, and perhaps even jeopardize the throne itself. The new king gave control of the Irish armed forces to one of his Irish Catholic cronies, Richard Talbot, soon afterwards created earl of Tyrconnell, commissioned a number of other Catholic officers, and ordered the disarming of the Irish militia following Protestant rebellions in England and Scotland in June 1685. The Catholic clergy, secular and regular, were allowed to go about their business wholly without interference. To achieve much more than this, Tyrconnell had to overcome the doubts of the king and the fierce resistance of his principal English advisers. By the first half of 1686 he had managed to get Catholics appointed to the Privy Council and one Catholic judge in each of the three common law courts. In the summer he carried out a radical restructuring of the Irish army, so that Catholics now made up two-thirds of the rank and file and 40 per cent of the officers. By February 1687 Tyrconnell had displaced the Protestant earl of Clarendon as viceroy, permitting further Catholic gains in the various branches of central and local government, in the lawcourts, the bureaucracy, and the army. In August, following a crucial meeting with James at Chester, he began to prepare a revision of the Restoration land settlement, in which Cromwellian and post-Cromwellian grantees would be required to restore one-half of their estates to the former owners. Such a measure would of course need the assent of an Irish parliament. But Tyrconnell had already begun a campaign to pack the city and borough corporations, by whose members the majority of MPs would be chosen, with solid Catholic majorities. Irish Protestants, it seemed, were on the point of losing all they had won in the upheavals of the mid-seventeenth century, and possibly a great deal more.[88]

Catholics responded to the accession of James II with undisguised euphoria. 'The Irish', Clarendon's secretary reported in June 1686, 'talk of nothing now but recovering their lands and bringing the English under their subjection, which they who have been the masters for above 400 years know not how well to bear.'[89] A Munster poet, writing in Irish, left a vivid account of what the Catholicization of the army meant in practice.

> Whither shall John turn? He has now no red coat on him,
> Nor 'Who's there?' on his lips when standing beside the gate.
> 'You Popish rogue' they won't dare to say to us,
> But 'Cromwellian dog' is the watchword we have for him.[90]

In time, however, it was to become clear that the interests of the new king and of these, the most enthusiastic of his subjects, did not always coincide. Early signs that this was so could be detected in the long campaign of court intrigue that Tyrconnell had to fight in order to achieve the power he needed in Ireland, battling both against the influence of English courtiers and against James II's own caution. But the real clash of interests came after James, now deposed in England, came to Ireland in person in March 1689, and two months later met his loyal Irish subjects in parliament in Dublin.

The Dublin parliament of 1689 had been elected by Tyrconnell's re-modelled constituencies. All but 6 of its 230 members were Catholics, about two-thirds Old English, the remainder 'Irish'. As such, it reflected closely the demands of the Catholic élite who were now James's chief supporters.[91] These were twofold: immediate legislation to undo the Restoration land settlement and measures to lessen Ireland's political dependence on Great Britain. James's response on both fronts was deeply disappointing. In the words of the Comte d'Avaux, the French diplomat who accompanied him to Ireland, 'his heart is too English for him to agree to anything that could displease the English. He still counts on being reestablished soon in the kingdom of England, and ... will do nothing to remove Ireland from its dependence on the English.'[92] He reluctantly accepted an act declaring that the English parliament had no right to pass legislation binding on Ireland, but blocked the repeal of Poynings's Law, the most important mechanism by which the proceedings of the Irish parliament were controlled from London. The same reluctance to prejudice his chances of being restored in England led him to oppose any attempt to overthrow the Act of Settlement. In the

[88] J. Miller, 'The Earl of Tyrconnell and James II's Irish Policy'; Simms, *Jacobite Ireland*, ch. 2.
[89] Rycaut to Cooke, 16 July 1686 (Melvin, 'Sir Paul Rycaut's Memoranda', 157).
[90] Ó Bruadair, *Poems*, iii. 97.
[91] Simms, 'The Jacobite Parliament of 1689', in *War and Politics in Ireland*, 65–90.
[92] Quoted in J. Miller, *James II*, 224.

end, the Commons had to threaten to withhold urgently needed financial legislation to extort his consent, and even then he refused demands that he immediately set up a court of claims to hear applications for restoration of confiscated lands. When the Commons went on to produce an Act declaring that over 2,000 named Protestants had forfeited life and property by their rebellion, James infuriated them by his comment: 'What, gentlemen, are you for another "41"?'[93] James II's lowly place in Irish folk history is conventionally linked to his dismal performance after defeat at the Boyne. But the seeds of a progressive disillusionment with Ireland's last Catholic sovereign had been sown much earlier.

The Catholic clergy were also to find the accession of James II something less than an unalloyed triumph. They may initially have revelled in the unaccustomed freedom to discharge their functions without harassment or the need for discretion. Before long, however, their spokesmen had begun to demand much more: the transfer to the Irish Catholic clergy of the lands and ecclesiastical buildings of the Church of Ireland, some sort of established status, and the formal repeal of all anti-Catholic legislation. Instead, they had to be content with a general Act for liberty of conscience and the exemption of non-Anglicans from the obligation to pay tithes to the Church of Ireland. The Acts of Uniformity remained on the statute book. The Church of Ireland not only retained possession of all temporal endowments; it was the Anglican bishops who were summoned to sit in the House of Lords in the parliament of 1689.[94] Meanwhile, the advent of a Catholic sovereign presented novel problems in church–state relations. As early as August 1685 it was said that the Catholic archbishop of Armagh was opposed by a faction among his clergy, who 'have already got the name of Whiggish Papists amongst them', because they took their appeals against the primate's judgements to the king rather than the Pope. James himself was not slow to assert his prerogatives. Archbishop Brenan of Cashel reported in 1691 that a chancery had been established in Dublin several years previously, 'through which the king would confer absolutely all ecclesiastical benefices according to the old system of investiture and regalia that prevailed in France'. To Brenan, at least, this extension to Ireland of practices normal in states ruled by Catholics was wholly unacceptable. He actively resisted the pretensions of two deans appointed by the chancery, one of whom had actually surrendered a papal bull in order to receive the king's presentment instead.[95]

For Irish Protestants the accession of James II meant subjection to a blatant and alarming Catholic triumphalism. As late as the very end of 1683 news that the nearest thing Charles II had to a Protestant heir, his illegitimate son

[93] Quoted in Bagwell, *Ireland under the Stuarts*, iii. 231.
[94] Simms, 'Jacobite Parliament', in *War and Politics*, 76–8.
[95] Archbishop Boyle to Ormond, 25 Aug. 1685 (HMC, *Ormonde Manuscripts*, NS vii. 354–5); Power, *Bishop of the Penal Times*, 98–9.

Monmouth, had been restored to favour had left Catholics downcast and
Protestants jubilant. In the summer of 1685, by contrast, news of Monmouth's
desperate rebellion against James II 'breeds a great deal of ill blood here
between the English and Irish, the latter charging this rebellion upon the
whole body of the English, and telling them that now their turn is come,
and that they will make the English of this country good subjects'.[96] The
disarming of the militia and the mass dismissals of Protestant soldiers were
grave blows to Protestant morale. In late 1686, Catholic soldiers in Dublin
disrupted the traditional Protestant celebrations of 23 October and 5
November, extinguishing bonfires and breaking glass windows in the lord
mayor's house.[97] Two contrasting incidents in the summer of 1686 seemed
further to confirm Protestant fears. Murtagh Magennis, who had stabbed
a Protestant officer after a quarrel, was bailed and taken to England by
Tyrconnell to receive a royal pardon. William Aston, a Protestant who stabbed
and killed a Catholic who he claimed had insulted his wife, was convicted
and hanged. Aston, who was said to have run his unarmed victim through as
he lay on the ground, seems to have deserved little sympathy. But then
Magennis's victim was apparently equally helpless, being held by several of
his attacker's friends.[98] To appreciate the impact of these two episodes on
Protestant opinion, it is important to recognize that the implications went far
beyond considerations of simple fairness. In a society in which gentlemen and
many others went armed and in which self-defence was still primarily a
personal responsibility, partisan justice could put a noose around the neck of
anyone who refused to be a passive victim.

Side by side with this growing insecurity was the steady erosion of
Protestant dominance in local government, the courts, and the civil administration. Sir Paul Rycaut, Clarendon's secretary, was an English royalist
whose political principles initially disposed him to accept without question the
changes in religious policy ordered by the new monarch. 'It is no strange
thing', he commented in July 1686, 'that the king, who is of the same
persuasion, should indulge some privileges to his Roman Catholic subjects,
and to put them in an equal condition with the Protestants.' Only a month
later, however, he was complaining bitterly of the blatant packing of freeholders' lists that had followed the order that Catholics were to be admitted to
corporations. 'But this will not satisfy these reasonable and modest men,
unless every one of that religion, fetched from the most remote parts of the
world, upon his claim and demand be admitted a freeman, which is the first
notion that I ever heard that religion gave any man a title to be made free of a
corporation.'[99] What incidents like these seemed to make clear was that no

---

[96] HMC, *Ormonde Manuscripts*, NS vii. 167; HMC, *Egmont Papers*, ii. 158.
[97] Melvin, 'Rycaut's Memoranda', 172, 175.
[98] HMC, *Egmont Papers*, ii. 185; Bagwell, *Ireland under the Stuarts*, iii. 160–2.
[99] Melvin, 'Rycaut's Memoranda', 160, 166.

compromise was possible between Catholic and Protestant interests. What had begun as an attempt to give Catholics a share in power had rapidly become a drive to replace one exclusive domination by another.

Despite these mounting pressures, Irish Protestants failed to put up any effective resistance to their Catholic monarch. The risings in England and Scotland in 1685, intended to secure a Protestant succession, evoked no response in Ireland. Over the next three years, the transfer of power into Catholic hands proceeded with remarkably little resistance, except for some minor incidents in the summer of 1686, when disbanded Protestant soldiers brawled both with the recruits who had replaced them and with the 'rabble' of the city. Catholics, not surprisingly, remained alert for signs of trouble. In November 1686 rumours of an imminent descent by Ulster Protestants and disbanded soldiers threw the common people of the counties of Westmeath, Longford, and Roscommon into panic, 'and caused them to lie out of their cabins and hide themselves in woods and ditches'. There were also other accounts of treasonable words or suspicious activities. None of these alarms, however, appears to have had much foundation. Instead, the response of the Protestant middle and upper classes to Catholic rule was at most passive resistance. Already by the middle of 1686 there were reports of a collapse of trade, as wealthy Protestants held back from tying up their money in livestock, rented land, or commerce while the future remained so uncertain. There was also a rise in emigration: 'Those who can fly out of the country, either to Pennsylvania, Virginia or other places, hasten away.'[100]

At first sight—when set, for example, against their conduct in late 1659 or during the period when the Restoration land settlement was being finalized— the supine behaviour of Irish Protestants may seem surprising. The lack of regular meetings of parliament, prorogued since 1666, took away the main potential forum for opposition. Some Protestants were undoubtedly restrained by an unwillingness to oppose a legitimate monarch. James Bonnell, a pious Anglican layman who had retained his post in the Irish customs, praised those Protestants remaining in the Irish army who had laid down their arms 'resolving not to fight against their religion nor against their king. We seem to wish that the army had done so in England, rather than deserted; and do not see how any Englishman can oppose the government here, where the king's commission abides in full force.' Even for those who did not share such scruples, there was little point in resisting James II in Ireland, where they were heavily outnumbered by his supporters, as long as he was securely established in Britain. Once James had lost power in England, it became possible for Protestants in Ulster, numerically strong and at a safe distance from Dublin, to declare against him. But elsewhere, little had changed. The Anglican congregation at Cork found itself in danger from the Jacobite

[100] Ibid. 155, 175, 178, 168, 157.

garrison when word got round that it had omitted to pray for the king by name. Protestants who considered opposing Tyrconnell's administration had also to ask themselves what the alternative might be. As early as April 1688, Bonnell believed that, if by any chance the king should die, 'we can expect nothing but a massacre' from the Irish army.[101]

Whether such practical and prudential considerations wholly explain the reaction of Irish Protestants to James II's regime is another matter. There is a curious passage in William King's *State of the Protestants of Ireland*, written just after the Williamite triumph, criticizing James for not having done more to retain the good will of his Protestant subjects, who were initially prepared to believe that he had learned a lesson from his misfortunes in England.[102] Four bishops of the Church of Ireland took their seats in the parliament of 1689, along with five or six Protestant MPs and five lay lords. One of the bishops, Anthony Dopping of Meath, acted as chief spokesman for the Protestant opposition, but he did so in terms that presupposed continued loyalty to James. 'Is it now a time for men to seek for vineyards and olive yards,' he demanded in his speech against the repeal of the Act of Settlement, 'when a civil war is raging in the nation and we are under apprehension of invasions from abroad?'[103] Just over a year later, Dopping was to lead the procession of clergy who went to declare their loyalty to William after his victory at the Boyne; he went on to become a leading opponent of the Treaty of Limerick. Such a career would seem to make him an equivalent of Bishop Henry Jones forty years earlier. And, in this respect at least, the political situation of Irish Protestants had not in fact changed very much. Surrounded by a hostile Catholic majority, they could ill afford the luxury of independent political judgement. Their main concern was rather with the political stability that alone could guarantee them some security. Faced with a well-established structure of authority, however distasteful its proceedings, they would be slow to take action on their own account. If an existing government was seriously challenged, the only rational strategy, given their dependent position, was to protect their interests as seemed best in the short term and in the long run to side with whichever of the contending parties emerged victorious.

A further explanation for the lack of effective resistance to James II may be found in the nature of the threat which Protestants faced. The packing of the army, local government, and the judiciary with Catholics was galling and in some ways alarming. But the long-term political future would depend, not on these reversible appointments, but on the land settlement. Both sides were aware of this. Among the reasons for welcoming Clarendon's appointment in 1685 was the belief that 'he will befriend the settlement of Ireland, which

[101] James Bonnell to Revd J. Strype, 21 Jan. 1689, 10 Nov. 1690, 17 Apr. 1688 (Strype Correspondence, I, fos. 82–3, 84, 78).
[102] King, *State of the Protestants*, 48.
[103] Simms, 'Jacobite Parliament', in *War and Politics*, 72.

was a work that passed while his father was chief minister, and for which the Irish have sufficiently maligned him'.[104] James II's Protestant servants, like Clarendon and Sunderland, worked hard to have him issue a declaration confirming the settlement, as the measure which more than any other would reconcile Protestants in both kingdoms to his rule. The Catholics too appreciated the primacy of the land question. 'Nothing can support Catholic religion in that kingdom', the lawyer Richard Nagle argued in October 1686, 'but to make Catholics there considerable in their fortunes, as they are considerable in their number. For this must be the only inducement that can prevail upon a Protestant successor to allow them a toleration as to their religion, and a protection as to their estates.'[105] Long before the Jacobite parliament met in 1689, it was clear that moves would eventually be made to overturn the Restoration land settlement. But until that moment actually arrived, Protestants could continue to hope that Catholic ascendancy would be a temporary affliction, better ridden out than actively resisted.

There was, of course, a point at which such calculations lost all relevance. It came when Protestants were faced with the immediate prospect of being delivered into the physical control of their Catholic enemies. For the Ulster Protestants who openly declared against James II in late 1688 and early 1689, this in fact turns out to have been the moment of decision. Derry's resistance began on 7 December 1689, when the citizens were faced with the prospect of having a regiment of Irish and Scottish Highlanders quartered among them, to replace soldiers earlier sent to England. Elsewhere in the north-west, Protestants were moved to form defensive associations on learning that commissions had been issued for the raising of several thousand Catholic soldiers with no provision for their support. Instead, they were 'all to be maintained at the expense of their officers (who were not able to support themselves) for the space of three months'. William King also emphasized the essentially defensive character of the initial Protestant mobilization, provoked by the upsurge in robberies and the raising of troops who could have no means to support themselves except plunder.[106]

Between 1689 and 1691 Ireland was one centre of a major European conflict. Irish, English, French, Dutch, German, and Danish troops confronted one another in a series of engagements. In terms of Irish history, the Williamite victories at the Boyne (July 1690) and Aughrim (July 1691) and the eventual surrender, on terms, of the Jacobites in October 1691 are often presented as a major turning-point, marking the final victory of Protestant over Catholic. Such an interpretation is difficult to sustain. By 1691, Protestants had for forty years been the unchallenged rulers of Irish society. Their power

---

[104] Southwell to Perceval, 3 Sept. 1685 (HMC, *Egmont Papers*, ii. 161).
[105] Nagle to Tyrconnell, 26 Oct. 1686 (HMC, *Ormonde Manuscripts*, NS vii. 464–5).
[106] Walker, *Siege of Londonderry*, 13; King, *State of the Protestants*, 114–19.

was based partly on religious discrimination, but mainly on their ownership of some four-fifths of the country's land and on control of the greater part of its trade. Protestant opponents of James II's religious policies were genuinely outraged, not just by his promotion of Popery but by what they saw as the removal of power from the hands of the natural rulers of society.

What struggle exact really about for this group.

One that a few days before was no other than a cowherd to his Protestant landlord, perhaps was set above him on the bench as a justice of the peace; and preferred to command as captain in the field, or a deputy lieutenant in the county.... Twas intolerable to [Protestants] to live under the government of their footmen and servants, which many must have done.[107]

This of course was polemical exaggeration. But in 1686 even the loyal Sir Paul Rycaut was worried that 'there will be some more than ordinary difficulty to find out men of that nation [i.e. Catholics] either of sufficient parts, learning or estates' to take the office of justice of the peace.[108] What James II and his Irish allies were attempting was to reverse a progressive transfer of power and property that had begun in the sixteenth century and had been largely completed by 1660. Their aim was counter-revolution, and the Williamite victories of 1690–1 were less the triumph of a new order than the re-establishment of one that had already existed for more than thirty years.

---

[107] King, *State of the Protestants*, 29, 92.
[108] Melvin, 'Rycaut's Memoranda', 153.

An Élite and its World

Let us turn from events to context. This chapter seeks to describe some of the main features of the world in which the events just described and the continuing political, religious, and social conflicts that will be discussed in the chapters that follow took place. It begins with a short account, descriptive and then interpretative, of the economic system. Next it discusses the question, by no means as straightforward as appears at first sight, of who exactly made up the ruling élite of early and mid-eighteenth-century Ireland. Finally there is an attempt, brief but necessary, to account for some of the distinctive features of the social and cultural life of that élite. The other half of the picture, the relationship between the governing class and other ethnic, religious, and social groups within Irish society, will be explored in a later chapter.

1. Uneven Development

Ireland in the late seventeenth and early eighteenth centuries was a society poised between two economic worlds. The seventeenth century, and in particular the thirty years or so following the Restoration, had seen a marked broadening of the country's economic base. It was only from the 1750s, however, that a second, dramatic phase of economic expansion, continuing into the early nineteenth century, completed the transformation of both town and countryside. Up to that point, the dominant characteristics of the Irish economy remained those of underdevelopment: a pattern of trade in which imports of manufactured goods were paid for by the export of a narrow range of basic products, a sparse population, recurrent subsistence crises, and widespread poverty.

Underdevelopment was most immediately obvious in the appearance of the landscape. The woods which had earlier covered a large part of the country-side had by the late seventeenth century been drastically reduced. The only substantial areas of forest remaining were some parts of Ulster and the south-west, where problems of transport made commercial exploitation less attractive. But there were nevertheless substantial trackless areas, where outsiders ventured only with difficulty. The Whig lawyer Alan Brodrick, travelling from Cork to Tralee for the autumn assizes in 1704, recorded that his party had had to cross eight miles of mountain on horseback with only a succession of posts set in the ground at intervals to mark out a path between areas of bog. Wolves, extinct in England since around 1500, survived in parts of Ireland for two centuries more. As late as the 1660s they preyed on the sheep belonging to Lord Conway's estate on the County Antrim shore of Lough Neagh. In the south-west, bounties were paid to those who killed them up to around 1710. Some accounts, of doubtful reliability, put the death of the last wolf as late as the 1770s.[1]

Even in less remote parts of the country, the condition of the landscape varied sharply. Areas of intensive cultivation alternated with stretches of common and waste, as patterns of settlement, the natural fertility of the soil, or the strength of market demand dictated. John Stevens, marching out of Limerick city into County Clare with the Jacobite army in 1691, found the countryside 'all very bare, there being in this way scarce any corn or meadow, but only a hilly common in some places boggy, everywhere covered with fern and rushes, which is all it produces'. Yet later, coming back into the city from a different direction, they passed through 'lanes, cornfields and meadows on both sides, all enclosed as in England'.[2] In the first half of the eighteenth century, visitors continued to comment on the lack of cultivation and the absence of enclosures. Samuel Molyneux, travelling through County Kildare in 1709, found 'the lands generally meadow; some corn, with very ill enclosures, and no hedges'. In County Westmeath, 'as we went further from Dublin, no enclosures or trees to be seen, but little scrubs in the bogs here and there'. County Tipperary, in 1717, was 'open country ... where you seldom have fences or hedges for bounds'. In some cases the absence of enclosures meant simply that holdings were not marked off from each other by the hedgerows and fences common in England; Molyneux, for example, commented elsewhere on the frequency of stone walls. Sir Henry Piers, writing of Westmeath in 1682, referred contemptuously to the manner in which a local farmer would fence his corn 'slightly and without any manner of quick ... if at any time he makes a fence likely to hold out a whole year, he triumphs, and with confidence pronounceth it a year's ditch, which among them passeth for a very strong fence'. In other cases there were in fact no physical boundaries. In the barony of Ards in County Down in 1744, 'they have no fences ... but to preserve their corn from trespass they fold their cattle within enclosures raised of sods'.[3] In still other cases the absence of enclosure marked the survival of open-field farming, with each tenant working

---

[1] E. McCracken, *Irish Woods*, 54–6, 112; Alan Brodrick to St John Brodrick, 7 Sept. [1704] (Midleton MS 1248/2, fo. 146); Sir George Rawdon to Viscount Conway, 3 Sept., 6 Oct. 1665 (*CSPD 1663–5*, 637, 649); Fairley, *An Irish Beast Book*, 180–7.

[2] Stevens, *Journal*, 152, 163.

[3] Molyneux, 'Journey to Connaught', 161–2, 164; Midleton to Thomas Brodrick, 30 Mar. 1717 (Midleton MS 1248/3, fo. 417); Piers, *County of Westmeath*, 59–60; P. S. Robinson, 'Spread of Hedged Enclosure', 59.

strips distributed across a single large tract of arable land and sharing access to a substantial area of common grazing.[4]

The absence of intensive cultivation was directly linked to the thinness of population. According to the latest estimates, the population of Ireland was somewhere close to 2 million in the late 1680s, had perhaps not increased at all by 1706, and was only slightly higher in the early 1740s (see Table 2.1). Contemporaries had no doubt that Ireland was seriously underpopulated. 'The country of Ireland', Mrs Delany noted in 1732, 'has no fault but want of inhabitants to cultivate it.' According to Charles Smith, writing in 1746, 'this kingdom is not above a fourth part peopled'. The lord chief justice reported in 1726 that 'some parts of the north are very well cultivated, but the southern parts are very thinly inhabited, and scarce a tree or hedge to be seen for twenty miles together'. As late as the early 1760s, in fact, Judge Edward Willes, a regular traveller on the different legal circuits, reported that 'the country in general, except in large trading towns, is very thinly inhabited'.[5]

Underdevelopment was equally, if not so immediately, obvious in the character of the country's towns. Urban life in Ireland, as in most pre-industrialized societies, was dominated by a single administrative and commercial centre. Dublin was, by any standards, a major European city. During the late seventeenth and early eighteenth centuries, when national population

TABLE 2.1. Estimates of Irish population, 1687–1821

Year	Population (millions)
1687	1.97
1706	1.75–2.06
1712	1.98–2.32
1725	2.18–2.56
1732	2.16–2.53
1744	1.91–2.23
1749	1.95–2.28
1753	2.20–2.57
1791	4.42
1821	6.80

Source: Dickson *et al.*, 'Hearth Tax, Household Size and Irish Population Change', 156.

---

[4] The whole question of open-field and partnership farming is a complex one. Understanding is not helped by the undeclared war between economic historians and a school of Ulster-based geographers. For a brief review of the problems, see J. H. Andrews in *NHI* iv. 241–5.

[5] Delany, *Autobiography and Correspondence*, i. 352; Smith, *Antient and Present State of Waterford*, ix; Thomas Wyndham to Robert Pitt, 8 Feb. 1726 (HMC, *Fortescue Manuscripts*, i. 75); Willes, in Crawford and Trainor (eds.), *Aspects of Irish Social History*, 2.

was stagnant or only slowly expanding, the city grew spectacularly, from 45,000 inhabitants in 1685 to 92,000 in 1725. By 1744 Dublin's population had risen to 112,000, making it Europe's eleventh largest city.[6] Growing size and wealth were gradually reflected in improved physical appearance. Sir Cyril Wyche, returning to Ireland after five years' absence in 1700, was told that a house available for rent 'looks fairly enough to the street for a Dublin house, though we are much improved here in sash windows and other ornaments of building since your honour left us'. Over the next four decades some new streets of élite housing were laid out. By the 1720s the creation of Dawson, Molesworth, Duke, and Anne Streets had filled in much of the space between Trinity College and St Stephen's Green, while the construction around 1730 of Henrietta Street marked the beginnings of what was to be a major expansion to the north-east. The same period saw the completion of major public buildings: the new parliament house on College Green in 1729, the Linen Hall on the northern outskirts of the city in 1728, and the Library in Trinity College in 1732. Yet the physical transformation of the city was a gradual process. Mrs Delany, making her first visit in 1731, was impressed by the public amenities. The Phoenix Park was 'far beyond St James's or Hyde Park', while St Stephen's Green 'I think... may be preferred justly to any square in London'. At the same time she found the town 'bad enough, narrow streets and dirty-looking houses, but some very good ones scattered about'. It was not until the middle and later decades of the century, when the pace of public and private construction quickened, and the Wide Streets Commissioners began to lay down a pattern of broad, straight thoroughfares and spacious squares, superimposed like a stencil on the existing network of crooked narrow streets, that the Tudor and Stuart city was finally transformed into Georgian Dublin.[7]

Dublin's importance and growth were in part a result of its political and social dominance. After 1692, meetings of the Irish parliament became much more frequent, eventually settling down to a regular session of five to eight months' duration every second year. The necessary residence of the lord lieutenant added a social dimension to these occasions. Even when parliament was not sitting, Dublin remained the centre of government and administration and also the scene of an increasingly highly developed winter season, which brought aristocracy and gentry crowding into the city for a round of social and cultural events.[8] But Dublin's dominance also had an economic foundation.

[6] Dickson, 'The Place of Dublin in the Eighteenth-Century Irish Economy', 179; Hohenberg and Lees, *The Making of Urban Europe*, 227.

[7] Christopher O'Bryan to Wyche, 25 Apr. 1700 (Wyche Papers, 1/1/172); Delany, *Autobiography and Correspondence*, i. 294, 300. This account of Dublin owes a great deal to the pioneering work of David Dickson and his students. See Dickson, 'The Place of Dublin', and Dickson (ed.), *The Gorgeous Mask*. See also Cullen, *Princes and Pirates*, ch. 1.

[8] Tighernan Mooney and Fiona White, 'The Gentry's Winter Season', in Dickson (ed.), *The Gorgeous Mask*, 1–16.

The city was a major centre of manufacturing industry. Well over half the sugar consumed in Ireland was refined in Dublin, and there was also a substantial work-force engaged in silk and wool production, textile printing, and the manufacture of luxury goods. In addition, Dublin dominated foreign trade, accounting for more than half the shipping entering Irish ports and half the country's customs receipts. Perhaps the most striking indication of the city's economic primacy was its dominance of the linen industry. In the first half of the eighteenth century, more than three-quarters of Ireland's linen exports, manufactured almost exclusively in east and central Ulster, were shipped through Dublin, 100 miles or more to the south.[9]

What all this meant was that the undoubted grandeur of eighteenth-century Dublin was in sharp contrast to—and indeed to some extent responsible for—the much less developed character of most Irish towns. There were a number of other significant centres: Cork, Waterford, Limerick, and Galway were all major ports, as were the Ulster towns of Belfast, already by 1700 rated as the fourth port in Ireland, and Derry. Cork, by now clearly established as the country's second city, managed, like Dublin, to grow substantially even during the period of national demographic stagnation up to the 1740s. By the mid-eighteenth century it had perhaps 50,000 inhabitants. With this one exception, however, even the second-rank towns were, by international standards, small. Lisburn, with a population of perhaps 4,000 in 1725, was the eighth largest town in Ireland.[10] But it was the minor provincial centres that made the deepest impression on English visitors. John Stevens, in 1690, thought the town of Killaloe in County Clare 'the meanest I ever saw dignified with that character ... it has nothing beyond many villages in England, nor is it equal to some'. The new archbishop of Tuam, in 1752, found the chief town of his diocese 'what you would reckon in England a village of no good appearance ... and yet they tell me the town is in a thriving way, and so I believe it is compared with the other towns I have seen, which in truth are no better than so many nests of filthy cabins inhabited by miserable and half starved creatures some of them scarce with human appearances'.[11]

Such conditions were not confined to the smaller towns. Visitors to Ireland were generally appalled by the poverty they saw all around them. Three-quarters of the Catholic population, Petty claimed in 1672, 'live in a brutish nasty condition, as in cabins, with neither chimney, door, stairs nor window [and] feed chiefly upon milk and potatoes'. 'If you peep into forty cabins,' John Dunton maintained in 1699, 'they are as spacious as our English hogsties, but not so clean; you will scarcely find a woman with a petticoat can touch her knee; and of ten children not one has a shoe to his foot.' Mrs

---

[9] Dickson, 'Place of Dublin', 181–4; Cullen, *Anglo-Irish Trade*, 14–16.

[10] Cullen, *Economic History of Ireland*, 84.

[11] Stevens, *Journal*, 152; John Ryder to Sir Dudley Ryder, 29 May 1752 (PRONI T3228/1/53).

Delany, arriving in Ireland for the first time in 1732, wrote that 'the poverty of the people as I have passed through the country has made my heart ache. I never saw greater appearance of misery.' Berkeley's *Querist*, three years later, enquired 'whether there be upon earth any Christian or civilized people so beggarly, wretched and destitute as the common Irish'. Nor was it only by comparison with the prosperity of England that Ireland appeared unusually poor. Bishop Nicolson of Derry, travelling for the first time through the mountains of south Ulster in the summer of 1718, had 'never beheld, even in Picardy, Westphalia or Scotland, such dismal marks of hunger and want as appeared on the countenances of most of the poor creatures that I met with on the road'. In 1738 George Whitefield, just returned from missionary work in America, observed 'the meanness of the poor people's living' as he passed through County Clare. 'If my parishioners at Georgia complain to me of hardships, I must tell them how the Irish live.'[12]

Poverty was most apparent, to contemporaries at least, in the houses of the common people. Petty estimated that 160,000 out of a total of 200,000 houses 'are wretched nasty cabins, without chimney, window or door shut'. Other accounts of housing were broadly similar: walls made of sods or mud mixed with straw, generally without windows; earthen floors; thatched roofs without chimneys, so that the smoke escaped through the door or else seeped through the thatch, 'so that you would think the cabin were on fire'.[13] As late as 1753 it was claimed that people frequently pulled down such simple constructions when the hearth-tax collector approached, rebuilding after he had left.[14] Furnishing was sparse. The better sort of cabins, John Stevens noted, commonly had one flock-bed, for the head of the household and his wife, other members of the family sleeping on straw spread on the floor. A County Kerry cottier who claimed in 1692 to have been robbed of his whole 'worldly substance' itemized his losses: '8 goats, 45 gallons of potatoes, 7 gallons of meal, 2 do. of groats, 4 pecks of oats, one iron pot containing 7 gallons, one hatchet, one spade, one reap hook, and $4\frac{1}{2}$ lb. of wool and yarn'.[15]

Evidence regarding other aspects of living conditions is less clear-cut. Petty noted that the poorer classes, though wretchedly housed, had clothing 'far better than that of the French peasants, or the poor of most other countries', because of the cheapness and abundance of wool. Early eighteenth-century

---

[12] Petty, *Political Anatomy*, 27; Dunton, 'Conversations in Ireland', in *Life and Errors*, ii. 615–16; Delany, *Autobiography and Correspondence*, i. 353; J. Johnston, *Bishop Berkeley's Querist*, 136; Nicolson to Wake, 24 June 1718 (Gilbert MS 27, 179); Whitefield, *Journals*, 180.

[13] Petty, *Political Anatomy*, 116–17; Dunton, *Letters*, in MacLysaght, *Irish Life*, 356. See also idem, *Life and Errors*, ii. 606; [Madden], *Reflections and Resolutions*, 34–5.

[14] Diary of Nathaniel Ryder, 25 July 1753, recording a conversation with his father, Sir Dudley Ryder (PRONI T3228/2/1). The same claim had been made the previous year by Pococke (*Tour*, 55), but this was not published at the time.

[15] Stevens, *Journal*, 139; Hickson, *Old Kerry Records*, 119.

observers, by contrast, repeatedly referred to rags and semi-nudity.[16] Tobacco had by the second half of the seventeenth century become firmly established as the main luxury of the Irish lower classes. Yet here too the impression is of a scarce commodity greatly prized. According to Stevens, 'a pipe an inch long serves the whole family several years, and though never so black or foul is never suffered to be burnt. Seven or eight will gather to the smoking of a pipe and each taking two or three whiffs gives it to his neighbour, commonly holding his mouth full of smoke till the pipe comes about to him again.'[17] Petty's comment on the widespread ownership of horses—'every man now keeping a small garran to ride on'—has been interpreted as evidence of modest prosperity. It can equally be seen, however, as a by-product of economic underdevelopment, reflecting the abundance of free or cheap grazing and the limited demand for draught animals. A report in 1665 noted that Ireland had a surplus of horses, some of which were exported 'and many more which we kill as being neither worth their grass to keep nor freight and custom to send abroad'.[18]

Contemporaries generally believed that the common people were poorly fed. According to the Anglican bishop of Meath, writing in 1697, 'the Irish, especially the poorer part of them, make little or no consumption of corn, but live wholly upon potatoes'. The most recent study of diet argues strongly that such comments should not be taken at face value, as reflecting the total dependence on the potato that was to be common among the poorer classes by the early nineteenth century. The varieties of potato in use at this period did not keep well enough to permit the use of the potato as an all-year-round food. Instead, it was combined with the cheaper grains and with large quantities of dairy produce.[19] A survey of County Kildare in 1683 describes a 'very mean and sparing' diet consisting of 'milk, roots and coarse, unsavoury bread'. Stevens, a few years later, also noted the high consumption of milk, 'which they eat and drink above twenty several sorts of ways'. Otherwise the main foods were oats and barley, coarsely ground by hand and cooked in flat cakes rather than baked as loaves in an oven. 'The meaner people', meanwhile, 'content themselves with little bread but instead thereof eat potatoes, which with sour milk is the chief part of their diet, their drink for the most part water, sometimes coloured with milk.'[20]

In addition to a generally low level of diet, housing, and overall consumption, the population remained vulnerable throughout this period to periodic

[16] Petty, *Political Anatomy*, 81; Stevens, *Journal*, 139; Nicolson to Wake, 24 June 1718 (Gilbert MS 27, 179); [Madden], *Reflections and Resolutions*, 34–5.

[17] Stevens, *Journal*, 139.

[18] Petty, *Political Anatomy*, 41, 56; Cullen in *NHI* iii. 401; *CSPI 1663–5*, 693.

[19] Brady, 'Remedies Proposed for the Church of Ireland, 1697', 166; Cullen, *Emergence of Modern Ireland*, 144–6.

[20] MacLysaght, *Irish Life*, 315; Stevens, *Journal*, 139.

crises of subsistence. The thirty years after 1660 were marked by recurrent hard seasons. In at least one of these, 1674, dearth turned into famine. A wet autumn the previous year had cut grain stocks, while freezing weather prevented spring sowing. Cattle, sheep, and horses died in their thousands. By June 1674, according to Oliver Plunkett, 'you can see hundreds and hundreds of starved skeletons, rather than men, walking the roads'. By September more than 500 inhabitants of the diocese of Armagh had died of hunger.[21] The three decades following the Williamite war were relatively free of such disasters. Harvest failure in 1708–9 brought some hardship in Munster, but nothing on the scale seen in continental Europe. The 1720s, on the other hand, brought the beginnings of a series of crises. In 1721–2 poor harvests, combined with the economic depression precipitated by the collapse of the South Sea Company, brought spectacular hardship. William Nicolson, who had come from England to the see of Derry three years before, was shaken by what he saw:

One of my coach horses, by accident, was killed in a field within view of my house. Before the skin could be taken off, my servants were surrounded with 50 or 60 of the neighbouring cottagers, who brought axes and cleavers, and immediately divided the carcass, every man carrying home his proper dividend for food to their respective families.[22]

Worse was to follow. The late 1720s brought a succession of bad harvests; estimates suggest that population was actually slightly lower in 1732 than it had been seven years before.[23] Then, during 1739–40, a sequence of a wet summer, a winter frost, and a summer drought destroyed both grain and potato crops, causing the most serious demographic crisis of the eighteenth century. An estimated 13 per cent of the population died of fever and starvation. In Munster, where the crisis was concentrated, the proportion may have been as high as one-fifth.[24] Ulster, which escaped comparatively lightly in 1739–41, bore the brunt of a second, though less serious, crisis in 1744–5, when crop failure and mortality among livestock pushed up death rates among both adults and children.

How are conditions of this kind to be accounted for? The central issue is that which confronts the historian of poverty in other regions of pre-industrialized Europe. Were hardship, deprivation, and recurrent subsistence crises the inevitable consequence of a 'society of scarcity', in which technological backwardness meant that there were simply not enough resources to go round? Or

---

[21] Plunkett, *Letters*, 404, 407, 410, 414, 416, 428.
[22] Nicolson to Wake, 2 June 1721 (Gilbert MS 27, 287).
[23] Dickson *et al.*, 'Hearth Tax, Household Size and Population Change 1672–1821', 164. Large-scale emigration from Ulster to America, beginning *c.*1717, was also a factor here.
[24] Ibid. 165–8; Drake, 'The Irish Demographic Crisis of 1741'.

is it also necessary to look at the role of political relationships, both within and beyond the society in question?[25]

Contemporary explanations of the poverty of Ireland tended to focus first of all on the shortcomings of the country's agriculture. One frequent complaint concerned the extension of pasture at the expense of tillage. In fact, climate and topography had always made Ireland more suitable for pasture. Even at the beginning of the eighteenth century, cattle and cattle products accounted for more than 50 per cent of exports, sheep and sheep products for another 30 per cent. A further shift towards pasture in the early decades of the eighteenth century undoubtedly brought hardship to smallholders in some regions. But the central contention, that neglect of tillage left Ireland vulnerable to recurrent famine, was unfounded. Tillage continued in the areas best suited to it, for example in Leinster counties like Louth, Meath, Kilkenny, and Wexford, on a sufficient scale to meet the greater part of the country's needs.[26] Contemporary critics were on stronger ground when they lamented the technical backwardness of Irish agriculture. Lord Molesworth, in 1723, bemoaned the absence of

the English customs in the make and fashion of their ploughs, harrows, plough gear, carts, tumbrils, wains and wagons in their broad ridges, ploughing with oxen, drains, beast houses, hovels, stand racks, folds in their way of laying down land to grass, even folding of sheep in pens upon their corn lands, and forty other things necessary to the good management of our farms.[27]

Nine years later, Samuel Madden complained in similar terms of inferior ploughing equipment and techniques, failure to manure, inefficient harrows, and the use of hooks instead of scythes in harvesting.[28] Some recent studies have argued that such criticisms, based as they were on the assumption that the most advanced English practice was automatically the best, failed to take into account specific Irish conditions. The reaping hook, for example, lost less grain than the scythe, and was better suited for work on uneven ground and where crops had often been flattened or twisted by rain and wind. Even ploughing by the tail, generally presented as the epitome of Irish agricultural primitiveness, was a sensible way of restraining an animal as it negotiated stony soil.[29] But all such arguments for the effectiveness of traditional Irish techniques tend to rest on certain key assumptions: that the soil was only crudely worked and that labour was the most plentiful resource. Irish farming

---

[25] Lis and Soly, *Poverty and Capitalism in Pre-Industrial Europe*, xi–xvi.

[26] Cullen, *Economic History*, 67–70. For resistance to the spread of pasture, see Connolly, 'The Houghers'. For the economic development of County Sligo, see O'Hara's Account of County Sligo (NLI MS 20,397).

[27] [Molesworth], *Some Considerations for the Promoting of Agriculture*, 21.

[28] [Madden], *Reflections and Resolutions*, 130–2.

[29] Bell, 'Improvement of Irish Farming Techniques'; Gillespie, 'Migration and Opportunity', 93.

practices, in other words, were more rational than was often supposed. But their rationality was that of a poor, underdeveloped society.

Behind this technical backwardness lay an agrarian system dominated by fragmented and undercapitalized holdings. There were some areas where this was not so. In Kilkenny in the late 1740s, for example, wheat was raised on farms of from 40 to 100 acres. But these were the exception. 'In a great part of this kingdom,' it was noted in 1728, 'the bulk of the farmers have but four, six, eight or ten acres, and a farmer of 20 acres is a great farmer.'[30] In some cases the solution to the dearth of solvent tenants with capital was to lease land in large blocks to middlemen, who then sublet to smallholders. In others, smallholders themselves took a substantial holding in partnership, 'four or five to a plough land of 100 acres, but they subdivide down to five or six acres'.[31] In either case the result was to put the bulk of agricultural production in the hands of a peasantry living close to subsistence level. John Dunton, in 1699, recorded his impression of the typical rural household:

Behind one of their cabins lies the garden, a piece of ground sometimes of half an acre, and in this is the turf stack, their corn, perhaps two or three hundred sheaves of oats, and as much peas. The rest of the ground is full of their dearly beloved potatoes, and a few cabbages which the solitary calf of the family that is here pent from its dam never suffers to come to perfection.[32]

Along with the deficiencies of agriculture, contemporaries commented on the weakness of Irish manufacturing industry. 'In general,' a report in 1665 noted, 'it may be observed that manufacture thrives very little in Ireland, we exporting so little wrought commodities, so much unwrought.' Charles Smith, eighty years later, made essentially the same point: the chief exports of most parts of Ireland, such as beef, butter, corn, and worsted yarn, were 'the natural growth of the country' in an unfinished or semi-finished state, so that great quantities had to be exchanged for 'small parcels of goods completely wrought'.[33] Pamphleteers and orators bemoaned their contemporaries' preference for imported, particularly English, manufactured goods. Yet the central problem was not one of fashion or lack of patriotism. Where luxury goods, such as glass or the finer fabrics, were concerned, the circle of élite consumers was too small to support a strong local industry. In other cases the difficulty was lack of raw materials. During the seventeenth century abundant supplies of timber had allowed Ireland to become a net exporter of iron. Once the forests had receded, however, iron smelting became rare in a country without its own ore. Dependence on imported coal further limited the

---

[30] William Colles to Thomas Carter, 14 Oct. 1747 (Prim MS 87, 18); Boulter, *Letters*, i. 214.
[31] Young, *Tour*, i. 234.
[32] Dunton, in MacLysaght, *Irish Life*, 356.
[33] 'Some observations upon the commodities of Ireland', 25 Dec. 1665 (*CSPI 1663–5*, 693); Smith, *Waterford*, 279.

possibilities for manufacture, particularly in inland towns. Greater opportunities existed in the processing of agricultural produce for a mass market. Brewing and flour milling were two of the better established Irish industries of the early eighteenth century. Even here, however, there were signs of undercapitalization and technical backwardness. Irish beer was both expensive and of notoriously poor quality, while rising imports of flour in the 1740s and 1750s testified to a failure to keep pace with the rapidly advancing milling technology of Great Britain.[34]

Ireland's main manufacturing industry in the second half of the seventeenth century was wool. Exports of frieze, the coarse woollen cloth worn in Ireland itself, rose significantly between the 1660s and the 1680s, while over the same period the country also began to export growing quantities of higher-quality 'new draperies'. The prohibition in 1699 on exports of wool or woollen cloth to any country except England, from which Irish woollens were already excluded by heavy import duties, cut off this rising export trade. Yet wool remained a major local industry, supplying the domestic market. The manufacture of woollen cloth was concentrated in a group of towns in Leinster and Munster, for which it provided a more secure economic base than that enjoyed by most Irish centres. In 1746, for example, it was noted that Carrick-on-Suir in County Waterford

has been for many years famous for the making of ratteens, a woollen manufactury ... which that town has brought to a great perfection, so as to make them equal to the finest of cloth.... It is incredible what numbers are employed in that little town in this manufactury, men, women and children finding sufficient work.[35]

Yet wool was also a major rural manufacture, with tens of thousands of women engaged in spinning woollen and worsted yarn. Some of this went to supply local weavers. The rest was sent to Great Britain, where sales of Irish yarn, already substantial in the first four decades of the century, soared to new levels in the thirty years after the import duty was removed in 1739.[36]

During the first decades of the eighteenth century, wool, while remaining a substantial manufacture, increasingly took second place to linen. Linen spinning and weaving, established in the Lagan valley from the 1660s, grew rapidly from the 1690s. Exports rose from 300,000 yards in 1700 to 1.7 million by 1710, 6.6 million by 1740, and more than 11 million ten years later.[37] By 1729 it was claimed that linen manufacture was well established in the equivalent of ten out of the thirty-two Irish counties: spinning and

---

[34] Malcolm, *'Ireland Sober, Ireland Free'*, 24–5; Cullen, 'Eighteenth-Century Flour Milling in Ireland', 8.

[35] Smith, *Waterford*, 281.

[36] Dickson, *New Foundations*, 124–5; Cullen, *Anglo-Irish Trade*, 35–6, 55–8.

[37] Cullen, *Anglo-Irish Trade*, 60. These figures are based on the English customs records; the exports recorded at the Irish end were 5–10% higher (ibid. 59).

weaving in Antrim, Down, Armagh, Tyrone, and Derry; spinning only in Donegal, Monaghan, and Cavan; and as much spinning and weaving else- where as might add up to the population of a further two counties.[38] In the eastern counties of Ulster, where weaving was most strongly established, linen increasingly replaced agriculture as the principal support of a growing section of the population. Already by 1708 a landlord in Ballyclare, County Antrim, was warned that 'the poor people's rent' on his estate 'depends on their cloth'. By the 1730s the region was becoming heavily dependent on imports of food from south Ulster.[39] The western counties remained self-sufficient in food, but there too, spinning, with a lesser amount of weaving, became central to the local economy. In 1720 the trade of Derry city had been brought to a standstill by the recession in Manchester, 'whence we used to have an annual demand for all the yarn we could spin'. In County Donegal it was reported in 1739 that the typical farmer 'generally contents himself with no more land than is necessary to feed his family, which he diligently tills, and depends on the industry of his wife and daughters to pay by their spinning the rent, and lay up riches'.[40]

The spectacular expansion of the linen industry was the most conspicuous economic development of the first half of the eighteenth century. But it was not the only one. Agriculture, whatever its failings, managed to sustain a slow but steady growth in exports, as Ireland benefited from the growing demand for provisions both from the French and British colonies of the West Indies and from transatlantic shipping. Exports of cattle and beef in the second half of the 1730s were 87 per cent higher than they had been at the start of the century. There had also been some growth in pig and butter exports.[41] All this was achieved by a variety of means. The piecemeal process of enclosure, drainage, and reclamation gradually increased productivity. Equally important was the growth in regional specialization: an increasingly clear distinction between areas of poor or medium-quality pasture, where young cattle were reared; the best grassland, where they could be fattened; and areas devoted more to tillage. In the greater part of County Sligo, for example, demand for cattle from the graziers of Munster led to a rapid expansion from around 1720 in stock raising and a decline in small-scale tillage. In the more fertile valleys, on the other hand, wheat, oats, and barley continued to be grown for the surrounding counties; the single barony of Tireragh was described in 1739 as 'a granary for the counties of Leitrim and Fermanagh', both overwhelmingly

---

[38] Dobbs, *Essay on Trade*, i. 32–3.

[39] James Hutchinson to Agmondisham Vesey, 16 Mar. 1708 (Sarsfield-Vesey Papers, 88); Crawford, 'Economy and Society in South Ulster', 244–5.

[40] Nicolson to Wake, 6 Dec. 1720 (Gilbert MS 27, 270); Henry, 'Hints' (Nat. Arch. Ire. MS 2533, 69).

[41] Crotty, *Irish Agricultural Production*, 276–7; Cullen, *Anglo-Irish Trade*, 60; idem, *Economic History*, 54.

devoted to grazing. The growth of fairs and markets was further evidence of the division of rural Ireland into interlocking regions.[42]

The combined effect of growth in linen and agriculture was significant: total exports in 1740 were 50 per cent higher than they had been in 1700.[43] This expansion in trade brought developments in infrastructure. Banking services improved rapidly, especially in the 1720s. Roads were improved and extended, especially after the introduction of turnpiking in the early 1730s. Stage-coach services gradually came to link the major towns. The Newry canal, cut between 1731 and 1742, was the first major waterway of its kind in the British Isles. Designed to bring coal from County Tyrone to Dublin, its main importance was in practice to open up central Ulster to wider markets. Meanwhile the physical fabric of Georgian Ireland as we know it today was gradually beginning to take shape, as the first landlords rebuilt their country houses along new and more ambitious lines, planted trees, and laid out parks and formal gardens. Already by the early 1740s Sir Richard Cox could assure two English visitors that 'if a person could but rise from the dead, who was entombed forty years, he would not know the spot where he was born, or his surrounding neighbourhood, for the face of nature, with the help of art, had entirely altered every feature'.[44]

All this brings us back to the problem of identifying the underlying causes of the poverty that so shocked observers of early eighteenth-century Ireland. Low productivity, in both agriculture and manufacturing, was clearly part of the problem. But it cannot have been the whole story. For this was not a conventional underdeveloped economy. Ireland's capital was one of the major cities of Europe. It had a significant and growing manufacturing sector, an increasingly sophisticated infrastructure, and a market-oriented agriculture. Yet none of these seemed to be reflected in the living standards of the great majority of its inhabitants. In fact, the Ireland of the 1720s and the 1740s, with a population only slightly higher than it had been in the reign of Charles II, was if anything more vulnerable to recurrent crises of subsistence. Two or three years before Sir Richard Cox's proud boasts, one-eighth or so of the population had died of fever and starvation. Other explanations, besides mere scarcity of resources, are clearly needed.

To see what these may be, it is necessary to look again at the general character of Irish economic development in the late seventeenth and early eighteenth centuries. Recent accounts have emphasized the rapid commercialization of the Irish economy during this period, a development

---

[42] O'Hara's Account of County Sligo (NLI MS 20,397); Henry, 'Hints' (Nat. Arch. Ire. MS 2533), 9; O'Flanagan, 'Settlement Development and Trade in Ireland', in Devine and Dickson (eds.), *Ireland and Scotland*, 147.

[43] Cullen, *Economic History*, 54.

[44] [Chetwood], *Tour through Ireland*, 98.

reflected in growing regional specialization, in the multiplication of fairs and markets, and in improvements in roads and banking.[45] But it is also important to notice that this commercialization rested on a narrow base. Geographical proximity and political subordination alike ensured that Ireland's economic development was closely directed towards the needs of the larger, better endowed, and more developed English economy. Commercialization thus rested on a growing export trade, largely though not exclusively directed towards England and its overseas possessions, rather than on an increase in the circulation of goods and services within the national economy. Already by the beginning of the eighteenth century, Irish exports have been estimated at around 6s. per head, compared with 4s. in the otherwise very similar economy of contemporary Scotland.[46] The needs to be met by the export trade, moreover, were highly specialized. The twin pillars of the Irish economy in the early and mid-eighteenth century were linen and cattle products, between them accounting consistently for more than four-fifths of the country's exports.[47] This narrow focus on the export of two staple products helps to explain the peculiarly uneven nature of Ireland's economic growth, with increasing sophistication in some areas coinciding with continued backwardness in others.

The second point that needs to be made regarding the commercialization of the Irish economy is its impact on the rural poor. The day-to-day transactions of this section of the population continued to take place largely within the framework of a barter-oriented subsistence economy. The great majority of occupiers, it was claimed in 1753, lived off the produce of their holdings, 'without perhaps touching a piece of money from year's end to year's end. They pay their rent in stock or else in labour.'[48] Yet the demands of an increasingly sophisticated market economy nevertheless reached deep into their lives. The extent to which this was so is vividly illustrated in Cullen's account of the dietary revolution that took place in the late seventeenth and early eighteenth centuries, as dairy products, which had acquired a commercial value, were replaced as the chief food of the rural lower classes by the less marketable potato.[49] In other respects too, surplus agricultural production, over and above what was needed for subsistence, was diverted to domestic and even more to export markets. 'The bulk of the people in Ireland', the Speaker of the Irish Commons observed in 1747, 'live so mis-

---

[45] See the discussion in Dickson and Devine (eds.), *Ireland and Scotland*, 265–6.

[46] Cullen and Smout (eds.), *Comparative Aspects*, 4.

[47] Dickson, *New Foundations*, 101.

[48] PRONI T3228/2/1 (see above, n. 14). As late as 1773 a visitor to Dawson Grove in County Monaghan noted that the outgoings of Lord Dartrey's residence there accounted for 'nearly all the hard money expended in the neighbourhood. The traffic of life is here chiefly carried on by exchange.' Burrows Tour (PRONI T3551), 54.

[49] Cullen, *Emergence of Modern Ireland*, 141–9.

erably that no two million of people besides of any country in Europe con-
sume so little of the commodities which they raise themselves.'[50]

Why did commercialization have these effects? One possible answer is
suggested by recent studies that have emphasized the limits which custom and
tradition imposed on the scope of landlord exploitation in pre-industrialized
Europe. Customary tenure, restricting the rents that could be charged for a
holding and ensuring its transmission to the next generation on payment of a
fixed fine, protected the small tenant from the full impact of market forces.
Use rights such as gleaning, access to commons, and entitlements to collect
wood or to take certain types of small game guaranteed the local poor some
share in the fruits of local agriculture.[51] In Ireland, such conventions seem to
have played little part in the economy of the countryside. An English judge,
writing in the 1750s, commented with surprise on the freedom of landlords
to seek the maximum possible rent for their lands, even by treating simultaneously with several potential tenants.[52] In the same way, customary entitlements of any kind, from access to common land to gleaning and similar
practices, are conspicuous by their absence, both in accounts of day-to-day
rural life and—even more revealingly—in the agrarian conflict that recurred
decade after decade from the 1760s.[53] Both sets of circumstances can be
explained in terms of the radical redefinition of property rights that took
place in the sixteenth and seventeenth centuries. What was important was
not, as is often assumed, the replacement of one set of proprietors by another.
The example of Highland Scotland should be enough to cast doubt on the
assumption that an indigenous landed élite would somehow have been less
responsive to the pressures and allurements of a more market-oriented
agrarian economy.[54] The point is rather the fracturing of that continuity on
which custom, by definition, depends. As a result, the rural lower classes
became subject to the same broad body of property law as in England, but
with none of the multiple accretions of use rights and customary entitlements
that offered the population there and elsewhere a measure of protection from
the pressures of a rapidly developing market economy.

The poverty that observers saw almost everywhere in early eighteenth-
century Ireland thus had a multiplicity of causes. Technical backwardness,
both in agriculture and in most areas of manufacturing, meant that overall
levels of wealth were low. Proximity, physical and political, to Great Britain

---

[50] 'Observations' in the handwriting of Henry Boyle, *c.*1747 (PRONI D2707/A1/12/3).

[51] For use rights, see Bushaway, *By Rite*, and E. P. Thompson, *Whigs and Hunters*, 240–1. For traditional tenure in France, see Brenner, 'Agrarian Class Structure and Economic Development', 69–71, and in England, Searle, 'Custom, Class Conflict and Agrarian Capitalism'.

[52] Willes, Observations on Ireland (PRONI T2855/1, 12).

[53] e.g. Even disputes over common land tended to be a matter not of communities asserting their customary entitlements, but rather of squatters defending relatively recent gains. See Andrews, 'The Struggle for Ireland's Public Commons'.

[54] Withers, *Gaelic Scotland*, 222–58.

enforced a close integration into the stronger British economy that accen-
tuated the consequences of this relative backwardness; with the exception
of linen, Ireland was locked into an inherently unequal pattern of trade,
exchanging primary or half-finished products for manufactured goods. High
levels of commercialization combined with the absence of customary restraints
on the operation of market forces to create unusually effective mechanisms
for syphoning off the surplus production of the majority of rural workers.
The result was the coexistence of an increasingly sophisticated and market-
oriented agriculture with miserably low living standards for the great majority.
In 1773, at a time when conditions even for the rural poor were a great deal
better than they had been thirty years before, a visiting English clergyman still
considered it 'one of the most unaccountable circumstances I have noticed in
my travels',

that when you see a very large extent of country covered with corn, your eye cannot
discover one farmhouse, or one rick of last year's produce, either of hay or corn. When
you ask where the tenants live of such demesnes, you are shown a hovel or two of a
cabin, which seem incapable of containing a thousandth part of the produce.[55]

All this has been a discussion of the Irish economy as seen from without,
and in a long historical perspective. To complete the picture, it is also
necessary to look at the way in which contemporaries perceived the economic
conditions and prospects of the society in which they lived.

Formal assessments were for the most part gloomy. Observers in the late
seventeenth century had been relatively optimistic: the poverty and backwardness of the society were undeniable, but there was also a sense of rapid
and progressive social change, opening up the prospect of future prosperity.[56]
From the first decade of the eighteenth century, the tone changed sharply.
Archbishop King of Dublin, writing in 1703, saw Ireland as 'a miserable
enslaved country without money or trade'. A year later the Whig politician
Alan Brodrick predicted that 'in a little time . . . estates in Ireland will be of no
other use to the owners but to eat, drink and clothe themselves on the spot
out of the produce of them'.[57] Such pessimism essentially reflected the
stagnation of Irish exports, commencing once the post-war recovery of the
1690s had run its course and continuing up to the 1740s. But it was powerfully
reinforced by political grievances. The Woollen Act of 1699, the continued
prohibition of cattle exports to Great Britain, and other commercial restric-

[55] Burrows Tour (PRONI T3551, 99).
[56] Optimism may be detected in Petty's *Political Anatomy*, written in 1672, as well as in the
county surveys collected in 1683–5 by William Molyneux (TCD MS 883). For a general review
of economic thinking in the late seventeenth and early eighteenth centuries, see P. Kelly, 'Ireland
and the Critique of Mercantilism'.
[57] King to Edward Southwell, 16 Feb. 1703 (TCD MS 1489/2, 156); Alan Brodrick to
Thomas Brodrick, 21 Oct. 1704 (Midleton MS 1248/2, fo. 152ᵛ).

tions were all cited as evidence that England would never allow Ireland to enjoy prosperity. High levels of taxation, some of the proceeds of which went to pay for pensions and grants to English courtiers and clients of the great, were seen as further blocking any prospect of economic improvement. The entire stock of money in the kingdom, it was claimed, passed through the Treasury each year.[58] Irish economic literature in the 1720s reveals what has been described as a 'paranoiac' fear that taxation would be still further increased.[59] In other respects too, the 1720s saw economic pessimism reach new depths. The famine of 1728–9 inspired Swift's notorious *Modest Proposal* (1729), which argued that Ireland should develop its one remaining economic resource by fattening children for export as food. Between 1735 and 1737 George Berkeley, bishop of Cloyne, published his *Querist*, with its despairing appeal for Ireland to cut itself off from external trade and seek to live in frugal comfort on its own produce. By the mid-1740s some observers, like Sir Richard Cox, had become more positive. But it was only in the following decade, as the boom in demand for both agricultural and manufactured goods became unmistakable, that contemporaries began to express real confidence in the country's economic prospects.

Even in the first half of the eighteenth century, however, pessimism was not total. Despite the general gloom, some members of the Irish élite, particularly in their role as landlords, attempted to find practical remedies for the economic backwardness they saw around them. Their projects tended to follow a recognizable pattern. In agriculture the main methods favoured were to develop demesne farming, both as a show-ground for improved techniques and to provide employment; to reclaim, enclose, or redistribute land; and to import English or Scottish tenants who could supply the capital and skills lacking in the indigenous population. Attempts at industrial development generally centred on textiles, again often taking the form of importing colonies of weavers from the established linen areas of Ulster. Where opportunity existed, other manufactures could also be encouraged; the most striking example is the complex of enterprises—a colliery, saltworks, a tannery, ironworks, a brewery, and bleach green and glass works—built up from the 1730s by Hugh Boyd at Ballycastle in County Antrim. The extent of interest in schemes for social and economic development was further reflected in the establishment in 1731 of the Dublin Society, formed to encourage experiment and to disseminate knowledge of the best techniques in agriculture and manufacturing. This attracted an initial membership of more than 300. The direct impact of attempts to promote economic change from above is difficult to assess. Landlords probably played a significant role in the process of

[58] King to Bladen, 27 Aug. 1717 (TCD MS 2534, p. 296). Interestingly, the same claim was accepted by at least one lord lieutenant: Bolton to ——, 8 July 1719 (SP 63/377/171).
[59] Lein, 'Jonathan Swift and the Population of Ireland', 449–52.

enclosure and reorganization of field systems; more ambitious attempts to transform a local economy appear to have achieved little except where circumstances were already reasonably favourable. Whatever their outcome, however, the number and distribution of such enterprises suggest that the belief that Ireland could be developed and radically improved, evident in the late seventeenth century, had not wholly disappeared even in the bleaker years that followed.[60]

One further key to the way in which contemporaries perceived their society is provided by the comparison that came spontaneously to so many when they found themselves confronted with one of the country's occasional more favoured corners. After his rugged journey across the mountains of Cork and Kerry in 1704, Alan Brodrick at last descended into what he described as 'very pleasant country, much like England'. 'Here is a great deal of wood and hedges hereabouts,' Swift wrote from King's County in 1714, 'so that in summer it would be a sort of England, only for the bogs.' County Armagh, a proud resident observed in 1737, was 'the best improved part of Ireland, not inferior to many parts of England'. Nor was it only natives who felt such comparisons appropriate. They also occurred repeatedly to Mrs Delany on her first visit to Ireland in 1732. Coote Hill in County Cavan was 'like a pretty English village, well situated; and all the land about it cultivated and enclosed with cut hedges and tall trees in rows'. Aire's Court, near Banagher in King's County, had 'a great many fine woods and improvements that looked very English'. If other Irish gentlemen would attempt the same improvements she had seen in County Tipperary, 'Ireland would soon be as beautiful as England.' Another English-born lady, the countess of Leinster, offered similar praise in 1759 of Lord Jocelyn's seat in Queen's County:

> You can't imagine anything more like the country of England than it is all around us here; shady lanes with oak trees in the hedges, a river just under the windows, fields and meadows with paths through them, no stone walls, no miserable looking cabins near it—in short, just this spot is vastly pretty.[61]

Such comparisons are of course natural enough, given the origins and cultural connections of the Irish élite. Nor should one mistake a figure of speech for a programme of action. But two points are nevertheless significant. Contemporary observers, even in the gloomiest days of the early eighteenth century, continued to see about them signs that something better was possible. And the summit of their aspirations, the image that haunted them, if only in their

---

[60] For landlord-sponsored enterprise, see Cullen, *Emergence of Modern Ireland*, 75; Kirkham, '"To Pay the Rent"', 96–7; Crawford, 'Ulster Landowners and the Linen Industry'. For Ballycastle, see Dallat, 'Ballycastle's Eighteenth-Century Industries'.

[61] Alan Brodrick to St John Brodrick, 7 Sept. [1704] (Midleton MS 1248/2, fo. 146); Swift, *Correspondence*, ii. 145; Sir Arthur Acheson to George Dodington, 2 Apr. 1737 (HMC, *Eyre Matcham Manuscripts*, 68); Delany, *Autobiography and Correspondence*, i. 376, 385, 387; countess of Leinster to earl of Kildare, 6 May 1759 (Leinster, *Correspondence*, i. 76).

dreams, was that of an Ireland whose fields and hedgerows, and by implication its people, would be those of a second England.

2. Gentlemen and Others

Who were the ruling class of eighteenth-century Ireland? The question is less
easily answered than at first sight might be expected. In part this is because
Ireland shared with Great Britain a status system different from those found
in most parts of continental Europe in that it gave only a limited role to the
legal distinction between noble and commoner. Instead, social position was
determined by complex criteria of wealth, parentage, and life-style that social
historians still struggle to define satisfactorily.[62] But there were also other
factors, distinctive to Ireland, that further complicate the task of deciding who
should, and who should not, be counted as part of the country's élite.

In both societies, of course, the most clear-cut social boundary was
ownership of land. Possession of a landed estate brought with it self-evident
benefits: control over the doings of tenants and dependants, prestige in the
eyes of inferiors and equals alike, eligibility for local office, and the opportunity to participate in national politics. There were also the less tangible, but
no less real, satisfactions of dynastic continuity. The County Westmeath peer
Lord Delvin, in 1746, congratulated his son-in-law on having escaped from
pressures to sell off part of his property: it was 'a glorious thing to save an
estate for a family, and eternize your name'.[63] In this sense the 5,000 or so
landed families of eighteenth-century Ireland can be seen as the core of the
country's élite.[64] The extent to which this was the case was particularly
evident in the composition of parliament. Of the 669 men who sat in the Irish
House of Commons during the reign of George II, over half were landed
gentlemen. The two other principal groups, the 128 lawyers and the 88 past
or current holders of commissions in the army, also represented occupations
overwhelmingly recruited from land-owning families. Even the much less
numerous representatives of non-landed wealth—the 30 to 35 merchants
and bankers—would have included some at least with landed connections.[65]

The landed class was not of course a homogeneous body. In the case of
eighteenth-century England, recent work has made it possible to distinguish
between a national élite of landed magnates, many though not all of them
aristocrats; a 'county élite' of landed gentry, distinguished by their collective
monopoly of local office and their individual occupancy of substantial country

---

[62] For a general discussion, see Stone, 'Social Mobility in England 1500–1700'; Corfield,
'Class by Name and Number in Eighteenth-Century Britain'.
[63] Delvin to Savage, 8 July 1746 (PRONI D552/A/2/6/8).
[64] For the figure of 5,000, see *NHI* iv. 34.
[65] McCracken, 'Central and Local Administration', 110.

seats; and the minor landowners or 'parish gentry'.[66] Similar distinctions must
have existed in Ireland, although their precise outlines remain to be properly
explored. There is some evidence to suggest that the late seventeenth and
early eighteenth centuries saw a rise in the importance of the middling and
smaller landed gentry compared to the largest proprietors. Dickson's study
of Munster shows a number of large estates, particularly those owned by
absentees, being sold in whole or in part in the decades after 1700, with
smaller local landowners the main purchasers.[67] Throughout the country,
meanwhile, the transition from the court-centred politics of faction and
clientage that had characterized seventeenth-century Ireland to the parliamentary politics of the post-Revolution era reduced the prominence of the
great provincial magnates, the heirs to Orrery and Ormond, and boosted both
the importance and the self-esteem of the gentry. But there remained a world
of difference between the great landed families, the Kildares, Downshires,
Abercorns, and their like, whose members could deal on equal terms with the
upper levels of English society, and the provincial gentry. One advantage of
the diocese of Raphoe, William King observed in 1701, was that it had 'no
very topping noblemen or gentlemen'. The gentry who did reside there
'generally are conformable plain men and are easily obliged, a dish of good
meat and a glass of moderate drink being all they expect'.[68]

The composition of parliament, then, confirms what every schoolboy
knows: property, and in particular landed property, was the basis of political
power. Yet this proposition should not be taken too literally. A certain level of
status and wealth were certainly essential to participation in the political
system. But the actual business of managing the affairs of the kingdom was
another matter. In the second half of the eighteenth century, as Malcomson
has shown, offices of real political influence were awarded, not on the basis of
acres owned, or even of parliamentary seats controlled, but for talent and
performance.[69] Earlier too, the men who dominated public life were not
necessarily the wealthiest. Indeed, some seem to have had modest or even
precarious fortunes. Sir Charles Porter, the English lawyer who served as lord
chancellor under James II and again under William III, died in 1696 leaving 'a
miserable family, and it is said no sort of provision for two daughters'.[70] When
Henry Boyle was being considered in 1734 for the Speakership of the House
of Commons, and in effect the role of chief manager of government business,
one of the objections raised against him was that 'if he has not got some

---

[66] Stone and Stone, *An Open Elite?*
[67] Dickson, 'Property and Social Structure in Eighteenth-Century South Munster', 130–1.
[68] King to John Pooley, bishop of Cloyne, 1 June 1701 (TCD MS 750/2/2, 158). For the rise
of the middling gentry, see Cullen, *Emergence of Modern Ireland*, 39–40.
[69] Malcomson, *John Foster*, 193–208.
[70] *CSPD 1696*, 461, 470.

valuable employment, his coming to town, his altering his manner of living, his equipage will be occasion of so great expense that he won't well bear it'.[71]

Boyle was nevertheless a man of a least some estate. In other cases prominence was achieved wholly on the basis of office. The Church of Ireland, at a time when bishops had important political functions, and the practice of the law both provided routes by which men of undistinguished origins could from time to time achieve both modest prosperity and political power. William King, archbishop of Dublin from 1703 to 1729 and twice a lord justice, was the son of a tenant farmer. Sir Richard Cox, born in the same year as King, 1650, was almost as much a self-made man. The son of an army officer killed in 1651, he inherited an interest worth £150 and £26 a year from property received in lieu of his father's arrears of pay. When he left school at 15, there was not enough money for him to go on to Trinity College, Dublin; it was only with difficulty, and through the help of friends, that he qualified as an attorney. His subsequent rise to the position of lord chief justice of the Common Pleas and then lord chancellor between 1703 and 1707 was achieved through successful legal practice, through local government office as recorder of Kinsale, and through the fortunate accident of being included in the entourage that William III brought with him to Ireland in 1690.[72] If substantial landowners made up the core of the country's political élite, it is also necessary to take account of men like King and Cox: office-holders in church, civil establishment, or armed services, who by ability or luck had managed to achieve a position of status and influence.

Or at least they did so for themselves. Some families managed to translate a temporary foothold in the establishment into assets that could be passed on to subsequent generations. Between 1712 and 1761, for example, the Cust family of County Armagh used modest local appointments in the revenue service to build up a landed estate worth more than £1,600 a year; in 1769 one of their number served as high sheriff of the county.[73] But others were all too aware that their status would not necessarily be passed on. Alan Brodrick, younger son of a County Cork landowner, was eventually, through his legal earnings, the profits of office, and speculation in forfeited lands, to build up a substantial estate of his own. In 1704, however, when a change of government had thrown him back wholly on his legal earnings, he directed that his eldest son should be kept strictly to his studies, for 'I cannot see but that he and all my children may chiefly depend on their own industry'. Twelve years earlier, John Vesey, archbishop of Tuam, had addressed his son Agmondisham, then apprenticed to a London merchant, in very similar terms:

---

[71] Coghill to Southwell, 5 Apr. 1733 (BL Add. MS 21,123, fo. 33).
[72] Cox, *Autobiography*, 7–13.
[73] Clarkson and Crawford, *Ways to Wealth*.

God knows how long I may live, and if I should live, how long I shall be able to maintain you and the rest of your brothers and sisters. You must not therefore think of any thing but making your own fortune by God's providence, praying for his blessing on your honest industry: for I am not likely to leave estates to my children unless in a virtuous education.[74]

Sir Richard Cox, in 1708, when he was already a prominent figure, was happy to marry his daughter to a man of £300 a year, 'a discreet, industrious, genteel man, very well bred at university and inns of court, and capable of any manner of business'.[75]

Nor was it only those whose dependence was primarily on office who had to think in these terms. Even the owner of a landed estate could not expect to pass on his status to more than one offspring of each sex: the inheriting son and the most generously portioned daughter. Many younger sons found their way into the gentleman's professions of the army, the law, or the church. Others, however, were directed into trade. Of the five non-inheriting sons of Alexander Cosby of Queen's County, for example, three began their careers with minor commissions in the army. The other two were apprenticed, one to a wholesale grocer, the other to a merchant, though both were in the end also to opt for military careers. One daughter married a landed gentleman from County Waterford, and one a Welsh army captain. One of the sons married an innkeeper's daughter. Of his three daughters, Alexander Cosby's grand-children, one married a tanner, and another a farmer. The third, who was left unprovided for at her father's death, was apprenticed by her uncle, the inheritor of the family estate, to a mantua-maker. Later, this uncle established her and her sister, now a widow, in a house in Waterford, where he expected them to maintain themselves by that trade. The Cosbys were substantial proprietors. The annual rent roll on the family estate rose from £1,000 in 1716 to £2,000 by 1725. Alexander's son Dudley served as MP for the county. Yet his close family connections reached down to the level of farmer, shopkeeper, and artisan.[76] This is not to suggest that family ties somehow co-opted such relatives into the Irish élite. On the contrary, as the case of the mantua-maker makes clear, a poor relation was precisely that. What the example of the Cosbys illustrates is, rather, the weakness of a social analysis conceived solely in terms of horizontal layers. From another point of view, Irish society, like English, consisted of a set of vertical networks of kinship, patronage, and clientage, linking greater landlords to lesser ones and middle and smaller gentry to the trading and even the manufacturing classes.

In a society constituted in this way, social boundaries, although of enor-

---

[74] Alan Brodrick to St John Brodrick, 25 Oct. 1704 (Midleton MS 1248/2, fo. 154); John Vesey to Agmondisham Vesey, 24 Dec. 1692 (Sarsfield-Vesey Papers, 15).
[75] Cox to Southwell, 4 Dec. 1708 (BL Add. MS 38, 156, fo. 33).
[76] Cosby 'Autobiography', 317–24, 423–30.

mous importance, could never be absolutely rigid. At the upper levels of the social hierarchy, matters were clear enough. The status of a gentleman, implying shared background, tastes, and code of conduct, linked the duke and the country squire, whatever the difference between them in terms of income and day-to-day life-style. Lower down the scale, on the other hand, came a misty territory in which the minor landed proprietor rubbed shoulders with those whose claim to gentility was at best provisional: the downwardly mobile man of good family reduced to dependence on some employment that was not trade or manufacture and the upwardly mobile office-holder or middleman. Of twelve 'gentlemen', mainly from Tipperary and King's County, who signed depositions in a serious criminal case in 1745, two were able to give the evidence they did because they manned collection points on particular turnpike roads; their status as gentlemen appears to have depended on the fact that they had purchased the right to collect these particular tolls, rather than work for a salary.[77] Archbishop King advised a young relative to keep his cornet's place in the army, because 'whilst you have such a place you are entitled by it to gentlemen's company', and cautioned him against indulging a preference for 'poor mean scullog's conversation, where you may be the best in the company'.[78]

The undefined gradations within landed society, the ambiguous status of the man of non-landed wealth, an interchange of personnel between the worlds of land and trade: all these were features common to English and Irish society in the late seventeenth and early eighteenth centuries. At the same time there are some grounds for suggesting that such ambiguities were more prominent in post-Restoration Ireland than they were in England. In the first place, there were the complexities created by the widespread letting of land through middlemen, permitting what one writer in 1728 described as 'the younger sons of our gentlemen, and the sons of our wealthy country men', to adopt the life-style and position of small and middling landed gentry. A reformist periodical in 1729 denounced 'this motley generation of half land-lords, half tenants' which was 'in constant emulation with our gentry to keep up a rank and character to which they are in no way entitled'. Arthur Young, half a century later, left a memorable pen-picture of what he called 'the class of little country gentlemen; tenants, who drink their claret by means of profit rents; jobbers in farms; bucks; your fellows with round hats, edged with gold, who hunt in the day, get drunk in the evening and fight the next morning'. The abolition of middleman tenures, he believed, would drive such individuals to more suitable careers in the army or navy 'or sink them into plain

---

[77] SP63/407/109–32. The case was that of the priest Dougan; see below, ch. 4, sect. 3.
[78] King to Cornet Abney Parker, 29 Dec. 1707 (TCD MS 750/3/2, 168–9). A 'scullog' was a tenant farmer.

farmers, like those we have in England, where it is common to see men, with much greater property, without pretending to be gentlemen'.[79]

The second distinctive feature of Ireland's social structure was the apparently greater scope it offered for upward mobility. The latest study of England has emphasized just how limited was the interchange between the worlds of land and commerce and how few newcomers penetrated the county élite at any time during the eighteenth century.[80] No equivalent systematic study of social mobility has been attempted for Ireland. At the same time, it is impossible not to be struck by the number of self-made men, or their sons, who appear in eighteenth-century public life. The classic example in the first half of the eighteenth century was of course William Conolly. Conolly was not, as tradition has it, the son of an innkeeper raised to great heights in the aftermath of the Glorious Revolution. Already before 1688 both he and his father were important enough to be included in the Act of Attainder passed by the Jacobite parliament.[81] At the same time it is clear that the huge personal fortune that Conolly eventually came to possess was built up through his own endeavours, by a combination of legal practice and shrewd dealing in land. Other self-made men prominent in the first half of the eighteenth century were Sir Richard Cox, whose case has already been discussed, and Luke Gardiner and Nathaniel Clements, whose fortunes were based on a combination of urban property speculation, banking, and exploitation of the profits of office. Lord Charlemont, writing around 1789, was to describe Gardiner's son as the grandson of a footman.[82] By the second half of the century, the list of self-made men or members of newly risen families had swelled to include a large proportion of the leading politicians of the age.[83]

Two main reasons can be suggested for this apparent prominence of self-made men and members of new families. First, there were the opportunities created by the large-scale forfeiture and redistribution of land in 1653–65 and again after 1691. The disposal all at once of so much confiscated land, in some cases to grantees who had no desire to remain in Ireland, created a buyer's market. Uncertainties regarding the status of these grants, in the 1660s and again in the 1690s, further depressed prices, creating openings for the speculative and the strong-nerved. Later there were further gains to be made from grantees or purchasers who failed to make good or to reconcile themselves to life in Ireland. It was, after all, through his dealings in the post-Revolution land market that William Conolly acquired a fortune and Alan Brodrick, a non-inheriting younger son, laid the foundations of an estate for

---

[79] Anonymous letter to earl of Burlington, 1 May 1728 (PRONI D2707/A1/1/11B); *Tribune*, quoted by Lecky, *History of Ireland*, i. 293 n.; Young, *Tour*, ii. 155.

[80] Stone and Stone, *Open Elite?*

[81] Boylan, 'The Conollys of Castletown'.

[82] Eamon Walsh, 'Sackville Mall: The First Hundred Years', in Dickson (ed.), *Gorgeous Mask*, 30–50; HMC, *Charlemont Manuscripts*, i. 70.

[83] Malcomson, *Foster*, 5–6.

himself. Secondly, there was the small overall size of the landed élite. There were simply not enough persons qualified by birth and ability to meet the needs of central and local government.[84] It was this shortage of manpower, for example, that gave the bishops of the Church of Ireland a prominence in politics and civil administration that their English counterparts never had. The same circumstance presumably made it that much harder to deny a man of abilities and fortune his place in public life simply because of his family's origins.

None of this is to suggest that social distinctions had ceased to matter. The criticisms levelled at the pretensions of middlemen make clear that they had not. Political opponents, equally, were quick to draw attention to the origins of self-made men. Sir Francis Brewster, a leading troublemaker in the parliament of 1692, was dismissed by one hostile contemporary as 'the barber's son of Tralee'. In 1717 Alan Brodrick, now Lord Midleton, objected to the suggestion that he be made lord justice on an equal footing with his former political and business partner William Conolly, on account of the latter's 'birth and education'. Earlier he had argued that if Conolly were to be granted a peerage, it should not be at a level that would give offence to other lords, 'who may be piqued at seeing one of his birth and condition put over their heads'. Pole Cosby denounced Ephraim Dawson, who in 1727 had prevented him from succeeding his father as MP for Queen's County, as 'a mean, very mean upstart, for his father kept an ale house, the sign of the cock, in Belfast'. Even in a more neutral context, Cosby dismissed a neighbour, Judge Parnell, as 'but a mushroom, a man of no family at all at all'. In the 1760s a conservative like the Revd Philip Skelton, son of a farmer and tanner, could reject the suggestion that a university education had made him a gentleman: 'He only was a gentleman as Lord Burghley defines it, who has riches derived from ancestors that possessed them from time immemorial.'[85] Just as in the case of England, however, and probably to an even greater extent, all such attempts to define and keep up clear-cut social boundaries were abstractions imposed on a more complex and far less tidy reality.

3. Manners

Fashions, in history as in real life, regularly change. The last few years have seen historians of English society return their attention from its lower levels

---

[84] Hayton, 'Ireland and the English Ministers', 5–7. The same point is made by Ehrenpreis, *Swift*, i. 79.

[85] John Richards to Wyche, 8 Jan. 1693 (Wyche Papers 1/1/65); Midleton to Thomas Brodrick, 29 Jan. 1717 (Midleton MS 1248/3, fo. 403); same to same, 7 Nov. 1717 (Midleton MS 1248/4, fo. 90ᵛ); Cosby, 'Autobiography', 174, 254; Burdy, 'Life of Skelton', in Skelton, *Works*, I, pp. ix–x.

to its top. A range of new and revealing work has anatomized the lives of the landed classes: their amusements, their sexual behaviour and family relationships, their distinctive institutions and assumptions. Little of this new interest has as yet reached Ireland. The comparable work, in fact, can be listed in one breath: an impressive study of marriage by A. P. W. Malcomson, some valuable comments on diet and hospitality by L. M. Cullen, and some rather specialized pieces on domestic architecture.[86] This means that any attempt to sum up the main features of the élite culture of late seventeenth- and early eighteenth-century Ireland can hardly be other than speculative and superficial. Yet the attempt must be made. For if detailed study has been lacking, interpretation has not. Central features of upper-class Irish life—its financial extravagance, its drinking customs, its quarrelsomeness—have been seen, not just as local peculiarities, but as evidence of a collective neurosis, arising out of the undistinguished origins of many landed families or alter- natively from the identity crisis of the conquistador.[87] Such interpretations, it will be suggested here, are misconceived. What was involved is more con- vincingly seen as an example of the uneven penetration of a provincial élite by the standards of metropolitan society. In this respect Ireland was not radically different from Scotland, Wales, or the more settled of the American colonies, or indeed from more remote parts of provincial England. In Ireland, as elsewhere, moreover, the early and mid-eighteenth century saw the pro- gressive extension among the upper classes of new standards of refinement and self-discipline.

The feature of Irish polite society that most forcibly struck contemporaries was its high consumption of alcohol. John Bowes, an Englishman newly appointed to legal office in Ireland, complained in 1727 that the people among whom he found himself 'have no notion of the pleasure of conversation. Drinking is the business of their leisure hours.' Lord Chesterfield, lord lieutenant from 1745 until 1747, repeatedly lectured his subjects on their consumption: 'Nine gentlemen in ten in Ireland are impoverished by the great quantity of claret which, from mistaken notions of hospitality and dignity, they think it necessary should be drunk in their houses.'[88] Such comments are apparently borne out by the available statistics. In the 1720s legal imports of wine amounted to 12.4 million gallons per year, an astonishing level for what must have been a relatively small circle of élite consumers. By the 1790s this

---

[86] Malcomson, *The Pursuit of the Heiress*; Cullen, *Emergence of Modern Ireland*, ch. 3, 7, 8. On architecture, see Crookshank in *NHI* iv, ch. 15, 16.

[87] To V. G. Kiernan, e.g., Ireland offers 'an instructive case study in the natural history of ruling classes established by force' (*The Duel in European History*, 106–8). To R. F. Foster, 'the ascendancy caste' was characterized by 'a certain savagery of mind, amplified by a subconscious recognition of the fundamental insecurity of their political and social position' (*Modern Ireland*, 176).

[88] Bowes to Sir Dudley Ryder, 12 July 1727 (PRONI T3228/1/1); Chesterfield to Bishop Chenevix, 18 June 1747 (Chesterfield, *Letters*, iii. 945); cf. ibid. 765–6, 771–2, 924.

had risen to 15 million gallons.[89] In 1762 a County Clare gentleman who complained of a nervous disorder was advised to stop 'bumping away all night' and to 'stint yourself to three pints instead of a gallon'.[90]

High consumption of alcohol, however, should not be viewed simply as reflecting compulsive drunkenness. Drinking was part of a wider social pattern, in which prestige was upheld and social bonds maintained by lavish hospitality and conspicuous excess. The earl of Orrery, taking up residence in Ireland in the early 1730s, was shaken by the consumption of food and drink alike.

Nonsense and wine have flowed in plenty, gigantic saddles of mutton and Brobding-naggian rumps of beef weigh down the table. Bumpers of claret and bowls of white wine were perpetually under my nose. . . . [Our entertainments] are esteemed according to the quantity, not to the quality, of the victuals. Be the meat good or be it bad, so that there is as much as would feed an army, the esquire thinks he comes off with honour.[91]

Other visitors commented on the extent to which provision of food and drink took precedence over the maintenance of even a minimal level of display in housing and furniture. 'The people of this country', the future Mrs Delany observed in 1732, 'don't seem solicitous of having good dwellings or more furniture than is absolutely necessary—hardly so much, but they make it up in eating and drinking.' One gentleman she visited in County Mayo lived in a thatched 'cabin', yet had been known to give 'entertainments of twenty dishes of meat'. The English-born wife of William Ponsonby was quoted in 1757 as having observed 'that everybody in Ireland spend all they have in eating and drinking, and have no notion of any other sort of comforts in life; they don't care whether their houses or anything in them is fit to receive company—provided they can stuff them that's enough.' In such a society consumption was not just a matter of private indulgence; it was a central ritual of sociability. 'Drunkenness', Orrery commented bitterly, 'is the touchstone by which they try every man, and he that cannot or will not drink has a mark set upon him.' John Bowes found that his refusal to join in tavern drinking sessions had led people to wonder 'how I preserve my rank in business'.[92]

With heavy eating and drinking went a certain lack of refinement. Orrery, an English-educated aesthete, left horrified accounts of the company he found himself keeping at Irish tables: 'Filth, obscenity and rudeness of every sort is the wit of the day, and he that can be most beastly, most impudent and most absurd, carries off the laurel of the triumph.' Elsewhere he complained of the

---

[89] Malcolm, '*Ireland Sober, Ireland Free*', 22.
[90] Edmund Sexton to Sir Edward O'Brien, 15 Nov. 1762 (*Inchiquin Manuscripts*, 186).
[91] *Orrery Papers*, i. 215.
[92] Delany, *Autobiography and Correspondence*, i. 351; countess of Kildare to earl of Kildare, 7 July 1757 (Leinster, *Correspondence*, i. 59); *Orrery Papers*, i. 157; Bowes, as above, n. 88.

failure of even Dublin booksellers to supply his needs: 'Scarce a gentleman in Ireland...goes further in literature than Urban's *English Magazine* or Faulkner's *Irish Journal.*' Others too lamented the lack of a reading public. Ireland, Archbishop King maintained in 1713, was 'an unfortunate country as to learning'. A man who wished to publish a work had to pay for the printing and distribute copies free, 'there not being scholars enough to take off an impression'. Archbishop Synge of Tuam confirmed in 1721 that 'there are very few books indeed of which an impression will go off in this kingdom'. Lord Molesworth, two years later, complained that the best education of many landed gentlemen reached 'no higher than to know how to make the most of a piece of land'. Of the 699 men who sat in the Commons between 1727 and 1760, only just over a quarter had attended a university.[93]

The other notorious vice of the Irish landed class, right through the eighteenth century, was duelling. The Revd Samuel Madden, in 1738, complained of 'that dreadful indulgence which through the whole kingdom is shown to fair and honourable murders of all denominations.... In general, it is safer to kill a man than steal a sheep or a cow.'[94] Most modern accounts of duelling tend to emphasize its stylized character, as a formal proof of courage and a ritualized reparation for insult or injury. Yet what is striking about Irish duels in the first half of the eighteenth century is their ferocity and the fragility of the conventions surrounding the central act of violence. Consider, for example, the way in which two County Cork combatants in 1733 resolved a dispute over a greyhound:

They entered the lists on horseback with sword and petronel. The former having discharged at and missed the latter, the other rode up to his breast but missed fire, whereupon he immediately dismounted and drew, as Newell did the like, and having made some sasas at each other, both received some slight wounds, but still the combat lasted, till at length one of Raymond's spurs got hold of his stockings, whereby he fell on his face to the ground, at which the other stabbed him through the back, and [he] not long after expired.[95]

In other cases too, what is conveyed is less an exaggerated concern with the niceties of personal honour than a murderous aggression. In 1729 two gentlemen who had quarrelled while staying at Lord Ferrard's house in County Louth were sufficiently reconciled to share a room that evening. 'But in the night their dispute rose so high that they fought with their fists in their shirts', and had to be dragged apart by the servants. They met next morning at a nearby churchyard and agreed to fight, one man getting off his first shot while the other was still removing his greatcoat. When Hamilton George

[93] *Orrery Papers*, i. 215, 319; King to John Woodward, Gresham College, 12 Sept. 1713 (TCD MS 750/4/1, 206); Synge to Wake, 6 Mar. 1721 (Gilbert MS 28, 156); [Molesworth], *Some Considerations*, 28–9; McCracken, 'Central and Local Administration', 112.
[94] [Madden], *Reflections and Resolutions*, 151–2.   [95] HMC, *Puleston Manuscripts*, 314.

quarrelled with Harry St Lawrence at a house party in 1737 over a supposed insult to St Lawrence's niece, the two men shot it out alone in a bedroom, after St Lawrence had refused to wait for the morning.[96]

Episodes of this kind suggest what is confirmed by other incidents: that duelling was only one, specialized manifestation of a general disposition towards aggression and ready violence. In 1738, for example, five men in Roscrea, County Tipperary, 'men of good circumstances and reputed gentlemen (as gentlemen go in this part of the world)', drew their swords on Lieutenant Hume, an English army officer with whom they had quarrelled in a public house, pursuing him from room to room and inflicting a total of sixteen or seventeen wounds before he died. They then fought a pitched battle with some soldiers who had come to the officer's aid, wounding several before making their escape.[97] A parallel case, which escalated into a sectarian *cause célèbre*, was the killing of Lieutenant Jolly by the Catholic gentleman Richard Martin in Galway city three years earlier.[98] Nor was it only social equals who were on the receiving end of spontaneous violence of this kind. The earl of Roscommon, attending a funeral in 1667, was enraged when a junior earl, Clancarty, did not move quickly enough to give him precedence. He 'came out of his coach in great heat and, falling amongst the footmen, wounded two or three of the earl of Clancarty's footmen and killed one of his coachhorses'. In 1744 a gentleman who got into a dispute with a ballad singer on a Dublin street ran him through and wounded another man before making off.[99]

Such episodes were, of course, unusual. They are of significance only for what they reveal of a wider social context. The memoirs of the bookseller John Dunton, who visited Dublin in 1699, offer a more direct glimpse of what that context was. Dining in a cook's shop in Crane Lane,

I perceive in these ordinaries, if a man makes a noise, laughs in fashion, and has a grim face to promise quarrelling, he shall be much observed; ... When we had filled our bellies, we all began to talk, and made as great a noise as Dover Court, for every man was willing to say something, though it was nothing to the purpose, rather than be thought to have nothing to say.[100]

In such loud, boisterous, competitive company, where men were expected to jostle for attention and esteem, it is hardly surprising that trivial disputes could be magnified into points of honour and verbal aggression could give way suddenly to physical violence.

---

[96] *Dublin Intelligence*, 25 Feb. 1729; HMC, *Puleston Manuscripts*, 312–13, wrongly dated 1731 (cf. *Dublin Gazette*, 4–8 Jan. 1737).

[97] HMC, *Polwarth Manuscripts*, v. 152–8.   [98] See below, p. 126.

[99] *CSPI 1666–9*, 493; *Faulkner's Dublin Journal*, 6–9 Oct. 1744.

[100] Dunton, *Life and Errors*, ii. 545–6. Dunton went on to give some idea of the type of company this represented. When dinner had ended, each went his own way, 'some to the college, some to the play house, others to court, a few to their shops, and Dunton to his auction'.

None of this should be taken as implying that drunkenness, brawling, and general disorder were universal. Quite clearly they were not. A reader of the voluminous correspondence of Alan Brodrick, later first Viscount Midleton, for example, will search in vain for duels, abduction, and debauchery. The prevailing tone is, if anything, of a rather sanctimonious respectability. One of the greatest concerns of his life, Brodrick told his teenage son Alan in 1718, was to have him 'bred up virtuously, according to my best wishes'. He had taken him once to Newmarket,

and hope you have seen enough of the cockpit, chocolate house and course to make you hate cockfighting, gaming and its attendant vices, desperate oaths, distraction, nay blasphemy, and that you see that horse racing is an introduction to cheating, sharping, hypocrisy, and lying, and ends in the ruin of men's estates as well as the loss of their characters gradually.[101]

Brodrick's tastes, it is true, set him apart from other members of his family. In 1702 he wrote disapprovingly of his brother William's fondness for gambling, watching others play cards, and talking news and politics, rather than spending his time in his legal chambers, 'or in reading law, which he much needs to do'. He was also critical of his brother Thomas's heavy spending on horse breeding and racing, and by 1720 he was noting with alarm young Alan's growing addiction to the same sport.[102] At the same time his correspondence reveals the other face of the early eighteenth-century Protestant élite: sober, restrained, and, as in the comments on brother William, possessed of a proper sense that prosperity was partly at least the reward of industry and self-discipline. Nor was Alan Brodrick alone in all this. Pole Cosby recalled that his father, Dudley, who had died in 1729, was 'a sober man [who] did not care at all for drinking above a pint, or generally half a pint, of wine, and that he liked very well'. In 1748 Lady Kildare recorded that her husband, 'who naturally hates drink, was obliged on account of some country gentlemen that dined with him, to sit very late at table'. The result was that he was 'so excessively sick (not being used to it) and his head so much disordered the next morning, that he was not able to settle to anything nor did not dare to ride or walk as usual'.[103]

This last example, with its implied contrast between the temperate aristocrat and the 'country gentlemen' he felt obliged to entertain, suggests one possible explanation for the roughness which contemporaries detected in much upper-class life. The peculiarities of the social structure of eighteenth-

---

[101] Midleton to Alan Brodrick, jun., 10 Apr. 1718 (Midleton MS 1248/4, fo. 150).
[102] Alan Brodrick to St John Brodrick, 5 May 1702 (ibid. 1248/2, fo. 61); Alan Brodrick to Thomas Brodrick, 3 May 1704, 12 June 1705 (ibid., fos. 135, 209); same to same, 20 Apr. 1720 (ibid. 1248/4, fo. 247).
[103] Cosby, 'Autobiography', 179–80; Lady Kildare to Anne Hamilton, 11 July 1748 (Leinster, *Correspondence*, i. 28).

century Ireland—the greater acceptability of the self-made or at least newly made family, the smallness of the social élite, the ambiguities of status created by the existence of a rural pseudo-gentry of middlemen—have already been discussed. All three, it may be suggested, must have contributed to the admission into polite society of men whose status and breeding would have excluded them from equivalent circles in England. This was certainly the implication of Arthur Young's denunciation of the middleman class in 1780. It is also implied in the characterization of the killers of Lieutenant Hume at Roscrea in 1738: 'men of good circumstances and reputed gentlemen (as gentlemen go in this part of the world)'. To this less exclusive definition of gentility may be added the preference of many larger proprietors for spending all or most of their time in London or on landed estates in England, rather than on their Irish property. The economic damage resulting from such absenteeism is nowadays largely discounted by historians.[104] Its social effects remain to be considered. A rural society whose natural leaders were only intermittently, or not at all, resident may have been one in which the lesser gentry, unchecked by influence or example from above, set the tone of manners and behaviour in a way that would not otherwise have been possible.

Finally, and most important, it is necessary to set the behaviour of which contemporaries complained in a wider historical perspective. By the early eighteenth century the Irish gentry seemed to their English counterparts to be unduly prone to violent aggression. Yet in England itself, very similar habits of violence had been common among the upper classes throughout the sixteenth and for most of the seventeenth century.[105] Likewise, other aspects of upper-class Irish behaviour—the central role of hospitality (defined in terms of conspicuous generosity and the creation of lavish profusion, rather than any calculated display of refinement) as both a badge of status and an essential social cement, an intense concern with personal honour, assertive behaviour giving way readily to violence—were typical of a pattern to be found throughout the greater part of early modern Europe.[106] By the beginning of the eighteenth century, it is true, such behaviour was becoming increasingly archaic. To say this, however, is only to say what should in any case be fairly obvious: that the Irish gentry were a provincial élite, whose behaviour lagged some distance behind that seen in the main centres of taste and refinement.[107] Nor were they unique in this. In Wales, it has been suggested, it was only during the late seventeenth century that the gentry abandoned the great halls, where they had feasted with their retainers, in favour of the privacy of a

---

[104] Malcomson, 'Absenteeism'; Cullen, *Economic History*, 45, 83.
[105] Stone, 'Interpersonal Violence in English Society', 25–6, 29.
[106] P. Burke, *The Historical Anthropology of Early Modern Italy*, 9–14.
[107] It is significant that Mrs Delany found the 'heartiness' and 'great sociableness' she encountered in Ireland reminiscent of Cornwall, a region of England where old habits would have died out more slowly than elsewhere: *Autobiography and Correspondence*, i. 291. The whole question of hospitality is discussed in Cullen, *Emergence of Modern Ireland*, ch. 8.

manor-house, thus catching up with fashions that had been established in England perhaps two centuries earlier. In Scotland, too, manners lagged behind those of England; it was in fact the middle decades of the eighteenth century that appear to have been the decisive period in the anglicization of the Highland gentry. A similar transition was apparent in colonial Virginia, where the planter élite only gradually developed a distinctive gentry life-style, expressed in increased refinement in dress, housing, and styles of entertainment and in the replacement of vicious hand-to-hand fighting as a means of settling disputes by the formalized and disciplined violence of the duel.[108]

The Irish gentry did not have as far to travel as their counterparts in Virginia or the Scottish Highlands. But for them too, the early and mid-decades of the eighteenth century saw a progressive reform of manners, bringing them closer to the standards of metropolitan society. The change was perhaps most apparent in housing. From the 1720s, fortified tower houses and the single-storey thatched cabins that had so struck Mrs Delany were increasingly replaced by country houses, large or small as family fortunes dictated, but conforming in their design and in the life-style they implied to prevailing English norms. Interiors were similarly transformed; the 1740s and 1750s saw the beginnings of a marked improvement in the quality of Irish plasterwork, glassware, furniture, and other decorative arts.[109] Meanwhile there was a general quickening of intellectual life. Newspapers, for example, became both more numerous and more stable. Of 37 titles launched between 1704 and 1714, only 6 lasted long enough to be considered successful. Of 33 papers launched between 1714 and 1727, on the other hand, 15 can be counted as successes. Most of these titles were published in Dublin, but there were also some provincial ventures. Cork had its first newspaper in 1715, while successful titles were launched in Belfast in 1737 and in Limerick two years later. The number of printers at work in Dublin rose from 3 in 1690 to 33 by 1760, the number of booksellers from 13 to 46. Much of the business conducted by both was in the vigorous trade in reprints of English works, produced for sale in Ireland and also for (illegal) export to Great Britain and America. But there was also a marked growth, from the 1720s, in the volume and vigour of pamphleteering on Irish issues. The establishment in 1731 of the Dublin Society, along with the shorter-lived Physico-Historical Society in the 1740s, was further evidence of a new spirit of enquiry and debate.[110]

There were parallel changes in standards of behaviour. Even the dyspeptic Orrery testified to the changing face of social life. 'We are imitating you', he told an English correspondent in 1737, 'as fast as poverty and native simplicity

---

[108] Morgan, 'From a Death to a View', 50; Smout, *History of the Scottish People*, ch. 14; Isaac, *The Transformation of Virginia*, 73–4, 94–8, 302–3; Gorn, 'Gouge and Bite', 21–3.

[109] Crookshank in *NHI* iv. 499–519.

[110] Munter, *History of the Irish Newspaper*, 18, 132–3; Cole, *Irish Booksellers and English Writers*; Cullen, *Emergence of Modern Ireland*, 30–1.

of manners will permit us . . . we are in some danger of growing errant south-Britons at last, for we are already arrived at ridottos, horse races and a whimsical sort of vehicle called a quadrille.' Ten years later he was more positive:

I have known this kingdom fifteen years. More improvements than I have visibly observed of all kinds could not have been effected in that space of time. Duels are at an end. Politeness is making some progress. Literature is close behind her. Industry must follow. As Popery decreases, cleanliness and honesty will find place.[111]

Orrery exaggerated. Duels were not at an end in Ireland, any more than Popery was decreasing. But there had been a change. Edward Willes, writing in the 1750s, reported that duels were less frequent than they had been. The backyard of Lucas's coffee-house was still the scene of frequent meetings, but it was some years since the house had been 'jocosely compared to surgeon's hall, a dead body usually on the table'.[112] Other visitors over the next thirty years or so agreed that drinking and duelling, though more common than in England, were less so than formerly or than they had been led to believe.[113] The Irish gentry of the late eighteenth century continued to be in many ways looked down on by their English counterparts. Yet the criticism directed at them was increasingly to be the condescension and mild scorn reserved for country cousins, rather than the mixture of alarm and disapproval inspired by a frontier society.

---

[111] Orrery to Thomas Southerne, 28 May 1737 (*Orrery Papers*, i. 227–8); Orrery to Birch, 26 May 1747 (ibid. i. 320–1).

[112] Willes, Observations on Ireland, 1750–60 (PRONI T2855/1), 41.

[113] Twiss, *Tour*, 10; Campbell, *Philosophical Survey*, 39–41; Young, *Tour*, ii. 152; Latocnaye, *A Frenchman's Walk through Ireland*, 32.

3
The Structure of Politics

What are Irish politics in the eighteenth century about? Historians have found it difficult to decide. The theme which most immediately seems to offer itself is the conflict between English government and Irish patriotism. Yet this way of looking at it has obvious limitations. Even in the last decades of the eighteenth century, the era of Grattan, the Volunteers, and the 'constitution' of 1782, an analysis focused on patriotism and its opposite must exclude from consideration much that was central to Irish political life. Applied to earlier decades, it becomes even more the arbitrary highlighting of what was at best a subsidiary theme. Yet what is to take its place? For the most part, the answer has been a reductionist interpretation, in which politics is seen as essentially the pursuit of private gain: the competition of individuals and factions, operating in an ideological vacuum, for the benefits to be gained from office or government favour. To present a more rounded picture, it is necessary, not to deny the importance of patronage and profit, but rather to recreate something of the cultural context within which they were pursued. First, however, we must say something about an earlier period still, one in which politics did in fact revolve around serious conflicts of political and religious principle.

1. A Company of Madmen: The Politics of Party 1691–1714

Two central developments combined, from around the beginning of the eighteenth century, to transform the character of Irish politics. The first was the new importance of parliament. Ireland had inherited from the Middle Ages a House of Lords and a House of Commons precisely modelled on those of England. But, prior to the 1690s, these had played only a limited role in the government of the kingdom. Between the death of Elizabeth I and the fall of James II they had in fact been summoned only four times, the last in 1661–6. Thereafter, however, the soaring cost of government combined with the heightened expectations aroused by the Glorious Revolution to give the Irish parliament a wholly new sense of its own purpose and consequence. The second development, commencing in the early 1700s, was the appearance of an increasingly clear-cut division between two rival parties, Whig and Tory. These labels, and much of the original impetus towards partisan division, came from England. But the issues involved were to become of deepest concern to Irish Protestants.

The rise to new prominence of the Irish parliament began in 1692. William III and his ministers had been under no obligation to summon the assembly that met in the autumn of that year. Indeed, there had been suggestions at the time of the Revolution that this might be a good moment to abolish the Irish parliament altogether, transferring full control of Irish affairs to England. But it was nevertheless decided to go ahead, 'for the quiet of the people and the settlement of the kingdom'.[1] The outcome was not what had been anticipated. Almost as soon as it met on 5 October, the Commons embarked on a spectacular revolt: members, the lord lieutenant, Viscount Sydney, complained twelve days into the sitting, 'have begun like a company of madmen'.[2] In quick succession the Commons threw out most of the legislative programme prepared by the executive; launched an investigation into alleged corruption, involving senior office-holders, in the disposal of forfeited estates; and mounted a violent attack on official policy towards the defeated Jacobites and the Catholic population generally. On 3 November, after a session of only four weeks, Sydney seized on the most provocative of the Commons' acts, their claim that they had the 'sole right' to initiate legislation relating to finance, as an excuse to suspend the proceedings by a prorogation.

Behind this parliamentary revolt lay a combination of principle, short-term grievance, and self-interest. To some extent members were staking their claim to share in the liberties which they saw as having been secured in England by the Glorious Revolution. Thus the Commons threw out bills relating to the army and the militia on the grounds that these placed too much power in the hands of the executive, and some members went on to demand the introduction of a bill for habeas corpus. The demand for 'sole right', equally, reflected a concern with parliamentary control of taxation that went back to the constitutional conflicts of the reign of Charles I. Alan Brodrick, one of the leading spokesmen for the opposition, justified the Commons' stand on the issue by pointing to the case of France, where an acceptance that the executive could raise funds on its own authority had led in the long run to the extinction of the Estates General.[3] Agitation over constitutional matters inevitably extended also to Anglo-Irish relations. Sydney reported in amazement that MPs talked 'of freeing themselves from the yoke of England' and in particular of removing Poynings's Law, the late fifteenth-century statute that subjected all Irish legislation to the approval of the English Privy Council.[4]

---

[1] Sydney to Portland, 29 July 1692 (Portland Papers, PwA 1345).
[2] Sydney to Nottingham, 17 Oct. 1692 (*CSPD 1695*, Addenda, 213). For a general account of these events, see McGuire, 'The Irish Parliament of 1692'.
[3] Alan Brodrick to St John Brodrick, 26 June 1693 (Midleton MS 1248/1, fos. 261–2).
[4] *CSPD 1695*, Addenda, 213.

What gave these constitutional demands their impetus, however, was a feeling of concrete grievance: resentment at apparent corruption in high places and a real belief that Catholics were being shown a dangerous degree of tolerance, even favour. Added to this was the pursuit of factional advantage and personal advancement. Among those who opposed the administration most vigorously were said to be several lawyers who had been passed over for office or favour, while other prominent troublemakers had links with the Whig opposition in England.

The importance both of practical grievances and of political self-interest was made clear by what followed. Parliament did not meet again until 1695. By this time Sydney's successor, Sir Henry Capel, had worked out a settlement with some of the leading troublemakers of the earlier session. Two of their number, Robert Rochfort and Alan Brodrick, became respectively attorney- and solicitor-general, and several others were also given office or added to the Privy Council. Meanwhile, the main concrete grievance that had fuelled the revolt was met by two new anti-Catholic bills, as well as by a general sense that affairs were now in the hands of more reliable men. On the key question of financial legislation, there was a careful compromise. The crown preserved its right to initiate money bills by sending over a bill drawn up by the English Privy Council to raise the token sum of £14,000. But the rest of what was needed, estimated at £200,000, was to be raised by legislation initiated in the Commons. Not everyone approved of this compromise. Rochfort and others were attacked by a former ally 'as men quitting their country's interest, by taking to be the king's servants'.[5] Later there were renewed demands for habeas corpus and a bill of rights. But all these attempts to revive the principles that had been put forward in 1692 were beaten off with little difficulty.

What made it necessary to conciliate the rebellious Irish parliament in this way was the unprecedented strain imposed by war on the public finances of both Ireland and Great Britain. Charles II's Irish parliament of 1661–6 had voted permanent revenues sufficient to meet all the needs of government and even to permit the transfer of significant surpluses from Ireland to England. Lost income and military spending during the crisis of 1688–91 wholly destroyed this equilibrium. Then came the cost of continued war with France, until 1697 and again from 1702 until 1713, followed by the decision that Ireland should continue to house and support a substantial portion of the peacetime standing army. All this could be paid for only by supplementing the hereditary revenue by additional duties, on alcohol, tobacco, and other goods, and these had to be voted by parliament.[6] The parliament of 1695 granted the

---

[5] Capel to Shrewsbury, 25 Aug. 1695 (PRONI T2807/5).

[6] In the absence of a recent study of public finance in this period, I have relied on T. J. Kiernan, *History of the Financial Administration of Ireland*, 160, 216–17; and O'Brien, *Economic History of Ireland in the Eighteenth Century*, 325–7.

necessary funds, but only for a period of two years: a move of much greater practical importance than its retreat on the principle of 'sole right'. This ensured that parliament met again in 1695, 1697, and 1699. Thereafter, rising receipts from the hereditary revenue, reflecting an expansion in trade, permitted government not to summon parliament for four years. When it did finally meet, there were pessimistic predictions that members might be asked to vote taxes for four or five years to come. In fact, what the Commons offered was additional duties for two years only, and they did not ratify these until other pieces of legislation, notably the major act against Catholic landed property, had been completed to their satisfaction.[7] Parliament met again in 1705, 1707, 1709, 1710, 1711, and 1713. From 1715 it became standard practice for it to meet every second year, to secure its recall by voting taxes for a period of two years only, and to pass the required financial bills only after the Commons had scrutinized the public accounts and considered other proposed legislation.[8]

The second major development to contribute to the reshaping of Irish politics was the rise of party. Divisions along lines of religious and political principle already existed in the 1690s. Indeed, the parliaments of 1695 and 1697 saw a power struggle between two quite clearly defined groups. On one side were those former 'sole right' men who had come to an arrangement with Capel and who continued, even after the lord deputy's death in May 1696, to be referred to as 'my lord Capel's friends'. On the other were the followers of the lord chancellor, Sir Charles Porter. Porter had been one of the main targets of the opposition attack in 1692, on account of his alleged Jacobite and Catholic sympathies. He and his followers continued to resist demands for a punitive anti-Catholic policy, and he also deplored what he saw as Capel's betrayal of the royal prerogative, in making terms with men who had obstructed the king's government. These, of course, were very much the issues that were to run through the Whig–Tory conflict of the next two decades. And indeed it has been pointed out that the majority of those MPs who remained in politics after 1703 did in fact follow a consistent allegiance, Porter's supporters becoming Tories and Capel's Whigs.[9] Yet Ireland was still some distance from fully fledged party politics. The very designation of the two groups by the names of their leaders makes this clear. So does the absence of a clear-cut alternation in power. Some of Porter's friends were removed to make way for Brodrick, Rochfort, and their followers in 1695, but

---

[7] Alan Brodrick to St John Brodrick, 29 Nov. 1702 (Midleton MS 1248/2, fos. 74–5); Simms, 'The Making of a Penal Law', in *War and Politics in Ireland*, 268–70.

[8] In 1724 Archbishop King noted that no public bill of any significance had passed in the recent parliamentary session, 'and some say we deserve to be so served for passing the money bill before we saw what we were to have for it': King to Edward Southwell, 8 Feb. 1724 (TCD MS 2537, 74).

[9] Hayton, 'Beginnings of the "Undertaker System"', 44.

others, including Porter himself, remained in office. The power struggle of
1695–7 in fact took place within the Irish executive. Even at the point where
Porter's opponents were trying to have him impeached, first in England and
then in Dublin, accusers and accused were all nominally members of the
court party. Clear-cut groupings came to an end in any case with Porter's
death in December 1696. His successor, John Methuen, reported the following June that 'the parties, which I find were even to a greater height than
I believed, are much broken'. 'My lord Capel's friends' were 'very easy,
believing the government such as they could wish', whereas Porter's former
supporters, deprived of a leader, were seeking to disown the very idea that
they constituted a party.[10]

   The transition to true party politics came about only gradually. A predominantly Tory administration came to power in England with the accession
of Queen Anne in March 1702. Initially, however, it held back from recon-
structing the Irish executive along party lines. Alan Brodrick, contrary to
his own expectations, remained solicitor-general, and the administration
accepted without demur his election as Speaker of the Commons. During the
parliamentary session of 1703–4, however, Brodrick and others systematically
sought to obstruct government business. In doing so they made use of constitutional issues—parliamentary control of finance and the amendment of
Irish bills by the English Privy Council—similar to those employed in 1692.
But their motives were clearly those of party.[11] The lord lieutenant, the
second duke of Ormond, responded by dismissing Brodrick and others in the
spring of 1704 and replacing them with reliable Tories. It was at this point
that the terms 'Whig' and 'Tory' began to come into use in an Irish context.[12]
Just at the time that Ormond took this step, however, Queen Anne broke with
the high Tories who had dominated her first ministry, and installed a mixed
administration. Pressure from the Whig faction within this ministry brought
about the recall of Ormond in 1707, but his successor, the earl of Pembroke,
was a neutral choice who made one last attempt at non-party government in
Ireland. It was a failure. The Whigs readmitted to office remained dissatisfied
that they did not have total control, while Tories resented the dismissals that
had been necessary to make way for the new appointments.[13] Meanwhile, in
England, the Whigs were increasingly coming to dominate the ministry. At the
end of 1708 Pembroke was recalled, to be replaced by the Whig earl of
Wharton. The parliamentary session of 1709 was a straightforward duel

---

[10] Methuen to Somers, 26 June 1697 (PRONI T2807/16).
[11] Account of the Conduct of the Speaker (BL Add. MS 9715, fo. 69).
[12] For the earliest recorded use of the terms, see Hayton, 'Beginnings of the "Undertaker
System"', 44.
[13] 'Some Considerations upon the Change of the Government of Ireland' (PRONI D638/
147); Saunders to ——, 4 Nov. 1707 (BL Add. MS 9715, fo. 225).

between parties, with Whigs supporting Wharton's executive and Tories in opposition.[14]

What did these increasingly clear-cut and emotive party divisions involve? In England the major issues were clear enough. Whigs supported full religious and political toleration for Protestant Dissenters along with an aggressive foreign policy to contain the threat of France. Most of all, they were enthusiastic supporters of the principles of the Revolution. Tories sought to uphold the exclusive claims of the Church of England, opposed involvement in European power struggles, and were more likely to regard the removal of James II as a regrettable necessity.[15] To some observers it was incomprehensible that these English political debates should divide Irish Protestants. 'You are sufficiently laughed at here', Archbishop King wrote from London in 1710,

for concerning yourselves in the factions of England. It may mischieve you but can do you no good and yet I hear that you are abundantly higher there than the parties are here which is reckoned an effect of Irish understandings.[16]

But this was a pointless appeal. Some of the issues that divided Tory and Whig in England, notably those of foreign policy and the cost of the continental war, were to arouse little passion in Ireland. Others were to be modified or partially redefined. Once translated into Irish terms, however, the party debate reflected real differences of political principle and real disagreements about how the security of the kingdom could best be safeguarded.

The first major issue dividing the parties was religion. Indeed, it has been suggested that the main reason for the sudden intensification of party conflict in the years after 1703 was the rise of a militant High Church party among the clergy, whose demand was that the state preserve and extend the exclusive privileges of the established church.[17] Irish Tories, like their English counterparts, were committed defenders of those privileges. Whigs, on the other hand, sought to protect Protestant Dissenters from the assaults of the High Church party. At the same time—and here the continuity with the divisions of the 1690s was particularly clear—Whigs advocated strong repressive measures against Catholics, while Tories were less hostile. These differences were reflected in popular and electoral support. The clergy of the Church of Ireland overwhelmingly supported the Tories, while Presbyterian votes made Ulster a major Whig power base. Tories also generally benefited from the electoral support of Catholics, where these were permitted to vote,

---

[14] Dralle, 'Kingdom in Reversion'. This whole account draws heavily on David Hayton's pioneering study, 'Ireland and the English Ministers'.

[15] Holmes, *British Politics in the Age of Anne*; Szechi, *Jacobitism and Tory Politics*.

[16] King to Stearne, 16 Feb. 1710 (TCD MS 2531, 145).

[17] Hayton, 'Ireland and the English Ministers', 125–6.

and from the influence which propertied Catholics could exercise over their enfranchised Protestant dependants. 'Though the Papists hate both,' Archbishop King noted in 1711, 'yet they expect more moderation from one than from the other.'[18]

In all these cases, hostility and sympathy were relative terms. The great majority of active members of both parties were Anglicans, and their first loyalty was to their own church. Irish Whigs, while prepared to protect Dissenters from direct attack, did not necessarily advocate their elevation to equal rights with members of the Church of Ireland. In 1707, for example, a Whig administration in England found its Irish allies overwhelmingly opposed to the repeal of the sacramental test, which excluded Presbyterians from local government and public office. After 1714, when the Catholic and Jacobite threat had receded, Irish Whigs were to be even more inclined to see Dissenters kept in their place.[19] Nor, despite Whig smears, were Irish Tories sympathetic to, or even tolerant of, Catholics. The Tory administration of 1710–14 may not have introduced any new penal laws against Catholics. It did, however, respond to alarmist reports of the doings of regular clergy in the autumn of 1712 by launching a nationwide drive against unregistered and non-juring priests. Forwarding copies of the proclamation that initiated this drive, Joshua Dawson, secretary to the lords justices and Tory MP for Wicklow, expressed the hope that gentlemen would exert themselves 'to put the laws in execution against those vermin that are always contriving the destruction of our constitution'.[20] The difference between Whig and Tory was not a matter of positive favour towards either of the two non-Anglican denominations. Instead, the debate was over which of the two presented the greater threat to the position of the Church of Ireland.

The second major issue dividing Whig and Tory in early eighteenth-century Ireland was their differing views of the implications of what had taken place in 1688. It is true that Irish Protestants, a minority in a predominantly Catholic country, were less well placed than their English counterparts to indulge in scruples about the legitimacy of having removed a Catholic monarch and his successors from the throne. This applied even to those who on religious issues would have been counted as Tories. 'We have one happiness,' King told an English bishop in 1709,

that generally speaking the most hearty persons for the Church are likewise most cordial for the Revolution, which I believe is partly due to the great sufferings they underwent in King James's reign, and I am apt to think that if in England they had tasted a little more of our treatment, there would have been as few non-jurors with you as with us.[21]

---

[18] King to Southwell, 13 Mar. 1711 (TCD MS 2531, 322–3).
[19] See below, ch. 5.
[20] Dawson to Forth and Moore, 23 Sept. 1712 (Country Letters, fo. 44ᵛ).
[21] King to bishop of Bangor, 8 Feb. 1709 (TCD MS 2531, 49–50).

To the extent that Ireland produced few Protestant Jacobites, King's claims were valid enough. But matters of constitutional principle nevertheless played a crucial part in the party conflict of the early eighteenth century. The issues involved were not very often directly debated. Statements of general principle, in fact, tended to come most commonly from clergymen, whose sense of theological certitude, or habitual pulpit dogmatism, sometimes took them further than most others would have wished. Thus an army chaplain who had preached in 1707 on the traditional High Church themes of passive obedience and divine right was attacked, not just by Whigs, but by Tory leaders also, for 'a very foolish sermon . . . overturning all Revolution principles'. Two years later it was the turn of the Whigs to be embarrassed by a sermon preached on the anniversary of the execution of Charles I, which had 'condemned the king, justified the traitors in everything but their barbarous way of killing him and . . . concluded with a tragical exclamation and curse on all such as believe passive obedience or the divine right of kings'.[22] Outside the pulpit, differences of constitutional outlook were more commonly expressed in skirmishing over trivial but symbolic issues. In 1709, for example, when Trinity College, Dublin, received a grant of £5,000 to build a library, Tories reacted angrily to a resolution of the House of Commons declaring this to be a reward for the college's 'steady adherence . . . to the late happy Revolution' and its action in expelling a student accused of insulting the memory of William III.[23] In a case like this, party conflict can be seen to have taken on its own momentum. Issues were elevated, regardless of their actual content, into symbols of what each side opposed in the other and sought to defend against it. Because so much conflict took place at this symbolic level, moreover, it was easy for each party to attribute to the other principles more extreme than the majority at least of its members actually supported.

The constitutional debate between the two parties, then, was an ambiguous combination of exaggerated mutual suspicion and real differences in outlook. Tories regarded Whigs, with their emphasis on the glories of the Revolution, as well as their patronage of Dissenters, as threatening to subvert the whole religious and social order. Sir Richard Cox, writing in 1714, described himself—truthfully—as having played a 'perfectly Hanoverian' part in the recent succession crisis. But he nevertheless insisted that he was, 'and to my dying day shall be, an anti-Whig. I hate their canting, lying and hypocrisy and I know too many of them aim at mutiny and schism.' Elsewhere he fell back on the vocabulary of the English civil war, referring to the 'fanatics and republicans' who longed for the overthrow of loyal men and their replacement

---

[22] Cox to Southwell, 4 Feb. 1707 (BL Add. MS 38,154, fo. 150ᵛ); King to Southwell, 16 Feb. 1709 (TCD MS 2531, 61): 'The Whigs . . . are as angry as can be and look on it as a mischievous libel on them.'
[23] Cox to Southwell, 4 June 1709 (BL Add. MS 38,156, fo. 79); cf. Dralle, 'Kingdom in Reversion', 404–5, 428.

by 'saints'.[24] Opponents of the Tories, for their part, claimed that they could not be trusted to place religion ahead of monarchical principle and uphold the Protestant succession. One reason why this charge was more credible than it might at first seem was that it was not, in the end, the political principles of Irish Tories themselves that were at issue. The disposition of the crowns of both Great Britain and Ireland would be decided, not in Dublin, but in London. So even if the Irish Tories did not themselves make very credible Jacobites, their alliance with Queen Anne's last English ministry was enough to convict them, in the eyes of many, of endangering the Protestant succession.

Differing degrees of enthusiasm for the general principles of the Revolution might logically be expected to have gone hand in hand with differing attitudes to day-to-day relations between executive and parliament. In practice, this was less and less the case. In England a growing association with the grievances of the country gentleman meant that, already from the 1690s, the Tories, the former supporters of the Crown, had become increasingly concerned with limiting the power of the executive. Conversely, the Whigs, the former defenders of parliamentary control and private liberties, became proponents of strong government.[25] In Ireland the position is less clear. There too the Whigs were the party who had earlier, in the 1690s, been associated with the defence of parliamentary privilege, the Tories the former supporters of the Crown. In the years that followed the Tories continued to use some of the language of a court party. In 1707, for example, their leaders responded to the appointment of Pembroke by presenting themselves as the natural supporters of the executive, who could serve the new man as they had his predecessor, 'without changing one principle'. The Whigs, on the other hand, could do nothing for him 'without running counter to everything they pressed for in both the last sessions'.[26] Whigs, for their part, still used some of the language of principled opposition. As late as 1713, Alan Brodrick could complain of a fellow MP that 'in every question of importance, where the court and country interest came in competition, he is a sure dead vote against the country'.[27] In Ireland, of course, such arguments had an additional twist, in that the potential confrontation was between the Irish parliament and an English-appointed executive. The Whigs, Sir Richard Cox claimed, 'maintain their popularity . . . by clamour against the jurisdiction, shall I say oppression, of England'; he, on the other hand, took as his maxim 'that 'tis the true interest of Ireland to retain the protection and affection of England, and I

---

[24] Cox to Southwell, 14 Aug. 1714 (BL Add. MS 38,157, fo. 108); same to same, 11 Sept. 1714 (ibid., fo. 121).

[25] Plumb, *Growth of Political Stability*, ch. 5.

[26] Saunders to Southwell, 10 June 1707 (BL Add. MS 9715, fo. 162ᵛ).

[27] Alan Brodrick to Alan Brodrick, jun., 26 Dec. 1713 (Midleton MS 1248/3, fo. 149ᵛ).

think it foolish to dispute their jurisdiction'. Another Tory leader listed the principles of his party as being 'to support the government with honour, not to quarrel with England, and to get all the good laws they could for the country'.[28]

All this, however, was increasingly so much rhetoric. On the Whig side the compromise of 1695 was to be several times repeated. In 1707, for example, Whig leaders who had earlier argued that parliament should maintain maximum control over the executive by never granting taxes for more than one year dropped this principle when the Tory Ormond was replaced as lord lieutenant by the more acceptable earl of Pembroke. In 1709 the Whigs were required to retreat even further from earlier principles when a Whig ministry in London altered the preamble to a money bill. On this occasion former 'sole right' men like Thomas Brodrick appeared as speakers for the altered money bill, while Tories denounced the alteration as an attack on 'the poor remains of our constitution'.[29] In 1715, with solidly Whig executives installed in both kingdoms following the accession of George I, it was once again a Tory opposition that took up the 'sole right' issue, arguing that the Commons should accept no finance bill that had not originated with themselves.[30] On both sides, it seems clear, the pursuit of party advantage had come to count for more than any theoretical commitment to a particular set of political principles.

The final stage in the development of party politics in Ireland began in August 1710, with the coming to power of the Tory administration headed by Robert Harley and Henry St John. Ormond returned to Ireland as lord lieutenant, Whig office-holders were dismissed and replaced by Tories, and the Church of Ireland commenced a new offensive against Dissenters. By this time, however, matters had gone beyond mere partisan politics. The queen was middle-aged, childless, and in poor health. The question of the succession would have to be decided shortly. Even as the new ministry took office, Alan Brodrick had reported that 'both parties looked just as in the beginning of eighty-eight', and that he himself could see 'nothing drawing on,

---

[28] Cox to Southwell, 27 May 1707 (BL Add. MS 38,155, fo. 51); Saunders to Southwell, 5 July 1707 (BL Add. MS 9715, fo. 170). Cox later had plans to write a reply to Molyneux's assertion of Ireland's constitutional independence: Cox to Southwell, 16 Oct. 1714 (BL Add. MS 38,157, fo. 136).

[29] Anderson Saunders to [Southwell], 5 July 1707 (BL Add. MS 9715, fo. 170); Addison to Godolphin, 10, 12 Aug. 1709 (Addison, *Letters*, 174, 176); Archdeacon W. Perceval to Sir John Perceval, 4 Aug. 1709 (HMC, *Egmont Papers*, ii. 238). There were also claims in 1709 that Alan Brodrick was seeking support for a British Act of Parliament to repeal the sacramental test in Ireland (James, *Ireland in the Empire*, 70). This would indeed have been a spectacular betrayal of Whig principles. However, it is so much at variance with Brodrick's private comments on the claims of the Presbyterians at this time (see below, p. 168) that the report, from a hostile source, is difficult to credit.

[30] Lords justices to Stanhope, 23 Nov. 1715 (SP63/373/256).

but what we have for twenty years past been (in all appearance) endeavouring to prevent'.[31] Over the next four years the proceedings of the executive ensured that such fears came to be shared by growing numbers. Its law officers prosecuted outspoken Whigs, yet dropped proceedings against a Jacobite printer, Edward Lloyd. There were claims of undue favour shown to recent converts from Catholicism and that the militia, the chief means by which Irish Protestants could hope to ensure their own security, was being run down. By the closing months of 1713 the political system had been brought to the edge of breakdown. A general election in November was bitterly contested. In Dublin, Tory supporters, many of them allegedly Catholics, rioted in support of their candidates, while at least nine recent converts were returned as Tory members. When parliament met, the Whig majority voted supplies for a period of only three months. In January 1714 attempts by the duke of Shrewsbury, who had replaced Ormond as lord lieutenant in September, to negotiate a compromise between the two sides collapsed.[32]

By this time the management of Ireland had become one issue in the power struggle taking place within the Tory party between moderates, led by Harley, now earl of Oxford, and extremists, led by St John, now Viscount Bolingbroke. In the summer of 1714 the hard-liners finally triumphed. Dissent, in Ireland as in England, immediately came under renewed attack. Payment of the *regium donum* was suspended, there was a rash of prosecutions under the Act of Uniformity, and Anglican mobs attacked meeting-houses. Meanwhile, fears regarding the succession grew as the queen's health failed. To add to the general tension, large numbers of Catholics were found to be enlisting with agents supposedly raising troops for the Pretender. When some of those arrested were sentenced to death, Thomas Lindsay, the Tory archbishop of Armagh and one of the lords justices, appeared to obstruct the execution of the sentence, while at the same time calling for action against Whig gentlemen who had begun to arm themselves in case of trouble. Even when the government, in July 1714, issued a proclamation calling for the seizure of the Pretender if he should land in the kingdom, there were claims that this had been deliberately worded in such a way as in fact to protect him from attack.[33] 'Matters seem to look cloudily,' Archbishop King wrote in June 1714; 'God only knows when they will clear up. Men's hearts melt for fear, and many are at their wits end what course to take.'[34]

---

[31] Alan Brodrick to Thomas Brodrick, 12, 15 Aug. 1710 (Midleton MS 1248/3, fos. 11, 13).
[32] Simms, 'Irish Parliament of 1713'; Hayton, 'The Crisis in Ireland'.
[33] King to bishop of Clogher, 3 July 1714 (TCD MS 750/4/1, 312).
[34] King to Samuel Molyneux, 17 June 1714 (TCD MS 750/4/1, 305).

2. 'Little Employments . . . Smiles, Good Dinners'

In the end, in Ireland as in Britain, the crisis never happened. When Queen Anne died on 1 August 1714, George Lewis, elector of Hanover, was proclaimed king without opposition. His accession was followed in all three kingdoms by an unprecedented purge of central and local government, replacing Tories with Whigs. Brodrick, promoted to the peerage as Viscount Midleton, became lord chancellor, while William Conolly became first commissioner of the revenue. Tories were dismissed from the judiciary, the Privy Council, the revenue service, and other offices held during pleasure.[35] In County Clare it was reported that the Whigs 'are resolved not one Tory shall be as much as a high constable'.[36] A general election in 1715 produced a large Whig majority; in many cases, it was reported, Tories did not even stand.[37] When parliament met, the Whigs made the very best of their advantage. Members of the fallen Tory administration were censured as enemies of the Protestant succession, and those who had supported them were forced to make humiliating public retractions. In four Tory-controlled boroughs the government intervened directly—twice by special act of parliament—to create new Whig-dominated corporations. The Tory hold on the House of Lords was broken by the creation in 1715 of eleven Whig peers; in the years that followed, the Whig majority thus created was strengthened by the appointment of reliable men to vacant bishoprics. Tory newspaper proprietors were imprisoned, fined, or driven into exile by a series of prosecutions.[38]

This transfer of power, unlike earlier shifts in the position of the parties, was to be permanent. After 1714 Tories never again held office, in either Ireland or Great Britain. At the same time there was a notable difference in their fortunes in the two countries. In England the Tories, despite exclusion from office, accusations of Jacobitism, and the curtailing of their popular support by means of the Riot Act and other repressive measures, remained a major force in national politics. In fact, it is now argued that the two-party system remained right up to the 1750s central to English parliamentary politics.[39] In Ireland too, a recognizable Tory party survived after 1714, its members joining dissident Whigs in opposing the government. Midleton, in 1717, sought to attach the label 'Tory' to all opponents of the ministry, 'whatever they formerly have been, or may pretend now to be'. In 1723, on

---

[35] Hayton, 'Ireland and the English Ministers', 304–8; Joseph Griffin, 'Parliamentary Politics in Ireland during the Reign of George I', 8–10; James, *Ireland in the Empire*, 85–7.

[36] *Inchiquin Manuscripts*, 121.

[37] Charles Delafaye to ——, 3 Nov. 1715 (SP63/373/207); King to Samuel Molyneux, 3 Nov. 1715 (TCD MS 2533, 116).

[38] Munter, *Irish Newspaper*, 128–9.

[39] Colley, *In Defiance of Oligarchy*; Cruickshanks, 'The Political Management of Sir Robert Walpole', in Black (ed.), *Britain in the Age of Walpole*, 32–3.

the other hand, when Midleton was in conflict with the lord lieutenant, it was he who found parliamentary support among the Tories. Two years later, when the Brodricks had progressed to open opposition, Tories 'to a man' allied with a group led by Midleton's son, St John Brodrick, to oppose the government over irregularities in the public accounts.[40] By the end of the 1720s, however, old animosities had begun to lose their force. In 1728 Bishop Bolton of Elphin believed that a proposed new parliamentary manager, Marmaduke Coghill, would be able to attract the support of the Tories, as long as they were not driven into another alliance with dissident Whigs by the 'unaccountably narrow' notions of some, who 'almost look upon a man as a deserter that shows common civility to those they call Tories'. By 1733 Coghill himself could dismiss the argument that one of the candidates for the Speakership of the Commons was a Tory while the other was a Whig with the comment: 'I thought these names were pretty well over and forgotten amongst us.'[41] Lord Chesterfield, writing as lord lieutenant of Ireland in 1745, confirmed that 'here are no parties of Whigs and Tories, no formed opposition'.[42]

Why did the Irish Tory party fall apart so much more quickly than the English? The Whig attack at the time of the accession of George I had been a ferocious one, but then English Tories suffered a similar proscription and an even more unscrupulous pillorying of their leaders. One answer would be that these imported party divisions had never made quite as much sense in Ireland as they had in England. This is not to say that the conflict between Whig and Tory had not involved real differences of principle. But the events of 1714, highlighting as they did the gap between political doctrine and what could in reality be lived with, may well have brought a more acute crisis of conscience for Irish Tories than for English. Certainly, subsequent allegations of Jacobitism or of Jacobite fellow-travelling, damaging enough in England, were much more so in Ireland. In England, furthermore, the defence of the established church continued to give Tories an effective rallying call. In Ireland, by contrast, the apparent threat of an expanding Presbyterianism receded from the early 1720s, if not before. There were later attempts, inspired from London, to abolish the sacramental test. But on these occasions the majority of rank and file Whigs proved as ready as the Tories had ever been to support the privileges of the Church of Ireland.

[40] Midleton to Thomas Brodrick, 11 Nov. 1717 (Midleton MS 1248/4, fo. 92ᵛ); Boulter to Newcastle, 28 Oct. 1725 (*Letters*, i. 49); Coghill to Southwell, 30 Oct. 1725 (BL Add. MS 21,122, fo. 24).

[41] Theophilus Bolton to [Carteret?], 16 July 1728 (PRONI D562/92); Coghill to Southwell, 5 Apr. 1733 (BL Add. MS 21,123, fo. 33). Old labels did not die out entirely, however. In 1744 Tories were reported to be greatly pleased by the appointment of Patrick Delany as dean of Down. Delany, according to his new bishop, was 'a distinguished high churchman but has affected to be thought a Whig for a few years past': John Ryder to Sir Dudley Ryder, 21 May 1744 (PRONI T3228/1/11).

[42] Chesterfield to Newcastle, 12 Sept. 1745 (*Letters*, iii. 664–5).

With party divisions now of peripheral importance, what gave shape to Irish parliamentary politics? The usual answer is faction and the pursuit of profit. Hayton, for example, sees the Whig and Tory parties of Queen Anne's reign giving way after 1714 to 'associations of men bound together in pursuit of power, place and profit rather than believers in a common ideology'. Dickson writes in similar terms of 'informal associations of MPs, which were held together by family connection or personal loyalty to the leading member, the common objective being to maximise the group's access to government patronage'. Elsewhere he summarizes the political objectives of the land-owners who dominated the Irish parliament from the 1710s to the 1760s. These were, 'in descending order of priority, . . . collective security of their property and social position, private profit from places, offices, employments and contracts in the gift of the state, low taxes, and . . . the creation and maintenance of an economic order that would aid and protect their estates and their incomes'.[43]

It would, of course, be pointless to deny the role of profit and self-advancement in eighteenth-century public life. Commissions in the army, places in the Church of Ireland, office in central or local government, membership of public corporations, sinecures, pensions, and peerages: all these were part of the common currency of politics. At the same time an analysis conducted wholly in such terms presents certain problems. The first is that it depends on a severely reductionist view of human motivation. A degree of scepticism concerning motives is, of course, no bad thing in a historian, particularly where politicians are concerned. But there is nevertheless a whiff of the pejorative in even recent writing on mainstream Irish politics in the mid-eighteenth century that seems to go beyond mere healthy cynicism. One recent commentator, for example, draws on a single case study of profiteering in the revenue service in order to characterize the lower levels of the Protestant establishment as a whole in terms that it is difficult to imagine being applied, today at least, to any other group within society: 'the grubby minor gentry—the second eleven of the ascendancy—who singlemindedly devoted themselves to increasing their store in this life and who sought to perpetuate both their name and their fortune after their death'.[44] A similar disposition to concentrate on the lowest common denominator, in terms of motivation, may be seen in the frequent attempts—discussed in a later chapter—to interpret penal legislation against Catholics solely in terms of the economic advantages to their persecutors.[45]

---

[43] Hayton, 'Beginnings of the "Undertaker System"', 47; Dickson, *New Foundations*, 63, 72-7.

[44] Thomas Bartlett, review in *IHS* 25 (1986), 101. The case study which Bartlett is reviewing, Clarkson and Crawford, *Ways to Wealth*, bears out his description well enough; it is the readiness to generalize from it in such strong terms that is suspect.

[45] Below, ch. 7, sect. 4.

A second weakness of the prevailing image of political life in Hanoverian Ireland is that it fails to take account of the important reassessment of the role and limitations of patronage developed (for a slightly later period) by Malcomson. In the first place, not all official patronage was employed for the purchase of parliamentary support. In reality, any substantial proprietor who was not in systematic opposition could expect to be permitted to nominate to minor local appointments and to solicit the occasional favour for himself or his dependants. Such benefits were an acknowledgement of a proprietor's social importance and a recompense for his work as the unpaid local agent of government; they in no way made him a client of the court. Secondly, and more important, patronage was not omnicompetent. Promotion in the peerage or a legal appointment for a relative or friend might secure an individual's compliance on a given occasion; it could not guarantee loyalty for the future. To work efficiently, patronage had to be constantly renewed. But in practice the supply was never equal to the demand, so that for every temporarily grateful recipient there were likely to be several disappointed and quite possibly troublesome supplicants.[46]

Malcomson's analysis is developed in the context of the late eighteenth and early nineteenth centuries. But in earlier decades too there are indications that the role of patronage as a political cement has been exaggerated. In 1732, when the government was actively seeking the removal of the sacramental test, Archbishop Boulter warned that it could not count on its influence over office-holders to help push the measure through, 'since in this and the last session many who have places under the Crown have voted wrong, where the Crown was directly concerned'. When a removal of the test had been attempted in 1719, Boulter recalled, 'not above 10 out of 50 in places' had voted for it.[47] A detailed analysis of the membership of the Irish parliament compiled in 1769, at the height of a bitter power struggle between the lord lieutenant and the leading political interest headed by Lord Shannon and the Ponsonby family, shows that even at this moment of maximum mobilization on both sides, over half the MPs listed were categorized as independents. This included no less than 55 of the 112 members reckoned as certain government supporters.[48] The different purposes, apart from the crude purchase of parliamentary support, which the granting of official favours could serve may also be seen in the list of names which Lord Chesterfield in 1746 proposed for admission to the Privy Council. Of the eight names he forwarded, one was a son-in-law to the Speaker of the House of Commons, who 'makes it a point', two others had 'relations' of 'credit and influence' who had solicited on

---

[46] Malcomson, *Foster*, 236–43. Malcomson's cautions regarding the importance of patronage are interestingly confirmed in a study of early and mid-eighteenth-century Scotland: J. S. Shaw, *Management of Scottish Society*, ch. 5.

[47] Boulter to Newcastle, 15 Jan. 1732 (SP63/395/3ᵛ).

[48] Large, 'The Irish House of Commons in 1769'.

their behalf, and a further two were 'what we call here *Castle-men*—that is, they meddle with no cabals or parties, but they belong to the lord lieutenant'. On the other hand, Lord Kildare and Lord Kerry were to be included because their rank and estate made it impossible to refuse them, while the reason for proposing Lord Limerick was that he 'applies himself much to the business of this country [and] promotes the manufactures'.[49]

The final and most important reason for dissatisfaction with the interpretation of early and mid-eighteenth-century Irish politics as amounting to no more than the self-interested pursuit of office and profit is that such a perspective repeatedly fails to do justice to the manner in which individuals actually behaved. Consider, for example, a political career that extended from the accession of William III to the last years of George I. Alan Brodrick, Viscount Midleton, is at first sight a perfect illustration of the expediency and self-aggrandizement concealed behind the political rhetoric of his age. A leading troublemaker in the parliament of 1692, he was one of those who came to terms with Capel in time for the session of 1695. In the reign of Queen Anne he continued to be the epitome of a court Whig, supporting government, altered money bills and all, while his party was in office, but seeking during periods of Tory government to revert to the rhetoric of patriotism.[50] After 1714 he pursued similar tactics in a new environment. Instead of party conflict, there was now a struggle for supremacy between two Whig factions, that of Midleton and that of his former ally, William Conolly. Faced with a series of lord lieutenants disposed to favour Conolly, Midleton, working through his son St John in the House of Commons, carried on a covert opposition. For this purpose his faction once again took up the stance of patriots. In the session of 1715–16, for example, Brodrick led the attack on the government's financial legislation, focusing in particular on the issue of pensions. Midleton, in private correspondence, claimed to be the spokesman of the 'country gentlemen', as opposed to Conolly's 'junto'.[51] In 1717, on the other hand, when a lord lieutenant favourable to Midleton was in power, he sought to prevent the House of Lords from pursuing the issue of its appellate jurisdiction in the case of *Sherlock* v. *Annesley*.[52] In 1727, after Midleton had finally been forced out of office, one of Conolly's lieutenants offered a harsh summary of his whole political career. A proposal by some of Midleton's supporters to delay passing the money bill until the committee of accounts had reported was, he imagined,

made with an intention to try if a party could be formed, upon some topic of patriotism, wherewith you know he often deceived young members (of which I have

[49] Chesterfield to Newcastle, 11 Mar. 1746 (*Letters*, iii. 742–4).
[50] See above, pp. 76, 78, 83.
[51] Midleton to Thomas Brodrick, 21 Nov. 1719 (Midleton MS 1248/4, fo. 170ᵛ).
[52] Griffin, 'Parliamentary Politics in . . . the Reign of George I', 52–5.

been one) which in the end have always proved mischievous to the country, and a means only to help designing men to what they aim at; witness the sole right, and the taxes for one year.[53]

All this is Brodrick's career as seen from the outside, in bald, factual summary, and through the eyes of his political opponents. Seen from within, through his private correspondence, his behaviour takes on a somewhat different aspect. The twists and turns are still there, but there is also, throughout his letters, a concern to justify his conduct that fits uneasily into the picture of an unashamedly mercenary political culture. Nor are his attempts to refute allegations of inconsistency or bad faith entirely without substance. On the question of money bills, for example, his original defence of the 'sole right' had been closely linked to his intense distrust of the administration of the day. It was thus not wholly inconsistent two years later, when the government was in the hands of men whom he considered 'sincerely friends to the true interest of this kingdom', for him to take a more flexible line. 'Good laws', he told his brother Thomas, 'will be an equivalent and be a good exchange for our money, and for ought I know our sole right of preparing heads of bills for money.'[54] In 1707, justifying his retreat from the principle of a one-year money bill which he had enunciated under the Tory lord lieutenant Ormond, he put the point more explicitly: 'Our principle was and always will be to do what was most for the service of our country; and it was so to do as little as possible for one chief governor, and not to be equally close handed to another.'[55]

In most of these cases, of course, Brodrick/Midleton remains open to the charge that he was concerned solely to rationalize his self-interest. There is, however, one episode in his political career that cannot be interpreted in such terms. In March 1719 Midleton announced his intention of voting, in his capacity as a member of the British House of Commons, against the government's Peerage Bill.

I am not at all a stranger to the probable consequences of men's speaking and acting according to their own sentiments in a certain affair; on the contrary have had broad hints, nay plain indications what is determined to follow. I have put honour and integrity in one scale and find it vastly to outweigh convenience, and am determined

---

[53] Coghill to Southwell, 8 Dec. 1727 (BL Add. MS 21,122, fos. 35–6).

[54] Alan Brodrick to Thomas Brodrick, 5 May 1694 (Midleton MS 1248/1, fos. 268–9).

[55] Alan Brodrick to a sister, 5 Aug. 1707 (Midleton MS 1248/2, fo. 316ᵛ). Brodrick was also consistent in another respect. In 1693 he justified his opposition to the measures of an executive in which he held minor legal office by arguing that such office did not bind him to a 'servile compliance': Alan Brodrick to [St John Brodrick], 6 May 1693 (ibid. 1248/1, fo. 259). Thirty years later he argued that his salary and perquisites as lord chancellor left him 'at liberty to act, vote and speak in parliament (as a lord) just in the same manner while I was on the woolsack, as I should have done on one of the benches': Midleton to Thomas Brodrick, 15 Mar. 1725 (in Walpole, *Memoirs*, ii. 417).

never to purchase the latter by parting with the former. This is a fixed resolution now, when it is in my power to do the convenient thing if I please.[56]

The tone of the declaration, carefully copied out and filed away in Midleton's papers with an explanatory note for posterity, is unpalatably self-righteous. But in this case at least, it is difficult to find reasons to suggest that his protestations concealed any ulterior motive. The Peerage Bill, intended to limit future ennoblements to the filling up of vacancies caused by the extinction of existing titled families, was indeed a party measure. It was proposed by the ministry of Sunderland and Stanhope, as a means of making permanent their faction's dominance in the House of Lords. It was opposed by their Whig rivals, Walpole and Townshend, who had gone out of office in 1717. Midleton, however, was an associate of the Stanhope–Sunderland faction; the lord lieutenant they had appointed for Ireland, the duke of Bolton, was his personal friend. All this makes it difficult to see his opposition to the bill as motivated by anything other than genuine principle. And in fact his stand was to lead to a permanent breach with both Bolton and Sunderland and a consequent revival in the fortunes of his rival Conolly.

Brodrick/Midleton was not the only politician of this era to profess, and on some occasions at least to demonstrate, that his conduct was motivated by something more than the pursuit of personal advantage. In fact, as Malcomson has shown, the theme of honour recurs constantly in Irish political correspondence throughout the eighteenth century.[57] Thus a letter from Edward Southwell in 1733 concerning a proposed accommodation with a rival for control of the borough of Kinsale is devoted mainly to his obligations 'in honour' both to his dependants in the borough and to other gentlemen to whom he had made promises regarding the disposal of his interest. A similar concern with reputation and integrity runs through the remarkably modest general statement that Marmaduke Coghill, no retiring backbencher but an aide and eventual heir to William Conolly, offered in 1733:

I have no other ambition but to go through the world with some sort of credit, to be in such a station only as becomes a private gentleman, to have as much business as may take up a reasonable part of my time, and to be able to serve my friends on proper occasions and that I may preserve the character of an honest man.[58]

Again, as in the case of Midleton, such professions cannot always be dismissed as posturing or self-delusion. In 1755, for example, the politically minded countess of Kildare welcomed the news that the struggle against the lord lieutenant in which her husband and others had been engaged seemed

---

[56] Midleton MS 1248/4, fos. 144–5.
[57] Malcomson, '"The Parliamentary Traffic of this Country"', 150–61.
[58] Southwell to Coghill, 11 Oct. 1733 (BL Add. MS 21,123, fo. 55); Coghill to Southwell, 31 Mar. 1733 (ibid., fo. 30ᵛ).

likely to end. At the same time, she instructed her husband, 'rather than be dirty or do any thing that had the appearance of being bought off, I would renounce all expectations and oppose as violently as ever'. Yet the Kildares were not at this time well off, and the £1,500 a year which the earl was to receive as Master General of the Ordnance after he had eventually made his peace with government was to mean a great deal to them. A less heroic but equally striking illustration of the motivating power of honour is provided by the case of Thomas Burgh, a minor office-holder who in 1729, after a night's hard drinking with members of the opposition, promised them 'in his cups' to vote against the money bill. Burgh kept his promise, and was punished by being refused the leave he had applied for to sell his office.[59]

All this, of course, related essentially to honour in personal conduct. What sense of obligation existed in relation to the public interest is more difficult to assess. The concept of 'patriotism' was already well established by the first decade of the eighteenth century, in both a laudatory and a derogatory sense. A supporter of Alan Brodrick commiserated with him in 1704 on having been dismissed from office for no other reason 'but your hearty espousing your country's interest and appearing as became a true patriot'. Three years later a political opponent noted derisively that Brodrick, having been appointed attorney-general by Pembroke, 'fell in now with the demands of the court, though he was too great a patriot to do it in the duke of Ormond's government'.[60] Patriotism had a specifically Irish meaning, as the defence of local or national interests against English interference. But it could also be used in the same sense as in contemporary England to mean a defence of the public interest against corruption, mismanagement, or abuse of power by the executive. In many cases, of course, the two senses overlapped. In addition, patriotism was associated with a wider concept of civic virtue. A speech in the Irish Commons in October 1729, for example, jumbled together political grievances and social ills in a single litany of complaint, lamenting

our want of public spirit, the poverty of the kingdom, the ill consequences of our people going to America, occasioned by pretendedly the oppression of landlords by setting their lands too high, and the hardships of collecting tithes, by the luxury of the better sort of people, by the extravagance of the ladies in their silks, laces and other vanities, by the irregular and uncertain state of our coin, by the tricks of bankers and merchants, by our excess in drinking French wines, by our gentlemen and ladies going abroad and living out of their native country, by the neglect of our laws for tillage, by the continual adding to our establishment.

The speaker concluded with a classic statement of the political philosophy of

[59] Countess of Kildare to earl of Kildare, 12 May 1755 (Leinster, *Correspondence*, i. 14); Coghill to Southwell, 25 Dec. 1729 (BL Add. MS 21,122, fo. 102ᵛ).

[60] William Cairnes to Alan Brodrick, 18 Apr. 1704 (Midleton MS 1248/2, fo. 133); Archdeacon William Perceval to Sir John Perceval, 7 Nov. 1707, in HMC, *Egmont Papers*, ii. 217–18.

the independent member, exhorting younger MPs 'not to be seduced by the flattery of courtiers to give up their country, nor by the insinuations of ill designing men (who intend to raise themselves on their shoulders) to go into any peevish or ill humoured measure to make the government uneasy'.[61]

Patriot sentiments were consistently espoused by only a small minority of MPs. At the same time they were capable, at least intermittently, of motivating a much larger group. If this had not been so, after all, opportunistic politicians out of office would hardly have thought it to their advantage to take up a patriot stance. The resonance of such themes over a wider cross-section of the political nation was most dramatically demonstrated in the great set-piece constitutional battles of the early and mid-eighteenth century, like the campaign against William Wood's patent for minting a new Irish copper coinage. But they could also come to the surface on less dramatic occasions. Thus a leading government manager, in 1728, noted with concern a threatened motion on the subject of pensions payable to private individuals out of public funds: 'This, you know, is a popular topic, and might create a disturbance in the king's affairs here.' Boulter, four years later, complained that 'we have so many young giddy members in the house, under no direction and full of a false patriotism, who are too likely even to throw out a thing they liked, merely for its coming from England'. Even leading members of the political establishment made gestures, whether politic or genuinely felt it is hard to tell, towards favourite patriot themes. The scarves distributed to mourners at the funeral of William Conolly in 1729, it was noted, were all of Irish linen. Six years later Luke Gardiner, vice-treasurer of the Irish exchequer, was savaged at a dinner party by Jonathan Swift for 'talking like a great patriot' and declaring that 'no gentleman of this country should be forgiven that wore anything but the manufactures of it'.[62]

Not only self-advancement, then, but honour and some sense of the public interest, could play a part in individual political motivation. What about collective behaviour? The House of Commons contained 300 members. Some of these belonged to what were by contemporary standards sizable factions or connections. Yet even the largest of these accounted for only a fraction of the house. Midleton, in the session of 1715–16, had a personal following of around thirty members; Henry Boyle in the early 1750s had around forty.[63] The great majority of MPs belonged to much smaller groups or else acted alone. What, then, determined which measures were and were not adopted? What, indeed, gave sufficient coherence to the proceedings to allow the dispatch of business at all?

---

[61] Coghill to Southwell, 23 Oct. 1729 (BL Add. MS 21,122, fo. 88).
[62] Coghill to Southwell, 15 Feb. 1728 (BL Add. MS 21,122, fo. 59); Boulter to Delafaye, 4 Jan. 1732 (SP63/395/18ᵛ); Coghill to Southwell, 8 Nov. 1729 (BL Add. MS 21,122, fo. 92ᵛ); Sir Arthur Acheson to George Dodington, 23 Oct. 1735 (HMC, *Eyre Matcham Manuscripts*, 65).
[63] Griffin, 'Parliamentary Politics', 48; J. L. McCracken, 'Undertakers in Ireland', 169.

One partial answer is effective argument. In an assembly without party divisions, large numbers of members were left to make up their own minds on particular issues. Rhetoric and reason thus had an important role, which the current emphasis on patronage has helped to obscure. In 1721, for example, Archbishop King complained of the progress being made by the bill to establish a bank of Ireland. 'All the speaking men in the House of Commons are for it, being concerned as subscribers. Many are against it, but can't speak their minds.'[64]

Secondly, and more important, most accounts of the 'management' of the Irish parliament tend to overlook the role of personal contacts. Yet these were of crucial importance. The landed élite from which the overwhelming majority of MPs were drawn was a small one. Extended close contact during each parliamentary session, both in parliament itself and in the winter social season that coincided with the session, would have created greater intimacy still. Under these conditions, without the countervailing influence of strong party loyalties, personal solicitation and persuasion played a major part. Here, for example, is how Alan Brodrick in the session of 1703, just before the beginning of the era of rigid party allegiances, sought to build up a majority for the granting of supplies for one year only:

The Speaker, being among the negatives, went from man to man in several parts of the house, and with earnest entreaties laboured to get them over on his side, and those that went over he openly saluted, saying welcome, welcome, and calling others over by their names, whom he saw stay behind, with so great passion as if the sum of affairs depended on that vote.[65]

In 1715, immediately after the short era of party had ended, a harassed chief secretary described how he had spent each day of the session just concluded 'running about to solicit the members and keep our forces to-gether, whom Brodrick [this time the former Speaker's son St John] with as much diligence endeavoured to debauch'. Direct lobbying of this kind was supplemented by informal social contact. 'My back', another chief secretary complained at the end of his parliamentary labours in 1731, 'is almost broke with bowing and my belly with eating, and what will become of my head I can't tell.' Archbishop Bolton of Cashel, two years later, was said to enjoy great influence in the Commons because 'he takes care to cultivate friendships and intimacies with the gentlemen of the country'. Lord Molesworth, in 1723, summed up the 'snares and temptations' that undermined the public spirit of the lesser Irish gentry as consisting not only of 'little employments for themselves or relations', but also of 'smiles, good dinners, threatenings etc'.[66]

---

[64] King to John Stearne, bishop of Clogher, 5 Oct. 1721 (TCD MS 750/7, 6).
[65] 'Account of Some Matters in the Session of 1703'. (BL Add. MS 9715, fo. 62).
[66] Charles Delafaye to ——, 17 Dec. 1715 (SP63/373/336); McCracken in *NHI* iv. 71; Coghill to Southwell, 5 Apr. 1733 (BL Add. MS 21,123, fo. 32); [Molesworth], *Some Considerations*, 29.

The personal touch was all the more vital because of the nature of the task which those charged with managing the Irish parliament had to accomplish. In addition to the obvious difficulties of mediating between a metropolitan government and a local assembly, there was the problem of easing sometimes complex business through the hands of a provincial squirearchy. The Irish gentry of the early and mid-eighteenth century, it was suggested earlier, were not a particularly well read or highly educated group. It is hardly surprising, then, that a body drawn mainly from their ranks had only a limited appreciation of the technicalities of legislation and government business. Privy Councillors met criticisms that they made excessive use of their power to amend heads of bills sent up from the Commons with the reply that the originals were commonly so badly drafted that they could not be left as they stood. In 1730, similarly, government supporters claimed that they had had to use 'the utmost diligence' to explain to younger members the restrictions which Poynings's Law imposed on their freedom of manœuvre in relation to a disputed money bill.[67]

Such a body, politically unsophisticated yet keenly aware of its own dignity, was easily alienated by the wrong sort of handling. In 1730, for example, members voted down a riot bill energetically promoted by Archbishop Boulter of Armagh and Sir Ralph Gore, 'for sometimes people have a mind to show them, that they shall govern but by the people of Ireland, with whom at present they have little correspondence or confidence, nor endeavour to have any, and yet seem desirous to carry everything as they have a mind'. Three years later a government defeat was blamed on a speech made by one of its own supporters 'which was in a sort of bullying manner, and accusing the house of disrespect to my lord lieutenant'.[68] The most successful managers of the Commons, by contrast, were those whose manner did least to arouse either the suspicions or the resentment of its members. Henry Boyle, for example, who became Speaker of the Commons in 1733, was described just before his election as 'a country gentleman of great good nature and probity, well beloved but not of extraordinary abilities, or much used to public business'. Even his friends, it was claimed, 'think him very unfit for that station [the Speakership], by reason of his natural modesty, and his little application to the knowledge of parliamentary proceedings'. His first speech from the chair did little to change this image. It 'was spoke, or rather read, with as much indifference and as little concern as if he had been at a tavern amongst a few of his friends, and indeed he read it as a schoolboy does his lesson'.[69] Yet despite, or perhaps because of, this modesty and lack of oratorical skills,

---

[67] King to Southwell, 8 Nov. 1707 (TCD MS 750/3/2, 160); Coghill to Southwell, 22 Jan. 1730 (BL Add. MS 21,122, fo. 107); Coghill to Southwell, 3 Jan. 1730 (ibid., fo. 103).

[68] Coghill to Southwell, 18 Apr. 1730 (BL Add. MS 21,123, fo. 1); Coghill to Southwell, 20 Nov. 1733 (ibid., fo. 66).

[69] Coghill to Southwell, 15 Mar., 20 Oct. 1733 (BL Add MS 21,123, fos. 26, 62).

Boyle was to serve as Speaker for over two decades and to be without question the most influential political figure of the middle decades of the century.

There was, of course, more to it than this. Henry Boyle was not, despite appearances, a simple country gentleman. He began his career as a member of the opposition Whig faction led by Midleton, taking over the leadership after the latter's death in 1728. In a truculent moment during his difficult first session as Speaker he declared that he had 'set up on the foot of the Country party' and owed nothing to the court.[70] In practice, however, Boyle soon settled into the role of the government's chief parliamentary manager, using his influence to steer its business through successive sessions. Chesterfield, whose period as lord lieutenant came when Boyle was at the height of his influence, left an acid description of the terms on which this service was rendered.

> Your Excellency or Your Grace wants to carry on His Majesty's business smoothly, and have it to say when you go back that you met with no difficulties; that we have sufficient strength in parliament to engage for, provided we have the favour and countenance of the government; the money, be it what it will, shall be cheerfully voted; as for the public, you shall do what you will, or nothing at all, for we care for that no more than we suppose Your Grace or Excellency does, but we repeat it again, our recommendations to places, pensions, etc. must prevail, or we shall not be able to keep our people in order. These are always the expressed, or at least the implied, conditions of these treaties.[71]

What Boyle became, in fact, was the most spectacularly successful of the 'undertakers': those local politicians who, from the collapse of party politics after 1714 onwards, became the chief means of bridging the gap between an Irish parliament and an executive whose personnel and policies it had had no direct role in choosing.[72] The undertakers used their influence to ensure that government business had majority support in the Irish parliament. In return, as Chesterfield noted with such distaste, they expected a substantial share of official patronage, both as a reward for their services and as part of the means by which they would discharge their side of the bargain.

The disjunction between Boyle's self-image as an honest country gentleman and his position as the leading player in a competitive political system came most clearly into the open when, in the early 1750s, two formidable rivals, the rising and well-connected Ponsonby family and the politically ambitious archbishop of Armagh, George Stone, sought to dislodge him from his position of power. To meet this threat, Boyle was able not just to employ the control of the machinery of government he had built up over two decades; he was also able to mobilize substantial support, both within parliament and

---

[70] Coghill to Southwell, 4 Dec. 1733 (BL Add. MS 21,123, fo. 12).

[71] Quoted in McCracken, *Irish Parliament*, 16–17.

[72] For the most recent account, see Hayton, 'Beginnings of the "Undertaker System"'.

outside, by presenting his struggle as a defence of Irish against English interests.[73] This may have been no more than a tactic. But its success is striking evidence of the extent to which Boyle, even after twenty years as the government's parliamentary manager, had not forfeited his credentials as a patriot and a man of principle. Most revealing of all, perhaps, is the bitter disillusionment expressed by so many when Boyle, after three years of hard political battle, made fresh terms with the government, accepting a peer-age and a sizable pension in return for sharing power in future with the Ponsonbys. If Boyle and his ally Lord Kildare had not abandoned 'the glorious cause of liberty', one correspondent lamented, 'their memory would have been engraved on the hearts of a free people, and their names would have been transmitted down to latest posterity with a Hampden and a Russell'. As it was, Boyle, 'whom we in a manner adored', had brought 'his grey head with infamy to the grave'. Michael Ward, an old associate of Midleton's, consoled himself with the thought that 'the patriot, alias the Protestant, alias the Whig interest is and must be the natural interest of Ireland, and every new session will bring forth new heads, and some unforeseen accidents administer new opportunities'.[74]

A full analysis of the parliamentary politics of the early and mid-eighteenth century, then, needs to be, not naïve or uncritical, but multi-dimensional. It must certainly take account of patronage and personal ambition. But it must also take in other points. It must note the limitations imposed on the pursuit of self-advancement by ideas of personal honour and public interest. It must acknowledge the role of personal obligation and connection. Most of all, perhaps, it must recognize the importance of a political style, such as Henry Boyle's image as a plain, unaffected country gentleman, in helping to resolve the central contradictions—between a legislature of provincial squires and an executive answerable to the English cabinet, between vague but pervasive 'country' instincts and the necessary exercise of power—that were built into the very structure of political life.

3. Politics and the People

All this relates to the political attitudes and behaviour of the élite: the landed class first and foremost, and along with it the ill-defined circle of office-holders and professional men, with a sprinkling of financial and commercial interests, described in an earlier chapter. To round off the discussion, it is necessary to say something about the political culture of the remainder of the

[73] J. L. McCracken, 'Conflict between the Irish Administration and Parliament'; D. O'Donovan, 'The Money Bill Dispute of 1753'.
[74] Robert Maxwell to [Bernard Ward], 13 Mar. 1756 (PRONI D2092/1/8/62); Michael Ward to Bernard Ward, 9 Mar. 1756 (PRONI D2092/1/8/57).

Protestant population, those whom the élite themselves would have recognized as 'the people'.[75] (The outlook and aspirations of the Catholic lower classes, which of necessity lay outside the limits of constitutional politics, will be examined in a later chapter.)

Popular participation in parliamentary politics was limited. The reasons for this lay partly in the electoral system. The franchise itself appears to have been as representative, if not more so, as that of contemporary England. In 1793 there was a total of around 60,000 voters in the Irish counties and boroughs, amounting to about 5.5 per cent of the Protestant population, or something like one adult male out of every five.[76] This compares with an electorate of around 5.5 per cent of total population in England in 1715, falling to 2.6 per cent on the eve of the Reform Act of 1832.[77] At the same time, the exclusion of Catholics from voting—substantial from 1704 and complete from 1728—meant that, even in the larger county constituencies, electorates, outside Ulster, were often small. In the late eighteenth century, when population was twice that of the early 1700s, there were still at least five counties in which the electorate numbered less than a thousand. In a hotly contested election in County Kerry in 1743, only 300 persons voted.[78]

More important than the absolute number of voters was the structure of Irish constituencies. Of the 300 parliamentary seats, 182 were for boroughs in which the franchise was restricted to members of the corporation or to corporation members and freemen. By the mid-eighteenth century all these constituencies, with the sole exception of Derry city, had come under the thumb of a single patron, whose control of the corporation allowed him in effect to nominate the MPs returned. In the reigns of William III and Anne the process may not have been quite so tightly closed to competition. With regular sittings of parliament commencing only in 1692, there had not always been time for dominant proprietorial interests to establish the control they were eventually to enjoy. Opportunities for electoral contests were also more common: there were five general elections between 1692 and 1714, compared with only two in the fifty years that followed. Certainly it seems to have been less common than it later became for a single family or individual to control the returns to several boroughs.[79] But where contests did occur, the struggle

---

[75] Below, p. 119.

[76] The figure of 60,000 freeholders in 1793 is that suggested by Cullen, 'Scotland and Ireland 1600–1800', 242. I have estimated a Protestant population of 25% of 4.4 million in the 1790s. Adult males would, at a rough estimate, have made up one-quarter of the total population.

[77] Speck, *Stability and Strife*, 16. Speck follows Plumb in arguing that the early eighteenth-century electorate was not only larger, but more independent than that of the period after 1714. J. C. D. Clark (*English Society*, 15–26) argues that the large numbers voting in the reign of Queen Anne were a consequence, rather than a cause, of the intensity of party conflict, and that most voters, then as later, were in fact acting under the direction of social superiors.

[78] McCracken, *Irish Parliament*, 8; Edmund Spencer to Francis Price, 22 Nov. 1743 (HMC, *Puleston Manuscripts*, 327).

[79] Hayton, 'Ireland and the English Ministers', 114–18.

was generally for the votes of a handful of electors, themselves men of substance. The complaints of Archbishop King, vainly seeking to negotiate some legal business in the middle of the election campaign of 1713, capture the intimate, personalized nature of electioneering under such circumstances:

They are all mad on elections, hurrying from place to place, so that I can hardly get one to speak to, and when I begin to talk to any of business, their answer is, 'How goes such an election? I must be so tomorrow at the Naas, the next day at Wicklow, next God knows where. Do you think I may depend on such a one's vote?' Then he hears some body is come to town and away he flies to secure him.[80]

Other constituencies—the thirty-two counties, the eight county boroughs centred on large towns, the potwalloping and manor boroughs where the voters were householders or freeholders within a limited geographical area— had larger and more popular electorates. Here the key factor was the control which social superiors could exert over the votes of tenants and other dependants. Again, it is possible that the deep ideological divisions running through the politics of the period up to 1714 made some voters less passive and less deferential than was to be the case in the calmer decades that followed. At the same time it is clear that proprietors took it for granted that their tenants and dependants would vote as instructed. In the general election of 1692, the managers of the Ormond estate as a matter of course instructed freeholders in the counties of Tipperary and Kilkenny on how to vote. Lord Ranelagh, learning with displeasure 'how refractory my tenants at Roscommon had been in choosing my friend Will Robinson for one of their burgesses', promised grimly 'that I will endeavour to be even with them'. In 1714, similarly, Lord Shannon and Lord Doneraile both had freeholders entitled to vote in County Cork 'who all wait to know their sentiments'. In other cases, complex electoral deals could be based on the premiss that significant bodies of voters would act as instructed. In 1702, for example, Lord Molesworth was willing to instruct his tenants at Swords, County Dublin, to vote for a candidate on condition that Lord Meath's tenants in Dublin county were instructed to vote for him.[81]

The electoral system, then, left little room for real popular participation. Whether this exclusion was resented, or even felt as such, is another matter. More direct expressions of the outlook of lower-class Protestants suggest a popular political culture that was limited in its aspirations, even deferential. In 1729, for example, a Dublin newspaper hailed the 'new and laudable custom' of public processions by the city's artisans. These seem to have begun, in fact,

---

[80] King to Mrs Marion King, 31 Oct. 1713 (TCD MS 750/4/1, 219).

[81] Longford to Ellis, 10 Oct. 1692 (Melvin, 'Letters of Lord Longford', 99–101); Ranelagh to Coningsby, 4 Oct. 1692 (PRONI D638/6/15); Alan Brodrick to Thomas Brodrick, 23 Feb. 1714 (Midleton MS 1248/3, fo. 166); Robert Molesworth to Lettice Molesworth, 26 Nov. 1702 (HMC, *Various Collections*, viii. 227).

the previous year, with separate processions of bricklayers and masons, spinners, wool-combers, butchers, bakers, tailors, and draymen, each celebrating the anniversary of the proclamation of George I. These were not guild events, dominated by the employers and large manufacturers. Those taking part were journeymen, men 'who daily labour', 'poor tradesmen, who now take pride to live sober all the year on purpose to enable themselves to appear genteel on their public day'.[82] As such they provided evidence that in Dublin, at least, the skilled workers had by this time developed both a collective consciousness and a capacity for independent organization. But the sense of identity they expressed was that of respectable tradesmen and loyal subjects. Their processions mirrored, rather than challenged, the image of the social order presented in state-organized celebrations of military victories, royal birthdays, and similar occasions of public festivity.

This is not to suggest that the collective consciousness of those concerned was necessarily tame or passive. Two years later, in 1731, the woollen-weavers of the city staged a rather more pointed piece of political theatre. They arranged for the public hangman to be presented with a suit of imported flowered fustian, which he duly wore when he carried out a public execution, ramming home the point by loudly addressing any similarly dressed persons whom he saw in the crowd around him 'by the affectionate name of brother'. When the execution was over, the hangman, still in his finery, 'made a tour to the Coombe, with his bloody cleaver etc'.[83] At the same time, even this expression of a popular grievance, aimed directly at the affluent consumer, could claim the sanction of élite political rhetoric; it was only two years, after all, since Irish-made linen scarves had been ostentatiously distributed at the funeral of William Conolly. The same broad point, that protest took place within the assumptions of the existing social order, could be made even of more direct and openly illegal forms of popular action. Artisans and other urban workers who rioted against forestallers and profiteers, who sought by threats and intimidation to regulate entry into particular occupations, or who struck in defence of customary wages and conditions of work could all claim to be operating within a moral and legal framework recognized by the state's own paternalist legislation.[84] In a revealing episode in 1734, a group of weavers out to track down imported goods dispersed voluntarily after they had encountered Jonathan Swift, who 'exhorted them to be quiet, and not to do things in a rash manner, but to make application in a peaceable way, and he did not make the least doubt but proper means would be found to make them all easy etc.'.[85]

It is hardly surprising, given this background, that direct popular inter-

[82] *Dublin Intelligence*, 3 Aug. 1728, 29 July, 16 Aug. 1729.
[83] Ibid., 9, 14, 16 June 1731.
[84] Below, ch. 4, sect. 4; ch. 6, sect. 3.
[85] *Dublin Journal*, quoted in Nokes, *Swift*, 384.

vention in national politics came only when those involved were given a firm lead from above. This happened on any great scale only during the period of conflict between rival Whig and Tory parties. In 1718, for example, a mainly Presbyterian crowd paraded through the streets of Armagh city, and beat up a couple of local Tory gentlemen, to cries of 'Scour the Tories and Papists, for they are much alike, and damn the Church of England people, for the most of them are Jacobites'.[86] In Dublin, on the other hand, it seems to have been Tory mobs who were most active. In 1713 the windows of houses that were not illuminated to celebrate the Peace of Utrecht, negotiated by the Tories against fierce Whig opposition, were smashed. Four months later, to the bafflement of the Tory administration itself, a crowd attacked the house of the archbishop of Tuam, in the mistaken belief that he was a Whig. At the general election in November, Tory supporters who believed they were being excluded from the Tholsel, where polling was taking place, attacked the building, and subsequently fought with soldiers. Alan Brodrick, writing from Dublin to his brother Thomas, claimed to find 'the insolence of the mob and rabble that very obsequiously attend one side' more threatening than anything he had witnessed in 1688.[87] In Dublin, at least, this popular partisanship continued into the 1720s, with regular clashes between the crowd, apparently including Protestants as well as Catholics, who turned out to celebrate the Pretender's birthday on 10 June, and a 'Whig mob' that appeared to oppose them.[88]

Episodes of this kind, born out of a bitter political struggle within the traditional ruling élite, may be contrasted with the absence of popular political action on other occasions, when the élite was not similarly divided. The obvious comparison is with the resistance to Wood's halfpence in 1723–5. This did involve some demonstrations of popular feeling. In September 1724 a ship carrying seven casks of the new halfpence arrived in Cork harbour. 'The whole country took all the boats and lighters they could get and went with a resolution to burn the ship and its cargo.' In the end, the ship was permitted to unload its other goods and sail away, still carrying the halfpence. In Dublin the same month, groups of one and two hundred strong twice paraded wooden effigies of William Wood through the streets, 'in order as they cried out to hang him, begging money as they went along to pay for a coffin'. These incidents make clear that there was substantial hostility to the proposed coinage. Yet, despite some wild claims to the contrary by English observers, these appear to represent the only two significant popular

---

[86] Brief of examinations relating to a riot in Scotch Street, Armagh, 17 Mar. 1718 (PRONI Dio 4/5/3/84).

[87] Margaret Dean to Henry Boyle, 23 June [1713] (PRONI D2707/A1/2/1B); W. Ellis to Swift, 20 Oct. 1713 (SP63/369/142–3); Alan Brodrick to Thomas Brodrick, 7 Nov. 1713 (Midleton MS 1248/3, fo. 132).

[88] Below, ch. 6, sect. 4.

4

Relationships

So far we have been concerned primarily with the Protestant population, and more particularly its upper levels. It is time to turn to a consideration of the wider framework of social and political relationships within which this élite existed. In doing so, however, we enter a zone of some confusion. To see this, it is only necessary to look at some of the different ways in which the governing class of eighteenth-century Ireland has been defined in recent historical writing. Its members appear variously as the 'Anglo-Irish', the 'Anglo-Irish ascendancy', the 'Protestant ascendancy', and 'colonists'. Behind each of these terms lies a very different set of assumptions regarding both the character of the élite itself and its relationship to other parts of the population. Yet these differences are rarely considered, much less debated. What one enters, in fact, is less a minefield than a fun-fair.

Take, for example, the term 'Anglo-Irish'. Ostensibly, this is an ethnic definition: it should refer to all those descended from the successive waves of migrants who, from the twelfth century, came to Ireland from England. In practice, however, it generally means something rather different. The 'Anglo-Irish', according to Beckett, were 'the Protestant community that dominated Ireland in the eighteenth century and those who inherited and maintained its tradition in the changed and changing circumstances of a later age'.[1] This raises two problems. First, it substitutes a religious for an ethnic definition: the term 'Anglo-Irish' now includes Protestant families of Irish descent, like the O'Haras of County Sligo and the O'Briens of County Clare, and excludes Catholic families of English descent, like the Butlers and Mathews of County Tipperary. Secondly, it introduces the question of distinctions of power and status. Were the Protestants who 'dominated' Ireland really part of the same community as the lower-class Protestants over whom they ruled? Beckett emphasizes the bonds of common identity and interest between Protestants of different social and economic backgrounds and the relatively good prospects for advancement enjoyed by even the poorer among them. But the fact remains that his study of the 'Anglo-Irish tradition' is in practice a study of the Protestant propertied classes and, above all, the landed élite. For other writers, too, 'Anglo-Irish' carries inescapable connotations of status, wealth, and power. Malcomson, an honourable early exception to the general un-willingness to probe these matters too deeply, recognizes both these problems. His suggestion is that the phrase should in fact be 'Anglo-Irish ascendancy',

---

[1] Beckett, *Anglo-Irish Tradition*, 11.

and that this should be 'defined along social and political, rather than ethnic, lines'.[2] But that brings us back to the question of why, in that case, one should retain an ethnic label at all.

Malcomson's 'Anglo-Irish ascendancy' of course recalls the more common 'Protestant ascendancy'. Here ethnicity is replaced by religion as the defining characteristic of the social élite. This resolves some problems, but leaves others. The phrase 'Protestant ascendancy' has now been traced back to the year 1782, when it was employed by a supporter of the Catholic relief bill to define the limit to which such relief should go. It came into more general use from 1787, during the violent religious polemics provoked by the anti-tithe disturbances in Munster, and was firmly established as a political slogan during the vehement opposition mounted against proposals for a further measure of Catholic relief in 1792–3.[3] In this original usage, however, 'Protestant ascendancy' was a state of affairs, the superiority of Protestants over Catholics. It was only later that the phrase came to refer instead to a social group: *the* Protestant ascendancy. Along with this reification, moreover, there developed new connotations of social exclusiveness. A term that owed much of its original popularity to its employment by the stridently anti-Catholic, and irredeemably bourgeois, corporation of Dublin now came to be thought of as referring specifically to the Protestant landed class.[4] At this point the problems begin to multiply. If we refer to the rulers of eighteenth-century Ireland as 'the Protestant ascendancy', to what extent are we implying that their dominant position was a result of their Protestantism, rather than of their ownership of land and the prestige, power, and economic advantage it conferred? And what, if anything, do we mean to imply regarding the position of those Protestants who were not landowners or their close relatives? Once again, the unexamined conflation of labels, in this case social and religious, obscures our image of the society.

'Anglo-Irish' and 'Protestant ascendancy' are both terms peculiar to Ireland. Some historians have preferred instead to apply a vocabulary drawn from the language of European overseas expansion. Ireland, in this version, was a colony of England (later of Great Britain). The Protestant population were 'colonists'. When it developed a political stance of increasingly confident defence of the rights of the kingdom of Ireland against English interference, this was 'colonial nationalism'. One recent essay seeks to compare the emergence of an 'Anglo-Irish identity' with changes in self-image and political

---

[2] Malcomson, *Foster*, xvii–xix.

[3] These points have emerged gradually in a series of writings by McCormack, beginning with *Ascendancy and Tradition*, and concluding, for the moment at any rate, with 'Eighteenth-Century Ascendancy', which includes a bibliography of earlier items.

[4] McCormack, *Ascendancy and Tradition*, 88. J. Kelly ('The Genesis of "Protestant Ascendancy"', 126–7) suggests that McCormack has overstated the urban and commercial origins of the slogan. But his essential point—the narrowing of the term to a social and political élite—stands.

loyalties among settlers in societies as different as the Spanish colonies of Central and South America, the West Indies, and the English and French colonies further north.[5] Compared to the specifically Irish alternatives available, such an approach has the virtues of precision and clarity; there are no hidden assumptions or implications. But there remains the problem of whether Ireland can in fact be fitted into a theoretical framework built on the expansion of Western Europe to other continents.

How, then, should the structure of post-Restoration Ireland be characterized? Should the main focus be on ethnic identity, religion, or—as elsewhere in *ancien régime* Europe—distinctions of wealth and status? Or should analysis concentrate instead on the tensions, internal and external, of a colonial society? This chapter will begin with the last of these options, examining the relationship between the kingdoms of Ireland and England. From this it will go on to discuss the relationships between groups—ethnic, religious, and social—within Irish society itself.

1. Kingdoms

Irish Protestants of the late seventeenth and early eighteenth centuries indignantly rejected the suggestion that they lived in a colony. Their argument was essentially a legal and historical one. Ireland, it was claimed, had been constituted in the Middle Ages as a separate kingdom belonging to the English crown, and it retained the title, the institutions, and the status of a kingdom. In the words of William Molyneux, writing in 1698:

Does it not manifestly appear by the constitution of Ireland, that 'tis a complete kingdom within itself? Do not the kings of England bear the style of Ireland amongst the rest of their kingdoms? Is this agreeable to the nature of a colony? Do they use the title of kings of Virginia, New England or Maryland? Was not Ireland given by Henry the Second in a parliament at Oxford to his son John, and made thereby an absolute kingdom, separate and wholly independent on England, till they both came united again in him, after the death of his brother Richard without issue? Have not multitudes of acts of parliament both in England and Ireland declared Ireland a complete kingdom? Is not Ireland styled in them all the kingdom or realm of Ireland? Do these names agree to a colony? Have we not a parliament and courts of judiciature? Do these things agree with a colony?[6]

Ireland's status as a kingdom was crucial to the opposition mounted by Irish Protestants against the claims of the Westminster parliament to ultimate authority over their affairs. 'Although Ireland is both a poor and an annexed kingdom,' Archbishop Synge of Tuam told the archbishop of Canterbury in 1719, 'yet still it is a kingdom, modelled according to the constitution of

[5] Canny, 'Identity Formation in Ireland'.   [6] W. Molyneux, *Case of Ireland*, 115–16.

England: and within itself, and in those matters where itself is only concerned, has all the courts, powers and jurisdictions which belong to the kingdom of England, *as a kingdom*.'[7] Jonathan Swift, a few years later, dismissed the idea that Ireland could be a kingdom and yet subject to the authority of an English parliament. 'A dependent kingdom is a modern term of art; unknown . . . to all ancient civilians and writers upon government.'[8]

However passionately it was articulated by Irishmen, however, this idea of Ireland as an autonomous kingdom was increasingly a meaningless archaism. It depended on the claim that the connection between Ireland and Great Britain lay in the person of the monarch: Ireland was not a dependency of England, but a separate possession of the English crown. In the seventeenth century, this assertion still had some meaning. The lords lieutenant who governed Ireland in the name of Charles II after 1660 were in a real sense his representatives, carrying out his instructions. Even when Irish interests were sacrificed to those of England, as happened with the Cattle Acts of 1663 and 1667, this was a case of the ruler of both kingdoms choosing (admittedly on no better basis than their relative ability to cause him trouble) which of the two he would favour. From the 1690s, however, the personal rule of the monarch progressively gave way to parliamentary government. As this happened, claims for Ireland's status as a separate possession of the crown amounted to less and less.[9]

The problem here lay not just in the change in the character of government in England, but in the way in which it was carried out. There was no formal definition of the new political order. The so-called Revolution settlement was more concerned to mask than to define the constitutional implications of what had happened. The form which change took was rather that ministers, representing the dominant faction within the English parliament, increasingly came to direct the monarch in the exercise of his or her prerogative powers. These, of course, included the direction of affairs in Ireland. It was this absence of formal constitutional change that allowed Irish Protestants to go on rejecting any suggestion of subordination to the English parliament, while professing their attachment, through the person of the monarch, to England. In doing so, however, they were building their case around a constitutional myth created to reconcile the more conservative-minded among the English ruling class to what had happened in 1688–9, a myth of diminishing relevance to the government of either England or Ireland.

After 1689, then, the government of Ireland, whatever the aspirations of its political élite, depended increasingly on the parliament of England. The head of the Irish executive was the lord lieutenant, chosen by the English ministry

---

[7] Synge to Wake, 17 Dec. 1719 (Gilbert MS 28, 140).
[8] Swift, *Prose Works*, x. 62.
[9] A similar development may be seen, though less acutely, in relations between England and her American colonies: Greene, *Peripheries and Centre*, ch. 4.

of the day and sent to Ireland to execute that ministry's policies. Many of the lesser positions within the civil, military, and ecclesiastical establishments were also held by Englishmen. The Irish parliament was a subordinate legislature. Poynings's Law, dating from 1494, required that all proposed legislation be submitted to London for approval before being considered. Since approval was to be by the English Privy Council, this was not in itself incompatible with Irish claims to be an autonomous kingdom; after 1689, however, approval by the Council came increasingly to mean approval by the English ministry, rather than by the monarch and his personal advisers. In 1720, meanwhile, the whole elaborate structure erected on the flimsy foundations of Ireland's status as a distinct possession of the crown was swept away by the Declaratory Act. Confirming a series of legal precedents, this formally asserted the right of the English parliament both to act as a final court of appeal in Irish cases and to pass, if it chose, legislation binding on Ireland.[10]

Added to this constitutional and political subordination, there were the restrictions imposed on Irish economic life. These dated back to the Restoration period. The Cattle Acts of 1663 and 1667 excluded Irish livestock from England and Scotland, in order to protect the profits of English graziers. The Navigation Acts of 1663 and 1671 broke with earlier practice, which had been to treat English and Irish trading interests as identical, by excluding Irish ships from direct trade with the colonies.[11] None of these measures was welcome. At the same time, such prohibitions, excluding Irish goods from England and from England's overseas possessions, were not a direct attack on Ireland's status as a kingdom. That came only after the Revolution. The Woollen Act of 1699 prohibited the export of wool or woollen cloth from Ireland to any destination other than England. Later English statutes, of 1710 and 1746, further encroached on Ireland's control of its own economic affairs, the first prohibiting the import of hops from any country other than England, the second the export of glass.

To enumerate in this way the elements in Ireland's political subordination is not to imply that its affairs were wholly under the control of English politicians. It is true that successive English ministries gave every sign of being ready to govern Ireland with minimal regard to the wishes of any section of its inhabitants. In this, however, they came up against a growing determination on the part of Irish Protestants not to be taken for granted. The disastrous parliamentary session of 1692 and the compromises with key Irish politicians that followed over the next three years were a clear indicator of the impracticality of governing Ireland by fiat from London.[12] The lesson, of course, was

[10] Victory, 'The Making of the 1720 Declaratory Act'.

[11] The novel implications of the Acts of 1663 and 1671 are noted by Lammey, 'The Free Trade Crisis', 70–1. For commercial restrictions in general, see Edie, 'The Irish Cattle Bills'; P. Kelly, 'The Irish Woollen Export Prohibition Act of 1699'; Cullen, *Economic History of Ireland*, 34–40.

[12] Above, ch. 3.

not learned overnight. The thirty years after 1690 saw a series of constitutional clashes—the 'sole right' campaign of 1692, the storms aroused by the Woollen Act of 1699 and the Forfeitures Resumption Act of 1700, the debate over the powers of the Irish House of Lords that culminated in the Declaratory Act in 1720, the Wood's halfpence dispute of 1723–5—as both sides sought to discover the full extent of their power in a transformed political environment. Where the dispute was over issues of constitutional principle, as in 1719–20, the Irish parliament was inevitably the loser: its members could do little more than rage while Westminster acted as judge in its own case. Where pragmatic matters of administration were concerned, the outcome was more balanced. In 1692–5 the Irish parliament successfully asserted its claim to be more than a ratifying body for legislation drawn up by the executive. And in 1723–5 the sustained opposition of virtually the whole political establishment to the patent granted to the English ironmaster William Wood to mint copper coin for Ireland eventually forced the government into a humiliating retreat.[13]

The Wood's halfpence affair was a turning-point in Anglo-Irish relations. The traditional view—that the crisis of 1723–5 led English ministers to introduce a new system of government through Irish 'undertakers'—has been undermined by the work of Hayton. In fact, undertakers—local politicians who, in exchange for a share in patronage and a say in the making of policy, undertook to manage the House of Commons on behalf of the government— had been part of the Irish political system ever since the 1690s.[14] Yet, if the change in the system of government was less clear-cut than has been claimed, a change nevertheless occurred. There were no further cases, after the 1720s, of the sort of provocative use of power that had been seen in measures like the Declaratory Act and the granting of Wood's patent. On the contrary, English ministers took care to avoid giving unnecessary offence to Irish opinion. Proposals for legislation coming from the House of Commons were treated with respect, and sparing use was made of London's extensive powers to veto Irish bills or to impose legislation on Ireland through Westminster. There were aggressive noises in the late 1720s about the need to curb a supposed tendency towards independence by appointing Englishmen to positions of importance in church and state. But in practice, the demand of the Protestant élite for a reasonable share of the patronage of their own country was respected. By 1760 the proportion of Irish bishoprics held by natives was the same as it had been when George I died in 1727, while the proportion of Irish judges was significantly higher.[15]

From the 1690s, then, and more particularly after the 1720s, the Irish political élite enjoyed a substantial degree of self-government. Although

[13] Goodwin, 'Wood's Halfpence'.
[14] Hayton, 'The Beginnings of the "Undertaker System"'; idem, 'Walpole and Ireland'.
[15] James, *Ireland in the Empire*, 131, 170–1, 258.

the nominal head of government was the lord lieutenant, representing the English cabinet, he was an absentee, residing in Ireland only during the biennial sittings of parliament. The day-to-day management of affairs lay instead in the hands of local politicians. The real power which these men possessed was amply demonstrated in Henry Boyle's success, during 1753–6, in bringing government to a virtual halt until he was at length bought off on highly favourable terms.[16] In normal circumstances managers like Boyle could ensure a parliamentary majority for financial and other legislation. But the Irish parliament was not a tame assembly. This was made clear, for example, in 1731–3, when the undertakers wholly failed to deliver the repeal of the sacramental test.[17]

The practical control over their own affairs which the Irish propertied classes had thus achieved was partly due to the growing financial needs of government and the consequent rise in the status of parliament. But this was not the whole explanation. In theory, English ministers could, after 1720 at least, have dispensed with the Irish parliament altogether, passing whatever Irish legislation was required—including finance bills—at Westminster. In practice such a move, apart from one brief period in 1720, was never seriously considered.[18] The truth, of course, was that the day-to-day government of Ireland required the co-operation of the Protestant middle and upper classes. Only they could staff the bureaucracy, maintain law and order, and act as intermediaries between central government and the localities. This alone was enough to ensure that ministers in London, after an initial attempt to ascertain just what they could get away with, found it necessary to pay serious regard to Irish prejudices and demands.

None of this, however, undermines the central point of Ireland's political subordination to Great Britain. Irish Protestants may have achieved substantial control over the day-to-day running of the country. On the other hand, they had to abandon the more exalted claims that had been made in the 1690s and early 1700s for Ireland's status as an autonomous kingdom. In this sense the smoother working arrangement achieved between Dublin and London after the mid-1720s required compromise on both sides. The practical autonomy which Ireland enjoyed, moreover, must be seen in perspective. In the American colonies too, practical considerations of distance, dependence on grants of taxation voted by local assemblies, and government's reliance on unpaid local agents meant that theoretical subordination to the metropolis was in practice modified to permit considerable local independence. One historian, indeed, suggests that by the mid-eighteenth century there had evolved an unwritten 'imperial constitution', extending to both

---

[16] McCracken, 'Conflict between the Irish Administration and Parliament'; O'Donovan, 'The Money Bill Dispute of 1753'.
[17] Below, ch. 5, sect. 3.
[18] Hayton, 'Walpole and Ireland', 102.

Ireland and America, whereby the metropolitan government managed defence and external affairs, while leaving domestic matters wholly in the hands of the local authorities.[19]

Was Ireland then a colony, its much vaunted parliamentary constitution no more than a practical freedom to manage purely local affairs that had also been conceded to Jamaica and Virginia? Some historians, surveying the clear evidence of political and economic subordination, have been convinced that it was. According to Cullen:

The relationship between Ireland and England was of course colonial—profoundly colonial in fact, not only because Ireland was subservient politically and economically, but because Ireland received civil and ecclesiastical administrators, more humble immigrants and ideas from England, and in turn many Irish migrated to London in search of fame or fortune.[20]

As an account of Ireland's many-sided subordination, this is fair enough. But does it in fact establish the existence of a colonial relationship? Intellectual and cultural dependence—the movement of ideas in one direction and of ambitious Irishmen in the other—does not prove very much: by those criteria, Ireland remains a colony of England today, as indeed England is increasingly becoming a colony of the United States. Political subordination is more to the point. But again it is necessary to be precise. *Ancien régime* Europe offers many examples of territories or historic nations under the domination of foreign rulers. Southern Italy was ruled first by Austria and then by Spain, Norway by Denmark, Finland by Sweden, Scotland and Wales (and Hanover) by England. Poland, by the end of the century, had been partitioned between Prussia, Austria, and Russia. Then there were the multinational empires: Austrian rule over Italians, Czechs, Magyars, and various Slav peoples; Russian rule over Lithuanians, Georgians, and others; and Ottoman rule over the various Balkan nationalities. In the nineteenth century many of these territories were to be the scene of nationalist revolts and wars of liberation. Yet none of them is normally described as a case of colonial rule. Why then should Ireland, alone in Western Europe, be considered for that status?

In general, two points serve to distinguish colonialism proper from the various examples of rule by foreigners that existed within early modern Europe. One is settlement, the other geographical separation. The two were closely related. While it was feasible for a strong state to exercise dominion over a weaker neighbour by bureaucracy and military force alone, possession of a distant territory, in Africa, Asia, or America, could in general be maintained only by also settling it with natives of the metropolitan power. Geographical distance and the racial and cultural inferiority that could be imputed to non-Europeans, equally, made it possible to legitimize the dispossession

---

[19] Greene, *Peripheries and Centre*, 64–6.   [20] Cullen, *Emergence of Modern Ireland*, 35.

of local peoples that such settlement necessarily involved, as well as the subjugation of territories to which no geographical claim could conceivably be laid. Race, in fact, counted for more than mere distance. In the two most notable cases in which what was clearly colonization did not in fact involve very great physical distance—French and Spanish control of Algeria and other parts of North Africa—domination extended across the frontier between continents, and involved a racial difference between colonist and colonized.

This is where the ambiguity of the Irish case becomes apparent. The conquest of Ireland in the sixteenth and seventeenth centuries involved a process of expropriation and settlement by natives of the metropolitan power that had no parallel in the many examples of conquest and subordination occurring within the boundaries of Western Europe. By 1700 roughly a quarter of the population of Ireland was of English or Scottish descent, all but a tiny proportion tracing their connection with Ireland no further back than the sixteenth century. Equally important, virtually the whole of the Gaelic landed class had been dispossessed and replaced by proprietors from the settler population. No comparable dispossession of the native élite had taken place in Wales, Scotland, or other parts of Europe. The 'humble emigrants' mentioned by Cullen thus turn out to be of potentially greater importance than any of the other badges of colonial status he enumerates. At the same time Ireland was neither a physically distant nor a racially separate possession. It was a neighbouring island, whose inhabitants were European in physical appearance, culture, and religion. And it is this which makes the colonial label less than satisfactory.

Physical proximity to England affected all levels of Irish society. For the Protestant élite it meant an opportunity to participate in English affairs in a way that none of the true colonists of India, America, or elsewhere could hope to do. Some made a career in politics. In all, sixty-six Irishmen sat in the British House of Commons between 1715 and 1754, one or two achieving some prominence. Thomas Brodrick, MP for Stockbridge 1713–22 and for Guildford 1722–7, was chosen in 1721 to head the Commons' enquiry into the South Sea scandal; John, Viscount Perceval, MP for Harwich 1727–34, was a leading supporter of Walpole's administration.[21] For others, the opportunities lay in theatre or letters. Indeed, it has been argued that the intellectual and literary interchange between Ireland and England was such that it is not possible to speak of a distinct Anglo-Irish literature during any part of the eighteenth century.[22] Members of the Irish élite also intermarried regularly with English propertied families, although a suitor whose lands lay in Ireland could expect to pay something over the odds in the English marriage market. As always in this complex area, it is important not to push the

---

[21] Sedgwick, *History of Parliament*, i. 156–7; ii. 336–8.   [22] Beckett in *NHI* iv. 424–70.

distinctions too far. A recent comparative study of Britain's Atlantic possessions during the eighteenth century suggests a general process of cultural convergence with the metropolitan centre, affecting Virginia, Barbados, and other Caribbean and North American colonies as much as Ireland.[23] But it seems clear, nevertheless, that geographical closeness and the constant face-to-face interchange it permitted must to some extent put Ireland in a different category from these other territories.

For those who were not members of the Protestant élite, the situation is less clear. Physical proximity must be set against formidable barriers of language, religion, and culture, as well as a history of military conflict. At the same time it is evident that wars, conquest, and plantation had for centuries been accompanied by less structured and less contentious movements of people in both directions. By the early eighteenth century there was already a significant Irish community in Great Britain, as well as large numbers of seasonal migrants. As with other immigrant groups, the relationship of these Irish with the host community was not always easy. There were riots in London in 1736 against Irishmen undercutting the wages of building workers and weavers. Local authorities made provision for the repatriation of Irish vagrants.[24] At times of political tension, Irishmen could become objects of suspicion. In 1696 Lord Inchiquin blamed the temporary detention at Gravesend of a relative's two sons on the shortcomings of their tutor, a Mr Connor: 'the Teigishest fellow I ever saw', whose 'accent will always declare what country he is of'.[25] In 1745, similarly, numerous Irish Catholics living in England were questioned or detained.[26] It is possible, however, that glimpses of this kind present an unduly bleak picture. The administrative records from which they come—criminal proceedings and accounts of suspect persons, the policing of vagrancy, accounts of riots—are by their nature ones which present their subjects as a problem. Instances of quiet assimilation or co-existence, by contrast, are passed over in silence. A rare glimpse of the other side of Irish life in England is provided by the search in 1700 for a Captain Turlough McMahon, wanted for his involvement in an attempted fraud in County Clare. McMahon was not traced in England, but two men of the same name were located and eliminated from the search. One was purser to a man of war, 'and lives in good esteem at Portsmouth'. The other, son of Bryan Rua McMahon of Ennis, 'lives in very good credit and keeps an inn at Kingston upon Thames'.[27]

---

[23] Greene, *Pursuits of Happiness*.

[24] Rude, '"Mother Gin" and the London Riots of 1736', in *Paris and London in the Eighteenth Century*, 201–21. For vagrants, see e.g. HMC, *Kenyon Papers*, 470–1.

[25] *Inchiquin Manuscripts*, 44.

[26] McLynn, '"Good Behaviour"'. Unfortunately, this article is stronger on hyperbole than evidence. In particular, the suggestion that 'to be an Irish Catholic in 1745 was much like being a Jew *and* a communist in Nazi-occupied Europe' (p. 46) is in no way substantiated by the scanty list of incidents cited.

[27] *Inchiquin Manuscripts*, 231.

Even more important than physical proximity was the absence of a racial barrier between settler and native. In the sixteenth and early seventeenth centuries, it is true, attempts were made to equate the Irish with the native races of America and other non-European possessions. Once the sharp clash of arms and cultures that accompanied the Tudor conquest was over, however, such claims became increasingly untenable. The wild Irishman rampaging at the frontiers of English settlement gave way in English folklore to the comic provincial.[28] The penal laws which distinguished Catholic from Protestant during the eighteenth century have been compared to the apartheid system of twentieth-century South Africa. But this is misleading. The barrier created by the penal laws could be crossed, in a way that no barrier based on colour could ever be, by a change of religious allegiance. The O'Briens of County Clare, the O'Haras of County Sligo, and the O'Neills of County Antrim were all Gaelic families whose leading male members at least conformed to the Church of Ireland in time to save both their estates and their political prominence. The career of William Conolly, meanwhile, provides evidence that a Catholic, Gaelic ancestry was no bar to spectacular upward mobility. Lower down the social scale, also, there were examples of persons of Catholic and Irish descent being absorbed into the Protestant community, as well as more common instances of isolated Protestant families being assimilated over time—despite the loss of legal rights involved—into the majority Catholic population.[29]

The precise significance of all this is open to debate. Whatever striking exceptions can be quoted, it remains true that the great majority of the Protestant landed class that dominated late seventeenth- and eighteenth-century Ireland was of English or Scottish origin, descendants of relatively recent settlers who had dispossessed the native élite. Kean O'Hara, it was noted in 1683, was 'the only mere Irishman' in County Sligo to have kept his estate during the upheavals of the 1640s and 1650s.[30] On the other hand, race, language, and culture were not in themselves the basis on which that dispossession, or the subsequent exclusion of a large majority of the population from power and privilege, were carried out. And this of course is the nub of the problem. A history of conquest followed by plantation and the expropriation of native proprietors gave Ireland some of the features of a

---

[28] Below, p. 121.

[29] For the assimilation of members of the pre-plantation population into Presbyterian congregations in east Ulster during the seventeenth century, see P. S. Robinson, *Plantation of Ulster*, 187–8. For later converts, see below, ch. 7, sect. 3. For a Protestant community established in County Westmeath in 1745 that had almost disappeared 65 years later, see Wakefield, *Account of Ireland*, ii. 626. Archbishop Boulter complained in 1728 of 'the descendants of many of Cromwell's officers and soldiers here being gone off to Popery': *Letters*, i. 223. The most spectacular case is of course the population of the Aran Islands, off the coast of Galway, a last bastion of traditional Gaelic culture, whom blood tests suggest to be in fact of English descent: A. T. Q. Stewart, *The Narrow Ground*, 27–8.

[30] Robert Downing, 'Account of County Mayo' (Molyneux Papers, 883/2, 53).

colony. Yet geography and ethnography ensured that the indigenous population, at any social level, could not in the long term really be treated as the native peoples of colonies generally were. For this reason the idea of Ireland as a colony, however attractive as an analytical tool, will never be wholly convincing.

2. Nations

This being the case, we must look at alternative systems of classification and analysis. Perhaps the best starting-point is the language that contemporaries used to describe themselves and others. This cannot be a static analysis. The major social and political changes of the seventeenth century were reflected in new ways of describing the different groups that made up Irish society. Yet this was a gradual process. Indeed, the reluctance of contemporaries to adopt new terminology to match changed social and political circumstances is in many ways as revealing as the changes they eventually made.

In the first half of the seventeenth century, writers on Ireland generally categorized its population under three main headings: Old English, descendants of pre-Reformation settlers who remained Catholic in religion; New English, who had come to Ireland since the Reformation and were Protestants; and Old, or native, Irish, Catholic in religion and of Gaelic descent and culture. In fact, matters were not always so straightforward. 'Old English' was in practice a cultural label, extending to some families of Gaelic Irish origin who had become wholly anglicized. The so-called New English, equally, included some, like the young James Butler, earl of Ormond, whose family had been in Ireland for centuries but who were Protestants. There were also ambiguities about the status of the 'native' Irish. The general presumption was that they were disloyal, or at least unreliable. Yet individual native Irishmen, of Gaelic ancestry and Catholic religion, were integrated into the social and, at local level at least, the political élite. There were also frequent marriage alliances between Old English and native Irish and between New and Old English families. At the same time, the terms 'Old English', 'New English', and 'native Irish', understood as religious and cultural, rather than simply ethnic, categorizations, have been found by modern historians to offer the best way of approaching the complexities of Tudor and early Stuart society.[31]

After the 1640s these subtle but readily comprehensible labels lost much of their application. Common participation on the losing side in the wars of the 1640s and 1650s meant that the Old English and the Irish were now categorized together as Catholic rebels. In the same way the divisions that

---

[31] Clarke, 'Ireland and the General Crisis', 80–90; Moody in *NHI* iii. xlii–xliii.

had existed between 'old Protestants', whose Irish interests dated from before 1641, and the 'new Protestants' who had come to the country since that date were forgotten at the Restoration, as the two groups joined in a defence of their common interests.[32] On both sides, religious affiliation, previously one of several components in a complex pattern, thus assumed a new primacy. Fundamental change of this kind should have meant the development of a whole different language to express the new lines of social and religious division. But in practice the adjustment of thinking and terminology to changed political and social realities was to take the best part of a century. Sir William Petty, writing in 1672, saw clearly enough that political divisions had been fundamentally altered by the events of the previous thirty years:

> The people of Ireland are all in factions and parties, called English and Irish, Protestant and Papists: though indeed the real distinction is vested and divested of the lands belonging to Papists, ann. 1641. Of which the Irish that are vested by restoration, seem rather to take part with the divested.... The differences between the Old Irish and Old English Papists is asleep now, because they have a common enemy.[33]

This would imply that ethnic terminology ('Old English', 'native Irish', 'New English') should give way to religious terminology: Catholic and Protestant. Yet Petty himself did not follow through the logic of his observations. The phrase 'Irish that are vested by restoration', for example, seems to refer to all Catholics who had regained land after 1660. And elsewhere too, Petty clearly equates 'Irish' and 'English' with 'Catholic' and 'Protestant'.[34]

Among other writers of the Restoration period the same equation was standard usage. A report from Dublin in 1663, at the time the court of claims was sitting, complained that 'the English are discontented and the Irish do not carry themselves prudently, being too much puffed up'. In 1683 Lord Longford reported that he had been invited to dinner by the 'Irish merchants' of Galway city, in order to hear their requests for a toleration of discreet Catholic worship.[35] Three years later Sir Paul Rycaut, the English Protestant royalist who served as secretary to the lord lieutenant, observed that 'the English are unreasonably timorous and fearful of being overrun with the Irish ... and the Irish are so silly as to believe what the English fear'. Elsewhere Rycaut lamented the dismissal of 'old English soldiers' to make way for Catholics and the economic difficulties caused by the unwillingness of the 'English dealers' of Munster to lay out their coin at a time of such political uncertainty. He even referred, on one occasion, to Irish Catholics as a

---

[32] Above, ch. 1, sect. 1.

[33] Petty, *Political Anatomy*, 42–4.

[34] At one point Petty notes that the sheriffs of counties are 'English for the most part, and most commonly Protestants' (p. 44). Elsewhere, however, he clearly equates his figure of 800,000 'Irish' with an identical number of Catholics (p. 8).

[35] *CSPI 1663–5*, 120; HMC, *Ormonde Manuscripts*, NS vii. 115–16.

'nation'.[36] In accounts of the war of 1689–91 the two sides are most commonly referred to simply as 'English' and 'Irish'.[37]

This continued use of the terms 'English' and 'Irish' was not just a matter of the survival of archaic terminology. The events of 1641–53 may have given religious allegiance a new primacy, but they did not wholly wipe out other divisions. On the Catholic side, in particular, the distinction between Old English and native Irish remained important. It played a central part in the bitter divisions, at one stage erupting into military conflict, within the Catholic Confederation, with the majority of the Old English anxious to reach a compromise with the king, while the Irish generally supported the papal nuncio, Rinuccini, in holding out for what would have amounted to virtual established status for the Catholic church. The same divisions between Old English royalism and the more militant posture of the native Irish reappeared in the controversy over the loyal Remonstrance, drafted by a group of Old English clergy and laity and most bitterly opposed by the native Irish members of certain religious orders. In the internal affairs of the Catholic church political and ethnic hostility was reinforced by the impact of the Counter-Reformation, as a predominantly Old English episcopate sought to bring the religious orders, representing the fervent but undisciplined piety of Gaelic Ireland, under tighter control. The appearance of several Gaelic Irish Franciscans as prosecution witnesses at the trial of the Old English and reforming prelate Oliver Plunkett was symptomatic of wider tensions.[38] Even during 1685–91 the composition both of the officer class of Richard Talbot's remodelled army and of the parliament summoned in 1689 indicates clearly that it was the Old English rather than the Irish who benefited from the short period of Catholic ascendancy.[39]

As in earlier periods, however, this social and political tension between Old English and Irish was no more than one strand in a complex pattern. Some of the complexities are evident in the Munster poet David Ó Bruadair's celebration of the changes taking place under James II. In the army, Ó Bruadair gloatingly noted, 'George' and 'John' are being pushed aside by 'Niall Og' and 'Tadhg from the mountain', and 'Cia súd?' has replaced 'Who's there?' as the sentry's watchword. Meanwhile in the courts:

---

[36] Melvin, 'Rycaut's Memoranda', 150, 152, 168, 153. For Catholics as a 'nation', see above, p. 40.

[37] Thus, an official letter on the question of when the war was to be considered as having started, for the purposes of the Act of Attainder, refers to the 'Irish armies' that marched on Bandon and Derry and the treatment of 'the English' who were captured in those engagements: Sydney to Nottingham, 28 Sept. 1692 (*CSPD 1695*, 206).

[38] This point is well brought out in Fitzpatrick, *Seventeenth-Century Ireland*, 77.

[39] Miller, 'The Earl of Tyrconnell and James II's Irish Policy', 804, n. 7; Simms, 'The Jacobite Parliament of 1689', in *War and Politics in Ireland*, 68.

> On the bench now are seated the Dalys and Rices
> And a sage of the Nagles is urging them
> To listen to the plea of the man who can't speak
> The lip dry and simpering English tongue.[40]

At first sight this is a straightforward celebration of the triumph, both linguistic and political, of Irish over English. But things are not that simple. All three of the surnames mentioned, those of the judges Daly and Rice and the barrister Nagle, are in fact Old English. Yet Ó Bruadair is willing not only to celebrate their new status, but to associate them by implication with a distaste for the English that would have been their first, and quite possibly only, language.

What Ó Bruadair was doing, in fact, was to combine a cultural, and more particularly a linguistic, definition of identity with a political outlook that treated Old English and native Irish as a single group. The result was inevitably inconsistency. Where race and culture could form the basis of abuse, as in Ó Bruadair's celebrations of the downfall of 'Robin', 'Digby', and 'John', they were used with gusto. In other cases, however, the realities of ancestry and cultural affiliation were tactfully ignored. In May 1682 Ó Bruadair even addressed a poem to Lord Chief Justice John Keating. Keating was of course a Protestant, and it is doubtful whether he understood Irish. Certainly the letter that accompanied the poem was composed in English. But this did not prevent Ó Bruadair from praising him at length for having presided over the acquittal of Catholic gentlemen accused of complicity in the Popish Plot. Indeed, Keating, like the Catholic Old English lawyers of a few years later, was implicitly co-opted into the Gaelic tradition by means of a passage linking him to his illustrious namesake, the Old English but hibernoscript historian of the 1630s.[41]

Irish Protestants were in general less concerned than Catholics with the division between Old English and native Irish. Indeed, the common use of the term 'Irish' for 'Catholic' ignored the distinction entirely. Yet there remained, even after 1660, at least occasional signs of an awareness that not all Catholics in Ireland were in fact 'Irish'. In 1672, for example, Captain George Mathew, manager of the duke of Ormond's estates, was reassured that allegations that he had, as a Catholic, obstructed the settlement of a Protestant colony on part of the property were not taken seriously:

Your near relation to that noble family [Ormond], with your English education and great concernedness in the English interest by your estate, doth sufficiently satisfy me your parts and ingenuity are too high to subject civil interest to the interest of a particular opinion in religion.[42]

---

[40] Ó Bruadair, *Poems*, iii. 129–33, 89.   [41] Ibid. ii. 257–9, 265–87.

[42] Laurence to Mathew, 25 Sept. 1674 (HMC, *Ormonde Manuscripts*, NS iii. 349).

Where Lord Chief Justice Keating had become an honorary Gael, Mathew, because of his family ties—he was in fact Ormond's half-brother—and his possession of an estate under the Restoration land settlement, was co-opted into 'the English', in the sense of Protestant, interest. Later still, in 1699, the lord chancellor, Sir Richard Cox, giving judgment in favour of the claim of certain citizens of Galway to come under the articles agreed at the end of the Jacobite war, observed that 'there are not in Europe any Papists better affected to the English interest than the inhabitants of Galway. Their town is an English plantation, every one of them is of English extraction, their estates are not only held by English titles but most of them derive under the very Act of Settlement.'[43]

A discussion of ethnic divisions in late seventeenth- and early eighteenth-century Ireland cannot, of course, focus on English and Irish alone. There was also the substantial and rapidly growing Scottish population of Ulster. For most of the later seventeenth century, the cultural differences that marked the Ulster Scots off from most other Irish Protestants were reinforced by religious hostility and political suspicion. In the 1690s mortal danger in the face of a common enemy led to some change in attitude. Although most discussions of the war of 1689–91 followed the precedent set in the 1640s by speaking of the two sides as 'English' and 'Irish', a few observers testified to the new sense of solidarity among Protestants by referring instead to the 'British'.[44] A little later, in 1694–5, some of the group that had aligned themselves with Capel seem to have made an attempt to promote the use of the term 'British' in place of 'English' interest—much to the disgust of Lord Chancellor Porter, whose own view was that it might at some time be necessary to arm the Irish Catholics in order to put down a rebellion by the Ulster Scots.[45] All this, however, was a response to the particular tensions of the immediate post-war years. By the early 1700s, 'English' had once again reasserted itself as the normal synonym for 'Protestant' among Whig as well as Tory members of the Church of Ireland.[46] The Scots themselves, meanwhile, held on to their own distinctive sense of identity. Ulster Presbyterians attending the University of Glasgow during the eighteenth century were entered on its rolls as 'Scotus Hibernus'. In 1722 there were bitter protests when the lord-advocate referred disparagingly to two such students who had appeared before him as 'Irishmen'.[47]

---

[43] BL Add. MS 38,153, fo. 21.

[44] e.g. Dolan MS 26; PRONI T924.

[45] Porter to Trumbull, 9 July 1695 (HMC, *Downshire Manuscripts*, i. 500); Justice Samuel Eyre to ——, 12 May 1695 (ibid. 468–9); Alan Brodrick to Thomas Brodrick, 5 May 1694 (Midleton MS 1248/1, fo. 268ᵛ). A declaration of loyalty by Ulster Presbyterian ministers in 1707 referred to 'the honour and safety of the Protestant religion, government, and British interest in this kingdom': *Dublin Intelligence*, 29 July 1707.

[46] e.g. Alan Brodrick to Thomas Brodrick, 11 Mar. 1702 (Midleton MS 1248/2, fo. 57).

[47] A. T. Q. Stewart, '"The Harp New Strung"', 261–2.

The real change in self-definition that took place in the period after 1691 concerned the use of the term 'Irish'. The traditional equation with 'Catholic' continued for several decades. A Major Steeres of County Kerry was heartily praised in 1693 by the Anglican bishop of Limerick 'for his courage and zeal for opposing the Irish faction there and most industriously promoting the Protestant and their Majesties' interest'. In 1708 a magistrate in the same county reported the detention during an invasion scare of 'several Irish gentlemen' who had refused to take the oath of abjuration, listing among those held the very definitely English name of 'Nicholas Browne, called Lord Kenmare'. Others blundered into even more obvious contradictions. A critic of Porter's administration complained around 1694 that 'the people of Ireland think themselves treated like enemies, while the Irish with their spoils make themselves favourites to men of public employments'. Archbishop King, during the invasion scare of 1708, wrote in similar terms: 'the Irish according to their laudable custom are insolent and foolish'; on the other hand, the emergency 'has given the people of Ireland a fresh opportunity to show their hearty and unanimous zeal for the Revolution'.[48]

Absurdities of this kind were evidence of the tenacity of long-established usage. By this time, however, the traditional terminology was nearing the end of its life. Already in May 1692 a government order had shown a new precision in its use of ethnic and religious labels when it called on the governors of counties to organize the seizure of arms held by 'the Irish and other Roman Catholics'. Sir Francis Brewster, writing in 1698, felt obliged to offer an explicit justification for his continued use of the traditional language, referring to 'the Irish Papists, as they consist of Popish English families, as well as of the ancient natives of that kingdom, in which sense I desire to be understood all along, when I mention the Irish'.[49]

The change, like most new developments in language, was a protracted and uneven process, impossible to date precisely. But from around the beginning of the 1720s it seems to have become more common to refer to threats to the establishment in church and state as coming from 'Papists' rather than from 'the Irish'. This did not mean, however, that Irish Protestants had become ready to apply the term 'Irish' to themselves. The Revd Samuel Madden, writing in 1738, was still anxious to argue that 'the children of those Englishmen, who have planted in our colonies in America, [may] be as justly reckoned Indians and savages, as such families, who are settled here, can be considered and treated as mere *Irishmen* and aliens'.[50] Even in the late

---

[48] Nathaniel Wilson to Bishop Moreton of Kildare, 3 Nov. 1693 (Wyche Papers, 1/1/96); Capt. Richard Hedges to Joshua Dawson, Apr. 1708 (in Hickson, *Old Kerry Records*, 134); PRONI T3222/1/10; King to Southwell, 13 Mar. 1708 (TCD MS 750/312, 194); King to bishop of Clogher, 20 Apr. 1708 (ibid. 205).

[49] *CSPD 1695*, 187; [Brewster], *Discourse Concerning Ireland*, 13.

[50] [Madden], *Reflections and Resolutions*, 107–8.

eighteenth-century golden age of Protestant patriotism, as Hayton has pointed out, an astonishing range of circumlocutions was to be pressed into service in order to avoid the use of a term so long associated with Catholicism, disloyalty, and cultural inferiority.[51]

At this point we move beyond the question of terminology to the more complex, and more disputed, issue of the way in which Irish Protestants chose to define their own identity. By the beginning of the eighteenth century the traditional self-image as 'the English in Ireland' had begun to appear less satisfactory. This was partly because of the passage of time. Families which at the Restoration had been headed by English-born or the sons of English-born could now trace their Irish roots back over two or three generations. Secondly, and more important, there was the growing estrangement of Protestants in Ireland from English government. The potential for conflict had always been there. As early as 1663, Charles II's secretary of state, Henry Bennet, who had just been granted the Clanmalier estates in King's and Queen's counties, was warned that 'the English that have been some time here hate as much that anything should come amongst them as the Creolians of Mexico and Peru do the natives of Spain that go every year to the Indies'.[52] But from the 1690s the heightened expectations created by the Glorious Revolution, along with a more secure position at home, encouraged Irish Protestants to assert themselves more consistently than before. They were all the more ready to do so because the different types of subordination of which they complained—the inferior status of the Irish parliament, the restrictions imposed on Irish trade, the substantial share of Irish public patronage disposed of for English political purposes—were no longer mediated through the personal rule of the monarch.

This is not to suggest that the immediate response of Irish Protestants to their assorted constitutional grievances was to cultivate an Irish patriotism. More commonly, in fact, their first instinct was to base their appeal for better treatment on their English ancestry and loyalties. Ireland, an opponent of the proposed prohibition on woollen exports claimed in 1698, was an 'enlarged part of England . . . to be reputed no more separate from the care of the monarch of Great Britain than Yorkshire, Cheshire or any other part of England'. William Molyneux, in 1698, based his case for Ireland's legislative independence mainly on the claim that Gaelic Ireland had voluntarily accepted English constitutional government, but hedged his bets by arguing, in a famous passage, that 'the great body of the present people of Ireland' were in fact descended from successive waves of settlers, so that 'there remains but a mere handful of the ancient Irish at this day, I may say not one

---

[51] Hayton, 'Anglo-Irish Attitudes', 151.
[52] Sir Thomas Clarges to Bennet, 1 May 1663 (*CSPI 1663–5*, 73).

in a thousand'.[53] With the passage of time, however, such a stance became steadily less attractive. Repeated rebuffs and instances of high-handed behaviour from London both demonstrated the ineffectiveness and diminished the attraction of the appeal to English blood. In the early years of George I's reign, as opinion was once again inflamed by a protracted dispute over the powers of the Irish House of Lords, English-born bishops like John Evans of Meath complained repeatedly of the 'rage and fury' expressed against 'everything that is English'. For Evans the kingdom now contained four parties: the 'Popish', the 'Scots', a weak 'English interest', and what he called the 'Irish, who (though Protestant and originally English) are more divided in their inclinations from [England] than those who are 10,000 leagues off'. Another English bishop, Henry Downes of Killala, commented on how 'we foreigners ... are railed at by the natives of one, two or more descents', while Bishop Nicolson of Derry wrote sardonically of the 'quarantine' imposed on persons born in England, after which 'our posterity (of the very next generation) will be as true born Irish men as if they had been brought out of Egypt in Scota's lap'.[54]

If political tensions encouraged a growing estrangement from England, so did the changing perception of Irish Protestants within England itself. Hayton, analysing literary representations during the late seventeenth and early eighteenth centuries, has traced the process whereby the English stereotype of the comic Irishman was extended to include the Protestant Irish gentry as well as the Catholic lower classes. Teague, the slow-witted servant, was joined in the gallery of stock characters by Captain O'Blunder and Sir Lucius O'Trigger, who shared with Teague the characteristics of outlandish accent, propensity to comic illogic, and absurdly overdeveloped national and family pride, while also exhibiting the more socially exclusive vices of a fondness for duelling and an obsession with the entrapment of English heiresses.[55] This image of the comic Irish gentleman was of course a literary creation, the frequent combination of a Gaelic name and pride in a 'milesian' ancestry with ownership of land, a military career, or membership of the Irish parliament revealing a blithe lack of concern with the realities of Irish society. Nor was the stereotype necessarily a hostile one. On the contrary, the artless honesty of the Irish gentleman was frequently contrasted with the insincerity and frivolity of the English, while his eloquent protestations of loyalty to Great Britain flattered and reassured English audiences.[56] At the same time mockery and

---

[53] *A Discourse on the Woollen Manufactury of Ireland*, 16, 10–11; W. Molyneux, *Case of Ireland*, 35.

[54] Evans to Wake, 18 Sept. 1719 (Wake MS XIII, 109); same to same, 25 Oct. 1716 (ibid. XII, fo. 80); Henry Downes to Nicolson, 20 Feb. 1720 (in Nicolson, *Letters*, ii. 509–10); Nicolson to Wake, 19 Mar. 1721 (Gilbert MS 27, 282).

[55] Hayton, 'From Barbarian to Burlesque'.

[56] Leerssen, *Mere Irish and Fior-Ghael*, ch. 3.

condescension inevitably came to play their part in political debate. During the Regency crisis of 1789, for example, the commissioners sent to London by the Irish parliament were met by a barrage of hostile cartooning, in which the traditional iconography of bulls, brogue, and potatoes played a prominent part.[57] And, even where done in a more neutral spirit, the lumping of Irish Protestants along with Catholics into a single Hibernian stereotype reflected a new perception of them as separate and even foreign.

One further development made it possible for Irish Protestants to think in new ways about their identity. This was the changing image, both political and cultural, of the Catholic lower classes. At the Restoration it had still been possible to see Gaelic Ireland as an alien and threatening entity. But such a perception was already anachronistic. By the middle decades of the seventeenth century the last vestiges of nomadic pastoral agriculture were giving way to an English tenurial structure. Dress and sexual behaviour were being assimilated to English models. The spread of bilingualism was breaking down the cultural isolation of all but the most remote regions.[58] In addition, as was made clear in the 1650s and again in 1678–9, the Catholic lower classes had become an essential part of the labour force in town and country alike.[59] None of this produced any great surge of fellow feeling. To Protestant observers the Catholic masses remained uncouth, disaffected, in thrall to a dangerous religious system. But economic integration and cultural assimilation nevertheless encouraged a transition from the image of Ireland as a territory inhabited by settlers and natives to that of a single society divided along lines of religion and class.

In the longer term, the military and cultural taming of Gaelic Ireland also made possible a more balanced, and even romanticized, view of its qualities. This did not happen on a large scale until the last decades of the eighteenth century, when Charlotte Brooke's *Reliques of Irish Poetry* and the deliberations of the Royal Irish Academy offered a literary and academic backing to the patriotic fervour surrounding the constitution of 1782.[60] But already in the 1720s and 1730s antiquarian and historical writers were showing a greater interest in pre-Norman Ireland and a new willingness to acknowledge its cultural achievements.[61] More favourable presentations of the Gaelic past also made their appearance on the Dublin stage, in Charles Shadwell's *Rotherick O'Connor* (1720) and William Philips's *Hibernia Freed* (1722), an account of the defeat of the Vikings.[62]

---

[57] N. Robinson, 'Caricature and the Regency Crisis'.

[58] On language, see Petty, *Political Anatomy*, 196; Piers, *Country of Westmeath*, 198–200; Williams (ed.), *Pairlement Chloinne Tomais*, 97–8, 101, 105, 109–10, 165. For landholding, see Andrews in *NHI* iii. 464–6, and for the imposition of a tighter sexual discipline, Corish, *Catholic Community*, 69.

[59] Above, p. 32.   [60] Vance, 'Celts, Carthaginians and Constitutions'.

[61] Hill, 'Popery and Protestantism', 102–4. See also Ó Catháin, 'Dermot O'Connor'.

[62] W. S. Clark, *Early Irish Stage*, 170–4; Leerssen, *Mere Irish and Fior-Ghael*, 378–9.

How is the new self-image of Irish Protestants in the early and middle decades of the eighteenth century to be defined? 'Colonial nationalism', another of the unexamined terms that litter modern writing on the period, is clearly not the answer. Ireland was not in any very clear sense a colony. Nor were its Protestant inhabitants nationalists, in the sense of pursuing the political expression of a collectivity defined in terms of ethnicity, language, and culture. A more satisfactory approach, as Leerssen has pointed out, is provided by the eighteenth-century concept of patriotism, defined in terms of a commitment to civic virtue and active citizenship. In defending the political institutions of their community from encroachment, Irish Protestant activists were in the same category as those Dutch patriots who resisted the pretensions to political supremacy of the House of Orange or the French *parlements* who sought to defend regional privileges and immunities against the claims of the central government.[63]

Even in these terms it is as well not to define too much. An analysis of political writings, from William Molyneux's *Case of Ireland* to Swift's *Drapier's Letters*, can be made to indicate the progressive development of a fully fledged political ideology. But it seems likely that the attitudes of ordinary men and women, even of the educated classes, would have been less clear-cut and consistent than any such synthesis of the loudest and most coherent voices would suggest. Nor did all Protestants necessarily move in the same direction. Bishop Evans of Meath may have complained at length of the hostility to England he perceived all around him. But he was also able to recommend to the archbishop of Canterbury a certain Benjamin Parry, a member of the Irish Privy Council, whose 'good sense, and the advantage of seeing the world abroad has given him a right turn, and cleared him of all narrow national partialities'. There was also Dr Owen Lloyd, than whom 'I know no native here so heartily in the English interest, for he has often laughed at their foolish complaints of being an oppressed nation'.[64] Nor was such aloofness confined to the sphere of politics. On her first visit to Dublin, in late 1731, the future Mary Delany was irritated by a Mr Barnard, who 'thinks to recommend himself to me by rallying Ireland and all its diversions'.[65] The provincial ostentatiously scornful of his own background is of course a familiar enough figure at any time. For the historian, however, he is easier to overlook than the admirer of Molyneux or Swift.

Above all, perhaps, it is important not to seek significance, or even coherence, where none existed. For a variety of reasons, Protestants in the early

---

[63] Leerssen, 'Anglo-Irish Patriotism'. For the use of the term 'colonial nationalism', see e.g. J. L. McCracken and R. B. McDowell in *NHI* iii, chs. 5 and 8 respectively. The phrase originated with J. G. Simms; see the brief comments of Hayton and O'Brien in their introduction to Simms, *War and Politics in Ireland*, xiii–xiv.

[64] Evans to Wake, 24 Dec. 1716, 4 Jan. 1717 (Wake MS XII, 104, 106).

[65] Delany, *Autobiography and Correspondence*, i. 315, 328.

eighteenth century were both pushed towards and attracted by a stronger sense of themselves as Irish. This meant accepting, in some vague way, an identity that overlapped with that of the native population, past and present. In 1739, for example, a Dublin newspaper praised the lord mayor of the city, who had intervened to help a visiting English woman who was ill-treated and imprisoned by her landlady, for having displayed 'that ancient and glorious characteristic of the inhabitants of this island, kind and courteous to strangers'. At the same time it noted that the landlady and her accomplices 'are some of those who highly value themselves on account of their not being descended from the old inhabitants of this kingdom'. But comments like this were essentially literary flourishes. The same was true even of the same paper's account, a few weeks later, of the bravery shown by Irish Catholic officers in the Austrian army during fighting against the Turks.[66] For some Protestants the logic of acceptance of an Irish national identity shared with Catholics was eventually to lead to the committee rooms of the society of United Irishmen and the battlefields of County Wexford. But that was never true of more than a minority, and even then only at a time of domestic crisis and international revolution. Half a century earlier, in the context of a stable political order and a supine Catholic population, Protestants who, for whatever reason, chose to play with the idea of themselves as Irishmen were under no real pressure to think through either the logic or the implications of the gesture.

3. Communities

So far we have discussed labels and concepts: the ways in which contemporaries thought and spoke of the different groups into which Irish society was divided. But what were the relationships between these groups, defined first in ethnic and later in religious terms, actually like?

This question, unfortunately, is easier to ask than to answer. Contemporary observers were inevitably concerned with the threat, real or imagined, that the Catholic lower classes, under the leadership of their social superiors, might pose to the state. But they had little interest in what went on as part of the day-to-day coexistence of ordinary Catholics and Protestants. Even when large-scale denominational feuding, which was eventually to lead to the emergence of the Defender and Orange societies, began in County Armagh in the early 1780s, it was a couple of years before the establishment came to realize that these plebeian brawls could not simply be ignored.[67] Records of law enforcement and court proceedings might have made it possible to

[66] *Dublin Daily Post*, 22, 23 Aug., 11 Sept. 1739.
[67] Connolly, *Religion and Society*, 18–20; D. W. Miller, 'The Armagh Troubles', 165–9.

recover what contemporaries saw as beneath their notice, but these have not survived.

What, then, can we say? We know, to begin with, that the large-scale settlement of Scots and English during the seventeenth century created predictable tensions. In Ulster these came bloodily into the open in the autumn of 1641, when the attempt by Catholic leaders to secure their position at a time of impending political crisis degenerated into apparently unplanned plunder and massacre. Later in the century, hostility to a Protestant population of relatively recent settlers remained evident as one of the motives behind the depredations, both in Ulster and elsewhere, of outlaw bands of tories.[68] By 1700 the great era of plantation and settlement was over, but the appearance of Protestant newcomers could still lead to trouble. Ephraim Dawson, who in 1709 settled some eighty Protestant refugees from the Rhineland palatinate on his estate in County Kilkenny, complained five years later that they had been driven away 'by the menaces of their Popish neighbours'.[69] In County Limerick, where the majority of the Palatines settled, hostility towards them was still evident over a century later.[70] In Erris, County Mayo, Protestant settlers introduced by Sir Arthur Shaen likewise complained of the efforts of the local Catholic population to 'ease themselves, and more effectually ruin us ... by the more secret artifices of stealing our cattle, to the number of 75, within the space of nine months, besides sheep without number, not to mention the plundering of our gardens, stealing our corn, both of the field and haggard, etc.'.[71] In Armagh the continued movement of Protestants, particularly Presbyterians, into the predominantly Catholic south of the county also caused difficulties. In 1743 the meeting-house founded near Crossmaglen by a newly established minister, Alexander McCoombe, was burnt down. A woman who had been on her way to join his congregation reported how she had been stopped on the road and told that 'she had better stay at home on 8s. an acre than go there and pay 4s., for the meeting house was burned, the people's cattle houghed, and that they (the Papists) would burn herself; that Mr McCoombe thought to be a little king in that country, but he must or would be holden in'.[72]

[68] For 1641 see Gillespie, 'End of an Era'; Nicholas Canny, 'In Defence of the Constitution? The Nature of Irish Revolt in the Seventeenth Century', in Bergeron and Cullen (eds.), *Culture et pratiques politiques*, 23–40. For the Tories see below, ch. 6, sect. 2.

[69] Ephraim Dawson to R. Piggott, 27 Aug. 1715 (TCD MSS 1995–2008/1714). For the Palatines, see also below, ch. 7, sect. 3.

[70] Cullen, *Emergence of Modern Ireland*, 205–6; Donnelly, 'Pastorini and Captain Rock', 129–30. A Methodist observer noted in 1829 that 'our county societies are composed exclusively of Palatines, the descendants of men driven from Germany on account of their religion, they do not amalgamate with the native Irish and are all Brunswickers': quoted in Hempton, 'The Methodist Crusade in Ireland', 42.

[71] The petition, undated but clearly belonging to the reign of Queen Anne, is reproduced in facsimile in Knight, *Erris in the 'Irish Highlands'*, facing p. 174. I have corrected a number of errors in Knight's transcription of the document (ibid. 64).

[72] Examination of Elenor Mulligan, 11 Oct. 1743 (PRONI T1392).

Even where tensions were not thus kept alive by the continued introduction of outsiders, there is clear evidence of a continuing hostility between
religiously and culturally defined groups. An English traveller visiting
Waterford in the early 1740s observed that 'the people that come to market
here, I mean of the native Irish, seem not to like the people of Waterford,
though they take their money, for they look upon them as English'. Near
Youghal he heard himself and his companions referred to as 'bugs', and was
'informed I might take the word *bug* in the English literal sense; for by that
the vulgar of this kingdom entitle all of our nation'.[73] More complex divisions
were reported in the barony of Forth in County Wexford, where the descendants of medieval English settlers, 'who retain the language and the manners of
the old English', exhibited 'an excessive antipathy to the native Irish', while at
the same time, as 'very bigotted Papists', being 'not much fonder of the
modern English inhabitants'.[74] In Dublin sectarian animosity played at least
some part in the vicious brawls between the predominantly Catholic butchers
of the Ormond market and the predominantly Protestant weavers of the
Liberties.[75] Elsewhere specific issues brought hostilities into the open. Thus
Catholics in Timahoe, County Kildare, burnt down the Quaker meeting-
house in 1740, following reports—later denied—that the Quakers had
burned an effigy of the Virgin Mary at their 5 November celebrations.[76] Five
years earlier the trial of the Galway Catholic Richard Martin, who had used
his sword to kill an unarmed officer with whom he had quarrelled in a public
billiard-room, was attended by a 'numerous and insolent . . . rabble, who
showed their joy upon the acquittal of Martin by loud exclamations in the
Four Courts, and bonfires in the Popish quarters of the town'.[77] A lesser
episode in County Meath the following year, when a recent convert named
Nugent challenged a magistrate who had arrested one of his servants, was
likewise reported to be 'understood to be a dispute between Protestant and
Papist'.[78]

Episodes of this kind confirm the existence of an underlying conflict
between Catholic and Protestant, readily brought to the surface by particular
incidents. At the same time it is clear that the division between the two camps
was bridged by a range of contacts. Intermarriage, for example, took place at
every social level. In the 1730s the parish of Navan in County Meath contained thirty-six Protestant families and no less than twelve Protestant women

---

[73] [Chetwood], *Tour through Ireland*, 161–2, 125–6.
[74] Willes, Observations on Ireland (PRONI T2855/1, 2–3).
[75] Fagan, 'Dublin Catholic Mob', 138–41.
[76] *Pue's Occurrences*, 2–5 Feb. 1740.
[77] Lords justices to Dorset, 25 Apr., 12 May 1735 (PRONI D2707/A/1/7, 26, 28–9); *Dublin Gazette*, 6–10 May 1735.
[78] Lords justices to Devonshire, 23 May 1736 (PRONI D2707/A/1/8, 6–9). See also Boulter to Devonshire, 7 June 1737 (*Letters*, ii. 228).

married to Catholics.[79] There were also other business and personal relationships. In 1709 Sir Richard Cox wrote to Edward Southwell to introduce
'Mr Dowdall (a Rom Cath)... a very ingenious man if you have a mind to be
informed how the world goes here'. Lord Midleton, in an earlier period one
of the strongest advocates of a tough anti-Catholic policy, took advice in 1719
on the letting of land from Standish Barry, 'a Papist, but the best of the kind I
ever knew, and very much inclined to do any service to our family'.[80] In 1751
Mary Delany, wife of the dean of Down, exchanged social visits with a nun
from the convent in King Street, Dublin, 'an agreeable, entertaining creature,
and seems to have good principles and pretty sentiments', even though 'I
don't call upon her so often as I should like to do, as people are so offended
here if these nuns are much taken notice of, that I should be thought
disaffected'.[81]

A more extended insight into the commonplace—and hence often
unrecorded—relationships that could cut across the division between Catholic
and Protestant is provided by a set of affidavits collected during 1745 on
behalf of a County Clare priest, James Dougan. Dougan had been charged
with going to England five years earlier to enlist men for the Spanish service.
Out of thirty-three witnesses who came forward to testify to Dougan's con-
tinuous residence in Ireland during the period concerned, twenty were
Protestants. In County Clare, for example, Thomas Wilkinson testified that he
had seen Dougan regularly at his inn during 1740 and also at the funeral of
Wilkinson's sister, 'and remembers to have helped him to some refreshment
on that occasion'. William May, who farmed the turnpike gate at Toomevara
in Tipperary, where Dougan had moved in 1741, deposed that he and the
priest 'very often ate and drank with each other... [and] had frequently been
in company with each other at funerals and other places'. William Lewis,
'gentleman', of Clash in the same county, had been in the company of
Dougan at the fair of Toomevara in October 1742, 'for five or six hours
at least'. Richard Branton, also claiming the status of gentleman, had
had Dougan in his house 'above twenty times'. In King's County, Rebecca
Minchin recalled that one night in January 1742 she had sent for Dougan to
baptize her dangerously ill nephew, 'having no clergyman of the Church of
Ireland as by law established convenient'. Dougan had come, baptized the
child, and eaten and drunk with the family for some two hours before taking
his leave.[82]

A final glimpse of the complexity of relationships at a personal level is

---

[79] Visitation of the diocese of Meath *c.*1733 (RCB GS 2/7/3/10, 48).
[80] Cox to Southwell, 29 Jan. 1709 (BL Add. MS 38, 156, fo. 48); Midleton to Thomas
Brodrick, 11 Dec. 1719 (Midleton MS 1248/4, fo. 183).
[81] Delany, *Autobiography and Correspondence*, iii. 9, 38.
[82] SP63/407/52–71, 109–32.

provided by the experiences of the Queen's County gentleman Pole Cosby. Travelling about during his vacation from the University of Leiden in the summer of 1723, Cosby was entertained 'with very great civility' at the Irish monastery in Prague, 'and four score Irish priests there were as glad and full of joy to see us as if we were their own kin'. Later, at Munich, he once again 'met with several Irish priests who were joyful to see a countryman'. It would be too much to say that either experience led Cosby to rethink his definition of nationality, much less his attitude to Catholicism. On the contrary, he found the church at Prague richly ornamented, but the other premises 'but ordinary and Irish all over, very dirty', while the priests were 'most extremely ignorant and very zealous of their superstitious religion'. At the same time it is clear that a bond of some kind was established. 'Many arguments I had with them. It is well they did not destroy me for being a heretic, as they often called me, and told me I would be infallibly damned, but when we did not talk of religion we were very fond.'[83]

4. Orders

From relationships that were in one way or another peculiar to Ireland, we turn to one that preoccupies historians everywhere: the relationship, that is, between rich and poor, propertied and propertyless, governing élite and common people. The traditional historical picture emphasizes the divisions between the upper and lower levels of Irish society: the cultural gulf separating English or anglicized landlord and Gaelic peasant, the built-in economic, religious, and political conflicts, the substantial sums extracted in rent from a desperately poor tenantry. None of these issues can be ignored. Yet a model built wholly around conflict fails to do justice to a complex reality. In Ireland, as elsewhere in early modern Europe, the authority of some and the sub-ordination of others existed within a framework of shared expectations and a degree of mutual accommodation, and vertical relationships of clientage and patronage, however unequal the terms, were an important part of how the society worked.

Let us start with the question of economic relationships. Members of the Irish ruling class, like their counterparts in England and elsewhere, conceived of the workings of the ideal society as paternalistic. The County Down landlord Michael Ward, in the letter of advice which he drew up in 1738 for the benefit of his son, recommended a careful combination of firmness and generosity towards tenants and employees:

Be just and kind with prudence to your servants. Reward long and faithful services to your family or yourself. Regard your tenants as part of your own family; you live by

[83] Cosby, 'Autobiography', 97–8.

their labour, therefore let them live comfortably by their industry. But if they become idle and dishonest, and you can't reform them, get quit of them as soon as you can.[84]

Dean William Henry, in 1739, offered an equally idealized picture of society in the improved areas of Ulster: the landscape 'tilled like a garden, crowded with industrious Protestant inhabitants, the happy landlord living in the midst of this numerous family as a true father of his country, at once watchful of their good and advancing thereby his own; while the flourishing tenants rejoice under his wing and pay him no less honour and love than to a natural parent'. But Henry went on to contrast these favoured northern counties with the rest of Ireland, where the landlord 'reigns as a petty tyrant over an herd of beasts and a few slaves more wretched than the beasts'. Other observers too suggested that the traditional ideal of landlord and tenant, master and servant, as bound together by mutually acknowledged ties of interest and obligation, was rarely realized in practice. Archbishop King, in 1712, complained of 'the cruelty of the landlords, who rack their tenants so that they can neither render to God, to the public, or their children what is due to them. . . . I am persuaded neither the peasants in France nor the common Turks live so miserably as the tertenants in Ireland.' Chesterfield declared that 'the poor people in Ireland are used worse than negroes by their lords and masters, and their deputies of deputies of deputies'.[85]

It is, of course, on comment of this kind that the prevailing image of Ireland as a society composed of wholly antagonistic strata is based. Yet the contrast with other eighteenth-century societies that is implied may be misleading. It was not only in Ireland, after all, that a theoretical commitment to paternalism failed to restrain landlords and others from maximizing their profits at the expense of their supposed dependants. To see this, it is necessary to look no further than the continued progress of enclosure in rural England or the drastic restructuring of tenurial relationships that took place from the mid-eighteenth century in the Scottish Highlands. Indeed, it can be argued that paternalism was always more potent as a rhetoric serving to legitimize inequalities of wealth and status than as an actual determinant of behaviour.[86] In addition, of course, paternalism could at times make economic sense. When Lord Midleton advised his brother in 1719 to give 'reasonable encouragement', as opposed to 'a bare preference at a rack rent', to 'an honest, old, English, Protestant improving tenant', he recommended no more than enlightened self-interest. The problem was that in Ireland tenants of this kind were hard to come by. Instead, landlords let to middlemen and large farmers, who in turn sublet to smaller tenants. In these circumstances, as even

[84] PRONI D2092/1/7/121.
[85] Henry, 'Hints' (Nat. Arch. Ire. M2533), 70–1; King to Nicolson, 20 Dec. 1712 (TCD MS 250/4/1, 85–6); Chesterfield, *Letters*, vi. 2617.
[86] For a useful, short discussion, see Wrightson, *English Society 1580–1680*, 57–65.

Archbishop King recognized, there was no point in landlords taking it upon themselves to let out land on good leases, 'for he that has it, sets it to another and he to another and the tertenants often hold from the fourth, who screws and racks them to death'.[87] Such comments prefigure the direction of recent historical work, which has been to emphasize just how limited was the control which the Irish landlord class of this period could exercise over any part of the workings of agrarian society.[88]

The complexity of rural social relationships is further confirmed by the evidence of the one major outbreak of agrarian protest to take place during the first half of the eighteenth century. This was the campaign of cattle maiming and intimidation, conducted by a group known as the Houghers, that spread through Galway, Mayo, Clare, and some other western counties during 1711–13. These events made clear that rural conflict, in a multi-layered tenurial system, could not in fact be reduced to a simple opposition between predatory landlords and exploited tenants. Instead, the Houghers directed their attacks at all those, whether landlords, middlemen, or large farmers, who sought to promote the further expansion of stock rearing at the expense of large-scale tillage farming. Like later agrarian movements, from the 1760s on, moreover, the Hougher campaign was defensive, even conservative, in character. Its purpose was not to challenge the structure of rural property ownership, but rather to appeal to social superiors to live up to their moral obligations, by letting land at reasonable rates and by not allowing commercial considerations to override the subsistence needs of the local agrarian population. 'Tenants', a proclamation by the Galway Houghers declared, 'have as right a title to the tenancy of the lands as the landlords to be landlords, for God made the earth and all the creatures thereupon for the use of man.'[89] Such sentiments were of course at the heart of popular protest everywhere in pre-industrialized Europe. Nor can they necessarily be taken as any indication of how things had really been, even in less contentious times. Yet, considered even as rhetoric, the appeal to ideas of reciprocity and mutual obligation remains important. However harsh the reality of economic life in the Irish countryside, these remained the terms in which the common people, no less than a thoughtful man of property like Michael Ward, felt that social relations should be discussed.

If the economic dimension of the relationship between rulers and ruled is less clear-cut than is often assumed, the same is true of the cultural dimension. The events of the sixteenth and seventeenth centuries had imposed a landed class overwhelmingly of relatively recent English descent on a popula-

---

[87] Midleton to Thomas Brodrick, 11 Dec. 1719 (Midleton MS 1248/4, fo. 183); King to Nicolson, 20 Dec. 1712 (TCD MS 750/4/1, 85–6).

[88] Roebuck, 'Landlord Indebtedness'. For the inability of landlords to get the tenants they would like, see Dickson, 'Middlemen'.

[89] Connolly, 'The Houghers'.

tion that, outside parts of Ulster, remained predominantly Gaelic in language and culture. Yet the importance of these divisions is easily overstated. Where language is concerned, it is important to remember that it was by no means only in Ireland that the upper and lower levels of society spoke different tongues. In Russia and parts of Italy, the educated and wealthy spoke French, in Bohemia German, in Norway Danish and in Finland Swedish, leaving the indigenous language in each case to the common people. Nearer to home, in highland Scotland and Wales, anglophone landlords presided over Gaelic- and Welsh-speaking rural populations.[90] Even in France, it has been esti- mated, almost half the population spoke a local dialect, rather than standard French, as their principal or—for about one person in four—only language.[91] Differences in language were not, in any case, an impenetrable barrier. Residence in a predominantly Irish-speaking countryside meant that even newcomers could pick up at least a smattering of the language. On the eve of the Restoration a Cromwellian army captain, drinking at the Sign of the Bear in Mallow, County Cork, was able to tell a Catholic gentleman at the same table, 'in broken Irish', that the sea would be red with blood before the king was again admitted to the throne.[92] The children of landed families, con- signed to the care of locally recruited servants and nursemaids, had even greater linguistic opportunities: a daughter of Lord Nugent, writing from Westmeath in 1744, reported that 'my little boy speaks nothing but Irish', and so was not yet ready to begin formal schooling.[93] By the end of the eighteenth century some knowledge of Irish appears to have been common enough among the Protestant middle and upper classes. In 1798 Thomas Judkin Fitzgerald, high sheriff of County Tipperary and the scourge of the county's United Irishmen, was able to harangue a crowd for three hours, part of the time in English and part in Irish.[94] William Kirkwood, the merchant who commanded the yeomanry at Killala, County Mayo, in 1798 at the time of the French invasion, was 'a good humoured man, well versed in the Irish language'.[95]

As with language, so with culture generally. The Irish gentry of the late seventeenth and early eighteenth centuries, like their counterparts elsewhere in pre-industrialized Europe, participated freely in a variety of amusements and performances that were shared with their social inferiors.[96] Music is an obvious example. Pipers and harpists, performing both Irish tunes and adapta- tions of English compositions, found audiences and patrons in the houses of

---

[90] P. Burke, *Popular Culture in Early Modern Europe*, 272.
[91] Muchembled, *Popular Culture and Élite Culture in France 1400–1750*, 42.
[92] HMC, *Egmont Papers*, ii. 33.
[93] Barbara Reilly to Andrew Savage, 21 Aug. 1744 (PRONI D552/A/2/7/11).
[94] McDowell, *Ireland in the Age of Imperialism and Revolution*, 580.
[95] Stock, *A Narrative of What Passed at Killala*, 9. For other examples, see Ó Cuiv in *NHI* iv. 383.
[96] Burke, *Popular Culture*, ch. 8, 9.

the gentry. The support which the great harpist Turlough O'Carolan (1670–1738) received from a range of families, Protestant as well as Catholic, English as well as Gaelic in origin, is well known. In the same way, Arthur O'Neill, making his first tour as an itinerant harper in County Antrim in 1760, was received both by his namesakes, the O'Neills of Shane's Castle, and by the much more recently established Boyds of Ballycastle.[97] Similar patronage was extended to games and festivals. In 1732, for example, the wife of the Church of Ireland bishop of Killala presided over the local fair-day sports, first riding in her coach to see horse races on the strand, then returning to her own house to watch 'dancing, singing, grinning [by old women for a prize of tobacco], accompanied with an excellent bagpipe, the whole concluded with a ball, bonfire and illuminations'. William Farrell, born in Carlow town in 1772, remembered the factions that in his youth had organized rival May Day celebrations: 'Every gentleman they had influence on, they went to him for a Maypole and were never refused.'[98]

Commercial entertainment also involved a regular mingling of classes. The Dublin theatre, John Dunton noted in 1699, 'gives entertainment as well to the broom man as the greatest peer', and dramatists ruefully commented on the difficulty of writing material that would appeal simultaneously to the journeymen and servants in the upper gallery and to the more refined audience seated in other parts.[99] Horse races and prize fights attracted a similar social mix.[100] The same was true of the more distinctively Irish game of hurling, which by the start of the eighteenth century had become established as a well-developed spectator sport, in which skilled performers competed, sometimes for substantial money prizes, before audiences from all social levels. In August 1746, for example, the venue of a proposed match, to be played near Gort in County Galway for a prize of forty guineas, was moved 'for the better accommodation of the ladies and gentlemen, and the benefit of a good road for carriages'. Nine years later a match between players from counties Kildare and Dublin was watched by the lord lieutenant, as well as 'a most brilliant appearance of nobility and gentry'.[101]

Nor was patronage of hurling and other sports confined to spectatorship and the heavy betting that inevitably, by the habits of the age, went with it. Pole Cosby of King's County recalled with pride the accomplishments of his father, who had died in 1729: 'He would follow ... a pack of fleet hounds from morning till night and keep closer in with the hounds than anyone on horseback; he danced on the ropes as well as any rope dancer that ever was; he was a fine tennis and five player, a most extraordinary fine hurler.' In

---

[97] O'Sullivan, *Carolan*, i. 43–5; ii. 145–6.
[98] Delany, *Autobiography and Correspondence*, i. 369, 373; McHugh (ed.), *Carlow in '98*, 23–4.
[99] Dunton, *Life and Errors*, ii. 563; Fagan, *Second City*, 68–70; Clark, *Early Irish Stage*, 144–6.
[100] e.g. Leinster, *Correspondence*, i. 61; *Dublin Intelligence*, 17 May 1731.
[101] *Pue's Occurrences*, 15–19 July, 9–12, 23–6 Aug. 1746; Ó Maolfabhail, *Camán*, 138.

County Kilkenny John Cuffe, Baron Desart (1730–67), was commemorated in popular song for his exploits on the hurling field; his nickname was Sean a' Chaipin ('Jack of the cap'), after the red cap he wore when leading his team. The Cocloughs of County Wexford were likewise remembered in the late nineteenth century as 'always fine fellows for sporting and hurling, and no gentleman in the county could equal them for throwing away money like chaff'.[102] Such comment may of course be affected by the rosy glow of distance. But overall, it seems clear that the roughness and lack of sophistication that contemporaries complained of in the Irish gentry of the early and mid-eighteenth century permitted a degree of cultural interaction with social inferiors that was not to be seen among their more refined descendants.

In addition to this patronage of the normal run of popular amusements, there were also the festive events which the élite organized for those below them on the social scale. Important political anniversaries, the monarch's birthday, military victories, the formal entry of the lord lieutenant into the kingdom: all these were celebrated by elaborate public ritual. This had two central elements. First, there was the dramatic representation of power, authority, and social hierarchy: the firing of vollies, the ringing of bells, the solemn processions of civic and ecclesiastical dignitaries. Secondly, there was the distribution of food and drink to all or part of the population. In Killarney, at the celebrations of the accession of George I organized by Captain Hedges, the local gentry set up a table by the bonfire 'set with bottles of claret and glasses to drink His Majesty's health', while providing 'barrels of beer for the soldiers and inferior company'. In Derry, the civic authorities celebrated the reconciliation between the king and the prince of Wales in 1720 by inviting 'all estates of men, women and children in this town (and very numerous they are) to a splendid entertainment of sweetmeats, etc., at the Guildhall'. At Carrickfergus, on 5 November 1728, the governor gave 'to the footsoldiers an hogshead, and to the dragoons a barrel of excellent punch, and the mob as much strong malt liquor as they could make away with'.[103]

The most elaborate such gestures, needless to say, were those in the capital. When the duke of Ormond entered the city in October 1665, the authorities erected 'a conduit in the corn-market whence wine ran in abundance'. At the celebrations for George II's birthday in 1733, the lord lieutenant invited the leading gentry to a banquet in Dublin Castle, 'placed in a surprising manner round a fountain in the council chamber, which flowed with wine all the night, from whence several hogsheads of wine were also set a running to the common people, who crowded below to see the illuminations'. In the troubled year of 1745 the hydraulics of collective festivity became more elaborate still.

---

[102] Cosby, 'Autobiography', 179; Ó Caithnia, *Scéal na hIománá*, 27–9, 36.
[103] Capt. Richard Hedges to ——, 23 Aug. 1714 (Hickson, *Old Kerry Records*, 148; see above, Introduction); Nicolson to Wake, 3 May 1720 (Gilbert MS 27, 260–1); *Dublin Intelligence*, 9 Nov. 1728.

At the entrance to the supper room at the Castle, on the night of the king's birthday,

were several statues which poured a perpetual flow of the choicest wines of all sorts into nick basins properly placed to receive them, from whence the liquor was conveyed into the lower Castle Yard where it played off in several fountains of wine during the whole of the entertainment, to give the populace an opportunity to drink His Majesty's health and long life and confusion to his enemies.[104]

The dominant note on these occasions of official festivity was deference: the grateful acceptance of favours from above in exchange for demonstrations of enthusiastic loyalty. The device of having wine flow from the formal banquet to the crowds gathered outside and the seating arrangements at Captain Hedges' Killarney celebrations, no less than the formal processions that preceded them, carefully combined communal celebration with the theatrical reinforcement of social distinctions. There was, however, another side to some of the rituals involved. A visitor to Cork city in the early 1740s observed how, on the day of the installation of a new mayor, 'those that are not concerned in the assembly procure large quantities of bran, which they throw into the eyes of every person they meet, not forgetting the new mayor, his officers and retinue'. Lord Orrery, a few years before, had to escape down an alley to avoid being pelted by 'a most despicable set of wretches':

These mayoralty honours have been paid to all Christian souls from time immemorial. The higher your rank, the greater your quantity of meal: so that if his sacred Majesty was to walk on this day from North Gate to South Gate in his black velvet coat, his black cravat and his black feather, he would only fulfill the Merlinean prophecy of the white king.[105]

Such displays were less a repudiation of the deference shown by the loyal crowd lining the route of official processions than its obverse. What they offered was a temporary escape from the normal constraints on behaviour: more specifically, an opportunity to express, in a ritualized manner, a degree of hostility towards social superiors. Similar occasions of licensed aggression and disorder, permitting a controlled release of the frustrations and resentments inevitable in a hierarchical society, were built into popular culture throughout the pre-industrialized world: the carnivals of southern Europe, with their motif of the world turned upside down; the Shrove Tuesday riots of London apprentices; and the aggressive demand for hospitality associated in some cases with a custom like Christmas mumming.[106] The custom observed at state banquets in Dublin Castle, whereby after the company had finished,

---

[104] Carte, *Ormonde*, iv. 225–6; *CSPI 1663–5*, 651; *Dublin Gazette*, 30 Oct.–3 Nov. 1733; *Faulkner's Dublin Journal*, 29 Oct.–3 Nov. 1745.

[105] [Chetwood], *Tour through Ireland*, 56–7; Orrery to Swift, Oct. 1735 (*Orrery Papers*, i. 137–8).

[106] Burke, *Popular Culture*, ch. 7; Sider, 'Christmas Mumming'.

the crowd outside was permitted to come in and carry off whatever food remained, comes midway between the two extremes of grateful acceptance and licensed plunder.[107]

Less spectacular than these officially organized celebrations, but in aggregate almost certainly more important, were those arranged by individual members of the élite for their tenants and dependants. When Pole Cosby returned to Queen's County in 1724, after three years at the University of Leiden, he was met at the county boundary 'by several gentlemen, friends and tenants, and garlands and long dancers, and my father invited them all home to dine with him, and gave drink and money to the common people and dancers'. When Cosby senior died five years later, his funeral was equally elaborate: 'Every creature that came that had the least tolerable appearance had scarves and gloves, 100 poor were served at the door with bread and ale, and great quantities of victuals of all sorts within, with plenty of wine.' In County Monaghan in 1773 Lord Dartry celebrated his son's fifteenth birthday 'in a very hospitable and princely manner, 150 poor people to dinner, a most magnificent bonfire, a grand dinner and supper, a brilliant ball and . . . very elegant fireworks'. Twenty children from the school run by Lady Dartry attended in their new uniforms, while '160 workmen of several kinds made a solemn procession round the bonfire, with each the instruments of his employment on his shoulder'. Here, no less than in the state-sponsored festivities in Dublin and elsewhere, paternalistic benevolence was combined with the ritualized depiction of social gradations.[108]

Nor was it only landowners who sponsored popular festivities on appropriate occasions. The proprietor of a new windmill completed at Mullingar in 1736 followed up a public dinner for the gentlemen, merchants, and traders of the town with his own version of the fountains of Dublin Castle: 'Two boxes or chests of lemons and oranges, with the just proportion of spirits etc were thrown to the mill stones, the mill being set going, the same ingredients were immediately ground down to punch through a conduit prepared, which conveyed the liquor into a cistern without-side for the use of the populace.' More robust entertainments were seen when the employees of Hugh Faulkner, of Wellbrook in County Tyrone, completed the construction of a weir and mill-race at eight o'clock on a May evening in 1765. 'From eight to nine o'clock we drank whiskey, and from nine to near eleven fought, yet by my management no blood drawn, but several shirts and waistcoats torn.' In all, the construction of the weir had taken '110 men and 20 horses and 15 gallons of whiskey'.[109]

[107] Delany, *Autobiography and Correspondence*, ii. 481; John Ryder to Sir Dudley Ryder, 25 Oct. [1743] (PRONI T3228/1/10).
[108] Cosby, 'Autobiography', 168, 181–2; Burrows Tour (PRONI T3551, 90).
[109] *Dublin Daily Advertiser*, 27 Dec. 1736; Hugh Faulkner to Samuel Faulkner, 12 May 1765 (PRONI Mic 21/1).

Other occasions for the entertainment of social inferiors were provided by the organization of the militia and the contesting of elections. Service in the militia was in many ways a perfect expression of vertical social bonds. Tenants and other dependants enlisted, not under an impersonal commander, but under their landlord and patron. 'Your tenants', an absentee Cork landowner was told in 1708, 'will suffer extremely now the country is arraying, for want of somebody to serve under.' The personal bond was reinforced by hospitality. A militia captain in County Down was severely criticized when he baulked at paying 6*d*. rather than 4*d*. a head for a dinner for the company he had raised during the 1745 emergency.[110] Elections were also the occasion of elaborate displays of generosity. A member of the Molesworth family commemorated in a song to 'a Fingall tune' the hospitality dispensed in 1727 to tenants and voters on the family estate near Swords, County Dublin:

> My Lady Molesworth she welcomed them all
> Where tables were laid in the large summer hall
> Well furnished with roast meat and hollow fowl
> And oceans of punch in a plate bowl.

The two candidates in the city of Dublin by-election two years later were reported to have 'continued these three or four weeks past to give the citizens music at Stephen's Green and the Bason, but as yet no open house has been kept to treat the poor freemen'. Closer to the contest, however, they began 'to bestir themselves properly', one of them spending more than £200 on food and wine for a gathering of more than 100 freemen. In County Kerry in 1743 the losing candidate provided '4 tuns of wine, 2 ditto ale, 2 ditto cider, 2 ditto beer, 40 sheep, 20 bullocks, 60 hams, 40 pigs, a hogshead of shrub, 600 fowls, venison, veal &c' for an electorate of only 300. In the borough of Kinsale in County Cork, Agmondisham Vesey in 1765 paid some £645 to four publicans, along with £5. 13*s*. 9*d*. for a fiddler and £14. 9*s*. 'for beer to the populace'.[111]

To patronage of popular amusements and the provision of treats and entertainments must be added an element of active paternalism. This was both official and unofficial. The official variety centred on the policing of markets for basic necessities. In Dublin and other cities the price and size of a loaf of bread was regularly fixed at the assizes, and the mayor and his officials made periodic tours of the public markets to confiscate underweight loaves, spoilt meat, and other defective goods.[112] There was also action against those who sought to manipulate the market for their own benefit. In 1709, for

---

[110] Alan Brodrick to Thomas Brodrick, 4 May 1708 (Midleton MS 1248/2, fo. 326); Charles Brett to Michael Ward, 4 June 1746 (PRONI D2092/1/17/21).

[111] HMC, *Various Collections*, viii. 398–9; *Dublin Intelligence*, 23 Aug., 20 Sept. 1729; HMC, *Puleston Manuscripts*, 327; Sarsfield-Vesey Papers, 54(d).

[112] e.g. *Dublin Daily Advertiser*, 28 Oct., 27 Nov. 1736.

example, the lord mayor of Dublin issued a proclamation calling on the toll collectors and constables to take action against 'a sort of people called sky farmers', speculators who bought up supplies of corn before they could reach the city markets. In January 1734, similarly, the mayor appeared in person on the coal quay to force merchants to release their stocks at a fixed price of 16s. per ton, at the same time ordering that no person be allowed to buy more than half a barrel. An appeal five years earlier by the colliers against the legality of such price-fixing had been dismissed by the Privy Council. In 1756 it was the rates charged by carmen and porters that were fixed by law, but again the reason was that 'the poor, it is hoped, will be eased from those extortions which have hitherto caused them loudly to complain'.[113] This sort of intervention was naturally most common in the city of Dublin, with its large consumer market. But similar action was taken elsewhere. In 1727 the grand jury of County Antrim reimbursed the sheriff for serving the county's magistrates with a letter from the lords justices 'commanding them to take care of the markets and persons forestalling and regrating'.[114]

Paternalist regulation was not confined to prices. Municipal and national authorities also rejected, in principle at least, the proposition that wages should be fixed by supply and demand alone. This could work both ways. In 1712 the grand jury of Antrim, lamenting that 'the blessing of plenty doth in this county occasion idleness and much raise the demands and wages of workmen and labourers', set out maximum wages for a range of trades. In 1740, on the other hand, the master and wardens of the weavers' corporation of Dublin condemned the practice of some masters who '(taking an advantage of [their workers'] wants and necessities) make them accept of less for their labour than the usual price given for such work, whereby they are rendered incapable of supporting themselves and families'. Nine years later a committee of the House of Commons upheld the complaints of the journeymen broadweavers concerning a deterioration in their wages and hours of work, and recommended that in future wages be regularly fixed by the city's magistrates.[115] The significance of all this should not, of course, be overstated. The committee's report was accepted by the Commons, but no legislation followed; parliament, like the various trade guilds and corporations, consistently proved more active in repressing combinations of workmen than they were in protecting the rights of employees. Even effective action against forestalling seems generally to be reported at times of exceptional hardship; 1708–9, 1734–5, and 1756–7, for example, were all years of poor harvests and high prices. But then paternalism is by definition an unequal relationship. And

---

[113] *Dublin Intelligence*, 8 Mar. 1709; *Dublin Gazette*, 22–5 Oct. 1709; *Dublin Intelligence*, 15, 22 Feb. 1729; *Faulkner's Dublin Journal*, 15–19 Jan. 1734; *Belfast News Letter*, 17 Feb. 1756.
[114] Antrim Grand Jury Presentment Book (PRONI ANT 4/1/3, 4).
[115] Ibid., ANT 4/1/1, 11; Papers relating to journeymen weavers, PRONI D562/1333, 1334, 1336.

even intermittent intervention to protect society's poorest members from the unrestrained operation of the market gave the rhetoric of reciprocity a substance it would not otherwise have had.

Practical favour might also be expected, on some occasions at least, from individual social superiors. Vertical relationships of clientage and patronage were important at every level of society. At the top, leading magnates channelled to their relatives and followers the choice pickings of the political system. Lower down, young men of education but no fortune polished up whatever personal or family connections they could muster as the key to a secure future in the civil or religious establishment. The case of Jonathan Swift, drawing on a long-standing family connection to obtain a post in the household of the retired diplomat Sir William Temple, to whom he then looked to find him a suitable appointment in the wider world, was in this respect typical. Patronage in its different forms was not of course unique to Ireland. But contemporaries do seem to have felt that it was even more important there than elsewhere. 'As it will be hard in that litigious country to live without some broils', the young Sir John Perceval was advised in 1702, he should retain the attorney-general by a standing fee, pay careful attention to visiting bishops, judges, and similar dignitaries, and maintain 'a fair correspondence' with other leading officials, 'for there is no quiet for any man there who is not known to have good friends and of every sort'.[116]

All this, of course, relates to the privileged or relatively privileged. More humble individuals might also in some cases count on the favour of a great man. In 1711, for example, the duke of Ormond, back in office as lord lieutenant, restored one of his former chairmen to a place in the Battleaxe Guards from which he had been dismissed during the period of Whig ascendancy.[117] More commonly, however, the dependence of the ordinary man or woman was on a local patron. This could take various forms. A resident landlord offered employment, in his house and on his demesne. Some at least dispensed charity. Some, like Lord Dartry, maintained free schools or other local services. A tenant in good standing had a certain claim to economic favour, if only the lax enforcement of covenants in leases and similar obligations. In other cases landlords could use their political and personal influence for the benefit of individuals or of the area as a whole, for example by lobbying the Linen Board for grants of spinning-wheels and other equipment or by influencing the location of army barracks, bridges, roads, and similar amenities.[118] Clientage also entered into the workings of the law.

---

[116] Sir Robert Southwell to Perceval, Sept. 1702 (HMC, *Egmont Papers*, ii. 210–11).

[117] Country Letters, fo. 3ᵛ.

[118] For the Linen Board, see Kirkham, '"To Pay the Rent and Lay Up Riches"', 97. For competition over the location of barracks, see St John Brodrick to Thomas Brodrick, 22 Feb. 1715 (Midleton MS 1248/3, fo. 215). For other activities, see e.g. Crawford, 'The Influence of the Landlord in Eighteenth-Century Ulster', 200; Malcomson, *Foster*, 349.

There were recurrent complaints of the willingness of landlords and others to shield even serious offenders from criminal prosecution.[119] Maria Edgeworth, writing at the end of the century, contrasted 'I'll have the law on you', 'the saying of an Englishman who expects justice', with 'I'll have you before his honour', 'the threat of an Irishman who hopes for partiality'.[120]

Favour of these different kinds was of course part of an inherently unequal exchange. Benevolence, whether symbolic or practical, was available only to the deferential and the compliant. Lord Donegall, angered by what he considered the insubordinate conduct of his tenants in Belfast, announced in 1739 that he intended to suspend plans to build a Linen Hall there until 'I am convinced they have a due sense of my intended favour to them'.[121] A tenant who declined to vote as his landlord wished could likewise find himself held rigidly to the covenants in his lease, refused rent rebates in hard years, or converted into an 'English tenant' by being required to pay his rents in the May and November they fell due, rather than the customary six months in arrears.[122] At this point he would realize quickly enough that the withdrawal of a rich man's favour counted for rather more than the withdrawal of a poor man's deference.

At the same time relationships of clientage, however unequal the terms, had a real meaning for those involved. In some cases at least, the dependants of landlords and other men of substance were willing to give not just mechanical obedience or an outward show of deference, but also active support. This happened, for example, at disputed elections, where control of the streets could be one factor in determining the outcome and candidates sometimes mobilized crowds of lower-class supporters armed with cudgels, stones, and even firearms to uphold their claims and intimidate their opponents.[123] The same fierce partisanship was seen on other occasions. Pole Cosby of Queen's County recorded indignantly in his autobiography how in 1738 Hunt Walsh of Ballykillcavan had celebrated a legal victory over another local gentleman by sending 'his people to my town of Stradbally to buy drink and drink about a bonfire' until sent away by a cousin of Cosby's. Two years later, after the judgment had been upheld on appeal, 'Mr Walsh's servant and people came to Stradbally with garland, piper and long dance', but were met by a group of the townspeople, who 'bid them go rejoice on Walsh's estate and not come into Stradbally'. A brawl followed, in which Cosby's tenants 'beat all the Ballykillcavan folks very heartily and made them return very shamefully'.[124]

---

[119] Below, pp. 224–5.

[120] Edgeworth, *Castle Rackrent*, 75.

[121] Donegall to ——, 28 {?} 1739 (PRONI D562/701).

[122] Malcomson, *Foster*, 311.

[123] e.g. John Bourke to Henry Boyle, Jan. 1731 (PRONI D2707/A1/2/57); Sir Richard Meade to Boyle, 18 June 1731 (PRONI D2707/A1/2/63).

[124] Cosby, 'Autobiography', 435–6.

The role of such vertical relationships points up the similarities, too often overlooked, between eighteenth-century Ireland and contemporary England, where the role of carefully nurtured relationships of deference and clientage in the maintenance of social order has long been recognized. Yet there were also important differences between the two societies. In both cases the few ruled the many. Yet contemporaries had the clear impression that in Ireland authority was more absolute and its exercise more brutal. The comments of Henry and Chesterfield, comparing the Irish lower classes to slaves, 'used worse than negroes', have already been quoted. Young, in 1780, was also struck by 'the subordination of the lower classes, degenerating into oppression'.[125] Authoritarianism above, moreover, was matched by submissiveness below. A pamphleteer in 1698 commented on the 'tame and cowardly' disposition of the common people. A visitor in the early 1740s noted their extravagant verbal obsequiousness. Paying a boatman who had taken them fishing off the coast of Cork, 'we had ten thousand "Good luck to your Honours, Long life to your Honours", a sort of compliment the vulgar Irish are very free of'. An English clergyman, thirty years later, reported the absence of 'that surly sturdiness in the yeomanry, which you may see in many parts of England. . . . All is misery, beggary, and prostration.'[126]

Perhaps the most striking single feature of Irish social relations, in the eyes of visitors, was the casual manner in which blows were dealt and accepted. According to Young:

A landlord in Ireland can scarcely invent an order which a servant, labourer or cottar dares to refuse to execute. Nothing satisfies him but an unlimited submission. Disrespect or anything tending towards sauciness he may punish with his cane or his horsewhip with the most perfect security; a poor man would have his bones broke if he offered to lift his hand in his own defence. Knocking down is spoken of in the country in a manner that makes an Englishman stare.[127]

Edward Wakefield, attending the Carlow races in 1809, was appalled to see a gentleman strike at a man who was unwittingly blocking his way 'with less ceremony than an English country squire would a dog' and lay open his cheek, without any response from the bystanders. Scattered earlier references make clear that such habits of casual violence towards social inferiors were of long standing. The dean of Down in the 1720s occasionally chastised a drunken schoolteacher with his cane. Swift referred casually to cuffing his servant. Nor were such exchanges confined to a domestic setting. A Dublin newspaper reported in 1727 that a gentleman who was offended by the 'unmannerly language' of a chairman 'drew his sword and in correcting him

---

[125] Above, n. 85; Young, *Tour*, ii. 53–4.

[126] [Brewster], *Discourse Concerning Ireland*, 20; [Chetwood], *Tour*, 117–18; Burrows Tour (PRONI T3551, 51).

[127] Young, *Tour*, ii. 54.

by chance gave him so desperate a cut on the right hand [that] 'tis believed he will lose some of his fingers'. In other cases the law relieved gentlemen of the necessity of thus physically enforcing a due measure of deference. In 1730 a porter was whipped 'for giving offence to some person who employed him, persuant to a clause for that purpose in the new act relating to the coachmen and such cattle'.[128]

Several explanations may be offered for the casual brutality revealed in reports of this kind. One English visitor blamed the structure of rural society, which left 'no middle rank between the great man and the beggar'. For others the problem lay in the origins of the ruling élite. Charles O'Hara, head of a Gaelic family turned Protestant, complained that the Irish resident gentry 'are mostly the descendants of adventurers', who had inherited from their ancestors a 'spirit of domination'. Young placed the blame partly on the religious inequalities enshrined in the penal laws and partly on the pettiness and narrow aspirations of the minor gentry who dominated rural society.[129] All these are valid points. At the same time it is important to recognize that authoritarian social relationships were not wholly imposed from outside. They also had roots in the culture of the Irish lower classes themselves. Traditional Gaelic society had been built around the personal bond between lord and follower. English observers frequently contrasted the unlimited obligations imposed by this bond with the strictly circumscribed duties imposed by the lease or contract. More perceptive commentators, however, observed that there was another side to the picture. Traditional landlords in County Westmeath, Sir Henry Piers noted in 1682, were 'great oppressors of their tenants and followers'. At the same time 'they are very industrious to preserve them from the wrongs and oppressions of others' and even from the settlement of their just debts. For this reason their exactions were willingly accepted, their tenants summing up their outlook in the slogan 'Defend me and spend me'.[130]

The strength of vertical attachments within the traditional social order may be seen in the prestige that members of the old ruling families continued to command long after military defeat and confiscation had destroyed the economic foundations of their power. Oliver Plunkett reported to Rome in 1670 that, although the Catholic landed families of County Armagh had been dispossessed and 'are rent payers on their own property...', their ancient vassals, although themselves paying rents to the Protestants, are none the less so well disposed to their former overlords that they always give them some

---

[128] Wakefield, *Account of Ireland*, ii. 773; Stevenson, *Two Centuries of Life in County Down*, 224; Nokes, *Jonathan Swift*, 402; *Dublin Intelligence*, 9–13 May 1727, 25 Apr. 1730.
[129] Burrows Tour (PRONI T3551, 51); O'Hara's Account of County Sligo (NLI MS 20,397); Young, *Tour*, ii. 53–4.
[130] Piers, *County of Westmeath*, 114. For Protestant perceptions of Gaelic lordship, see also King, *State of the Protestants*, 35–6.

contribution'. Sir Robert Southwell, in 1702, advised his protégé Perceval that if he must take Irish tenants, they should be 'such as are not of any clan, or obliged, as they think, to maintain the old proprietor'. Two visitors to Callan, County Kilkenny, in the early 1740s, were struck by the 'extraordinary respect' shown to a descendant of one of the ancient Gaelic families as he rode through the fair mounted on a small horse. 'The old Irish', they were told, gave such a man 'the title of his ancestors, make him and his lady (if he has one) little presents, cultivating his spot of ground, not suffering him or his to do the least work to degrade his airy title.'[131] In 1757 a member of the O'Flaherty family led a rebellion of tenants on the St George estate, claiming that the land was rightfully his.[132] Almost thirty years later, in 1786, a certain Roderick O'Connor, 'known as the king of Connacht', was able to raise a force of four or five hundred armed men to occupy Ballintober Castle.[133]

Seen in this light, the submission of the Irish lower classes to harsh treatment at the hands of social superiors takes on a slightly different meaning. What seemed to outsiders their cringing deference reflected not so much an externally imposed tyranny as the incorporation of a largely new landed class into traditional ideas of lordship and superiority. In County Kildare it was even claimed that 'the ordinary sort of people take a sort of pride in prostituting their daughters or kinswomen to their landlords' sons or kinsmen', cherishing any products of such unions as much as legitimate offspring. A similar receptiveness to the sexual attentions of gentlemen is hinted at in later accounts.[134] Even the beatings and knockings-down that so horrified Young and others may not have seemed to the recipients so very extraordinary. John Stevens, the English royalist serving with King James's Irish army, found that the soldiers 'not only fear, but respect and love the officer much more that beats them daily without mercy, than him that cherishes and carries a light hand over them'.[135] Against this background, the harshness that contemporary observers perceived in relations between rulers and ruled complements, rather than contradicts, the picture of a society ruled by vertical relationships of clientage, dependence, and the acceptance of strong personal authority.

None of this is intended to suggest that the network of vertical relationships did not have its structural weaknesses. With the benefit of hindsight, the fault lines along which Irish society was to split in the 1790s and after are apparent throughout. To see this, it is only necessary to look back at the various

---

[131] Plunkett, *Letters*, 74; see also ibid. 247; Southwell to Perceval, Sept. 1702 (HMC, *Egmont Papers*, ii. 209); [Chetwood], *Tour*, 147–8.

[132] Edward Willes to earl of Warwick, *c.*1759 (PRONI Mic 148, 17); 'Calendar of Church Miscellaneous Papers', 87, 89.

[133] HMC, *Rutland Manuscripts*, iii. 279, 284.

[134] Account of County Kildare (1683), in MacLysaght, *Irish Life*, 317. See also Cullen, *Emergence of Modern Ireland*, 244–5.

[135] Stevens, *Journal*, 63.

manifestations of reciprocity and mutual accommodation discussed earlier. Some of these—patronage of popular amusements and paternalistic regulation of the market—were equally open to all sections of plebeian Irish society. Others, however, were not. Catholic farmers, labourers, and tradesmen may have been happy enough to join in the cheering, fuelled by free drink, for the birthday of a landlord's son or the state entry of a lord lieutenant into Dublin. They are likely to have been less enthusiastic on other occasions of government-sponsored festivity: the accession of George I in 1714, for example, and the various military victories achieved against France or Spain. And there were some festivals, such as 5 November and the anniversary of the discovery of the supposed conspiracy of 1641, towards which they can hardly have been anything other than openly antagonistic.[136] In the case of two other important occasions for the display of reciprocity and vertical attachments, elections and service in the militia, Catholics were excluded by law, up to 1793, from taking any part. In economic matters too, the preference given, where feasible, to Protestant tenants and dependants can hardly have gone unnoticed. Such points have been largely overshadowed by what are, at first sight, the more important legal disabilities imposed on Catholics: the denial of voting rights, restrictions on land ownership, and exclusion from office. But this is to project the rhetoric of Catholic democracy, developed by O'Connell and others in the 1820s, back into the eighteenth century. If we are to ask what mattered to people at the time, rather than to later generations, then it can be suggested that the real flaw in the structure of eighteenth-century Irish society was not that it excluded a large section of the population from democratic freedoms. It was rather that it debarred them from taking on as fully as they might otherwise have done the role of deferential subordinates.

[136] Cf. the action taken against both anniversaries by soldiers in Tyrconnell's army: above, p. 36.

5

The Inventions of Men in the Worship of God: Religion and the Churches

1. Numbers

It is unlikely that we will ever know with certainty the absolute, or even the relative, size of the different religious denominations in late seventeenth- and early eighteenth-century Ireland. Contemporaries offered widely varying estimates. Sir William Petty, in 1672, suggested that there were 300,000 Protestants in Ireland and 800,000 Catholics. Oliver Plunkett, two years earlier, had claimed that there were twenty Catholics for every Protestant. Sir Richard Cox, arguing in 1706 that the Catholics no longer constituted a serious threat, maintained that they outnumbered Protestants only by two to one or less. Lord Coningsby, in the course of a more pessimistic review of the state of Ireland in 1714, put the Catholic superiority at eight to one; while in 1708 the Whig Lord Chancellor Richard Freeman maintained that it was 'by the best information I can get...at least ten to one through the whole kingdom'. Archbishop Boulter in 1731 believed that Catholics outnumbered Protestants by at least five to one; others, he noted, put the figure as high as seven to one.[1]

The one attempt at a national religious census during this period was undertaken in 1732–3, when collectors of the hearth tax were required to state the number of Catholic and Protestant families in their districts, as it was in 1732, classifying each household according to the religion of its head. The collectors returned a total of 386,902 families, of which 281,401, or 73 per cent, were Catholic.[2] Like most early modern tax returns that historians have sought to exploit for demographic purposes, the hearth-tax returns seriously understated the true number of households: the most recent survey puts the average deficiency in the first half of the eighteenth century at between 14 and

---

[1] Petty, *Political Anatomy*, 8; Plunkett, *Letters*, 103, 106; Cox to Southwell, 24 Oct. 1706 (BL Add. MS 38,154, fo. 86ᵛ); Report on the State of Ireland *c*.1714 (PRONI D638/145); Freeman to Somers, 16 Oct. 1708 (PRONI T2807/42); Boulter, *Letters*, i. 210; ii. 70.

[2] *Abstract of the Number of Protestant and Popish Families*. The hearth-tax returns seem generally to have enumerated tax-paying units, which in practice meant households, rather than houses. There is some indication that an extra effort was made in 1732 to enumerate families rather than houses. See Dickson *et al.*, 'Hearth Tax, Household Size and Irish Population Change', 131–2 and n. 27.

34 per cent.[3] Underregistration did not affect all denominations equally. Of the major likely causes of the shortfall—incompetence, corruption, the exemption of poorer houses, and the inaccessibility or obscurity of some dwellings—the last two at least would undoubtedly have affected proportionately more Catholics than Protestants. If one takes the maximum correction factor that has been suggested for the 1732 returns and assumes that all the houses missed were inhabited by Catholics, then there would have been some 409,000 Catholic houses, or 79 per cent of a total of 514,500. If, as seems more likely, the deficiency was less than this and some Protestant households were also missed, the Catholic proportion would have lain somewhere between 73 and 79 per cent. This still leaves the problem of converting houses to people. Catholics may have had larger families than Protestants: Archbishop King in 1718 described them as 'a breeding people', while the abstract of the 1732–3 returns conceded that the poor had more children than the rich.[4] Protestant households would have been enlarged by a greater proportion of servants, but some of these would have been Catholics. All in all, the most it seems safe to say is that Catholics in the first half of the eighteenth century probably made up somewhere between three-quarters and four-fifths of the population.

The deficiencies of the hearth-tax returns also affect any attempt to determine the regional distribution of the different denominations (see Fig. 5.1). In particular, the proportion of Catholics returned for parts of Ulster, such as the counties of Donegal and Londonderry, appears unrealistically low. Given that the likely bias is towards understating the Catholic share of the population, however, the returns for the other three provinces are of value in indicating just how weak the Protestant presence was. Nor could it even be claimed that Protestant numerical strength was related to the level of economic development. It was true that the highest proportion of Catholics was to be found in the western counties of Connacht and Munster. Yet, outside the city of Dublin—where one-third of the Protestants in the province lived—the proportion of Catholics in Leinster was not significantly lower. In the counties of Kildare, Kilkenny, and Meath, probably three of the richest in the country, nine households out of every ten returned were Catholic.

In the late seventeenth century the numerical weakness of the Protestants had to some extent been compensated by their strong position in the towns. Although Catholics were far more numerous in the countryside, the Catholic bishop of Waterford and Lismore reported in 1672, 'in the cities the heretics are of equal number with the Catholics'. In Waterford itself, fifteen years later, Protestants still comprised up to half the population.[5] Elsewhere the

---

[3] Dickson *et al.*, 'Hearth Tax', 149. This replaces an earlier estimate, by Connell, of a 50 per cent deficiency: *The Population of Ireland 1750–1845*, 24.

[4] King to Wake, 6 Feb. 1718 (TCD MS 2535, 80); *Abstract*, 11.

[5] Power, *Bishop of the Penal Times*, 29, 91.

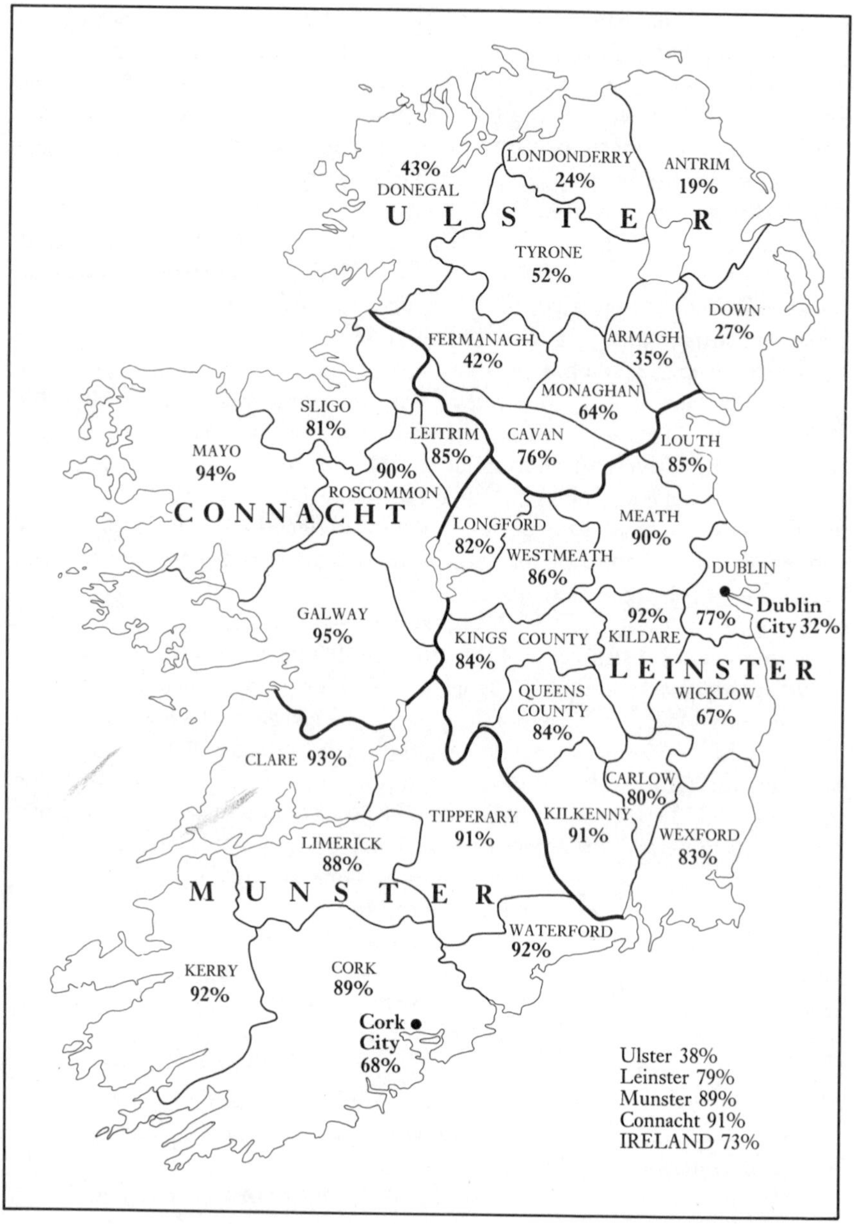

LONDONDERRY
24%
ANTRIM
19%
43%
DONEGAL
U L S T E R
TYRONE
52%
DOWN
27%
FERMANAGH
42%
ARMAGH
35%
MONAGHAN
64%
SLIGO
81%
LEITRIM
85%
CAVAN
76%
LOUTH
85%
MAYO
94%
90%
ROSCOMMON
CONNACHT
LONGFORD
82%
MEATH
90%
WESTMEATH
86%
DUBLIN
Dublin
City 32%
GALWAY
95%
92%
KILDARE
77%
KINGS COUNTY
84%
LEINSTER
QUEENS
COUNTY
84%
WICKLOW
67%
CLARE 93%
CARLOW
80%
TIPPERARY
91%
KILKENNY
91%
WEXFORD
83%
LIMERICK
88%
MUNSTER
WATERFORD
92%
KERRY
92%
CORK
89%
Cork
City
68%
Ulster 38%
Leinster 79%
Munster 89%
Connacht 91%
IRELAND 73%

Fig. 5.1. Map of Irish counties showing Catholic households as percentages of total, 1732.

Protestant position was even stronger. Drogheda, for example, was reported to be predominantly Protestant in 1670, while in Dundalk Catholics made up only a quarter of the population.[6] By the early eighteenth century, this numerical superiority had in most cases been eroded, as expanding urban centres drew in people from the surrounding countryside and earlier attempts to exclude Catholics from walled towns and other strategic centres were abandoned. By 1732–3 only a quarter of the population of Drogheda, and just under one third of the population of Cork, were Protestants.[7] Bandon in County Cork was an increasingly conspicuous exception to the national trend, regularly singled out as a wholly Protestant town, whose inhabitants refused to permit a Catholic to settle among them, or even, it was reported, a Catholic piper to play in the street.[8] In Dublin, things were more finely balanced. The hearth-tax collectors' returns of 1732–3 suggested that Protestant households were in a comfortable two-thirds majority. Recent work, however, suggests that the Protestant share of the population was in fact closer to 50 per cent.[9] Yet even this is a figure to take note of. When a gentleman left his town house or an MP the parliament building on College Green, he stepped out onto the streets of what could still, if only just, be considered a Protestant city.

Numbers were only part of the story. A comparison in terms of property and status yielded very different results. This was particularly true of landownership. Confiscations of land not protected by the Articles of Limerick reduced the Catholic share of profitable land from 22 per cent in 1688 to 14 per cent in 1704. Thereafter Catholic landownership was further reduced by the operation of penal laws.[10] In two respects, however, these figures are potentially misleading. In the first place, much of the fall in Catholic landownership after 1704 was due to the conformity of proprietors or their heirs to the established church. Some of these converts became fully integrated into the Protestant élite; others were only nominal conformists, or at least retained strong links with the religion they had formally renounced. Secondly, there was the substantial amount of land held on long leases by Catholic middlemen and tenant farmers: a less prestigious asset than outright ownership, but nevertheless one that brought with it economic advantage, social authority, and also—where there were Protestant undertenants—political influence.[11]

---

[6] Plunkett, *Letters*, 73.

[7] David Dickson, '"Centres of Motion": Irish Cities and the Origins of Popular Politics', in Bergeron and Cullen (eds.), *Culture et pratiques politiques*, 106.

[8] Burke, *Irish Priests*, 382; [Chetwood], *Tour*, 110; Smith, *Antient and Present State of the Country and City of Cork*, i. 239; Pococke, *Tour*, 119.

[9] Dickson, '"Centres of Motion"', 107.

[10] Most accounts, following Simms, *Williamite Confiscation*, 160, cite Young's supposed estimate that in 1780 Catholics owned only 5 per cent of the land in Ireland. But this derives from a throw-away comment ('Upon the whole nineteen twentieths of the kingdom changed hands from Catholic to Protestant': *Tour*, ii. 59) that hardly supports the weight placed on it by repeated quotation. For the figures for 1688 and 1703, see Simms, *Williamite Confiscation*, 195.

[11] Cullen, 'Catholics under the Penal Laws', 27–35. See also Dickson, 'Middlemen', 171–2.

There was also a substantial Catholic merchant class. Samuel Molyneux reported in 1709 that the trade of Galway was 'wholly' in Catholic hands; over forty years later the city's trade was still carried on mainly by Catholics, who 'are jealous of others coming into any share with them'. In Limerick in the 1750s a Catholic priest complained of the willingness of Catholic merchants to take Protestant apprentices, thereby endangering their own near monopoly of the city's trade.[12] Both Limerick and Galway, however, were stagnant or declining ports. Elsewhere, in larger and more dynamic trading centres, the Catholic share of mercantile wealth, though still significant, was considerably smaller. Even in the second half of the eighteenth century, at a time when their relative importance in trade was probably increasing, Catholics made up less than one-third of wholesale merchants in Dublin and less than one-quarter in Cork.[13] An analysis compiled by Theophilus Bolton, Anglican bishop of Elphin, apparently based on some variant of the 1732–3 returns, calculated that of those houses—a little under one-seventh of the total—with more than one hearth, about half belonged to Catholics and half to Protestants.[14] Of the six out of every seven houses with only one hearth, on the other hand, 70 per cent were headed by Catholics (Table 5.1). These figures, if in any way reliable, would confirm that the Catholic propertied class was a substantial one in relation to the nation's wealth, yet grossly undersized in relation to the Catholic share of the total population.

Social inequalities below the level of the gentry and merchant classes are harder to measure. In Ulster the Catholic population, initially fairly evenly distributed on land of all qualities, was by the later seventeenth century being relegated to the poorer and less advantageously situated areas. This was partly due to the greater economic dynamism of the English and Scots settlers, but also to some extent to direct discrimination.[15] With almost no landed proprietors of any standing and with urban trade almost entirely in Protestant

---

[12] Molyneux, 'Journey to Connaught', 172; Pococke, *Tour*, 104; White, 'Annals of Limerick' (NLI MS 2714), 169–70.

[13] Dickson, 'Catholics and Trade in Eighteenth-Century Ireland', in Power and Whelan (eds.), *Endurance and Emergence*, 90; idem, *New Foundations*, 121.

[14] PRONI D207/3/18B. These rough working notes do not distinguish between single and multiple hearths in so many words. They refer to 56,176 houses that 'may be reckoned to have one with another 3 hearths', with an average of eight inhabitants, and the remaining houses 'that are computed to have but $4\frac{1}{2}$ to a house'. However, it seems safe to assume that this is what was meant. The average of 3 hearths per multiple-hearth house was earlier used by Petty, and the ratio of multiple- to single-hearth houses in 1706 was 1:7.7, close to that in Bolton's calculations. See Dickson *et al.*, 'Hearth Tax', 158–9. Bolton's calculations give a total of 392,355 houses, 5,453 more than the published total for 1732, but with Catholic houses accounting for only 68 per cent of the total.

[15] Cunningham and Gillespie, 'An Ulster Settler and his Manuscripts', 30. See also the comments of Oliver Plunkett in 1675: 'The Catholics being, as a rule, lease-holders, often lose their leases, which are then given to Protestants or Presbyterians or Anabaptists or Quakers. These are the dominant sects here, and every time a new colony of them arrives, the poor Catholics are set aside' (*Letters*, 454–5).

TABLE 5.1. Religion and house type, *c.*1732

House type	Protestant	Catholic
Multiple-hearth	27,553	28,623
Single-hearth	99,633	236,546
Total	127,186	265,169

Source: PRONI D207/3/18B; see n. 14.

hands, Ulster Catholics were thus a clearly disadvantaged group. In the diocese of Derry, Bishop Nicolson reported in 1722, 'There are not three Papists rich enough to bear the office of high constables.'[16] Elsewhere, Catholic disadvantage was less extreme, but nevertheless apparent. The religious census of the Connacht diocese of Elphin in 1749 shows the Protestant population to have been concentrated in the towns and on the more fertile lands to the east of the diocese. In the towns of Sligo and Athlone, Catholics made up only a third of the retailers and small manufacturers, just over half the skilled tradesmen, but more than 80 per cent of the labourers.[17] By this time Catholic social inferiority was beginning to be mitigated by the emergence in some parts of the country of a Catholic tenant-farmer class possessing livestock and other capital resources that set them clearly apart from the mere peasantry.[18] But the economic and social superiority of even humbler Protestants over their Catholic neighbours was to remain for much longer, not only in Ulster but also in the other three provinces.

2. Catholics

The Catholic church of the early and mid-eighteenth century was a post-Counter-Reformation institution. In the seventeenth century, two major periods of reform, the first extending from the 1590s to the 1630s, the second during the 1670s and 1680s, had reshaped ecclesiastical structures and religious practice along the lines prescribed by the Council of Trent. A clear parochial and diocesan organization replaced a decentralized system based largely on ties of kin; a 'civic religion' whose observances had primarily social and communal functions gave way to a new code of personal religious

---

[16] Nicolson to Wake, 4 Mar. 1722 (Gilbert MS 27, 314).

[17] Nat. Arch. Ire. M2466. A proper analysis of this important document is long overdue. In the meantime, I am most grateful to Mr Colm Trainor of the Library of the University of Ulster for allowing me to see the results of a partial analysis carried out by him, from which the figures above are derived.

[18] Dickson, *New Foundations*, 98–9, 113–14.

practice.[19] In addition, from the early seventeenth century, clerical intel-
lectuals formulated a new, more combative Catholic political philosophy, in
which Irish affairs came to be interpreted as part of the international struggle
against heresy.[20] In a century of political upheaval and sudden dramatic
changes of fortune, Irish priests and bishops at different times played the part
of courtiers, warlords, and martyrs. After 1691, all this was over. Final,
irreversible military and political defeat left no realistic option for the future
other than passivity. In internal management too, the era of heroic endeavour
gave way to the more or less conscientious maintenance of the existing system.

On two occasions during the first half of the eighteenth century the government collected information on the Catholic church establishment. In 1704
priests were required to register with the authorities and give securities for
good behaviour. This was meant to apply only to secular priests exercising no
ecclesiastical jurisdiction, but analysis of the 1,089 persons who registered
under the Act reveals that many regulars, as well as the three bishops then in
the country, registered themselves under the guise of secular parish priests. At
the same time it must be assumed that other regulars, and possibly some
secular priests also, preferred to remain technically outside the law, rather
than bring themselves to the attention of the authorities. If so, the true total of
Catholic priests would have been somewhere above 1,100.[21] This was at a
time when several hundred regular clergy had recently left or been expelled
from the country, along with most of the bishops who alone could ordain new
priests. As attempts to enforce the Banishment Act of 1697 fell off, numbers
rose. When the House of Lords in 1731 compiled a report based on returns
from magistrates and Anglican clergy throughout the country, it found that
there were 1,445 secular priests and 254 friars.[22] Again, this is almost certainly an underestimate. There was no return from the diocese of Kerry or
from some parishes in other dioceses, and it is likely that even where returns
were made, some clerics, more obscure or more cautious than the rest, were
left out. The figure for regulars is clearly deficient: other evidence would
suggest that, by 1750 at least, the true number was around 800.[23] The return
of secular priests, more visible in their functions and in general less disliked
by the Protestant establishment, is probably more accurate. But it too provides
at best a minimum estimate.

Overall it is clear that the Catholic church in Ireland was thinly manned by
comparison with that in the Catholic countries of Europe. Taking the total

---

[19] Corish, *Catholic Community*, ch. 1–3; Bossy, 'The Counter-Reformation and the People of
Catholic Ireland', 155–69.

[20] Cunningham, 'Native Culture and Political Change in Ireland 1580–1640', 165–70;
Canny, 'The Formation of the Irish Mind', 95–104.

[21] Ó Fiaich, 'The Registration of the Clergy in 1704'.

[22] 'Report on the State of Popery, Ireland 1731', 1 (1912), 10–11.

[23] Fenning, *Undoing of the Friars*, 44.

number of priests, secular and regular, in 1731 as 2,300 and the Catholic population as 1.8 million, there was one clergyman to every 783 Catholics. In France and Spain, by contrast, male ecclesiastics made up more than 1 per cent of the population. At the same time it is important to remember how many of the latter fulfilled pastorally unproductive roles, as cathedral canons, private chaplains, or members of the less active religious orders. If we confine ourselves to the 1,445 secular clergy known to have been working in Ireland in 1731, there was a maximum of 1,245 Catholics to every parish priest or curate. This does not compare at all badly with the ratio of 1,110 to 1 that was to be recorded in 1901, in the heyday of Irish Catholic triumphalism. Contemporary observers, Catholic as well as Protestant, believed that in the first half of the eighteenth century Ireland had in fact more priests than it needed or than the population could support.[24]

Straitened circumstances were more apparent in the material possessions of the church. Conditions naturally varied. Catholic churches in the city of Dublin appear, even in the first half of the eighteenth century, to have been solid and in good repair, with pews and galleries and a reasonable level of altar furnishing, paintings, and other decorations.[25] Accounts of some fifty churches in the visitation records for the diocese of Cashel and Emly in the 1750s reveal a more modest level of provision: simple rectangular structures, one-third with walls of mud, all thatched and with almost no internal decoration.[26] Earlier in the century and in regions in which the Catholic population was less prosperous, conditions were much worse. In the diocese of Derry, it was reported in 1731, there were only nine Catholic churches, 'mass being said in most places sub dio, or under some sort of shed, built up occasionally to shelter the priest from the weather'. In Down and Connor, there were only five churches, mass being said elsewhere 'upon mountains or in private houses'. In the diocese of Cloyne there were seventy mass houses, but these were 'generally mean thatched cabins, many or most of them open at one end'. Even the Leinster dioceses of Leighlin and Ferns had, respectively, three and eleven 'moveable altars in the fields'.[27]

In addition to mass houses of varying quality, the 1731 inquiry returned a total of 549 Popish schools.[28] Since such institutions were illegal, the figure is

[24] The figure of 1.8 million represents 76 per cent of a total population midway between the upper- and lower-bound estimates offered by Dickson *et al.*, 'Hearth Tax'. For France and Spain, see Callahan and Higgs (eds.), *Church and State in Catholic Europe of the Eighteenth Century*, 15, 36, 55. For Ireland in 1901, see Connell, *Irish Peasant Society*, 160. For some of the many complaints about excessive numbers of priests in the first half of the eighteenth century, see Fenning, 'Some Problems of the Irish Mission', 62–3; idem, 'Clerical Recruitment 1735–83', 1, 5; Giblin, '*Nunziatura di Fiandra*', 10 (1967), 90.

[25] Fagan, *The Second City*, 113–21, 127–32.

[26] Whelan, 'The Catholic Church in County Tipperary 1700–1900', 225–7. For the original returns, see O'Dwyer, 'Archbishop Butler's Visitation Book'.

[27] 'Report on the State of Popery', 1 (1912), 17, 18; 2 (1913), 127; 4 (1915), 165, 170.

[28] Ibid. 1, 11.

once again almost certainly an underestimate. 'Popish school', of course, meant simply a school run by a Catholic teacher. Yet it is likely that a substantial proportion provided some religious instruction. Some were in fact conducted in Catholic parish chapels.[29] The visitation records of the diocese of Cashel in the 1750s indicate that, by then at least, Catholic schoolmasters were expected to teach the catechism and were liable to be cited to appear before the bishop if they failed to do so.[30] Although most such schools would presumably have provided only elementary instruction, some went much further. The Anglican bishop of Ossory noted in 1731 that he had met 'the son of a poor man that dwells in a cabin', whose 14-year-old brother was one of six pupils (out of a total of thirty) learning Latin from a local schoolmaster.[31] The maintenance of this network of schools, capable of producing both a Catholic intelligentsia and some level of basic instruction among the laity as a whole, stands out as one of the main reasons for the resilience of Irish Catholicism in the eighteenth century.

Historians of the Irish Catholic church have sought the key to its long-term success in retaining a unique hold on the minds and hearts of its followers in its disadvantaged political and social circumstances. As a persecuted church, it was not embarrassed by too close an identification with the state or the ruling class; the clergy attracted to a church without wealth or prestige were drawn from social backgrounds similar to those of their congregations. The same point was noted by some contemporaries. Berkeley, in 1735, queried 'whether it be not of great advantage to the church of Rome that she hath clergy suited to all ranks of men . . . whether her numerous poor clergy are not very useful in missions, and of much influence with the people'.[32] Yet it is important to recognize that this was a situation into which the church settled only gradually. Oliver Plunkett, in the 1670s, argued that the church could not afford a bishop in every diocese: but he had in mind a standard of living that would allow those so appointed to mix with peers and large landowners.[33] Within twenty years, such aspirations had become meaningless; most eighteenth-century bishops were to have little choice but to accept what was at best a modest middle-class life-style. Yet, even at this point, wealth and birth did not become wholly irrelevant. Some bishops were undoubtedly of humble background: Mrs Delany, in 1758, found Edmund O'Doran, bishop of Down

---

[29] 'Report on the State of Popery', 2 (1913), 116, 132; 4 (1915), 158.

[30] O'Dwyer, 'Archbishop Butler's Visitation Book', 34 (1976–7), 25. See also ibid. 5, 6, 15, 31, 39; 33 (1975), 63, 68, 69, 73.

[31] State of the Diocese of Ossory (Nat. Arch. Ire. M2462, 21).

[32] J. Johnston, *Bishop Berkeley's Querist*, 147.

[33] See e.g. his letter of 15 Sept. 1677: 'Bishops here have to carry on in a manner which brings shame upon the mitre and crozier. . . . No bishop in Ireland has two servants; it is one and the same who acts as his valet and his stable boy, and it is his stable boy who serves his mass, and if the bishop has a nose at all he won't fail to notice a trace of the odour of the stable at the altar' (Plunkett, *Letters*, 498). See also ibid. 457, 495.

and Connor, do be 'the quintessence of an Irish brogueneer'.[34] Yet members of influential and still wealthy Catholic families, like the Butlers, the Blakes, and the Bellews, continued to be well represented at the upper levels of their church. In addition, surviving Catholic proprietors continued in some cases to enjoy formal or informal rights of presentation to particular parishes. Successive Viscounts Kenmare, for example, presented throughout the eighteenth century to the parish of Killarney, while Lord Fingall had the right, confirmed as late as 1782, to present to at least one parish in the diocese of Meath.[35] In 1726 Archbishop O'Gara of Tuam renounced his predecessor's opposition to Lord Athenry's claim to nominate to the parish of Dunmore, promising to 'load' an alternative claimant with ecclesiastical censures if he did not give way to Athenry's nominee.[36] In cases like these, the Catholic church, no less than its established counterpart, made the necessary concessions to a world of hierarchy and privilege.

In other respects too the church was a mixture of the archaic and the new. The reforms of the seventeenth century had introduced the essential elements of the Tridentine system, with its rigid territorial divisions, hierarchical command structure, and bureaucratic procedures. But the detailed workings had still to be perfected. Evidence from the diocese of Ferns in 1722 suggests that the ability of the bishop to direct the work of his clergy within a fixed parochial system had still not been unambiguously established.[37] The presence of a large body of regulars offering pastoral services largely outside episcopal control was another flaw in the structure of church government, remedied only by tight new regulations enacted by Rome in 1751.[38] Nor did the new system prove wholly effective in dealing with negligence or delinquency. One complaint, throughout the early and mid-eighteenth century, was the number of bishops who failed to reside in their dioceses, preferring to live either elsewhere in Ireland or, in some cases, in one of the more pleasant corners of Catholic Europe. A report in 1739 listed no less than six habitual absentees, three of whom were said not to have lived in their

---

[34] Delany, *Autobiography and Correspondence*, iii. 503. O'Doran, Mrs Delany reported, had lived 24 years in Spain and 'speaks hardly any language'. The nineteenth-century historian of the Catholic diocese suggests, on the basis of a letter from O'Doran which he prints in full, that he was in fact more at home in Irish than in English: O'Laverty, *An Historical Account of Down and Connor*, v. 546.

[35] Kenmare's right to present to Killarney was confirmed in 1722: Brady, *The Episcopal Succession in England, Scotland and Ireland*, ii. 61. For its continuance into the later eighteenth century, see O'Shea, 'Bishop Moylan's Relatio Status 1785', 35; Kenmare, letter of presentation, 4 Sept. 1797 (Cashel Diocesan Papers, Bray Papers 1797/19); C. Sughrue to Bray, 5 Sept. 1797 (ibid. 1797/20). For Fingall, see Cogan, *Ecclesiastical History of the Diocese of Meath*, i. 416–20.

[36] Bryan O'Gara to Athenry, 6 June 1726 (PRONI D207/3/24). Cf. 'Calendar of Church Miscellaneous Papers', 72.

[37] J. Brady and Corish, *The Church under the Penal Code*, 28.

[38] Fenning, *Undoing of the Friars*.

dioceses for ten years or more.[39] There were also complaints of indiscriminate ordinations. In the 1720s two bishops, Eustace Brown of Killaloe and Thomas Flynn of Ardagh, were suspended by Rome for having ordained large numbers of priests in order to receive the fees paid by the candidates.[40] Dominic Daly, bishop of Achonry, was alleged in 1734 to visit his diocese only once a year, to collect money from his priests and, while there, to ordain any candidate who came forward with the necessary fee.[41]

Among the lower clergy, too, discipline was far from perfect. The most common moral offences complained of concerned sexual misbehaviour, drunkenness, and neglect of pastoral duties. A visitation notebook kept by Bishop Nicholas Sweetman of Ferns in 1753 contains numerous complaints of dilapidated church buildings, damaged altar equipment, and torn or shabby vestments. One parish priest visited by the bishop was not 'very zealous or diligent in his duty', another 'neither very industrious or edifying to his flock', while a third apparently 'minded dogs and hunting more than his flock'.[42] There were also priests who resisted episcopal authority, relying on their local backing to defy disciplinary action or attempts to transfer them to another parish. In one case in 1755, supporters of a Limerick city priest who had been suspended after two women had apparently given birth to children of his used firearms to prevent the bishop from taking possession of the parish chapel.[43]

Observers of Irish Catholicism in the late seventeenth and early eighteenth centuries were generally impressed by the level of popular religious devotion. This was true even of the bishops sent direct from Rome to commence the reconstruction of the Irish church at the end of the 1660s. Thus Oliver Plunkett in 1670 was consoled for his other difficulties by having 'found in the people such devotion, such piety and such constancy in the faith ... that one could not ask for anything more in this world'. A colleague in Waterford reported that 'the people, generally speaking, are very religious and pious, leading a Christian life without great faults or many scandals'.[44] Protestants were in general more impressed by the influence which the clergy appeared to wield. 'The main of their religion', John Dunton noted in 1698, 'consists in a blind and total adhering to what is delivered to them by their oracles their clergy.' A visitor in the early 1740s thought the crowd at an open-air mass near Waterford seemed 'very solemn and sincere in their devotion', but noted

[39] Fenning, 'John Kent's Report on the Irish Mission 1742', 59–62; Giblin, '*Nunziatura di Fiandra*', 5 (1962), 123–4; 9 (1966), 30–2; Carrigan, *History and Antiquities of the Diocese of Ossory*, i. 155–6.

[40] Fenning, *Undoing of the Friars*, 41.

[41] Giblin, '*Nunziatura di Fiandra*', 9 (1966), 35–7. The charges appear to have had at least some basis: see Fenning, *Undoing of the Friars*, 114.

[42] Flood, 'The Diocesan Manuscripts of Ferns during the Reign of Bishop Sweetman', 2 (1913).

[43] White, 'Annals of Limerick' (NLI MS 2714), 130–48.

[44] Plunkett, *Letters*, 69; Power, *Bishop of the Penal Times*, 34.

with concern that 'their priests have a very despotic power over them'. The people of the Mourne mountains, a judge on circuit noted in 1759, 'seem to be much upon a rank with the American natives, excepting that they have some notion of making the sign of the cross, and stand much in awe of their priests'. On Cape Clear Island off the coast of Cork, it was reported nine years earlier, the priest 'is temporal as well as spiritual judge in his parish, and is absolute governor of the island'.[45]

Evidence regarding the level of popular religious practice is mixed. In the diocese of Cashel the visitation book of James Butler I makes clear that even in the 1750s the rosary was well established as a popular devotion, and was said in the churches before mass on Sunday. In Ossory, on the other hand, diocesan regulations drawn up in 1748 complained that large numbers did not meet even the minimum requirement of confessing and receiving communion at least once a year, around Easter.[46] Evidence from the early nineteenth century suggests that by that time total attendances at Sunday mass may have amounted to no more than 40 per cent of the total Catholic population. These figures cannot necessarily be projected back into earlier decades. Average standards of religious practice may have declined in the late eighteenth and early nineteenth centuries as the supply of priests and places of worship increasingly failed to keep pace with a rising population. At the same time these figures add to the suspicion that the Tridentine ideal of regular religious observance was never wholly established in Ireland.[47]

Whatever the level of formal religious practice, it is clear from the comments both of Protestant observers and of the church authorities that popular Catholicism diverged in important respects from the official variety. Orthodox doctrine and ritual existed side by side with a wide range of magical beliefs and practices: traditions of prophecy and divination, calendar custom marking out important turning-points in the agricultural year, charms to cure illnesses or to ensure good luck and protection, and belief in fairies and other supernatural beings. In some cases religion and magic were inextricably combined, as in the patterns celebrated at holy wells, where prayers to a Christian saint were combined with a variety of protective or propitiatory rituals. Alternatively, Catholic ritual was reinterpreted in magical terms: in the diocese of Ferns, priests had to be forbidden in 1771 'to act the fairy doctor in any shape', by reading 'exorcisms or gospels over the already too ignorant' or blessing water 'to sprinkle sick persons, cattle, fields with'.[48] Other prac-

[45] Dunton, *Letters*, in MacLysaght, *Irish Life*, 341; [Chetwood], *Tour*, 163; Edward Willes to Sally Wise, 1 May 1759 (PRONI Mic 148); Smith, *Ancient and Present State of Cork*, i. 279.

[46] O'Dwyer, 'Archbishop Butler's Visitation Book', 34 (1976–7), 24, 29, 40; Carrigan, *History and Antiquities of Ossory*, i. 153.

[47] For differing views, see D. W. Miller, 'Irish Catholicism and the Great Famine'; Corish, *Catholic Community*, 107–8.

[48] Flood, 'Diocesan Manuscripts of Ferns', 3 (1914), 117.

tices, such as the hugely popular pilgrimages to Lough Derg, attracting an estimated 3,000 to 4,000 visitors a year, revealed a basically contractual approach to religious obligation, conceived of in terms of a more or less arbitrary set of rules, compliance with which would secure benefits and ward off evil consequences.[49]

Protestant observers inevitably seized on these features of Irish Catholicism—the low status of its clergy, the weakness of internal discipline, the mingling of religion and magic—to legitimize its proscription. For the Catholic poor, Petty maintained in 1672, adherence to their religion 'is rather a custom than a dogma'. The archbishop of Armagh in 1745 denied that 'popery in the gross' could be called a religion, and referred to 'their absurd doctrines (which may be wondered at, and pitied)'.[50] What is more remarkable, however, is the reluctance of most Protestants, even in the seventeenth century, to carry such arguments to their logical conclusion. When a Franciscan friar was seized as he was about to celebrate mass in Dublin in 1665, some of the arresting party proposed to smash his portable altar and light their pipes from the candles. The friar, however, was able to appeal successfully to the mayor 'that if he were a Protestant, and therefore admitted that the Body of Christ was really present on the altar, then he could not in conscience profane that altar on which that body had been consecrated'. Archbishop King, writing in 1723, accepted that 'the communion of saints' required him to take as valid the orders of Catholic priests who had conformed to the Church of Ireland, provided they could produce proof of having been ordained by a properly qualified person.[51] The civil law also accepted the validity of Catholic orders, in that it recognized marriages between Catholics celebrated by a priest as valid, even though marriages performed by Protestant Dissenting clergymen were not. Catholicism, in other words, was culturally and intellectually inferior, but its rituals and orders, however much despised, were nevertheless accorded a certain validity.

The main justification for the suppression of Irish Catholicism, of course, lay not in its religious failings, but in the political dangers that it posed: Catholics, bound in conscience to obey the Pope and his agents and to advance by all means the interests of their church, could never be other than potential enemies of a Protestant state. Such charges are most commonly dismissed out of hand, as examples either of paranoia or of the spurious legitimation of

---

[49] 'An Account of Lough Derg', in Skelton, *Works*, v. 15–20. For a fuller discussion of popular religion and popular magic, drawing on evidence from the late eighteenth and early nineteenth centuries, see Connolly, *Priests and People in Pre-Famine Ireland*, ch. 3; idem, *Religion and Society in Nineteenth-Century Ireland*, 47–58.

[50] Petty, *Political Anatomy*, 96; Brady, *Catholics and Catholicism*, 69–70.

[51] Millett, *Irish Franciscans*, 292; King to Timothy Godwin, bishop of Kilmore, 11 Apr. 1723 (Mant, *Church of Ireland*, ii. 211).

exploitation and confiscation. But what were the political principles of Irish Catholic clergymen in the late seventeenth and early eighteenth centuries?

The period in which Irish Catholic churchmen might be expected to have given the clearest indication of their political outlook was during the reign of James II, and more particularly in the years 1688–90. Even then, however, the picture is not wholly clear. The actions of the Jacobite government in Ireland represented an uneasy compromise between the wishes of the king, anxious not to prejudice his chances of regaining power in England, and those of his Irish Catholic supporters. Among the acts of the parliament of 1689, for example, was a measure rendering Catholics and Ulster Presbyterians liable to pay tithes to their own clergy rather than to the established church. What the Irish Catholic bishops had actually wanted was a transfer of church land and buildings from the Church of Ireland to themselves. Given more time and a more co-operative monarch, would they have gone on to seek recognition as the established church and the creation of a Catholic state? Much has been made of the Act of 1689 guaranteeing liberty of conscience, 'a landmark of religious toleration in an environment hostile to it'.[52] In reality, however, the purpose of the Act was not to light a beacon of religious liberty, but rather to get around a practical problem: how to nullify the provisions of the Act of Uniformity, which gave the Church of Ireland its privileged status, and made non-attendance at its services punishable by law, without embarrassing the king by too direct an attack on the Anglican establishment.[53]

After 1691 the Irish Catholic church adapted to changed political circumstances. Owing to the lack of explicit political discussion in the surviving sources, the precise process by which it did so remains unclear. Already in 1691 the defeated Jacobites had accepted a clause in the Treaty of Limerick requiring them to take the oath of allegiance to William III and his successors. When the Catholic clergy were required to register with the authorities in 1704, the requirement that they take this oath appears to have caused no difficulty. When oaths of allegiance were being tendered in 1714 to the newly crowned George I, a priest in Macroom, County Cork, wrote to a local magistrate 'that he might be the first to give an example to the Papists, and after he had taken the oath declared it to be his and all persons' indispensable duty to do the same'.[54] Declarations of this kind were backed up by exhortations to the Catholic population to remain both docile and loyal. The statutes of the diocese of Limerick, in 1721, ordered all priests to admonish their flocks, both publicly and privately, to show honour and obedience to temporal superiors, whether Catholic or Protestant.[55] Where popular disturbances did

---

[52] Corish, *Catholic Community*, 72.
[53] Simms, 'Jacobite Parliament of 1689', in *War and Politics in Ireland*, 76–7, 14–16.
[54] Hickson, *Old Kerry Records*, 149–50.
[55] White, 'Annals of Limerick' (NLI MS 2714), 91.

occur, they were immediately and unequivocally condemned. In Dublin, for example, crowds who plundered wrecked ships near the city in 1725 and sought to liberate stocks of grain during the famine year of 1729 were threatened with excommunication.[56] In 1745, equally, priests exhorted their congregations 'to behave themselves peaceably and quietly like good subjects'.[57]

The obvious problem with these apparently impeccable declarations of obedience was of course that they came from a defeated and precariously tolerated church whose sincerity was thus open to question. Beyond this question of credibility, moreover, lay two more serious issues. The first was the old problem of whether the duties of the citizen in a Protestant state could ever be reconciled with the claims of the papacy. Issues that had split the Irish Catholic élite in the remonstrance debate of the 1660s continued, even in the more secularized political and international order of the eighteenth century, to create genuine difficulties. In the reign of George I plans for an address of loyalty from the Catholics of Great Britain and Ireland collapsed when the government insisted that this should include a denial that the Pope could interfere with the temporal jurisdiction of princes. When George II came to the throne in 1727, a group of Irish Catholic laymen presented an address declaring that their loyalty was 'a religious duty, which no power on earth can dispense with'. But even this oblique repudiation of papal power gave rise to 'great heats and divisions' among Catholics.[58] Thirty years later, when Archbishop O'Reilly of Armagh proposed an address repudiating, among other things, the supposed deposing power of the Pope, he still found his three fellow archbishops unwilling to join him.[59]

The second major difficulty, of course, was that the church of which the Irish Catholic clergy were a part continued to recognize the Stuarts as rightful monarchs of Great Britain and Ireland. When the Irish Catholic clergy were called on in 1709 to repudiate the Stuart claim by taking the oath of abjuration, all but a handful refused, even at the price of forfeiting the legal recognition conferred on them by the Registration Act of five years earlier.[60] For more than half a century longer, until the death of the Old Pretender in 1766, all but a handful of the bishops appointed to vacant Irish sees were chosen on the nomination of the Stuarts.[61] This power, along with the patronage it dispensed from its own funds, made the Jacobite court the focus of much lobbying and intrigue. In 1711, for example, the government inter-

[56] Brady, *Catholics and Catholicism*, 43, 49.   [57] Ibid. 67–8.

[58] Boulter to Carteret, 20 July 1727 (*Letters*, i. 188–9); Giblin, '*Nunziatura di Fiandra*', 5 (1962), 121–2. For the address, see Brady, *Catholics and Catholicism*, 45–7.

[59] O'Reilly to other metropolitans, 5 Sept. 1757 (Cashel Diocesan Papers, James Butler II Papers 1757/1); White, 'Annals of Limerick' (NLI MS 2714), 148–53; Wall, 'Catholic Loyalty to King and Pope', 17–24.

[60] Below, p. 276.   [61] Giblin, *Irish Exiles in Catholic Europe*, 47–52.

cepted a petition from the Catholic clergy of the diocese of Derry asking the Pretender to nominate one of their number to the bishopric.[62] In 1753 an opponent of the reform-minded party among the clergy of Dublin known as the *zelanti* wrote anonymously to 'James III' to complain that these low-born priests talked openly of ending his power of nomination, a development which 'has alarmed very much all the ancient families of Ireland, who will never think of putting an Italian cardinal instead of their lawful king'.[63]

There was nothing inconsistent in all this. The distinction between a *de jure* and a *de facto* right was one which conscientious Protestant clergymen in both England and Ireland had used to rationalize their acceptance of William III and his successors. Whether or not the Pretender had a right to the thrones of Great Britain and Ireland, the Dublin priest Cornelius Nary explained in 1724, 'I am no way concerned at taking the oath of allegiance, which the law of nature and the common practice of all nations allows me to take with a safe conscience to any prince who conquers me and the country of which I am a member, though he be never so great a tyrant or usurper, even to the Zar of Muscovy or the Grand Turk.'[64] Yet this, even apart from the unflattering comparisons, was hardly the sort of profession of loyalty likely to win a ruler's heart. And scepticism was surely justified. For the problem regarding a theory of political obedience grounded on the obligation to accept *de facto* authority is that the obligation disappears once that authority is effectively challenged. In Ireland, during the period in which Jacobitism remained a live issue, this never happened. But Protestants could legitimately have asked where the Catholic clergy would have stood if it had.

3. Dissenters

The historian seeking a rounded view of Irish Protestantism in the late seventeenth and early eighteenth centuries must begin by confronting what seems to be a largely unacknowledged problem. Whatever became, outside Scottish Ulster, of Irish Dissent? According to Sir William Petty, writing in 1672, the Protestant population consisted of 100,000 Scots, who were Presbyterians, and 200,000 'English', of whom 'above 100,000 [are] legal Protestants or conformists, and the rest are Presbyterians, Independents, Anabaptists and Quakers'.[65] Petty's figures are suspiciously round; but his unwillingness to put the proportion of conformists even among the English population at more than something above half is nevertheless striking. During the 1660s and 1670s the Irish authorities periodically expressed concern over

---

[62] Dartmouth to Ormond, 6 Apr. 1711 (Dartmouth Papers, D (W) 1778/III/o/10, 82–4).
[63] Fenning, 'Clerical Recruitment', 13–14.
[64] Nary, *The Case of the Roman Catholics of Ireland*, 130.
[65] Petty, *Political Anatomy*, 8.

the doings of 'fanatics' or 'anabaptists'.[66] Oliver Plunkett reported in 1673 that the bishop of Waterford had taken refuge with him 'because his city is full of fanatics and mad Presbyterians'. In Dublin, too, old loyalties survived. When one of the ministers ejected at the Restoration died there in 1666, 'men stood amazed at the number that accompanied his hearse. The lord mayor and aldermen, lord chief baron, judges, brief men of great and small rank, made his followers no less (as some think) than 3,000.'[67]

After the 1670s this southern Dissenting population appears suddenly to recede into the background. It did not disappear entirely. In Dublin there is clear evidence of the existence in the early eighteenth century of an intellectually active Presbyterian circle, and there were also Baptists, Quakers, and other smaller groups.[68] John Dunton, visiting the city in 1698, found 'several large meeting houses, large and conveniently ordered within'. This in turn reflected a solid presence in the city's middle ranks. The Anglican movement for religious and moral revival of the later 1690s, as one of its leading members admitted, had the support of a few gentlemen, 'but of inferior ranks we have few or none, except the lowest of all, ordinary handicraftsmen, whereas the Dissenters have substantial shopkeepers and tradesmen'.[69] Yet overall, numbers were small. A survey of the parish of St Michan's in 1723 showed only 1,000 Dissenters out of a Protestant population of 6,000 and a total population of 14,000. Even within the limited circle defined by the property-based parliamentary franchise, an attempt in 1728 to capture one of the city's two seats served only to show, in the words of an opponent, that 'their strength is not so great as they would have the world believe'.[70] Elsewhere, there are no precise figures before 1833, when Protestant Dissenters (excluding Wesleyan Methodists) made up well under 1 per cent of the population outside Ulster. But it seems clear that, already in the eighteenth century, numbers were very small. The Quaker population in the middle of the century has been estimated at between 3,000 and 5,000; Baptists in 1800 numbered only about 500, in five congregations grouped in the south and south-east.[71]

This decline was not specific to Ireland. In England too, radical Protestantism lost its momentum after 1660, and numbers continued to fall in the first half

---

[66] HMC, *Ormonde Manuscripts*, iii. 124–9, 135, 243–4, 321; *CSPI 1663–5*, 565–6, 621, 644, 663, 679; *CSPI 1666–9*, 87, 92–3, 771; Irwin, 'The Earl of Orrery and the Military Problems of Restoration Munster'.

[67] Plunkett, *Letters*, 387; Toby Bonnell to J. Johnson, 23 Oct. 1666 (Strype Correspondence, III, fo. 42).

[68] M. A. Stewart, 'John Smith and the Molesworth Circle'.

[69] Dunton, *Life and Errors*, ii. 555–6; James Bonnell to Strype, 25 Jan. 1699 (Strype Correspondence, I, fo. 126ᵛ).

[70] Return of the population of St Michan's 'from an actual computation', 1723 (Gilbert MS 35, 389); Coghill to Southwell, 12, 27 Jan. 1728 (BL Add. MS 21,122, fos. 46, 55ᵛ).

[71] *NHI* iv. 42; Gribbon, 'Irish Baptists in the Nineteenth Century', 4–5.

of the eighteenth century. But the collapse in Ireland of non-Presbyterian Dissent, plunging from a supposed one-third or so of the Protestant population to an insignificant minority, was on a wholly different scale. The reasons, at this stage, can only be guessed. Although the Catholic threat did not do anything to bring Anglicans and Presbyterians in Ulster together, the pressure for Protestant unity in the face of the common enemy may have been more effective in the overwhelmingly Catholic south. The sects in Ireland, moreover, had always been heavily dependent on the army. Many former soldiers had left within a few years of the Restoration (with consequences for Dissenting numbers that Petty may have failed to take fully into account), and others would have continued to drift away over a longer period. The social and economic environment was also distinctly less favourable. Towns, the main centres of Dissent in both Ireland and Britain, were fewer and smaller in Ireland, and non-agricultural employments less common. Whether or not there was any inherent connection between involvement in trade and a propensity to religious Dissent remains a matter of debate. But if nothing else, a smaller urban sector meant fewer people sufficiently free of the economic and social authority of the landlord class to exercise private judgement in religious matters.

For practical purposes, then, Irish Protestant Dissent meant Ulster Presbyterianism, based on the Scottish immigrants who had been entering the province in irregular waves since the early seventeenth century. An estimate based on hearth-tax returns and on the poll tax of 1659 suggests that already by the late 1660s Scots made up 60 per cent of the British inhabitants and around 20 per cent of the whole population of Ulster.[72] An anonymous memorandum drawn up around the same time proposed that Scots in Ulster should be required to wear hats instead of bonnets, partly in order to promote a local manufacture at the expense of imports, but also to raise the morale of the English of the province, 'who in all fairs and markets see a hundred bonnets worn for one hat'.[73] The main Presbyterian strongholds were the counties of Antrim and Down. But even in Armagh, as Oliver Plunkett reported in 1679, 'one could travel twenty-five miles . . . without finding half a dozen Catholic or Protestant families, but all Presbyterians i.e. strict Calvinists'.[74] Continued immigration in the 1670s and 1680s brought in English as well as Scots. But the 1690s saw a last great surge of purely Scottish immigration that tilted the balance even more in favour of Presbyterians. By 1718 the parish of Derry, with two Dissenters to every Anglican, was reported to be 'one of the most conformable of the province of Ulster. In some parishes (even of this diocese) the Nonconformists are forty to

---

[72] Macafee, 'The Population of Ulster 1630–1841', 85–7. See also Macafee and Morgan, 'Population in Ulster 1660–1760'.
[73] *CSPI 1660–2*, 164–5.　[74] Plunkett, *Letters*, 530.

one.' In Belfast in 1752 Bishop Pococke found only 60 Church of Ireland households out of 400, the rest being Presbyterians.[75] Even in the 1830s, when their relative numbers had been reduced by over a century of emigration, there were almost three Presbyterians to every two Anglicans in Ulster.[76]

This Presbyterian numerical superiority, even if confined to Ulster, was clearly a challenge to the Anglican establishment in church and state. The response of that establishment is, in outline at least, well known. Policy under Charles II had been marked by the same anomalies and sudden shifts as were seen with regard to Catholics. Spasms of repression alternated with periods of relative tolerance, while from 1672 the ministers of a technically illegal church received a royal grant, the *regium donum*. After the Revolution, English governments were no longer prepared to order or sanction even intermittent campaigns of repression directed against the Dissenting population as a whole. But plans to introduce a Toleration Act, similar to that in England, which would formally guarantee freedom of worship to all Protestants, were dropped in the face of overwhelming opposition.[77] Although the civil authorities were no longer prepared to interfere seriously with established Presbyterian congregations, they continued to lend their aid in preventing the creation of new ones. In 1708, for example, Archbishop King wrote to Captain Oliver McCausland of County Donegal asking him to help prevent the establishment of a Presbyterian congregation in his district. Five years later a magistrate in Macroom, County Cork, reported proudly: 'We had a Presbyterian minister attempted lately to set up here, but he found no rest for the sole of his foot and is travelled.'[78] Meanwhile, from the end of the 1690s, Anglican church courts began a campaign against Presbyterian weddings, citing ministers for marrying without a licence and the couples concerned for fornication.[79]

To this continued harassment in religious matters was added a major civil grievance. Since 1673 holders of offices of trust or profit under the crown in England had been required to qualify themselves by taking communion in the established church. No such requirement existed in Ireland: its absence, and the consequently weaker position of the established church, had been one of the reasons urged against the proposed Toleration Acts of 1692 and 1695.[80] In 1703–4, however, someone—most probably the High Church earl of

[75] Nicolson to Wake, 1 Aug. 1718 (Gilbert MS 27, 186, 189); Pococke, *Tour*, 21.

[76] In the dioceses of Raphoe, Derry, Connor, Down, Dromore, Armagh, Clogher, and Kilmore in 1834 there were 474,394 Anglicans and 636,935 Presbyterians: *Report of the Commissioners of Public Instruction, Ireland* (Brit. Parl. Papers 1835, XXXIII).

[77] Beckett, *Protestant Dissent in Ireland*, 31–4.

[78] King to McCausland, 2 Oct. 1708 (TCD MS 750/3/2, 249); Richard Hedges to Joshua Dawson, 23 Apr. 1713 (Hedges Letters).

[79] Beckett, *Protestant Dissent*, 117.

[80] Sydney to Nottingham, 18 Oct. 1692 (*CSPD 1695*, 214); HMC, *Buccleuch and Queensberry Manuscripts*, ii. 209–10.

Nottingham—took the opportunity to add a clause imposing a similar sacramental test to the major Popery Bill being considered by the English Privy Council.[81] The precise impact of this new restriction has never been studied in detail. Spokesmen for the Anglican interest argued that the number of Presbyterians actually qualified to hold the positions from which they were now excluded was in any case negligible. Archbishop King claimed in 1706 that only twelve justices of the peace in the whole of Ulster had refused to take the test, and that several of these were men who 'came in surreptitiously in the Revolution, when the gentry of the country were absent'. Archbishop Boulter, who supported the repeal of the test, also reported in 1732 that Dissenters were 'not proprietors of much land or wealth. I have been assured that, if the test were taken off, there are not 20 persons amongst them qualified for substance to be justices of the peace.'[82] This claim that there were in any case few Dissenters qualified to form part of the governing élite is to some extent borne out by the evidence of representation in parliament. Even in the absence of any direct legal barrier, there were no more than 10 Presbyterian MPs in 1703, 7 in 1713, and 12 in 1715.[83] It is also unlikely that the test made much difference in terms of salaried public employment, access to which depended largely on the patronage of a solidly Anglican élite. Certainly there is no evidence of a purge of office-holders after 1704. Where the test did clearly make a difference was in local government, where prominence in commerce and manufacture would otherwise have entitled Presbyterians to a significant share of power. In Belfast, for example, 7 or 8 of the 12 burgesses had by 1707 been disqualified for not having taken the test. Derry, not quite so seriously affected, lost 2 out of 12 aldermen and 12 out of 24 burgesses.[84]

The test was imposed at a time when Tories were in power in both kingdoms. The shift to Whig government between 1707 and 1710 brought some improvement for Presbyterians. Thus, in 1708, when the archbishop of Armagh attempted to suppress a new Presbyterian congregation in Drogheda, his action was openly disowned, and the archbishop was soon reported to be trying to extricate himself from the whole business.[85] The Tory administra-

---

[81] Simms, 'The Making of a Penal Law', in *War and Politics in Ireland*, 271–4, reviews the inconclusive evidence on the identity of the person or persons responsible for the inclusion of the test clause.

[82] King to bishop of Killaloe, 30 Oct. 1706 (TCD MS 750/3/2, 62–3); Boulter to Newcastle, 15 Jan. 1732 (SP63/395/4). See also Cox to Southwell, 24 Oct. 1706 (BL Add. MS 38,154, fo. 87); Synge to Wake, 3 Feb. 1716 (Gilbert MS 28, 38); Nicolson to Wake, 2 July 1719 (Gilbert MS 27, 222).

[83] Hayton, 'Ireland and the English Ministers', 39–40.

[84] King to Southwell, 8 Nov. 1707 (TCD MS 750/3/2, 161); Anderson Saunders to Southwell, 18 Oct. 1707 (BL Add. MS 9715, fo. 205); Robert Rochfort to Ormond, 3 Aug. 1704 (HMC, *Ormonde Manuscripts*, NS viii. 103–4).

[85] Richard Freeman, lord chancellor, to Somers, 16 Oct., 2 Nov. 1708 (PRONI T2807/42, 43); Lord Drogheda to Coningsby, Dec. 1708 (PRONI D638/167/14).

tion of 1710–14, by contrast, brought the high point of the post-Revolution offensive against Irish Dissent. High-Churchmen assembled in Convocation, along with their allies in parliament, clamoured for action to stem what they saw as the unchecked spread of Presbyterianism. In 1712 the government sanctioned the prosecution of ten ministers who had come to help establish a congregation at Belturbet in County Cavan. Over the next two years, denunciations of Presbyterianism became more virulent, and legal harassment of ministers and congregations more common. In 1714, responding to what had been one of the most common Tory demands of the preceding few years, the government suspended payment of the *regium donum*.

The death of Queen Anne, and the Whig monopoly of power that followed, put a permanent end to direct interference in the religious life of Irish Dissenters. This did not happen overnight. In particular, the church courts, which were outside the direct control of the government, provided the opportunity for a rearguard action by the more militant Anglican clergy on the subject of Presbyterian marriages. Proposals in 1723 for a bill to offer legal protection to marriages where both the minister and both parties were Dissenters were rejected because of fears that this would leave the way open for clandestine marriages. But the threat of legislation that might weaken the church's control over marriages in general led the bishops to order their clergy to become more discreet. By the end of the 1720s prosecutions in the church courts had largely ceased. An act of 1737 confirmed the legality of marriages performed by Presbyterian ministers, as long as both partners were also Presbyterians.[86]

The granting of political rights was a different matter. Here it was clear, even before 1714, that Irish Whigs were ambivalent, if not positively hostile. The imposition of the test in 1704 had been strongly opposed. But this seems to have been due more to dislike of the way in which the thing had been done, along with partisan hostility to a Tory measure, than to any great concern for the Dissenters themselves.[87] The true Whig attitude was made clear three years later, when the appointment of Pembroke raised expectations of an attempt to repeal the test. Amendments to Commons addresses intended to close off any hint of willingness to accept repeal were carried by majorities of three and five to one. A jubilant Sir Richard Cox compared 'the zeal which appeared on this occasion' with that aroused by the failure of James II's

---

[86] Nicolson to Wake, 18 Dec. 1719, 17 Jan. 1720 (Gilbert MS 27, 249, 251–2); Grafton to Carteret, 15 Nov. 1723 (SP63/382/18); same to same, 12 Feb. 1724 (SP63/383/63ᵛ); King to William Walkington, 15 Aug. 1724 (TCD MS 2537, 146–7); Beckett, *Protestant Dissent*, 120–3.

[87] Memorandum on the conduct of the Speaker *c.*1704 (BL Add. MS 9715, fos. 69–70). See also p. 168 for Brodrick's distinctly unsympathetic comments only 5 years later. For his ambiguous stance in 1719, see n. 92.

prosecution of the seven bishops in 1688.[88] The hopes and fears of the Dissenters and their opponents were revived when Pembroke was succeeded in 1708 by the Whig earl of Wharton. This time the scheme proposed to get round the clear objections of the Irish parliament was a repeat of the tactics of 1704: a clause to repeal the test tacked on to a strong anti-Popery bill. In the event, Wharton's English colleagues lost their nerve, and no further attempt was made to raise the question during what was to prove the high point of Whig power under Queen Anne.[89]

After 1714, with the Tories safely consigned to the political wilderness, the lack of real sympathy for Presbyterianism among Irish Whigs became even clearer. In 1716 supporters of the Dissenters, skilfully capitalizing on the invasion scare of the previous year, introduced heads of a bill to exempt officers in the militia and army from taking the sacramental test. However, this was rejected. Instead, the Commons brought in a resolution declaring anyone who prosecuted a Dissenter for accepting a commission an enemy of the Protestant interest, thereby allowing Dissenters to contribute to the defence of the state, while at the same time avoiding concession on the principle of the test.[90] Despite this defeat, Dissenters returned to parliament in 1719 with high expectations. 'They will have all or nothing', Bishop Evans of Meath reported; in particular, they 'despised' the suggestion of a mere guarantee of religious freedom, without access to political office, such as Nonconformists in England enjoyed.[91] The executive agreed that Sir Ralph Gore, chancellor of the exchequer, should introduce a bill to allow Dissenters to be justices of the peace and to hold certain civil and military offices. Before he could do so, however, St John Brodrick and others introduced an alternative measure. This exempted Protestant Dissenters and their ministers from the penalties, still in force under the Acts of Uniformity but in practice long forgotten, for non-attendance at church and for officiating without proper authority. Dissenters were still to be required to pay tithes and other dues to the Church of Ireland, and the authority of the ecclesiastical courts was explicitly restated. The involvement of Brodrick in this cleverly designed pre-emptive measure gave rise to allegations that the whole business was an attempt by the Midleton faction to display its parliamentary strength.[92] But if

[88] Cox to Southwell, 15 July 1707 (BL Add. MS 38,155, fo. 79). See also Saunders to Southwell, 10 July 1707 (BL Add. MS 9715, fo. 174); Cox to Southwell, 31 July 1707 (BL Add. MS 38,155, fo. 87).

[89] Hayton, 'Divisions in the Whig Junto'.

[90] King to Wake, 24 Mar. 1716 (TCD MS 2533, 160–70); Godwin to Wake, 11 Feb., 3 May 1716 (Wake MS XII, fos. 16–17, 45ᵛ).

[91] Evans to Wake, endorsed 27 June 1719 (Wake MS XIII, 71); Bolton to ——, 27 June 1719 (SP63/377/234).

[92] 'A brief account of some proceedings in the parliament of Ireland', 16 July 1719 (Wake MS XIII, 90). Midleton, who was still lord chancellor, denied that he had encouraged his son's action. There had even been a public argument between them on the issue. Bolton, on paper at least, claimed to accept Midleton's assurances: Bolton to Craggs, 8 July 1719 (SP63/377/167).

so, it had chosen its ground well. Attempts to expand the provisions of the bill, by adding clauses to permit itinerant teachers, to legalize Dissenting marriages, and to prevent landlords from blocking the erection of meeting-houses on their estates, were voted down by majorities reported to be as high as 200 to 20. Gore announced that he would not proceed with his proposed bill, and the Presbyterians were left with the bare formal toleration they had been reported to despise.[93]

In the same year, 1719, parliament also passed what was to be the first in a series of Indemnity Acts for officers in paid civil employment who had not taken the sacramental test. This is normally interpreted as a concession mitigating the practical effects of parliament's refusal to repeal the test.[94] But if so, it would hardly have passed with so little discussion. A more likely explanation is that the bill was intended to save persons who had neglected to qualify within the strict time limits laid down by the Act of 1704 from falling foul of the law. The practical irrelevance of the Indemnity Acts is revealed in their disjointed chronology. Although they were renewed many times between 1719 and 1780, there were also quite lengthy intervals during which they were not in force, without anyone seeming to be greatly concerned.[95]

The next—and, as it happened, the last—major drive to remove the test began in 1731, when representatives of the Irish Presbyterians successfully appealed to the English ministry to take up their cause. Initially there were plans to attach a clause abolishing the test to the Popery Bill laid before the parliament of 1732; but this second attempt to repeat in reverse the events of 1704 was abandoned as the level of opposition became clear. Instead, the lord lieutenant was instructed to seek a straightforward bill to remove the test in the parliament of 1733. The plan was to avoid bringing the issue forward until after the recess, when the money bill would be safely through and 'it was probable, that the number of gentlemen who declared against it might be lessened, or their zeal be abated'.[96] Opponents of repeal, however, forced the issue by introducing a resolution fixing a deadline after which no bill to repeal any part of the Popery acts should be received. Support for the resolution was so strong that the government's managers surrendered without a division; Boulter estimated that the majority against removing the test would have been three to two. A few days later, leading members of the Irish executive met

---

[93] Evans to Wake, 16 July 1719 (Wake MS XIII, 88); Bolton to Craggs, 16 July 1719 (SP63/377/139ᵛ).

[94] Beckett, *Protestant Dissent*, 80. Cf. James, *Ireland in the Empire*, 93: 'The events of 1719 did in a sense constitute the first breach in the Anglican monopoly.'

[95] The first Indemnity Act, e.g., extended the time for taking the test to 25 Mar. 1720. The next Act was not passed until 1725. It set a deadline of 1 Aug. 1726, but no further Act followed until 1729. See table in Beckett, *Protestant Dissent*, 81.

[96] Dorset to Newcastle, 14 Dec. 1733 (SP63/396/121ᵛ).

representatives of the Presbyterians to tell them that there was no hope of carrying a repeal bill.[97]

Behind this consistent refusal to admit Protestant Dissenters to full civil rights lay a changing mix of religious and social motives. In the period up to 1714, attempted repression was founded on a real fear that Presbyterians would succeed in establishing themselves as the dominant religious group. Presbyterians could not be admitted to government, Sir Richard Cox declared in 1706, 'because assuredly if they were in, they would put us out'.[98] Already by the 1690s Presbyterians outnumbered Anglicans in Ulster, and throughout that decade and for some years after they were being reinforced by further immigration from Scotland. The number of ministers and congregations seems to have grown by up to half between 1689 and 1707 and by another 30 per cent between 1707 and 1716.[99] In addition, Anglicans had before them the dreadful example of Scotland, where Presbyterianism had only a few years before supplanted episcopacy as the established religion. A pamphleteer in 1698 alleged that the clergy of the former established church in Scotland had been subjected to greater indignities than those Protestant clergy who had remained in Ireland during the worst period of Jacobite rule.[100]

Presbyterians were alarming, not just on account of their numbers, but also because of their discipline and cohesion. Ulster Presbyterianism, especially after the establishment of the Synod of Ulster in 1691, was an autonomous and highly organized ecclesiastical polity.[101] The discipline which the kirk session exercised over its members was both strict and broadly defined. Members could be called to account not only for sabbath-breaking, neglect of religious duty, drunkenness, and sexual or other immorality, but also for engaging in disputes with neighbours, for dishonesty in business dealings, or for applying to a landlord for land held by another member.[102] As a result, William King alleged in 1716, Presbyterians 'are under an absolute slavery' to the ministers and elders of their church. 'They are in a manner obliged only to buy and sell with such as these order them to deal with. They dare not so much as join in partnership or set up a plough, which is common in the north, with a neighbour that offends their ministers and elders.' Where Presbyterians had succeeded in gaining control of trade and of local government, 'they refused to admit any apprentices or servants that would not indent or covenant to go to the meetings with them and refused the common offices

---

[97] Boulter, *Letters*, ii. 109–12.
[98] Cox to Southwell, 24 Oct. 1706 (BL Add. MS 38,154, fo. 86).
[99] Hayton, 'Ireland and the English Ministers', 36; idem, *Ireland after the Glorious Revolution*, 7.
[100] [Brewster], *Discourse Concerning Ireland*, 24–5.
[101] Brooke, *Ulster Presbyterianism*, 112.
[102] Stevenson, *Two Centuries of Life in Down*, 173–83; Barkley, 'The Presbyterian Minister in Eighteenth-Century Ireland', 52–3.

of neighbourhood to such as were not of their persuasion'. Bishop Nicolson of Derry likewise insisted to the archbishop of Canterbury that Ulster Presbyterians 'have been accustomed to act in conformity to the whole discipline of the Kirk of Scotland', so that they could not be satisfied by a mere measure of religious toleration.[103]

In addition to the threat it posed to the Church of Ireland, the tight discipline of the Ulster Presbyterians had political implications. Irish Dissenters, King explained to the archbishop of Canterbury in 1716, were not like their English counterparts:

They are a people embodied under their lay elders, presbyteries and synods and come to their sacraments in crowds of three or four thousand from 20 or 40 miles about, and they make laws for themselves and allow not that the civil magistrate has any right to control them and will be just so far the king's subjects as their lay elders and presbyteries will allow them.[104]

Four years earlier the lord chancellor, Sir Constantine Phipps, complained in similar terms that Presbyterian ministers 'convene assemblies, call synods, exhibit libels, summon witnesses and proceed in form to pronounce sentences'. In Belfast they had gone so far as to set up a Society for the Reformation of Manners, 'of which about fifteen are sworn once a month before the sovereign of the town, in the nature of a grand jury', which then despatched constables to enter houses and arrest persons accused of moral offences.[105] Nor was it only Tories like Phipps who found the assertiveness of the Presbyterians in these years alarming. Alan Brodrick complained in 1709 that their behaviour in attempting to set up a new congregation in Drogheda and a sermon against episcopacy recently preached by the Dublin minister Joseph Boyse, 'savours of a temper that affects more than liberty of serving God in such manner as their conscience allows of, and that aims at dominion and power'.[106]

The fear that their numbers or their cohesion might allow Presbyterians eventually to achieve religious supremacy was slow to die completely. As late as 1718, Bishop Nicolson of Derry predicted that if the ban on occasional conformity were lifted, 'presbytery will forthwith extirpate episcopacy in the province of Ulster'. Their numbers were already superior, so that they 'want nothing but the sword, either of justice or iniquity, for the establishment of

---

[103] King to bishop of Clogher, 8 Feb. 1716 (TCD MS 2533, 132–6); King to Wake, 24 Mar. 1716 (ibid. 160–70); Nicolson to Wake, 17 Jan. 1720 (Gilbert MS 27, 252).

[104] King to Wake, 24 Mar. 1716 (TCD MS 2533, 165).

[105] Phipps to Oxford, 26 Dec. 1712 (HMC, *Portland Manuscripts* V, 254–6).

[106] Alan Brodrick to Thomas Brodrick, 13 Jan. 1709 (Midleton MS 1248/2, fos. 350–1). Archbishop King singled out the Drogheda affair and Boyse's sermon as having alienated many of the Dissenters' former supporters, claiming that he could name 40 gentlemen who had changed their mind about the test as a result: King to Southwell, 16 Feb. 1709 (TCD MS 2531, 61); King to Annesley, 27 Jan. 1709 (ibid. 44–6).

their own discipline in all that quarter', and ultimately in the whole of Ireland.[107] By this time, however, such dire predictions were beginning to seem unrealistic. The flow of migrants from Scotland had died away in the early 1700s, while the commencement from around 1718 of large-scale emigration from Ulster to America held out the prospect that from now on Presbyterian numbers would decline rather than rise. Then, from the mid-1720s, came the first in a series of doctrinal splits. To William Conolly, the politician most closely associated with the cause of the Ulster Presbyterians, the internal divisions that followed were 'downright madness', which 'will render them less formidable and consequently less considerable in all matters'. Nicolson, by contrast, welcomed the way in which the Presbyterians were 'distracted and disjointed' by their internal disputes.[108]

By the time of the last attempt to remove the test, in 1733, the change of tone is evident. A substantial majority of members in both houses were clearly determined to block any attempt to repeal the test. At the same time there were none of the apocalyptic predictions of disaster that had been common twenty years before. Indeed, Marmaduke Coghill told the lord lieutenant that one reason for maintaining the test was 'the further prospect I had of all Protestants coming to church.... Let us continue in the state we were in, I durst venture to say, we shall not have a Dissenter of £100 per ann. left in Ireland in twenty years time.'[109] Two decades of Whig ecclesiastical appointments ensured that on this occasion the bishops no longer led the defence of the sacramental test, as they had done in the days of Queen Anne. The lower clergy, by contrast, remained as determined as ever. 'The bishops here', Boulter warned the government in January 1732,

who are for letting the Dissenters live unmolested, have at present that weight with their clergy, as to keep them from any unreasonable warmth against Dissenters in their sermons. But if those bishops can once be run upon as persons who would bring Dissenters into power, they will soon lose their present weight, and both they and the Dissenters will be the subject of angry discourses from the pulpit.[110]

When a vote on the issue was expected the following year, 'many of the clergy from the several parts of the kingdom' came up to Dublin for the start of the parliamentary session. Yet even here there was a cooling of former passions. As soon as the bill was rejected, Boulter was confident that 'the heat among the churchmen here will, I think, be soon over'.[111]

For the Anglican gentlemen who dominated the parliament and who were the real obstacle to the removal or modification of the restrictions imposed

---

[107] Nicolson to Wake, 15 Sept. 1718 (Gilbert MS 27, 192–3).

[108] Conolly to ——, 7 July 1723 (SP63/381/61); Nicolson to Wake, 27 Aug. 1725 (Gilbert MS 27, 374–5).

[109] Coghill to Southwell, 18 Oct. 1733 (BL Add. MS 21,123, fos. 58–59).

[110] Boulter to Newcastle, 15 Jan. 1732 (SP63/395/4).

[111] Boulter, *Letters*, ii. 109, 114.

on Dissenters, a desire to uphold the supremacy of their own church was reinforced by strong social and political objections to Nonconformity in general, and to Ulster Presbyterianism in particular. One focus of suspicion was the Scottish origins of most Irish Dissent. 'Though the Irish might be mischievously inclined,' an Irish earl was quoted as saying in 1695, 'yet they wanted the Scots' power and their neighbourhood to their countrymen in Scotland.'[112] Under Charles II and James II the fear had been that Ulster Presbyterians might link up with anti-episcopalian forces in Scotland. Between 1690 and 1707, concern shifted to the increasingly bitter constitutional conflict between England and Scotland, and there was anxious speculation about which side the Ulster Presbyterians would take in any military conflict.[113] There was in addition the widespread belief that dissent in religious matters was likely to be associated with, or to encourage, undesirable political principles. Opponents were able to point, for example, to the inclusion in Presbyterian catechisms of the Solemn League and Covenant, with the echoes this revived of civil-war radicalism and the withdrawal of obedience from a monarch who was held not to fulfil his obligation of upholding true religion.[114] Such suspicions became less urgent in the long era of political stability that began in 1714, before being reawakened, most notably in Ireland, by the American and French revolutions. But they did not disappear. At the time of the great anti-union riot in Dublin in 1759, the lord lieutenant, the duke of Bedford, blamed the disturbances on the influence of 'new light' Presbyterians, 'totally republican and averse to English government'. His chief secretary also reported that there were groups of Dissenters whose hostility to both monarchy and the established church made them require 'equal watching with the Papists'.[115]

Hostility to Ulster Presbyterians can also be better understood in the light of the different character of the English and the Scottish migrations to Ulster in the seventeenth century. The majority of English settlers, it has been suggested, were without independent economic resources. Many, in fact, were sponsored migrants, and most settled into positions of economic dependence on landlords or employers. Scottish settlers, by contrast, were for the most part independent migrants, with capital resources of their own. By the early eighteenth century, Scots were displacing not only Catholics but also Anglicans from the more fertile lands in areas of previously English-dominated settlement such as Londonderry, Tyrone, and east Donegal.[116] The same economic independence, it can be suggested, made the Scots less ready than the

---

[112] HMC, *Downshire Manuscripts*, I: *Papers of Sir William Trumbull*, 508.
[113] HMC, *Ormonde Manuscripts*, NS viii. 74, 78, 112, 132.
[114] Evans to Wake, 23 June, 7 July 1719 (Wake MS XIII, 69, 80).
[115] Murphy, 'Dublin Anti-Union Riot', 59, 61.
[116] Cullen, *Emergence of Modern Ireland*, 55–6.

English to fit into the structure of a hierarchical and deferential society. Observers in the early nineteenth century were to comment on the blunt manners of the Presbyterian population of County Antrim, their 'notion that they have no superiors and that courtesy is but another term for servility'.[117]

Finally, of course, there was the continued maintenance by Presbyterians of their own ecclesiastical organization. This may no longer have appeared as formidable as in the days when there had seemed to be a real possibility that presbytery would displace episcopacy in Ireland as it had already done in Scotland. But Presbyterianism, in Ulster at least, remained a tightly organized system whose authority was wholly independent of both the state and the landed élite. According to King, writing in 1719 to the archbishop of Canterbury, this was the central issue underlying the whole debate:

> The true point between [the Dissenters] and the gentlemen is, whether the Presbyterian ministers with their synods, presbyteries and lay elders in every parish shall have the greater influence over the people to lead them as they please, or the landlords over their tenants. This may help Your Grace in some degree to see the reason why the parliament is so unanimous against the taking off the test.[118]

4. Churchmen

The Church of Ireland of the early eighteenth century was an institution torn between an exalted vision of its potential role and a circumscribed, demoralizing, and, in places, sordid reality. Historians have, in general, done less than justice to the former, while at the same time unconsciously applying its improbably high standards to their assessment of the latter.

The vision was of a church that would play a central part in the organization of society: acting as the acknowledged custodian of religious doctrine and morals, upholding by its teaching both social order and the authority of government, and in return being supported by the coercive sanctions of the civil power. A document of 1693, calling for a regal visitation to promote ecclesiastical reform, summed up this concept of church and state as interlocking and mutually reinforcing parts of a single, organic whole:

> It is most evident from the principle of religion, the dictates of natural wisdom and policy, and the observation of regular practice, that there is such a golden chain of participation of symbols linking the ecclesiastical state with the civil, in all well-ordered constitutions of Christian governments, and consequently so great a connection of interest and concern betwixt them, that the due administration of the jurisdiction of the one, doth as mainly conduce to the advancement and establishment of the other, as

---

[117] Connolly in *NHI* v. 21.
[118] King to Wake, 1 Aug. 1719 (TCD MS 750/5, 192).

abuses, neglects and corruptions growing in the one produce inconveniencies and disturbances to the other.[119]

Such ideas had of course been part of orthodox Christian doctrine for centuries. In the 1690s and early 1700s, however, they acquired a new resonance, with the rise in England of what came to be called the High Church party. In part this was a response to the crisis of confidence created by the events of 1688, when churchmen had been forced into an undignified scramble to reconcile their doctrines with a radically new political reality. In part it reflected the dismay felt by devout Anglicans at the sudden collapse of the quite effective social and ecclesiastical discipline that had been maintained since the Restoration. The Toleration Act of 1689 had not only recognized the right of Dissenters to worship in their own manner. It had also permitted large numbers to abandon religious practice altogether, and had fatally weakened the coercive discipline exercised through the ecclesiastical courts. Meanwhile, the suspension in 1695 of the system of obligatory licensing of publications had opened the way for what seemed to be a tide of rationalist and infidel literature. Against this background, it seemed to many that the only salvation, for religion and civil society alike, lay in a restoration of the church's lost authority in matters of belief and morals. This was to be achieved partly through a revival of Convocation, the representative body of bishops and lower clergy, and partly by winning the support of the state, through an alliance with the Tory party, for the reimposition of orthodoxy and social discipline.[120]

The Irish High Church party was in some respects a direct extension of the English. It was the English High Church militant Francis Atterbury who in 1703 used his influence with the Tory ministry to have the Irish Convocation, dormant since the 1660s, recalled, thereby opening up an ecclesiastical second front across the Irish Sea. Atterbury was assisted by William Perceval, archdeacon of Cashel, whom the Whig chief secretary Joseph Addison described in 1709 as the High Church party's 'principal agent' in the kingdom. William King too blamed the disputes that followed on 'such clergymen as, having been educated in England, have taken their measures from some of the most forward in that country'.[121] As with party politics, however, labels initially imported from England quickly became passionately felt causes. Once Convocation got under way, the demand for a vigorous reassertion of the rights of the established church drew an enthusiastic response from a substantial section of Irish clerical opinion. The militants included a number of

---

[119] 'Reasons offered to promote the speedy holding of a regal visitation' (Portland Papers, PwA 2374).

[120] Holmes, *Trial of Doctor Sacheverell*, ch. 2; Bennett, *The Tory Crisis in Church and State*, ch. 1, 7.

[121] Addison to Sunderland, 13 June 1709 (*Letters*, 148); King, quoted in Beckett, 'The Government and the Church of Ireland under William III and Anne', 298.

bishops. Addison named Thomas Lindsay of Killaloe and Charles Hickman of Derry as among those who 'do underhand inflame the inferior clergy', and also attacked John Pooley of Raphoe, 'a man of ungovernable passions inflamed with the most furious zeal and generally passes for mad'.[122] But in general, it was in the lower house that High Church principles, as in England, were most vigorously articulated.

The extent to which High Church principles had caught the imagination of a substantial section of the clergy was made clear in 1703, when the lower house of Convocation introduced resolutions calling for a stricter enforcement of public morality, including legal action against sabbath-breaking and swearing, and tighter censorship, to restrain 'the profaneness and immorality of the stage, and the indecent and immodest behaviour too frequent in the play house'. Members also called for an assault on irreligion, demanding that churchwardens should present to the bishop the names of all those in their parishes who did not attend some place of worship at least once a month.[123] In addition, Convocation followed the example of its English counterpart in showing a high sense of its own importance. In 1705, it denounced a bill to encourage the manufacture of linen by reducing the tithe on flax and hemp as an invasion of the clergy's privileges, arguing instead for the right of the clerical order to tax itself in Convocation. In 1709 some members attempted to censure Ralph Lambert, dean of Down, for having questioned the right of the lower house to meet independently of the bishops. Since Lambert was chaplain to the lord lieutenant, this provoked a dangerous political quarrel. Even Queen Anne was snubbed in 1711, when Convocation refused to accept a letter similar to that sent earlier to its English counterpart, on the grounds that it was a national rather than a provincial synod (the English body technically represented only the province of Canterbury) and because it had never, as in England, surrendered its rights by an act of submission to the crown.[124]

In England the claims of the Highflyers were opposed by a smaller Low Church party, whose members saw the means of improving the position of the church less in the restoration of its coercive authority than in higher standards of pastoral efficiency and moral leadership.[125] A similar division may be suggested for Ireland: certainly the High Church militants of Queen Anne's reign are not the men who stand out as advocates of internal reform. But the distinction should not be pressed too far. Recent research has shown that even

[122] Addison to Sunderland, 20 July 1709 (*Letters*, 168); Addison to Godolphin, 30 June 1709 (ibid. 162).
[123] Journals of the Upper House of Convocation, 1703–13 (PRONI Dio 4/10/3/2, 142–7). Cf. Phillips (ed.), *Church of Ireland*, iii. 178–9, 184–5.
[124] Winnett, *Peter Browne*, 37–47; Dralle, 'Kingdom in Reversion', 412–14; Addison to Sunderland, 13 June 1709 (*Letters*, 167); Theophilus Harrison, dean of Clonmacnoise, to Strype, 4 Aug. 1711 (Strype Correspondence, III, fo. 812).
[125] Bennett, 'Conflict in the Church', 164–5.

in England the Low-Churchmen who became the dominant party in the long period of Whig ascendancy after 1714 were neither as wholly subservient to the state nor as willing to abandon the claims of their church to a special status as their opponents claimed.[126] In Ireland the opponents of the High Church party were, if anything, even slower than their English counterparts to abandon traditional ideas of the church's proper role. Archbishop King of Dublin, for example, may have played a crucial part in defusing the High-Church offensive in the Convocation of 1709. But he was able to do this so effectively precisely because he was himself a noted defender of the church's privileges, 'looked upon as the oracle of the church party in this kingdom'.[127] His vision of his role was summed up in his pamphlet *A Discourse Concerning the Inventions of Men in the Worship of God* (1694), in which he addressed the Presbyterian inhabitants of his diocese of Derry 'in the spirit of meekness (as one that is appointed by the providence of God and the care of a Christian magistracy to watch over your souls)'.[128] In his visitation the previous year he had put this conception of his own authority into practice, declaring his intention of proceeding vigorously against the large number of cases of incest, whoredom, and adultery, mostly by non-Anglicans, that had been reported to him.[129]

In other respects too, Irish churchmen of the early eighteenth century, and not just the Highflyers among them, revealed their continued commitment to the coercive maintenance of religious orthodoxy. Demands for repressive measures against Presbyterianism may be explained in terms of the very real threat posed by the tight organization and numerical near equality of a rival group. But the smaller Nonconformist sects, contrary to what is often claimed, also attracted hostile attention. Quakers, in particular, were suspect, to some extent as a powerful economic interest, but mainly on the grounds that their rejection of such fundamental doctrines as the resurrection of the body, the Trinity, and 'the satisfaction purchased by the literal blood of Christ... make[s] their case very different from the case of other schismatics'.[130] In 1697 a bill to permit Quakers to affirm, rather than take oaths, in certain types of legal action was blocked by the votes of the bishops in the House of Lords. As late as 1724 a bill to the same effect was opposed by four out of sixteen bishops voting.[131] Both Archbishop King and Bishop Moreton of Kildare also

---

[126] Taylor, 'Sir Robert Walpole, the Church of England and the Quakers' Tithe Bill of 1736'.

[127] Addison to Godolphin, 26 May 1709 (*Letters*, 144).

[128] Quoted in Brooke, *Ulster Presbyterianism*, 64.

[129] King to Foley, 9 May 1693 (TCD MSS 1995–2008/274). This declaration of intent seems to contradict Beckett's suggestion that in King's dealings with Dissenters during this phase of his career, 'common sense (if no other motive) prevented his zeal from carrying him into a policy of coercion' ('William King's Administration of the Diocese of Derry', 171–2).

[130] King to Lindsay, 19 May 1698 (TCD MS 750/1, 235); King to Archdeacon Thomas Parnell, 29 Jan. 1708 (TCD MS 750/3/2, 183).

[131] Beckett, 'Government and the Church of Ireland', 292; Nicolson to Wake, 27 Jan. 1724 (Gilbert MS 27, 337); King to Wake, 1 Feb. 1724 (TCD MS 2537, 68).

brought pressure to bear on the small congregations of French Protestants established in Dublin and elsewhere from the 1690s.[132] The Toleration Act of 1719, introduced in order to block any attempt at real concessions to Protestant Dissenters, was nevertheless vehemently opposed both by King and by Edward Synge, archbishop of Tuam and another prominent Whig churchman, on the grounds that it did not require those wishing to qualify for its protection to make even the most basic profession of Christian faith or to submit to any inspection of their tenets. The result, both bishops argued, would be to open the way for wild and dangerous sects of the kind that had appeared in England during the interregnum, as well as to remove all restraint from 'those that are resolved to trouble themselves with no religion'.[133] Nor was this commitment to the repression of religious error purely theoretical. In 1697 the deist John Toland, a well-established figure in English philosophical and literary circles, returned to his native Ireland, only to be forced to make a hurried retreat in order to escape prosecution. Six years later, in another celebrated case, the Dublin Presbyterian minister Thomas Emlyn was imprisoned for two years for having published a book that questioned the orthodox doctrine of the Trinity.[134]

Why were Irish churchmen, even those who were not Highflyers, so committed to the repression of heresy and irreligion? One recent study argues that the defence of rigid doctrinal orthodoxy was necessary to uphold the privileges of the Anglican élite. 'Free thought, as a tolerant, demystifying and counter-divisive force, could insidiously undermine the privileged status of the ascendancy.' 'With the Christian mysteries intact,' on the other hand, 'the division between Anglican and Catholic, Anglican and Dissenter, could be maintained.'[135] Yet it is difficult to see by what psychological mechanism, other than an improbable level of conscious hypocrisy, this particular motive of shoring up the Anglican establishment behind barriers of deliberately created unreason could have operated. A simpler explanation would be that support for old ideas and intolerance of new ones lasted longer in a provincial society than in the metropolis. Ireland, in this respect, was not very different from Scotland, where an Edinburgh student convicted of having ridiculed the Scriptures was hanged, despite having recanted, in 1697, and where pro-

---

[132] King to Southwell, 24 Mar., 7 Apr. 1705 (TCD MS 750/3/1, 121–2, 138); King to M. de Galenière, 7 Apr. 1705 (ibid. 137); King to bishop of Ferns, 24 Oct. 1710 (TCD MS 2531, 211); King to Southwell, 29 Aug. 1704 (TCD MS 750/3/1, 24); Caldicott *et al.* (eds.), *The Huguenots and Ireland*, 310–11.

[133] King to Lord Southwell, 10 Nov. 1719 (TCD MS 750/5, 203); King to Wake, 1 Dec. 1719 (ibid. 220); Archbishop Synge's speech on the Toleration Bill, 1719 (Gilbert MS 28, 121–38). Other Irish bishops also opposed the bill. All five of those who voted for it, as King pointed out with some bitterness, were Englishmen recently appointed to Irish sees: King to Arthur Charlet, 7 Jan. 1720 (TCD MS 750/5, 241); King to Annesley, 10 Nov. 1719 (ibid. 200).

[134] Simms, 'John Toland (1670–1722), a Donegal Heretic', in *War and Politics in Ireland*, 38; Brooke, *Ulster Presbyterianism*, 79–80.

[135] David Berman, 'The Culmination and Causation of Irish Philosophy', 271.

secutions for witchcraft continued for several decades after they had been abandoned in England.[136]

Even in relation to their larger and more formidable rivals, Presbyterians and Catholics, the attitudes of early eighteenth-century churchmen were determined by religious as well as political considerations. In the case of the former, both King and Edward Synge seem genuinely to have believed that the points of theology and liturgy on which Presbyterians differed from the established church were not sufficiently distinctive to explain their refusal to remain within it. Rather, Presbyterian insistence on maintaining a separate establishment was to be explained in terms of the self-interest of their ministers and the rigid discipline these maintained over their congregations. King claimed to know hundreds 'that would not be Presbyterians if they durst be otherwise'.[137] The Anglican assault on Presbyterianism, following this logic, placed little emphasis on doctrinal controversy, but instead concentrated on attempting, with the help of the state, to break the organizational and social structures that were seen as giving Presbyterianism its power. Catholicism, by contrast, was perceived not just as a political and social system, but as a formidable body of erroneous doctrine, which should be met by constant counter-argument as well as political repression. Among the points of which the parish clergy should be reminded during a visitation, King noted in 1720, was the necessity of preaching against Popery, so that 'when any occasion offers of confuting any point of false doctrine advanced by the Church of Rome, . . . they would lay hold on it and . . . show as briefly as they can the falsehood thereof'. In 1735 Archbishop Boulter responded enthusiastically to plans to reprint a selection of anti-Catholic writings from the reign of James II: 'We are very much troubled with Popery here, and the book cannot but be very useful.'[138] The same concern was shared by religiously minded laymen. In 1709 Sir Richard Cox reported that he had completed *An Enquiry into Religion*, whose aim was 'to confound Popery without railing . . . All I will yet say of it is that it has silenced several very bigotted Papists whom I have showed it to, and made them stagger.' Judge Michael Ward advised his son in 1738 not to trouble with polemical theology, but to study those points that separated Protestants from Catholics, 'that their numbers and temporal greatness may not tempt us to submit to their many errors and superstitions'.[139]

One further manifestation of the continued claim of the church to a coercive authority was the operation of the ecclesiastical courts. These had

[136] J. C. D. Clark, *English Society 1688–1832*, 284–5; Larner, *Enemies of God*, ch. 6.

[137] King to James Bonnell, 4–18 Jan. 1695 (TCD MSS 1995–2008/396); Synge to Wake, 22 Mar. 1716 (Gilbert MS 28, 55). See also King to bishop of Clogher, 24 Mar. 1702 (Mant, *Church of Ireland*, ii. 125): 'Very few are so weak as to think it a sin to conform.'

[138] King to Synge, 24 Apr. 1720 (TCD MS 750/6, 67); Boulter, *Letters*, ii. 143, 244.

[139] Cox to Southwell, 1 Nov. 1709 (BL Add. MS 38,156, fo. 99); Judge Ward's 'Last advice' to his son, 19 Nov. 1738 (PRONI D2092/1/7/121).

jurisdiction over all matters relating to tithes and ecclesiastical fees, as well as over wills and marriages. In addition, they were empowered to try and to punish cases of heresy, blasphemy, non-attendance at church, sabbath-breaking, defamation, and sexual immorality. In practice, by the later seventeenth century, the courts seem to have largely confined themselves to dealing with the enforcement of the church's financial claims and the harassment of its religious rivals. Of 102 persons standing excommunicated in the diocese of Derry in 1667, 14 had refused to pay tithes or contribute to the repair of their parish church, 27 had refused to attend the parish church or submit to the ecclesiastical court, and 37 had been excommunicated for 'nonconformity', defined as including 'not only absence from the church but baptising children by unlicensed ministers'. Even at this time, however, the excommunicates also included a farmer found ploughing on Christmas Day and two men who had refused to appear in a case of defamation.[140] In Dublin Mary Collins was arraigned before the consistory court in 1713 for having called James Conran 'a whore's son and a son of a whore and a rogue' and Conran's wife Elizabeth a 'whore and bastard'. A 'notorious and villainous sodomite' arrested in 1726 was said to have tried to silence his accusers by threatening to bring charges of defamation against them in the same court.[141] There was also some enforcement of sexual morality. In 1711 King recommended to the bishop of Clogher that an adulterer be required 'to stand in a white sheet, bare footed and bare legged, in every church in the diocese Sunday after Sunday for a year, and if this do not mend him enlarge it into two or three as many as you please till he mend'. Nine years later he sought to force the unfortunate parson of Blessington, County Wicklow, to initiate formal proceedings against Lord Blessington for maintaining a lewd woman.[142]

The main weapon available to the church courts to back up their judgments was the threat of excommunication. This involved exclusion not just from the church's services, but also from the society of its members. When a man was excommunicated in Roscrea in 1727 for repeatedly failing to answer summonses in a case involving tithes, the rector was instructed to publish the sentence to the congregation 'and to forbid them upon pain of the law to deal, correspond or keep company with the said excommunicate person'. For a practising member of the church, such ostracism, combined with exclusion from religious services, would have been a serious penalty. Where the offender was a Catholic or a Dissenter, on the other hand, neither sanction is likely to have counted for very much. Bishop Dopping of Meath complained in 1697 of 'the general slight and contempt there is put upon excommunica-

---

[140] PRONI Dio 4/5/3/10. There were also 14 persons excommunicated for adultery or fornication, but these may have included Dissenters who had been married by their own clergy.
[141] RCB GS2/7/3/34; *Dublin Intelligence*, 17 Sept. 1726.
[142] King to bishop of Clogher, 7 Aug. 1711 (TCD MS 2531, 350); King to Mr Welsh, 20 Nov. 1719, 20 Jan. 1720 (TCD MS 750/5, 214).

tion which is the highest act of censure of the church'. Boulter, in 1728, confirmed that Catholics and Dissenters, the great majority of the population, were indifferent to excommunication.[143] For persons of any property, on the other hand, the sentence could involve serious civil penalties. An excommunicated man could not serve on a jury, be a witness in any court, or bring an action to recover land or money due to him.[144] Further, the clergy could apply to the civil authorities for a writ *de excommunicatio capiendo*, under which the offender would be committed to gaol until he submitted to the authority of the court. Nor was this wholly a dead letter. In 1699 the government's law officers indicated their willingness to issue writs for the imprisonment of any Dissenting ministers whom the church authorities chose to excommunicate for performing marriages, while around the same time a Mrs Lenthall of the diocese of Meath, whose husband refused to appear to answer her suit for maintenance, was able to have him excommunicated 'and thereon committed'.[145]

These were the aspirations. The day-to-day reality, however, could be a grim experience. 'You'll have but a melancholy time of it,' William King told the newly appointed Bishop Evans of Meath, about to set out on his first visitation in 1717, 'to see the desolation of churches and the thinness of your congregations.' Queen Mary, in 1690, had pronounced the Church of Ireland to be 'the worst in Christendom'.[146] Such judgements have been echoed by modern writers. One historian has dismissed the whole Anglican establishment in Ireland as a 'simulacrum of a church'. J. L. McCracken, in a more measured survey, concludes that 'the Church of Ireland possessed power and wealth in ample measure, but for a number of reasons it was singularly ineffective as a religious organisation'.[147]

The deficiencies that gave rise to such comments, both at the time and since, are well known. The report on the 'present disorders' of the church drawn up in 1697 by Anthony Dopping, bishop of Meath, neatly summed up the major problems: '1. want of ministers; 2. want of Protestants; 3. the great pluralities and non-residence of the clergy who are there; 4. the ruinous condition and want of churches in that kingdom'.[148] Part of the difficulty lay in the depletion of material resources: the large proportion of churches in ruins or in bad repair, the absence in most parishes of what should have been

---

[143] Excommunication of Michael Bergin, 19 Jan. 1727 (NLI MS 1562); Brady, 'Remedies Proposed for the Church of Ireland', 172; Boulter, *Letters*, i. 212–13.
[144] Lea, *Present State of the Established Church*, 66.
[145] St George Ashe, bishop of Clogher, to King, 28 Oct. 1699 (TCD MSS 1995–2008/632); Harrison to Strype, 13 Oct. 1697, 16 July 1698 (Strype Correspondence, III, fos. 424, 431).
[146] King to Evans, 2 Mar. 1717 (TCD MS 2534, 99–100); Queen Mary, quoted in Landa, *Swift and the Church of Ireland*, 189.
[147] V. G. Kiernan, *The Duel in European History*, 180; J. L. McCracken in *NHI* iv. 86–8.
[148] Brady, 'Remedies', 164.

the standard provision of a residence for the minister and an allotment of glebe land to supplement his table or his income, the shortage of parish clergy, and the inability of the parochial revenues available to provide adequate support even for those there were. Archbishop King, replying to a request in 1710 for contributions towards the support of missionaries in Britain's overseas colonies, maintained that in Ireland 'we are in little better circumstances, as to a competent provision for supplying the duties of religion, than the foreign plantations themselves'.[149] To this was added the damage done by human neglect: the bishops who failed to pay more than an occasional visit to the dioceses committed to their care; the holders of rich benefices who spent all or most of their time in Dublin or in England, entrusting their pastoral responsibilities to poorly paid and unsupervised curates; the pluralists who held two or more livings, again relying on curates to discharge the duties of all or—at best—all but one of these.

All this adds up to a formidable charge sheet. But it is necessary to question some of the premisses on which it is drawn up. The spectacle of a countryside dotted with ruined churches, while many parishes remained without a resident clergyman or a functioning place of Anglican worship, undoubtedly shocked contemporaries. McCracken quotes the comments of William Nicolson, just after he had gained his first experience of an Irish diocese by accompanying the bishop of Meath on a visitation in 1718:

The churches are wholly demolished in many of their parishes; which are therefore called non-cures; and several clergymen have (each of them) four or five, some six or seven of these. They commonly live at Dublin; leaving the conduct of their Popish parishioners to priests of their own persuasion.[150]

To Nicolson, fresh from a church which, despite its failings, still had real claims to be a national institution, all this was of course deplorable. Yet we may question whether the 'Popish parishioners' of these 'non-cures', whatever their other grievances, felt anything like as strongly about the absence from their lives of their nominal spiritual shepherds. Similarly, the 600 incumbents and 200 curates who were estimated to be serving in Ireland in 1728 were indeed wholly inadequate for a total population of some 2.5 million. But for an Anglican population of at most 250,000 they provided a perfectly respectable ratio of one clergyman to every 312 church members.[151] As for the ruined churches that so depressed the English visitor, these were the relics of a pre-Reformation church that had ministered to the population as a whole. The diocese of Meath in 1697 had indeed only 43 churches in repair out of a

[149] King to John Chamberlaine, 7 Oct. 1710 (TCD MS 2531, 207).

[150] Nicolson to Wake, 17 June 1718 (Gilbert MS 27, 177–8); McCracken in *NHI* iv. 87–8.

[151] Boulter to archbishop of Canterbury, 13 Feb. 1728 (*Letters*, i. 210); Boulter to Newcastle, 7 Mar. 1728 (ibid. 223). Even if we assume, unrealistically, that all 200 of the curates were deputizing for absentees, then the 600 serving parochial clergy would have provided 1 cleric for every 417 faithful.

total of 197. But with an Anglican population of perhaps 15,000, this meant that there were just under 350 potential worshippers to every church in repair. In the same way, Charles Smith's return of 126 churches in repair out of a total of 340 in the Munster counties of Waterford, Cork, and Kerry, another proof of ineffectiveness cited by McCracken, in fact translates into a provision of one functioning place of worship for every 300 to 350 Anglicans.[152]

In order to assess the pastoral effectiveness of the Church of Ireland, then, it is necessary to begin by shedding the assumption, common among contemporaries and unconsciously absorbed by more recent historians, that this should be measured in terms of potential provision for the population as a whole. It might, of course, be argued that this is too indulgent an approach. The Church of Ireland, after all, was not a voluntary body, but an established church, whose rivals were disadvantaged by law and to whose upkeep the whole population was required to contribute in fees and dues. But this is not really relevant. In the first place, it would be wrong to overstate the significance of the church's privileged status. In 1832 the gross parochial revenue of the Church of Ireland amounted to £610,653, of which more than £100,000 was in the hands of laymen. By contrast, landlords in the last years of the Napoleonic Wars are estimated to have received some £12 million a year in rents.[153] Similar calculations cannot be made for the early eighteenth century. But the £2,000 or so per year brought in by the most profitable Irish dioceses in the 1720s (see Table 5.2) was no more than the rent roll which a middle-ranking landowner like Dudley Cosby of Queen's County was able to achieve, through careful management, around the same time, and rather less than the £3,000 that a highly successful barrister, Anthony Malone, was reportedly earning within a few years of being called to the bar in 1726.[154] The number of clerical high earners, moreover, was small. King claimed in 1716 that not more than 200 out of the 600 beneficed clergy had incomes of more than £100 per year.[155] If the legal privileges of the Church of Ireland made it one of the predators that appropriated part of the wealth generated by

---

[152] For Meath, see Brady, 'Remedies', 164. The data from Smith's surveys are brought together in Mant, *Church of Ireland*, ii. 574, and are quoted by McCracken, *NHI* iv. 87. The population estimates are inevitably crude. They were obtained by using the following data from Dickson *et al.*, 'Hearth Tax': (1) Numbers of houses in counties Meath and Westmeath in 1706 and in counties Cork, Waterford, and Kerry in 1752, as returned by the hearth-tax collectors. (The diocese of Meath in fact takes in almost all of County Meath, most of Westmeath, a smaller part of County Kildare, and a very small part of County Dublin.) (2) A multiplier to correct for underrecording of houses. Since the aim is to test the possible inadequacy of Anglican pastoral provision, the upper-bound multiplier of 1.34 was chosen. (3) Regional estimates of average household size: Leinster (1706), 5.2; Munster (1749), 4.7. The Anglican share of the total population has been taken as the proportion of Protestants indicated by the *Abstract* of 1736. See Fig. 5.1 above.
[153] Akenson, *Church of Ireland*, 94; Cullen, *Emergence of Modern Ireland*, 44.
[154] Cosby, 'Autobiography', 171; Malone in *DNB*.
[155] King to Wake, 29 Mar. 1716 (TCD MS 2533, 181).

TABLE 5.2. Some gross episcopal revenues (Church of Ireland)

Diocese	Revenue (£)
Ardagh and Kilmore (1714)	1,600
(1727)	2,000
Clonfert (1727)	1,200–1,500
Derry (*c.*1720)	2,200
Dromore (1717)	900–1,000
Dublin (1723)	2,200
(1727)	2,650
Elphin (1720)	1,400–1,600
Ferns (1727)	1,600
Kildare + deanery of Christ Church (1727)	1,600
Killala (1717)	1,000
(1720)	900
Killaloe (1714)	800
(1745)	1,200
Raphoe (1714)	1,200
Waterford (1745)	1,400

Sources: Figures for 1714 for Ardagh and Kilmore, Killaloe, and Raphoe, King to archbishop of Canterbury, 30 Sept. 1714 (Mant, *Church of Ireland*, ii. 284–5); for Ardagh and Kilmore 1727, King to Carteret, 6 June 1727 (TCD MS 750/8, 204); for 1727 for Clonfert, Ferns, Kildare and deanery of Christ Church, Boulter to Newcastle, 18 Feb. 1727 (*Letters*, i. 139), and Boulter to bishop of London, 18 Feb., 16 Mar. 1727 (ibid. 142, 149); for Derry *c.*1720, *NHI* iv. 84; for Dromore 1717, Godwin to Wake, 31 Jan. 1717 (Wake MS XII, fo. 119); for Dublin 1723 and 1727, Kennedy, 'Administration of the Diocese of Dublin', 32–3; for 1720 for Elphin and Killala, Synge to Wake, 12 Apr. 1720 (Gilbert MS 28, 142–3); for Killala 1717, Godwin to Wake, 4 Jan. 1717 (Wake MS XII, fo. 106ᵛ); for 1745 for Killaloe and Waterford, Chesterfield to Newcastle, 29 Nov. 1745 (*Letters*, iii. 707–8).

the labouring masses, in other words, its share of the pickings was a fairly modest one. Secondly, and more important, a political or moral critique of the privileges enjoyed by the Church of Ireland, however valid in itself, can have no real bearing on an assessment of the quality of the pastoral services that the church provided to the minority who were its members.

From this revised perspective, contemporary perceptions of the Church of Ireland as crippled by inadequate resources are revealed as to some extent misleading. This is not to deny that there were genuine difficulties. In some

western dioceses, where revenues were at their lowest, the Anglican population especially thin, and the life-style offered to the resident clergyman
particularly uncongenial, the level of provision was by any standards inadequate. Kilmore, taking in most of County Cavan and part of Leitrim, had 28
beneficed clergy and 7 curates in 1697, but only 17 of these lived in the
diocese, and there were only 9 churches in repair. In Tuam in 1717 Edward
Synge found 14 resident clergymen, out of a total of 18 benefice-holders, and
only 10 churches, including the cathedral at Tuam, so that in two or three
parishes services were held in private houses.[156] In most cases, however, it is
likely that complaints of inadequate resources referred to difficulties of access,
rather than the level of overall provision. Archbishop Boulter in 1728 wrote of
'parishes eight and ten, twelve and fourteen miles long, with it may be only
one church in them, and that often at one end of the parish'.[157] But this
problem would have affected any denomination seeking to cater for a small
population scattered across a large area. And in these circumstances an
unestablished church that had nevertheless managed to provide a purpose-
built place of worship and a clergyman for every 3–400 of its members
across a large part of the country would probably have felt that it was doing
reasonably well.

If the material deficiencies of the Church of Ireland have been overstated,
what of the problems of absenteeism and neglect supposedly current among
the clergy at all levels? Here too it can be suggested that historians have not
always chosen their evidence as carefully as they might. The negative picture
of the Anglican clergy generally presented relies heavily on the comments of
two groups of observers: committed supporters of ecclesiastical reform on
the one hand and English clergymen experiencing their first taste of Irish
conditions on the other. Neither type of comment can be taken wholly on
trust. Newcomers like William Nicolson were likely to be struck initially by all
the ways in which the Irish church fell short of the standards of its English
counterpart. Once over the initial shock, however, they tended to adopt a
more balanced outlook. Certainly Nicolson quickly went on to take quite a
positive view of conditions in his new diocese of Derry.[158] Where reformers
are concerned, William King's voluminous, colourfully expressed, self-
righteous letters, spanning more than three decades, provide an irresistible
fund of quotation regarding the deficiencies of his fellow clergymen. Yet,
when King was not beating the drum of internal reform or sulking after
another initiative had not gone as he had wished, his comments on the clerical
rank and file were in fact more favourable than might be expected. In Derry,
during a visitation in 1693, 'I observed the clergy looked well, and are many of
them good men; I should not desire to change above four or five, if it were in

---

[156] Brady, 'Remedies', 164; Synge to Wake, 27 Sept. 1717 (Gilbert MS 28, 90–4).
[157] Boulter to archbishop of Canterbury, 13 Feb. 1728 (*Letters*, i. 210).
[158] Nicolson to Wake, 8 July 1718 (Gilbert MS 27, 181).

my power.' After visiting the whole province of Ulster on behalf of the primate in 1700, he reported: 'I do believe the clergy in the north were never more numerous, more industrious, and more learned than at this time. . . . Except in one diocese, I hardly found any liable to exception.' In Kildare, Leighlin, and Ossory, which he visited in his capacity as archbishop in 1712, 'I find the clergy very regular and diligent, but in a most miserable condition as to their maintenance.'[159]

In addition to being aware of the limitations of contemporary comment, it is necessary to place some of the disciplinary problems most frequently complained of in context. Plurality, for example, the simultaneous occupation of more than one benefice, was not always a consequence of greed. In many parishes, some or all of the tithes were either 'appropriate' (payable to senior officers of the church) or 'impropriate' (payable to laymen). In the diocese of Ferns in 1712 there were 99 parishes with tithes impropriate or appropriate, leaving only 32 whose income was available for the support of a ministering clergyman.[160] In such circumstances pluralities were the only way to make up even a barely adequate income. In Kildare, Leighlin, and Ossory, King reported, some of the clergy held eight, nine, or ten parishes while enjoying annual incomes of less than £40.[161]

Non-residence, too, was by no means always evidence of a lack of commitment. Ireland, as Archbishop Boulter pointed out, had 'few market towns that supply convenient food for the neighbourhood, nor farmers that can supply the common necessaries of life, which may be had at most farmers in England'. Hence, even committed reformers accepted the fact that it was often not practical to expect the clergy to reside in their parishes unless provided, as most were not, with parsonages and glebe land.[162] In addition to these practical difficulties, the rigours both of travel and of life in an underdeveloped countryside were a real deterrent. No less a person than Archbishop King warned his friend Edward Synge against travelling to his diocese of Tuam in winter, when 'want of lodgings will hinder you, and two or three nights ill lying . . . may be of ill consequence to you'. Philip Skelton, frequently cited as the exemplar of a conscientious parish clergyman, began, in his mid-sixties, to spend the winters in Drogheda and later in Dublin, rather than in his rural parish in County Tyrone. For the last seven years of his life, when he could no longer endure the twice-yearly journey, he lived

---

[159] King to Samuel Foley, 9 May 1693 (TCD MSS 1995–2008/274); King to Sir Robert Southwell, 19 Nov. 1700 (TCD MS 750/2/2, 17); King to Annesley, 3 June 1712 (TCD MS 750/4/1, 29).

[160] King to Annesley, 7 June 1712 (ibid. 34).

[161] King to Annesley, 3 June 1712 (ibid. 29).

[162] Boulter, *Letters*, i. 210. See also King's comment on Kildare, Leighlin, and Ossory: 'There's hardly a glebe in ten parishes, and where there is they are so small and lie so inconveniently that the clergy cannot reside or build on them, which they are well inclined to do' (King to Annesley, 3 June 1712, TCD MS 750/4/1, 29).

entirely in Dublin. Nor was it only the middle-aged and elderly who found the hardships of residence in rural Ireland more than an inconvenience. Edward Synge the younger recalled to his daughter how as a young child she had fallen ill during her first journey to his diocese of Elphin: 'The night you came here I would have given half I was worth that I had not brought you from town.'[163]

A degree of perspective is also necessary in considering another feature of the Church of Ireland that has attracted much negative comment. This is its involvement in the network of political patronage. The use of ecclesiastical appointments as prizes within the spoils system of both British and Irish public life, as well as to ensure the smooth management of government business in the Irish House of Lords, had obvious drawbacks. Archbishop King complained in 1715 of the difficulty of inducing the lower clergy to reside in their parishes and discharge their duties conscientiously, 'whilst that is not the way to ingratiate the practisers to the government and give them the views of great preferments'.[164] But the assumption that political appointees were necessarily either corrupt or negligent is a twentieth-century prejudice. Eighteenth-century patronage, precisely because it was neither shamefaced nor furtive, had its own rules of conduct, one of which was that persons appointed to offices that were more than sinecures should be at least competent to perform the duties involved. The duke of Grafton, forwarding a list of suggested episcopal appointments at the time of the Wood's halfpence crisis, felt obliged to apologize for the unusual dominance of considerations of political reliability: 'The times, I fear, are not so happy . . . as to allow of so much regard to that merit which is not accompanied with such qualifications as might otherwise be due.'[165] Even at this low point in the history of ecclesiastical patronage, furthermore, political and pastoral efficiency were not mutually exclusive. Theophilus Bolton, bishop of Clonfert, whom Grafton recommended for promotion as a man 'endowed with active parts applicable to business', was also a former protégé of Archbishop King, and was to go on combining an active political role with a high reputation as an ecclesiastical administrator.[166] In the same way, Hugh Boulter, appointed around the same time as a politically reliable archbishop of Armagh, combined his role as chief ecclesiastical champion of the English interest in Ireland with efforts to promote legislation favourable to the church, as well as giving vital support to the launching of the Charter Schools and at his death leaving most of his personal fortune for the provision of glebe lands and the augmentation of small benefices.

---

[163] King to Synge, 10 Sept. 1716 (TCD MS 2533, 299); Samuel Burdy, *The Life of the Rev. Philip Skelton*, in Skelton, *Works*, i. cvii–cviii, cxv; Edward Synge, Jun., to Alicia Synge, 9 May 1747 (Synge Papers).

[164] King to St George Ashe, 15 Sept. 1715 (TCD MS 2533, 83).

[165] Grafton to Carteret, 22 Mar. 1724 (SP 63/383/105ᵛ).

[166] Grafton to Carteret, 4 Mar. 1724 (SP 63/383/164ᵛ).

Having said all this, we are still left with the question of just how serious the problems of neglect, indifference, and delinquency complained of by contemporaries really were. The small number of reports of bishops' visitations surviving from the late seventeenth and early eighteenth centuries suggests that serious delinquency was in general less common than is often assumed. The diocese of Connor, for example, was inspected in 1693, just after the bishop, Thomas Hackett, had been deposed in the most serious ecclesiastical scandal of the period, following allegations of the sale of livings and a range of other offences.[167] Yet the findings were undramatic. One incumbent was admonished to adopt a more reserved dress, and one curate a more sober life; one vicar was to reside in his parish and take better care of the church; two were to provide curates, and two were said to keep curates who were inadequately qualified.[168] In Limerick a succession of blandly uneventful visitations from 1698 until 1704 was followed by what was clearly a much tougher inspection in 1707. Clergymen in no less than seventeen parishes were instructed to take better care of church buildings, furnishings, or the parish records. This, however, represented the greater part of the delinquency uncovered in the diocese. The only other offenders noted were a clergyman who was instructed to take up residence in his parish, two others who were required to provide Protestant schoolmasters, and one who was ordered to pay his curate by a specified date.[169] Other information on the specific question of non-residence also indicates that the problem, though real, should not be overstated. Of 50 beneficed clergymen in the diocese of Meath in 1693, 9 lived outside the diocese, 7 of them in Dublin. In Clogher 3 out of 22 incumbents recorded in 1700 lived outside the diocese, while in Raphoe the following year 18 out of 22 incumbents were resident.[170]

Any full assessment of pastoral effectiveness must take account of consumers as well as producers. Unfortunately, evidence regarding the religious attitudes and practice of the ordinary Anglican population is scattered and often difficult to assess. A Protestant pamphleteer of 1698 admitted that, although 'the generality' were wholly reliable in their hostility to Popery, 'very many of them can't in any tolerable order lay down their own principles'. By contrast, the evangelist George Whitefield, not yet the leader of a breakaway sect, was favourably impressed by the response when he visited Ireland in 1738. In Limerick he preached 'to a very numerous audience, who seemed universally affected'; in Dublin 'the people . . . not only hung upon me to hear me in the morning, but also flocked to the church where I preached in the

---

[167] King to Revd Samuel Foley, 14 Mar. 1694 (TCD MSS 1995–2008/340); King to James Bonnell, 21 Mar. 1694 (ibid. 341); abstract of charges against Hackett (PRONI T545/7).
[168] Visitation of Connor, 20 Feb. 1694 (RCB 31/5, 297–300).
[169] Visitation of Limerick, 28 Aug. 1707 (RCB D13/1/9).
[170] Loupes, 'Bishop Dopping's Visitation', 138–9; Visitation of Clogher, 1700 (RCB 61/6/3); King to Pooley, 1 June 1701 (TCD MS 750/2/2, 158).

afternoon, so that it was like a London congregation'.[171] A popular loyalty of some kind to the established church was also reflected in the violent hostility shown to Dissenters. Proposals to pillory Emlyn after his conviction for heresy in 1703 were turned down on the grounds that 'by reason of the great abhorrence the people had to his doctrine, this would be equal to death'. In 1726 a crowd wrecked what was described as the Bradelonian meeting-house in Dublin and badly beat up the preacher. Early Irish Methodists, like their English counterparts, also endured their share of mob violence.[172]

Some indication of levels of religious practice is provided by two visitation books from the early 1730s that note both the number of Anglicans in particular parishes and the number of Easter communicants (see Tables 5.3 and 5.4). Little weight can be placed on the figures for specific parishes, since many people, particularly given the prevalence of pluralities, would have taken communion outside the parish in which they lived. Also, it is not clear whether population totals, when expressed in terms of individuals rather than families, include children. Overall, however, the figures would suggest that around one person per household, or one-third to one-half of the adult Anglican population, took communion at Easter. This was well below the level to which churchmen aspired; but it nevertheless suggests something more than a merely vestigial popular piety. The figure of some 500 communicants at major festivals in Derry city cannot be related to any reliable population figure. But it compares favourably with the 300 Easter communicants that Bishop Nicolson recorded in the city nine years earlier. This in turn had been a marked improvement on conditions under Nicolson's absentee predecessor, when '74 were reckoned a vast number'.[173]

These statistics from Derry bring us to the final point to be considered: the question of change over time. Any account of either actions or mentalities must distinguish two periods: the reigns of William III and Anne on the one hand and the years after 1714 on the other. The first of these saw a concerted campaign for internal reform. As the Jacobite war came to an end, hopes were high that government could be persuaded to include in its programme of settlement and reconstruction a general overhaul of the Church of Ireland. Official and personal papers of the early and mid-1690s contain numerous suggested schemes, all built around the same basic points: a reorganization of church finances, a rationalization of parish structure, and the imposition of tighter internal discipline.[174] By the end of the decade, however, it had become clear that the government, despite the inclinations of some highly

---

[171] *Discourse on the Woollen Manufactory of Ireland*, 4; Whitefield, *Journals*, 182, 184.

[172] Harrison to Strype, 30 June 1703 (Strype Correspondence, III, fos. 118–19); *Dublin Intelligence*, 13 Sept. 1726; Fagan, *Second City*, 125–6.

[173] Nicolson to Wake, 10 Apr. 1724 (Gilbert MS 27, 346).

[174] e.g. TCD MSS 1995–2008/115a; Portland Papers, PwA 2374; Brady, 'Remedies'. For a general discussion of reform efforts, see Beckett, 'The Government and the Church of Ireland under William III and Anne'.

TABLE 5.3. Easter communions in the diocese of Ossory, 1731–2

Parish	Number of persons	Number of families	Number of communicants
St Mary's, Kilkenny	397		120–30
Comer	80		40
Eirke		23	15
Donoghmore		5	5
Aghavo		30	7
Skirke		7	7
Offerelane		42	40
Attanagh		5	20
Kiltranine		5	30
Callan		40	80
St Canice's, Kilkenny		50	150

Source: State of the diocese of Ossory, 1731–2 (Nat. Arch. Ire. M2462).

TABLE 5.4. Communicants in the diocese of Derry, *c*.1733

Parish	Number of persons	Number of families	Number of communicants
Templemore			500
Culdaff		40	50
Donagh	50		20
Clonleigh		80	80
Ardstraw		104	100–16
Kilcronaghan		13	15

Source: Visitation book, diocese of Derry *c*.1733 (RCB GS 2/7/3/34). The figure for Templemore refers to communicants 'at great festivals'. The figures for other parishes refer simply to communicants, the sacrament being said in each case to be administered four times a year.

placed individuals, would never be brought to undertake anything as burdensome and contentious as a general programme of church reform. Attention turned instead to the prospect of change from within, to be achieved through Convocation. Again, expectations were initially high. In 1705 William King offered the prolocutor of the forthcoming session a detailed list of the reforms he believed could be enacted: measures to enforce clerical residence, to limit pluralities, and to punish delinquent clergymen; better provision for the maintenance of curates in large parishes and in appropriated and impropriated livings; and closer scrutiny of the character and qualifications of those seeking ordination. In the event, however, Convocation proved more interested in the increasingly shrill defence of the church's privileges against parliament, Dissenters, and Whig lords lieutenant than in self-scrutiny or self-improvement. The whole practical outcome of the four Convocations that met between 1703 and 1711 consisted of some canons relating to the workings of the ecclesiastical courts and three new forms of prayer to be used by those visiting prisoners.[175]

After 1714 the Church of Ireland, like its English counterpart, had to adjust to a radically different climate. With the eclipse of the Tories, the grandiose notions of the church's status built up by their High Church allies lost credibility. Convocation, the visible symbol of earlier pretensions to the status of a self-governing corporation, was not recalled in either kingdom after the death of Queen Anne. As well as expecting churchmen to know their place, the Whig ministries that monopolized power under the first two Georges made unprecedentedly systematic use of their control of church appointments, from the point of view of both the exploitation of ecclesiastical patronage and the extension of political control. The result was a definite change in outlook, at least at the church's upper levels. Already by the 1730s, as was seen earlier, the bishops could no longer be counted on to lead the lower clergy against the proposed repeal of the test. Two decades later, Archbishop Ryder of Tuam, expressing his approval of the English Marriage Act of 1753, offered vivid testimony to just how far episcopal attitudes had changed since the days not just of Highflyers like Perceval and Lindsay, but also of William King or Edward Synge.

Religion as you say can have nothing to do with the question, what forms shall be submitted to in order to a valid marriage, but whenever religion is dragged into a question it seldom fails with some men to darken what would be otherwise plain and obvious.[176]

Meanwhile, the apparently united front of theological conservatism that had been maintained in the reigns of William III and Anne had also been weakened. By the mid-1730s the bench of bishops now included at least three men of reputed heterodox views: John Hoadley, archbishop of Dublin; Thomas Rundle, dispatched to Derry after his appointment to an English diocese had been blocked on account of his dubious opinions; and Robert Clayton, bishop of Cork and Ross and later of Clogher, against whom formal proceedings for heresy had actually begun at the time of his death in 1758.[177]

---

[175] King to Samuel Synge, 16 Jan. 1705 (TCD MS 750/3/1, 67–72); Mant, *Church of Ireland*, ii. 230–3.

[176] Ryder to Sir Dudley Ryder, 31 July 1753 (PRONI T3228/1/56).

[177] Johnston, 'Problems Common to both Catholic and Protestant Churches', 24–8. For Clayton, see Winnett, 'An Irish Heretic Bishop'. Johnston suggests that Irish sees were to some extent used to limit the influence of Latitudinarianism in the English church, by providing

In the decades after 1714, then, the Irish church became both less rigidly orthodox and more erastian in outlook. It would be easy to assume that the impulse towards internal reform that had been evident in the years after 1690 had likewise dwindled and died away. But in fact this was not the case. If committed churchmen no longer aspired to a total pastoral and moral renewal of the kind envisaged in the aftermath of the Revolution, concern for the improvement of standards continued to be expressed. In 1728 the Irish executive, working closely with Boulter, introduced legislation to facilitate the provision of chapels of ease, glebes, and clerical residences; to permit the division and union of parishes; and to provide for the better maintenance of curates. There were also unsuccessful attempts between 1724 and 1732 to introduce bills to penalize non-resident clergy. Outside parliament, Boulter obtained some support in 1724 for a scheme by which voluntary contributions from bishops and clergy throughout the country could be used to augment the fund for the purchase of glebes and impropriations, although the project eventually collapsed through lack of support.[178] Such initiatives were more limited in scope than the projects of an earlier generation; but that may be seen as a reflection of greater realism rather than of diminished commitment.

In some respects, indeed, it is possible that the general level of interest in reform and improvement grew rather than diminished in the years after 1714. William King, the key figure in the reform movement of the post-war years, maintained in 1723 that the church was in a better state than when he had become a bishop in 1691. 'I have now the archbishop of Tuam and several other bishops that join heartily with me, whereas at first I had hardly any who durst own my schemes, and several who not only opposed them violently but made it their business to expose and ridicule them.' The following year he noted at the end of his triennial visitation that the province of Dublin was 'in much better condition' than it had been three years before.[179] Evidence of increased expectations may also be seen in the comments of the recently appointed bishop of Down and Connor, who reported in 1746 that he had taken a house in Rasharkin, County Antrim, partly to benefit his own and his children's health, but also because he 'found it was unavoidable not to reside some considerable part of my time in my diocese, in regard to the expectations of my clergy'.[180] More detailed information available for the diocese of Dublin confirms that, although the most dramatic expansion in pastoral provision came in the first three decades of the eighteenth century, there was further

---

appointments for candidates whose principles were suspect but who could not be passed over because of their personal or political connections. Something of the kind certainly happened in the case of Rundle: see Mant, *Church of Ireland*, ii. 537–9.

[178] Boulter, *Letters*, i. 5–6, 210–25; Mant, *Church of Ireland*, ii. 474–82, 430–4.

[179] King to Wake, 8 June 1723 (TCD MS 750/7, 349–50); King to Josiah Hort, bishop of Ferns, 29 Dec. 1724 (TCD MS 2537, 174).

[180] Ryder to Sir Dudley Ryder, 11 Feb. 1746 (PRONI T3228/1/22).

improvement thereafter. In Dublin city, for example, 6 new parishes had been created by the 1740s to meet rising demand, while the number of churches fit for use rose from 9 in 1729 to 18 by 1766. In the diocese as a whole the number of clergy rose from between 87 and 100 in the early eighteenth century to between 115 and 120 by 1753.[181] None of this, of course, came near to realizing the self-imposed ideal of a national church. But it does confirm that the ambitious reform schemes of the 1690s and early 1700s gave way, not to apathy and stagnation, but to a quieter concern with the maintenance and gradual improvement of pastoral services.

5. Christians

The habit of thinking in centuries is pernicious but hard to break. The seventeenth century is the age of faith and religious wars, the eighteenth of secularization and the Enlightenment. Yet it has long been clear that any such simple division is wholly inadequate. In the case of Catholicism we now know that it was only in the early or even the middle decades of the eighteenth century that the high tide of a regenerated Counter-Reformation piety reached some regions. Protestantism, too, showed a continued capacity for renewal, in the Pietism that flourished in Prussia and elsewhere from the late seventeenth century, in the surge of enthusiasm for missionary efforts overseas and for evangelization and moral improvement at home that appeared among English Protestants in the 1690s and early 1700s, and in the later attempts at regeneration that eventually developed into Methodism. The eighteenth century as a whole did indeed see a secularization of attitudes, among the educated at least, in Catholic and Protestant countries alike. But in the first half of the century in particular it would be wrong to underestimate either the strength of conventional beliefs and attitudes or the capacity for real religious enthusiasm.

What is true of Western Europe in general applies also to Ireland. The continued hold of Catholicism on the hearts and minds of the majority of the lower classes is well known. Irish Presbyterianism also appears to have maintained both a strong communal identity and a firm social discipline throughout the eighteenth century. Even in the Church of Ireland, as we have just seen, levels of religious practice were higher than has often been assumed. And if we turn from the population as a whole to the social and political élite, all the signs are that there, too, conventional Christian religious belief continued to play a central role in the lives of men and women.

Two reasons may be suggested to explain why the religious life of the élite

---

[181] Kennedy, 'The Administration of the Diocese of Dublin', 45, 47–51, 102, 156–7, 160–2, 172–3.

has tended to be ignored or undervalued. The first is the undue credence that has been given to the literary stereotype of the Irish landed class as drunken, violent, and licentious.[182] The second is the distinctly unfriendly attitude that a large section of that class displayed towards its own church. To some extent this hostility reflected a straightforward economic rivalry between landlord and parson for the tenant farmer's profits. In 1736, for example, observers of the vigorous and ultimately successful agitation of the country gentry against the levying of tithes on cattle reported 'a rage stirred up against the clergy that they thought equalled anything they had seen against the Popish priests, in the most dangerous times they remembered'.[183] But two other considerations helped to legitimize the self-interest of landlord and middleman. First, the partisan Tory politics of the great majority of the lower clergy in the years immediately before and after 1714 contributed to their unpopularity with a predominantly Whig gentry. Alan Brodrick was alleged to have told Bishop Lindsay early in the reign of Queen Anne that 'he hoped to live to see the day when there should not be one of his order in the kingdom'.[184] Secondly, there was the contrast between the privileges claimed by the Church of Ireland and its all too obvious moral and pastoral failings. William King, while complaining bitterly of parliamentary encroachments on the rights of the church, nevertheless admitted that the real reason why the laity 'are so hard upon us' was 'our acting so much as men of the world'.[185]

Hostility to the church and its servants, however, was not the same as religious indifference. Such indifference did of course exist. John Dunton, attending a service in Christ Church, Dublin, in 1698, professed to be shocked to see 'all sorts of men walking in the aisles' and 'some rustling, powdered beaus swearing with as little concern as in a coffee house', while 'men of business make it too often their Sunday exchange'. In the late 1730s there were complaints of a Hell-Fire club devoted to blasphemy and debauchery.[186] Yet it is also clear from casual references that formal prayer was a standard part of the domestic routine of many upper-class households in the early and mid-eighteenth century. 'Prayer time' in the Kildare household at Carton on a Monday in 1748 was one o'clock; the widow of William Conolly 'had prayers every day at twelve'; a visitor to the Rawdons at Moira, County Antrim, in 1758 reported 'constant prayers'. In the same way, Dudley Cosby of Queen's County, who died in 1729, 'held the keeping of the Christian Sabbath, seldom or never missed public worship and had most every night worship in his own family, reading the scriptures of the Old and New

---

[182] See ch. 2, sect. 3.

[183] Boulter to earl of Anglesey, 8 June 1736 (*Letters*, ii. 192).

[184] Mant, *Church of Ireland*, ii. 185–6.

[185] King to Ashe, 17 Aug. 1704 (TCD MS 750/3/1, 15–16); same to same, 7 Apr. 1705 (ibid. 136).

[186] Dunton, in MacLysaght, *Irish Life*, 381; Lecky, *History of Ireland*, i. 323–4.

Testament, and on Sabbath days other good books, and singing of psalms and reading of prayers'.[187] Despite widespread hostility to tithes, equally, laymen were prepared to contribute to religious causes. Even Archbishop King was led to admit in 1713 that 'charity is not lost out of the hearts of men', instancing the £14,000 sterling that had been contributed for church building since he had come to the diocese of Dublin ten years earlier.[188]

Such gestures were not, of course, motivated by piety alone. The utility of religion as a support for social order was after all a commonplace of the age. Bishop Dopping of Meath, in the 1670s, recommended to masters of families that they conduct regular prayers, 'upon the score of profit and peace (if for no other motive) . . . that this will be the way to make their children dutiful . . . ; that servants will be more faithful and diligent, when they do their duty out of conscience and not for profit'. 'I am sure you will have a sober family,' the young Sir John Perceval was advised a few years later, 'and to have prayers constantly said will, besides the great benefit, keep them regular.'[189] Participation in public or household worship could also be an assertion of status. Dudley Cosby, for example, not only financed substantial improvements to the local parish church, but also erected a gallery with five pews, 'the middle for himself, and the two on the east for his maidservants and the two on the north side for his menservants'.[190] No doubt his leadership of regular household prayers had the same effect of reinforcing his patriarchal authority.

At the same time the tone of private correspondence indicates that upper-class religiosity was more than a façade for the benefit of servants and underlings. Sir St John Brodrick appears to have been a fairly hardliving County Cork gentleman, and his sons were Whig politicians, lawyers, and businessmen. Yet his daughter's account of his last days, in February 1712, is of a model Christian deathbed:

He talked as well upon most things as any man, and not upon any better than religion. The season of the year made that the subject when Mr Edgley visited him. He did not foresee his death, but however he desired him to pray by him which he did. He in his illness was prayed with by several. . . . He died with a thorough faith in Jesus Christ and sincere repentance and has a great many good works to follow him.[191]

In 1738 Michael Ward, another Whig office-holder, began a letter of advice intended to be given after his death to his son with the reminder that 'your only business in this world is, first, to secure to yourself eternal happiness in

[187] Fitzgerald, *Emily, Duchess of Leinster*, 28; Delany, *Autobiography and Correspondence*, iii. 159, 526; Cosby, 'Autobiography', 180.

[188] King to Thomas Wentworth, 13 Oct. 1713 (TCD MS 750/4/1, 213–14).

[189] 'Rules proposed to myself in the visiting of my parishioners' (MS Dopping Notebook, 232–3); Sir Robert Southwell to Sir John Perceval, 16 May 1682 (HMC, *Egmont Papers*, ii. 114).

[190] Cosby, 'Autobiography', 170. For a similar arrangement in County Down, see John Savage to ——, 24 Sept. [1733] (PRONI D552/A/2/2/46).

[191] K. Whitfeld to Alan Brodrick, 13 Feb. [1712] (Midleton MS 1248/3, fo. 68ᵛ).

the next life, and secondly as far as it is consistent with this, to endeavour to obtain the comforts and conveniences of this world'. He went on to offer several paragraphs of exhortation on virtue and religious duty, before turning to advice on financial affairs, estate management, and marriage.[192]

Alongside such expressions of a conventional but to all appearances genuine piety must be set the appearance in Ireland of the same movement for spiritual renewal and moral reform that was seen among English Protestants in the 1690s and early 1700s. Around 1695 four or five 'societies of young men ... after the manner of those in London' were established in Dublin, meeting on Sunday evenings for prayer and discussion.[193] By 1697–8 those involved had, like their English counterparts, moved on from pious exercises to a campaign for the reform of manners, concentrating their efforts against prostitution and swearing. 'Vice', a High-Church clergyman reported, 'is prosecuted very vigorously among us', and there had been 'a visible decrease of all lewdness and profaneness'.[194] These efforts received at least some support from the civil authorities. Parliament in 1695 had enacted new penalties for swearing, while John Dunton praised the recorder of Dublin for 'severely putting the law in execution against lewd and wicked people, without regard to any degree of quality or riches'. Swearers were fined or put in the stocks, while 'many of the strolling, courteous ladies of the town have by his orders been forced to expose their lily white skin down to the waist at a cart's tail'. A poem written a few years later noted similar efforts, though with rather less confidence than Dunton in the impartial application of the law: 'Poor Paddy swears his whole week's gains away/While my young squires blaspheme and nothing pay.'[195]

If the influence of religion in the lives of the Protestant élite of the late seventeenth and early eighteenth centuries has been too often underestimated, the same may be said of their Catholic counterparts. The main reason in this case has been the eventual willingness of the majority of Catholic landowners to conform to the Church of Ireland. The spectacle of mass apostasy, combined with the self-image subsequently developed by Catholic historians of a church uniquely dependent on the poor and oppressed, encourages the impression of a cynical and religiously indifferent landed élite. But that does little justice to the complexity of the motives and attitudes involved. If considerations of material opportunity had been enough in themselves to destroy the Catholicism of the propertied classes, Catholic landownership

---

[192] PRONI D2092/1/7/121.

[193] Bonnell to Strype, 6 May 1695, 6 May 1696 (Strype Correspondence, I, fos. 117–18, 121ᵛ).

[194] Theophilus Harrison to Strype, 16 July 1698, 13 Oct. 1697 (Strype Correspondence, III, fos. 431ᵛ, 424ᵛ).

[195] Dunton, *Teague Land*, 70; Revd James Ward, 'The Smock Race at Finglas' (n.d. but clearly written in the reign of Anne), quoted in Fagan, *Second City*, 83. See also Bonnell to Strype, 25 Jan. 1699 (Strype Correspondence, I, fo. 126).

would have ceased to exist long before 1689. In 1694 Kean O'Hara of County Sligo reported to a highly placed relative that there was no prospect of finding a young man among 'our Roman Catholic friends of our name' for the latter to take under his protection: 'I am afraid their natural principles are such, that they had rather have their children live miserable all their days than consent to have them bred Protestants and be preferred in the world.'[196] The Popery Act of 1704, threatening not just disadvantage but the destruction, through subdivision or alienation, of entire family estates, was a different matter. The Catholic aristocracy and gentry were now forced to choose between two essential elements in their social identity, religion and land. That they generally chose the latter should not be taken to mean that they were indifferent to the claims of the former. In 1732 John Savage of County Down, himself part of a family containing many converts, wrote feelingly in support of an acquaintance who had conformed in order to preserve an estate that had been in his family for 600 years, 'in hopes that God might pardon it on such an emergency, as we trust He will our other daily transgressions'. Edward Rice conformed on the death of his father Sir Stephen Rice in 1716, in order to inherit the family lands intact. Yet witnesses later testified that before his death in 1720 he had declared his intention of selling the estate and going to France 'to live comfortably a Roman Catholic'.[197]

This is not to say that the Catholic upper classes were uniform models of piety and moral behaviour. No doubt standards varied. The English middle-class Jacobite John Stevens was shaken by the licentiousness he witnessed in Dublin during the time it served as King James's last capital in the winter of 1689–90. On the other hand, Viscount Sarsfield, in the field with the Jacobite army in September 1689, instructed his wife that 'there may be a mass said to the Holy Ghost daily desiring the exaltation and maintaining of the Roman Catholic church and our good return with victory'. Writing in 1726 to John Savage, who was depressed by the charges encumbering the family estate, the Catholic lawyer Edward Malone offered, with apparent sincerity, a religious consolation: 'I am the worst of doctors for prescribing any worldly remedy or cure for such a distemper, but I can put you in mind of the answer made by our Saviour to the rich young gentleman or nobleman in the gospel.'[198] Some credit for active religious commitment, even if mixed with the quest for prestige, must also be given to those merchants in Limerick, Dublin, and elsewhere who endowed Catholic churches with lavish altars and other expensive accessories.[199]

---

[196] Kean O'Hara to Sir Charles O'Hara, 5 Jan. 1695 (PRONI T2812/8/2).

[197] Savage to ——, 22 Mar. 1730 (PRONI D552/A/2/2/18); notes on Norton V. Rice (PRONI D562/707).

[198] Stevens, *Journal*, 92–3; Simms, 'Lord Kilmallock's Letters to his Wife', 138; Malone to Savage, 28 May 1726 (PRONI D552/A/2/2/3).

[199] White, 'Annals of Limerick' (NLI MS 2714), 166; Pococke, *Tour*, 175; Fagan, *Second City*, 127–32.

If the conventional piety of many members of the élite, both Catholic and Protestant, undermines any idea that this was a secularized society, so too do the more exotic beliefs that circulated at all social levels. Ireland, like England, was affected by the wave of millenarian excitement introduced in the first years of the eighteenth century by Protestant refugees from France. In 1709 Jane Bonnell reported the appearance in Dublin of two 'prophets', although she did not expect them to last long, 'for we are pretty severe upon things that are out of the common road'.[200] The following year the city's life was further enlivened by the arrival of Sir Richard Bulkeley. Bulkeley, though a Fellow of the Royal Society and a member of the Irish parliament, was already noted for his eccentricities, among them his plan of a few years before to establish a university on his estate at Dunlavan, County Wicklow. He had now come under the influence of a French-inspired prophet, who was engaged in persuading him to sell his property and give the proceeds to the poor and who was also reported to have promised him supernatural protection if he would burn his house and walk through the flames.[201] Others were infected by the same spirit. Archbishop King had to reprimand a clergyman in County Sligo for having 'raised up the condemned heresy of the millenaries and infected many with it, and occasioned great disorders in the minds of some and prejudices against their teachers'.[202] Later unorthodox movements included a sect established in 1704 by a tradesman named Bradley (apparently the same one that had its meeting-house wrecked twenty-two years later) and a group reported in 1730 whose members paraded the streets naked.[203]

These, of course, were the more exotic fringes of contemporary belief. But educated and in some cases influential men also revealed in less dramatic ways their willingness to accept the direct, literal intervention of the supernatural in daily life. The description of Iar Connacht prepared in 1684 for William Molyneux by the Catholic antiquary Roderick O'Flaherty includes an account of the fatal consequences which befell two sailors who had refused to pay the customary respect to a local saint as their boats passed his shrine. O'Flaherty also noted the numerous sightings of the mysterious island of O Brasil: 'Whether it be real and firm land kept hidden by special ordinance of God as the terrestrial paradise, or else some illusion of airy clouds appearing on the surface of the sea, or the craft of evil spirits, is more than our judgements can sound out.' Another of Molyneux's correspondents, John Keogh in County Roscommon, sent a detailed account of one of the stone

---

[200] Jane Bonnell to Strype, 25 Oct. 1709 (Strype Correspondence, III, fo. 270).

[201] John Stearne to King, 16, 25 Feb. 1710 (TCD MSS 1995–2008/1352, 1354). For Bulkeley's career, see *DNB*; Harrison, *Second Coming*, 25–6. For the university at Dunlavan, see TCD MS 883/2, 87.

[202] King to Edward Nicolson, 24 May, 12 June 1707 (TCD MS 750/3/2, 122, 128–9).

[203] King to Revd Charles Whittingham, 31 Oct. 1704 (TCD MS 750/3/1, 48); *Dublin Intelligence*, 10 July 1730.

darts with which the fairies were reported 'to strike man or beast with some occult wound or distemper'. He went on to ask Molyneux's opinion on 'the true cause of this phenomenon strange to me, and to inform me if it be commonly received by the learned in experiments as a certain and undoubted experiment [*sic*] of the operation of spirits or of other causes'.[204] Archbishop King argued in 1713 that the misfortunes recently endured by France and Spain were in part a punishment for the participation of those kingdoms in the slave trade: 'Such violence, oppression and murder must bring the curse of God on the guilty.' Alan Brodrick believed that he had been forewarned, by dreams and other signs, of the death of his brother St John in 1707.[205]

There was one area in which popular and élite conceptions of the workings of the supernatural came together. This was with regard to witchcraft. Ireland, even in the sixteenth and seventeenth centuries, did not have a well-developed tradition of witchcraft prosecutions. Yet the handful of cases that did occur, such as the trial of Florence Newton at Cork in 1661, make clear that this was not because of any lack of belief on the part of the authorities. Acceptance of the reality of witchcraft persisted in fact to the end of the seventeenth century and beyond. When a gentleman's son in Cork was attacked by dangerous convulsive fits in 1686, his mother and several others believed that he had been bewitched by a woman whom his father had recently imprisoned, although the father himself had 'not faith to believe it was anything but the hand of God'.[206] In 1693 Bishop King drafted a letter to the authorities at Salem, Massachusetts, suggesting that the outbreak of witchcraft there was a result of the inhabitants having abandoned the formula of renouncing the devil and his works at baptism.[207] A witch is said to have been executed in County Antrim in 1699, although the legal records that would confirm the report do not survive. If so, this was fourteen years later than the last legal execution for witchcraft in England, though seven years earlier than the last such event in Scotland.[208]

Any remaining doubt regarding official acceptance of the reality of witchcraft is dispelled by the celebrated trial that took place in County Antrim in 1711. This arose out of the allegations of a teenage girl, Mary Dunbar of

[204] TCD MS 883/1, 16–17, 121–2, 129–30.

[205] King to Francis Annesley, 14 Apr. 1713 (TCD MS 750/4/1, 141–2); Alan Brodrick to ——, 5 Aug. 1707 (Midleton MS 1248/2, fo. 316).

[206] Christopher Crofts to Sir John Perceval, 15 Mar. 1686 (HMC, *Egmont Papers*, ii. 181–2).

[207] King to ——, n.d. (TCD MSS 1995–2008/300). The letter was intended to be sent anonymously. Salem is not mentioned by name, but it seems clear that this was what King was referring to.

[208] Lecky, *History of Ireland*, i. 412–13. Lecky's source is Thomas Crofton Croker, writing in *Dublin Penny Journal*, 1 (1843), 341, who in turn draws on a contemporary pamphlet account. For England and Scotland, see Thomas, *Religion and the Decline of Magic*, 537; Larner, *Enemies of God*, 78.

Island Magee, who blamed her convulsions, temporary loss of speech, and a range of other symptoms, on a group of women who came by supernatural means to torment and threaten her. Eight women whom she identified were tried and convicted, being sentenced to a year's imprisonment and to stand four times in the pillory; the husband of one of the eight was also later convicted as an accomplice. Exactly what lay behind these events remains unclear. The local population seems to have been convinced of the guilt of the accused; one observer's reference to their 'frequent vaunts and threats of their own revenge and power' suggests that they may, like other victims of witchcraft accusations, have brought their fate on themselves, by seeking to cultivate a reputation as persons possessing some sort of magical abilities. But whatever the background, the response of the authorities, civil and religious, was unambiguous. A Presbyterian minister and at least one local landlord took an active part in the investigation of Mary Dunbar's accusations. William Tisdall, vicar of Belfast, accepted the supernatural nature of the happenings, although he believed that the accused should not have been convicted, since it was perfectly possible for the Devil to have assumed the shape of innocent persons. Of the two judges who presided at the trial, one accepted that the events reported had been of supernatural and diabolical origin, but argued that the accused could not be convicted 'upon the sole testimony of the afflicted person's visionary images'. The other told the jury that the evidence was sufficient to allow them to find the accused guilty of witchcraft.[209]

[209] [McSkimmin, ed.], *Narrative of Some Strange Events*, 53–7; copies of depositions relating to the case of Mary Dunbar (TCD MS 883/2, 273–84); Samuel Molyneux to Thomas Molyneux, 14 May 1711 (TCD MS 889, fo. 30). Samuel Molyneux, who sent the depositions to his uncle, reported that, in addition to their evidence, 'the judges related to me several much more convincing circumstances which appeared on the trial' and which made clear that 'many supernatural appearances did happen to Mrs Dunbar'.

6

Law and the Maintenance of Order

'There is no doubt, that if the poor should reason, "We'll be the poor no longer, we'll make the rich take their turn", they could easily do it, were it not that they can't agree.'[1] The issue raised by Samuel Johnson has become a central concern of the modern social historian. A steadily expanding literature on crime, law, and social control has sought to explore the ways in which, in societies marked by enormous inequalities, the few were able to maintain their rule over the many. In the case of Ireland, the question has an added point. The seventeenth century had seen the overthrow of one élite by another. In the struggles by which that overthrow was accomplished, the common people had overwhelmingly taken the side of the losers. So how did the victors maintain their position, once the fighting was over? Was Ireland a conquered country, held down by force? If so, what were the means of coercion? If not, how was order in fact maintained?

1. Resources

For most of the eighteenth century the maintenance of order was based on the institutions, transplanted from England, of the self-policing society. The backbone of the system was the service of men of property as justices of the peace, acting both as the lowest level of the judiciary and as the main agents of local law enforcement. A return in 1760 counted 2,024 justices,[2] although evidence from the early nineteenth century would suggest that only a minority of these, perhaps as few as one in five, would have taken an active part in routine law enforcement.[3] Two hundred and twenty of those listed were clergymen of the Church of Ireland; another 6 were attorneys. The great majority of the remainder were presumably landed gentlemen. Urban areas, meanwhile, had their own commissions of the peace, giving executive and judicial powers to the mayor and aldermen, as well as empowering a salaried lawyer to preside, as recorder, in the local court.

To assist them in the discharge of their duties, justices of the peace and urban magistrates could call on local constables and watchmen. Medieval

---

[1] Boswell, *Life of Johnson*, 423.   [2] Gilbert MS 34, 181.
[3] Palmer, *Police and Protest*, 60; 622, n. 102.

legislation, revised and supplemented by an Act of 1715, required each parish to appoint a constable, with, in addition, a high constable for each barony. Towns were also required to appoint an adequate number of watchmen to patrol the streets at night, at least during the months from September to March. In some cases at least, these would be armed with halberds, half-pikes, or similar weapons.[4] Rural parishes were also supposed to have a night watchman, though it is doubtful whether many actually did.[5] In theory, all Protestant heads of household were eligible to take their turn as constables and watchmen. In practice, the latter were usually paid employees, although the wage was in general too low to make service a full-time employment.

For more effective support in the exercise of their duties, magistrates and other officials could look to the army and the militia. An English Act of 1699 fixed the size of the regular army at 12,000 men in Ireland and 7,000 in England. These figures, however, should not be taken at face value. The limits were imposed following a major parliamentary confrontation, in which opposition politicians had successfully appealed to traditional Country principles to frustrate King William's plans to maintain a substantial force under arms following the end of the war with France in 1697. In the case of Ireland, the limit first proposed had been 8,000 men, but this was objected to as too low, given the disaffection and numerical superiority of the Catholics and the threat of a French or Spanish invasion. MPs who had estates in Ireland were said all to be in favour of a higher limit.[6] To what extent such fears were genuine and to what extent supporters of the ministry were simply trying to maximize the overall military resources left to the crown remains unclear. But in practice, at least, the Irish military establishment quickly came to be used as a reserve, to be drawn on for service wherever troops were needed.

Those soldiers who were stationed in Ireland were there to defend against both foreign invasion and domestic rebellion. Under a scheme approved by parliament in 1698 and implemented over the next few years, the entire Irish army was housed in barracks, rather than quartered among the civilian population, as was often the case in England. This was partly a response to the practical difficulties of finding satisfactory private accommodation in a country where the towns were small and the quality of housing poor. 'There is not a public house in the kingdom', it was pointed out in 1692, 'able to give an officer credit for a week', while ordinary troops, scattered in ones and twos in the cabins of the peasantry, were vulnerable both to attack and to the erosion

---

[4] Starr, 'The Enforcing of Law and Order in Eighteenth-Century Ireland', 26–100; McDowell, *Ireland in the Age of Imperialism and Revolution*, 67.

[5] Cf. the complaints of the government during the Hougher outrages of 1711–12 that 'watch and ward' were not kept nightly 'as the nature of the case shall require, and the laws of the land do appoint and permit': Connolly, 'Law, Order and Popular Protest', 54.

[6] For an account of the debate, see Hayton, 'Debates in the House of Commons 1697–1699', 366–7.

of discipline.[7] But the need to protect against internal troubles also played a part. English barracks were concentrated along the south coast, where an invading army was most likely to appear. Those in Ireland, on the other hand, were distributed throughout the country. But the contrast with England should not be pushed too far. The Irish barracks built around 1700 were plain residential buildings, quite different from the fortified structures being erected about the same time as part of the pacification of the Scottish Highlands.[8]

Although the Irish army was seen as having a more important role in internal security than was the case in England, furthermore, this did not necessarily imply its use for day-to-day law enforcement. The duke of Bedford, in 1758, was 'sorry to be obliged to say' that the internal peace of the kingdom 'cannot well be secured without a strong military force'. What this meant in practice, however, was the maintenance of substantial garrisons in the major towns 'for the security of the Protestant inhabitants'.[9] To use soldiers for routine policing was more problematic. At least some Irish gentlemen shared the traditional English view that standing armies were a threat to the liberty of the subject. Opponents of the Barracks Bill of 1699 objected that 'barracks and redoubts were French engines of slavery and platforms for arbitrary power'. As late as 1756 a writer defending proposals to build a series of fortresses along the south coast felt obliged to counter the argument that 'the consequence of such strongholds in the hands of the government must be more terrible to a land of freedom than the ravages of a transient invader'. The earl of Charlemont, pressed to send for troops to quell an outbreak of trouble in County Armagh in 1779, replied that 'there is nothing from which I am more averse than the interference of the military in matters of a civil nature', and refused to act until 'every possible constitutional method' had first been tried.[10]

More important than Whig scruples of this kind was the attitude of government itself. Putting troops on active service and quartering them away from their usual barracks was expensive. There was also the risk that making military aid too easily available would encourage magistrates and gentry to

---

[7] Sydney to Nottingham, 2 Sept. 1692 (*CSPD 1695*, 198); Orrery to Ormond, 22 Nov. 1678 (Wyche Papers, 1/1/25); Joshua Dawson to Major Francis, 5 Apr. 1712 (Country Letters, fo. 29ᵛ).

[8] Palmer, *Police and Protest*, 62; Ferguson, 'The Army in Ireland', 79–80. The only exceptions were the fortified 'redoubts' built in remote areas during the campaign against the tories, and mainly abandoned by *c*.1720.

[9] Bedford to Pitt, 29 Aug. 1758 (Bedford, *Correspondence*, ii. 363). See also Bedford to Archbishop Stone, 22 May 1759 (ibid. 374).

[10] King to——, 2 Feb. 1699 (TCD MS 750/2/1, 63); *Belfast News Letter*, 20 Feb. 1756; Smyth, 'The Volunteer Movement in Ulster', 29–31; HMC, *Charlemont Manuscripts*, i. 350–2. Charlemont also criticized as 'by no means necessary' the drafting in of troops to suppress the Oakboy disturbances in the county in 1763: ibid. 141.

send for soldiers as a first, rather than a last, resort. Thus, where troops were supplied, as in the case of the Hougher disturbances of 1711–12, central government was at pains to make clear that these were intended only to supplement the efforts of local authorities.[11] Ready resort to military force was further discouraged by the requirement that all troops remain under central control. When the County Sligo landowner Kean O'Hara applied in 1693 for an order that troops in the county be quartered as the local justices of the peace directed, to help deal with an outbreak of banditry, he was told that no such arrangement could be considered. An officer in County Cork in 1704 refused a request for soldiers to assist in tracking down tories, 'not having, as he thinks, a warrant for it'. A magistrate in the same county ten years later complained that although the Protestant population was hopelessly outnumbered by Catholics, 'I dare not apply military force without a particular order where provision is made by the civil power'.[12]

The other military force available for peacekeeping duties was the militia. This had a varied, and in many ways still obscure, history.[13] The force raised in 1666 had been disbanded early in the reign of James II. A new Protestant militia was raised from the summer of 1690, but by 1694 this was said to be 'now almost quite laid aside'.[14] There was some sort of general review in 1702, but when militia companies were again organized to meet the threat of invasion in 1708, contemporaries seem to have perceived this as the creation of a new force rather than the mobilization of an existing one.[15] This militia was allegedly run down by the Tories during 1710–14, but revived and rearmed by the Whigs to meet the invasion scare of 1715.[16] An Act of 1716 provided for a more regularly constituted force, involving all Protestant males aged between 16 and 60 and mustered on four days each year. Yet this was never fully implemented. The militia was arrayed in 1719, and there were further large-scale mobilizations, though without a formal commission of array, in 1739–40 and in 1745. On these occasions it is clear that companies actually met for training, display, and festivity. The last major array, in 1756, on the other hand, seems to have gone no further than the appointment of

---

[11] Connolly, 'Law, Order and Popular Protest', 58–9.

[12] Percy Gethin to Kean O'Hara, 27 Aug. 1693 (PRONI T2812/4/82A); Aldworth to O'Hara, 5 Sept. 1693 (PRONI T2812/4/84); John Davie to Edward Southwell, 11 Feb. 1704 (BL Add. MS 34,744, fo. 36); Capt. Richard Hedges to Dawson, 8 June 1714 (Hickson, *Old Kerry Records*, 144).

[13] For general accounts, see J. O'Donovan, 'The Militia in Munster'; Ferguson, 'Army in Ireland', 102–6; Smyth, 'Volunteer Movement in Ulster', ch. 2.

[14] Capel to Trenchard, 14 July 1694 (HMC, *Buccleuch and Queensberry Manuscripts*, ii. 99).

[15] 'I am afraid 'tis not the humour of some to secure us by a militia, and therefore it is our interest to take this opportunity to form one': King to John Bolton, 7 Apr. 1707 [recte 1708] (TCD MS 750/3/2, 201).

[16] King to Sunderland, 31 Dec. 1714, 8 Jan. 1715 (TCD MS 750/4/2, 27, 29a); King to Delafaye, 25 July 1715 (ibid. 58–9); lords justices to——, 14 Nov. 1715 (SP63/373/242–3).

officers and the swearing in of men.[17] Nor is it clear what happened outside these years of general mobilization. In the city of Dublin, militia companies seem to have had a permanent existence and to have been taken seriously as a peacekeeping force. Elsewhere there are occasional indications that individual companies continued to function at some level, but little to show how common this was.[18]

The effectiveness of the militia was also limited by lack of arms. A magistrate in Lifford reported in August 1715 that although County Donegal would be able to array something like 7,000 men, he had been unable to find 'thirty men tolerably armed' to pursue a group of tories. Archbishop King, the dominant figure among the three lords justices, had strong views on the value of a militia, and in October he and his colleagues ordered that 14,750 muskets be issued from the king's stores. Even this, however, was calculated to be sufficient for only two-fifths of the force, and there was no ammunition available to go with it.[19] In 1739 and 1745 parliament voted sums of just over £35,000 in each case to buy arms for the militia. But in fact, just over 5,000 muskets and bayonets were issued in the period 1745–56.[20] Some militia companies remained wholly unequipped. In 1741 Sir Edward O'Brien, just appointed colonel of a militia regiment in County Clare, discovered that his men had neither pistols nor firelocks, 'so that we can't be of either ornament or service to the country'. He appealed to no less a figure than Henry Boyle to get him some arms from those recently called for by parliament. Yet, when the same regiment was arrayed in 1756, it contained 24 officers and 138 rank and file, but 'no fire locks—bayonets—pistols—swords or any kind of arms— drums—or accoutrements'.[21]

Military force did of course have a part to play in the maintenance of law and order. Regular soldiers and militia were both employed in the suppression of banditry in the south-west and in south Ulster. Most major urban riots seem to have ended with the calling out of troops. Excise men pursuing smuggled goods or other officials engaged in unpopular duties were on

---

[17] *Dublin Courant*, 26 Aug. 1719; *Dublin Daily Post*, 24, 27 May 1740; *Faulkner's Dublin Journal*, 12–15 Oct., 19–22 Oct. 1745. See also Smyth, 'Volunteer Movement in Ulster', 32–3. A Commission of Array is generally said to have been issued in 1745, but there seems to be no concrete evidence of this: McAnally, 'The Militia Array of 1756', 98 n. 24.

[18] Thus it was reported from Dublin in 1728 that several companies of foot guards had been drafted for service overseas, 'and our militia have done duty in their stead': *Dublin Intelligence*, 27 Jan. 1728. See also Stone to Bedford, 28 May 1759 (Bedford, *Correspondence*, ii. 382). For militia activity elsewhere, see the comments of Sir Edward O'Brien upon taking up command of a militia regiment in County Clare in 1741 (below, n. 23), and also the complaints made in County Down that the militia could be required to exercise on only 4 days of the year: Robert Ward to Michael Ward, 14 Apr. 1744 (PRONI D2092/1/6/83).

[19] Frederick Hamilton, Lifford, to King, 9 Aug. 1715 (TCD MSS 1995–2008/1700); lords justices to——, 14 Nov. 1715 (SP63/373/242–3). The Order in Council of the lords justices is printed in Prim, 'Documents Connected with the City of Kilkenny Militia', 270–1.

[20] Smyth, 'Volunteer Movement in Ulster', 32.

[21] O'Brien to Boyle, 5 June 1741 (PRONI D2707/A/1/11/69); *Inchiquin Manuscripts*, 649.

occasion escorted by soldiers, as were tax collectors transporting large sums in cash. Military guards were provided for particularly dangerous prisoners, such as the men sentenced to death in Dublin for enlisting in the Pretender's service in the summer of 1714. All these, however, were cases in which the normal resources of the law were, for one reason or another, inadequate. Routine law enforcement remained, as in England, in local civilian hands: which in practice meant the recognized officials charged with keeping the peace—justices, constables, and watchmen—supported when necessary by whoever else volunteered or could be persuaded to assist them. Thus Francis Eustace, wanted for the murder of his wife in Dublin in 1710, was apprehended as he tried to leave the city by a group consisting of his father-in-law, a constable, and three other men. In 1744 Viscount Buttevant set off in pursuit of a group who had abducted a woman in Cork city, 'accompanied by several gentlemen with a great number of his lordship's servants, well mounted and armed'. In County Kilkenny in 1739 local gentlemen came together to track down a band of robbers who had been terrorizing the surrounding region.[22]

What sort of order did these different forces, civil and military, formal and informal, maintain? The historian of these matters must maintain a precarious balance between sensationalism and blandness. A focus on those occasions when law and order broke down most spectacularly provides a colourful but hardly representative portrayal. Yet criminality and lawlessness can hardly be omitted entirely. The discussion that follows will take the question in two stages. First, it will look at some areas in which the normal machinery of law and order was clearly unable to cope. The aim here is not to present the conditions described as typical, but to see what such extreme cases reveal of the system of law enforcement as a whole. After this, there will be an attempt to assess the overall level of crime and violence in Restoration and post-Revolutionary Ireland.

2. The Limits of Order

Perhaps the most striking example of the breakdown of conventional methods of maintaining order is seen in the survival of banditry. In Ireland this had its own distinctive terminology. The term 'tory', probably from an Irish word for 'raider', was first used in the late 1640s and 1650s. It continued to be applied to the outlaw bands that operated after the Restoration, as well as being attached, by derisive extension, to the English opponents of the Exclusionists in the crisis of 1679–81. During the war of 1689–91 a new term, 'rapparee',

---

[22] *Dublin Gazette*, 25–8 Mar. 1710, 15–18 Apr. 1710; *Faulkner's Dublin Journal*, 14–18 Feb. 1744; *Dublin Gazette*, 13–16 June 1739.

apparently a corruption of the Irish word for a half-pike, came to be applied to groups of Jacobite irregulars who plundered Protestant houses and carried out guerrilla raids on the Williamite army. After the war the two terms 'tory' and 'rapparee' were both used to refer to outlaw bands. William Montgomery, writing around 1700, referred to the killing of an ancestor at the start of the preceding century by 'Irish woodkerns', adding that 'we now call such robbers, if on foot, tories, if on horseback rapparees'.[23]

Toryism was a major problem in Restoration Ireland. From the 1660s to the 1680s, reports from all four provinces regularly spoke of armed bands holding up travellers and robbing houses. In October 1686 the secretary to the lord lieutenant referred resignedly to 'tories and robbers which at this season of the year, when the days are short and the nights long, do always infest the country'.[24] The problem continued in the years immediately following the end of the Williamite war. Large-scale tory activity was reported not just in remote parts of the south-west and Connacht, but even in more settled counties. In Tipperary, for example, there were complaints in 1694 that the tories 'are in several parties, sometimes 10, 20, 30 or more in a company, and not only rob houses and travellers but strip, beat or kill the people. They also surround the fairs etc. and set upon persons going to or coming from them, so that trade or commerce in this county is almost totally damped.'[25] By the summer of 1696, however, a vigorous campaign of suppression, assisted by soldiers, was reported to have largely cleared the country of robbers.[26] Thereafter, bandit activity on any scale appears to have been confined to two main areas. In the south-west, in counties Cork and Kerry, there were further waves of tory activity in 1702–4, around 1707, and in 1711.[27] In Ulster there was an alarming upsurge of robberies in 1714–15 and another, more prolonged outbreak commencing at the beginning of 1718 and continuing into the early 1720s (see Table 6.1). Ulster tories were most active in the mountainous region on the borders of County Monaghan and south County Armagh, but others were based in the Sperrin Mountains of Tyrone and Londonderry, in the wilder parts of County Donegal, and also on the

[23] *NHI* iii. 375; *Montgomery Manuscripts*, 357.

[24] Rycaut to Cooke, 16 Oct. 1686 (Melvin, 'Rycaut's Memoranda', 171). For a general account, see Duffy, 'Redmond O'Hanlon and the Outlaws of Ulster'.

[25] P. Moore to——, 20 June 1694 (Wyche Papers, 2/122). See also Longford to Ellis, 27 Oct. 1692 (Melvin, 'Letters of Lord Longford', 103); Aldworth to O'Hara, 5 Sept. 1693 (PRONI T2812/4/84); Porter to Coningsby, 13, 19 Nov. 1694 (PRONI D638/18/28, 29); abstracts of reports *c.*1694 (Wyche Papers, 2/123); Barton to——, 3 Nov. 1694 (ibid. 2/125).

[26] Porter to Coningsby, 7 Feb. 1695 (PRONI D638/11/19); Porter to Coningsby, 15 July 1696 (PRONI D638/18/73); Porter to Vernon, 6 Aug. 1696 (*CSPD 1696*, 328).

[27] *Dublin Intelligence*, 1 Sept. 1702; Sir John Peyton to Kean O'Hara, 20 Mar. 1703 (PRONI T2812/5/76); Hedges to Cox, 20 Oct. 1704; Hedges to Joshua Dawson, 28 June, 8, 15 July 1707; Hedges to Thomas Browne, 26 Feb. 1711; Hedges to——, 22 Apr. 1711 (all in Hedges Letters).

TABLE 6.1. Numbers of rewards paid for the apprehension or killing of tories, rapparees, and other offenders in counties Louth and Antrim, 1712–49

Year	Louth	Antrim	Year	Louth	Antrim
1712	—	0 (1)	1731	0	3
1713	1	2	1732	1	2
1714	1	0 (1)	1733	0	0
1715	1	3	1734	—	1
1716	8	6 (9)	1735	—	0
1717	3	3 (8)	1736	—	0 (1)
1718	0	5 (8)	1737	—	2
1719	9	2	1738	—	0
1720	14	17 (19)	1739	—	1 (3)
1721	1	6 (12)	1740	—	0
1722	5	—	1741	—	3 (10)
1723	6 (7)	—	1742	—	0
1724	1	—	1743	—	5
1725	1	—	1744	—	1
1726	7	—	1745	—	3 (9)
1727	4	0	1746	—	1 (3)
1728	2	2 (3)	1747	—	0 (14)
1729	1 (2)	2 (3)	1748	—	0
1730	0	0 (3)	1749	—	0 (1)

Note: Figures show the number of offenders described as tories or rapparees for whose killing or capture a reward was ordered to be paid. Where rewards were also paid for offenders not so described, the total number of rewards is given in brackets. In 1716, for example, the County Antrim grand jury ordered payment of rewards for six tories, two 'notorious rogues', and one horse-stealer.
Source: Louth Grand Jury Presentment Book, 1713–33; Antrim Grand Jury Presentment Books, 1711–21, 1727–67.

Antrim plateau, whose greatest tory, Eneas O'Haghian, was hanged in 1721 with a guard of no less than sixty men in attendance.[28]

The gravity of the problem presented by the tories is evident not just in the concern expressed at their activities, but in the methods employed for their

---

[28] For references to Ulster toryism in this period, see the various comments by King: TCD MS 750/4/2, 27, 34; MS 2533, 111; MS 2535, 56–7. See also F. Hamilton to King, 9 Aug. 1715 (TCD MSS 1995–2008/1700); Nicolson to Wake, 17, 24 June 1718, 9 Aug. 1720 (Gilbert MS 27, 176–7, 179, 266–7); 'Calendar of Church Miscellaneous Papers', 58, 79. The dimensions of the outbreak are confirmed by entries in the Antrim Grand Jury Presentment Book (PRONI ANT 4/1/1), summarized in Table 6.1. For the execution of O'Haghian, see ibid. 300.

suppression. Patrols and searches by regular troops and locally raised forces were supplemented by secret negotiations, in which tories who were willing to surrender themselves and bring in either the live bodies or the severed heads of their accomplices were offered rewards and pardons for their own offences. Such deals had a dual importance. They neutralized individual tories, and at the same time created divisions among those still in the field. Sir Charles Porter was able to report in 1695 that some of the tories recently active had been killed or taken, 'and the rest are dispersed in so great fear of one another by reason of the impunity and rewards to those of them who shall destroy any of their accomplices that at present we do not hear of any robberies they commit'. In July 1707, similarly, tories in County Kerry were said to be 'now so divided that they cannot long stand. . . . Each of them wants only an opportunity to cut off his fellow's head to save his own life.'[29] Central government was never altogether happy with this crude frontier justice, by which men who had been the terror of the countryside received rewards, safe conducts, and pardons in exchange for the severed heads of their former comrades. But it recognized the utility of such methods, and confined its interference to an insistence that all negotiations have official approval and that the terms of surrender should not be unduly generous.[30]

Who were the tories? Observers in the Restoration period believed that they consisted mainly of those who had lost out in the upheavals of the 1640s and 1650s. Oliver Plunkett, writing to Rome in 1671, explained that the tories of Tyrone and Armagh were 'certain gentlemen of the leading families of the houses of O'Neill, MacDonnell, O'Hagan etc., up to twenty-four in number, together with their followers', who had taken to 'assassination and robbery on the public highway' after they had lost their properties. An account of Kildare in 1683 suggested that most of the 'robbers, tories and wood-kernes' who lurked in the mountains, bogs, and forests were 'the offspring of gentlemen that have either misspent or forfeited their estates' and who were unwilling to demean themselves by turning to a useful trade.[31] Concrete support for this image of Restoration toryism as a campaign of vengeance and resistance directed against the new political and social order is provided by the case of two of the most formidable tories of the period, Edward Nangle and Dudley Costello, who terrorized Leitrim and the surrounding counties during 1666–7. Both men had lost estates after 1641, and had failed to regain them at the Restoration: a detailed statement of the wrongs suffered by Catholic landowners at the hands of the court of claims was found on Nangle's body

---

[29] Porter to Coningsby, 7 Feb. 1695 (PRONI D638/11/19); Hedges to Dawson, 8, 15 July 1707 (Hedges Letters).

[30] Hedges to Dawson, 7 Apr. 1711 (Hedges Letters); Dawson to Major Lawrence Clayton, 19 Feb. 1712 (Country Letters, fo. 19ᵛ); Cox to Edward Southwell, 21 Sept. 1704 (BL Add. MS 38,153, fo. 88).

[31] Plunkett, *Letters*, 160; Account of County Kildare, 1683, in MacLysaght, *Irish Life*, 316.

after he was killed during an attack on the town of Longford in July 1666. During the attack, it was noted, their followers had 'burnt most of the English houses but none of the Irish in the town'. In addition it was reported that the two men claimed to be acting on the authority of a commission from the French king. By these means they appear to have won substantial support from the local Catholic population. 'By his pious insinuations', it was claimed, Nangle 'grows exceedingly into the kindness and wonder of the common Irish, insomuch that in some parts they fall down on their knees at sight of him.'[32]

All this would suggest that the tories of Restoration Ireland should be compared, as indeed they have been more than once, to the 'social bandits' famously characterized by Eric Hobsbawn: outlaws who acted as the poor man's champion against an oppressive social and political order and were rewarded with his support and hero worship. More recent work, however, has suggested that the 'social bandit' was in general a figure out of mythology rather than life. In reality, most bandits preyed indiscriminately on rich and poor (though they may have chosen, for purely prudential reasons, to leave the inhabitants of their home base unmolested, and even to allow them a modest share in their spoils). Where the bandit did take on a social or political role, in fact, it was more likely to be as client or strong-arm man to a local landowner or other magnate than as defender of the poor and the weak.[33] It is of course possible that in Ireland, with its distinctive religious and political conflicts, the concept of banditry as a form of social and political revolt has a greater relevance than elsewhere. But there is other evidence to suggest that tory activity cannot in fact be interpreted in any straightforward way as a struggle by dispossessed Catholic against new Protestant proprietor. In one case, in 1668, it was reported that 'several tories have lately got out in the north here of Ireland, both Irish, English and Scots'. And even where tories were Catholics, as the great majority of course were, there are indications that they did not confine their attentions to Protestants. The Anglican archbishop of Armagh assured the earl of Orrery in 1679 that all Catholics had been disarmed, 'but such as are particularly licenced for the security of themselves and of their houses against the tories'. Nor was it only the well-to-do who required such protection. The celebrated south Ulster tory Redmond O'Hanlon, killed in 1681, was said to have 'kept two or three counties almost waste, making the peasants pay continual contributions'. One of his followers, Shane Donnelly, still active in County Tyrone in 1706, issued a proclamation calling on English, Scots, and Irish alike to pay him protection money.[34]

---

[32] *CSPI 1666–9*, 137, 158–9, 176, 249, 306, 312, 315–16; HMC, *Ormonde Manuscripts*, NS iii. 225, 227.

[33] See in particular Lewin, 'Oligarchic Limitations of Social Banditry'. For a useful general review of the debate, see B. D. Shaw, 'Bandits in the Roman Empire', 4–5, 25, 38.

[34] *CSPI 1666–9*, 612; Michael Boyle to Orrery, 18 Mar. 1679 (Wyche Papers, 1/1/30); Carte, *Ormonde*, iv. 618; Hutchinson, *Tyrone Precinct*, 79.

Toryism in the 1690s and after retained the same ambiguous character. Once again religious and political animosities played at least some part in its depredations. During the war of 1689–91 a Danish observer noted that the rapparees 'give no quarter to English Protestants, but they spare the Danes, Dutch and French'.[35] Most observers of post-war toryism, similarly, presented it primarily in terms of attacks by Catholics on Protestants. They also pointed to the support it received from the wider Catholic population. One report in the mid-1690s claimed that the tories of County Kerry had 'above 5,000 relations and friends within their ranges'. Sir Francis Brewster, writing from Killarney in 1704, complained of 'the daily rescues, the insolence of the old proprietors, this whole side of the country sheltering and siding with the tories at one time by whom they are protected at another'.[36] Lists of suspected harbourers of tories in Cork and Kerry, drawn up around 1694, include the names of a number of surviving gentry and substantial middlemen.[37]

Once again, however, these indications of a clearly defined political and religious purpose may be to some extent misleading. The County Kerry magistrate Richard Hedges, a hostile but well-informed observer, presented the local tories not as the forces of a resurgent Jacobitism, but as drawn from a floating population of the tough and the desperate: deserters from the army, 'some rogues that come back from beyond sea in privateers, with the loose idle fellows of the country'.[38] Nor is it necessary to see the connivance or active co-operation that the tories received from local communities as evidence of a shared political purpose. Ties of family and neighbourhood, local hostility of outside authority, social tensions within a region, and a judicious distribution of the spoils of outlawry could all have been influential here, as they were in other societies in which banditry flourished. Even the patronage apparently shown by local men of property had its parallels elsewhere, from Sicily to the Brazilian backlands. Lord Chancellor Porter, writing in 1694 on Counties Cork and Kerry, saw local support for toryism as economically based:

the country [are] very backward to do their parts, but on the contrary it is plain they have rather been encouragers and harbourers and given them monies to save their own stocks, by which means tenants are discouraged to plant there and the present

---

[35] Danaher and Simms, *Danish Force in Ireland*, 96–7.

[36] 'Proposals for Reducing the Tories', c.1694 (Wyche Papers, 2/120); Francis Brewster to Alan Brodrick, 4 Jan. 1704 (Midleton MS 1248/2, fo. 117).

[37] Wyche Papers, 2/124. It is on this basis that Cullen suggests that toryism in the south-west retained a political and 'military' character marking it out from banditry elsewhere: 'Social and Cultural Modernisation of Rural Ireland', 205. See also the testimony of two tories in 1711 that they were sheltered by the substantial Catholic middleman Daniel Mahony: Hickson, *Old Kerry Records*, 137–8.

[38] Hedges to Thomas Browne, 26 Feb. 1711 (Hedges Letters). See also the comments of Archbishop King (below, p. 219).

inhabitants take the lands at much lower rates than they would otherwise let for, and make their advantages by compromising with the tories for a small matter.[39]

Another report from Kerry at about the same time suggested that it was in fact the Protestant magistrates of the county who were to blame, for selling protections and safe conducts to local tories, some of whom 'impudently own that it has cost them £50 to get these safeties'.[40]

The disappearance of banditry is impossible to date precisely. Use of the term 'tory' was perpetuated into the middle years of the eighteenth century by a distinctive legal procedure whereby a wanted man could be presented by a grand jury as a tory, a robber, or a rapparee, 'out in arms and on his keeping'. He would then be named as such in a proclamation by the Privy Council, the force of which was to render him guilty of high treason and liable to be killed on sight unless he surrendered for trial by a specified date. The last such proclamation was issued in 1753.[41] But long before then it seems clear that for a man to be proclaimed in this way meant only that he was armed and on the run. The essential distinction from the point of view of the historian of crime is between the bandit living permanently outside the bounds of settled society and the criminal who leaves its shelter only long enough to carry out a particular operation. And here it remains difficult to draw a clear line between the tories of late Stuart Ireland and the substantial groups of outlaws who continued to operate in different regions at least until the 1740s. In 1729, for example, 'a gang of highwaymen' of about 18 strong, commanded by three brothers named O'Neill, was reported in the area round Dungannon, County Tyrone. In 1738 a gang of 30 was said to be active in Counties Antrim and Down.[42] Between 1738 and 1740 the Kellymount gang, said to number 30 or more, terrorized Kilkenny and the surrounding counties, robbing in such numbers 'that there was no resisting them' and extorting supplies from the local gentry 'as soldiers do in an enemy's country'.[43] In 1746 a gang of 12 robbers who 'go armed, with their faces blackened' were reported to be 'out' in County Kildare.[44]

If these outlaw gangs resembled the tories of a generation earlier in their manner of operation, they also on occasion received some of the same sort of popular support, or at least connivance. Fergal McVeagh, who went on the run after a botched housebreaking escapade in Ballycastle, County Antrim, in

[39] Porter to Coningsby, 19 Nov. 1694 (PRONI D638/18/29).
[40] Barton to——, 3 Nov. 1694 (Wyche Papers, 2/125).
[41] Dutton, *Justice of Peace*, 360; 'Catalogue of Proclamations, 1618–1875'.
[42] *Dublin Intelligence*, 2 Sept. 1729; *Dublin Gazette*, 3–7 Jan. 1738.
[43] [Chetwood], *Tour*, 173, 206, 213. See also *Dublin Gazette*, 16–19 Dec. 1738, 13–16 Jan. 1739; *Dublin Daily Post*, 22 Oct. 1739, 11, 21 Apr. 1740; George Ross to Barrymore, 22 Aug., 13 Sept. 1740 (HMC, *Puleston Manuscripts*, 321–2).
[44] *Pue's Occurrences*, 14–18 Oct. 1746.

1724, was 'much encouraged by some idle vagrant persons who reside in that corner of the country called the Low Glens'.[45] The highwayman 'Captain' James Freney, operating in Leinster in the 1740s, appears to have enjoyed a wider fame, which he cultivated, if his own best-selling memoirs can be credited, by sparing poor or 'worthy' victims.[46] The most that can be said is that the outlaw bands of the 1720s and after seem not to have enjoyed quite the same territorial dominance, or perhaps the same life expectancy, as the tories of an earlier era. Even the Kellymount gang, probably the closest in its scale of operations to the earlier tories, appears to have lasted only about two years before its members were killed, taken, or scattered.

Banditry in whatever form was of course only part of a wider problem: its existence depended on there being substantial territories that were not fully under the control of government and its agencies of law enforcement. The precise nature of the challenge provided by such areas varied from case to case. In the mountains of south Ulster the problem seems to have been geographical and cultural isolation: a rugged, trackless region with a strong surviving Gaelic tradition and a population fiercely resistant to outside interference. Similar conditions existed in the other major area of tory activity, the south-west. But here there was also the disruptive influence of members of the traditional Gaelic ruling families, like the MacCarthys and the O'Donoghues of Glenflesk, who had either succeeded in holding on to at least part of their estates through the troubles of the previous century or else retained a local prominence by acting as middlemen to the new proprietors. Captain Hedges, writing in 1714, complained that 'some heads of Irish clans' had 'gained the ascendant over the civil power by their insolence and number, so that the ordinary course of the laws cannot be put in force against them, without hazard to the lives of such as go about to do it'. A report in 1720 singled out the thrice-yearly fairs at Millstreet in County Cork as occasions on which 'the clans of Glenflesk' came in great numbers 'to create quarrels and revenge former ones to the great discouragement of dealing people that do come a great way to buy and sell there'.[47] Over the next few years the authorities in Dublin received a whole series of lurid reports concerning Daniel Mahony of Dunloe. A substantial Catholic middleman claiming to pay £1,500 a year in rents to Lord Shelburne and other head landlords, Mahony was reported to have 'contrived a way to make himself great and dreadful in this country', by organizing his tenants and clients into a body known as 'Daniel Mahony's fairesses'. These roamed at night, 'smocked and black in

---

[45] PRONI T808/14895, fo. 5ᵛ.

[46] Freney, *Life and Adventures*, 27, 29–30, 32, 45, 49.

[47] Hedges to Dawson, 8 June 1714 (Hickson, *Old Kerry Records*, 144); Henry Wallis to Midleton, 19 May 1720 (Midleton MS 1248/4, fo. 264a). See also *Kenmare Manuscripts*, 45, 48.

their faces', and their influence was such 'that none dare to execute any judicial orders against the said Mahony's fairesses or himself'.[48]

This is not to suggest that the disorders of the south-west were wholly the work of survivals of the old Gaelic order. What made the problem of exercising effective control over the region so intractable was that those Protestant gentlemen who had managed to establish themselves there had also tended to be drawn into powerful local networks of personal and family connections and in some cases at least exhibited the same open disregard for central government and its laws as their Gaelic neighbours. A correspondent in 1696 complained of seeing 'most of the English courting and making friends with the Irish'.[49] Captain Robert Topham, a magistrate and joint agent of the extensive Shelburne estates, was alleged to have driven away a group of tenants who had complained of their cattle being seized by the O'Sullivans in lieu of rents claimed under the short-lived Jacobite land settlement 'and bid them all begone to the [Devil] for a company of churls, and told them he would not for forty pounds have the ill-will of O'Sullivan Mor upon account of such rascals'. Francis Eager, grandson of an English army officer who had come to Ireland in the 1640s but now married to a daughter of the O'Donoghue, was described in 1712 as 'Captain General, in conjunction with his brother Tim, of all the rapp[eree]s of Glenflesk'. There was also Francis Herbert, shot dead in 1734, a member of a cadet branch of the Shropshire-based landed family who appears to have joined with followers of MacCarthy Mor in attacks on the main Herbert estate and other properties in the vicinity.[50]

The third region which remained notorious for its lawlessness up to the middle of the eighteenth century was Iar Connacht, the territory west of Galway city consisting of the baronies of Moycullen and Ballynahinch and the half-barony of Ross. Samuel Molyneux, who visited the area in 1709, found it a 'strangely stoney and wild' country, the home of 'multitudes of barbarous uncivilized Irish' united in 'the defence of any of their own or even other rogues that fly to them', so that 'the sheriffs of this county scarce dare appear on the west side of Galway bridge, which, though Ireland is now generally esteemed wholly civilized, may well be called the end of the English pale'.[51] In 1711–12 Iar Connacht was the centre of a series of attacks on livestock, the one major outbreak of agrarian protest to take place in Ireland prior to the 1760s. As in the south-west there was evidence that local gentlemen, both

---

[48] Hickson, *Old Kerry Records*, 137–8, 153–63, 178–86. Hickson suggests that the word 'fairesses' derives from an Irish word for 'men'.

[49] William Brewster to Sir William Trumbull, 24 Nov. 1696 (HMC, *Downshire Manuscripts*, i: *Papers of Sir William Trumbull*, 711).

[50] Hickson, *Old Kerry Records*, 119–22, 139–41, 147, 187–94.

[51] Molyneux, 'Journey to Connaught—April 1709', 171.

Catholic and Protestant, had obstructed attempts to investigate the disturbances, and in some cases had been directly involved in their planning and
execution.[52] By the middle of the century little had changed. A clerical
magistrate complained in 1749 that 'neither the law nor the gospel do ... in
the wild country of Eyre Connaught'. A few years later there was a new
outbreak of disturbances on the St George estates. Edward Willes, chief
baron of the Irish exchequer, noted in 1759 that Iar Connacht was still
a district 'inhabited by the ancient Irish, who never yet have been made
amenable to the laws. No sheriff dares go there to execute any process.'[53]

These three areas of lawlessness, Iar Connacht, south Ulster, and the
south-west, were in many ways similar. All were rugged and relatively impenetrable territories where traditional social structures and codes of behaviour remained substantially intact. But there was also one significant
difference. Iar Connacht, despite its fearsome reputation as a wild, uncivilized
territory, does not figure in accounts of toryism, either in the seventeenth
century or later. One reason is that it did not, like the other two regions, have
a lucrative raiding ground close at hand. The fertile lands of east Connacht
were cut off by the garrison town of Galway, while to the north lay only the
slender pickings offered by County Mayo. But there is another point to
consider. Banditry, it has been pointed out, is a product of one particular
stage in the development of the state. It occurs when there is a sufficiently
rigid system of civil law for a man to be able to place himself clearly outside it,
yet where there are not yet sufficient coercive resources to deal effectively
with such outlaws.[54] In south Ulster and the south-west, both these conditions were met. Elsewhere in Ireland, the second no longer applied after the
1690s. In the more self-contained and isolated Iar Connacht, on the other
hand, it was the first condition, the existence of a rule of law sufficiently clear
for certain types of offender to step incontrovertibly outside it, that was not
met. The inhabitants of Iar Connacht, the antiquarian and Gaelic scholar
Roderick O'Flaherty wrote in 1684, 'are so observant of law, that now for
above 30 years of peace, there was not one body executed out of the whole
territories for any transgression, and scarce any brought to the bar for mis-
demeanour'.[55] In light of the comments of some other observers, this might
be dismissed as a mere excess of local patriotism. Yet it might be closer to the
truth to see it as a reminder that banditry, like other forms of criminality,
exists only within the framework of a certain system of law.

The other main environment in which the normal resources available for
the enforcement of order regularly proved inadequate was the larger urban

[52] Connolly, 'The Houghers', 155–60; idem, 'Law, Order and Popular Protest', 59–60.
[53] 'Calendar of Church Miscellaneous Papers', 87; Edward Willes to earl of Warwick, c.1759
(PRONI Mic 148, 16–17).
[54] Shaw, 'Bandits in the Roman Empire', 49.
[55] O'Flaherty, Account of Iar Connacht 1684 (Molyneux Papers, 883/1, 102).

areas. The coercive resources available there were more formidable than in the countryside. In 1780, on the eve of the first steps towards a modern police system, Dublin had some 400 watchmen.[56] Military aid was quickly available from the garrisons in all the major towns. But these advantages were outweighed by the special problems of urban areas: the speed with which a large crowd could gather, the protection granted to offenders by the anonymity of town life, and the absence of the close personal supervision by social superiors that was possible in the countryside. Urban authorities thus lived with the constant threat of riot. In some cases this was a form of economic protest, provoked by high prices, food shortages, or the undercutting of local produce by imported goods.[57] In other cases urban crowds acted to resist the normal processes of law enforcement, obstructing arrests and even rescuing prisoners. In one incident in Cork city in 1733, a group of soldiers detailed to convey a butcher and noted local rough to gaol on a charge of assault came under attack from a crowd of several hundred, who continued to obstruct the party until two of their number had been shot.[58] In Dublin during 1729 there were recurrent street disorders involving a group based in Kevin Street, close to St Patrick's cathedral, who brawled with watchmen and carried out a series of assaults on persons who had in one way or another offended them. The group was known as Kevin's Bail, 'from their frequent rescue of prisoners out of the hands of the peace officers'.[59] The impotence of authority in the face of a determined urban crowd was further demonstrated by an episode in 1734. Around ten o'clock on the night of 23 August, Paul Farrell, popularly known as 'Gallows Paul', a city constable turned criminal, was being escorted to prison. He was rescued from custody, apparently by accomplices who believed he was about to give evidence against them, battered to death in the streets, and his body hanged on a tree in the Liberties area, where it remained until the authorities were finally able to remove it at three the following afternoon.[60]

Even outside the major towns, the resources of the state repeatedly proved inadequate to secure the enforcement of unpopular laws. Catholic clergymen arrested in the early period of serious enforcement of the penal laws were regularly rescued, sometimes even from the hands of soldiers.[61] Coastal

[56] Palmer, *Police and Protest*, 81.
[57] Above, p. 100; below, pp. 219–20.
[58] *Faulkner's Dublin Journal*, 1–5 Jan. 1734.
[59] *Dublin Intelligence*, 29 Apr., 23 Aug. 1729. See also, among other references, ibid., 26 Apr., 10 June 1729.
[60] Thomas Tickell to Walter Cary, 23 Aug. 1734 (PRONI D2707/A/1/7, 12–13). In July 1730 Farrell had been described as 'a noted, active constable' (*Dublin Intelligence*, 10 July 1730). The following March he was acquitted of charges of robbery, but convicted of assault (ibid., 8, 13 Mar., 12 Apr. 1731). At the time of his death the *Dublin Gazette* described him as a constable (20–4 Aug. 1734), but Tickell called him 'a notorious offender'.
[61] Below p. 297.

populations, as in Cornwall and other parts of England, regarded wrecked vessels and goods washed ashore as legitimate takings, and fiercely resisted attempts to secure them for the owners.[62] Revenue officials were regularly intimidated or obstructed in their pursuit of contraband and illicitly distilled or brewed liquors, and goods seized were frequently rescued.[63] In all these cases resistance was a reflection not of simple 'lawlessness', but of a denial of the legitimacy of particular laws. As such, it makes clear the extent to which other, more successful instances of law enforcement depended on some basic level of popular acceptance.

Resistance to the law was not confined to the lower classes. Smuggling, for example, was widely connived at by local landed gentlemen, encouraged by the cheapness of run goods, the increased rent-paying capacity of tenants involved in the trade, or even a share in the profits. Urban men of property were similarly implicated. In 1735, for example, 'several merchants of credit' were reported to have gone to Kinsale at the head of 'the mob of Cork weavers' and disrupted the trial of an alleged wool smuggler. Afterwards a man believed to be an informer 'had his ear cut and was scalped'.[64] In other cases too, popular obstruction of the law was most formidable when encouraged or directly led by social superiors. A collector of crown rents in County Kildare, attempting in 1699 to seize cattle in lieu of arrears owed by a Mr Seagrave, was 'beset by near 60 people, men and women, scullogs of the country and servants of Mr Seagraves, with staves and pitchforks'. In a similar incident in 1754 John Trimble, the chief tenant on a County Down estate bought by the Belfast merchant William Macartney, raised an armed party of thirty of his undertenants to resist all attempts to collect arrears of rent.[65] In County Antrim in 1729 two gentlemen, Richard Jalland and Kennedy Stafford, waged a more spectacular private war. Placing themselves at the head of 'about forty distracted country people', they took forcible possession of a house formerly belonging to the Stafford family but now sold, for what they regarded as an unduly low price, to the bishop of Down and Connor. When the sheriff attempted to put the bishop in possession, he was driven away by gunfire. Eventually, after an interval of five months, troops and artillery were brought to dislodge the two men and their followers from the

[62] e.g. *Dublin Intelligence*, 11 Jan. 1725, 4 Jan. 1729; George Ross to Francis Price, 18 Jan. 1734 (HMC, *Puleston Manuscripts*, 316–17); Robert Ward to Michael Ward, 3 Feb., 5 Jan. [recte Feb.?] 1740 (PRONI D2092/1/5/47, 51). For the English counterpart, see Rule, 'Wrecking and Coastal Plunder', which also has a short discussion of Ireland (pp. 174–5).

[63] For smuggling, see e.g. Hickson, *Old Kerry Records*, 169–77. For brewing, see the revenge taken on an informer at Loughrea, County Galway, in 1724 (*Dublin Intelligence*, 15 July 1724).

[64] Coghill to Southwell, 14 Jan. 1735 (BL Add. MS 21,123, fos. 84–5). A few years earlier Coghill, then himself a commissioner of the revenue, was worried that a recent seizure of tobacco and brandy near Kinsale might ruin some of Southwell's tenants in the area: same to same, 21 Apr. 1730 (ibid., fo. 5ᵛ).

[65] John Green to Agmondisham Vesey, 1 Jan. 1699 (PROI Sarsfield-Vesey Papers, 37); Smyth, 'Volunteer Movement in Ulster', 5–6.

house. In the interval they had also led an armed raid on a house belonging to the Jalland family, which they had burned down by firing red-hot slugs into the roof.[66]

The problem with incidents of this kind, of course, was that they involved precisely the social group, the Protestant propertied classes, on whom the day-to-day enforcement of the law depended. In many cases, indeed, it was the magistracy itself that most conspicuously subverted the rule of law. In 1700 the English creditor of a certain Mr Jones found himself unable, despite a promise of assistance from no less a person than the lord chief justice, to recover his money. The reason was that 'Jones being a great magistrate in Athlone he was so powerful there that he could not get the law to proceed against him'.[67] When defiance came at this level, central government was largely powerless. In 1712 the lords justices, faced with clear evidence that the sheriff of County Galway had helped his brother to abduct a widow whom the latter wanted to force into marriage, could respond with nothing more than a weak injunction 'for your own sake ... to have the gentlewoman sent home ... putting an end to a matter that will hereafter make a mighty noise to the prejudice of your reputation'.[68] Even the killers of Lieutenant Hume, despite the pressure brought to bear on the Dublin government by influential English relatives of the dead man, received largely effective protection from the county authorities. A witness was spirited away the day of the inquest. The coroner and the local magistrates delayed sending to Dublin the examinations needed for the issue of wanted notices. When formal arrest warrants were finally issued, duplicates were sent to Hume's military colleagues because of suspicions that the sheriff 'might be too favourable to his neighbours in the country'.[69]

Right up to the middle of the eighteenth century, then, there were segments of Irish society in which normal processes of law and order were largely ignored and others in which they operated at best imperfectly. To say this, however, is not to suggest that Ireland was in any way unusual. All the forms of disorder cited had their parallels elsewhere. Banditry remained a problem in most European states up to the mid-eighteenth century, and in some areas, like Corsica and southern Italy, for considerably longer.[70] Even within the British Isles, South Armagh, Iar Connacht, and the handful of baronies in the far south-west were isolated pockets compared with the Highlands of Scotland, where well into the eighteenth century feuding and cattle raiding

---

[66] 'Calendar of Church Miscellaneous Papers', 83; Tennison Groves Abstracts, County Antrim (PRONI T808/14896); *Dublin Intelligence*, 4, 11 Oct. 1729.

[67] William Glanville, jun., to Sir Cyril Wyche, 24 Sept. 1700 (Wyche Papers, 1/1/184); William Glanville, sen., to Wyche, 7 Nov. 1700, 4 Feb., 13 Mar., 5 Sept. 1701 (ibid. 1/1/191, 210, 215, 240).

[68] Dawson to sheriff of County Galway, 26 Jan. 1712 (Country Letters, fo. 16ᵛ).

[69] HMC, *Polwarth Manuscripts*, v. 152–8, 182.

[70] Lenman and Parker, 'The State, the Community and the Criminal Law', 40–3.

remained a way of life for a large part of the population. Nor were the exploits of the Irish tories so very much more dramatic than those of the smugglers who operated along the coast of Sussex throughout the 1740s and 1750s, in some cases fighting pitched battles with soldiers and revenue officers or taking over whole towns in order to rescue impounded goods or vessels.[71] The behaviour of sections of the Irish gentry may have been anarchic by comparison with their English counterparts. But it too had its parallels, in the American colonies, in Britain's Celtic fringe, and elsewhere.[72]

Spectacular though these different manifestations of Irish lawlessness could be, moreover, their day was, by the early eighteenth century, drawing to a close. Banditry, as already seen, had ceased to be a national problem by the end of the 1690s, and was gradually to die out over the next few decades. One important reason for its demise was the general embarracking of the army in the years after 1700, which provided the opportunity to locate barracks and redoubts at strategic points in formerly unpoliced areas. To this must be added the influence of gradual but progressive economic development, bringing with it improved communications, the creation of new relationships dependent on a degree of centralized law enforcement, and changes in the physical appearance of even the most remote areas. The Barnesmore Gap, for example, the only pass linking the north of Donegal with the south, was at one time 'much infested by robbers'. By 1739, however, 'the woods being cleared, it has been for these many years safe'.[73]

By the middle of the eighteenth century the forces of change had begun to penetrate even the most intractable regions. South Armagh was reported in 1759 to have been 'much civilized' over the previous twenty years, thanks to the stationing of soldiers, the building of a road through the mountains, and the efforts of landlords to plant their estates with English and Scots tenants imported from other parts of Ulster.[74] In the south-west too, a great deal had changed since the days of Daniel Mahony and Florence O'Donoghue. When Sir Thomas Denny organized a militia troop at Tralee during the crisis provoked by the Jacobite rising of 1745, a newspaper reported how 'MacCarthy Mor, the chief of the Milesian noblemen of this kingdom, to show his attachment to the present government, did Sir Thomas the honour to be arrayed in his troop, and came several miles from his own palace, though in extreme bad weather, to ride in the troop this day'.[75] Only Iar

---

[71] Smout, *History of the Scottish People*, 319–20; Winslow, 'Sussex Smugglers'.

[72] Above, ch. 2, sect. 3.

[73] Henry, 'Hints' (Nat. Arch. Ire. M2533), 66. For barracks, see Ferguson, 'Army in Ireland', 76–80.

[74] Willes to Sally Wise, 1 May 1759 (PRONI Mic 148); cf. Cullen, *Emergence of Modern Ireland*, 206–7.

[75] *Faulkner's Dublin Journal*, 19–22 Oct. 1745.

Connacht, more self-contained and with less potential for economic development, remained to be brought under control. And even there the government responded to the troubles on the St George estate by ordering the construction of a new barracks in the territory and a road to link it to the city of Galway.[76] Changes also took place among the Protestant gentry, as rising incomes and the gradual extension to even provincial Ireland of metropolitan standards of behaviour combined to modify the unruly behaviour common in earlier generations.[77] Government, too, became progressively less tolerant of delinquency. Already by the 1730s leading members of the Irish executive seem to have made a determined effort to prevent influential persons intervening on behalf of well-born offenders.[78] By the end of the eighteenth century, attitudes had become tougher still, particularly in the matter of abductions.[79]

The different kinds of lawlessness discussed here—the banditry of tories and rapparees, the general lack of discipline in remote corners like Iar Connacht and the far south-west, the sporadic eruptions of urban crowds, and the anarchic behaviour of sections of the gentry—thus have a twofold significance. In the first place they provide evidence, both in their survival into the early eighteenth century and in their rapid decline thereafter, of the nature and timing of important changes taking place in the character of Irish society. Secondly, there is the light they cast on the basis of social order. Toryism and urban riot cannot be taken as reflecting the prevailing state of affairs even in the early part of the century: they represent the extremes, the points at which the usual controls on behaviour broke down. For that very reason, however, they help to make clear what those controls were and how they operated. What emerges above all is that the maintenance of order did not depend primarily on physical repression. Whether challenged by serious resistance from below or by non-cooperation from the élite, the ramshackle apparatus of coercive discipline rapidly revealed its limitations. Samuel Johnson's observation, in other words, was as true of Ireland as it was of other parts of eighteenth-century Europe. Despite the recent history of conquest and warfare and the political and religious tensions that resulted, this was not a society held down by force. Instead, government depended on the continued willingness of the many, most of the time, to accept the domination of the few—even if this was only, as Johnson suggested, because they lacked the ability to establish, or possibly even to imagine, an alternative.

---

[76] Willes to earl of Warwick, *c.*1759 (PRONI Mic 148, 16–17).

[77] Above, ch. 2, sect. 3.

[78] Boulter to Carteret, 11 June 1730 (*Letters*, ii. 19); lords justices to Dorset, 25 Apr. 1735 (PRONI D2707/A/1/7, 26); lords justices to Devonshire, 23 May 1736 (PRONI D2707/A/1/8, 8–9).

[79] Cullen, *Emergence of Modern Ireland*, 245–8.

3. The Rule of Law

All this, of course, leaves the central issue unresolved. What in fact was the level of crime and disorder in late seventeenth- and early eighteenth-century Ireland? Contemporaries do not on the whole appear to have felt that they were living in a particularly violent or dangerous society. Although there were tories and robbers in the mountains and forests, one writer observed in 1683, 'yet the robberies, felonies, burglaries etc. usually committed in this kingdom are not so numerous but there are commonly sentenced to die in a monthly sessions at the Old Bailey more than in a half-year's circuit of Ireland'. A separate account in the same year characterized the people of County Leitrim as being most proud of their ancient chronicles and genealogies and 'as much abhorring theft'. Lord Orrery, coming to live in Ireland in 1732, found the inhabitants of County Cork 'exceeding honest': 'We lie with our doors and windows open, and strangers are going in and out of the house *ad libitum* all night long.' In County Down in 1744, few serious crimes were said to come before the courts. 'Men travel securely by day, and are afraid of little disturbance at night to keep them on their guard.' 'A comfortable circumstance belonging to this country', Mrs Delany told an English friend in 1750, 'is that the roads are so good, and free from robbers, that we may drive safely any hour of the night.'[80]

Where contemporaries did express concern regarding crime, it was often in terms of specific outbreaks, rather than of a permanent state of affairs. During 1665, for example, there were complaints of an upsurge in crime both in Dublin and in the country. In 1728 a newspaper reported the appearance of 'a new gang of desperadoes' who had begun robbing houses in the capital. Two years later 'the highways near this city begin to be so infested with rogues, that travelling late is held dangerous, especially by persons unarmed'.[81] Such outbreaks of crime were directly related, in the opinion of a great many observers, to economic conditions. Sir George Rawdon, writing from Lisburn at the end of 1667, commented on a recent rash of thefts: 'Poverty is so great that many run away from their farms and betake themselves to stealing.' In 1692 a visitor to Galway and Roscommon, both still suffering from the effects of wartime dislocation, found that 'many families have broke up and are turned beggars, thieves, or robbers, of which last number there is got together in the mountains of Slieve Murray about 30 or 40, but some say 100'. Archbishop King, in 1723, claimed that, owing to the rise in rents, 'so many poor tenants are broke, that not being allowed to go to foreign service, the

---

[80] Account of County Kildare, 1683, in MacLysaght, *Irish Life*, 316; Account of County Leitrim, 1683 (Molyneux Papers, 883/1, 138); *Orrery Papers*, i. 116; [Harris and Smith], *County of Down*, 110; Mrs Delany to Mrs Dewes, 10 Dec. 1750 (*Autobiography and Correspondence*, ii. 626).

[81] *CSPI 1663–5*, 550, 689; *Dublin Intelligence*, 19 Mar. 1728, 30 Sept. 1730.

strong turn robbers, tories and rapparees, and the weak beg'. The famine of 1741 had similar effects. In County Cork, 'there is now scarce a night passes without accounts from different parts of the country of cows, sheep or some kind of provisions being stole, and the jails are already so full that the consequence is greatly to be dreaded'. By the late 1750s, on the other hand, Charles O'Hara could list among the first benefits of rising living standards that 'there is much greater attention to home business, less riot and disorder'.[82]

There was one undoubted difference in terms of the state of law and order between the Ireland of the early and mid-eighteenth century and that of later decades. This was the absence of large-scale popular protest. In the countryside there was one serious outbreak of agrarian crime, the Hougher movement of 1711–12, when thousands of cattle were slaughtered in an organized protest against the extension of large-scale stock rearing into Galway, Clare, and other western counties. This had much in common with later agrarian outbreaks: a clandestine group acting with the connivance of a large section of the population, the issue of 'laws' and 'proclamations' in conscious imitation of the forms employed by the civil authorities, and association under a mythical leader, 'Ever Joyce'. Unlike later movements, however, the Houghers depended on a degree of leadership from above. Local gentlemen, whether motivated by religious and political grievances or, more probably, by their own dislike of a more commercialized agriculture, encouraged and in some cases took part in attacks on livestock.[83] In the absence of such leadership, the product of particular local circumstances, the Houghers had no successors. Crimes of protest continued. Newspaper reports and private letters over the next fifty years refer occasionally to threatening letters, the maiming of cattle, the levelling of fences, and similar occurrences.[84] But it was not until the emergence of the Whiteboys in 1761 that there appeared another concerted expression of agrarian discontent.

Organized protest was more common in the towns. Trade disputes, food shortages, and the import of manufactured goods could all be the occasions of formidable disturbances. Yet, even on these occasions, violence was rarely random or uncontrolled. Urban crowds responded to economic and other

---

[82] Rawdon to Conway, 24 Dec. 1667 (*CSPI 1666–9*, 530); Dean John Trench to King, 12 Apr. 1692 (TCD MSS 1995–2008/220); King to Gen. Gorge, 6 Apr. 1723 (TCD MS 750/7, 332); William Conner to Henry Boyle, 5 May 1741 (PRONI D2707/A1/4/3); O'Hara's Account of County Sligo (NLI MS 20,397).

[83] Connolly, 'The Houghers'.

[84] For examples, see Hickson, *Old Kerry Records*, 187–9; Robert Ward to Michael Ward, 4 Nov. 1738 (PRONI D2092/1/5/43); *Dublin Intelligence*, 1 July 1729; *Dublin Gazette*, 27 Apr.– 1 May 1736; *Faulkner's Dublin Journal*, 13–17 Sept. 1743, 29 May–2 June 1744; *Esdall's News Letter*, 24 Apr. 1751, 27–9 June 1753. There is a particularly vivid account of the troubles encountered with unruly tenants in County Cork during 1745–54 in the Ward Papers, PRONI D2092/1/7–8.

grievances by disciplined collective action informed by a clear perception of how society should be ordered. The 'mobs' that broke into corn warehouses in Cork and Limerick during the famine year of 1729, for example, did not loot the contents, but instead sold them off at what was regarded as a fair price. In Dublin, similarly, a crowd took over potato barges moored at Aston Quay, 'and sold the roots there for 3*d*. per peck, which was half price'. In Kilkenny in 1766 the inhabitants went to the houses of farmers and mealmen and carried any oatmeal they found there to the weighing house for immediate sale.[85] Even the great anti-Union riot of 3 December 1759, the most spectacular popular political demonstration to be staged prior to the rise of the Volunteers, was essentially an attempt to ensure that social superiors adhered to their duty by retaining an Irish parliament in Dublin.[86] Protest of this kind—defensive, ritualized, and in many cases a signal to those above that something had gone wrong—was common to all parts of pre-industrialized Europe.[87] It was only during the last years of the eighteenth century, in response to new economic, sectarian, and political tensions, that protest became a real threat to social order, and Ireland began to stand out, at least from the other regions of the British Isles, for the scale and ferocity of its popular movements.[88]

In a perfect world these impressionistic and anecdotal assessments of the state of law and order in early and mid-eighteenth-century Ireland would be checked against statistical evidence on the incidence of different types of crime and the way in which these were dealt with. In practice, the judicial records from which that might be done no longer exist. At the same time the fragmentary evidence that does survive from the 1760s and after generally bears out the suggestion that Ireland, by this period at least, was not a society in which serious crime was common. The two earliest assizes for which records survive are those for the counties of Antrim and Meath in the summer of 1766. Between them these heard four serious cases. In Antrim there was an accidental homicide involving a man who had pushed a woman during a quarrel, causing fatal injury to the baby she was holding, and two cases (possibly related) involving the theft of large quantities of spirits from merchants in Belfast. In County Meath six men were accused of having assaulted and disarmed a party of revenue officers and rescued some confiscated tobacco. The other cases heard at both assizes were relatively minor matters. In Antrim there were 15 assaults, 8 thefts, 2 cases of forcible rescue from

---

[85] Boulter, *Letters*, i. 285, 287–8; *Dublin Intelligence*, 18 Mar. 1729; William Colles to Barry Colles, 14 June 1766 (Prim MS 87, 71–5). See also *Dublin Daily Post*, 3 June 1740: 'The bakers having made but little household bread, the populace were so greatly enraged that they broke open their shops.... Some sold their bread and gave them the money, others took it away.'

[86] S. Murphy, 'Dublin Anti-Union Riot'.

[87] Hobsbawm, 'The City Mob'; Tilly, 'Collective Violence in European Perspective'.

[88] Bartlett, 'An End to Moral Economy'. See below, Epilogue.

custody, 2 of riotous assembly, 3 of arson or other damage to property, and 1 of taking forcible possession. In Meath there were 6 assaults, 7 thefts, 1 rescue, and 1 riotous assembly accompanied by assault.[89]

Both these assizes, of course, tried cases from what were mainly rural areas. Records from the city and county of Cork during 1789–90 reveal, as might be expected, a somewhat higher level of organized and professional crime: thefts of substantial quantities of goods, charges of receiving stolen property, a counterfeiter, and a whole series of indictments against someone who was clearly a fairly active highwayman. There was also rather more violence than in Meath and Antrim. The spring assizes of 1789, for example, heard three homicide cases, although one of these was clearly accidental. But once again the great majority of charges heard by the court related to lesser offences. Forty-nine out of eighty-three sets of charges, for example, were of theft, mainly single articles of clothing, small household utensils, or in some cases goods from shops. In almost half the cases the value of the goods stolen was under £1, and in only nine was it greater than £5.[90] It would of course be naïve to draw too many conclusions regarding the actual level of crime from the absence of prosecutions: one thinks of Roderick O'Flaherty's eulogy on the people of Iar Connacht. But unless there was a massive, systematic bias towards the prosecution of lesser offences, it seems clear that routine law enforcement, by this time at least, was overwhelmingly concerned with petty crime: mainly small-scale, probably opportunistic, theft and brawls arising from personal disputes. The relative infrequency of lethal violence is also revealing, especially when we consider that of all crimes homicide was the one likely to have been most vigorously pursued and least often settled outside the courts.

If assizes records offer only indirect evidence of crime levels, they provide more precise information regarding punishment. The Cork assizes of the spring of 1789 sentenced 17 convicted offenders. Of these, 6 were condemned to hang, 3 were to be transported, and 7 were to be imprisoned, 3 of them also standing in the pillory and another 3 being whipped. The remaining offender was required to pay compensation. In these respects 1789 appears to have been a fairly typical year. A return covering the forty years 1767–1806 shows a total of 130 persons condemned to death in County Cork (24 of these

---

[89] Crown Book, County Antrim assizes, summer 1766 (PRONI D207/19/109); Crown Book, County Meath assizes, summer 1766 (PRONI D207/1/9). Of the three assizes records cited here and in the next note, that for County Cork is the official crown book, the only such volume to escape the destruction of the national records in Dublin in 1922. Those for County Antrim and County Meath, along with a few others of slightly later date, are apparently copies of the crown book, preserved in the Foster–Massereene papers (PRONI) and presumably resulting from work by members of the Foster family as crown prosecutors.

[90] Crown Book, Cork assizes, 1789–90 (Nat. Arch. Ire., Crown and Peace records, County Cork). I am indebted for the figures to Mavis Bracegirdle. Where several indictments that clearly relate to the same episode are listed, these have been counted as a single case.

in 1798) and a further 202 transported.[91] This was not, by contemporary
standards, a high rate of capital convictions. In Surrey, with a population
probably not much more than half that of County Cork, 680 persons were
condemned to death between 1764 and 1802.[92]

Comparable statistics for Ireland in the first half of the eighteenth century
do not exist. However, there is fragmentary evidence to suggest that the
number of capital sentences was not significantly higher than that recorded in
Cork from the 1760s. Fairly tough justice was handed out in County Meath in
the spring of 1737, when 8 convicted prisoners were sentenced to death.
More still, 18, were 'condemned' at Cork in May 1731.[93] Elsewhere, however, death sentences were less common. An observer at the spring assizes for
County Clare in 1692 complained that only 1 man had been hanged, 'though
12 deserved death'. Two capital convictions were reported at the quarter
sessions for Dublin in December 1726. In County Down 5 or 6 prisoners
were awaiting trial on capital charges in March 1736, of whom 3 or 4 were
expected to be found guilty.[94] At Derry in 1742, 3 prisoners were capitally
convicted, and a prisoner who had been held over from the previous assizes to
allow him an opportunity to fulfil an offer to inform against his accomplices
was also ordered to hang. Other reports in the same year speak of several
death sentences in County Kildare, one in County Cavan, and one or two in
Queen's County.[95] Two men were sentenced to death at Wicklow assizes in
March 1731, one at Cork in 1729, one at Westmeath in 1744, and one at
Waterford in 1746.[96] Most of these reports, it should be emphasized, relate to
numbers sentenced to death. In eighteenth-century England only 40 per cent
or so of those capitally convicted were actually hanged.[97] No similar statistics
exist for Ireland, but there too it seems clear that by no means all death
sentences were actually carried out. Captain Hedges reported in 1711 that 3
tories had been condemned to die at Cork and 2 at Tralee, but 'I think they
are not all hanged, the judge having reprieved a boy or two of them'. Of two
men convicted in Dublin in 1729 for robbery, one, aged 18, was hanged
according to sentence, the other, 'being but 17 and very childish', was reprieved for transportation. Likewise, of the 3 men sentenced to hang at Derry

[91] Newenham, *View of the . . . Circumstances of Ireland*, appendix 43–7.
[92] Beattie, *Crime and the Courts*, 532–3.
[93] Brady, *Catholics and Catholicism*, 57; *Dublin Intelligence*, 5 May 1731.
[94] Laurence Chroe to Sir Donough O'Brien, 14 Apr. 1692 (*Inchiguin Manuscripts*, 35); *Dublin Intelligence*, 13–17 Dec. 1726; Robert Ward to Michael Ward, 6 Mar. 1736 (PRONI D2092/1/5/8).
[95] *Faulkner's Dublin Journal*, 31 Aug.–4 Sept., 4–7 Sept., 14–18 Sept., 28 Sept.–2 Oct. 1742.
[96] *Dublin Intelligence*, 29 Mar. 1731; *Dublin Weekly Journal*, 10 May 1729; *Faulkner's Dublin Journal*, 7–10 July 1744; *Pue's Occurrences*, 9–12 Aug. 1746.
[97] Beattie, *Crime and the Courts*, 433.

in 1742, only 2 were in fact executed, the third being recommended for mercy by the jury.[98]

The main alternative to hanging was transportation. Official returns for the period 1737–43 suggest that Ireland, with a population of around 2.5 million, transported on average around 227 persons each year to penal servitude in the American colonies. England, with a population of 5.5 million, transported an average of 620 per year. In fact, the contrast is greater than these figures suggest, for virtually all English transportees had been convicted of a felony. In Ireland less than half of those whose offences are known (459 out of 990) had been so convicted. The remainder were vagrants transported after they had failed to provide security for their future good behaviour.[99] Transportation as a punishment for crime (as opposed to the possible price of being poor and friendless) was thus between three and four times less common in Ireland than in England.

The relatively sparing use of the death penalty was evident even during periods of what was perceived as serious disorder. Archbishop William King, commenting on the epidemic of enlisting in foreign armies in the early 1720s, summed up the standard approach of government on such occasions: 'Half a score have been hanged for these treasonable practices, which we hope will put a stop to them, for it would be a massacre to execute all the guilty.'[100] A similar desire to make effective examples, while avoiding a 'massacre', was evident in the handling of the Hougher disturbances in Connacht ten years earlier.[101] The longer-lasting and more geographically extensive Whiteboy outbreaks of the 1760s, 1770s, and 1780s met with a rather more severe response. Twenty-six agrarian offenders were sentenced to death between 1762 and 1765, 48 in 1770–6, and 19 during 1786–8. Not all those sentenced, however, were actually hanged: at least 5 out of 30 prisoners condemned in 1776 and 6 of the 19 sentenced in 1786–8 were pardoned or escaped with some lesser punishment.[102] This would suggest a total of perhaps 60 or 70 executions during fourteen years of serious agrarian disturbance: a tough response, but well short of a judicial bloodbath.

All in all, the evidence that can be pieced together on the use of execution and transportation would suggest that social order in eighteenth-century Ireland cannot be seen as having been upheld by the ruthless application of legal terror. The law could be harsh, of course. In Dublin in 1726 a boy of 12

[98] Hedges to Dawson, 7 Apr. 1711 (Hedges Letters); *Dublin Intelligence*, 29 July 1729; *Faulkner's Dublin Journal*, 28 Sept.–2 Oct. 1742.
[99] Ekirch, *Bound for America*, 22–5. The annual average suggested for Ireland excludes the higher figures recorded in the famine years of 1741–2.
[100] King to Samuel Molyneux, 23 June 1722 (TCD MS 750/7, 143).
[101] Connolly, 'Law, Order and Popular Protest', 63–4.
[102] Donnelly, 'The Whiteboy Movement', 51; idem, 'Irish Agrarian Rebellion', 317, 324, 328; 'The Rightboy Movement 1785–8', 193–4.

was sentenced to death for having stolen a silver tankard.[103] In general, however, a bloody penal code was applied, as in England, to provide limited numbers of awful examples, rather than the forests of corpses its provisions seemed to imply. It is also important to remember that the penal codes of Ireland and England alike presented a sharp contrast with those that existed in most parts of eighteenth-century Europe. Both, for example, had by the second half of the seventeenth century abandoned the practice of judicial torture, standard in most parts of Western Europe for another century or more.[104] Public hangings, equally, were not a pretty spectacle. But an Irish medical student visiting France in 1781 was as shocked as any Englishman would have been at the spectacle of a criminal left to die slowly after being broken on the wheel.[105]

These earliest surviving assizes records reveal one further striking feature. This is the extraordinarily low proportion of cases that ended with the conviction of the accused. Of the 10 cases heard in County Meath at the summer assizes in 1766 for which an outcome was recorded, 1 bill of indictment was rejected by the grand jury, 4 ended in guilty verdicts, and 5 in acquittals. In County Antrim 7 bills were rejected by the grand jury, and 6 cases were dropped. In the remaining 14 cases there were 4 verdicts of guilty, all relating to charges of assault, and 10 of not guilty. Of 142 defendants coming before the Cork assizes in spring 1789, 26 had their bills of indictment rejected by the grand jury, 5 had their cases deferred, 31 were discharged without being brought to trial, and 43 were tried but acquitted. This left only 37 found guilty, a conviction rate of 26 per cent, as compared to the 60 to 70 per cent that appears to have been common in eighteenth-century England.[106]

How is the failure of so many criminal prosecutions to be accounted for? Equally low conviction rates in the early nineteenth century were attributed to popular alienation from the forces of law and order, combined with the pervasive intimidation of jurors and witnesses alike.[107] But this was after the traumatic events of the 1790s. Observers in the eighteenth century based their explanations of low conviction rates not on horizontal bonds of religious and political solidarity, but rather on vertical ties of patronage and clientage. In 1718 Archbishop King complained that 'the grand juries and gentlemen of

---

[103] *Dublin Intelligence*, 2 July 1726.

[104] Lord Orrery admitted in 1667 that he had threatened a prisoner with the rack and had lit matches tied to his fingers, though with orders that they be taken away before the flame reached his skin. Two years later there were allegations that he had again used matches, this time not merely as a threat, on a French sea captain: *CSPI 1666–9*, 476–8, 725–6. In London a few years later a commission was issued, though not apparently acted on, for the use of torture against two suspected Dutch spies: *CSPD 1672–3*, xvi.

[105] Robert Perceval to William Perceval, 1 Aug. 1781 (PRONI D906/147).

[106] PRONI D207/1/9, D207/19/109; Nat. Arch. Ire., Cork assizes. For England, see Sharpe, *Crime in Early Modern England*, 65–6.

[107] Palmer, *Police and Protest*, 196–7. See also Beames, *Peasants and Power*, 163–7, 178–9.

the country are too easy in making addresses for malefactors'. When a group of tories had recently been condemned at Dundalk, 'about six justices of the peace and 40 or 50 more' had signed a request for a pardon for 'the most mischievous and notorious person among them'. Samuel Madden, writing in 1738, blamed the difficulty of executing the laws even 'against the plainest crimes and the most confessed thieves and villains' not just on 'the corruption of prosecutors, as well as the villainy and perjury of bribed witnesses', but also on 'the interest of the landlords'. Forty years later Arthur Young complained of 'men of fortune' protecting 'all sorts of offenders' and 'making interest for their acquittal'.[108]

Just why the influence of social superiors should apparently have operated so much more frequently in Ireland to secure the acquittal of offenders remains unclear. In some cases the motive was straightforward corruption. The County Kilkenny highwayman James Freney claimed on one occasion to have paid five guineas to 'a man of power and interest' in order to ensure that a sufficient number of jurors would refuse to convict two of his associates awaiting trial in Kilkenny. In Dublin a public outcry in 1729 led to a purge of the city's constables, as well as action against certain magistrates who 'made a trade of binding and unbinding people, as they call it, and taking exorbitant fees'.[109] Yet corruption on the scale necessary to produce the conviction rates recorded in the surviving records would surely have received more explicit mention from contemporary critics. One obvious possibility is that ties of patronage and clientage were simply stronger in Ireland. Another is that the numerical and economic weakness of the Irish middle classes weakened the potential support for processes of bureaucratic rationality, leaving the way open for a more extensive and capricious use of influence by gentry and aristocracy.[110]

A second key element in the low level of convictions was the jury. Arthur Young, proudly informed that not one person had been hanged in County Fermanagh in the preceding twenty-two years, commented sourly that in that case 'there had been many a jury who deserved it richly'.[111] In civil cases contemporaries appear to have taken it for granted that juries would act with a greater or lesser degree of partiality, particularly as between outsiders and local men. Thus Lord Dartmouth, involved in a lawsuit over land in County Galway, was warned by his agent in 1701 that 'there's no justice to be expected for a stranger from a jury of that county' and that his only hope was

---

[108] King to Thomas Coote, 19 Nov. 1718 (TCD MS 750/5, 64); [Madden], *Reflections and Resolutions*, 151–2; Young, *Tour*, ii. 154.

[109] Freney, *Life and Adventures*, 24–5; *Dublin Intelligence*, 13 Sept., 1, 18 Nov., 13, 30 Dec. 1729; Coghill to Southwell, 3 Jan. 1730 (BL Add. MS 21,122, fo. 104).

[110] I owe this suggestion to a lecture given by John Styles to the Economic and Social History Society of Ireland in September 1988.

[111] Young, *Tour*, ii. 154.

to get his case heard elsewhere. In 1731 John Savage of Portaferry in County Down was dismayed when some Belfast merchants who were suing him arranged for the case to be tried at Carrickfergus, where they were 'sure to be favoured by a jury of their own pricking'. He was more satisfied with the outcome of another case, heard in County Down before a jury 'who were all gentlemen of good sense, mostly of my own choosing, by the interest I had in our high sheriff'.[112]

Both local partiality and the packing of juries could also happen in criminal cases. The judge at the Sligo assizes in 1703, outraged at the acquittal of a defendant against all the evidence, was reported to have openly declared 'that the subsheriff was but a shadow to Gallagher a Papist', and that this Gallagher 'has sold the jury'. In 1711 James Gildart, accused of communicating with the Pretender, was indicted in the county rather than the city of Dublin, 'the lords justices doubting whether the indictment could be found in the city where the merchants have so great influence, Gildart being a master of a ship'. The acquittal of Richard Martin in 1735 was attributed to the action of the sheriff in drawing up a panel of jurors consisting 'chiefly of relations of the prisoner, Papists, or such Protestants as were either actually confined to their houses by sickness or absent from the kingdom'.[113] One obvious solution to such problems would have been for the authorities themselves to have intervened in the selection of jurors. Some manipulation of jury lists is in fact known to have occurred, in the trial of the Whiteboys in Tipperary in 1776 and in proceedings against the United Irishmen in 1797.[114] But these were times of exceptional stress. On other occasions what is striking is the absence of any suggestion that either central government or local authorities should use this means to secure a higher rate of convictions.

If juries were sometimes influenced in their decisions by local or personal loyalties, they most commonly used their power, as in contemporary England, to mitigate the harshness of the criminal law. In some cases, as in Derry in 1742, a prisoner might be capitally convicted but recommended for clemency.[115] In others the declared value of goods stolen was reduced to eleven pence, making the offence petty larceny, punishable by whipping and imprisonment, rather than grand larceny, punishable by death.[116] The

---

[112] R. Ayleway to Dartmouth, 7 Sept., 21 Dec. 1701 (Dartmouth Papers, D(w) 1778/Iii/37, 39); Savage to——, 20 July 1731 (PRONI D552/A/2/2/25); Savage to Malone, 2 May 1731 (PRONI D552/A/2/2/21).

[113] Charles O'Hara to Kean O'Hara, 9 Mar. 1703 (PRONI T2812/5/71); Roger Smith to Kean O'Hara, 12 Mar. 1703 (PRONI T2812/5/73); Joshua Dawson to——, 20 Jan. 1711 (Dartmouth Papers, D(w) 1778/Iii/224); lords justices to Dorset, 12 May 1735 (PRONI D2707/A/1/7, 28).

[114] Donnelly, 'Irish Agrarian Rebellion', 328; McDowell, *Ireland in the Age of Imperialism and Revolution*, 547–8.

[115] *Faulkneor's Dublin Journal*, 28 Sept.–2 Oct. 1742.

[116] The verdicts recorded in the Cork assizes for 1789–90 confirm that this was a common practice in Ireland as well as England.

willingness of jurors to use their discretion in these ways depended on their own assessment both of the prisoner's character and of the gravity of the offence. When in 1726 'that memorable whore, thief, bawd, etc. known by the name of Old Hat' was sentenced to death for the theft of a chicken, 11s. 6d. in cash, a pair of gloves, and a pair of scissors, it was most probably her notoriety that sent her to the gallows on a charge that would probably have brought a different offender no further than the whipping post.[117] The ultimate exercise of discretion was of course for a jury which felt that the penalty faced by a particular offender was too severe simply to refuse to convict. Proposals in 1725 to make smuggling a capital offence were objected to on the grounds that in that event 'it would be very difficult to get a jury to find one guilty'. Samuel Madden, while condemning 'a false tenderness and mercy in some men', also recognized that the proliferation of capital statutes was one important reason why juries were so often unwilling to convict.[118]

The independence and discretionary power of juries make it impossible to regard the criminal law, in Ireland any more than in England, as a mere instrument of the ruling class. Men of substantial property ruled the country and made its laws. But it was juries, made up overwhelmingly of farmers, shopkeepers, and artisans, who decided to what extent and in what precise manner those laws were implemented. Indeed, some observers believed that the social bias of the law was in the opposite direction. Sir Robert Southwell in 1702 advised his young protégé Sir John Perceval to settle cases where possible out of court, since 'it is almost current there on any trial to give verdict against him that has most'. Molesworth, in 1723, complained of the folly of gentlemen who avoided service on petty juries, leaving their cases to be decided by 'those meaner ranks of men, who generally attend to serve upon juries, and find their account by doing so'. As a result, a landlord who took his tenant to court could expect no redress, 'the terms of *stiff*, *staunch*, and *tenantable* being to be explained by a jury of farmers, and the damages given seldom answering the bare costs of suit'.[119]

A final reason for the high level of acquittals recorded at assizes lay in the nature of the law itself. The English criminal law of the eighteenth century was distinguished by its insistence on high standards of proof, rigid procedures, and narrow definitions.[120] Detailed accounts of Irish criminal trials are rare, but there are indications that there, too, an insistence on the strict letter of the law could operate to the advantage of the accused. James Shirley, convicted of a rape in 1671, was granted a new trial on the grounds that in the

---

[117] *Dublin Intelligence*, 3 Sept. 1726.
[118] Robert Ward to Michael Ward, 3 Oct. 1725 (PRONI D2092/1/3/54); [Madden], *Reflections and Resolutions*, 151–2.
[119] Southwell to Perceval, Sept. 1702 (HMC, *Egmont Papers*, ii. 211); [Molesworth], *Some Considerations*, 6–7, 20, 10.
[120] Hay, 'Property, Authority and the Criminal Law', 32–3.

writ issued against him the word 'rapuit' had been written 'repuit' and that there was also a suspected erasure. Two men accused of murder in Dublin in 1730 had their trial postponed, the indictment 'having put Latin for a leg instead of a thigh'. The accused in this latter case were eventually convicted and hanged, but others were more fortunate. William Butler, tried at Carlow in 1754 for breaking into a dwelling and taking two yards of frieze, was acquitted on the grounds that the prosecution had proved only that he had broken into the house at night with an intention to rob, not that the goods were in fact taken.[121] In the case of Thomas Corr, a prisoner in the Marshalsea in Dublin tried in 1737 for stabbing a soldier detailed to put him in irons for a disciplinary offence, the court ruled that the order to put on the irons had not come from a duly authorized officer of the prison. This made the soldier guilty of an assault on Corr, and his death became manslaughter not murder. Corr accordingly escaped with a year's imprisonment and a branding on the hand.[122]

To insist in this way on the respect shown for the formalities of due legal process may seem perverse. After all, this was a legal system part of whose provisions systematically deprived three-quarters of the population of a range of basic liberties and entitlements. The chief baron of the Irish exchequer, in a much quoted judgement delivered in 1758, declared that Irish law did not presume a Catholic to exist, except for the purpose of punishment.[123] Such a pronouncement may seem to render the technicalities of individual cases, like those of Butler or Corr, irrelevant. Even where the criminal law is concerned, an insistence on the importance of strict procedure goes against the grain of recent writing, where two notorious cases, those of Sir James Cotter in 1720 and Nicholas Sheehy in 1766, have been cited as evidence of a system of justice readily perverted to political and sectarian purposes.[124]

There is no doubt that the cases of Cotter and Sheehy cast a somewhat different light on the workings of the criminal law in early and mid-eighteenth-century Ireland. But whether they bear the full weight that has been laid on them in recent years is another matter. Sheehy, parish priest of Clogheen, County Tipperary, was executed, along with four others, on a charge of involvement in a Whiteboy murder. He was possibly not a wholly innocent victim: he had, at the very least, given encouragement to those who resisted demands for tithes, and the Catholic vicar-general of his diocese refused to appear at his trial to testify to his loyalty. On the other hand, there seems no doubt that the charge of murder was a blatant fabrication designed

---

[121] *CSPD 1671*, 355, 383; *Dublin Gazette*, 21–4 Nov. 1730; Gilbert MS 34, 197.
[122] Gilbert MSS 32, 3–9; 39, 91–115.
[123] e.g. Fagan, *Second City*, 10; Corish, *Catholic Community*, 73.
[124] Cullen, *Emergence of Modern Ireland*, 199; idem, 'Catholics under the Penal Laws', 32; *NHI* iv. 401–2; Bartlett, 'A New History of Ireland', 216.

to get rid of a known troublemaker.[125] The real question is whether this one case of assassination by legal process can be taken as reflecting on the system as a whole. During the early 1760s the involvement of prominent Catholic and conformist families in County Tipperary politics had created deep religious divisions, which the Whiteboy agitation had inflamed to the point, on the Protestant side, of near hysteria.[126] The judicial murder of Sheehy was thus the high point of a particularly vicious local conflict, its very notoriety, both at the time and later, marking it out as an exceptional event.

The case of Sir James Cotter, hanged for the rape of Elizabeth Squibb, is less clear-cut. Cotter, like Sheehy, was undoubtedly a Catholic troublemaker: an alleged Jacobite who had played a leading part in the Dublin election riot of 1713 and whose father (a point of much greater weight with contemporaries than recent historians have allowed) had assassinated the regicide John Lisle at Lusanne in 1664. But here the similarities end. There was, in the first place, no local conspiracy to bring about Cotter's death. On the contrary, leading members of the County Cork Protestant establishment, from the sheriff and grand jury up to Lord Chancellor Midleton, made strenuous efforts to save him from the gallows. Responsibility for his death lay rather with the trial judges, who were said not to have shown him 'that tenderness . . . on his trial as is usual in cases of life and death'; with the English secretary of state, James Craggs; and possibly with some members of the Irish executive.[127] The second point is that Cotter had quite clearly been guilty of rape. Apart from Miss Squibb's own testimony, there were witnesses 'as to hearing her cry out, and being in a very ill condition after the act committed, and being found with her clothes up and very ill and vomiting violently when Cotter left her'.[128] The main arguments for a reprieve were compassion for Cotter's wife and children, combined with a feeling that Miss Squibb had, by

---

[125] O'Connell, 'The Plot against Father Nicholas Sheehy'; Lonergan, 'The Life and Death of Father Sheehy'.

[126] Cullen, *Emergence of Modern Ireland*, 122–3, 200.

[127] This discussion is based mainly on the long account of the case in Midleton to Thomas Brodrick, 28 Mar. 1720 (Midleton MS 1248/4, fos. 440–2). Midleton identifies one of those who argued that Cotter, as a political undesirable, should be shown no mercy as a Mr C——. This could refer to the English secretary of state, James Craggs, whose belief that Cotter should be hanged is noted in other sources, or alternatively to William Conolly. Even insiders remained unclear as to who had influenced the lord lieutenant against a reprieve: Thomas Brodrick to Midleton, 29 Apr. 1720 (Midleton MS 1248/4, fo. 256ᵛ). Bishop Evans of Meath later noted that he was accused by Catholics of having played a part in the decision: Evans to Wake, 22 Mar. 1723 (Wake MS XIV, 61). A further complication is that the lord lieutenant's wife was a grand-daughter of Lisle (information from D. W. Hayton).

[128] Midleton to Thomas Brodrick, 28 Mar. 1720 (Midleton MS 1298/5, fo. 441). See also Midleton to Thomas Brodrick, 20 Apr. 1720 (ibid., fo. 247); Midleton to Henry Boyle, 24 Mar. 1720 (PRONI D2707/A1/2/8A). These letters seem wholly to dispose of suggestions that Midleton, representing a Munster-based ultra-Protestant party, should be seen as the man behind Cotter's death. (See Cullen, 'The 1798 Rebellion in its Eighteenth-Century Context', 100.)

the double standard of the time, contributed to her own downfall by forward and indiscreet behaviour. If there was a complaint to be made about Cotter's treatment, in other words, it was not that an innocent man had been hanged, but rather that he had not been shown the indulgence that could normally have been expected by a well-born offender convicted of this particular crime. This does not alter the fact that Cotter's Catholic and Jacobite associations played a part in bringing him to the gallows. But the episode falls somewhat short of the judicial assassination that has been implied in recent work.

Just how inaccurate a paradigm these two notorious cases offer for the normal workings of the law in eighteenth-century Ireland may be seen by looking at the way in which the formidable body of discriminatory legislation affecting Catholic clergy and laity was actually implemented. In the case of the Catholic clergy, a return of persons brought before the courts as regulars or persons exercising ecclesiastical jurisdiction in the years 1699–1703 shows an outcome only slightly more decisive than in other criminal cases. Out of a total of 26 men listed, 11 had been convicted, 5 had been acquitted, 1 had been discharged when no indictment was framed against him, and 9 were awaiting trial, 4 on bail, the other 5 in custody.[129] More striking still, in terms of strict adherence to proper legal procedure, was the implementation of the post-war land settlement. Sir Richard Cox, giving judgement in 1699 on the claim of certain citizens of Galway to be protected by the articles agreed when the town had surrendered eight years earlier, subjected the appellants to a patronizing homily on their good fortune in coming before a court that operated on principles different from their own: 'You ought therefore to impute it to the honesty of Englishmen and the sincerity of Protestants, to the honour of a noble nation and the principles of a pure religion, that we have postponed our passions to our justice.'[130] But the fact remains that Cox's self-congratulatory rhetoric was for the most part justified. In sharp contrast to what had happened in 1663, the cases of those claiming the protection of the Articles of Limerick and Galway appear to have been heard impartially and according to proper rules of evidence. The courts in fact rejected only 15 or 16 out of a total of 1,283 cases. In addition the trustees who administered the sale of the forfeited estates during 1700–3 admitted the claims of substantial numbers of wives, children, and others pleading an interest in forfeited lands on the basis of leases, family settlements, and other property transfers. In all, some 12 per cent of the land held by Catholics in 1703 had been secured on the basis of such claims, some of them almost certainly based on the forgery or backdating of the necessary documents.[131]

---

[129] PRONI D207/1/2; Burke, *Irish Priests*, 155–61.
[130] Speech in the Court of Claims (BL Add. MS 38,153, fo. 18).
[131] Simms, *Williamite Confiscation*, 45–54, 136–46, 193. For the series of legal fictions produced by one Catholic claimant, see Troost, 'Letters from Bartholomew van Homrigh', 73–6, 85–7, 90, 97, 99, 101. The forging of backdated leases and settlements seems to have happened on a large scale in England and Scotland after 1715: Lenman, *Jacobite Risings*, 162–73.

The distinction between the discriminatory content of legislation and the manner of its implementation is further evident from the enforcement of the legal restrictions of Catholic landownership introduced by the Popery Bill of 1704 and later measures. The comments of Chief Baron Bowes to the effect that a Catholic had no legal existence are particularly misleading here. Bowes was giving judgment against a Catholic merchant who had tried to keep a young female relative away from other family members seeking to convert her to the Church of Ireland. His point was that Catholics could claim no rights as a corporate body, not that they did not as individuals have the same rights as other citizens.[132] And in fact it is clear that Catholic defendants, even in cases arising from the Popery acts themselves, had the same freedom as others to shelter from the penalties of the law within the undergrowth of its technicalities and procedural rules. It is true that the courts consistently ruled that the Popery laws should be considered as ameliorative, intended for the betterment of society, and therefore to be interpreted more broadly than penal laws, intended to impose penalties on particular classes of persons.[133] Within this framework, however, the laws were enforced with strict regard for rules of procedure and definition. Thus there was much debate on the issue, apparently never fully resolved, of the extent to which the Act of 1697 declaring a man married to a Papist to be himself a Papist 'for all intents and purposes' thereby left him open to the penalties of later Popery acts. Other rulings were clearly in the interest of Catholic defendants. A bill of discovery was rejected because the discoverer, though he had performed the public recantation required of converts from Catholicism, had not filed his certificate of having done so within six months. A covenant to renew a lease as often as the lessor's own lease was renewed was held not to be a discoverable interest, being contingent on the head landlord's good will. A bill of discovery against the purchase by some of the joint heirs of a Catholic landlord of the interest held by others was accepted; but the court rejected a claim that their action had made the whole estate discoverable, 'for their old right they still have as executors and under the will'. A decision of the House of Lords making a Catholic purchaser accountable for profits arising from the time of purchase was held to be 'on account of some extraordinary circumstances'. Consequently, a later defendant was not required to pay either costs or past profits, 'for that it was hardship enough on the defendant to lose his lands'.[134]

Religion was not, of course, the only source of potential injustice. Even in theory, the legal system was by no means blind to social distinctions. Sir

---

[132] Fagan, *Second City*, 10.

[133] W. N. Osborough, 'Catholics, Land and the Popery Acts of Anne', in Power and Whelan (eds.), *Endurance and Emergence*, 22.

[134] For men married to Papists, see Howard, *Several Special Cases*, 24, 47–9, 49–61; Cases on the Popery Acts (Gilbert MS 191, 10). For the other cases mentioned, see Gilbert MS 191, 2, 3, 11–12, 46, 50; Howard, *Several Special Cases*, 27, 69. See also Osborough, 'Catholics, Land and the Popery Acts of Anne', 34–8.

Richard Cox, supporting the appeal in 1704 of a certain Mr Power who had been convicted of manslaughter to be spared the usual penalty of branding, observed confidently that 'it was never meant to burn a gentleman in the hand, unless the fact had appeared villainous, as it did not'. A legal opinion drawn up around 1730 made clear that whipping, as a punishment generally considered shameful, was to be inflicted only on 'low mean rioters' and other offenders unable to pay a fine.[135] Persons presented as vagrants under the Act of 1706 were to be transported unless they could provide security for their good behaviour. The hundred or more persons shipped off to the American colonies each year were thus in effect being punished because they had neither resources of their own nor patrons to stand by them. When it came to individual cases, social distinctions became even more important. Well-born criminals could expect the systematic exertion of influence on their behalf; the poor man's fate was determined by more haphazard processes of patronage, by the impression he managed to make on a jury of small property-owners, and by impersonal calculations of the proper balance to be maintained between justice and clemency.[136] In England, defenders of the legal system could point to the example of Lord Ferrers, convicted and hanged in 1760 for the murder of his steward. Ireland had its potential equivalent in the case of Lord Santry, indicted in 1739 for the murder of his footman. Santry's trial was a major public event, the tickets sold to spectators carrying the promising motto 'Justice and no favour'. In the event, however, the sentence of death was followed by a timely reprieve and the restoration to Santry's family of the estate which he had forfeited as a condemned felon.[137]

Cases like this make clear that one should not idealize the workings of the criminal law. At the same time, important points remain to be considered. Eighteenth-century Ireland, despite its recent history of warfare and military conquest, was not a society ruled either by terror or by arbitrary power. This was not just because the apparatus of coercion available to central and local authorities was small-scale, informal, and decentralized. Even where offenders were brought before the courts, only a minority were convicted, and far fewer of these were executed than the harsh provisions of the law implied. It follows that judicial terror can have played only a limited role in the maintenance of order. To the extent that the sparing use of capital and other major penalties was due to the acceptance of strict formulas and rules of procedure, we have a demonstration that the rule of law, in Ireland as in England, was no mere

---

[135] Cox to Ormond, 25 May 1704 (HMC, *Ormonde Manuscripts*, NS viii. 79); Gilbert MS 35, 39–43.

[136] For English parallels, see Hay, 'Property, Authority and the Criminal Law', 44–9; Langbein, 'Albion's Fatal Flaws'; King, 'Decision-Makers and Decision-Making in the English Criminal Law'.

[137] Lavallin Nugent to Margaret Savage, 26 Apr. 1739 (PRONI D552/A/2/10/1); *Dublin Daily Post*, 28 Apr., 1, 17, 21, 25 May, 9 Aug. 1739.

slogan. The law may have served the interests of the ruling élite; but it also imposed real limits on their actions. To the extent that restraint in the implementation of a harsh penal code resulted from the discretionary granting of clemency or the invocation of vertical ties of clientship and patronage, we are once again reminded that government was no one-way process. In Ireland, as elsewhere in modern Europe, the rule of the few depended on constant accommodations to make it acceptable, or at least bearable, to the many.

4. Views from Below: Disaffection and the Threat of Rebellion

In the eyes of Irish Protestants, of course, the real threat to the social and political order came not from crime, or even from toryism, but from the disaffection of the Catholic masses. Sometimes what was envisaged was another 1641: a popular rebellion accompanied by wholesale plunder and massacre. More commonly the assumption was that a rising in Ireland would be part of an attempt, probably supported by one or more of the Catholic powers of Europe, to restore the exiled Stuarts. The reality that lay behind these assumptions has been little explored. Traditional historical writing on Irish Catholicism has been characterized by a marked telescoping of historical reality, in which the political principles espoused by late eighteenth-century campaigners for 'Catholic relief' have been projected backwards onto the Jacobites who laid down their arms, in the face of military defeat, in 1691. The result has been to present the Catholic Irish of the early eighteenth century as passive victims of the malice and paranoia of a victorious Protestant establishment.[138] The recent explosion of work on Jacobitism in early Hanoverian England has made such a perspective increasingly difficult to sustain.[139] But as yet there has been little attempt to investigate the character of political loyalties in any section of the Catholic population.

The essential starting-point for any such investigation is the recognition that the Irish supporters of James II did not see their surrender in 1691 as a permanent settlement. The Treaty of Limerick, far from enshrining the long-term political aspirations of Irish Catholics, set out the terms of a purely local truce, under which the defeated but still militarily formidable Jacobites laid down their arms and awaited the outcome of the general European conflict.[140] Throughout the next six years, hopes rose and fell with the military fortunes

---

[138] See e.g. Corish, *Catholic Community*, ch. 4, 6, which leaps from the Catholic defeat of 1689–91 to the apolitical character of rural protest in the 1760s and after, with clear, if unstated, implications for the intervening account of legal repression and discrimination.

[139] See e.g. B. Ó Buachalla, review of Evelyn Cruickshanks and Jeremy Black (eds.), *The Jacobite Challenge*, in *Eighteenth-Century Ireland*, 4 (1989), 186–90. For a selection of recent work on England, see below, n. 245.

[140] P. Kelly, 'Lord Galway and the Penal Laws', 254 n. 51.

of France. Thus, in May 1692, when a major invasion of Great Britain had been widely expected, Lord Longford reported from Dublin that 'the Irish (the most considerable of which have been for some time in town) the last week carried their noses high and looked big'. But the latest packets, bringing news of the defeat of the French fleet at Barfleur, 'have made them crest-fallen'. By November of the following year expectations had recovered. The bishop of Limerick complained of 'the impudence of the Irish at this time, their confident expectation of a turn, and presumptuous carriage . . . which makes the Protestants despond'.[141] The Treaty of Ryswick in 1697 tem-porarily curtailed hopes of an early reversal in fortunes. On the other hand, the breakdown of relations between William III and his parliament in 1701 left 'the Irish . . . very much up'.[142] With the resumption of war in 1702, the anxious scrutiny of distant battlefields resumed. Minor French successes in the early part of the 1704 campaigning season 'did so much exalt the Papists in this kingdom, that they grew insolent and took liberty of talking more largely than ever they durst since 1691'. After Marlborough's spectacular victory at Blenheim (2 August), on the other hand, 'the dejection some of the Irish (I mean such of them as I have seen) show on this occasion is incredible)'. In 1707 Captain Hedges was outraged by 'the insolent behaviour of the Irish' following news of the French victory at Almanza in Spain. Early the following year, with a French invasion fleet on its way to Scotland, 'the Irish, according to their laudable custom, are insolent and foolish'.[143]

The swings between anticipation and dejection that inevitably accompanied the ups and downs of a lengthy military conflict were intensified by a de-pendence on word of mouth to bring early news of distant events. A hostile pamphleteer in the mid-seventeenth century had already made the connection between the political circumstances of Irish Catholics and their constant quest for information. They were 'servile, crafty and inquisitive after news, the symptoms of a conquered nation'. A more friendly writer in 1683 found them to be 'great lovers of music and fond of news'.[144] After 1691 the progress of events outside Ireland assumed a more immediate relevance. Alan Brodrick thought it sinister that word of the victory at Blenheim was brought to Cork city on 12 August by persons coming from the western baronies of the county, although the official dispatch did not reach Dublin for another five days. In the same way, King, commenting in 1706 on reports current among the Catholics regarding a French defeat in Spain, complained that 'they have

[141] Longford to Ellis, 19 May 1692 (Melvin, 'Letters of Lord Longford', 94); Nathaniel Wilson to William Moreton, bishop of Kildare, 3 Nov. 1693 (Wyche Papers, 1/1/96).
[142] Alan Brodrick to Thomas Brodrick, 28 June 1701 (Midleton MS 1248/2, fo. 24).
[143] Coursey Ireland to Robert Harley, 18 July 1704 (HMC, *Portland Manuscripts*, iv. 103); Alan Brodrick to St John Brodrick, 11 July 1704 (Midleton MS 1248/2, fo. 141); Hedges to Dawson, 8 July 1707 (Hedges Letters); King to Southwell, 13 Mar. 1708 (TCD MS 750/3/2, 194).
[144] Leerssen, *Mere Irish and Fior-Ghael*, 62; Account of County Leitrim 1683 (Molyneux Papers, 883/1, 138).

news some ways unknown to us, a considerable time before we hear any thing of the matter'.[145]

After 1710, as the French war effort wound down preliminary to the opening of peace negotiations, attention shifted to English domestic politics. Jacobites and anti-Jacobites alike speculated on the succession to the childless Anne, and sought to divine the intentions of the Tory government. In January 1712 Alan Brodrick, travelling towards Dublin, 'was met by an Irish man (one Tirwhit of the County of Kilkenny)' who asked him if he knew that examinations had been taken by the Tory government against his son St John for some supposedly seditious remarks. Their meeting provides a brief glimpse of the sort of encounter that may have lain behind the constant complaints of 'insolence', at a time when members of the Catholic élite were both more numerous and more assertive than they were later to become. Archbishop King a few months later commented on the relationship between the 'despondence' of the Protestants, greater even than in 1686–7, and the 'strangely cheerful' appearance of the Catholics: 'I reckon that these mutually cause one another, as in a dropsy thirst causes drinking and drinking increases the thirst, in proportion as the one goes down the other rises, et vice versa.'[146]

The peaceful installation of George I was followed by one last surge of anticipation. In the summer of 1715 both sides believed that a Jacobite invasion was imminent. The Irish Catholics, King reported in July, 'could not conceal their expectations'. In November, after armed risings had begun in Scotland and the north of England, the lords justices complained of 'a greater spirit among the Papists and other disaffected persons than has yet shown itself in this kingdom since the Revolution'. A correspondent in County Kerry reported in January 1716 that 'the people here, I mean Papists, are so far advanced that they will pay no money'; 'the whisper' among them, apparently, was that soldiers from Irish regiments in the French army were about to start landing secretly, in small detachments, to prepare for a rising.[147] Later the same year, even after the English and Scottish risings had been crushed, Irish Catholics were still sufficiently convinced of the relevance of European diplomacy to their condition to lament the defeat of France's clients, the Turks, by England's ally, the Empire.[148] In April 1719, after another Jacobite invasion fleet had been scattered by a storm, Midleton once again complained that 'the Irish are very insolent in the remote parts of the kingdom, and they

[145] Alan Brodrick to St John Brodrick, 27 Aug. 1704 (Midleton MS 1248/2, fo. 145); King to Annesley, 17 Sept. 1706 (TCD MS 750/3/2, 51).

[146] Alan Brodrick to Thomas Brodrick, 18 Jan. 1712 (Midleton MS 1248/3, fo. 62); King to George Tollett, 28 Aug. 1712 (TCD MS 750/4/1, 46–7).

[147] King to Revd Robert Howard, 30 July 1715 (TCD MS 2533, 39); lords justices to Stanhope, 8 Nov. 1715 (SP63/373/236); extract from a letter from Tralee, 10 Jan. 1716 (SP63/374/49).

[148] Godwin to Wake, 4 Sept. 1716 (Wake MS XII, fo. 71); Evans to Wake, 30 Oct. 1716 (ibid., fo. 89).

as little believe that the designed invasion is in great measure defeated, as they formerly pretended to believe any such thing was intended'.[149]

By this time, however, the great age of Jacobite expectation was already over. A treaty concluded between France and England at the end of 1716 marked the start of two decades of unprecedented good relations between the two states. One consequence of this diplomatic revolution was the withdrawal of French support for the Pretender. Even the 1719 expedition, despite the hopes it aroused, was in reality a desperate venture, backed by the second-rate powers of Spain and Sweden. Yet, even in the bleaker international climate that now reigned, Irish Catholics continued to look to the world outside for signs of an imminent transformation of their condition. In 1722, with Louis XV about to come of age, Archbishop King found 'a notion got into the Papists' heads' that he would feel bound by his coronation oath, which obliged him to extirpate heresy, to renew French support for the Stuarts. 'They greatly please themselves with this and depend on it as certain.' During the short war with Spain in early 1727, 'the vulgar Papists' eagerly took up reports that Gibraltar had fallen or was about to fall. In 1734 Boulter reported that French successes against Austria in the War of the Polish Succession had made Protestants very uneasy, while 'the Papists here are more than ordinarily insolent on the occasion'.[150]

This account of Catholic political responses is of course derived wholly from the comments of Protestant observers. The constant references to 'insolence' are a reminder both of the hostility and of the preconceptions of such witnesses. Yet the image of an unreconciled, assertive Catholic party, constantly alert for signs of a possible reversal in fortunes, does not depend solely on the fears of Irish Protestants. There were also concrete manifestations of the continued attachment of substantial numbers of Catholics to the cause of the French and the exiled Stuarts.

One of these was privateering. The commissioning of private vessels to prey on enemy shipping was an integral part of French naval strategy, especially in 1689–97 and 1702–13. Privateering ventures were in many cases financed by Irish merchants based in France, acting on commissions either from Louis XIV or from the Jacobite court. The captains and crews of the vessels involved were also in many cases Irish.[151] Nor was it only expatriates who collaborated in this way with the enemy power. There were also repeated complaints that Stuart and French privateers operating off the coast of Ireland received active assistance from the local population, who supplied them with fresh provisions, help in navigating local waters, and information concerning the movement of potential prizes. Pierce Arnop, whose fortified house at Crookhaven was

[149] Midleton to Thomas Brodrick, 25 Apr. 1719 (Midleton MS 1248/4, fos. 242–3).
[150] King to Edward Hopkins, 6 Nov. 1722 (TCD MS 750/7, 235); *Dublin Intelligence*, 27–30 May 1727; Boulter to bishop of London, 9 Sept. 1734 (*Letters*, ii. 124–5).
[151] Beresford, 'Ireland in French Strategy', 72–9.

sacked by sixty or seventy French privateers in April 1704, blamed the local Irish for having informed the attackers of the weak state of his defences. Three years later privateers who landed near Ballycotton, County Cork, took sheep belonging to a local gentleman, 'but left all the Irish, which I suppose they knew by intelligence, or thought them to be Irish because they were not marked'.[152]

A further demonstration of Catholic disaffection was provided by the Irish regiments in the French service. The original nucleus of this force had been the 5,000 to 6,000 men brought over in 1690 in exchange for French troops sent to James II in Ireland, along with the 12,000 or so members of the Jacobite army who had exercised their right to go to France after the surrender of Limerick. Thereafter numbers were kept up by clandestine recruiting in Ireland. Prior to 1714 this regular export of young men destined for the forces of what was for most of the time a hostile power appears to have caused irritation rather than anxiety.[153] Presumably the authorities recognized that it could not be prevented or saw other threats as more immediate. It was not until 1714, at a time when the two kingdoms were in fact at peace, that the activities of French recruiters became an issue of real concern. Precisely why this happened remains unclear. One possibility is that the recruiters, now that the war was over, had become less discreet. Certainly the sheer numbers believed to have been recruited—10,000 to 20,000 according to some reports—was one of the reasons given for the sudden outcry. Added to this were persistent reports that those enlisting were intended not for the French army, but for the Pretender's service. All this, moreover, came at a time when Protestant nerves were already on edge as the queen entered her last illness. The result was a wave of arrests and the eventual execution of three men in Dublin on a charge of having enlisted recruits on behalf of the Pretender.[154]

Recruitment for the French service continued after 1714. Cullen puts the number enlisted in the 1720s and 1730s at somewhere under 1,000 men per year.[155] With England and France now on friendly terms, such activity was no longer as threatening as before. But in 1720 there were complaints that men claiming to be on their way to France were in fact heading for Spain, which the year before had backed a Jacobite invasion plan. Concern over Spanish

---

[152] Petition of Pierce Arnop, Sept. 1704 (HMC, *Portland Manuscripts*, iv. 123–4); Charles Crowe, bishop of Cloyne, to Sir Richard Cox, 25 May 1707 ('Calendar of Church Miscellaneous Papers', 74). See also *CSPD 1695*, 200; *Dublin Intelligence*, 8 Oct. 1709.

[153] See e.g. Addison to Godolphin, 21 May 1709 (*Letters*, 140).

[154] HMC, *Portland Manuscripts*, v. 460, 472, 473; BL Add. MS 38,157, fos. 55, 57ᵛ, 63, 65, 69ᵛ, 106. The number enlisted was hotly debated. In April, Cox rejected Alan Brodrick's figure of 4,000. 'I don't believe the tenth part of that number went hence since Christmas': Cox to Southwell, 20 Apr. 1714 (BL Add. MS 38,157, fos. 83–4). The lord lieutenant, just over 2 months later, put the number at 'not less than 4 or 5,000 men...some pretend 50,000': Shrewsbury to Prior, 1 July 1714 (HMC, *Portland Manuscripts*, v. 469). King wrote of 'at least 10,000; some think 20,000': King to Samuel Molyneux, 17 June 1714 (TCD MS 750/4/1, 305).

[155] Cullen in *NHI* iv. 161.

recruiting mounted during the next two years. By the summer of 1722 it was claimed that several thousand had left. Those involved were said to have 'appeared in companies of 4 or 500 and quartered themselves on the country'. In January parliament had rushed through a bill making it a felony to enlist in, or recruit for, any foreign service without licence. Over the next few months between six and ten men were hanged for their part in raising troops for Spain.[156] Even enlisting for the French army, despite the new diplomatic relationship, was not wholly acceptable. The Dublin government, on instructions from London, ignored the activities of French recruiting officers. If any were apprehended, the prosecution was dropped or else the accused was pardoned after conviction. Yet a proposal in 1729–30 to license French officers to raise 750 men aroused such opposition in Ireland that it had to be dropped.[157]

It would be naïve to see this recruitment of young Irish Catholics solely in terms of support for the Stuart cause. The export of surplus males as fighting men was a common feature of less developed regions in early modern Europe. By the early nineteenth century, Irishmen were to account for up to one-third of the forces of the British crown: there is no way of knowing how many of the 'wild geese' of earlier generations would just as readily have entered the service of King William, Queen Anne, or the first two Georges, had they been permitted to do so. Some Catholic Irishmen, after all, joined the army of England's ally Austria; this means that on occasion, as at Cremona in 1702, Irishmen fought on both sides. And in fact the great majority of Irish Catholics who entered the service of foreign powers did not by so doing become soldiers for the Stuart cause. Well-informed Protestant observers believed that the large numbers recruited in 1714 would in fact find themselves serving in the regular French army; the men recruited for Spain in 1720–2 were reputedly destined for service against the Moors. Yet the fact remains that French and Spanish recruiters found the promise of serving the Stuarts an effective way of gaining recruits. Men enlisted in Dublin in 1714 were told 'that they should immediately march to Lorraine and see the young king; and if they behaved themselves well, should soon return with preferment'. Others, signed up in County Wexford, were assured that 'they were to serve King James the Third and that they should not fight a battle till they landed in England or Ireland'.[158] Later recruits may have had a more realistic view of their prospects. Yet some sense of commitment to a cause

---

[156] Horatio Walpole to Delafaye, 15 Sept. 1720 (PRONI T2806, 34); Nicolson to Wake, 13 Jan. 1722 (Gilbert MS 27, 276); King to Molyneux, 23 June 1722 (TCD MS 750/7, 142–3); King to Annesley, 11 Dec. 1722 (ibid. 253). The term 'wild geese' appears to have originated at this time: see *Dublin Intelligence*, 3 Apr. 1722.

[157] Boulter, *Letters*, ii. 30–48.

[158] Information of Henry Murphy, 15 Jan. 1714 (Midleton MS 1248/3, fo. 157ᵛ); report by John Forster, 19 July 1715 (SP63/373/34–5).

remained. 'All recruits raised here for France or Spain', Archbishop Boulter told the duke of Newcastle in 1730, 'are generally considered as persons that may some time or other pay a visit to this country as enemies. That all who are listed here in those services hope and wish to do so there is no doubt.'[159] The commander of the Irish brigade at Fontenoy in 1745, leading his men into withering gunfire, urged them forward 'against the enemies of France and your own selves'. They responded with cries of 'Cuimhnigi air Luimneach agus feall na Sasanach' (remember Limerick and the treachery of the English).[160]

In addition to foreign recruitment and the co-operation of coastal populations with privateers, there were occasional more direct demonstrations of Jacobite loyalty. In Dublin during the 1720s there were regular gatherings at St Stephen's Green on 10 June, the date of the Pretender's birth. In 1724 the crowd made 'a sort of a procession round the Green, a thing like a woman dressed in white on horseback appearing to be the chief person in the same'. Some of the crowd wore white roses. There were cries of 'High Church and Ormond', 'Down with King George', and (as somewhat improbably phrased by a Whig newspaper) 'Long Live the Pretender'. A similar demonstration two years later was larger and more violent. Constables sent to break it up were driven away with stones and bricks, and the crowd dispersed only after soldiers had fired on them. Archbishop Boulter rejected suggestions that there had been plans for a Papist rising. 'At present I do not find that there was much more in it than the Popish rabble coming down to fight the Whig mob, as they used to do on that day, only that upon the prospect of a war, the Papists are better in heart, and so might come in greater numbers.' In 1729 a party once again turned out 'wearing white roses and abusing passengers who might from their appearances be thought to be of the Protestant interest, in a most barbarous manner'.[161]

Boulter saw the 10 June rioters as a 'Popish rabble'. Yet the slogan 'High Church and Ormond' suggests that a few at least were Anglicans. Elsewhere too there are occasional references to Protestant disloyalty. In Kilkenny, Ormond's city, there were complaints in 1715 that a Protestant crowd had played a seditious tune and insulted visiting judges, and that those responsible had been shielded by the grand jury. Archbishop Synge, in 1716, referred to 'strong parties' of disaffected Protestants in Kilkenny, Derry, Waterford, and Galway.[162] There were also repeated allegations that Trinity College, Dublin,

---

[159] Boulter to Newcastle, 14 Oct. 1730 (*Letters*, ii. 31).

[160] *NHI* iv. 635.

[161] *Dublin Intelligence*, 13, 17 June 1724, 11 June 1726; Boulter to Newcastle, 11 June 1726 (*Letters*, i. 80–1); *Dublin Intelligence*, 14 June 1729; Giblin, '*Nunziatura di Fiandra*', 9 (1966), 14–15.

[162] King to Robert Mossom, dean of Ossory, 10 Sept. 1715 (TCD MS 2533, 79–80); Synge to Wake, 9 Oct. 1716 (Gilbert MS 28, 70).

was a stronghold of Jacobite sentiment. In 1708 a student named Forbes was expelled and deprived of his degree for his derisive reply to a toast that had been proposed to the glorious memory. Two years later, three students were convicted of having defaced the statue of King William in the square before the college. Around the same time or shortly after, a student reproved for omitting any reference to the Revolution in a 5 November oration 'answered that he durst not say any thing of it, for his class fellows and all the scholars would hiss him if he said anything to its advantage, and he should not be able to live in the college'.[163] In 1715 there were new complaints regarding 'a nest of Jacobites' in the university. King William's statue was again defaced, while students openly celebrated the birthday of the duke of Ormond, the college's former chancellor. In 1719 three students got into a street brawl with two English footmen who had objected to hearing them sing 'The King shall enjoy his own again'.[164] There were repeated complaints that the college authorities made no effort to suppress these displays of disaffection. Addison, in 1715, went so far as to claim that some of the senior fellows sought 'to corrupt the principles of the young men in favour of Popery and the Pretender, with treasonable healths, riotous proceedings etc'.[165] The appointment in 1717 of a new Whig provost was seen as bringing the college under a measure of control. But as late as 1727 Archbishop Boulter defended the extensive powers of the provost, 'beyond anything any head of a college has in Oxford', as necessary 'to keep the college here from being a seminary to Jacobitism'.[166]

The other major centre of suspected Protestant disaffection was among the clergy of the Church of Ireland. In 1688 Irish churchmen, faced with the reality rather than the mere threat of Popish government, had been significantly more ready than their English counterparts to reconcile their consciences to the necessity of dethroning James II. Only one bishop, William Sheridan of Kilmore, and a handful of the lower clergy had refused to take the oaths of supremacy and allegiance under William III and Mary, as compared to six bishops and some 400 clergy in England.[167] Over the next two decades, however, the pressures on the Irish Anglican clergy became more complex. A growing number came under the influence of the High Church movement, in which extravagant claims for the prerogatives of the established church were inextricably tied up with the ideology of hereditary succession within a divinely ordained political and social order. If Irish

---

[163] King to——, n.d. [1712–14] (TCD MS 750/4/1, 341–2). For the other episodes, see McDowell and Webb, *Trinity College, Dublin*, 33–4.

[164] King to Addison, 7 July 1715 (TCD MS 750/4/2, 54); King to bishop of Dromore, 6 Oct. 1715 (TCD MS 2533, 97–8); King to Nicolson, 16 July 1715 (ibid. 15); King to Wake, 2 Aug. 1715 (ibid. 42–3); Synge to Wake, 3 May 1716 (Gilbert MS 28, 62); King to Wake, 8 May 1716 (TCD MS 2533, 231); Evans to Wake, 2 July [1719] (Wake MS XIII, 75).

[165] Addison to Delafaye, 4 June 1715 (*Letters*, 331–2).

[166] Boulter to Wake, 6 July 1727 (*Letters*, i. 179–80).

[167] McGuire, 'The Church of Ireland and the "Glorious Revolution"'.

Anglicans lived with a more real Popish threat than their English counter-parts, moreover, they also lived with the rivalry of a numerically much stronger Dissent. The result, as party divisions hardened during the reign of Queen Anne, was to turn the majority of the Irish clergy into openly partisan Tories. The Whigs, in response, became, in some cases at least, openly anti-clerical.[168]

All this helps to explain why the installation of George I in 1714 appeared to many churchmen less as a deliverance from catastrophe than as the triumph of the church's enemies. A sudden rash of sermons denounced the doctrine of consubstantiation and other aspects of Lutheranism, which some preachers allegedly presented as being 'as bad, if not worse, than Popery'. William Nicolson, arriving at his new see of Derry in 1718, was treated to a visitation sermon denouncing the doctrines of Benjamin Hoadly and other leading Whig divines in England and exhorting those present 'to stand manfully in the gap; to support with all our strength the tottering Church of Ireland; and to sound an alarm betimes in all the streets of our Jerusalem. In short, a stranger (as I was) could hardly avoid fancying, there was another Popish army at the gates of Derry, and that we were all to prepare for a new siege.'[169]

Faced with sentiments of this kind, some observers believed that the political allegiance of the clergy of the Church of Ireland was less certain after 1714 than it had been in 1688–91. Bishop Godwin of Kilmore declared in 1716 that he would be more comforted by the absence of non-jurors in Ireland were it not 'that we have so many swearing clergymen that favour the cause as much as the nonjurors'. The lords justices in the same year complained of 'the neglect of most of the clergymen here to mention his Majesty and their Royal Highnesses in the prayer before their sermons'.[170] In Derry Nicolson learned that four or five of his clergy had left out the customary collect used in times of war and tumult during the Jacobite risings of 1715 and 1719.[171] Nor was offence confined to acts of omission. In 1719 a clergyman in Kilkenny chose as his text for a sermon on the anniversary of George I's accession 'Thou shalt not set a stranger over thee'. Another, in County Cork a few years later, opted for 'Sufficient unto the day is the evil thereof'.[172]

None of these episodes of apparent Protestant disaffection can be taken wholly at face value. Vague references to 'disaffection' and even 'sedition' in

---

[168] Above, pp. 79, 191.

[169] King to bishop of Clogher, 19 Aug. 1714 (Mant, *Church of Ireland*, ii. 275); King to bishop of Dromore, 26 Aug., 10 Sept. 1714 (ibid. 276, 280); Nicolson to Wake, 8 July 1718 (Gilbert MS 27, 181).

[170] Godwin to Wake, 13 Dec. 1716 (Wake MS XII, 97ᵛ); lords justices to Stanhope, 22 Jan. 1716 (SP63/374/54).

[171] Nicolson to Wake, 7 June 1719 (Gilbert MS 27, 218–19).

[172] King to bishop of Down and Connor, 22 Jan. 1719 (TCD MS 750/5, 120); Nokes, *Swift*, 296.

places like Kilkenny and Galway cities can in many cases be dismissed as no more than a Whig smear directed at surviving centres of Tory loyalty. Even where crowds did make use of Jacobite symbolism, as in Dublin, this may have reflected little more than a desire to taunt the Whig establishment. In the case of the clergy, too, it is likely that some, at least, of what Whigs chose to regard as political disaffection amounted in reality to no more than continued Tory partisanship and genuine concern for the position of the established church. Even clergy who declined to pray for the new royal family or indulged in other forms of disrespect may have been motivated more by a dislike of Whig triumphalism than by any real attachment to the house of Stuart. Where Trinity College students are concerned, it is also necessary to make allowances for the combined influence of drink and an adolescent desire to shock.

Having said this, it must be assumed that in some cases at least the sentiments expressed were real enough. That some Irish Protestants were led, despite the possible implications for themselves and their church, to give even symbolic expression to doubts regarding the legitimacy of the Hanoverian succession is striking evidence of the continued importance of religious principle in the early eighteenth century; once again we are reminded of the inadequacy of interpretations based solely on the assumption of secular self-interest. At the same time the limitations of a Jacobitism that expressed itself in undergraduate pranks and studiously offensive sermon texts are obvious enough. Of much greater importance than the reservations of clergymen and academics was the practical stance taken by the aristocracy and the gentry. And here it was clear that few were prepared seriously to question the Revolution settlement. 'Not only our religion and liberty,' as Archbishop King put it in 1715, 'but estates depend on the Revolution.' It followed that while others 'may make terms with the Pretender, or imagine they may do so, . . . no Protestant in Ireland can have any hope or view that way'.[173] There were of course some exceptions. The second duke of Ormond had been active in the Jacobite wing of the Tory party for several years before the threat of impeachment forced him to flee to the Pretender's court in 1715. The earls of Orrery and Barrymore were heavily involved in Jacobite conspiracy, up to and including the rising of 1744–5.[174] All three of these men, however, were at least partially resident in England, and it was there, rather than in Ireland, that their conspiracies were acted out. Sir Richard Cox, in 1707, believed that 'there are not five Protestants in the kingdom of £300 per annum any way

---

[173] King to Wake, 2 Aug. 1715 (TCD MS 2533, 42–3); King to Lord Southwell, 8 Jan. 1720 (TCD MS 750/5, 243).

[174] Szechi, *Jacobitism and Tory Politics*, 39–40, 159, 162, 202; Cruickshanks, *Political Untouchables*, 18–20, 55, 59–61.

favourable to [the Jacobites]'. Bishop Ryder, in 1745, thanked God that 'we have scarce a Jacobite amongst the Protestants of this kingdom'.[175]

The real threat, then, in so far as there was one, came from Catholic loyalty to the exiled Stuarts. This had more than one possible basis. Jacobitism in its pure form was above all a religious ideology, based on loyalty to a divinely ordained hereditary succession. Such a religious underwriting of political propositions is certainly evident in the limited body of theoretical writing produced by early eighteenth-century Irish Jacobitism.[176] At the same time it is noticeable that Irish Jacobites did not confine their designs to a simple restoration of James II and his heirs to their rightful place on the throne of all three kingdoms of the British Isles. There were also projects for an independent Ireland or one under French control.[177] This suggests that the principle of indefeasible hereditary right counted for less, in the eyes of some at least, than the practical benefits to be hoped for from a Stuart restoration. From this point of view, those gentlemen who had retained their estates or had established some new position of relative security for themselves and their families had less incentive than others to risk their all in an attempted counter-revolution. Richard Hedges, in County Kerry, noted that some local Catholic gentlemen had 'very freely' taken the oath of abjuration, and singled out 'the proprietors and idle persons, and such as served King James and are poor' as the most active supporters of the Pretender's cause.[178] Yet even the best-endowed Catholic families had much to hope for from a Stuart restoration: political influence and access to patronage, an end to restrictions on their religious activities, and freedom from the threat to their landed property posed by the Popery laws. Hence it is not surprising that Jacobite agents visiting Ireland should have received at least verbal encouragement from leading Catholic proprietors such as the earl of Fingal, as well as from those who no longer had anything much to lose.[179]

The precise meaning of Jacobitism to the Catholic lower classes must necessarily remain obscure. For some, particularly in areas like the southwest, allegiance to the Stuarts was probably inseparable from loyalty to local social superiors. Hostility to Protestants, clearly documented in other contexts, was also an obvious motive. William Lahey, enlisted in County Waterford in January 1714, was told that he and his companions 'should all return for Ireland again in less than a year's time, with an army to destroy and root out

---

[175] Cox to Southwell, 15 July 1707 (BL Add. MS 38,155, fo. 79); Ryder to Sir Dudley Ryder, 17 Dec. [1745] (PRONI T3228/1/18). See also Willes's comment a few years later (PRONI T2855/1, 16).

[176] Kelly, ' "A Light to the Blind" '.

[177] Beresford, 'Ireland in French Strategy', 5–6, 138–40.

[178] Hedges to Dawson, Apr. 1708 (Hickson, *Old Kerry Records*, 134). 'Proprietors', in this context, means the dispossessed Gaelic landowners.

[179] Beresford, 'Ireland in French Strategy', 54–5.

the Protestants there'.[180] For others the main attraction of a Stuart restoration may well have been the prospect it seemed to hold out of radical
social upheaval. William Headen, tried at Wexford for having enlisted in the
Pretender's service in May 1714, declared that 'he would not stay to be a slave
here, since he was to return again in the harvest'. In Dublin a tanner named
Cusack was indicted for observing of those arrested for enlisting: 'Who would
blame them for endeavouring to get estates if they could, for that fellows
that came over in leathern breeches and wooden shoes now rides in their
coaches?'[181]

All this, of course, raises an obvious question. If significant numbers of
Irish Catholics remained committed to the cause of the Stuarts, why did that
commitment receive so little concrete expression? It was of course possible to
deny the legitimacy of the Hanoverian dynasty without feeling obliged to seek
its overthrow. That, after all, was the position of some High-Churchmen in
both England and Ireland, and a similar stance is implicit in the statement of
the Irish Catholic position offered by the Revd Cornelius Nary in 1722.[182]
Nor was it only in Ireland that professions of loyalty to the exiled dynasty were
made by men who in the event declined to risk their lives and fortunes for
anything less than a guaranteed Jacobite victory. Nevertheless, there were
Jacobite rebellions in Scotland in 1708 and in England and Scotland in 1715
and 1744–5, as well as a range of conspiracies of varying degrees of serious-
ness. Ireland played no part in any of the three uprisings, and there is little
evidence at any time of purposeful clandestine activity, as opposed to the
'insolence' and disaffection so frequently complained of.

One major reason for this absence of active opposition to the Hanoverian
regime was lack of leadership. In a few cases, such as Iar Connacht and the
south-west, the heads of traditional ruling families retained a significant
authority. But in general the progressive reduction of Catholic landed property had drastically weakened, as it was intended to, the vertical ties that might
have been called into service in any further mobilization of the Catholic
population, in the way that similar ties could still be employed in the Scottish Highlands up to 1745. Other restrictions, meanwhile, had placed the
Catholics, despite their numerical superiority, at a massive military disadvantage. The arsenals, the garrison towns, the army, the militia, and the
machinery of central and local government were all in exclusively Protestant
hands, and the Catholic gentry and common people alike had been at least
partly disarmed. As the earl of Mar put it in 1716, using the less than
impenetrable code adopted by Jacobite correspondents:

---

[180] Examination of William Lahey, 26 Jan. 1714 (Midleton Papers, 1248/3, fo. 159).
[181] Report by John Forster, 19 July 1715 (SP63/373/34–5); *Dublin Daily Post*, 21 July 1714,
in Brady, *Catholics and Catholicism*, 311.
[182] Above, p. 159.

You will not forget to think of Mr Jennings, for, if some commodities be not likewise sent to enable him to set up the trade, I see not how it will be in his power to do it to any purpose, for he is barehanded, and the other traders in his parts full of money and all necessary commodities.[183]

Finally, and most important, the small part played by Catholic Ireland in purposeful Jacobite conspiracy was a reflection of its strategic irrelevance. During 1688–9 Ireland had served as the base for a last-ditch attempt to prevent William III from establishing himself on the throne of England. But even at this point its role was at least partly to keep Dutch and English forces tied down on the periphery of the European conflict. Once the British Isles had been lost, there was no possibility of Ireland serving as the springboard for their recovery. Every Jacobite invasion plan in the decades that followed hinged on speed: a seizure of power accomplished before the British government could deploy its fleet to protect the coastline and bring reinforcements from overseas. An invasion of Ireland, even if wholly successful, would leave the conquerors trapped on the wrong side of the Irish Sea, deprived of the advantage of surprise. It was in recognition of this that the numerous Jacobite invasion plans devised during the early and mid-eighteenth century—even those drawn up by Irishmen—invariably focused on a direct attack on the British mainland, with Ireland being assigned at best a diversionary role.[184]

How long did Irish Catholic loyalty to the cause of the Stuarts continue? There is no doubt that the breakdown of the long Anglo-French *détente*, the coming of war in 1739, and the widespread belief in 1744–5 that a French invasion was imminent produced an immediate revival of traditional expectations. A pro-Hanoverian observer writing in August 1745 commented sardonically on the attention once again being paid to events on distant battlefields:

It is amazing how zealously our Roman Catholics are affected with the success of the French in Flanders. *Pue's [Occurrences]* is their paper, the Protestants prefer *Faulkner's [Dublin Journal]*, . . . and it is diverting how they fight each other with their different intelligences. One reads that the French have taken Ghent, the other falls upon him with a detachment from Buthiane, the Frenchman, again, cuts off our communication with Ostend, but this does not prevent the patriot from electing an Emperor. If our Catholics come to a march, made by those of his belief in Flanders, the other's table is informed of it and in confusion, till the other raises 20,000 in Holland to relieve us.[185]

Others revealed their aspirations more directly. A Catholic farmer in County Down was arrested for drinking the Pretender's health and declaring 'that he would drink it over and over again in spite of all present, who might kiss his

---

[183] Mar to Atterbury, 2 Oct. 1716 (HMC, *Stuart Manuscripts*, iii. 13).

[184] Beresford, 'Ireland in French Strategy', 129–33, 144–5, 179–80.

[185] Richard Edwards to Francis Price, 4 Aug. 1745 (HMC, *Puleston Manuscripts*, 333).

arse, for that if he was hanged for it 500 of them should hang along with him'.[186] On the estates of the archbishop of Cashel, 'some of the Papists, not only of the poorest but the middling sort, expect some strange revolution that makes them so unwilling to part with their money'. In County Cork, similarly, 'the common people expect to pay their rents by the invasion they wish for', and elsewhere too there were complaints that 'the Papists that owe money will pay none'.[187] There were also some, at least, who were prepared to do more than wait passively. Early in 1746 an emissary, Patrick Wall, arrived in Scotland with a message of support for Charles Edward on behalf of the Catholics of Ireland.[188]

Old loyalties and aspirations, then, had certainly not disappeared. At the same time, other evidence suggests that Catholic political allegiances were more divided than they had been in earlier decades. In October 1745, when the Pretender's supporters were in arms in both Scotland and England, a Dublin periodical reported that the Catholic clergy had for the past three weeks been recommending to their congregations to behave in such a way 'as to be worthy the favour and liberty which they now enjoy'. The report, moreover, had been inserted at the request of 'several Roman Catholic gentlemen . . . to show their peaceable disposition and loyalty at this time to the present government'. In the same month the lord lieutenant reported that 'the most considerable' men among the Catholics had come to assure him of 'their firm resolution not to disturb the government'. Despite 'very good intelligence', moreover, he had been unable to discover any evidence to the contrary.[189] Such professions of loyalty might, of course, be seen as no more than a prudent insurance against failure. But Patrick Wall was also to admit some years later that the group he represented had not even tried to obtain the support of the Catholic landed proprietors, 'because they are known to be attached to the present ruling dynasty, and any upheaval would be dangerous for them'.[190]

Several developments help to explain why leading Catholics at least should have been less enthusiastic than in the past at the prospect of another Franco-Stuart assault on the Hanoverians. The long period of peace between France and England after 1716 must have led some to recast their expectations and to lose the habit of scanning international horizons for signs of an imminent transformation of their position. There had also been a change both in generations and in personal circumstances. Men who had actively supported

---

[186] Robert Ward to Michael Ward, 10 Feb. 1746 (PRONI D2092/1/7/40).

[187] Henry Waylands to Anthony Foster, 4 July 1744 (PRONI D562/1376); Stephen Rolleston to Ward, 25 Jan. 1745 (D2092/1/6/106); Robert Jones to Francis Price, Dec. [1745] (HMC, *Puleston Manuscripts*, 333).

[188] Beresford, 'Ireland in French Strategy', 176–7.

[189] *Exshaw's Magazine*, in Brady, *Catholics and Catholicism*, 67–8; Chesterfield to Newcastle, 24 Oct. 1745 (*Letters*, iii. 686).

[190] Beresford, 'Ireland in French Strategy', 175–6, 423.

James II and retained personal memories of the brief period of Catholic ascendancy had been replaced by sons and grandsons who had known nothing other than life under a Protestant government. Families that in the 1690s or 1700s might have been concerned primarily with the recent loss of their lands had, by the 1740s, established new, if often less prestigious, places for themselves as merchants or middlemen. Meanwhile the legal position of Catholics had improved significantly. Restrictions on landed property and exclusion from political life remained, but harassment of priests, bishops, and even regular clergy had largely ceased. Equally important, there had for many years been no new legislation of any significance: Catholics no longer had cause to feel, as they must have done in the 1690s and early 1700s, that their position was becoming progressively worse.

Defeat in 1744–5 marked the beginning of the end for Jacobitism. In Scotland a series of reforms directed against the personal authority of the clan chiefs destroyed its military potential for ever. In England the Jacobite wing of the Tory party disappeared gradually over the next fifteen years, clearing the way, according to some accounts, for the restructuring of British party politics that took place in the 1760s.[191] Even the Pope took account of changing times. From 1760 the name of James III no longer appeared on the briefs appointing Irish bishops. With his death in 1766, the papacy dropped all support for Stuart claims. Against this background, the leaders of Irish Catholicism completed, during the 1750s, the redefinition of their political allegiances. As England and France drifted into a new war during 1755–6, official observers were more ready than on any previous occasion to express their belief that nothing was to be feared from the Catholics.[192] In April 1755, rumours of a French invasion planned for the west coast led Catholic gentlemen in Galway to present themselves to the governor to assure him of 'their inviolable attachment and sincere affection to his Majesty's sacred person and government'. In 1759, when defeat in other theatres had led French ministers to revive plans for an invasion of the British Isles, the printer George Faulkner cited as one reason against panic 'the Roman Catholics of all the great cities here addressing and entering into associations in support of his Majesty, his crown and his dignity'. The establishment of a Catholic Committee in 1760 marked the inauguration of what was to be for the next sixty years the principal political strategy of the Catholic élite: deferential petitioning for the removal of legal disabilities combined with declarations of unqualified loyalty to crown and government. Addresses offered in 1761 to the newly crowned George III went out of their way to advertise the break with the dynastic rhetoric of the Stuarts. The new king was welcomed on his

---

[191] J. C. D. Clark, *English Society*, 30–3, 184, 195–6; cf. Cruickshanks, *Political Untouchables*, 112–13.

[192] Below, p. 259.

accession 'to the throne of your ancestors'; in him his loyal Catholic subjects saw his grandfather's virtues, 'as hereditary as his crown'.[193]

All this applied only to the Catholic propertied classes, however. At the popular level the idea of foreign intervention to impose a whole new social and political order clearly retained something of its appeal. Archbishop Ryder of Tuam, in 1755–6, reported that the local Catholic gentry, while insisting that there were no plans for a rising, 'do not conceal from us their fears that the populace, of which 99 in 100 are Papists, would not be restrained from any violence on the landing of a foreign force'.[194] Yet this popular disaffection, deprived both of upper-class leadership and of a realistic European context, was very different from the Jacobitism of earlier decades. Gaelic poets in the second half of the eighteenth century may have continued to deploy the traditional themes of French or Spanish invasion and a Stuart restoration. But they did so in a spirit very different from the informed engagement with contemporary diplomacy and military strategy that had been among the most striking features of Catholic political aspirations in the half-century after the Treaty of Limerick. When the County Kerry labourer Eoghan Rua Ó Súilleabháin (1748–84) composed a poem on the American War of Independence, for example, his delight in the difficulties engulfing the Hanoverian dynasty was conveyed in a web of confused and inconsistent images, in which the American colonists were not mentioned at all, while 'the Emperor' was somehow imagined to be among Britain's enemies. The ritualistic references to a return of the rightful dynasty, similarly, confusingly linked predictions of a radical change in all three kingdoms ('All will be well again in Whitehall, in Ireland and Scotland') with images of a purely Gaelic triumph over 'the wretched troops who speak English'.[195]

Ideas so fossilized should perhaps be considered part of a society's folklore rather than its politics. Neither the overthrow of the ruling dynasty nor the recovery of lost ancestral lands played any detectable part in the thinking of the agrarian secret societies of the 1760s, 1770s, and 1780s.[196] The new forms of popular political awareness reflected in the spread of the United Irish and Defender movements of the 1790s, equally, had little or no connection with the Jacobite past. They were the product of change rather than tradition: of rising literacy, the shift from the Irish to the English language, and a new openness to influences from America, France, and elsewhere. Where the authorities of the early and mid-eighteenth century had envisaged popular

---

[193] *Pue's Occurrences*, 29 Apr. 1755, in Brady, *Catholics and Catholicism*, 86–7; Faulkner to Derrick, 18 Dec. 1759 (Faulkner, *Prince of Dublin Printers*, 57); Catholic addresses (1761) printed in Brady, *Catholics and Catholicism*, 99–101.

[194] Ryder to Sir Dudley Ryder, 20 May 1755, 24 May 1756 (PRONI T3228/1/69, 75).

[195] Ó Súilleabháin's poem is translated in F. Murphy, *The Bog Irish*, 24–6.

[196] Donnelly, 'The Whiteboy Movement', 30.

rebellion as most likely to take place in the south and the west, counter-insurgency in the 1790s was to be concerned principally with the more anglicized and commercialized east and north. Yet there was one episode that demonstrated the continuing vitality, even at the end of the eighteenth century, of older political loyalties. This was the arrival in County Mayo in August 1798 of a small French force under General Humbert. In Connacht, a province largely untouched by United Irish organization over the preceding decade, Humbert and his men were welcomed, not as the bearers of liberty, equality, and brotherhood, but in the name of the confessional and dynastic loyalties of the *ancien régime*. They were saviours 'come to take arms for France and the Blessed Virgin'.[197] If the more sustained and politically sophisticated risings that had occurred earlier in the summer in Leinster and Ulster can be taken as inaugurating the new nationalism of the nineteenth century, the small eruption that followed Humbert's landing in Mayo may be seen as the last rising of traditional Ireland. For a brief period, ghosts that had been born in the Ireland of Queen Anne and George I returned to haunt the age of Napoleon and Pitt.

5. Views from Above: Perceptions of the Catholic Threat

What are the implications of all this for an assessment of the outlook of the Protestant élite? Historians have characterized that outlook in radically different ways. For some, this was 'the great century of the Anglo-Irish', marked by a mood of 'confident expectation', when 'the Protestant ascendancy seemed to be firmly established'. Others have portrayed a minority ruling class tortured by 'irrational' and 'almost pathological' fears of rebellion and social upheaval. Others again attempt a compromise. 'In Ireland,' one writer suggests, 'the eighteenth century was for the élite an age of elegance, and for every section of the community an age of insecurity.'[198]

Two points may be made about these differing assessments. The first is that historians who write in terms of 'paranoia' tend to ignore the wider ideological context within which the views of Irish Protestants must be located. At the beginning of the eighteenth century most Englishmen still saw Catholicism as a powerful international force which threatened their religion and liberties; many also believed that Popery was gaining ground in England itself. By the mid-eighteenth century such fears had begun to moderate among the educated. But popular feeling remained strong. Serious riots in 1779 prevented the extension to Scotland of the English Relief Bill of the

---

[197] Elliott, *Partners in Revolution*, 224.
[198] Beckett, *Anglo-Irish Tradition*, 47; Berlatsky, 'Roots of Conflict', 46–7; E. M. Johnston, *Ireland in the Eighteenth Century*, 1.

previous year. In London in 1780 Lord George Gordon's demonstrations calling for a repeal of the same Act led to five days of rioting and a minimum of 285 deaths.[199] Against this background a perception of Catholicism as a powerful and insidious menace may be seen less as a neurosis specific to Irish Protestants than as part of the common political culture of the three British kingdoms. The second point is that the material assembled in the preceding section makes both the portrayals generally offered of Irish Protestant mentalities impossible to sustain. All the evidence is that the great majority of the Catholic population did in fact continue, for several decades after their defeat in 1691, to give their loyalty to the exiled Stuart dynasty and to welcome with open enthusiasm any apparent prospect that the government under which they lived was about to be overthrown. There was thus nothing paranoid about the fears repeatedly expressed of Popish conspiracy or insurrection. Nor, under these circumstances, does it make much sense to talk in terms of an age of untroubled security.

The problem, however, does not end there. The ill will of militant Catholicism, at home and abroad, was by no means solely a figment of overheated Protestant imaginations. But there were nevertheless strategic and military considerations—made clearer with hindsight but already recognized by contemporaries—that limited the practical threat to be anticipated from this Catholic disaffection. What this means in practice is that the outlook of Irish Protestants, as a well-entrenched but numerically weak élite, cannot be summed up in any simple formula. The confidence of the Protestants, like the hopes of the Catholics, rose and fell in response to changes in what was always a complex balance of political and strategic considerations. It follows that any assessment of either words or actions must take account of the precise context in which these arose.

The point may be illustrated by looking at the events of the years immediately following the end of the Jacobite war. In the early 1690s, many remained obsessed with what they saw as the continuing threat of a powerful Catholic interest. 'I look upon the Protestants here,' James Bonnell maintained in October 1692, 'to be the same as if they lived in New England among the natives, of whom they are always in danger.'[200] Such remarks were primarily inspired by resentment and alarm at the potentially disastrous leniency supposedly extended to the defeated Catholics since the conclusion of the war. But there was also genuine concern at the inadequacy of the resources available for the defence of the kingdom. 'I have taken the best care that is possible for our defence in case we are attacked,' Lord Deputy Sydney reported in December, 'but with all I can do we shall make a very ill one.'[201]

[199] C. Johnson, *Developments in the Roman Catholic Church in Scotland*, 18; Rude, 'The Gordon Riots', in *Paris and London in the Eighteenth Century*, 268–92.

[200] Bonnell to Revd J. Strype, 18 Oct. 1692 (Strype Correspondence, I, fo. 104).

[201] Sydney to Portland, 13 Dec. 1692 (Portland Papers, PwA 1352).

Yet by the time invasion was again seriously threatened, less than four years later, all had changed. The Irish executive had been remodelled to include some of the advocates of a tougher anti-Catholic policy. The seizure of arms and horses in Catholic hands, a major demand of the preceding five years, had been carried out under the provisions of a new Act. The militia had been extended. These developments produced a new confidence. 'I doubt not,' Henry Capel, Sydney's successor as lord deputy, assured the government in March 1696, 'but we shall be in a readiness should any attempt be made within this kingdom.' A few days later, he wrote: 'We are all here in great peace and quiet, and all the ferment we have here is amongst the Protestants in their forwardness to show who shall be most zealous in asserting his Majesty's right, and standing by his person.' Fresh reports of an impending descent in November left people equally undisturbed; according to Lord Chancellor Porter, 'there appears great cheerfulness in the generality, especially in the gentry, who are now in great numbers in town.'[202]

This general mood of confidence continued into the next decade. A newsletter reported in February 1705 that a letter had been found purporting to reveal plans for a general massacre of Protestants, 'but the thing is so improbable, the Romanists being all disarmed and the power in the Protestants' hands, that the same is little minded'.[203] By this time the association between partisan politics and differences in attitude towards the Catholic threat, already evident in the 1690s, had become more marked. In the party conflict that became increasingly clear-cut from the accession of Queen Anne, Whigs maintained that Catholics continued to represent a serious threat and that unity among Protestants of all denominations was consequently essential. Tories, on the other hand, argued that it was now Dissent, and in particular Ulster Presbyterianism, that was the real threat to the established order in church and state. Jonathan Swift, in a famous passage, enquired which a man would choose to have: 'either a lion at his foot, bound fast with three or four chains, his teeth drawn out, and his claws pared to the quick, or an angry cat, in full liberty at his throat'. In the same way Sir Richard Cox, writing in 1706, dismissed the arguments of Whig opponents of the sacramental test:

Their first and main cunning is to represent the Irish as formidable though they really despise them, and know that their youth and gentry are destroyed in the rebellion, or gone to France; that those who are left are destitute of horses, arms and money, capacity and courage; that five in six of the Irish are poor insignificant slaves, fit for nothing but to hew wood and draw water.[204]

---

[202] Capel to Portland, 12 Mar. 1696 (Portland Papers, PwA 268); Capel to Shrewsbury, 23 Mar. 1696 (HMC, *Buccleuch and Queensberry Manuscripts*, ii. 317); Porter to Vernon, 16 Nov. 1696 (*CSPD 1696*, 439).

[203] Newsletter, 27 Feb. 1705, in HMC, *Portland Manuscripts*, iv. 169.

[204] Swift, 'A Letter Concerning the Sacramental Test', in *Prose Works*, ii. 122; Cox to Southwell, 24 Oct. 1706 (BL Add. MS 38,154, fo. 86).

These rival views found their main expression, apart from debates on the sacramental test, in the controversy that took place in 1703–4 on disorders in Munster. Whig spokesmen vigorously promoted claims that Protestants in the south-west, and even in County Limerick, were being terrorized and plundered by tory bands. The Tory administration rejected these reports as alarmist propaganda, and (according to Whig accounts) tried to intimidate those responsible into silence.[205] Yet it is noticeable that even Whig spokesmen, whatever they said in public, did not at this time take the threat of a Catholic rising very seriously. Robert Molesworth regarded the supposed plot of 1705 as 'a very silly business, and which ought not to have been regarded by any man of sense, who might easily see that the Irish are in no manner of condition to do the least mischief, much less to massacre'. Even Alan Brodrick, the scourge of the allegedly pro-Catholic policies of the preceding decade, did not take the report of a planned massacre seriously. He believed the whole affair to have been fabricated in order to further plans to have Catholics excluded from the corporate towns—or, alternatively, to have been got up by the Papists themselves as part of an elaborate plot to discredit their opponents.[206]

This was the position when, in 1708, Ireland was suddenly faced with the very real prospect of a French and Jacobite invasion. The first reports of French preparations do not appear to have caused great concern. 'We are much amused here with an invasion intended from France,' Archbishop King reported in February. 'Some reckon it with the alarm of 3,000 Irish cutting all the throats in England at one and the same time.' Others believed that there had been a real danger; but even their concern, significantly, focused on suspicions of the intentions of Robert Harley, recently dismissed from the ministry in England, rather than on the military threat itself.[207] Attitudes changed quickly when a French fleet actually put to sea in March. 'People here', King wrote from Dublin, 'are almost frightened out of their wits.' By this time it was known that the French plan was for a landing in Scotland; but there were fears that if this failed, they would turn towards Ireland itself. The defences of the country, King admitted, were frighteningly weak: there were

---

[205] Alan Brodrick to Thomas Brodrick, 27 Jan., 21 Oct. 1704 (Midleton MS 1248/2, fos. 121, 153); Memorandum of what passed in Council, 12 Jan. 1704 (ibid., fos. 76–7); Col. Maurice Hussey to ——, 7 Aug. 1703 (BL Add. MS 34,773, fo. 116); Cox to Southwell, 2 May 1704 (BL Add. MS 38,153, fo. 50).

[206] Molesworth to Letitia Molesworth, n.d. (HMC, *Various Collections*, viii. 232–3); Alan Brodrick to St John Brodrick, 17 Feb. 1705 (Midleton MS 1248/2, fos. 169ᵛ–170).

[207] King to John Vesey, archbishop of Tuam, 28 Feb. 1708 (TCD MS 750/3/2, 189). In December 1707 William Greg, a clerk in Harley's office, had been found to be sending information to the French. Harley's fall in February 1708 was for other reasons: he lost a power struggle with Godolphin and Marlborough. But the Greg affair had clearly left him open to accusations of secret Jacobitism. See Gregg, *Queen Anne*, 256–8.

not more than 4,300 regular soldiers; stores of arms and ammunition were badly depleted; and the militia had been 'absolutely neglected'.[208]

At the same time the lords justices, of whom King was one, managed to avoid a general panic. When the bishop of Clogher wrote to ask for instructions, King told him to encourage the Protestant population: 'I do not mean that you should bear them in hand that there is no danger, but that there is none but what we may with the help of God and due care prevent.' Such efforts seem to have been generally successful. 'We find from all counties', King reported four days later, 'that the people are hearty and willing.'[209] Meanwhile the government had taken steps to ensure that the Catholic population remained quiet. The licences to keep arms held by a small number of individuals were revoked; priests and prominent laymen, especially those who had refused to take the oath of abjuration, were detained; and Catholics were expelled from the key cities of Limerick and Galway. At the same time there was a conscious desire to avoid overreaction. On 7 April, as soon as the crisis was over, those who had surrendered themselves were released on bail. The Catholics who had been turned out of Limerick and Galway were allowed to return after three and a half weeks. 'We have no more to do,' King wrote, 'than to arm ourselves as well as we can for our defence, and disarm our enemies, but in such a manner that we may not provoke them to desperation by harsh and unjust usage whilst they are quiet.'[210]

With the return to power of a Tory administration in 1710, the partisan debate concerning the extent of the threat from Catholicism at home and abroad was resumed with new intensity. Whigs sought to present the Hougher disturbances of 1711–12 as part of a Jacobite conspiracy; the government, correctly as it turned out, insisted on treating them as a local outbreak of social protest.[211] In 1713 a Cork Whig, Arthur Hyde, publicized alarming reports of the state of the county: Protestants, outnumbered fifty to one, lived in constant fear of attack; priests said mass openly, and paraded round the countryside wearing swords; and papers had been found revealing a treasonable conspiracy. The administration took the unusual step of publishing a lengthy rebuttal of these claims, and summoned Hyde himself before the judges of assizes to account for his conduct.[212] A few months later Lord Abercorn, a Tory sympathizer, circulated an open letter condemning

---

[208] King to Southwell, 13 Mar. 1708 (TCD MS 750/3/2, 194).

[209] King to Ashe, 23 Mar. 1708 (TCD MS 750/3/2, 196); King to Thomas Knox, 27 Mar. 1708 (ibid. 199).

[210] King to Crowe, 23 Mar. 1708 (TCD MS 750/3/2, 198). For the release of those held on bail, see ibid. 201. For the period of $3\frac{1}{2}$ weeks, see White, 'Annals of Limerick' (NLI MS 2714), 79.

[211] Connolly, 'Law, Order and Popular Protest', 65.

[212] Dawson to Hyde, 21 Feb. 1713 (Country Letters, fo. 59); Dawson to judges of assizes, 24 Mar. 1713 (ibid., fo. 62); *Dublin Gazette*, 10–14 Mar. 1713.

'designing, intriguing men, who invent scandalous insinuations wherewith they alarm the credulous' and who in his view were 'making a bugaboo of the Pretender'.[213] By this time many Irish Protestants were in fact in a state of deep anxiety. But their fears were not focused on the Catholics. Rather, they believed, along with many Englishmen, that the Tory administration of Oxford and Bolingbroke was plotting to bring back the Stuarts on the death of Queen Anne.[214]

The peaceful installation of George I in August 1714 did not immediately relieve the fears of Protestants. Observers over the next two years commented uneasily on the air of confident expectancy that they detected among the Catholic population.[215] In the summer of 1715 it was clear that some sort of Jacobite attack was planned. Bishop Stearne of Dromore reported that in some areas Protestants had been 'alarmed into extraordinary nightly guards by a rumour that the Irish and Jacobites intend to cut their throats'. This in turn had led local Catholics to fear that some attack was being prepared against them.[216] In general, however, removal of the fear of betrayal in high places brought a return of confidence. A report on the activities of magistrates in County Roscommon suggests a heavy-handed but not panic-stricken policy:

I find by many of them who were here this day with me, that neither the superiority of the Papists in number, nor the want of arms or ammunition among them, will cramp their spirits, but, notwithstanding the alert air of the Popish party, and the dodging and subtlety of their management, and even the assemblies of multitudes under the pretence of common sports (which is always among us understood as a forerunner of a rebellious design) are resolved to attack them on every hand, as far as the law can support them.[217]

Elsewhere too, according to Archbishop King, again one of the lords justices, the Protestants seem 'very zealous and hearty'.[218] By this time three regiments of regular troops had been transferred from Ireland to Scotland to repel the expected invasion, and others were to follow shortly. King, however, believed that internal order could safely be maintained without them. As long as Protestants remained united, 'the Papists, though more numerous, yet being poor, dispirited and unarmed, can't do us much mischief'. If the French were to land some men, with enough arms and ammunition, 'they might have twenty thousand hands in a little time to join them'. However they would have no horses, 'these being all in the hands of Protestants, and these new raised men must be so raw and unacquainted with arms, that the Protestant militia would be able I believe to give a good account of them[selves] if furnished

[213] Abercorn to ——, 23 Mar. 1714 (PRONI T2541/1K/1/14).
[214] See above, pp. 83–4.   [215] Above, p. 235.
[216] Stearne to King, 27 Aug. 1715 (TCD MSS 1995–2008/1713).
[217] W. Caulfield to Delafaye, 1 Aug. 1715 (SP63/373/58).
[218] King to Delafaye, 6 Aug. 1715 (TCD MS 750/4/2, 63).

with arms and ammunition'. A leading judge, Baron Pocklington of the Exchequer, agreed. Now that the Pretender was deprived of foreign aid, he suggested in October 1716, 'he would make a very ridiculous attempt, especially here, where his friends are disarmed, and besides our regular forces we have now (without boasting) as fine a militia for the number as has been seen anywhere'.[219]

The same confidence in the ability of Protestant Ireland to defend itself, at least against any domestic upheaval, was evident in the last major crisis of the early Hanoverian years, the Spanish-backed invasion project of 1719. ''Tis somewhat to the honour of the Protestants of Ireland,' King boasted in May 1719, 'that notwithstanding we have six or seven Papists for one of us, we have kept our country in quiet, where Britain is now under the fears of a second rebellion.'[220] Even the brief landing in the west of the country of a small party under the earl of Lucan, apparently hoping to raise a local insurrection that would divert British resources away from the main invasion planned for the west of England, failed to create much concern. In April, after Ormond's fleet had been dispersed by a storm, Midleton grumbled that 'the Protestants seem to be a little too secure, and not to apprehend as much danger as there certainly was and I doubt still is from their enemies'.[221] In July there were proposals to transfer yet more troops from Ireland. The lord lieutenant sent assurances that, as long as there was no risk of foreign invasion, this could be safely done:

I must own I think we have not much reason to apprehend intestine commotions from the Irish; the Protestants are so well affected and in such a condition as to be able, in conjunction with the remaining part of the army, to prevent any disturbances from the natives, while there may be a necessity of employing some of the forces of this kingdom in another place.[222]

Even when there were reports, at the end of the year, that the Jacobite fleet was being regrouped, the chief secretary remained unworried. All available troops had been brought together in a position from which they could engage any invading force soon after its landing. 'We are in no great doubt of being able to cope with the enemy, let their correspondence be what it will here, notwithstanding we are at this time so weak in foot.' The following year the bishop of Elphin expressed similar confidence. In Connacht, it was true, there were fifty Papists to every Protestant. 'But the north is strong enough to keep the west in awe, and the civil and military power is everywhere in honest

[219] King to Nicolson, 16 Sept., 30 July 1715 (TCD MS 2533, 84, 41); Pocklington to Wake, 5 Oct. 1716 (Wake MS XII, fo. 81).
[220] King to Nicolson, 28 May 1719 (TCD MS 750/5, 163).
[221] Midleton to Thomas Brodrick, 25 Apr. 1719 (Midleton MS 1248/4, fos. 242–3).
[222] Bolton to ——, 8 July 1719 (SP63/377/171).

hands.' The only threat to the security of the Protestant interest, in fact, came from the internal divisions created by 'the Tories and national men'.[223]

There was to be little in the next two decades to shake this sense of security. In 1722 troops were once again moved to England following the uncovering of a Jacobite plot there. This allowed Archbishop King to repeat his boasts concerning the ability of his countrymen to dispense with regular soldiers and still keep the country in perfect peace.[224] The plot itself aroused little anxiety.[225] The years that followed saw occasional scares. In 1726, for example, there was a sudden cluster of suspicious occurrences. A ship intercepted at Killybegs carried mysterious papers. There was an apparent surge in the numbers of those enlisting for foreign service. The Catholic clergy had called for unusual fasting and prayers. A sermon was preached on an allegedly inflammatory text. All this was seen as evidence of 'some mischievous design among the Papists'.[226] Yet such worries tended to be short-lived and never very acute. A clergyman of the diocese of Armagh, preaching the annual 5 November sermon before the House of Commons in 1731, told members that, though the intentions of their enemies were unchanged, their power was much broken. Samuel Madden, in 1738, argued that it was still to the advantage of Ireland that more of its inhabitants be won over from Popery. Nevertheless he believed that the 'terrible contests' that had taken place in the past were 'pretty well over, and humanly speaking can never disturb us more'. Although Catholics were numerically stronger, 'yet the advantages of arms, strength and power, is so entirely on the other [side], that there is not the remotest prospect of dangers from that quarter'.[227]

The war against Spain that ended the long period of peace was received in Ireland with enthusiasm rather than apprehension. One contemporary, Tory if not Jacobite in sympathy, sent a scathing account of the displays of militaristic excitement that followed the declaration of war in October 1739:

I cannot but take notice in particular of the Mayor of Carrickfergus and company, who no sooner the Declaration was read than they all and one mounted on their fiery horses, drew their swords, flung away their scabbards, made several parades to and from the Castle and round the city walls and often wished for a bridge to pass them over to Spain in order to pull Don Philip by his ears out of the throne.[228]

At the beginning of 1744, the war suddenly came closer to home, as it became clear that France was assembling a major invasion fleet. Yet the military

---

[223] Webster to Delafaye, 10 Nov. 1719 (SP63/378/141); Downes to Wake, 15 Oct. 1720 (Wake MS XIII, 200).

[224] King to Wake, 15 May 1722 (TCD MS 750/7, 109).

[225] King to Edward Hopkins, 4 June, 11 Dec. 1722 (ibid. 122–3, 247); Nicolson to Wake, 4 Apr. 1723 (Gilbert MS 27, 321).

[226] Boulter, *Letters*, i. 70–4; *Dublin Intelligence*, 7, 11 June 1726.

[227] Jenney, *A Sermon*, n.p.; [Madden], *Reflections and Resolutions*, 92.

[228] George Ross to Francis Price, 30 Nov. 1739 (HMC, *Puleston Manuscripts*, 320).

assessment of the Irish executive remained much what it had been in earlier crises. The lord lieutenant, the duke of Devonshire, warned at the end of January that to remove regular troops from Ireland too quickly 'might be of fatal consequence'. All that was needed, however, was time to 'arm the Protestants, who, if no regular troops invade us, will be able to keep the Papists quiet and so by degrees if there be occasion we might send over almost all our regular forces'. The following month, reports of ships off the south-west coast caused great alarm: 'Nothing is talked of here but an immediate invasion.' By March the French invasion force, intercepted by British ships and then damaged by bad weather, had been stood down. 'Everything is quiet here,' Devonshire reported, 'the Papists quite dispirited and the Protestants extremely zealous.'[229]

The crisis, it soon became clear, had been postponed rather than averted. In July of the following year Charles Edward Stuart landed in the Scottish Highlands; over the next six months he raised an army, defeated government forces at Prestonpans, and swept south as far as Derby, briefly seeming to threaten London itself. Throughout this sequence of disasters the earl of Chesterfield, who had replaced Devonshire as lord lieutenant in August, maintained that Ireland was not seriously at risk. In part, his confidence depended on the familiar strategic argument that the French were unlikely to divert valuable resources to an invasion of Ireland when it was in England that the final outcome would inevitably be decided. But Chesterfield also cast doubt on the likelihood of a Catholic insurrection, affecting a patrician disdain for the prejudices of 'my good subjects', who 'are in general still at the year 1689, and have not shook off any religious or political prejudice that prevailed at the time'.[230] There is no doubt that his attitude caused offence. Bishop Ryder of Down noted the uneasiness caused by 'his slighting the rebellion as he has done, and instead of encouraging, his ridiculing such as have been warm and active in opposition to it'.[231] Yet resentment at Chesterfield's insouciance went along with a general confidence that the kingdom could be defended from any likely threat. 'We are largely over-numbered by Papists,' Chief Baron Bowes wrote in October, 'and by withdrawing the troops are left to defend ourselves. But this may and will be done, if we are secured from abroad, for the Protestants here may be justly esteemed amongst his Majesty's best subjects.' The archbishop of Dublin agreed:

---

[229] Devonshire to [Newcastle], 31 Jan. 1744 (SP63/406/32–3); William Pearde to Francis Price, 26 Feb. 1744 (HMC, *Puleston Manuscripts*, 327); Devonshire to [Newcastle], 22 Mar. 1744 (SP63/406/143).

[230] Chesterfield to Newcastle, 5 Oct. 1745 (*Letters*, iii. 679–80); Chesterfield to David Mallet, 27 Nov. 1745 (ibid. 705).

[231] Ryder to Sir Dudley Ryder, 19 Dec. 1745 (PRONI T3228/1/19). See also Bowes to Sir Dudley Ryder, 1 Jan. 1746 (PRONI T3228/1/20).

There are but few disciplined forces in the kingdom, and the Papists, our professed enemies, are numerous. Yet the Protestants upon this occasion show an uncommon zeal for the defence of their civil and religious rights, [so] that I trust in God we shall be safe and soon free from the apprehension of any danger.[232]

A correspondent in County Down found 'a brave spirit in the common people', despite reports of an imminent invasion. Another 'never saw men more cheerfully determined to risk their lives and fortunes in defence of our King and country'.[233]

Responses to the crisis of 1745 had one significant new feature. Up to this time the belief that Irish Catholics were uniformly the 'professed enemies' of the state, only waiting for an opportunity to rise in rebellion, had been expressed without contradiction. Clearly in 1745 this remained the majority assumption. Yet, for what seems to have been the first time, there were some who took a different view. Mrs Delany, wife of the dean of Down, writing to her sister in October 1745, believed that Ireland had been in less danger of civil war than any other part of the British Isles. 'People in general are very well affected towards the present government, and even the Papists... seem to know their happiness in a quiet possession of what they have.' An anonymous pamphleteer, who in 1746 called for new powers of search and detention against Catholics, commenced his argument with a curiously roundabout justification of their necessity. The current generation of Irish Catholics, he conceded, had remained quiet and peaceable 'even at seasons when a very different conduct was generally expected from them'. It was therefore 'no more than common equity' to accept that 'they honestly and sincerely mean to persevere in their usual inoffensive conduct and peaceable submission to the present civil government'. The real danger, in fact, was that the Pope might be prevailed on by foreign powers to order them into rebellion against their inclinations.[234]

Evidence of changing attitudes may also be detected in the public letters, so similar in content as to suggest a concerted policy, drawn up by several bishops of the Church of Ireland. These, as might be expected, called on the clergy to make clear to their congregations the nature of the threat they faced and to mobilize them for their own defence. But in addition, in a striking new departure, the clergy were advised to address themselves to their Catholic parishioners also. To them they were to emphasize not only the harsh consequences that might follow yet another failed rebellion, but also the benefits they enjoyed under the existing regime: the 'mild and gentle government' and

---

[232] Bowes to Sir Dudley Ryder, 5 Oct. 1745 (PRONI T3228/1/17); Charles Cobbe to Rawdon, 15 Oct. 1745 (D2924/1, 24–6).
[233] Robert Ward to Michael Ward, 18 Nov. 1745 (PRONI D2092/1/7/47); Robert Ross to Michael Ward, 1 Nov. 1745 (PRONI D2092/1/6/120).
[234] Mrs Delany to Mrs Dawes, 3 Oct. 1745 (*Autobiography and Correspondence*, ii. 391); *Queries Humbly Proposed to the Consideration of the Public*, 3–4.

'free exercise of their religion' despite the existence of necessary penal laws, the 'equal benefit and protection of the laws', and the blessings of domestic peace and security. Catholics, the bishop of Clonfert agreed, 'may perhaps please themselves with the expectation of seeing their religion the established religion of the country'. But against this they should be reminded 'that if it should happen, it will be at the expense of their civil liberty', since Popery and tyranny were inseparable.[235] How such arguments would have been received by the Catholics to whom they were to be addressed is difficult to conceive. But the attempt, however inept, to convince Papists that their true interest lay in upholding the existing order was itself evidence of a major change in assumptions.

These signs of a reassessment of the likely response of Irish Catholics to any challenge to the existing political order were only the beginning. Over the next ten years, as Jacobitism ceased to be a serious political force and Irish Catholics began to offer increasingly explicit declarations of loyalty to the Hanoverian monarchy, long-standing assumptions began to be openly questioned. During the next major invasion crisis, in 1758–9, the duke of Bedford, now lord lieutenant, clung firmly to the traditional view of Catholic disloyalty. In the event of a French landing in the 'Popish and disaffected counties' of the south-west, he warned, 'the whole country is so full of disaffected inhabitants, that the enemy could not be in want either of supplies of provision or succours and intelligence of every kind'. Archbishop Stone of Armagh, on the other hand, was confident that there was 'little or no danger' to be feared from the Catholics. A French invasion force would no doubt be joined by 'many single vagabonds ... but I am almost confident the Roman Catholics of property, whether landed or monied, would not assist, but that they rather fear than wish such an attempt from the French, and that some of them would even give their assistance towards serving his Majesty'.[236] Over the next four decades, Protestant politics in Ireland were to become increasingly polarized between those who believed that there had been a fundamental change in Catholic political loyalties and those who claimed that Catholics remained as unfit as ever to be admitted to political power.[237]

This survey of changing Protestant attitudes to the threat of insurrection or invasion has been dominated, inevitably in view of the character of the surviving documentation, by voices close to the centre of government. As such it must risk creating a misleading image of unanimity. The example of the Hougher outbreak of 1711–12 reminds us that there was a considerable gulf between the attitudes of the Dublin executive, to whom the outbreak was a

---

[235] The letters are printed in Brady, *Catholics and Catholicism*, 68–73.

[236] Bedford to Pitt, 29 Aug. 1758 (Bedford, *Correspondence*, ii. 362–3); Stone to Bedford, 28 May 1759 (ibid. 379–80).

[237] See in particular J. Kelly, 'Genesis of "Protestant Ascendancy"'; idem, 'Inter-denominational Relations and Religious Toleration'.

manageable local emergency, and those of local Protestants, who took up wild stories of French agents moving among the peasantry.[238] There was also a broad regional division, with the Protestants of Connacht and Ulster—in the 1690s at least—revealing themselves as more strongly anti-Catholic than those of Munster and, more particularly, Leinster.[239] Then there is the distinction proposed in one important recent study of the late seventeenth century between the outlook of those Protestants whose lives were lived wholly in Ireland and those (the true 'Anglo-Irish') who moved back and forth between Ireland and England.[240] There was also, of course, the difference between the social and political élite and the Protestant lower classes. Even the most virulently anti-Catholic members of the landed gentry inhabited a different world from the farmers of County Tyrone, who convinced themselves that the fake classical statues installed by the earl of Orrery in his wife's demesne at Caledon were in reality Popish idols.[241]

Yet, even when they are recognized as the views of a small élite, the attitudes to the security of the kingdom expressed in the correspondence of politicians and administrators remain, across a period of half a century, remarkably constant. Catholics, who outnumbered Protestants three to one, were generally assumed to be hostile and potentially mutinous. But the threat they presented was for the most part seen as containable. Numerical strength, in a pre-democratic age, was less important than other considerations: the massive attrition of the Catholic leadership class, the economic and social superiority of the Protestant population, and the concentration in Protestant hands of military resources and expertise. From this came the confidence repeatedly expressed that the Protestant militia could defeat any purely local rebellion. Invasion by trained and well-equipped regular troops would of course be a different matter. But there were sound strategic reasons for doubting whether either the Jacobites or a hostile European force would really commit the substantial resources that would be necessary in return for the limited gains to be achieved by taking Ireland. Even if the provinces and the common people were at times more excitable than the great men of the metropolis, moreover, the contrast should not be overstated. A recurrent theme, from the 1690s to the mid-1740s, was the steadiness of nerve and purpose not just of the governing élite, but of the Protestant population as a whole.

There remained one further threat to the security of Protestant Ireland. This was that it might be destroyed not by frontal attack, but by betrayal from within. Nor was this seen as a mere theoretical possibility. For almost three decades after 1691 Irish Protestants were obsessed with the idea that their

---

[238] Connolly, 'Law, Order and Popular Protest', 65–6.
[239] Below, p. 266.   [240] Barnard, 'Crises of Identity', 47.
[241] *Orrery Papers*, i. 307–8.

victory might be undone by treachery in high places. Opponents of Sir Charles Porter in the early 1690s were convinced that his opposition to tough anti-Catholic measures and his determination to honour the full provisions of the Treaty of Limerick were evidence of secret Jacobite loyalties.[242] In the next decade the same charge was levelled by Whigs against Tories. When the Irish executive, in July 1714, issued a proclamation offering a reward for the taking of the Pretender, there were some who claimed that it had in fact been worded so as to preserve him from attack. And when, two years later, the Tory archbishop of Armagh, Thomas Lindsay, signed a declaration against the Pretender drawn up by the House of Lords, it was noted that he placed his signature at the bottom of the page, 'from whence his name might be cut off in time convenient'.[243] The term by which Irish Whigs, like their English counterparts, referred to themselves was, significantly, 'honest men'. A toast drunk at the Tholsel in Dublin during celebrations of George I's birthday in 1715—'To all those gentlemen who were honest in the worst of times'—summed up their view of the crisis they had just lived through.[244]

Fears of this kind are, once again, easily dismissed as irrational. Yet they must be seen in context. Ever since the 1660s, Irish Protestants had lived with the knowledge that the governments in whose hands they found themselves could not be trusted to protect their interests. First, there had been the ambiguous religious allegiances and constantly shifting policies of the court of Charles II. Next had come the nightmare of James II's reign, when a Catholic monarch, aided by Protestant collaborators, had come close to overturning the constitution in church and state alike. As regards the reign of Queen Anne, the belief that many Tories were secret Jacobites was common in England as well as Ireland. And, since modern historians have disagreed sharply in their assessment of the relationship between Toryism and Jacobitism in this period, contemporaries—with less information and more at stake—can hardly be criticized for having feared the worst.[245]

Paranoid or not, the fear of internal betrayal was a central feature of Protestant political culture. One aspect was an exaggerated respect for the behind-the-scenes influence supposedly exercised by representatives of the Catholic interest. The Irish, one observer wrote in 1691, 'have been a worming people, and have found the blind side of the courtiers'.[246] In 1719 and again in 1723 wild stories circulated of the sums of money raised and the

---

[242] Below, ch. 7, sect. 1.

[243] King to bishop of Clogher, 3 July 1714 (TCD MS 750/4/1, 312); King to George Walter Storey, 3 July 1714 (ibid. 315–16); Delafaye to ——, 24 Jan. 1716 (SP63/374/57).

[244] *Dublin Intelligence*, 31 May 1715.

[245] For the traditional view, that Jacobitism was a minority movement, see Speck, *The Butcher*, 54–70; Colley, *In Defiance of Oligarchy*, ch. 2. Cruickshanks, *Political Untouchables*, argues that, on the contrary, Jacobitism was the main ideological basis of the Tory party. The same view is taken in Clark, *English Society*, 30–3.

[246] James Bonnell to Robert Harley, 3 Nov. 1691 (HMC, *Portland Manuscripts*, iii. 479).

7

'Reasonable Inconveniences': The Theory and Practice of the Penal Laws

We come, finally, to the penal laws. An account of the legal restrictions, political, religious, and economic, imposed on Irish Catholics in the period after 1691 is a standard set piece in textbook accounts of the eighteenth century. For some, indeed, the whole period remains the 'penal era'.[1] Against this background, the present chapter has two main purposes. The first is to make clear the extent to which the legislation concerned was the product of a particular political context and of a complicated and often muddled legislative process. Far from being a systematic 'code' reflecting a consensus among the Protestant élite as to how its security could best be preserved, penal legislation against Catholics was in fact a rag-bag of measures, enacted piecemeal over almost half a century. These were drawn up in response to a variety of immediate pressures and grievances and to the accompaniment of continual disagreement over both the principle and the detail of the measures taken. The second purpose of the chapter, taken up in the final section, is to ask to what extent the penal laws, despite the importance accorded them both by contemporaries and by later generations, can really be said to have made the Ireland of Queen Anne and the first two Georges a radically different society from what it would have been otherwise.

The term 'penal laws' was not, of course, one that Protestants of the period would themselves have used. They preferred, most commonly, to speak of the 'Popery laws'. Archbishop King maintained in 1705 that Ireland had in fact no 'penal laws in matters of religion' apart from the fines for non-attendance at Anglican services imposed by the long-defunct Elizabethan Act of Uniformity.[2] King's point was that Catholics and Dissenters, though subject to a range of legal disabilities, were not forbidden by law to practise their religion. This was not wholly special pleading: the position of Irish Catholics may be contrasted with that of French Protestants, whose ministers incurred the death penalty simply by officiating, while their congregations became liable to a lifetime of imprisonment or service in the galleys. Yet the distinction between imposing on members of a religious group a range of disabilities that would continue as long as they remained loyal to their church and directly

---

[1] See the title of the excellent collection of essays edited in 1979 by Bartlett and Hayton.

[2] King to Cox, 6 Feb. 1705 (TCD MS 750/3/1, 81). For the separate question, affecting interpretation in the courts, as to whether the laws were ameliorative or penal, see above, p. 231.

forbidding them to keep up its doctrines and worship is, to say the least, a tenuous one. Despite King's claim to the contrary, moreover, the Irish Popery laws did, in theory at least, have implications for the long-term survival of Catholic religious practice. All in all, then, it seems best to follow established usage and to refer to the legal restrictions imposed from the 1690s on Catholic clergy and laity as 'penal laws'. But it is as well to remember that this is another example of a term belonging to later political and religious controversies being retrospectively applied to the Ireland of King William and his immediate successors.

1. 'Raw Head and Bloody Bones': Parliamentary Management and Penal Legislation

The origins of what were to become the penal laws lie in the intense passions of the years following the end of the Jacobite war. The foreshortening of hindsight encourages a perception of the restrictions eventually imposed on Catholic clergy and laity as the revenge of a securely victorious faction on a helpless and defeated enemy. But Irish Protestants in the early and mid-1690s saw themselves in no such terms. In their own eyes they remained dangerously exposed to the attacks of a formidable Catholic enemy, as well as to what some at least saw as the real threat of betrayal from within.

At the root of these fears lay the terms of the settlement that had concluded the Jacobite–Williamite war. The Treaty of Limerick, signed in October 1691, secured all those still under arms in support of James II in the possession of their estates, pardoned all acts of treason committed by such persons since the accession of James II, and prohibited all lawsuits against them for acts of trespass or plunder committed during the war. Catholics in general were to be granted the same religious freedoms as they had enjoyed in the reign of Charles II, on condition only of taking a simple oath of allegiance. To King William and his advisers, all this was a reasonable price to pay for the surrender of a well-entrenched enemy, permitting the return of men and resources to the continental theatres from which they had been diverted. To Irish Protestants, on the other hand, the Treaty was a betrayal of their deepest interests. Bishop Dopping of Meath, preaching at a service of thanksgiving on 26 November, cited the twenty-two general and forty-four local rebellions that had taken place since 1172 in order to argue that the Irish, 'from the first settling an English colony in this country, to this very day', had demonstrated an implacable intention 'of extirpating the English nation upon every fair opportunity'. They would go on doing so, 'notwithstanding all the articles of peace that are granted them, and all the obligation of oaths and promises that are laid upon them'. It followed that any settlement that left the estates and political power of a substantial section of the Catholic gentry intact could only mean that the contest for supremacy would at some stage be renewed. In the words of James Bonnell, writing just after the treaty had been concluded, ''tis plain the Irish are in much better condition than we hoped they would be in the end of this war, and by consequence the condition of the Protestants so much worse'.[3]

Resentment at the terms of the peace treaty was reinforced by the conduct of the Irish executive in the years immediately following the war. Executive power lay in the hands of two lords justices, Sir Charles Porter, the lord chancellor, and Thomas Coningsby, the vice-treasurer. Both men had been involved in negotiating the Articles of Limerick. They now showed what many regarded as an undue concern to see its provisions upheld. In May 1692, for example, they had responded to news of an imminent French invasion by ordering the confiscation of arms in Catholic hands, but had added a lengthy stipulation that those employed to enforce the order should not 'commit any insolency or violence to any of [the Catholics], nor make use of this service as a colour for plundering or otherwise injuring any of them, that it may not be a reproach to us that under a specious pretence we break our faith and violate the king's word and honour'.[4] Articles of impeachment drawn up against the two men in December 1693 alleged that they had 'openly favoured and supported the Papists in their robberies and their outrages committed upon the Protestants, refusing then to allow them liberty of taking their legal remedies against the Papists'.[5] This may have referred to events since October 1691. More probably, however, it reflects the intense resentment engendered by Porter's and Coningsby's determination to uphold the ban on lawsuits arising out of injuries done during the war. Sir Francis Brewster, as late as 1698, wrote bitterly of those who 'under the subterfuge of the articles of Limerick and Galway etc. have sheltered themselves from common justice, and live splendidly and securely upon the spoils of ruined Protestants'.[6]

If the scrupulous regard shown by Porter and Coningsby for the terms of the agreement with the defeated Catholics made them widely unpopular, some of their critics took their suspicions further than others. Both Sir Henry Capel, who joined Porter as a lord justice in 1693, and Alan Brodrick, one of the Irish politicians with whom Capel aligned himself, maintained that the lord chancellor was in fact secretly wedded to the cause of James II, and was supported by all those who shared the same loyalty: men 'that had sat in the Irish parliament [i.e. the Jacobite assembly of 1689], had served in employ

---

[3] Text of Dopping's sermon in Portland Papers, PwV 74, 223–65; James Bonnell to Robert Harley, 3 Nov. 1691 (HMC, *Portland Manuscripts*, iii. 479). For general statements of the case against the treaty, see Capel to Trenchard, 14 July 1694 (HMC, *Buccleuch and Queensberry Manuscripts*, ii. 101); Thomas Brodrick to Shrewsbury, 21 Nov. 1695 (ibid. 261–4).

[4] Lords justices to Nottingham, 14 May 1692 (*CSPD 1695*, 186–7).

[5] Articles against Coningsby and Porter, printed in Troost, *William III and the Treaty of Limerick*, 86.

[6] [Brewster], *Discourse Concerning Ireland*, 22.

civil or military under the late king since the abdication, had been suspected
for having too favourable an opinion of his proceedings, or almost lived in the
Irish quarters'. According to Brodrick, such persons in fact commanded a
majority, both within parliament and outside it: 'This is not very politic to
own, but to one that hath a concern in the kingdom and knows where the
majority of this nation lies, it will not seem strange that we are outnumbered
in the country as well as the house.'[7]

Alan Brodrick's assertion that the Irish parliament was in the hands of a
crypto-Catholic and Jacobite interest is a striking reflection of the overheated
atmosphere of the early and mid-1690s. The claim itself is of course nonsense. The proceedings of the parliament of 1692 make it clear that the
policies of the post-war administration were widely disliked. Sydney, shortly
before the session began, confessed that his greatest fear was of 'the violence
that will be against the Papists, for they do hate and despise them to the
greatest degree imaginable'.[8] It is true that when the Brodricks and others
tried in October 1695 to have Porter impeached in the Irish Commons, they
lost by a margin of 77 votes to 121. But this merely suggests what would
be in any case the common-sense conclusion: that the views of most Irish
Protestants lay somewhere between the two extremes, in disliking the Treaty
of Limerick and finding Porter and Coningsby too lenient, yet rejecting the
wilder allegations made against them.

The power struggle between Porter and his critics casts a rare light on the
differences that existed at this crucial period in the outlook of Protestants
living in different regions. An analysis of the Irish Commons drawn up in
August 1695 shows that supporters of the lord chancellor were most numerous in Leinster, and opponents in Connacht. Munster and Ulster were
more evenly divided, with a small pro-Porter majority in the former and a
small anti-Porter majority in the latter.[9] These regional differences may be
accounted for in several ways. It is likely, for example, that Catholic freeholders, still legally entitled to vote, would have given their votes to men
known to be sympathetic to the Treaty of Limerick, and Catholic landlords
and middlemen may in some cases have influenced their tenants, Protestant as
well as Catholic, to do likewise. The virtual absence of a Catholic interest of
this kind would help to explain why Porter's opponents did relatively well in
Ulster. They were also probably helped there, as their ideological descendants
the Whigs were later to be, by the Presbyterian vote, which would have been
strongly anti-Catholic. But it seems likely that the most powerful influence on

    [7] Capel to William III, 16 Oct. 1695 (Portland Papers, PwA 251); Alan Brodrick to St John
Brodrick, 13 Nov. 1695 (Midleton MS 1248/1, fo. 277).
    [8] Sydney to Nottingham, 28 Sept. 1692 (*CSPD 1695*, 205).
    [9] Troost, *William III*, 107. In Leinster, Porter had 89 supporters and 30 opponents, in
Munster 36 supporters and 20 opponents, in Connacht 11 supporters and 18 opponents, and in
Ulster 30 supporters and 38 opponents.

Protestant attitudes was the type of Catholic with whom different regional groupings had to deal: the tories, cattle-raiders, and Gaelic notables of the south-west and Iar Connacht would have been less reassuring neighbours than the Old English gentry and the relatively tame tenantry of the former Pale. There were also the different experiences of the two regions in the recent war: the east liberated early by King William's forces, the south and west longer under Jacobite control and the scene of something much closer to civil war between Catholic and Protestant.

The first penal laws, then, must be set in the context of the immediate grievances of Irish Protestants in the aftermath of the Jacobite war. Alongside these grievances must be set a second development, without which the resentment they created would have counted for little. This was the sudden rise in the status of the Irish Parliament. In earlier periods, in 1670–2 or to some extent in 1678–9, the executive had been able to conduct religious policy with little regard for the preferences of Irish Protestants. After the short, but important, session of 1692 this was no longer possible. Over the next three years, as Sir Henry Capel set about rebuilding the administration's links with the men who had emerged as leaders of Irish parliamentary opinion, an essential part of his task was to meet the complaints that had been made regarding Catholic policy. When parliament met again, in 1695, the necessary compromise on the question of the sole right was sweetened by the parallel introduction of bills to disarm the Catholic population and to prevent them either running schools or sending their children abroad to be educated. These two measures, Porter reported in July 1695, had been impossible to resist, 'the majority of the Commons being earnest for them and his Excellency [Capel] cooperating therein as if it had been part of the bargain upon which the new measures are taken'.[10]

The two bills introduced in 1695, the first of the penal laws, addressed the specific anxieties that Protestants had expressed over the previous four years. The retention of arms in the hands of Catholics had long been a contentious issue. The half-hearted measures of May 1692 had clearly been disliked: one of the resolutions passed during the short parliamentary session in the autumn had called on the lord lieutenant to seize arms and horses in Papist hands. A few weeks later, faced with reports of a possible invasion, the executive had in fact sanctioned a fresh seizure of weapons. However, it still refused to order the confiscation of horses fit for use in war, on the grounds that such orders had in the past been abused 'to the hindrance of tillage and robbing the country of all their garrans'.[11] The bill introduced in 1695 put an end to such disagreements: henceforth no Catholic was to be permitted to keep weapons

[10] Porter to Trumbull, 3 July 1695 (HMC, *Downshire Manuscripts*, vol. 1: *Papers of Trumbull*, 493). See also Capel to Portland, 5 July 1695 (Portland Papers, PwA 242).
[11] Resolutions of Irish Commons, 20 Oct. 1692 (*CSPD 1695*, 214); Porter to Coningsby, 23 Nov. 1692 (PRONI D638/18/3).

or a horse of more than £5 in value. The confiscation of Catholic arms and horses that followed the passage of the Act in September 1695 was mentioned as one reason why the invasion scare of the following year aroused less alarm than such threats had done earlier.[12] The second Act, relating to education, is more often misunderstood. The prohibition on Catholics teaching or running schools was to enter historical folklore as evidence that the real purpose of the penal laws was to deny to Irish Catholics every conceivable material advantage. In fact, the concern of the Act was not with schooling as such, but with the opportunity that the regular traffic in students provided for contact between Irish Catholics and their European co-religionists. The title of the measure was 'An act to restrain foreign education', and it was in these terms that those involved in its drafting consistently referred to it. Its purpose, Capel wrote, was 'to bring the Irish from their foreign correspondences and to dispose them to a dutiful obedience to the king'. The ban on Catholics teaching in schools, in reality no more than a reiteration of the established church's monopoly of education, appears to have been added as a supplementary provision and attracted little notice at the time.[13]

The change of policy signalled by the education and disarming Acts was generally popular. There were those, however, who felt that the executive had not gone far enough. Alan Brodrick, already under attack for his surrender on the sole right, was irritated to find himself berated for his failure to take a strong enough anti-Catholic line.

> The more hard things anyone moved against the Irish, the more popular they who moved them became by so doing; and when those who were concerned for the government showed the ill policy of pressing things to extremity and of demanding all things at once against Irishmen, they were represented as courtiers who had lost all regard for the [*page torn*] country.[14]

On one issue, the status of the Catholic clergy, the Commons succeeded in getting the executive to do more than it had originally planned. In the 1690s, as in the reign of Charles II, there was still no specific legislation restricting either Catholic religious practice or the activities of those in Catholic orders. Nevertheless, a committee set up in 1693 to consider what should be done with the regular clergy rounded up during the recent invasion scare had recommended that these be deported, along with the Catholic bishops. As precedents, its members cited the proclamations issued in 1673 and 1678. The proposal was first approved, then dropped after the king withdrew his consent.[15] Now, in October 1695, the Commons resolved to initiate legislation to banish members of religious orders and to prevent any more priests

---

[12] Capel to Portland, 12 Mar. 1696 (Portland Papers, PwA 268).
[13] Irish Statutes, 7 Wm III, c. 4; Capel to Portland, 5 July 1695 (Portland Papers, PwA 242).
[14] Alan Brodrick to St John Brodrick, 17 Dec. 1695 (Midleton MS 1248/1, fo. 279).
[15] *CSPD 1693*, 8–10, 15, 51, 141, 162, 179.

from entering the country. The Irish executive responded by drawing up its own heads of a bill on the matter, but the English Privy Council declined to give these the necessary approval.

By the time the Irish parliament met again, in 1697, its political complexion had further altered. The formidable parliamentary following that had gathered around the lord chancellor had broken up in disarray following his death in December 1696, leaving the former adherents of Capel (now also deceased) in uncontested control. In the draft legislation prepared by the Irish Council before the session began was the bill to expel regular clergy that had been dropped two years before. Later, after the session had opened, the measure was redrafted to include the banishment not just of members of religious orders, but also of bishops and all others exercising ecclesiastical jurisdiction. Despite this considerable widening of its scope and representations from the agents of King William's ally the Emperor, the bill was approved by the English Council and then passed by both houses of the Irish parliament.[16] Another bill successfully carried through the parliament of 1697 provided that the estate of a Protestant heiress who married a Catholic should pass to her Protestant next of kin and that a Protestant man marrying a Catholic was to be 'in law deemed and esteemed to all intents, constructions and purposes, to be a Papist': the status of 'constructive Papist' which was subsequently much debated in the courts.[17] Like the other bills of the 1690s, this was essentially a defensive measure, closing off one of the avenues by which Catholics might supposedly subvert the Protestant landed interest. But it also looks forward to the direct assault on Catholic landed property that was to constitute the main business of the next decade.

The Banishment Act and the law against intermarriage may be seen as further fruits of the bargaining that was now necessary if the executive was to secure the co-operation of the Irish Commons in financial and other matters. The other major bill relating to Catholics considered in 1697 was, by contrast, an unpalatable necessity. The Articles of Limerick had included a promise that William and Mary would use 'their utmost endeavours' to have the agreement as a whole ratified by the Irish parliament. But the disasters of the 1692 session and the delicate compromise achieved in 1695 had ruled out any attempt at so contentious a measure. In 1695 the English Privy Council had inserted a clause in the disarming Act to exempt those whose right to carry arms had been guaranteed in the Articles of Limerick, but had worded this in such a way as to avoid any specific mention of the hated Articles.[18] When a bill to ratify the Treaty was eventually introduced, in 1697, it made a series of important concessions to the continuing objections of Irish Protestants. The

---

[16] Simms, 'Bishops' Banishment Act', 187–8.
[17] Irish Statutes, 9 Wm III, c. 3; above, p. 231.
[18] Shrewsbury to Capel, 2 July 1695 (HMC, *Buccleuch and Queensberry Manuscripts*, ii. 198).

original fair copy of the Treaty had failed to include a clause extending its provisions not just to members of the Jacobite forces, but to non-combatants under their protection. King William had subsequently certified by letters patent that the omission was a clerical error, but the clause was nevertheless dropped from the version of the Treaty proposed for ratification. Also omitted were the articles stating that Catholics were to enjoy the religious freedoms that had been allowed them under Charles II, which Protestants had objected to as giving Catholicism a legal foundation in Ireland, and the stipulation that they were to be required to take no oath save the oath of allegiance. The ban on lawsuits arising out of wartime events was included, despite vigorous objections from members of the Irish Council, but the war was stated to have commenced on 10 April 1689, opening up the possibility of redress for acts of plunder before that date.[19]

This failure to ratify the full provisions of the Articles of Limerick and Galway is often seen as a key moment in the reduction of Irish Catholics to political and social inferiority. This is largely misleading. In the first place it is likely that at this point Catholics themselves still saw the Articles primarily as the terms of a temporary truce; it was only later that they came to be seen, mistakenly, as a catalogue of the terms on which Catholics would have accepted permanent subjection to a Protestant government.[20] In practice, moreover, the various omissions turn out to have been of limited significance. The dropping of the omitted clause, potentially disastrous, was not in the event followed up by a wave of prosecutions against those thereby exposed to prosecution and forfeiture.[21] The religious liberties enjoyed by Catholics in the reign of Charles II had been so ill-defined and so much a matter of connivance rather than entitlement that a guarantee of their continuance counted for little. After all, the Bishops' Banishment Act became law a few days before the ratification of the Treaty, and its provisions were based on precedents set in the 1670s. Perhaps the most important omission was the stipulation that Catholics should be required to take only a simple oath of allegiance. The oath of abjuration, in particular, was subsequently to be used to legitimize the detention of suspected persons, to exclude Catholics from voting, and to prevent them from practising law. But even here it is difficult to believe that other means could not have been used to achieve each of these ends. Overall it seems clear that the Ratification Act was of real significance only for the Protestant political élite. For them the outcome confirmed the new balance of power that had been established between executive and parliament, and finally laid to rest the dark fears of betrayal that had centred round the Treaty and its authors.

[19] Simms, 'The Treaty of Limerick', in *War and Politics*, 212–16; Troost, *William III*, 164–74.
[20] P. Kelly, 'Lord Galway and the Penal Laws', 254, n. 51.
[21] Simms, *Williamite Confiscation*, 63–5.

This is not to suggest that the Protestant élite was united in its attitude either to the Treaty or to the wider question of how the Catholic population was now to be dealt with. The Ratification Bill appears to have passed through the Commons without undue difficulty. In the Lords, however, it passed by only 23 votes to 20. Fourteen of its opponents, including 6 bishops of the Church of Ireland, went on to enter a formal protest against the bill's claims to ratify the Articles, when in fact 'no one of the said articles is therein, as we conceive, fully confirmed', and those in whose favour they had been granted were put 'in a worse condition than they were before'.[22] The Lords also rejected as too sweeping a bill, already passed by the Commons, to confirm all existing sentences of outlawries. Its members later accepted a revised bill, although Bishop King admitted that it still 'bears hard upon several'.[23]

On another measure the Lords stood firm. This was the draconian bill 'for securing the king's person and government' introduced in response to the attempt to assassinate William III the previous year. Its provisions permitted justices of the peace to summon before them any person and require him to take an oath denying the Pope's power to depose rebellious princes. Those refusing became liable to the forfeiture of all their goods. The bill passed through the House of Commons, but was rejected in the Lords by 18 votes to 14, 8 of those voting against being bishops. The reasons for its failure were complex. In addition to the influence of a crypto-Catholic interest ('the Irish new-converted lords, pardoned and restored by the king's mercy'), observers suggested that the Lords had been alarmed at the prospect of seeing their Catholic tenants bankrupted at the will of a local magistrate and that the bishops had rebelled against an over-generous clause in favour of Quakers.[24] Yet there were also objections in principle to the interference with Catholic civil and religious liberties. To subject four-fifths of the nation to the discretionary power of two justices of the peace in a matter involving life, liberty, and property was, in Bishop King's view, a breach of the Magna Carta, 'which is law in Ireland as well as in England'. In addition, he considered it 'a direct persecution' to impose on Catholics an oath to renounce an article of their faith, in this case the supremacy of the Pope. Catholics could legitimately be barred from offices of public trust, 'but [I] think it hard to take away men's estates, liberties or lives merely because they differ in sentiments of religion'.[25] A revised version of the bill was brought forward in 1699, but again rejected, this time in the Commons.

---

[22] Troost, *William III*, 182.

[23] King to Lord Clifford, 9 Oct., 20 Nov. 1697 (TCD MS 750/1, 106, 132–3).

[24] Methuen to Shrewsbury, 27 Nov. 1697 (HMC, *Buccleuch and Queensberry Manuscripts*, ii. 583–4); Drogheda to Coningsby, 2 Dec. 1697 (PRONI D638/167/13).

[25] King to Clifford, 20 Nov. 1697 (TCD MS 750/1, 134); King to archbishop of Canterbury, 30 Nov. 1697 (ibid. 136); King to Sir Robert Southwell, 21 Dec. 1697 (ibid. 147–50). Writing to the last of these, King also complained that 'men of no religion, nay that scoffed at all religion . . . should impose on men that had some, though an ill one'.

King explained this second defeat of the bill to preserve the king's person by suggesting that the arguments advanced against it in the Lords 'made such impression in the generality of the kingdom that it was thrown out by a great majority'.[26] But it was also true that by 1699 the intense debate that had surrounded all aspects of policy towards Catholics had considerably abated. The central issue of the Articles of Limerick had been resolved to the satisfaction of the majority, while grievances of a different kind—moves by the English parliament to restrict the Irish woollen industry and bitter disputes over the disposal of lands forfeited by those Jacobites not able to claim the protection of the Treaty—had come to the fore. Most important of all, expanding trade and a consequent rise in tax receipts permitted the government to avoid summoning the Irish parliament for four years after 1699. By 1702, however, it was clear that a session could not be put off much longer. In November the lords justices summoned Alan Brodrick, still in office as solicitor-general, along with the attorney-general and three senior judges, to discuss the prospects for a parliament that would grant additional taxes. Invited to suggest 'what good could be done for Ireland', Brodrick and the others responded with a range of demands: removal of restrictions on trade, compensation for Protestant purchasers of forfeited estates, and a reduction in Ireland's contribution to military expenditure. In addition, Lord Chief Justice Pyne suggested 'laws against the Irish inheriting while they continued Papists, and for admitting no priests into the kingdom'.[27] The lords justices took the hint, and a bill 'for preventing Protestants from turning Papists, and for any estate of Protestants to descend or come to any Papist, and to prevent Papists from disinheriting Protestants' was forwarded to the English Council for approval early in 1703.

What was proposed at this stage was a defensive measure, similar in intent to the Marriage Act of 1697. The aim was to regulate land transactions, and in particular family affairs, in such a way as to ensure that land did not pass from Protestant to Catholic hands.[28] By the time parliament opened in September 1703, however, the English Privy Council, concerned that the proposed legislation was too harsh and might contravene the Articles of Limerick, still had not given the necessary approval. The delay was to cost the Catholics in whose interest the Council acted dear. In the absence of a

---

[26] King to ——, 2 Feb. 1699 (TCD MS 750/2/1, 62).

[27] Alan Brodrick to St John Brodrick, 29 Nov. 1702 (Midleton MS 1248/2, fos. 73–5). Pyne was probably thinking of a measure considered, but not proceeded with, in 1698, 'to prevent the estates of Protestants to descend or come to Papists': *Journal of the House of Commons*, ii. 838, 28 Nov. 1698; Roger Smith to Kean O'Hara, 29 Oct. 1698 (PRONI T2812/4/253).

[28] Lords justices (Mountalexander and T. Keightley) to Rochester, 30 Jan. 1703 (BL Add. MS 9715, fo. 41ᵛ). The lords justices did, however, add that the bill of which they sent a draft would be more acceptable if it were extended to prevent Papists taking freeholds 'by purchase or descent'.

government-sponsored measure, the Commons set about framing its own Act to Prevent the Growth of Popery. This proposed to prohibit Catholics not just from inheriting land owned by Protestants, but also from purchasing such land or renting it on long leases. In addition, estates owned by Catholics were not to be transmitted intact on the death of the proprietor, but instead were to be divided equally among the male heirs. A primarily defensive measure had thus given way to a fresh attempt to accomplish what the Articles of Limerick had prevented happening at the end of the war: the destruction of the Catholic landed interest. The heads of a bill were duly transmitted to London, accompanied by more or less explicit threats that there would be no supply bill unless the measure was returned intact. In the event, the bill came back from London strengthened rather than weakened, the ban on purchasing or leasing land from Protestants having been extended to the acquisition of any land whatever. The Council had extracted its own price for this compliance, however, by adding the clause to impose the sacramental test on holders of crown and municipal offices.[29]

These complicated transactions confirmed the close relationship, already clear in 1695, between anti-Catholic legislation and the exigencies of parliamentary management. In the session that followed, that relationship became more blatant still. As early as May 1704, Sir Richard Cox pointed to the need to have 'some popular thing' ready if parliament should meet the following spring, 'not only to stop the mouths of enemies, but to oblige our friends and do good to the whole kingdom and consequently to ourselves'. At this stage Cox believed that a bill to establish a registry of property transactions would be sufficient to 'bring a ready compliance to continue the excise etc. two years more'.[30] Presumably he expected this to be attractive both as a means of facilitating land transactions generally and as an aid to the enforcement of the restrictions recently imposed on Catholic land dealings in particular. By the end of the year, with the new parliamentary session now imminent, men's minds had been further concentrated. A group of government managers met in mid-December to go through the bills that had been prepared for previous sessions but not proceeded with. They drew up a list of the most promising of these,

which in truth after all seem of very indifferent consequence, and therefore I proposed if they could think of some Brilliant to open the session withal that might have some relish with it for extraordinary good, like our last Popery Act or plus acres. Mr Solicitor [Sir Richard Levinge] in his merry way thought there must be some raw head

---

[29] For a detailed account of the passage of the Act, see Simms, 'The Making of a Penal Law'.

[30] Cox to Ormond, 20 May 1704 (HMC, *Ormonde Manuscripts*, NS viii. 75); Sir Richard Levinge to Ormond, 6 July 1704 (ibid. 94). A registry was in fact established, primarily for this purpose, in 1708: Roebuck, 'Irish Registry of Deeds'.

and bloody bones viz. some corroboration of the last Popish act, which as it now directs all priests to be registered so may make it penal for any priest hereafter to officiate who may have been ordained since.[31]

Once again, English ministers were unenthusiastic. The queen, Ormond was told, 'may be ready to gratify the people of Ireland in this point when she is not engaged in a big war with so many Roman Catholic allies. Yet at this time she fears it may occasion too great a noise abroad.' After the bill had passed through parliament and been sent to London for approval, Ormond himself indicated that he would be happy to see it dropped, now that it had done its work in easing the passage of the supply bill. In the end, however, the measure was sent back by the English Council and duly passed.[32]

That the 'Brilliant' fixed on by the executive should have been a further amendment to the law relating to Catholic clergymen is not at all surprising. Nowhere, in fact, is the lack of central planning—or even a coherent purpose—behind the anti-Catholic legislation of the post-war years more apparent than in the series of statutes on this subject. The Act of 1697 had required all regular clergy and those exercising ecclesiastical jurisdiction to leave the kingdom before 1 May 1698. Queen Anne's first parliament, in 1703–4, made it illegal for any Catholic clergyman to enter the kingdom after 1 January 1703, and required those already there to register their names and the parishes they served, and to give security for their good behaviour. What was pointed out in 1705 was a new loophole: the earlier measures did not apply to priests who had been ordained since their enactment or who might be ordained thereafter. The solution was to extend the provisions of the Banishment Act to all priests found in the kingdom after 24 June 1705 who had not been registered under the statute of 1704.

The purpose of this untidy accumulation of statutes was never made wholly clear. The preamble to the Banishment Act cited in justification the role of Catholic ecclesiastics in inciting discontent and rebellion. Looked at in these terms, the categories of person chosen for exclusion made sense. Bishops were both political and religious leaders. Regulars were more dangerous than secular clergy because the organizational structure of the orders to which they belonged placed them more clearly and directly under the control of foreign ecclesiastical superiors. (Most Protestants also found regulars more objectionable because their dependence on alms and lack of a clearly defined pastoral role made it easier to see them as wholly parasitic.)[33] At the same time the

---

[31] Edward Southwell to Ormond, 14 Dec. 1704 (HMC, *Ormonde Manuscripts*, NS viii. 125).

[32] Coningsby to Ormond, 21 Jan. 1705 (ibid. 135); ibid. xliv (editor's introduction). For the bill (4 Anne, c. 2), see below, p. 275.

[33] There was some disagreement on this point, however. Of two memoranda submitted to the government in 1691, one, probably by Bishop Moreton of Kildare, recommended banishing all regulars while providing pensions to four bishops. The other argued that regulars were for the most part 'harmless, ignorant poor men' and that it was the seculars who should be banished: *CSPD 1691–2*, 56, 68–9.

statute had another implication. If bishops were to be excluded from the kingdom, then there would be no one to ordain replacements as the existing parish clergy died out. Some contemporaries, like John Dunton, the English bookseller who visited Dublin the year after the Banishment Act became law, certainly got the impression that this was its real purpose.[34] Subsequent additions did little to clarify matters. Instead, each successive piece of legislation explained its existence by referring back to previous measures. The preamble to the bill against Catholic clergy entering the kingdom complained that bishops and regulars had been smuggling themselves in disguised as secular priests. Next, the Registration Act declared itself to be necessary to ensure that the provisions of the two earlier Acts were not being evaded. At the same time, the addition of a clause laying down that no parish priest was to keep a curate implied a separate purpose of limiting the number even of secular priests. The preamble to the Act of 1705 abandoned logic altogether. The existence of more recently ordained priests (who should not of course have been there at all, if the 1697 Act excluding all bishops from the kingdom had been enforced) was somehow an obstacle to the implementation not just of the Registration Act, but also of the other two statutes, that against bishops and regulars and that against priests entering the kingdom from abroad.[35]

The reason for this confusion is of course that the legislation relating to Catholic ecclesiastics did not reflect any single clear purpose. Like other anti-Catholic statutes, these were compromise measures, drafted and amended to achieve maximum support in a House in which opinions differed on how best to deal with the problem of Catholicism. From this point of view a certain vagueness as to ultimate purposes was an advantage. It meant that the bills could be supported by those who wished to see the Catholic church establishment limited in size and brought under supervision and also by those who wished to see it abolished altogether. It could also be supported, of course, by those—perhaps a substantial number—who felt that something needed to be done about the problem of Popish clergymen but did not trouble themselves greatly with the theoretical implications of alternative proposals.

For several years after the passage of the Bishops' Banishment Act, then, the ultimate fate intended for the Catholic church establishment remained, almost certainly by design, unclear. This was still the case when the whole position was transformed by what can only be considered a spectacular misjudgement on the part of the authorities. This was the Act, in 1709, requiring all registered priests to take the oath of abjuration, thereby accepting the Queen as *de jure* as well as *de facto* sovereign and denying the right of James III to the throne. The Act, sponsored by the firmly Whig executive headed by the earl of Wharton, was in part a response to the invasion scare of the

---

[34] Below, p. 296.
[35] Irish Statutes, 9 Wm III, c. 1; 2 Anne, c. 3; 2 Anne, c. 7; 4 Anne, c. 2.

preceding year. Addison noted that MPs were resentful of the 'insolent behaviour' of the Catholics, and in particular of the attacks made on a few priests who had come forward voluntarily at that point to take the oath.[36] In the event, however, the law proved impossible to enforce. Out of somewhere over 1,000 priests in the country, only 33 came forward to take the oath. The remainder, by their refusal, had now forfeited the legal status granted them under the Registration Act of 1704. There followed a short period of disruption, in which priests in many areas went into hiding and Catholic churches closed their doors.[37] But there was no sustained attempt to put the laws into effect against the non-juring majority. The government had, quite simply, overreached itself. In doing so, however, it had crossed an important threshold. Earlier legislation had defined which categories of Catholic ecclesiastic were to be prohibited and which tolerated. Now the whole Catholic church establishment was theoretically outside the law, and more or less enforceable prohibitions had been replaced by what could never in practice be more than a legal fiction.

The imposition of the abjuration oath on the Catholic clergy was only part of a much wider measure. In 1707 the Commons had considered heads of a bill to amend the 1704 Popery Act. These would have extended to annuities the existing prohibition on the purchase of land by Catholics, added to the provisions against unregistered priests and schoolteachers, and offered new protection to the Protestant wives and heirs of Catholic proprietors. By this time, however, legislators were beginning to trip themselves up on complexities of their own making. A clause confirming the right of a Catholic proprietor to sell his land to a Protestant, despite anything to the contrary in the Act of 1704, was objected to on the grounds that it would permit such a proprietor to deprive a Protestant heir of his entitlement, and the bill was rejected.[38] A second bill, introduced in 1709, was more successful. As eventually enacted, it imposed the oath of abjuration on priests wishing to claim the benefits of registration, and plugged a number of loopholes in the provisions relating to landed property enacted in 1704. Most important of all, it created a new figure, the Protestant discoverer, who by filing a bill in relation to any transaction in breach of the Popery laws became himself entitled to the Catholic party's share in that transaction. It was the introduction of this self-motivating agent of enforcement that gave the earlier legislation teeth, and

---

[36] Addison to Somers, 14 June 1709 (*Letters*, 151).

[37] Ó Fiaich, 'The Registration of the Clergy', 49; Burke, *Irish Priests*, 197; White, 'Annals of Limerick' (NLI MS 2714), 78. White lists several cases in which priests who took the oath then seized possession of parishes belonging to those who had gone into hiding after refusing to take it.

[38] Account of bills approved by the Privy Council, 1 Sept. 1707 (PRONI Dio 4/5/3/40); Saunders to Southwell, 18 Oct. 1707 (BL Add. MS 9715, fo. 205); Saunders to [?Southwell], 4 Nov. 1707 (ibid. 225ᵛ).

ensured that the laws relating to landed property would be the most effectively implemented of all the penal laws.

The Popery bills of 1707 and 1709 were, like their predecessors, the product of immediate political circumstances. In 1707 the earl of Pembroke was attempting to maintain an Irish executive free of the increasingly clear-cut party divisions of Whig and Tory, and it seems likely that new restrictions on Catholics were to some extent, at least, a device intended to attract a non-partisan government majority. In 1709 the aim was partly to create a measure so attractive that the Irish parliament would not risk its loss even when—as was initially intended—the Whig-dominated Privy Council in England repeated the Tory trick of 1704 by attaching to it a clause to repeal the sacramental test. Beyond this, a tough anti-Catholic line was clearly in keeping with Wharton's determination to build up a more firmly Whig administration. Certainly the promise of anti-Catholic legislation had not lost its role as a bargaining counter in the management of parliament. When MPs objected to amendments made to the money bill drawn up by the Commons, government supporters 'hinted at several inconveniencies that would attend the rejecting of it, as the case of all the other bills which had been made this session, and particularly that for preventing the growth of Popery'.[39]

If the gradual hardening of party divisions that was taking place at this time helps to explain the introduction of the bills of 1707 and 1709, it also helps to explain the stiff resistance these met with, not only in the Lords but also in the Commons. Whereas in the past, the main role of MPs had been to press government for tougher measures than it wished to sanction, their contribution in 1709 was significantly to weaken the measure before them. In particular, a clause that would have banned Catholics from trading as merchants and forbidden Catholic tradesmen from taking apprentices was dropped. A clause retrospectively invalidating all conveyances made by Catholics since 1704 was replaced by one invalidating only those made with an obvious intention of evading the provisions of the Popery Act of that year. Such opposition combined the principled and the tactical. For example, a clause to prevent Catholics—even those who had taken the oath of abjuration—from voting was objected to on the grounds 'that it was unreasonable so great a body of people should be bound by laws which were not made by their representatives'. But there were also fears that to disenfranchise Catholics would strengthen the Dissenting interest and weaken that of the established church.[40] The bill as a whole also encountered resistance in the Lords, so

---

[39] Addison to Godolphin, 12 Aug. 1709 (*Letters*, 176). See also 'Mr S.' to ——, 13 Aug. 1709 (BL Add. MS 34,777, fo. 65ᵛ). For the project of attaching a clause to repeal the test, see Hayton, 'Divisions in the Whig Junto'.

[40] Addison to Somers, 14 June 1709 (*Letters*, 151); B. Stapleton to William Butler, 27 Jan. 1709 (*Inchiquin Manuscripts*, 99), reporting the views of Bishop Lindsay of Killaloe.

much so that for a time there were fears that the bill might be lost there. In the end it passed narrowly enough: 15 lay peers and 6 bishops voted for the bill, 6 peers and no less than 8 bishops against it.[41]

Although policy towards Irish Catholics had thus become an issue in the deepening party conflict between Whig and Tory, it is important that the contrast between the two parties should not be overstated. It is true that Catholic clergymen welcomed the accession of a Tory administration in 1710 as rescuing them from the threat they were under because of their refusal to take the oath of abjuration. But the four years that followed made clear that tolerance, in this context, was wholly relative. Early in 1712 the lords justices ordered the arrest of all Catholic clergy in seven western counties, on the grounds that they were thought to have encouraged the recent outbreak of cattle maiming in the region.[42] In September of the same year the discovery of a nunnery in the city of Dublin and the seizure there of papers relating to regulars elsewhere in the kingdom led to a proclamation calling for a nation-wide drive to arrest members of religious orders and persons exercising ecclesiastical jurisdiction.[43]

Much the same point applies to legislation. The Tory Ormond had been quite happy in 1705 to offer a new law against priests in exchange for parliamentary co-operation. It is true that no further anti-Catholic statutes were enacted during the Tory administration of 1710–14. But there were other reasons for this. With politics now divided along rigid party lines, it was no longer necessary for the executive to construct its majority by bargains of this kind. Nor is it clear just what form new penal legislation could have taken at this stage. Most important of all, those most committed to the defence of Protestant Ireland against Popery had other things to worry about in the last years of Anne's reign. As long as there were real fears that the queen's death might be followed by a Stuart restoration, the question of further refinements to the Popery laws was hardly of great relevance. Thus it was not until after 1714 that Irish Protestants were disposed to look again at the legal position of Catholics. By the time they did so, both the circumstances and the terms of the debate had been subtly but unmistakably transformed.

---

[41] List of Lords voting in BL Add. MS 34,777, fo. 68. This is a fuller list than that given in Addison to Godolphin, 21 Aug. 1709 (*Letters*, 183).

[42] Connolly, 'Law, Order and Popular Protest', 56–7.

[43] *Dublin Gazette*, 771 (6–9 Sept. 1712); King to John Hartstong, bishop of Ossory, 18 Sept. 1712 (TCD MS 750/4/1, 48); Proclamation, 20 Sept. 1712, in Brady, *Catholics and Catholicism*, 18–19. For the enforcement of the proclamation, see Country Letters, fos. 44–50, and the material for 1712 scattered through the topographically arranged chapters of Burke, *Irish Priests*, 267–453.

2. Debate

At the beginning of January 1715 Archbishop William King, once again in office as a lord justice, addressed two letters to the lord lieutenant on the state of the law relating to Catholicism. His purpose was to emphasize the need for a new and more clearly defined policy. Severe laws—too severe, in King's view—existed to restrict the activities of Catholic ecclesiastics. Yet these were not being enforced. 'For want of a due execution of the laws', priests regularly landed from foreign parts, and there were Catholic bishops in the kingdom that ordained many more. Now that George I had been safely installed, people in Ireland expected a more effective policy. But this would be achieved only if government gave an unequivocal lead:

> The management towards them has been so uncertain for 50 years last past, in truth ever since the Reformation, that none dare trust the government so far as to exert themselves in earnest against them, for ten to one but in a few years that is imputed to him as a crime. I hope we shall have more steadiness for the future, but that must be signified to the kingdom and effectually inculcated and encouraged before we can expect any execution of the laws.[44]

What King wanted was for the new monarch to be asked to decide just how far the existing laws were to be enforced and for his decision then to be implemented consistently. The worst thing that could be done was to order strict measures and then fail to carry them out. Such empty gestures 'do a great deal of hurt, discourage the Protestants and animate the Papists, as has frequently happened formerly'.

King's indictment of the evasions and inconsistencies of past religious policies was formidable. Yet his plea for a new 'steadiness' under George I went unanswered. Some of the reasons were what they had always been. The resources available to enforce the law were wholly inadequate. Magistrates and others were held back by inertia, fear of reprisal, or perhaps a lack of conviction that particular laws were necessary or justified. Government in London was open to the same diplomatic pressures—the need to maintain good relations with Catholic allies, combined with concern for the fate of Protestant minorities abroad—that had operated in the reigns of William III and Anne. But there were also new developments. With George I safely installed on the throne, Protestants in both Great Britain and Ireland could feel more secure than they had done at any time in the last thirty years, and quite possibly for much longer. The defeat of the Jacobite risings of 1715 and the *entente* with France the following year considerably reinforced this sense of security.

---

[44] King to Sunderland, 1, 8 Jan. 1715 (TCD MS 750/4/2, 25–6, 29b). Mant (*Church of Ireland*, ii. 212–13), who reprints the first letter, gives the date as 21 Jan. My reading of the manuscript, however, is that King's clerk began to write 31 Dec., then changed this to 1 Jan.

None of this meant, however, that the problem of Irish Catholicism had ceased to matter. Three-quarters of the population remained openly hostile to the political and religious establishment, even if that hostility was for the moment denied effective expression. Even without this political threat, moreover, the existence of a substantial Catholic ecclesiastical organization was an anomaly in a Protestant state, and it became more so as that organization was slowly rebuilt and extended. Against this background, Protestant opinion, never united on the question of Catholic policy, became newly polarized. At one extreme were those who responded to the ineffectiveness of the Popery laws by demanding that they be made tougher. At the other were those who argued that the laws should be dismantled and replaced by something else. In the centre was the government, reasonably satisfied with the existing state of affairs, but responding to pressure when it felt obliged to do so.

Just how little concern there was to adopt a more consistent policy of the kind Archbishop King was advocating was made clear in the four or five years following the accession of George I. Gestures were certainly made. A party led by the sheriff of County Donegal raided the pilgrimage site at Lough Derg in August 1715—although even then there were allegations that the three priests arrested were deliberately allowed to escape. In October 1716 the lords justices issued a new proclamation calling for strict enforcement of the laws against regulars and other prohibited groups, including registered priests who had not taken the oath of abjuration. Yet there was no consistent effort to implement such orders. William Nicolson, recently arrived in Ireland, reported in June 1718 that the Catholic clergy 'are said to be now more numerous than ever'.[45] At the beginning of the same month the authorities had raided several houses in Dublin and arrested seven regulars and un-registered priests. Six of them were subsequently sentenced to transportation, but the prize catch, Edmund Byrne, archbishop of Dublin, was acquitted and released when the prosecution brought no evidence against him. Since the witness whose evidence had led to his arrest, the priest-hunter John Garzia, was at this time in protective custody in Dublin Castle, it seems clear that the collapse of the prosecution was deliberate, most probably reflecting another diplomatic intervention by England's Catholic allies.[46] The comments of a County Clare man visiting Dublin in April 1719 confirm that the authorities there—though not necessarily in other parts of the country—had largely given up attempting to enforce the letter of the law: '[I] do design to leave town next Sunday after hearing mass publicly at any of the known chapels, not knowing

[45] King to Dean Trench, 12 July, 30 Aug. 1715 (TCD MS 2533, 8, 69); Proclamation, 8 Oct. 1716, in Brady, *Catholics and Catholicism*, 25–7; Nicolson to Wake, 17 June 1718 (Gilbert MS 27, 178).
[46] McGrath, 'John Garzia', 496–504.

whether I should be allowed any such liberty in the county of Clare. There is no such thing as the least notion of trouble here.'[47]

The frustration caused by an increasingly visible Catholic ecclesiastical structure, and perhaps by the sort of official duplicity revealed in the Byrne case, helps to explain the notorious heads of a bill drawn up in the Commons in the parliamentary session of 1719. These provided, among other things, that regular clergy, unregistered priests, and other outlawed varieties of Catholic ecclesiastic found in the kingdom be branded on the cheek. When the heads came to the Irish Privy Council, this clause was amended: instead of being branded, priests illicitly in the kingdom should be castrated. A formal letter recommending the new clause was signed by, among others, the lord lieutenant, the duke of Bolton, Lord Chancellor Midleton, and Bishops Evans of Meath and Stearne of Clogher. The English Privy Council, in its turn, deleted the Irish Council's amendment, and apparently the whole clause.[48] When the bill was returned to Dublin, doubts were expressed about a completely different issue: a clause that not only prohibited leases in reversion but invalidated all such leases made since the Act of 1704. The Commons, reassured by the unanimous opinion of the judges that the clause merely confirmed a prohibition already implicit in the 1704 Act, passed the bill. The Lords, however, voted by a majority of fourteen to eleven to reject it, on the grounds that it constituted an attempt at retrospective legislation.[49]

Precisely what lay behind these events remains unclear. The reason given for the Irish Privy Council's amendment was, to say the least, thin: that where branding had been used as a punishment in the past (presumably the burning in the hand inflicted for non-capital homicides and some other offences), 'the rapparees in their robberies made it a common practice to brand innocent persons with that mark in order to destroy the distinction it was intended for'.[50] The penalty proposed did not exist in English or Irish law, raising the question of how exactly it would be inflicted. (Castration did of course form part of the death sentence in cases of high treason, but there, questions of surgical technique were largely beside the point.) It is true that castration of priests had been discussed in the English parliament in 1674 and in at least one pamphlet since.[51] But it is difficult, given the earlier vetoing of much

---

[47] J. Davoren to Mrs O'Brien, 28 Apr. 1719 (*Inchiquin Manuscripts*, 140).

[48] Most accounts, presumably following Lecky (*History of Ireland*, i. 163), suggest that the English Council restored the branding penalty. However, Bishop Godwin's claim that, in the final version, 'all sanguinary clauses were left out' (to Wake, 7 Nov. 1719, Wake MS XIII, 124) seems to cast doubt on this.

[49] Nicolson to Wake, 30 Nov. 1719, 23 Feb. 1720 (Gilbert MS 27, 245, 254); Synge to Wake, 19 Nov. 1719 (Gilbert MS 28, 120); Bolton to Craggs, 3 Nov. 1719 (SP63/378/133); Evans to Wake, 31 Oct. 1719 (Wake MS XIII, 120).

[50] Bolton to Craggs, 25 Aug. 1719 (SP63/377/42); Webster to Delafaye, 26 Aug. 1719 (SP63/377/44).

[51] Plunkett to Falconieri, 12 Feb. 1674 (*Letters*, 402); Lecky, *History of Ireland*, i. 163.

milder measures in England, to see how the experienced politicians and administrators who recommended its introduction in 1719 can possibly have expected the proposal to be approved. There were claims that the clause had been added by opponents of the bill, to ensure its defeat. But this does not fit what is known of the proposal's origins.[52] The most probable explanation is that members of the Irish executive, knowing that a bill prescribing that priests be branded on the face was not going to get past the English Council, were determined to make sure that the recriminations that would inevitably follow would be directed at London, not themselves. In changing the penalty to castration, they may have intended to make doubly sure that the clause would be struck out. Alternatively, and more probably, they sought to re-inforce the point that it was not they who were to be blamed for any failure to take more effective action against priests.

The second major attempt to tighten up the laws against priests came in 1723. During the previous year, complaints about the number and effrontery of the Catholic clergy had once again been building up. Bishop Nicolson in January 1722 bemoaned the 'daily increasing shoals of priests and friars from abroad'. Two months later the judge at the spring assizes for Derry pro-nounced that the number of priests was now six times greater than in Queen Anne's day. A Dublin newspaper offered similar inflated estimates: 'There are no less than 1,500 lately come hither from other countries who are not registered nor can be, which gives reason to the government to suspect some design extraordinary to be on foot.'[53] Concern at apparently increasing num-bers was reinforced by other considerations. The uncovering of Atterbury's Plot led the lords justices to call in April 1722 for a strict enforcement of the laws against Catholic clergy and the closure of chapels. Closer to home, and singled out specifically in the preamble to the bill of 1723, there was the alarm caused by the sudden wave of recruiting for the Spanish service.[54]

When parliament assembled in September 1723, the lord lieutenant, the duke of Grafton, recommended to the members as 'a matter deserving your serious attention to provide some laws for the further strengthening of the

---

[52] Pocklington to Wake, 3 Nov. 1719 (Wake MS XIII, 122): the archbishops were 'very fierce' against the bill in the Lords, 'which makes people say that their putting in the castrating clause to the bill against Popery was only with a view to have the bill lost in England'. Archbishops Synge and King had not signed the letter supporting the amendment, however; if they had played a part in the decision, it is hard to imagine, given their known views, that this would have escaped comment. The person who does appear both as a sponsor of the castration clause and as an opponent of the bill in the Lords is Midleton, who claimed that he had only become aware of the objectionable nature of the retrospective clause after the bill had come back (see Thomas Brodrick to Midleton, 27 Jan. 1720, Midleton MS 1248/4, fo. 206). But if Midleton did have an ulterior motive, it was that he had already fallen out with the lord lieutenant over the Peerage Bill (see above, ch. 3).

[53] Nicolson to Wake, 13 Jan., 4 Mar. 1722 (Gilbert MS 27, 276, 314); *Weekly News Letter*, 20 Mar. 1722, in Brady, *Catholics and Catholicism*, 35–6.

[54] Brady, *Catholics and Catholicism*, 36; above, p. 238.

Protestant interest of this kingdom, particularly for preventing more effectually the eluding of those in being against Popish priests'.[55] Grafton's motives
are obvious enough: discontent over William Wood's patent and the continuing feud between the Midleton and Conolly factions promised a difficult
session ahead. The Commons took the hint, and drew up heads of a new bill.
These provided that any regular or person exercising ecclesiastical jurisdiction
found in the kingdom after 25 March 1724 should be guilty of high treason.
This would make them liable to be hung, drawn, and quartered. The same
would apply to all unregistered priests found in the kingdom after that date,
except those who had taken the oath of abjuration before 14 November 1723.
Persons harbouring these ecclesiastics and also Catholic teachers, became
guilty of felony, which meant that they could be hanged.[56]

Once again, as in 1719, it is not safe to assume that draft legislation
represented in any straightforward way the intentions of the legislators. At
least one observer questioned whether the bloody provisions of the heads of
1723 were ever really intended to become law. According to Bishop Evans of
Meath:

I hear some members have openly declared that since you [i.e. the English govern-
ment] will have such a bill, or law, (the lord lieutenant having recommended it from
the throne) they would send you one, and whether you would pass, or reject it, majesty
itself must bear the blame either way.[57]

Other accounts, by contrast, suggest that in this case Evans's obsession with
the conflict he insisted on seeing everywhere between English and Irish
parties makes him an unreliable witness. The Commons, Nicolson reported,
'appear to have set their hearts' on the bill; and King used an almost identical
phrase.[58] MPs themselves demonstrated their commitment to the measure
by coming in a body, led by the Speaker, to present the heads to the
lord lieutenant. The Privy Council, on the other hand, was deeply divided.
According to Nicolson:

The Popery bill . . . has gone a fiery ordeal (as hot as purgatory itself) before our lords
of the council. They have made amendments, additions, subtractions, heard counsel,
etc. And at last cooked up the whole in such a manner that the lord lieutenant was
hard put to it for a quorum to subscribe. Many of us seem to be exceedingly afraid of
provoking our Roman neighbours.[59]

Grafton, reporting to London on the version agreed by the Privy Council,
conceded that it still contained clauses 'which at first sight may seem severe',

---

[55] *Commons Jn. Ire.* iii. 314, 5 Sept. 1723.
[56] Heads of the bill reprinted in Burke, *Irish Priests*, 455–60.
[57] Evans to Wake, 19 Nov. 1723 (Wake MS XIV, 119).
[58] Nicolson to Wake, 14 Dec. 1723 (Gilbert MS 27, 332); King to Southwell, 26 Dec. 1723
(TCD MS 2537, 43).
[59] Nicolson to Wake, 14 Dec. 1723 (Gilbert MS 27, 332).

but pointed to 'the vast swarm of Romish priests who infest and impoverish this kingdom' and the recent role of such clergy in enlisting men for foreign service.[60] Whether he really favoured the bill or whether, like Bolton four years earlier, he was going through the motions necessary to preserve good relations with the Commons remains unclear. Either way, the English Privy Council, as might have been predicted, refused to approve the bill.

The bishops of the established church were deeply divided in their attitude to the 1723 bill. Josiah Hort of Ferns was in principle favourable. His only objection was that the date by which priests could escape the provisions of the bill by taking the oath of abjuration would be already past by the time it became law. Even then, his concern was primarily with how the measure would be viewed abroad: given an opportunity, he felt, very few priests would in fact take the oath. In other respects his belief was that, if the bill became law, 'the coup de grace will be given to Popery here'.[61] Support for at least the principles of the bill may also be inferred from William Nicolson's criticism of those who seemed afraid 'of provoking our Romish neighbours'. Timothy Godwin of Kilmore, on the other hand, saw the bill, even in modified form, as 'a cruel one, and I could never have come into it'. William King, predictably enough, opposed it as 'in itself barbarous and, if I mistake not, at this time unseasonable'.[62] These were primarily objections to the harshness of the provisions. Others, however, showed a new willingness to question the very principle on which the bill was based. Edward Synge of Tuam believed that it was legitimate to exclude, on pain of death, any priest who would not provide security for his good and loyal behaviour, but 'must own that I cannot come into a law to put him to death (under the name indeed of high treason, but in reality only for adhering to an erroneous religion, and worshipping God according to it)'. Bishop Evans of Meath was more direct: 'I thought allowing no priests to above a million of people (how false soever their religion may be) was the worst of tyranny, and a very hard chapter, which I could never come into.'[63]

Objections from bishops of the established church to tough anti-Catholic measures were not of course new. Several of the key statutes introduced in the reigns of William III and Anne had found their strongest opponents among the bishops in the Lords. That opposition, however, had been directed at proposals affecting the Catholic laity: the incomplete ratification of the

[60] Grafton to Carteret, 15 Nov. 1723 (SP63/382/18ᵛ).
[61] Hort to Wake, 29 Nov., 14 Dec. 1723 (Wake MS XIV, 124, 132). Even Hort had earlier declared that it would be better to tolerate a reasonable number of priests 'under such qualifications as a Papist can with a good conscience submit to' than to seek 'to extirpate them all by capital punishment': to Wake, 19 Oct. 1723 (ibid. 105).
[62] Godwin to Wake, 24 Jan. 1724 (ibid. 152); King to Southwell, 2 Dec. 1723 (TCD MS 2537, 29).
[63] Synge to Wake, 13 Dec. 1723 (Gilbert MS 28, 193); Evans to Wake, 17 Dec. 1723 (Wake MS XIV, 133).

Treaty of Limerick, the summary procedures laid down by the bill to preserve the king's person, and the restrictions on landed property imposed in 1709. It is true that in the summer of 1714 William King was led to wonder, in the context of proposed legislation against Dissenting schools, 'whether severe laws against Dissenters ever be the way to support the church'. He had even considered the possibility that Catholics and Dissenters be permitted to run seminaries, where their members could be trained without being exposed to dangerous foreign influences, 'and make it death for any to be a Romish priest or Dissenter teacher that is not bred here'.[64] But this sudden rush of liberality may well have been a response to the apparently desperate situation of the Church of Ireland in the last months of Queen Anne's reign. King, after all, had shown a similar surge of tolerance towards Dissenters in the dark days under James II.[65] And in any case it was not until the 1720s that any other leading figure in the established church can be found expressing reservations about the laws relating to Catholic ecclesiastics.

It is important to be clear about what these reservations involved. Critics of the 1723 proposals or of the existing penal laws did not question the principle of imposing legal disabilities on Catholics. Archbishop Synge, for example, preaching before the Lords on 23 October 1721, distinguished between persecution solely on account of religious belief, which was contrary to the spirit of the Gospel, and the measures which could and should be used to contain those whose doctrines posed a danger to the state. His aim was to demonstrate that it was both legitimate and necessary to exclude Catholics from public employment and political influence, not because their beliefs were false, but because their church made it a religious principle to seek the destruction of heresy and required its members to give unlimited obedience to the Pope, regardless of their obligation to their temporal rulers. Synge's argument was essentially the same as that advanced thirty years previously by William King: 'It is no injustice to exclude a certain rank of men, that want such qualifications as may give the commonwealth confidence in them, from intermeddling in the government.'[66]

What was at issue, then, was not the exclusion of Catholics from civil life, but rather the extent to which that exclusion should be accompanied by

---

[64] King to George William Story, dean of Limerick, 19 June 1714 (TCD MS 750/4/1, 349); King to F. Annesley, 3 July 1714 (ibid. 310–11).

[65] Carpenter, 'William King and the Threats to the Church of Ireland'. Note, however, that in January 1689 James Bonnell reported that leading churchmen were drawing up plans for a new ecclesiastical establishment, 'if ever we should have a parliament', and mentioned proposals, similar to those being discussed in England, to accommodate Dissenters on the matter of ordination (Strype Correspondence, I, fo. 83). If the document Carpenter analyses was part of this effort, then it was compiled with an eye to the political changes that had already taken place in England, rather than as a desperate response to James II's attacks on the Church of Ireland. The accusation of bad faith on King's part thus becomes somewhat less compelling.

[66] Synge, *A Sermon against Persecution*; King, *State of the Protestants*, 42.

restrictions on their ecclesiastical organization. Here Synge had, by the early 1720s, undergone a radical change of mind. In 1715 he had argued that a proper enforcement of the laws against unregistered and regular clergy could eventually cause the whole Catholic church establishment to wither away.[67] By 1722, on the other hand, he had abandoned all such hopes. Instead, he had turned his attention to the possibility of devising a test of allegiance that would allow the state to extend a limited toleration to Catholic ecclesiastics and laymen alike. What he had in mind was a formula that would enable Catholics to swear allegiance to George I, to disclaim all intention of altering the succession, and to renounce specifically the Pretender and his heirs. In addition—and in light of later experience something that would almost certainly have condemned the scheme to failure—they would have to deny that the Pope had the power to depose princes or release subjects from their allegiance. What they were not to be required to do was to deny the Pretender's *de jure* right to the throne.[68] It was clearly this formula that Synge was thinking of when he referred in 1723 to priests providing security for their loyal behaviour as a condition of being permitted to officiate in the country.[69]

What Synge was proposing was thus the replacement of the existing, ineffective laws with a more realistic definition of the sort of Catholic church establishment that could be tolerated in a Protestant state. By the 1720s, others, possibly influenced by the controversy surrounding the Popery Bill of 1723, had begun to think along similar lines. A revenue official in County Galway submitted to the government an apparently unsolicited scheme to license one priest for each parish and require him to take a new oath that would be acceptable to his conscience. A pamphlet by Viscount Molesworth, who had been a prominent opponent of the 1719 bill, argued that 'to expect to have a numerous people, without allowing the exercise of a religion, is both tyrannical and impolitic'. The secular clergy, in fact, should be paid out of public funds, which would 'engage the priests ... in the true interests of the government'. Regulars, on the other hand, should be carefully excluded.[70] The next session of parliament, in 1725–6, saw a concerted effort to implement the idea of a licensed, officially regulated Catholic ecclesiastical establishment. The House of Lords passed a resolution in favour of permitting a sufficient number of licensed priests. Henry Downes, bishop of

---

[67] Synge to Wake, 13 Apr. 1715 (Gilbert MS 28, 23–7), printed (from another source) in Burns, 'Thoughts on Converting the Irish'. See below, p. 298.

[68] Synge to Wake, 27 Jan. 1722 (Gilbert MS 28, 166–76). For difficulties over the Pope's deposing power, see above, ch. 5, sect. 2.

[69] Synge to Wake, 13 Dec. 1723 (Gilbert MS 28, 193): 'If any Papist or Popish priest will not solemnly upon oath renounce the Pretender, and also the Pope's power of deposing princes, or absolving subjects from their allegiance, let him leave the kingdom or be dealt with as a traitor.'

[70] Charles Hogg, gauger, Loughrea, addressed directly to the king, 10 Dec. 1723 (SP63/383/55); [Molesworth], *Some Considerations*, 30.

Elphin, introduced more concrete proposals to permit a maximum of 600 priests, with one bishop to ordain replacements for those who died. Prospective priests should be permitted to attend Trinity College, Dublin, without being required to attend Anglican services. Meanwhile, Archbishop Synge revived his proposals for a new oath acceptable to conscientious Catholics.[71]

Synge's son, another Edward, also entered the debate. Preaching the annual sermon to members of the House of Commons on the anniversary of the rising of 1641, he took as his theme the text: 'Compel them to come in.' Both occasion and text were misleading. The first half of Synge's discourse closely echoed his father's sermon to the Lords on the same occasion four years before: it was legitimate to impose disabilities on Catholics, not because of their religious errors, but because their doctrines were inimical to the security of the state. The second part of the discourse, however, followed Synge senior's more recent thinking. Since the Gallican party within the Catholic church rejected the most dangerous of these doctrines—the Pope's deposing power and his ability to dispense subjects from their allegiance— then Irish Catholics should be given the opportunity to do the same, with some measure of greater toleration for those who did so. The younger Synge's sermon involved him in a pamphlet controversy with what he alleged was a Tory opponent motivated by party hostility. But no steps were taken to implement either his or Downes's suggestions.[72]

What was happening in the 1720s was that Protestant churchmen and laity alike were having to accept that the laws against Catholic ecclesiastics were not working. Whether the number of priests had increased as much as was claimed is not clear. But they had certainly become more visible, and ecclesiastical structures disrupted in the 1690s were being rebuilt. The demand for drastically harsher penalties and the proposals for a licensed and properly regulated Catholic clergy represented the two logical responses to these circumstances. Logic for its own sake, however, has rarely carried much weight with practical men of government. English ministers found the prospect of tougher measures against Catholicism diplomatically embarrassing and possibly distasteful in itself. If the demand for such measures from the Irish parliament had been strong enough to threaten serious disruption, they might have acted differently. But it was not: partly because of the tighter system of parliamentary management built up since 1714 and partly because Protestant demands no longer had the edge of real fear that had been evident in the reigns of William III and Anne. As for the calls of a handful of conscientious churchmen to bring the law into line with practical reality, these were of no weight at all compared with the battles that would have to be

---

[71] Nicolson to Wake, n.d. [*c.* Jan. 1726] (Gilbert MS 27, 390–2); Wall, *Catholic Ireland*, 97.

[72] Synge, jun., *The Case of Toleration Considered*; Edward Synge, jun., to Wake, 19 Mar. 1726 (Wake MS XIII, 330).

fought to stand established religious policy on its head. Of all the sleeping dogs in Sir Robert Walpole's dominions, the legal position of Irish Catholics had as good a claim as any to rest undisturbed.

The development and consolidation of Catholic church structures continued during the mid- and late 1720s. Archbishop King spent the last years before his death in 1729 raging against what he saw as the collapse of all attempts to keep Popery within bounds. The Catholics, he complained in 1727,

have more bishops in Ireland than the Protestants have, and twice (at least) as many priests. Their friaries and nunneries are public; it is in vain to pass laws against them, for the justices of the peace are no ways inclined to put such laws in execution; and, to help the matter, there is a notion prevails universally that the government is so engaged with the neighbouring Popish powers by treaties and confederacies that they are obliged to connive at the practices of their Popish subjects.[73]

King, of course, was an old man, a critic of the anti-Catholic policies of an earlier age now at length overtaken by history. But the essential truth of his observations was confirmed when the House of Lords in 1731 called on the clergy of the established church, along with magistrates, mayors, and other officials, to submit a return of the priests, mass houses, friaries, nunneries, and Catholic schools in their respective districts. Two things are immediately evident from the resulting reports. The first is the scale and level of Catholic ecclesiastical organization: a generous ratio of clergy to people; an uneven, but still extensive, provision of places of worship, ranging from crude cabins to solid and well-furnished urban churches; a network both of elementary and of more advanced schools; and large numbers of regular clergy, some of them living in settled communities.[74] The second is the general absence of concealment. The clergy and lay officials charged with making the return were all clearly well-informed as to the location of mass houses, schools, and communities of religious, as well as the identity not just of parish clergy, but of bishops, vicars-general, and other dignitaries.

It would be wrong to suggest that toleration was total. In some areas, particularly the provinces of Ulster and Munster, attempts were still being made to enforce the laws. In the diocese of Derry, it was claimed, Popish schools were still being effectively prevented: 'Sometimes a straggling schoolmaster sets up in some of the mountainous parts of some parishes, but upon being threatened, as they constantly are, with a warrant or a presentment by the churchwardens they generally think proper to withdraw.' In Clogher the Catholic bishop still lived under an assumed name, and 'disappears since these enquiries'. In Clonfert the recent prosecution of a schoolmaster had led

---

[73] King to Carteret, 22 June 1727 (TCD MS 750/8, 213–14). For other expressions of King's grave disquiet at this time, see ibid. 196, 214–15; Mant, *Church of Ireland*, ii. 487.
[74] Above, ch. 5, sect. 2.

others to make themselves scarce.[75] Even where Catholics were permitted to organize their religious life with relative impunity, they were expected to do so in ways that did not offend Protestant sensibilities or suggest that they took their freedom too much for granted. Magistrates at Cloyne and Charleville in County Cork prevented the erection of mass houses 'within view of the churches in those towns, and where no mass houses were before'. A Kildare rector, similarly, had a mass house pulled down, 'it standing in the direct road to my church, and not far from it'.[76] In other cases the laws were suddenly invoked following local conflicts or clashes of personalities. At Castle Lyons, County Cork, in 1733, one of the parties to a quarrel at a meeting of the turnpike commissioners retaliated against its opponents (presumably a convert family) by nailing up the mass house and warning the priest 'not to celebrate mass for the future, on pain of transportation'. The following year the bishop of Raphoe complained that his Catholic counterpart had removed 'a quiet, inoffensive priest and put a turbulent fellow in his place'. The county authorities promptly arrested the latter.[77]

Incidents of this last kind, of course, made nonsense of the idea of a law to be applied equally to all Catholic clergymen. But the advocates of a return to strict ecclesiastical prohibition had not yet given up. In 1730 the House of Lords threw out a proposal to register the secular clergy and expel regulars.[78] In the following session of 1731–2, the Commons passed heads of two bills for the same purposes. These were forwarded to England by the Irish Council, but not returned.[79] In January 1734 the lord lieutenant, at the request of parliament, issued a proclamation calling for a strict enforcement of the laws against Catholic ecclesiastics. This was done, according to the papal nuncio, in revenge for the success of the Catholics in inducing the English Council, partly by means of bribery, to drop the recent bills.[80] Yet even in parliament there were signs that opinion was shifting. Writing in December 1731, Boulter reported that the Disarming Bill could not be made as strong as he would like: 'Too many in the House of Commons show a disposition to favour the Papists more than is consistent with the Protestant interest here.' A month later he warned against proposals to attach a clause repealing the sacramental test to one of the bills approved in London. That was how the test had first been introduced; but 'there was then a very great spirit against Popery amongst the Commons, which I fear I cannot say now'.[81]

---

[75] 'Report on the State of Popery', i (1912), 17, 16; 3 (1914), 133.

[76] Ibid. 2 (1913), 127; 4 (1915), 159.

[77] George Ross to F. Price, 18, 21 Sept. 1733 (HMC, *Puleston Manuscripts*, 316); Burke, *Irish Priests*, 289.

[78] Boulter to bishop of London, 2 Jan. 1730 (*Letters*, i. 345).

[79] List of bills, 3 Feb. 1732 (SP63/395/44); Newcastle to Dorset, 24 Feb. 1732 (SP63/395/66).

[80] Giblin, '*Nunziatura di Fiandra*', 9 (1966), 38.

[81] Boulter to Newcastle, 4 Dec. 1731 (*Letters*, ii. 70–1); Boulter to Delafaye, 4 Jan. 1732 (SP63/395/18).

The sudden invocation of the laws with which parliament rescued its bruised pride in 1734 was no empty gesture. Churches closed their doors, and priests went into hiding. But the disruption was short-lived. By May reports from Ireland to the nuncio in Brussels suggested that life had largely returned to normal.[82] This jerking of the lead, moreover, was the last occasion of its kind. The law was still invoked from time to time in individual cases. In County Westmeath in 1742 a priest who had converted a woman to Catholicism was convicted as an unregistered cleric and transported. The rector of the parish of Fews in County Armagh, where a Presbyterian meeting-house was burned down in 1743, reported that 'the gentlemen of the country are determined no priest shall be suffered in it, unless a discovery be made'.[83] In general, however, priests, bishops, and even regulars who avoided drawing attention to themselves appear to have operated largely undisturbed. By 1743 even the preacher of the annual 1641 commemoration sermon before the House of Commons could present the non-enforcement of the law as a virtue rather than a failing. The Catholics 'enjoy the free exercise of their religion in a manner little differing in fact from a legal toleration . . . if any harshness appears in some of our laws with respect to their clergy, it is well known they were intended to prevent treason against the state, and are never executed on any account merely religious'.[84]

The laws that were thus being permitted to slide progressively into disuse were those relating to Catholic ecclesiastics. The absolute necessity of excluding Catholics from political power of all sorts, including that which would come with ownership of landed property, remained common ground among Protestants of all political views.[85] The legislation by which this was to be achieved was in place well before 1714. Yet minor additions continued to be made throughout the next three decades, as real or imagined loopholes were discovered. In 1726 a bill to prevent Protestants from acting as agents for Catholics in collusive discoveries and to prevent Catholic tradesmen evading the restrictions on the number of apprentices they could take on was submitted to London, but not approved. In 1728 concern at the large number of what were claimed to be purely nominal converts practising at the bar led to a bill to require lawyers to educate their children as Protestants and to impose a two-year 'quarantine' before converts could practice law.[86] The same year a clause in a bill to regulate parliamentary elections excluded Catholics from

[82] Giblin, '*Nunziatura di Fiandra*', 9 (1966), 41.

[83] Brady, *Catholics and Catholicism*, 64; Hugh Hill to [Hoadly], 24 Oct. 1743 (PRONI T1392).

[84] Bacon, *A Sermon Preached at St Andrew's, Dublin*, 13.

[85] See e.g. the views of Revd Philip Skelton, in an otherwise conciliatory pamphlet, 'The Chevalier's Hope', in *Works*, v. 310.

[86] Abstract of a bill, Feb. 1726 (BL, Southwell Papers, Add. MS 34,777, fos. 84, 86–7); Boulter to Newcastle, 7 Mar. 1728 (*Letters*, 226–8); Boulter to bishop of London, 7 Mar. 1728 (ibid. 229–31).

voting. Catholic participation in elections had already been sharply reduced by their exclusion from borough corporations and by the requirement, imposed in 1704, that voters take the oath of abjuration. But the real point was that the franchise, within the political framework of early Hanoverian Ireland, counted for relatively little—far less than membership of the oligarchic municipal corporations that returned the majority of members to parliament or the landownership that conferred control over the votes of freeholders in the counties and potwalloping boroughs. Once again, we are reminded that the enactment of the penal laws is not to be understood in terms of the political priorities of a century later.[87]

The session of 1733–4 brought two further measures aimed at bogus converts. Lawyers married to Catholics were debarred from practice, while converts whose wives and children remained Catholics became ineligible to act as justices of the peace.[88] Meanwhile, an embarrassing loophole had appeared in the Disarming Act of 1695. A judgment at the Galway summer assizes in 1731 was taken to mean that the provisions of the Act applied only to Catholics living at the time it had been passed and to the arms they had then held. Catholics responded quickly to the judgement: 'The Papists in Dublin have upon it put on swords, and those in the country in Connacht at least travel publicly with swords and firearms.' A new Disarming Act was approved in London, but did not pass into law.[89] Legislation to annul mixed marriages performed by priests, dropped in 1732, was finally passed in 1745, still resisted by some of the Privy Council but energetically pushed by the Speaker on behalf of the Commons. As late as 1748 the Lords considered a bill to tighten the law against education abroad.[90]

The legal immunity increasingly enjoyed by the Catholic clergy from at least the mid-1720s was, of course, at a time when the Anglo-French accord commenced in 1716 deprived Jacobitism of foreign backing and consequently of most of its credibility. The revival of a serious invasion threat in 1744 brought an abrupt return to traditional responses. When the lord lieutenant met his Privy Council in February to concert security precautions, its members called for the arrest of bishops and regulars and the suppression of monasteries and nunneries. The lord lieutenant objected that it was unwise to alarm the Catholic population before defence measures had been completed, 'but they were so set upon it, that I could not stop it without refusing to sign the order, which would have been improper at this time'.[91] A proclamation

---

[87] Simms, 'Irish Catholics and the Parliamentary Franchise', in *War and Politics in Ireland*, 232–3.

[88] Kenny, 'Exclusion of Catholics from the Legal Profession', 353–4; 7 Geo. II, c. 6.

[89] Boulter to Newcastle, 4 Dec. 1731 (*Letters*, ii. 68–71).

[90] Irish Statutes, 19 Geo. II, c. 13; Bernard Ward to Michael Ward, 29 Oct. 1745 (PRONI D2092/1/7/93); Ryder to Sir Dudley Ryder, 19 Jan. 1748 (PRONI T3228/1/42).

[91] Devonshire to Newcastle, 20 Feb. 1744 (SP63/406/89–90).

calling for the execution of the laws against Catholic ecclesiastics and offering rewards for their apprehension duly appeared on 28 February. Magistrates and other officials throughout the country were ordered to make returns of regulars and persons exercising ecclesiastical jurisdiction in their districts. In Louth and Queen's County known regulars were presented at the spring assizes. In Kilkenny the grand jury presented the Catholic bishop of Ossory, Colman O'Shaughnessy, as an enemy of the king, claiming that he had served as domestic chaplain to the Pretender. Churches, in the towns at least, were closed up. Searches for regulars and other prohibited persons brought some arrests: two friars and a secular priest in Dublin city and a few priests in County Cork. In general, however, local authorities reported that the clergy, secular and regular, had gone into hiding, and could not be found.[92]

This last, forcible shutting down of the Catholic church establishment continued for several months: it was not until January 1745 that the nuncio at Brussels reported that the storm had largely passed.[93] Only six months later the threat of invasion and rebellion reappeared, this time in more concrete form. But there was no attempt to repeat the closure of chapels or the attempted seizure of suspect ecclesiastics. Chesterfield, according to his own account, responded to assurances of good intent from leaders of the Catholic community by promising that they would be left in peace, while warning of the dreadful consequences if these assurances proved false. Chesterfield, of course, was to be severely criticized for his relaxed attitude to the crisis of 1745–6. But it is significant that those who attacked his apparently casual dismissal of Protestant fears and his spurning of offers to raise more troops did not also complain of the absence of a new drive against bishops and regulars. All in all, it would seem that even those who had been responsible for the measures taken in 1744 had come to see them as unnecessary, if not anachronistic.[94] Proposals to bring the law into line with a changed reality were another matter. The following year two bills were introduced in the Commons. One took up the familiar suggestion of a more realistic, and therefore more enforceable, scheme for registering Catholic priests. The other was more novel: a move to permit Catholics to take long leases. Despite Chesterfield's support, both were decisively rejected.[95]

By the 1750s the gap between law and practice had become wider still. In 1751 the government ordered the arrest of Nicholas Sweetman, Catholic bishop of Ferns, after a suspended priest had charged him with raising men and money on behalf of a foreign power. Five years later the archbishop of Armagh was arrested, along with eighteen of his priests, as they met to

[92] Burke, *Irish Priests*, ch. 7–10; Brady, *Catholics and Catholicism*, 65–7; White, 'Annals of Limerick' (NLI MS 2714), 113–14; W. Colles to his wife, 10 Mar. 1744 (Prim MS 87, 1); William Pearde to F. Price, 9 Mar. 1744 (HMC, *Puleston Manuscripts*, 328).
[93] Giblin, '*Nunziatura di Fiandra*', 10 (1967), 103.
[94] Above, ch. 6, sect. 5.   [95] Wall, *Catholic Ireland*, 116.

transact diocesan business. In each case the ecclesiastics involved were civilly treated and released immediately after questioning. Both encounters, in fact, had a curiously formal and ambiguous air: they could be used to demonstrate either the continuing legal menace hanging over Catholic churchmen or the extent to which the Bishops' Banishment Act and later statutes had ceased to have real meaning.[96] At the beginning of 1756 Lord Clanbrassil, the magistrate before whom the archbishop of Armagh and his priests were to be brought a few months later, introduced in the House of Lords a new attempt to replace unworkable prohibitions with a realistic system of regulation. Parish priests were to be required to register and give security for their good behaviour, under the Act of 1704. However bishops were to be permitted, and there was explicit provision for a succession to parishes without a priest. The Lords rejected the bill. In 1757 Clanbrassil, by now Lord Limerick, introduced an amended version, with the support of the lord lieutenant, Bedford. This time his heads of a bill passed the Lords, but were rejected, by fourteen votes to twelve, in the Irish Privy Council.

Clanbrassil/Limerick's registration bills of 1756–7 mark a turning-point in the history of attempts to deal by legislation with the existence in Ireland of a substantial Catholic church establishment. The stated premiss of the bills was the same as that of earlier statutes. 'That the Papists of Ireland are zealously attached to the cause of the Pretender', Clanbrassil wrote, 'is but too manifest, and that this zeal is fed and cherished by their priests is as notorious.' One object of offering some recognition to the secular clergy was to make it easier to exclude the regulars, 'those restless emissaries of France and the Pretender'. And even for the registered clergy the restrictions to be imposed were formidable: not only were they to take an oath renouncing belief in the Pope's deposing power and exhort their flocks to pray by name for the king and his successors; in addition, all priests registered were to be approved by the lord lieutenant.[97] On the other hand, the bills explicitly sought to replace the existing policy of tacit connivance with a formal recognition of the right of the Catholic clergy to operate under supervision. It was on this ground that both bills were eventually rejected.[98] The debate within the political establishment had changed. From this point on, controversy was to centre on attempts to take formal notice of the existence of Catholic ecclesiastics rather than—as in the past—on attempts to impose new restrictions on their activities.

The events of 1756–7 also revealed a change in the stance of the bishops

[96] Burke, *Irish Priests*, 315–19; Wall, *Catholic Ireland*, 37, 58, 98, 109; Brady, *Catholics and Catholicism*, 90.

[97] Clanbrassil to Bedford, 17 July 1757 (Bedford, *Correspondence*, ii. 263–4); text of the bill in Burke, *Irish Priests*, 204–6.

[98] Lord Drogheda was reported to have voted for the bill in the Lords, but to have opposed it in the Privy Council when he learned 'that Popish bishops were also to be established': Barry to Orrery, 24 Jan. 1758 (*Orrery Papers*, ii. 130–1).

of the Church of Ireland. From the 1690s to the 1730s the division had been between a section of the Protestant political classes, who had wished to enact tough anti-Catholic laws, and bishops like King and Edward Synge, who drew a distinction between legitimate self-defence and religious persecution. In 1756–7, on the other hand, it was the bishops, led by Archbishop Stone of Armagh, who took the lead in opposing Clanbrassil's bills. In doing so, they clearly did not envisage any return to an attempted enforcement of the existing laws. At the same time, they evidently felt, as their predecessors thirty years before had not, that any legal recognition of the existence of the Catholic clergy, however hedged about with precautions, would call into question the status of their own church. It was a subtle, but significant, change in outlook. Once, churchmen had considered religious policy in terms of how far the civil power should go in repressing their rivals. Now, they looked to a façade of unenforceable laws to uphold their pretensions in the face of a contrary reality.

3. The Conversion of the Natives

In any discussion of the differing approaches of Irish Protestants in the decades after the Jacobite war to the question of how best to secure their position, one theme requires special consideration. This is the view of those who believed that the ultimate aim of religious policy should be the conversion of the Catholic population to Protestantism. The issue was not a new one. Attempts to provide Irish-speaking ministers and teachers, along with the printing of key religious texts in Irish, began in the reign of Elizabeth. They were continued, by Bishop Bedell of Kilmore and others, in the 1620s and 1630s, and more sporadically under the Commonwealth in the 1650s. Robert Boyle had sponsored the reprinting of an Irish New Testament in 1681 and the first printing of an Old Testament four years later. He was encouraged in these efforts by Narcissus Marsh, provost of Trinity College, who also arranged for instruction in Irish, aimed at prospective ministers, to be provided in the college.[99] All these efforts ran up against the same problems: lack of resources, apathy, and a feeling that the Irish language should be discouraged rather than propagated. Most important of all, perhaps, was the sheer scale of the social change proposed, in a society where even routine governmental functions could not always be taken for granted. Increasing political stability after 1691 modified the last objection, but left the others untouched. Yet the question of converting the Catholic population refused to go away. At all times there were those who argued that real steps should be

---

[99] Barnard, *Cromwellian Ireland*, 171–82; Maddison, 'Robert Boyle and the Irish Bible'; McDowell and Webb, *Trinity College, Dublin*, 9–10.

taken to bring the Irish lower classes into the established church. And on occasion, possibly in the 1690s and certainly in the 1730s and 1740s, such projects had significant backing within the political establishment.

The reasons why Protestants should have been attracted by the idea of converting the Catholic population are evident enough. First, there was the question of security. In the words of an ambitious blueprint for the regeneration of the Church of Ireland drawn up while the Jacobite war was still being fought:

> the principal way to reduce the natives of Ireland (I mean the Irish) to civility, obedience and fidelity to the English government is to take the most probable way to make them Protestants, the difference in religion being a more prevailing cause of their hatred to the English language, customs and government, than the difference of nation.[100]

Secondly, there was the widespread conviction that Catholicism, with its parasitic clergy, its proliferation of holy days, and its stifling of individual responsibility, was inimical to economic development: schemes for the dissemination of Protestantism were closely linked to projects for economic development and general social improvement. To these secular motives must be added some element of religious duty. It is true that seventeenth- and eighteenth-century Anglicanism did not have a strong missionary tradition: there was no equivalent in England's American colonies of the work of French Jesuits and others among Amerindians and other non-European populations.[101] Closer to home, on the other hand, attempts were made, in the 1690s and after, to promote the reformation of manners and the religious education of the poor. Echoes of this movement reached Dublin, and it is likely that for some the conversion of the Irish was part of the same broader project as the suppression of prostitution and the tighter enforcement of sabbath observance. Jane Bonnell, widow of the most prominent figure in the movement of lay piety in the 1690s, argued in 1712 that 'it has been just in God to let the Irish be a scourge to us, because no care has ever been taken to convert them. We have made severe (to say no more) laws against them, and now would leave them to turn heathens by denying them the exercise of their own religion without instructing them in a better.'[102]

One way in which Catholicism could be made to give way to Protestantism was of course by forcible suppression. It was regularly claimed that this was in fact the purpose of the Popery laws. The comments of John Dunton, visiting Ireland in 1699, presumably reflect the terms in which the recent Bishops' Banishment Act had been presented to him there.

---

[100] 'The State of the Church of Ireland, 1690' (TCD MSS 1995–2008/115a).

[101] Monter, *Ritual, Myth and Magic*, 100–1.

[102] Jane Bonnell to King, 20 Mar. 1712 (TCD MSS 1995–2008/1422). For the movement to reform manners, etc. in Dublin, see above, ch. 5, sect. 5.

Our red-lettered gentlemen were never under such circumstances here, as now; for all their bishops and regular clergy are banished by act of parliament, which makes it death to find any of them returned again; so that now they are wholly depending on the seculars, and every parish is allowed his [*sic*] priest: but when he dies, there being none to ordain a new one, it must remain without; and this will be the state of the whole kingdom in a little time, when the present set of priests shall be extinct. They have also another law, that no Papist shall keep a school, nor any one native of a foreign education be admitted to dwell in the kingdom; so that by these acts, I think, it will appear plain enough, that the Romish religion is on its last legs in Ireland, and the present Romanists who survive their priests must conform to the Protestant religion or live and die without the exercise of their own.[103]

Archbishop King, writing nearly two decades later, was equally clear about the purpose of the Act: 'The design was that there should be no succession.' Joseph Addison, commenting on the Popery Bill of 1709, reported that large numbers of conversions were expected to follow the new restrictions proposed, 'for I don't see how a Papist with an estate will be able to live under it, when he is tied up from employing his money in purchases, mortgages, or trade'; indeed, by the time the existing generation of Catholic merchants, the last to be permitted, had died out, 'they hope the whole nation will be Protestant'. As late as 1719, members of the Privy Council supported the castration clause with the claim that 'the common Irish will never become Protestant or well affected to the crown while they are supplied with priests, friars etc.'.[104]

   Comment of this kind can easily be dismissed as so much rhetoric. In some cases, such as the last, this is most likely what it was. Indeed, it is tempting to assert, on the basis of the subsequent history of the laws relating to bishops, regulars, and others, that the idea of ridding Ireland of Catholic clergy was never really taken seriously. But this is to read history backwards. An examination of the first decade or so in which the laws against Catholic ecclesiastics were in operation suggests a more complex picture. The passing of the Banishment Act was followed by an immediate drive to fulfil its provisions. In the early months of 1698, 424 members of religious orders were transported from Ireland to continental Europe, while as many as 300 more left of their own accord. Two Catholic bishops also left voluntarily; a third, Bishop Sleyne of Cork, was arrested and kept in prison, since he was too ill to be sent overseas. All this seems to make clear that the Banishment Act was, initially at least, taken very seriously. So far, however, those removed from the country had either left of their own accord or given themselves up to be deported.[105]

---

[103] Dunton, *Life and Errors*, ii. 556–7.
[104] King to Sunderland, 1 Jan. 1715 (TCD MS 750/4/2, 25); Addison to Somers, 14 June 1709 (*Letters*, 151); Addison to Godolphin, 13 June 1709 (ibid. 148); Burke, *Irish Priests*, 200–1.
[105] Simms, 'Bishops' Banishment Act', 197–8; Burke, *Irish Priests*, 131–3; Wall, *Penal Laws*, 15–17.

There remained those who refused to co-operate: five bishops, perhaps a couple of dozen deans and vicars-general, and an unknown number—one modern account suggests about 200—of the regular clergy.[106] Over the next few years attempts were made to round up these fugitives. But the results were unimpressive. The returns submitted by six judges of the Catholic ecclesiastics brought before them, both on assizes and in the courts of Queen's Bench, Exchequer, and Common Pleas, between 1698 and 1703, list a total of only twenty-seven persons.[107]

Failure to act more forcefully against bishops and other clergy declared outlaws by the Banishment Act can certainly be attributed in part to lack of will. As early as August 1698 the imperial ambassador in London reported that officials in Ireland were 'not at all pleased when over-officious informers bring a priest to them'. Five years later the mayor of Derry complained that several gentlemen from County Donegal were using all their influence to secure the release of a priest who had been imprisoned for performing marriages contrary to the Act of 1697.[108] Yet there were also other reasons for failure to enforce the laws more rigorously. The limited machinery of coercive discipline available to even the most conscientious local magistrates has already been discussed. Added to this was the hostility of the majority of the population. Of the five fugitive bishops, for example, one, Bishop Donelan of Clonfert, was arrested in 1703, but was rescued by a group of nearly 300 persons, 'some whereof were mounted on good horses and well armed and others on foot'. Less dramatically, but perhaps more effectively in the long run, Richard Huddy of County Cork, who apprehended a regular clergyman in 1707, had his house burnt down soon after.[109]

However unsatisfactory the enforcement of some parts of the laws against Popery, moreover, some well-placed observers in the early years of their operation expressed considerable optimism regarding the potential of legal disabilities for winning those affected over to Protestantism. 'We have abundance of converts every day from Popery,' King reported in 1707. Sir Richard Cox the previous year put the number at 'at least 10,000 every year which turn Protestants to get service'. At a later stage, of course, doubts began to creep in regarding the value of changes of religious allegiance procured by such means. In 1723, plagued by informers offering evidence regarding enlistment for the Pretender, King tellingly compared such witnesses to Catholic converts: 'The first thing after the one's abjuration and the other's

---

[106] Fenning, *Undoing of the Friars*, 44.

[107] Burke, *Irish Priests*, 155–61. A copy of part of the return is preserved in PRONI D207/1/2.

[108] Ambassador quoted in Burke, *Irish Priests*, 145; Samuel Leeson to King, 23 July 1703 (TCD MSS 1995–2008/1035).

[109] Burke, *Irish Priests*, 136; Proclamation, 10 Dec. 1707, in Brady, *Catholics and Catholicism*, 8–9.

discovery is, "my friends have deserted me, pray let me have a maintenance".'
But here, as in other respects, disillusionment followed on earlier high
expectations.[110]

The claims of King and Cox are at first sight hard to reconcile with the
mere trickle of converts listed in the official records: only 36 in the period
1703–9, a further 668 up to 1731, and 3,360 more in the following forty
years. But these returns relate only to those whose landed or professional
concerns made it worth their while to file the necessary documents and obtain
a certificate of conformity. Of all the converts recorded between 1703 and
1838, some 1,700 were 'esquire', 'gentleman', or 'mister', compared with a
mere 300 other stated occupations. A better indication of the potential that
convert numbers could seem to show is provided by the local religious census
carried out by the hearth-tax collector for a district near Athlone in 1725.
This showed a total of 245 inhabitants born of Protestant parents and 42
converts. Both figures were of course dwarfed by the total of 3,816 Catholics.
But it is easy to see how conversion on a scale sufficient to increase the
Protestant population of a locality by one-sixth could be taken as evidence that
things were moving in the right direction.[111]

More direct evidence of a belief in the possibility of achieving religious
change through coercive legislation is provided by the proposals which
Edward Synge, bishop of Raphoe, outlined in 1715 to Archbishop Wake
of Canterbury. These involved levying a collective fine on the Catholic
inhabitants of every barony in which an unregistered or foreign-educated
priest was found, sufficient to pay a reward for his capture and to cover the
costs of shipping him overseas. This direct financial penalty on those who
harboured priests would, in Synge's view, effectively remove the Catholic
clergy, except for the declining group registered under the Act of 1704. But
that was only the first step.

Once remove their priests and place some Protestant ministers amongst them, who
may but be able to read our liturgy, and some few plain homilies composed in
Irish ... and they would all become Protestants in a little time. And when once they
come to embrace our religion, they will presently be willing to learn our language also,
and glad to become one people with us.[112]

---

[110] King to Southwell, 8 Nov. 1707 (TCD MS 750/3/2, 161); Cox to Southwell, 24 Oct.
1706 (BL Add. MS 38, 154, fo. 86ᵛ); King to Southwell, 8 Jan. 1723 (TCD MS 750/7, 278).

[111] Account of Protestant and Popish Inhabitants in Parishes of Moatgreenogue Walk, Athlone
district (PRONI D207/1/3). For legal records of conformity, see O'Byrne (ed.), *The Convert
Rolls*, vii–xvi. The casual attitude of some conformists to the formalities of registration is
indicated by the note attached to two certificates submitted in 1741 'by a person who pretended to
go downstairs for change but never returned or paid for them and therefore they were not
enrolled' (ibid. 281).

[112] Synge to Wake, 13 Apr. 1715 (Gilbert MS 28, 23–7, reprinted by Burns as 'Thoughts on
Converting the Irish').

Another of Wake's correspondents placed his faith more in the restrictions imposed on Catholic property-owners, lawyers, and others. The policy should be to encourage the sincere convert 'and at the same time to heap all reasonable inconveniencies upon Papists in general, to lay them (as it were) under a necessity to break those bonds of ignorance in sunder, which the policy of the court of Rome has loaded them with, and to enquire into the doctrine of our church, whose beauty and comeliness can never fail to engage the hearts of those who without prejudice consider them'.[113]

Bishop Synge's assessment of what his proposed change in the law would achieve and, even more, his projection of what would happen afterwards were, to say the least, optimistic. But he did at least recognize that the removal of the Catholic clergy would have to be seconded by an educational and pastoral effort that would surmount the barrier of language. Others took up the same point. In 1703–4 and again in 1709, both houses of Convocation supported resolutions in favour of providing preaching and religious instruction, along with basic religious texts, in Irish, in order to begin the work of converting the Catholic population.[114] For several years, starting in 1708, Charles Linegar, a convert, was employed to give lessons to students at Trinity College. In 1715 King drew up a list of forty-five students, all destined for the ministry, whom Linegar had taught to read Irish.[115] The refusal of the great majority of the Catholic clergy to take the oath of abjuration imposed on them in 1709 and their consequent loss of legal recognition appear to have been taken by some Protestant clergy as a signal to begin missionary work among the congregations these priests had served. In Armagh the archbishop and clergy agreed to subscribe £130 per year to support ministers who would preach to the Catholic population in Irish. A similar venture was reported in the diocese of Derry.[116]

It was out of the same new opportunities that briefly seemed to be opened up by the mass rejection of the oath of abjuration that there developed the most ambitious attempt yet to promote the conversion of the Catholic population. In March 1711 John Richardson, rector of Belturbet in County Cavan, arrived in London to solicit support for an elaborate programme of action. This had two main elements: the printing of an Irish New Testament, catechism, and Prayer Book and the establishment in each parish of a Charter School that would provide free instruction in the English language and

---

[113] John Browne to Wake, 26 Jan. 1727 (Wake MS XIV, 315).

[114] Richardson, *Short History*, 37–40; Journal of the Upper House of Convocation, 3 Mar. 1704 (PRONI Dio 4/10/3/2, 145–6); Revd Theophilus Harrison to Strype, 14 Sept. 1709 (Strype Correspondence, III, fo. 311).

[115] McDowell and Webb, *Trinity College, Dublin*, 10; King to Conolly, 16 Feb. 1715 (Mant, *Church of Ireland*, ii. 295–6).

[116] Burke, *Irish Priests*, 284; Richardson, *Short History*, 54.

Protestant doctrine. An incorporated society was to be established to receive subscriptions and distribute funds. Richardson had already at his own expense purchased the fount of Irish type that had been used for Robert Boyle's Bible in the 1680s. He went on to publish Irish versions of a catechism and the Book of Common Prayer. His proposals were supported by Bishop Wetenhall of Kilmore, by the earl of Anglesey, and by several other members of the nobility and gentry. In London they were recommended by Edward Southwell, the chief secretary, and by the lord lieutenant, Ormond. The Irish Commons passed resolutions in their favour, as did the lower house of Convocation. Yet, despite all this, the scheme came to nothing. No practical steps were taken to provide either schools or Irish-speaking ministers, and Richardson himself was left heavily out of pocket as a result of his expenditure on type and printing.[117]

There were several reasons for the failure of Richardson's scheme. A major objection raised against it, in Convocation and elsewhere, was the encouragement it would supposedly give to the Irish language. Indeed, it was claimed that to print even missionary literature in Irish would contravene a statute dating from the reign of Henry VIII. Some saw this as no more than a delaying tactic, but that may not have been entirely true. In 1697, Anthony Dopping, bishop of Meath, whose commitment in this area seems beyond question, gave exactly the same reason for dropping from his latest proposals for church reform the employment of Irish-speaking teachers, which he had earlier supported.[118] There also appear to have been objections to the intrusion of itinerant missionaries into the territory of the parish clergy.[119] This might help to explain why some of the strongest opponents of the scheme, in Convocation and among the bishops, appear to have been High-Churchmen. Richardson, in fact, may have fallen foul of the deepening party conflict within both English and Irish Anglicanism, in which Tories looked to a restoration of the church's legal monopolies and coercive authority, while missionary efforts tended to be associated with Whiggery.

Archbishop King, who had supported Richardson's scheme and quarrelled with his episcopal colleagues over their failure to do the same, had a simpler explanation. The bishops had opposed the scheme in case they might be required to pay for it. In addition, they 'resented a private clergyman's meddling with Irish things'.[120] Some responsibility may also attach to

[117] Richardson, *Proposal for the Conversion of the Popish Natives*; Richardson, *Short History*, 44–66; C. S. King, *A Great Archbishop of Dublin*, 291–8; Williams, *I bPrionta i Leabhar*, ch. 9. For Richardson's financial losses, see Boulter to Dorset, 3 Sept. 1730 (*Letters*, ii. 28–9).

[118] Brady, 'Remedies Proposed for the Church of Ireland', 163, 168. This was not Dopping's first change of mind. In the 1680s similar considerations seem to have led him to withdraw from his original support for Boyle's Irish Bible: Maddison, 'Robert Boyle and the Irish Bible', 86.

[119] W. Perceval to Gastrell, 1 Nov. 1711 (HMC, *Portland Manuscripts*, v. 105–6).

[120] King to St George Ashe, bishop of Clogher, 24 Feb. [recte Mar.] 1711 (TCD MS 2531, 326).

Richardson himself. Jonathan Swift, who met him in London in the spring of 1711, presented him as something of a crank: 'I am plagued with one Richardson, an Irish parson, and his project of printing Irish Bibles etc. to make you Christians in that country.' This may have been the cynicism of a political parson or another example of Tory and High Church prejudice. Yet King also expressed some criticism of Richardson's tactics, implying that he had been too precipitate in launching his scheme without adequate backing from above.[121]

Conversion, of course, was only one way of increasing the Protestant population of a given area. The other was to bring in Protestants from elsewhere. Efforts to establish colonies of Protestants, mainly recruited from Ulster, were made throughout the three southern provinces.[122] The motivation behind such ventures was largely economic. It was generally accepted that Protestant tenants, of English or Scottish cultural backgrounds, were both more reliable and more productive than 'Irish' ones. In many cases the importation of Ulster Protestants was also linked with attempts to introduce the spinning and weaving of linen. Added to this was the contribution such a boost in numbers could make to both the physical security and the morale of the local Protestant population. Finally, for those prepared to take a longer-term, more optimistic view, settlement could promote cultural and possibly religious change among the indigenous population. Thus, Archbishop King, in 1714, praised one County Wicklow landlord, a Mr Wentworth, not just for letting his whole estate to Protestant tenants, but also for having established on it 'several schools for teaching English'. All these themes—economic development, social and cultural improvement, and the religious assimilation of the indigenous population—come together in Archbishop Stone's eulogy, in 1759, on the work of Robert French near Athenry, County Galway.

He has brought the linen manufacture there, which is already in a flourishing state. He has also brought some Protestants there from other counties, but he has prevailed upon a far greater number of the old inhabitants to conform to the established religion; the consequence of which has been, that there is now a face of industry, sobriety and decency in that district unknown to any part of that province at least.[123]

The importation of Protestants from other parts of Ireland could transform the religious balance within a particular locality. It could not in itself do anything to improve the ratio of Protestants to Catholics in the country as a whole. For that it was necessary to look outside Ireland. The last surge of Scottish immigration in the 1690s marked the end of the huge inflow of people from Great Britain that over the previous two centuries had trans-

---

[121] Swift, *Journal to Stella*, i. 229; King to Annesley, 13 Nov. 1712 (TCD MS 750/4/1, 65).

[122] Cullen, *Emergence of Modern Ireland*, 193–5.

[123] King to Annesley, 3 July 1714 (TCD MS 750/4/1, 310); Stone to Bedford, 1 Jan. 1759 (PRONI T2915/7/1).

formed the character of Irish society. But there remained the possibility of attracting Protestant refugees from continental Europe. 'It is only by such,' a memorandum drawn up around 1694 warned, 'that kingdom can be made secure and profitable to England, by balancing the numbers of the Irish, for England can't spare many to plant in Ireland.'[124] Once again, religious considerations were seconded by economic ones. Immigration would bring an increase in numbers at a time when Ireland was still seen as underpopulated rather than the reverse, and might also introduce much-needed skills. The most successful scheme of this sort was the settlement of Huguenots during the 1690s. Here circumstances were favourable: England and Ireland were at war with France; William III had French Protestant regiments in his service, whose members when disbanded formed the nucleus of the settlements; the Huguenot magnate de Ruvigny was a leading figure at court, and for a time lord justice of Ireland. In all, there were five major Huguenot settlements set up after 1691 and at least fourteen minor ones.[125]

A later scheme, to bring in refugees from the German Palatinate, worked less well. Out of 3,073 Palatines brought to Ireland at the end of 1709, only just over 1,200 remained by late 1711. In the end, fewer than 200 families were to take up permanent residence, mainly in counties Limerick and Kerry. Archbishop King blamed the failure of the scheme partly on the Palatines themselves: 'I conceive their design 'tis but to eat and drink at her Majesty's cost, live idle, and complain against those that maintain them.' Against this were claims that the money allocated to aid the settlement had been misappropriated.[126] The real reason for the failure of the scheme was probably political. The introduction of foreign Protestants was a Whig enthusiasm. Tories were in principle hostile to foreign entanglements of any kind, and in this case suspected that the refugees were more likely to strengthen the forces of Dissent than those of the established church.[127] (The latter point would also, of course, help to explain King's undisguised lack of enthusiasm for the project.) In the case of Ireland the settlement of Palatines was initiated by the Whig lord lieutenant Wharton, and permitted to languish under his Tory successor.

Already by the early years of the eighteenth century, schemes of this kind belonged to a vanishing age. Protestants in the Catholic states of Europe continued to suffer harassment and legal disabilities. But religious refugees were something of an anachronism, as were ideas of an international conflict

---

[124] Paper on Ireland *c.*1694 (PRONI T3222/1/10).
[125] Caldicott *et al.* (eds.), *Huguenots and Ireland*, esp. 219–22.
[126] King to Dawson, n.d. [Feb. 1711] (TCD MS 2531, 311); King to Addison, 14, 31 May 1715 (TCD MS 750/4/2, 47–8); Robert Johnson to Ormond, 9 Nov. 1710 (NLI MS 2474, 29); T. J. Caesar to John Chamberlayne, 16 June 1712 (HMC, *Portland Manuscripts*, v. 183–4). For numbers coming and eventually settled, see Hick, 'The Palatine Settlement in Ireland'.
[127] Holmes, *British Politics in the Age of Anne*, 69.

between Protestantism and Popery. Ireland too was changing: having gradually become more settled and secure, it seemed less convincing as a site for colonization efforts. Yet the idea did not wholly die away. In 1745 Chesterfield considered the possibility of sponsoring a new immigration of French Protestants now coming under renewed pressure at home. The increase in population would, he believed, be 'a great advantage to any nation that is not already overstocked, which is by no means the case of Ireland at present'; moreover, 'such an increase by Protestants would be particularly advantageous to Ireland, considering the great number of Papists there'. In the early 1750s, when a new wave of persecution was launched in Languedoc, small numbers of Protestants were in fact settled in Ireland.[128] But there seems to have been little expectation that this would be more than a humanitarian gesture and an aid to strictly local social improvement.

This left the possibility of the conversion of the indigenous Catholic population. Convocation, the main forum through which major schemes of Protestantization could be put forward, did not meet again after 1713. The failure of Richardson's venture must also have discouraged excessive ambition. Yet the idea of a Protestant Ireland had certainly not died. Berkeley's *Querist*, published between 1735 and 1737, suggested Irish-speaking missionaries, along with charity schools, as methods by which 'our Irish natives should be converted, and the whole nation united in the same religion'.[129] Samuel Madden, in 1738, put his faith in a union of Ireland and England: 'We then would in a few years, by a mixture of people and interests, become as entirely an English and a Protestant country also as Wales.'[130] Several bishops also showed an interest in the issue. Bishop Hort of Kilmore, addressing his clergy in 1731, argued that coercive laws could restrain those whose principles threatened church and state, 'but they can never convince nor convert anybody. . . . This is only to be done by enlightening their minds, and making proper application to their understandings and consciences.' Nine years earlier, Francis Hutchinson, bishop of Down and Connor, had published a catechism for the use of the Irish-speaking population of Rathlin Island. This had parallel texts in English and Irish, both presented in a phonetic spelling of his own devising. Bishop Tennison of Ossory, who died in 1735, left a bequest of £40 a year to pay for the catechizing of Catholic children.[131] More co-ordinated efforts in the same direction came from the society established

---

[128] Chesterfield to —, 23 July 1745 (*Letters*, iii. 649–51); Cullen, *Emergence of Modern Ireland*, 78.

[129] Johnston, *Berkeley's Querist*, 147–8, 181–2. In a later edition (1752), Berkeley omitted the most direct reference to conversion, but other queries not deleted seem to contradict the suggestion that he had lost faith in the idea: ibid. 181 n.

[130] [Madden], *Reflections and Resolutions*, 122–3.

[131] Hort, quoted in Phillips (ed.), *Church of Ireland*, iii. 209; Williams, 'Thomas Williamson, Francis Hutchinson agus Litríu na Gaeilge'; King to Hutchinson, 6 Nov., 22 Dec. 1722 (TCD MS 750/7, 236–7, 260–1); Mant, *Church of Ireland*, ii. 507.

in Dublin in 1717 for promoting charity schools, where children could be instructed in religious doctrine and useful skills. By 1721 the society claimed to know of 130 schools, attended by 3,000 children.[132] These would have included children of poor Protestants as well as Catholics. But the basic purpose of the movement was clear: 'the conversion of Irish Popish natives by the method of English schools'.[133]

It was out of this charity school movement that there developed the single most important effort during the eighteenth century to promote a widespread change in religious allegiance. In 1730 Henry Maule drew up an appeal for a royal charter 'to incorporate a society for promoting Christian Knowledge among the poor natives of the kingdom of Ireland'. Maule, a long-standing advocate of charity schools, had been bishop of Cloyne since 1726; he was thus better placed to make an impact than the unfortunate rector of Belturbet had been fifteen years before. But the scheme had more substantial backing still. Hugh Boulter, archbishop of Armagh and the English government's leading agent in Ireland, had in his very first charge to the clergy of his diocese declared it 'a reproach to the Protestants of this country, that so few converts have been made from Popery in the several seasons of settled peace this nation has from time to time enjoyed'.[134] He now gave Maule's initiative his full support. Even with this backing, it took almost four years to steer the proposal through the various levels of the political process. Once the charter had been granted in February 1734, however, things moved more quickly. By 1748 the Incorporated Society in Dublin for Promoting English Protestant Schools in Ireland had a total of 30 schools, attended by 900 pupils. These were supported by voluntary subscriptions, by an annual grant from the crown, and from 1747 by funds voted by the Irish parliament.[135]

Assessment of the Charter Schools project has long been overshadowed by the grim subsequent reputation of these establishments. By the end of the eighteenth century, the schools run by the Incorporated Society had become little more than centres for the exploitation of captive child labour. Their inmates were poorly housed, clothed, and fed, remorselessly worked, and scantily schooled. Yet all this, as Kenneth Milne's important recent reassessment has made clear, represented a perversion of the spirit of religious and social commitment in which the scheme was originally launched. It is true that inmates of the Charter Schools were expected to do productive work. But this was not initially an end in itself. Instead, the aim of turning Catholics into Protestants was inextricably bound up, as in earlier schemes for conversion and plantation, with that of disseminating useful skills and habits of industry.

---

[132] Milne, 'Irish Charter Schools', 8–12.

[133] Maule to Wake, 26 June 1723 (Wake MS XIV, 80). Cf. King to Townsend, 3 Apr. 1717 (TCD MS 2534, 142): 'The charity schools have a very good effect towards converting the Papists, and on that account deserve to be encouraged.'

[134] Mant, *Church of Ireland*, ii. 440–1.   [135] Milne, 'Irish Charter Schools', 12–23.

In the words of Archbishop Boulter, 'the push now made by this society in erecting working schools for the education of the children of poor Papists, as well as of the meanest of the Protestants, both in Christian knowledge and some useful business, is the most rational method that has yet been attempted to bring about any reformation in this nation'.[136] It was this same aim of lifting Catholic children out of their environment of superstition and idleness and turning them into industrious, useful Protestants that lay behind the policy of boarding children in schools well away from their native districts. On leaving school, they were to be apprenticed to Protestant masters, who could be trusted to complete the work of cultural, economic, and religious transformation.

The enthusiasm of Protestants for the first Charter Schools and the widespread conviction that they had at last discovered an effective instrument of religious and social change are unmistakable. In 1742 Henry Maule, now bishop of Dromore, found it 'extremely edifying to hear the little Popish children giving by heart a perfect account of [the] catechism in the Charter Schools and in the public congregations at church where they attend divine service'. Two years later he remained profoundly optimistic:

We now want but five of five hundred children educated in these nurseries of labour and true religion. When we consider the produce of these, even in fifty years, what an increase and strengthening will this be to the Protestant religion in this part of his Majesty's dominions.[137]

A clergyman in south Armagh had higher hopes still: 'We have great reason to hope that this great and good work will prosper and will in the end tend to the downfall of Popery amongst us.' Walter Harris, writing in 1744, believed that 'the wit of man could not suggest a more effectual or rational scheme for making this a Protestant nation'. Even the earl of Orrery was moved to unwonted enthusiasm: 'As Popery decreases, cleanliness and honesty will find place. The Charter Schools will banish the former, and introduce the two latter.'[138]

Hopes of this kind lasted at least to the end of the 1750s. In 1758 two clergymen, Anthony Burke and Edmund Kelly, offered their services to the House of Commons as preachers skilled in Irish who were anxious to work among 'the natives'. Both had already begun preaching regularly in Irish, one in St Patrick's cathedral, the other in St Audeon's, both in Dublin, in each case to 'very numerous' congregations. The following year a correspondent in a Dublin newspaper republished the results of the religious census of 1731, to counteract what he saw as exaggerated claims regarding the numerical

---

[136] Boulter to Dorset, 24 May 1737 (*Letters*, ii. 225–6).

[137] Maule to James Payzant, 21 Aug. 1742, 15 Dec. 1744 (SP63/405/61–2, 63/406/234).

[138] Revd Hugh Hill to Archbishop John Hoadly, 24 Oct. 1743 (PRONI T1392); [Harris and Smith], *County of Down*, 17–18; Orrery to Birch, 26 May 1747 (*Orrery Papers*, i. 320–1).

superiority of the Catholics. His figures, showing a Protestant population of 105,501 out of 386,796, were, he admitted, poor enough. On the other hand, 'many noble, rich and valuable families have renounced and do daily renounce the errors of Popery,' while 'the Charter Schools work a reformation among the common people'.[139] Such comment would suggest that serious interest in the possibility of mass conversion faded away—if indeed it ever wholly did—only in the closing decades of the eighteenth century. Already by the end of the 1790s, moreover, it is possible to detect the first stirrings of the renewed interest in missionary work that was to expand into the Second Reformation of the early and mid-nineteenth century.[140]

From the reign of Elizabeth I to that of Victoria, then, a concern with the necessity of promoting the conversion of the Catholic population consistently played at least some part in Irish Protestant thinking. But how is the significance of that concern to be assessed? There is the obvious danger of being over-impressed by the energy, commitment, and self-publicization of what was never more than a zealous minority. In the case of the early and mid-eighteenth century, it is clear that many Protestants were indifferent, to say the least, to the conversionist schemes of men like Richardson and Maule. Some observers, in fact, believed that there was positive hostility to such ventures. Edward Synge senior complained in 1719 that there were 'too many amongst us who had rather keep the Papists as they are, in an almost slavish subjection, than have them made Protestants, and thereby entitled to the same liberties and privileges, with the rest of their fellow subjects'. King took the same view. Justices of the peace 'make no other use of our Popery acts but to oppress the poor people'. They had no desire to suppress Popery, 'nay take care to cherish and support it, alleging that Papists make the best tenants, as indeed they pay more rent and are greater slaves to their landlords than Protestants would ever be'. Laws against the Catholic clergy served the same purpose, as 'the gent[lemen] . . . govern their Popish tenants by their priests, and the more obnoxious those are to the laws, the more the poor people will be under their landlords' power'. It might be unwise to place too much weight on the grumblings of disappointed reformers. But almost exactly the same point was made by Sir Robert Wilmot, the long-serving, London-based secretary to successive lords lieutenant: the reason why so little progress was made towards converting the Catholics, he observed in 1758, was that the country gentlemen did not encourage such efforts, 'choosing rather to keep the countrymen in their present condition of Popery, ignorance and slavery, than to civilise them and to make them Protestant, which would tend in some measure to make them independent'.[141] Even if conscious calculation of

---

[139] Brady, *Catholics and Catholicism*, 93, 95, 96.
[140] Hempton, 'The Methodist Crusade in Ireland'; Bowen, *The Protestant Crusade in Ireland*.
[141] Synge to Wake, 19 Nov. 1719 (Gilbert MS 28, 120–1); King to Edward Southwell, 12 Nov. 1719, 26 Dec. 1723 (TCD MSS 750/5, 211; 2537, 43); diary of Nathaniel Ryder [1756] (PRONI T3228/2/2).

group advantage on the scale suggested seems inherently improbable, such comment leaves little doubt that support for conversionist schemes among the Protestant gentry was never very impressive.

What, then, can we say? The belief that Catholics could and should be brought into the established church had played some part in Protestant thinking ever since the Reformation had become firmly established in Ireland. In the two generations after the deliverance of 1689–91, it refused to go away. It had the serious support of a significant body, though still clearly a minority, within the clergy and of a much smaller section of the laity. A larger number declared their support for the principle, although showing little disposition to translate words into action. Even those who were indifferent found it difficult to say so openly. In this sense the conversion of the Irish can be compared to other long-term official goals—the creation of a socialist society in the post-war British labour movement or the restoration of the Irish language as the normal medium of communication in post-independence Ireland—which only a minority have ever believed to be feasible, but to which much larger numbers, especially among those in public life, have felt obliged to offer at least token support. Such goals can never be taken at face value. But a history of the societies concerned that omitted them entirely would nevertheless be seriously deficient.

4. Protestant Ascendancy? The Consequences of the Penal Laws

The comments of Archbishops Synge and King and of Sir Robert Wilmot raise a final, important point. Their contention was that the majority of Protestant gentlemen had no interest in schemes for the conversion of the Irish lower classes because it was to their advantage that these should remain Catholic. But what was the nature of that advantage? To what extent did religious divisions and the penal laws that grew out of them operate to create inequalities and forms of exploitation that would not have existed had the whole population been Protestant?

The question needs to be asked in this form because it has frequently been asserted that penal legislation against Catholics did in fact have precisely such an effect. Corish quotes with approval the comments of W. E. H. Lecky: penal legislation was designed 'to make [Catholics] poor and to keep them poor . . . to degrade them into a servile caste'. According to E. M. Johnston: 'The operation of the penal code created on a religious basis what was in many ways a typical colonial situation. . . . During the eighteenth century colour and slavery were not the only badges and methods by which a small minority kept a large majority in subjection.'[142] A number of writers, pursuing

---

[142] Lecky, *History of Ireland*, i. 152; Corish, *Catholic Community*, 73; E. M. Johnston, *Ireland in the Eighteenth Century*, 19.

the same line of argument, have compared anti-Catholic legislation in Ireland to the apartheid system of twentieth-century South Africa. According to the late Maureen Wall, for example, penal legislation 'operated to exclude the Catholic majority from all positions of importance in the country—from the professions, from parliament, and from the ownership of property—in the same way as the colour bar has operated to ensure white ascendancy in African countries in recent times'.[143] From this it follows that the majority of Protestants—just as Synge, William King, and Sir Robert Wilmot complained—would actually have been unwilling to see the lower classes converted. 'Protestant ascendancy, as applied to a small privileged group, must disappear if the whole population were to become Protestant.'[144] It is against the background of these extravagant claims that it becomes necessary to restate what should in fact be some rather obvious points regarding the penal laws and the society in which they operated.

Let us begin with the Catholic landed classes. These were both the main targets of penal legislation and, without question, its main victims. In the fifty years or so after the passage of the Act to Prevent the Growth of Popery, the majority of the surviving land-owning families conformed to the Church of Ireland. The precise mechanisms by which this was brought about remain to be properly investigated. Many accounts highlight the 'gavelkind' clause in the Act of 1704, under which estates had to be divided equally among the male heirs. Faced with this requirement, it is suggested, Catholic families either kept the estate intact through the conformity of the eldest son or else 'sank to the level of middle class farmers' as it was repeatedly subdivided.[145] In fact no case has yet been produced of a family permitting its property to be dismantled in this way. As for the gavel clause, this may not in practice have proved as effective as expected. Social pressures and a sense of family loyalty seem in many cases to have ensured that younger sons simply refrained from asserting their claims under the Act. Catholic proprietors who conformed to the established church, equally, may in many cases have been motivated less by a fear that their estates would be dismembered than by a desire to escape the numerous lesser burdens that Catholicism brought with it: inability to expand one's property by purchase or long leases, a restricted choice of marriage partners, and exclusion from local and national politics. In other cases again, as Cullen has pointed out, conformity was a short-term response by which Catholic gentlemen sought to secure themselves during a particular crisis, such as the invasion scare of 1745.[146]

---

[143] Wall, *Penal Laws*, 9. See also Brendan Bradshaw, review of Beckett, *The Anglo-Irish Tradition*, in *Studies*, 66 (1977), 242, in which Beckett is rebuked for his failure to make use of the analogy.

[144] Wall, *Penal Laws*, 9. See also Corish, *Catholic Community*, 55, 75.

[145] James, *Ireland in the Empire*, 25.

[146] Cullen, *Emergence of Modern Ireland*, 195–6.

Two other processes contributed to the decline of Catholic landownership. The 1720s and 1730s were a period of rapid turnover in the Irish land market. Small proprietors in particular lost out, as low prices and stagnant rents left them unable to cope with inherited debt and other burdens. This affected both Catholic and Protestant landowners. The difference was that where it was Catholic proprietors who went to the wall, the land they sold could be purchased only by Protestants.[147] In other cases, the change from Catholic to Protestant came about during a minority. Such was the case, for example, with the Antrim estates, the last substantial Catholic property in Ulster.[148] The importance of this particular route to Protestantism is evident from the tussles which repeatedly took place between Catholic families and Protestant guardians, supported by the government, over the custody of minors. In 1708 the dowager Lady Louth, 'a rigorous Papist', was alleged to have taken her son away from his Protestant uncle, ostensibly to buy him clothes. Instead, Lord Louth, 'a weakly child of about 10 years of age', had been shipped to Chester 'in as cold and tempestuous a season as any hath happened this winter', so that he could be sent on to France. His mother was arrested and released only on promising to bring him back. In 1725 Archbishop Synge of Tuam consulted Archbishop Wake regarding the 16-year-old heir to the Brown estates in Mayo, who was to be sent to Oxford 'that he may be secure from the insinuating attempts of his Popish kindred'. Darker fears were expressed for young Master O'Hara, heir to an estate of £1,400 a year in County Antrim. He was to be sent to Eton 'as his estate at his death would descend to Papists' and his Protestant relations 'are desirous to have him bred in England so as to be out of the way of them'.[149]

Such episodes provide vivid evidence of just how seriously the passage of land from Catholic to Protestant hands was taken by both sides. At the same time it is necessary to keep this aspect of the penal laws in perspective. We must recognize, in the first place, just how limited a quantity of land was involved. In 1685 Catholics owned 22 per cent of the country's profitable acreage. By 1780 this had fallen to an estimated 5 per cent. What was transferred to Protestant ownership, in other words, was about one-sixth of total landed wealth. Almost half of this, furthermore, was lost before the passing of the Popery acts, through the confiscation of estates not protected by the Articles of Limerick and Galway. The amount of land passing out of Catholic hands as a result of penal legislation was thus less than one-tenth of the country's profitable acres.[150] It is also necessary to be precise about what one means by a 'transfer' of land ownership. The confiscations of the

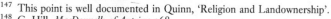

[147] This point is well documented in Quinn, 'Religion and Landownership'.
[148] G. Hill, *MacDonnells of Antrim*, 368.
[149] R. Freeman to Somers, 2 Mar. 1708 (PRONI T2807/41); Synge to Wake, 15 Apr. 1725 (Gilbert MS 28, 203–4); Ryder to Sir Dudley Ryder, 4 Mar. 1749 (T2338/1/48).
[150] For the figures on landownership, see above, ch. 5, n. 10.

seventeenth century, up to and including the Williamite settlement, were indeed cases of 'transfer': land was taken away from one set of owners and given to another. The decline in Catholic landownership after 1703, on the other hand, came about mainly through existing proprietors changing their religion.[151] The character of these conversions varied: some convert families identified themselves wholly with the Protestant establishment they had joined; others remained closely linked to their former co-religionists, to the extent that one recent writer has suggested that converts should be considered part of a continuing 'Catholic interest'.[152] This is probably to overstate the case. But the fact that the transfer was by conversion rather than confiscation certainly undermines still further any suggestion that penal legislation brought about a revolution in Irish landownership.

Penal legislation also imposed important economic restrictions on other groups. Concern for the fate of the Catholic heir to a landed estate has overshadowed the problems of his non-inheriting brothers, to whom the traditional careers open to the younger sons of gentlemen—government service, the army, the law, and of course a decently endowed church—were all closed. Middle-class Catholics also suffered from this exclusion from legal and official careers. Catholic manufacturers and merchants, too, incurred undoubted disadvantages. They were less likely to be awarded official contracts; they could not buy or take long leases on urban property; most important of all, perhaps, they could not defend or further their commercial interests through participation in local government and the guilds. Yet none of these disabilities was sufficient to prevent the survival—and possibly even the expansion—of a substantial class of Catholic merchants, traders, and manufacturers. It is true that the Catholic share of overseas trade remained well below the Catholic share of the total population. But this, it has been argued, was due not to direct restrictions on Catholic enterprise, but rather to the collapse of Catholic landownership, at a time when landed wealth remained the main source of capital for trade and manufactures.[153]

For the rural population below the level of the gentry, legal restrictions were of far less importance. For the labourer or small farmer, denial of the right to buy or inherit land or to marry a Protestant heiress were wholly theoretical disabilities. Nor is there any reason to suppose that, even without the penal laws, more than a small proportion of the children of a poor peasant society would have received even a rudimentary schooling. The clauses in the

---

[151] It is true that the Act of 1709 permitted Protestant 'discoverers' to appropriate to themselves assets illegally conveyed by Catholics. However, research by T. P. O'Neill of University College, Galway, indicates that most bills of discovery were in fact collusive, filed by agents of the supposed victims.

[152] Cullen, 'Catholics under the Penal Laws', 28–30.

[153] Dickson, 'Catholics and Trade in Eighteenth-Century Ireland', in Power and Whelan (eds.), *Endurance and Emergence*, 93–4.

less essential → gentry (handwritten)

Act of 1704 forbidding Catholics from taking a lease for longer than thirty-one years or at a rent of less than two-thirds of the yearly value had rather more meaning. The latter clause, however, was impossible to enforce effectively.[154] Where the length of leases is concerned, several points must be made. First, it was only a minority of the rural population who could expect to hold their land by lease, rather than from year to year. Secondly, a period of thirty-one years was not in fact a short lease, especially at a time of rapidly rising prices like the mid- and late eighteenth century. A Protestant tenant or middleman could of course do even better: the three life leases that were standard for Protestant tenants in mid-eighteenth-century Ulster lasted on average between fifty and seventy years.[155] Nevertheless, it was precisely at the time that the provisions of the Act to Prevent the Growth of Popery operated, the period between 1700 and the 1780s, that the social structure of rural Ireland was transformed by the emergence of a new class of substantial tenant farmers, overwhelmingly Catholic in composition, that was distinguished from the labourers and smallholders by its ownership of livestock and other capital resources and by the security and relative comfort these conferred.[156]

To economic restrictions must be added the denial of political rights. Catholics were barred from sitting in parliament, holding office in central or local government, and voting in elections. Yet all this took place in a society in which public life was in any case dominated by a small landed élite. Even the Protestant merchant classes were poorly represented in parliament. For the great majority of Protestant voters, equally, what the franchise conferred was essentially the right to vote as directed by a social superior. Even if Catholics had not been excluded from the political process, it is difficult to see how they could have achieved more than a marginal representation in parliament. If acres had been directly transferable into votes, then the owners of the 14 per cent of land still in Catholic hands after 1703 would have been able to elect just over 40 MPs, in a house of 300. But in fact more than two-thirds of MPs sat for borough constituencies which were under the control of a single patron. Even in the counties and the one or two open boroughs, furthermore, a franchise based on property qualifications would have given Protestants a decided advantage. William King, writing in 1692, believed that the Protestant overrepresentation among freeholders and among 'the trading industrious men of the kingdom' was such that even if 'a fair election' had been held, no Catholic would have been able to carry a county constituency.[157] And indeed,

---

[154] Cullen in *NHI* iv. 167. Cullen's suggestion that there is only one known instance of the clause being enforced is a slight overstatement. See Brady, *Catholics and Catholicism*, 44; Gilbert MS 191, 11, 46. But instances do seem to have been rare.

[155] Roebuck, 'Landlord Indebtedness', 146.

[156] Dickson, *New Foundations*, 98–9, 113–14.

[157] King, *State of the Protestants*, 88.

in the previous general election, in 1661, only one Catholic candidate, later to be unseated on petition, had been returned. Even after 1832, when Catholics were again permitted both to vote and to sit in parliament and when, in addition, the electoral system had been substantially reformed, Protestants were to continue for almost half a century to hold a majority of Ireland's parliamentary seats.[158]

Comparisons between the penal laws and the apartheid legislation until recently in force in South Africa, implying that institutionalized discrimination had a key role in creating inequality and exploitation, are thus misconceived. It was of course the case that Ireland in the late seventeenth and eighteenth centuries was an unequal and exploitative society, in which power and wealth were monopolized by a small group. But the same was true of contemporary England, and indeed of the whole of western Europe, regardless of the religious composition of the population. Ireland's penal laws operated mainly to exclude one segment of the country's natural ruling élite—by this time a small minority—from the advantages that would normally have gone with their economic and social position. They did not determine the relationship between that élite and the remainder of the population. If the penal laws had been removed or if the whole population had been transformed overnight into Protestants, then a few new faces would have made their appearance in the ranks of the ruling class. There is no reason to assume that land would have ceased to be the key to political power, that men would have become really equal before the law, that workers' combinations or other forms of popular collective action would have been legitimized, or that wealth would have been divided any more equitably.

All this, of course, is with the cold eye of chronological distance. That the penal laws did not have the influence that has been claimed in shaping the structure of Irish society does not mean that institutionalized religious discrimination was not experienced as a grievance. Indeed, we know that some of it was. Ordinary Catholics reacted fiercely to attempts, for as long as these were made, to enforce the laws against their clergy. Catholic soldiers in 1686–7 left little doubt as to their dislike for the triumphalist rituals of the Protestant state.[159] The right to vote may in practice have been exercised under orders, but it was nevertheless a badge of citizenship, whose loss may well have been resented. Certainly that was the case with the right to carry arms, which emerged as a central issue in the sectarian warfare that developed in south Ulster from the 1780s.[160] Hypothetical calculations regarding the likely composition of parliaments elected under different conditions, equally, take us only so far. What mattered to ordinary men and women was not the

---

[158] Hoppen, *Elections, Politics and Society*, 264.
[159] Above, p. 36.
[160] D. W. Miller, 'The Armagh Troubles', 182–3.

doings of MPs assembled on College Green, but the exercise of local power, by magistrates, constables, bailiffs, and other officials. Here the Protestant monopoly may well have had practical consequences. Certainly the abuse of local power, though admittedly in the very different circumstances of a politicized community, was to be one of the major grievances behind the Catholic agitation of the 1820s.[161] We must also consider informal social relations. The legal inferiority of the Catholic lower classes may well have operated, as King and others suggested, to encourage habits of petty tyranny in their social superiors.

Or again they may not. An alternative explanation, it was suggested earlier, is that such 'tyranny' reflected the expectations and values of the Catholic lower classes themselves. It is one of the things about the operation of the penal laws that we need to find out. If we are to have any hope of doing so, however, we must begin by locating our inquiry within a realistic context. First we must recognize that the penal laws enacted after 1691 were only a part, and not the most important part, of a much wider process by which power and wealth had over a long period been transferred from Catholic to Protestant hands. Secondly, we must see the whole structure of confessionally based inequality as itself existing within a wider structure of hierarchy and privilege that Ireland shared with other societies of the *ancien régime*.

[161] Connolly in *NHI* v. 26–7.

Epilogue

Ireland at the end of the 1750s was a society whose worst problems seemed to be behind it. The high hopes of a complete religious and cultural transformation that had been reawakened by the launching of the Charter School movement had, it is true, begun to fade. On the other hand, the problem of Catholicism no longer seemed so urgent, now that Jacobitism was a spent force and Catholics had begun to offer unqualified assurances of loyalty to the ruling dynasty. On a day-to-day basis the country was peaceful. The last centres of lawlessness, in south Ulster, the south-west, and even Iar Connacht, had been brought under control. Levels of crime, especially violent crime, were low. Among the upper classes too, habits of violence, debauchery, and disregard for law were being progressively modified by the spread of metropolitan standards of behaviour. Meanwhile, the signs of economic prosperity were everywhere to be seen: in the continued growth of Dublin and the expansion of other towns, in the country houses being built or extended, and in the roads, enclosures, and plantations that were transforming the appearance of the landscape. Manners, economic development, and most of all the religious composition of the population continued to fall well short of the ideal of a second England across the Irish Sea. But Ireland was nevertheless more settled and more prosperous than it had ever been before.

It was not, of course, to last. Already by the early 1760s, the appearance in parts of Munster and south Leinster of the Whiteboy movement marked the beginnings of the endemic rural violence that, for over a century to come, was to make Ireland a byword for lawlessness and terror. Politics too began to take an alarming turn, as advocates of reform showed a new willingness to enlist popular support in order to achieve their aims. In 1779–82, against the background of the American Revolution, such tactics succeeded in bringing about what at the time looked like a major transfer of power from London to Dublin. But by the 1790s frustrated radicals, facing an increasingly alarmed and consequently repressive establishment, had begun to look to popular revolt, supported by revolutionary France, as the only means of achieving political change. Meanwhile, there had been a resurgence, at every social level, of suspicion and hostility between Catholic and Protestant. Social protest, political radicalism, and sectarian animosity all came together in a vicious cycle of disaffection and official repression, culminating in the bloody civil war of 1798.[1]

---

[1] The best recent account of this period is Elliott, *Partners in Revolution*. For an important analysis of the 1790s as marking a turning-point in relations between rulers and ruled, see Bartlett, 'An End to Moral Economy'.

Various explanations can be offered for this rapid disintegration of an apparently orderly society. External events—the American and French revolutions—clearly had an important impact. Secondly, there was a new instability at the level of high politics. When in 1753–6 Henry Boyle and his associates turned a struggle for personal power into a contest between 'Irish' and 'English' interests, they lifted political conflict out of the restricted circles to which it had previously been confined. In the 1770s and 1780s the appeal to out-of-doors opinion became more reckless still. Meanwhile some reformers had begun to add to their programme a relaxation of the legal restrictions affecting Catholics. The British government, motivated partly by its own strategic and military interests and partly, perhaps, by a growing impatience with the political antics of the Protestant gentry, showed signs of wanting to move in the same direction. But suggestions that the legal foundations of Protestant power might be weakened, coinciding as they did with the continued agitation of the Catholic lower classes against rents, tithes, and a range of other grievances, provoked a powerful conservative Protestant reaction.[2]

There was also the impact of economic change. Irish agriculture at the end of the eighteenth century was still enjoying the benefits of the long period of rising demand and buoyant prices that had begun in the 1740s, and manufacturing industry had not yet begun to crumble under the pressure of English and Scottish competition. But population was already rising alarmingly, swelling the ranks of the least secure sections of the rural population, the labourers, cottiers, and smallholders. Even in prosperous areas, moreover, commercialization disrupted established economic relationships, and exposed a steadily widening section of the population to the vicissitudes of the market economy.[3] Economic improvement also had direct political consequences. It boosted both the size and the self-confidence of a middle class still largely excluded from real political power. It also permitted a section of the working population, in both town and country, to achieve the modest prosperity that gave them the means and the will to develop their own political movements. The rapid growth in elementary education and the resulting rise in literacy were of particular importance here.[4]

None of this, of course, was unique to Ireland. Other societies also experienced the shock waves of the American and French revolutions, the disruption of traditional economic relationships, the rise of middle-class and plebeian radicalism, and repression by the forces of a suddenly insecure and

[2] J. Kelly, 'The Genesis of "Protestant Ascendancy"'; idem, 'Interdenominational Relations and Religious Toleration in Late Eighteenth-Century Ireland'.
[3] Clark and Donnelly (eds.), *Irish Peasants*, 25–35.
[4] See Daly and Dickson (eds.), *The Origins of Popular Literacy in Ireland*, in particular the valuable case study by Kirkham, 'Literacy in North West Ulster 1680–1860'. See also Cullen, *Emergence of Modern Ireland*, ch. 11.

frightened establishment. Yet in few countries were the consequences as explosive as in Ireland. The extra ingredient was, clearly enough, religious conflict. The existence of substantial numbers of Catholics and Protestants sharing the same territory was itself unusual in a Europe in which either the Reformation or the Counter-Reformation had generally achieved more or less total victory in any one area. But the real problem was the peculiar circumstances that had made a religious minority the dominant political and social group. In the early and mid-eighteenth century the problem had been containable. In a pre-democratic age, numbers counted for less. The leadership class that in the past, in the 1640s or in 1689–91, had mobilized the Catholic masses had now been decisively broken; in its absence, poverty, illiteracy, linguistic isolation, localism, and an authoritarian culture all combined to preclude effective political action. By the end of the century, however, all this had changed. On the one hand, popular discontent had found new leadership among radical elements in the upper and middle classes. On the other, movements like the Whiteboys and later the Defenders testified to the beginnings of a new capacity for organization lower down the social scale. At this point the Protestant élite could no longer see its control of the levers of government and its near monopoly of landed wealth as more than adequate compensation for numerical weakness.

It is, of course, the events of the 1790s, casting their shadow backwards over earlier decades, that give an analysis of the eighteenth century as an age of conflict and insecurity its conviction. From another point of view, however, it is the 1790s themselves that need to be re-evaluated with the benefit of hindsight. After that decade, relations between rulers and ruled, landlord and tenant, above all Catholic and Protestant, were never to be the same. There was a new bitterness on one side and a new insecurity on the other. The threshold of violence, in disputes of all kinds, became significantly lower.[5] Yet none of this was reflected in the country's political structures. For twenty-five years after the Act of Union the landed élite continued to monopolize parliamentary representation, through the votes of a deferential—or at least obedient—electorate that now included Catholics as well as Protestants. It was only in the 1820s that the first inroads, limited and impermanent, were made into this monopoly.[6] In the 1850s and 1860s, with parliamentary nationalism in disarray and a shrinking population enjoying the benefits of modest economic growth, the political influence of the landlord class was to make a dramatic recovery, before going into decline in the 1870s.[7] By 1885 the Land War and the rise of Parnellism had brought about a spectacular collapse of

---

[5] The extent to which Ireland in the early and mid-nineteenth century was in fact an unusually violent society remains somewhat unclear, however. See Connolly, review of Palmer, *Police and Protest*, in *IHS* 25 (1989), 307–9.

[6] Connolly in *NHI* v, ch. 4.

[7] Hoppen, *Elections, Politics and Society*, ch. 2.

landed political power everywhere except in Protestant Ulster. But even then, it has been argued that landlords remained important, influential figures in the Irish countryside for at least another quarter of a century.[8]

In this, as in other respects, the experience of Ireland is less unusual than is generally supposed. The political order, rule by a Protestant landed class that had been established at the Restoration and confirmed in the war of 1689–91, was badly shaken by the events of the late eighteenth century. But it was to hold its ground for the best part of another century. By the time it finally disintegrated, landed and aristocatic power was everywhere coming under attack. The collapse, in the Irish case, came a generation earlier than in Germany and other parts of central Europe, where aristocratic dominance of public life continued up to the First World War.[9] It was more precipitate than in England, where the erosion of landed supremacy in central and local government was spread over half a century or more.[10] But these were variations in what was essentially the same process. In Ireland, as elsewhere, moreover, the social groups to whose challenge the landed classes eventually succumbed were of relatively recent emergence. The hostile polemicists who gathered round the Protestant élite in its declining years emphasized the religious, cultural, and political barriers that set it apart from the rest of Irish society. But in reality its members were no more distant from the traditional Ireland over which they had ruled for more than two centuries than were the Catholic bourgeoisie to whom they now surrendered power.

[8] Vaughan, *Landlords and Tenants in Ireland*, 36–40.
[9] Blum, *The End of the Old Order in Rural Europe*, 420–9.
[10] F. M. L. Thompson, 'Britain', in Spring (ed.), *European Landed Élites*, 23–9.

Bibliography

MANUSCRIPT SOURCES

A List of Popish Clergy in the Diocese of Derry, 1694–6: typed copy from records (diocesan collections) no longer extant in Public Record Office of Ireland, PRONI T924.

Antrim Grand Jury Presentment Books, 1711–21, 1727–67, PRONI ANT 4/1/1/, 4/1/3. No book survives for 1722–6.

Armagh Diocesan Papers: records of the Church of Ireland diocese of Armagh, PRONI Dio 4.

Burrows Tour: diary of a tour through Ireland by Revd J. Burrows, 1773, PRONI T3551; original in NLI.

Cashel Diocesan Papers: papers of the Catholic archbishops of Cashel, NLI microfilm P5998–6013, originals in Archbishop's House, Thurles.

Castleward Papers: personal and estate papers of the Ward family, County Down, PRONI D2092.

Country Letters: out-letter book of the lords justices of Ireland, 1711–13, Bodleian Library, Oxford, MS Eng. Hist. b125 (31,758).

Dartmouth Papers: papers of the earl of Dartmouth, including some official correspondence relating to Ireland and some papers relating to property there, Staffordshire Record Office.

De Ros Manuscripts: papers of Thomas Coningsby, lord justice of Ireland 1690–2, lord treasurer 1692–1710, PRONI D638.

Dolan Manuscript: MS history of County Fermanagh compiled by John Dolan, 1718–19, NLI MS 2085.

Dopping Notebook: notebook, dating probably from the 1670s, of Anthony Dopping, bishop of Meath 1682–97, Cambridge University Library Add. MS 711.

Elphin Census: religious census of the diocese of Elphin, 1747, Nat. Arch. Ire. M2466.

Fews informations: modern typed copies of informations etc. relating to the destruction of the Presbyterian meeting-house at Fews, County Armagh, 1743, PRONI T1392.

Foster/Massereene Papers: political and personal papers of Anthony and John Foster, PRONI D207.

Gilbert MSS: including eighteenth-century copies of letters from Archbishops King and Synge and Bishop Nicolson to Archbishop Wake of Canterbury (the originals of which are in the *Wake MSS*), as well as miscellaneous papers on legal affairs, Dublin Municipal Library, Pearse Street, Dublin.

Harrowby Papers: Irish correspondence of Sir Dudley Ryder, successively British solicitor-general, attorney-general, and lord chief justice of King's Bench, PRONI T3228.

Hedges Letters: early twentieth-century typescript copies of letters of Capt. Richard Hedges 1703–14, Nat. Arch. Ire. M757.

Henry, 'Hints': 'Hints towards a Natural and Topographical History of the Counties

Sligo, Donegal, Fermanagh and Lough Erne', by Revd William Henry, 1739, Nat. Arch. Ire. M2533.

King Papers: correspondence of William King, bishop of Derry 1691–1703, archbishop of Dublin 1703–29. King's letter books are TCD MSS 750/1–8; some not now fit to be handled must be read in the early twentieth-century transcripts, MSS 2531–7. Letters to King, with some of his papers, are TCD MSS 1995–2008.

Louth Grand Jury Presentment Book, 1713–33, NLI MS 11,949.

Midleton MSS: correspondence of Alan Brodrick, later Lord Midleton, and Thomas Brodrick, Surrey Record Office, Guildford Muniment Room.

Molyneux Papers: papers of William, Samuel, and Thomas Molyneux, including accounts of Irish counties collected for a proposed atlas of Ireland c.1682–4, TCD MSS 883, 888, 889.

O'Hara Papers: personal and estate papers of the O'Hara family, County Sligo, PRONI T2812.

O'Hara's Account of County Sligo: account of the county's economic development since 1700, compiled in 1753, with a year by year account of the period 1754–73 appended, NLI MS 20,397.

Portland Papers: papers of William Bentinck, first earl of Portland, Nottingham University Library.

Prim MSS: Nineteenth-century copies of the letters of Alderman William Colles, Kilkenny 1742–68, Nat. Arch. Ire.

Sarsfield-Vesey Papers: papers of Agmondisham Vesey, Nat. Arch. Ire.

Savage Papers: personal and estate papers of the Savage family, County Down, and their relatives by marriage, the Nugents of County Westmeath, PRONI D552.

Shannon Papers: personal and official papers of Henry Boyle, first earl of Shannon, PRONI D2707.

Somers Papers: Irish papers of Sir John Somers, lord keeper and then lord chancellor of England 1693–1700, lord president of the Council 1708–10, PRONI T2807; originals in Surrey County Record Office, Kingston-upon-Thames.

Southwell Papers: Irish correspondence of Edward Southwell, British Library Add. MSS 9715, 21,122–3, 34,773–8, 38,153–7.

The State of the Diocese of Ossory: modern typescript copy of a visitation notebook of Bishop Edward Tennison, 1731–2, Nat. Arch. Ire. M2462.

State Papers (Ireland): Public Record Office, London, SP63. These have been used in conjunction with *CSPD* and *CSPI* for the period 1660–1704 and in conjunction with the typescript calendars in PRONI T448, etc. for the period after 1714.

Strype Correspondence: letters mainly to Revd J. Strype from members of the Bonnell family and others in Ireland c.1659–c.1711, Cambridge University Library, Baumgartner Papers.

Synge Papers: modern typescript copies of letters of Edward Synge, jun., bishop of Raphoe, to his daughter Alicia, 1744–7, in the possession of Ms M.-L. Legg.

Tennison Groves Abstracts: taken from County Antrim assizes and quarter sessions records now lost, PRONI T808/14895–6.

Trumbull Papers: Irish correspondence of Sir William Trumbull, PRONI T3222.

Tyrone Grand Jury Indictment Book, 1745–1809, PRONI Tyr 4/2/1.

Visitation Records: records (including both originals and modern copies of documents now lost) of episcopal visitations of the dioceses of Clogher, 1700 (61/6/3); Connor, 1693 (31/5); Derry *c.*1733 (GS2/7/3/34); Limerick 1693, 1698–1704 (D13/1/1–15); Meath, *c.*1733 (GS2/7/3/10), Representative Church Body Library, Dublin.

Wake MSS: correspondence of William Wake, archbishop of Canterbury, Christ Church, Oxford.

Walpole Letter Book: out-letter book of Horatio Walpole as secretary to the duke of Grafton, lord lieutenant 1720–1, PRONI T2806; original in Lincolnshire Archives Office.

White, 'Annals of Limerick': 'Annals of the city and diocese of Limerick' compiled *c.*1755–68 by Revd J. White, NLI MS 2714, photostat; original in St Patrick's College, Maynooth.

Willes Papers: letters and memoranda relating to conditions in Ireland *c.*1750–*c.*1762, PRONI T2855 and Mic 148.

Wyche Papers: papers of Sir Cyril Wyche, lord justice 1693 and a trustee for forfeited estates 1700–3, Nat. Arch. Ire.

NEWSPAPERS

Belfast News Letter
Dublin Courant
Dublin Daily Advertiser
Dublin Daily Post
Dublin Gazette
Dublin Intelligence
Dublin Journal
Dublin Weekly Journal
Esdall's News Letter
Faulkner's Dublin Journal
Pue's Occurrences

PRINTED WORKS

Abstract of the Number of Protestant and Popish Families in the Several Counties and Provinces of Ireland (Dublin, 1736).

ADDISON, JOSEPH, *The Letters of Joseph Addison*, ed. Walter Graham (Oxford, 1941).

AKENSON, D. H., *The Church of Ireland; Ecclesiastical Reform and Revolution 1800–1885* (New Haven, 1971).

ANDREWS, J. H., 'The Struggle for Ireland's Public Commons', in O'Flanagan *et al.* (eds.), *Rural Ireland 1600–1900*, 1–23.

ARNOLD, L. J., 'The Irish Court of Claims of 1663', *IHS* 24 (1985), 417–30.

BACON, BENJAMIN, *A Sermon Preached at St Andrew's, Dublin* (Dublin, 1743).

BAGWELL, RICHARD, *Ireland under the Stuarts* (3 vols., London, 1909–16).

BARKLEY, J. M., 'The Presbyterian Minister in Eighteenth-Century Ireland', in J. L. M. Haire *et al.*, *Challenge and Conflict: Essays in Irish Presbyterian History and Doctrine* (Antrim, 1981).

BARNARD, T. C., 'Crises of Identity among Irish Protestants 1641–1685', *Past & Present*, 127 (1990), 39–83.

—— *Cromwellian Ireland: English Government and Reform in Ireland 1649–1660* (Oxford, 1975).

—— 'Planters and Policies in Cromwellian Ireland', *Past & Present*, 61 (1973), 31–69.

BARTLETT, THOMAS, 'An End to Moral Economy: The Irish Militia Disturbances of 1793', *Past & Present*, 99 (1983), 41–64.

—— 'A New History of Ireland', *Past & Present*, 116 (1987), 206–19.

—— and HAYTON, D. W. (eds.), *Penal Era and Golden Age: Essays in Irish History 1690–1800* (Belfast, 1979).

BEAMES, MICHAEL, *Peasants and Power: The Whiteboy Movements and their Control in Pre-Famine Ireland* (Brighton, 1983).

BEATTIE, J. M., *Crime and the Courts in England 1660–1800* (Oxford, 1986).

BECKETT, J. C., *The Anglo-Irish Tradition* (London, 1976).

—— *Confrontations: Studies in Irish History* (London, 1972).

—— 'The Government and the Church of Ireland under William III and Anne', *IHS* 2 (1941), 280–302.

—— 'The Irish Armed Forces 1660–1685', in John Bossy and Peter Jupp (eds.), *Essays Presented to Michael Roberts* (Belfast, 1976), 41–53.

—— *Protestant Dissent in Ireland 1687–1780* (London, 1948).

—— 'William King's Administration of the Diocese of Derry 1691–1703', *IHS* 4 (1944), 164–80.

Bedford, Duke of, *Correspondence of John, Fourth Duke of Bedford*, ed. Lord John Russell (3 vols., London, 1842–6).

BELL, JONATHAN, 'The Improvement of Irish Farming Techniques since 1850', in O'Flanagan *et al.* (eds.), *Rural Ireland 1600–1900*, 24–41.

BENNETT, G. V., 'Conflict in the Church', in Holmes (ed.), *Britain after the Glorious Revolution*, 155–75.

—— *The Tory Crisis in Church and State 1688–1730: The Career of Francis Atterbury, Bishop of Rochester* (Oxford, 1975).

BERESFORD, M. DE LA POER, 'Ireland in French Strategy' (unpublished M. Litt. thesis, TCD, 1975).

BERGERON, LOUIS, and CULLEN, L. M. (eds.), *Culture et pratiques politiques en France et en Irlande XVIᵉ–XVIIIᵉ siècle* (Paris, 1991).

BERLATSKY, JOEL, 'Roots of Conflict: Colonial Attitudes in the Age of the Penal Laws', *Eire-Ireland*, 18/4 (1978), 40–56.

BERMAN, DAVID, 'The Culmination and Causation of Irish Philosophy', *Archiv für Geschichte der Philosophie*, 64/3 (1982), 257–79.

BLACK, JEREMY (ed.), *Britain in the Age of Walpole* (London, 1984).

BLUM, JEROME, *The End of the Old Order in Rural Europe* (Princeton, 1978).

BOLTON, F. R., *The Caroline Tradition of the Church of Ireland, with Particular Reference to Bishop Jeremy Taylor* (London, 1958).

BOSSY, JOHN, 'The Counter-Reformation and the People of Catholic Ireland 1596–1641', in T. D. Williams (ed.), *Historical Studies*, viii (Dublin, 1971), 155–69.

BOSWELL, JAMES, *Life of Johnson*, ed. R. W. Chapman (Oxford, 1970).

BOTTIGHEIMER, K. S., *English Money and Irish Land: The 'Adventurers' in the Cromwellian Settlement of Ireland* (Oxford, 1971).

—— 'Kingdom and Colony: Ireland in the Westward Enterprise 1536–1660', in K. R. Andrews *et al.* (eds.), *The Westward Enterprise: English Activities in Ireland, the Atlantic and America 1480–1650* (Liverpool, 1978), 45–64.

—— 'The Restoration Land Settlement in Ireland: A Structural View', *IHS* 18 (1972), 1–21.

BOULTER, HUGH, *Letters Written by his Excellency Hugh Boulter D. D. Lord Primate of all Ireland, to Several Ministers of State in England and Some Others* (2 vols., Oxford, 1769–70).

BOWEN, DESMOND, *The Protestant Crusade in Ireland 1800–1870: A Study of Catholic–Protestant Relations between the Act of Union and Disestablishment* (Dublin, 1978).

BOYLAN, LENA, 'The Conollys of Castletown, a Family History', *Irish Georgian Society Bulletin*, 11/4 (1968), 1–46.

BRADY, CIARAN, and GILLESPIE, RAYMOND (eds.), *Natives and Newcomers: Essays on the Making of Irish Colonial Society* (Dublin, 1986).

BRADY, JOHN, 'The Arrest of Oliver Plunkett', *Irish Ecclesiastical Record*, 81 (1954), 81–92.

—— *Catholics and Catholicism in the Eighteenth-Century Press* (Maynooth, 1965).

—— 'Oliver Plunkett and the Popish Plot', *Irish Ecclesiastical Record*, 89 (1958), 1–13, 340–54; 90 (1958), 12–27.

—— 'Remedies Proposed for the Church of Ireland (1697)', *Arch. Hib.* 22 (1959), 163–73.

—— and CORISH, P. J., *The Church under the Penal Code*, iv. 2, in P. J. Corish (ed.), *A History of Irish Catholicism* (Dublin, 1971).

BRADY, W. M., *The Episcopal Succession in England, Scotland and Ireland* (Rome, 1876).

BRENNER, ROBERT, 'Agrarian Class Structure and Economic Development in Pre-Industrial Europe', *Past & Present*, 70 (1976), 30–75.

[BREWSTER, Sir FRANCIS], *A Discourse Concerning Ireland, and the Different Interests Thereof, in Answer to the Exon and Barnstaple Petitions* (London, 1698).

BRIDGES, JOHN; WARREN, EDWARD; and WARREN, ABEL, *A Perfect Narrative of the Grounds and Reasons Moving Some Officers of the Army to the Securing of the Castle of Dublin* (London, 1660).

BROCKLISS, L. W. B., and FERTÉ, P., 'Irish Clerics in France in the Seventeenth and Eighteenth Centuries: A Statistical Study', *Royal Irish Academy Proc. C*, 87/9 (1987), 527–72.

BROOKE, PETER, *Ulster Presbyterianism: The Historical Perspective* (Dublin, 1987).

BURKE, NUALA, 'A Hidden Church? The Structure of Catholic Dublin in the Mid-Eighteenth Century', *Arch. Hib.* 32 (1974), 81–92.

BURKE, PETER, *The Historical Anthropology of Early Modern Italy: Essays on Perception and Communication* (Cambridge, 1987).

—— *Popular Culture in Early Modern Europe* (London, 1979).

BURKE, W. P., *The Irish Priests in the Penal Times 1660–1760* (Waterford, 1914).

BURNS, R. E., 'The Irish Penal Code and Some of its Historians', *Review of Politics*, 21 (1959), 276–99.

—— 'The Irish Popery Laws: A Study in Eighteenth-Century Legislation and Behaviour', *Review of Politics*, 24 (1962), 485–508.

—— 'Thoughts on Converting the Irish 1715', *Irish Ecclesiastical Record*, 98 (1962), 142–4.

BUSHAWAY, BOB, *By Rite: Custom, Ceremony and Community in England 1700–1880* (London, 1982).

CALDICOTT, C. E. J.; GOUGH, H.; and PITTION, J.-P. (eds.), *The Huguenots and Ireland: Anatomy of an Emigration* (Dublin, 1987).

'Calendar of Church Miscellaneous Papers', Public Record Office of Ireland, *Report of the Deputy Keeper*, 58 (1951), 71–92.

Calendar of State Papers Preserved in the Public Record Office, Domestic Series (81 vols., London, 1856–1972).

Calendar of the State Papers Relating to Ireland, 1509–1670 (24 vols., London, 1860–1912).

CALLAHAN, W. J., and HIGGS, DAVID (eds.), *Church and Society in Catholic Europe in the Eighteenth Century* (Cambridge, 1979).

CAMPBELL, THOMAS, *A Philosophical Survey of the South of Ireland* (Dublin, 1778).

CANNY, NICHOLAS, 'The Formation of the Irish Mind: Religion, Politics and Gaelic Irish Literature', *Past & Present*, 95 (1982), 91–116.

—— 'Identity Formation in Ireland: The Emergence of the Anglo-Irish', in N. Canny and A. Pagden (eds.), *Colonial Identity in the Atlantic World* (Princeton, 1987), 159–212.

—— *The Upstart Earl: A Study of the Social and Mental World of Richard Boyle, First Earl of Cork 1566–1643* (Cambridge, 1982).

CARPENTER, ANDREW. 'William King and the Threats to the Church of Ireland during the Reign of James II', *IHS* 18 (1972), 22–8.

CARRIGAN, WILLIAM, *The History and Antiquities of the Diocese of Ossory* (4 vols., Dublin, 1905).

CARTE, THOMAS, *History of the Life of James, First Duke of Ormonde*, 2nd edn. (6 vols., Oxford, 1851).

'Catalogue of the Proclamations Issued by the Lord Lieutenant and Council, 1618–1875', Public Record Office of Ireland, *Report of the Deputy Keeper*, 23 (1891), 25–74.

CAULFIELD, RICHARD (ed.), *The Council Book of the Corporation of the City of Cork* (Guildford, 1876).

Chesterfield, Earl of, *The Letters of Philip Dormer Stanhope, 4th Earl of Chesterfield*, ed. Bonamy Dobree (6 vols., London, 1932).

[CHETWOOD, W. R.], *A Tour through Ireland in Several Entertaining Letters... by two English Gentlemen* (Dublin, 1746).

CLARK, J. C. D., *English Society 1688–1832: Ideology, Social Structure and Political Practice during the Ancien Régime* (Cambridge, 1985).

CLARK, SAMUEL, and DONNELLY, J. S., jun. (eds.), *Irish Peasants: Violence and Political Unrest 1780–1914* (Madison and Manchester, 1983).

CLARK, WILLIAM SMITH, *The Early Irish Stage: The Beginnings to 1720* (Oxford, 1955).

CLARKE, AIDAN, 'The Genesis of the Ulster Rising of 1641', in Peter Roebuck (ed.), *Plantation to Partition* (Belfast, 1981), 29–45.

—— 'Ireland and the General Crisis', *Past & Present*, 48 (1970), 79–99.

CLARKSON, L. A., and CRAWFORD, E. M., *Ways to Wealth: The Cust Family of Eighteenth-Century Armagh* (Belfast, 1985).

COGAN, A., *The Ecclesiastical History of the Diocese of Meath, Ancient and Modern* (3 vols., Dublin, 1862–70).

COLE, R. C., *Irish Booksellers and English Writers 1740–1800* (London, 1986).

COLLEY, LINDA, *In Defiance of Oligarchy: The Tory Party 1714–60* (Cambridge, 1982).

CONNELL, K. H., *Irish Peasant Society: Four Historical Essays* (Oxford, 1968).

—— *The Population of Ireland 1750–1845* (Oxford, 1950).

CONNOLLY, S. J., 'The Houghers: Agrarian Protest in Early Eighteenth-Century Connacht', in C. H. E. Philpin (ed.), *Nationalism and Popular Protest in Ireland* (Cambridge, 1987), 139–62.

—— 'Law, Order and Popular Protest in Early Eighteenth-Century Ireland: The Case of the Houghers', in P. J. Corish (ed.), *Radicals, Rebels and Establishments* (Belfast, 1985), 51–68.

—— *Priests and People in Pre-Famine Ireland 1780–1845* (Dublin, 1982).

—— *Religion and Society in Nineteenth-Century Ireland* (Dundalk, 1985).

CORFIELD, P. J., 'Class by Name and Number in Eighteenth-Century Britain', *History*, 72/234 (1987), 38–61.

CORISH, P. J., *The Catholic Community in the Seventeenth and Eighteenth Centuries* (Dublin, 1981).

COSBY, POLE, 'Autobiography of Pole Cosby of Stradbally, Queen's County, 1703–37', *Kildare Archaeological & Historical Society Journal*, 5 (1906–8), 79–99, 165–84, 253–73, 311–24, 423–36.

COX, RICHARD, *Autobiography of the Rt. Hon. Sir Richard Cox, Bart.*, ed. Richard Caulfield (London, 1860).

CRAIG, MAURICE, *Dublin 1660–1860: A Social and Architectural History* (Dublin, 1969).

CRAWFORD, W. H., 'Economy and Society in South Ulster in the Eighteenth Century', *Clogher Record*, 8/3 (1975), 241–58.

—— 'The Influence of the Landlord in Eighteenth-Century Ulster', in Cullen and Smout (eds.), *Comparative Aspects*, 193–203.

—— 'Ulster Landowners and the Linen Industry', in J. T. Ward and R. Wilson (eds.), *Land and Industry* (Newton Abbot, 1971), 117–44.

—— and TRAINOR, BRIAN (eds.), *Aspects of Irish Social History 1750–1800* (Belfast, 1969).

CROTTY, R. D., *Irish Agricultural Production, its Volume and Structure* (Cork, 1966).

CRUICKSHANKS, EVELYN, *Political Untouchables: The Tories and the '45* (London, 1979).

CULLEN, L. M., *Anglo-Irish Trade 1660–1800* (Manchester, 1968).

—— 'Catholics under the Penal Laws', *Eighteenth-Century Ireland*, 1 (1986), 23–36.

—— *An Economic History of Ireland since 1660* (London, 1972).

—— 'Eighteenth-Century Flour Milling in Ireland', *Irish Economic & Social History*, 4 (1977), 5–25.

—— *The Emergence of Modern Ireland 1600–1900* (London, 1981).

—— *Princes and Pirates: The Dublin Chamber of Commerce 1783–1983* (Dublin, 1983).

—— 'Scotland and Ireland 1600–1800: Their Role in the Evolution of British Society', in R. A. Houston and I. D. Whyte (eds.), *Scottish Society 1500–1800* (Cambridge, 1989), 226–45.

—— 'The Social and Cultural Modernisation of Rural Ireland 1600–1900', in Cullen and Furet (eds.), *Ireland and France*, 195–212.

—— 'The 1798 Rebellion in its Eighteenth-Century Context', in P. J. Corish (ed.),

Radicals, Rebels and Establishments (Belfast, 1985), 91–113.

—— and FURET, F. (eds.), *Ireland and France 17th–20th Centuries: Towards a Comparative Study of Rural History* (Paris, 1980).

—— and SMOUT, T. C. (eds.), *Comparative Aspects of Scottish and Irish Economic and Social History 1600–1900* (Edinburgh, 1978).

CUNNINGHAM, BERNADETTE, 'Native Culture and Political Change in Ireland 1580–1640', in Brady and Gillespie (eds.), *Natives and Newcomers*, 148–70.

—— 'Seventeenth-Century Interpretations of the Past: The Case of Geoffrey Keating', *IHS* 25 (1986), 116–28.

—— and GILLESPIE, RAYMOND, 'An Ulster Settler and his Manuscripts', *Eigse*, 21 (1986), 27–36.

CURTIS, EDMUND, and McDOWELL, R. B., *Irish Historical Documents 1172–1922* (London, 1943).

DALLAT, CAHAL, 'Ballycastle's Eighteenth-Century Industries', *Glynns*, 3 (1975), 7–13.

DALY, M. E., and DICKSON, DAVID (eds.), *The Origins of Popular Literacy in Ireland* (Dublin, 1990).

DANAHER, KEVIN, and SIMMS, J. G. (eds.), *The Danish Force in Ireland 1690–1691* (Dublin, 1962).

DAVIES, GODFREY, *The Restoration of Charles II 1658–1660* (Oxford, 1955).

DEANE, SEAMUS, 'Swift and the Anglo-Irish Intellect', *Eighteenth-Century Ireland*, 1 (1986), 9–22.

DELANY, MARY, *The Autobiography and Correspondence of Mary Granville, Mrs Delany*, ed. Lady Llanover, ser. 1 (3 vols., London, 1861).

DEVINE, T. M., 'The English Connection and Scottish and Irish Development in the Eighteenth Century', in Devine and Dickson (eds.), *Ireland and Scotland*, 12–29.

—— and DICKSON, DAVID (eds.), *Ireland and Scotland 1600–1850* (Edinburgh, 1983).

DICKSON, DAVID, 'Middlemen', in Bartlett and Hayton (eds.), *Penal Era and Golden Age*, 162–85.

—— *New Foundations: Ireland 1660–1800* (Dublin, 1987).

—— 'The Place of Dublin in the Eighteenth-Century Irish Economy', in Devine and Dickson (eds.), *Ireland and Scotland*, 177–92.

—— 'Property and Social Structure in Eighteenth-Century South Munster', in Cullen and Furet (eds.), *Ireland and France*, 129–38.

—— (ed.), *The Gorgeous Mask: Dublin 1700–1850* (Dublin, 1987).

—— O GRADA, CORMAC; and DAULTREY, STUART, 'Hearth Tax, Household Size and Irish Population Change 1672–1821', *Royal Irish Academy Proc. C*, 82/6 (1982), 125–81.

A Discourse on the Woollen Manufactury of Ireland, and the Consequences of Prohibiting its Exportation (n.p., 1698).

DOBBS, ARTHUR, *An Essay on the Trade and Improvement of Ireland* (Dublin, 1729).

DONNELLY, J. S., jun., 'Hearts of Oak, Hearts of Steel', *Studia Hibernica*, 21 (1981), 7–73.

—— 'Irish Agrarian Rebellion: The Whiteboys of 1769–76', *Royal Irish Academy Proc. C*, 83/12 (1983), 293–331.

—— 'Pastorini and Captain Rock: Millenarianism and Sectarianism in the Rockite Movement of 1821–4', in Clark and Donnelly (eds.), *Irish Peasants*, 102–39.

DONNELLY, J. S., jun., 'The Rightboy Movement 1785–8', *Studia Hibernica*, 17–18 (1977–8), 120–202.

—— 'The Whiteboy Movement 1761–5', *IHS* 21 (1978), 20–54.

DOWNIE, J. A., *Jonathan Swift: Political Writer* (London, 1984).

DOYLE, WILLIAM, *The Ancien Régime* (London, 1986).

DRAKE, MICHAEL, 'The Irish Demographic Crisis of 1741', in T. W. Moody (ed.), *Historical Studies*, vi (London, 1968), 101–24.

DRALLE, L. A., 'Kingdom in Reversion: The Irish Viceroyalty of the Earl of Wharton 1708–10', *Huntington Library Quarterly*, 15 (1951–2), 393–431.

DUFFY, R. Q., 'Redmond O'Hanlon and the Outlaws of Ulster', *History Today*, 32 (Aug. 1982), 9–13.

DUNTON, JOHN, *The Life and Errors of John Dunton* (2 vols., London, 1818).

—— *Teague Land, or a Merry Ramble to the Wild Irish*, ed. Edward MacLysaght (Dublin, 1982).

DUTTON, MATTHEW, *The Office and Authority of a Justice of Peace for Ireland* (Dublin, 1718).

EDGEWORTH, MARIA, *Castle Rackrent and the Absentee*, Everyman edn. (London, 1972).

EDIE, C. A., 'The Irish Cattle Bills: A Study in Restoration Politics', *American Philosophical Soc. Trans.* 60/2 (1970), 1–66.

EHRENPREIS, IRVIN, *Swift: The Man, His Work and the Age* (3 vols., London, 1962–83).

EKIRCH, A. R., *Bound for America: The Transportation of British Convicts to the Colonies 1718–75* (Oxford, 1987).

ELLIOTT, MARIANNE, *Partners in Revolution: The United Irishmen and France* (New Haven and London, 1982).

FAGAN, PATRICK, 'The Dublin Catholic Mob (1700–1750)', *Eighteenth-Century Ireland*, 4 (1989), 133–42.

—— *The Second City: Portrait of Dublin 1700–1760* (Dublin, 1986).

FAIRLEY, J. S., *An Irish Beast Book: A Natural History of Ireland's Furred Wildlife* (Belfast, 1975).

FAULKNER, GEORGE, *Prince of Dublin Printers: The Letters of George Faulkner*, ed. R. E. Ward (Lexington, 1972).

FENNING, HUGH, 'Clerical Recruitment 1735–83', *Arch. Hib.* 30 (1972), 1–13.

—— 'John Kent's Report on the Irish Mission, 1742', *Arch. Hib.* 28 (1966), 59–102.

—— 'Some Problems of the Irish Mission 1733–1744: Documents from Roman Archives', *Coll. Hib.* 8 (1965), 58–109.

—— *The Undoing of the Friars of Ireland: A Study of the Novitiate Question in the Eighteenth Century* (Louvain, 1972).

FERGUSON, K. P., 'The Army in Ireland, from the Restoration to the Act of Union' (unpublished Ph.D. thesis, TCD, 1980).

FINLEY, M. I., 'Colonies—An Attempt at a Typology', *Royal Historical Society Transactions*, 26 (1976), 167–88.

FITZGERALD, BRIAN, *Emily, Duchess of Leinster: A Study of her Life and Times* (London, 1949).

FITZPATRICK, BRENDAN, *Seventeenth-Century Ireland: The War of Religions* (Dublin, 1988).

FLOOD, W. H. GRATTAN, 'The Diocesan Manuscripts of Ferns during the Rule of

Bishop Sweetman', *Arch. Hib.* 2 (1913), 100–5; 3 (1914), 113–23.

FOSTER, R. F., *Modern Ireland 1600–1972* (London, 1988).

FRENEY, JAMES, *The Life and Adventures of James Freney* (1754), ed. Frank McEvoy (Kilkenny, 1988).

GALE, PETER, *An Enquiry into the Ancient Corporate System of Ireland* (London, 1834).

GIBLIN, CATHALDUS, 'Catalogue of Material of Irish Interest in the Collection *Nunziatura di Fiandra*, Vatican Archives', *Coll. Hib.* 3 (1960), 4 (1961), 5 (1962), 9 (1966), 10 (1967), 11 (1968), 12 (1969), 13 (1970), 14 (1971), 15 (1972).

—— *Irish Exiles in Catholic Europe*, iv. 3, in P. J. Corish (ed.), *A History of Irish Catholicism* (Dublin, 1971).

GILLESPIE, RAYMOND, 'The End of an Era: Ulster and the Outbreak of the 1641 Rising', in Brady and Gillespie (eds.), *Natives and Newcomers*, 191–213.

—— 'Migration and Opportunity: A Comment', *Irish Economic & Social History*, 13 (1986), 90–5.

GOODWIN, ALBERT, 'Wood's Halfpence', *English Historical Review*, 51 (1936), 647–74.

GORN, E. J., 'Gouge and Bite, Pull Hair and Scratch: The Social Significance of Fighting in the Southern Backcountry', *American Historical Review*, 90/1 (1985), 18–43.

GREAVES, R. L., *Deliver us from Evil: The Radical Underground in Britain 1660–1663* (New York, 1986).

GREENE, J. P., *Peripheries and Centre: Constitutional Development in the Extended Polities of the British Empire and the United States 1607–1788* (Athens, Ga., 1986).

—— *Pursuits of Happiness: The Social Development of Early Modern British Colonies and the Formation of American Culture* (Chapel Hill, N.C., 1988).

GREGG, EDWARD, *Queen Anne* (London, 1984).

GRIBBON, H. D., 'Irish Baptists in the Nineteenth Century: Economic and Social Background', *Irish Baptist Historical Society Journal*, 16 (1983–4), 4–18.

GRIFFIN, JOSEPH, 'Parliamentary Politics in Ireland during the Reign of George I' (unpublished MA thesis, University College, Dublin, 1977).

HALEY, K. H. D., *Politics in the Reign of Charles II* (Oxford, 1985).

[HARRIS, WALTER, and SMITH, CHARLES], *The Antient and Present State of the County of Down* (Dublin, 1744).

HARRISON, J. F. C., *The Second Coming: Popular Millenarianism 1780–1850* (London, 1979).

HAY, DOUGLAS, 'Property, Authority and the Criminal Law', in Hay *et al.*, *Albion's Fatal Tree*, 17–63.

—— LINEBAUGH, PETER; RULE, J. G.; THOMPSON, E. P.; WINSLOW, CAL, *Albion's Fatal Tree: Crime and Society in Eighteenth-Century England* (Harmondsworth, 1977).

HAYTON, D. W., 'Anglo-Irish Attitudes: Changing Perceptions of National Identity among the Protestant Ascendancy in Ireland *ca.*1690–1750', *Studies in Eighteenth-Century Culture*, 17 (1987), 145–57.

—— 'The Beginnings of the "Undertaker System"', in Bartlett and Hayton (eds.), *Penal Era and Golden Age*, 32–54.

—— 'The Crisis in Ireland and the Disintegration of Queen Anne's Last Ministry', *IHS* 22 (1981), 193–215.

HAYTON, D. W., 'Debates in the House of Commons 1697–1699', *Camden Miscellany*, 29 (1987), 343–407.

—— 'Divisions in the Whig Junto in 1709: Some Irish Evidence', *Institute of Historical Research Bulletin*, 55/132 (1982), 206–14.

—— 'From Barbarian to Burlesque: English Images of the Irish *c.*1660–1750', *Irish Economic & Social History*, 15 (1988), 5–31.

—— *Ireland after the Glorious Revolution 1692–1715* (Belfast, 1976).

—— 'Ireland and the English Ministers 1707–16: A Study in the Formulation and Working of Government Policy in the Early Eighteenth Century' (unpublished D.Phil. thesis, Oxford, 1975).

—— 'An Irish Parliamentary Diary from the Reign of Queen Anne', *Analecta Hibernica*, 30 (1982), 97–149.

—— 'Walpole and Ireland', in Black (ed.), *Britain in the Age of Walpole*, 95–119.

HEMPTON, D. N., 'The Methodist Crusade in Ireland 1795–1845', *IHS* 22 (1980), 33–48.

HICK, VIVIEN, 'The Palatine Settlement in Ireland: The Early Years', *Eighteenth-Century Ireland*, 4 (1989), 113–31.

HICKSON, M. A., *Selections from Old Kerry Records, Historical and Genealogical*, ser. 2 (London, 1874).

HILL, GEORGE, *An Historical Account of the MacDonnells of Antrim* (Belfast, 1873).

HILL, J. R., 'Popery and Protestantism, Civil and Religious Liberty: The Disputed Lessons of Irish History 1690–1812', *Past & Present*, 118 (1988), 96–129.

Historical Manuscripts Commission, *Manuscripts of the Duke of Buccleuch and Queensberry*, 2 (1903).

—— *The Manuscripts and Correspondence of James, First Earl of Charlemont*, 1 (1891).

—— *Downshire Manuscripts*, 1: *Papers of Sir William Trumbull* (1924).

—— *Papers of the Earl of Egmont*, 2 (1909).

—— *Manuscripts of Miss M. Eyre Matcham* (1909).

—— *The Manuscripts of J. B. Fortescue, esq. Preserved at Dropmore*, 1 (1892).

—— *Manuscripts of Lord Kenyon* (1894).

—— *Leyborne–Popham Manuscripts* (1899).

—— *Manuscripts of the Marquis of Ormonde* (3 vols., 1895–1909; NS, 8 vols., 1902–20).

—— *Manuscripts of Lord Polwarth* (5 vols., 1911–61).

—— *Manuscripts of the Duke of Portland* (5 vols., 1891–9).

—— *Manuscripts of Rev. Sir T. H. G. Puleston, Bart.* (1898).

—— *Manuscripts of the Duke of Rutland*, 3 (1894).

—— *Stuart Manuscripts*, 3 (1907).

—— *Various Collections*, 8 (1913).

HOBSBAWM, E. J., *Bandits* (Harmondsworth, 1972).

—— 'The City Mob', in idem, *Primitive Rebels* (London, 1959), 108–25.

HOHENBERG, P. M., and LEES, L. H., *The Making of Urban Europe 1000–1950* (London, 1985).

HOLMES, GEOFFREY (ed.), *Britain after the Glorious Revolution* (London, 1969).

—— *British Politics in the Age of Anne* (1967), rev. edn. (London, 1987).

—— *The Trial of Doctor Sacheverell* (London, 1973).

HOPPEN, K. T., *Elections, Politics and Society in Ireland 1832–1885* (Oxford, 1984).

The Horrid Conspiracy of Such Impenitent Traitors as Intended a New Rebellion in the Kingdom of Ireland (London, 1663).

HOWARD, G. E., *Several Special Cases on the Laws aganist the Further Growth of Popery in Ireland* (Dublin, 1775).

HUTCHINSON, W. R., *Tyrone Precinct: A History of the Plantation Settlement of Dungannon and Mountjoy to Modern Times* (Belfast, 1951).

HUTTON, RONALD, *Charles II: King of England, Ireland and Scotland* (Oxford, 1989).

—— 'The Making of the Secret Treaty of Dover 1668–70', *Historical Journal*, 29/2 (1986), 297–318.

—— *The Restoration: A Political History of England and Wales 1660–1667* (Oxford, 1985).

Inchiquin, earls of, *The Inchiquin Manuscripts*, ed. John Ainsworth (Dublin, 1961).

INNES, JOANNA, 'Jonathan Clark, Social History and England's "Ancien Régime"', *Past & Present*, 115 (1987), 165–200.

IRWIN, LIAM, 'The Earl of Orrery and the Military Problems of Restoration Munster', *Irish Sword*, 13/50 (1977), 10–19.

—— 'Politics, Religion and Economy: Cork in the Seventeenth Century', *Cork Historical & Archaeological Society Journal*, 85/241–2 (1980), 7–25.

—— 'The Suppression of the Irish Presidency System', *IHS* 22 (1980), 21–32.

ISAAC, RHYS, *The Transformation of Virginia* (Chapel Hill, N.C., 1982).

JAMES, F. G., 'The Active Irish Peers in the Early Eighteenth Century', *Journal of British Studies*, 18/2 (1979), 52–69.

—— 'The Church of Ireland in the Early Eighteenth Century', *Historical Magazine of the Protestant Episcopal Church*, 48/4 (1979), 433–51.

—— 'Derry in the Time of George I: Selections from Bishop Nicolson's Letters', *Ulster Journal of Archaeology*, 17 (1954), 173–86.

—— *Ireland in the Empire 1688–1770* (Cambridge, Mass., 1973).

—— *North Country Bishop: A Biography of William Nicolson* (New Haven, 1956).

JENNEY, HENRY, *A Sermon Preached at St Andrew's, Dublin . . . on Friday, the 5th of November 1731* (Dublin, 1731).

JOHNSON, CHRISTINE, *Developments in the Roman Catholic Church in Scotland 1789–1829* (Edinburgh, 1983).

JOHNSTON, E. M., *Ireland in the Eighteenth Century* (Dublin, 1974).

—— 'Problems Common to both Protestant and Catholic Churches in Eighteenth-Century Ireland', in Oliver MacDonagh *et al.* (eds.), *Irish Culture and Nationalism 1750–1950* (London, 1983), 14–39.

JOHNSTON, JOSEPH, *Bishop Berkeley's Querist in Historical Perspective* (Dundalk, 1970).

JONES, G. H., 'The Irish Fright of 1688: Real Violence and Imagined Massacre', *Institute of Historical Research Bulletin*, 55/132 (1982), 148–53.

JONES, J. R., *The First Whigs: The Politics of the Exclusion Crisis 1678–83* (London, 1961).

Journals of the House of Commons of the Kingdom of Ireland, 2nd edn. (23 vols., Dublin, 1763–86).

KELLY, JAMES, 'The Genesis of "Protestant Ascendancy": The Rightboy Disturbances of the 1780s and their Impact upon Protestant Opinion', in O'Brien (ed.), *Parliament, Politics and People*, 93–127.

—— 'Interdenominational Relations and Religious Toleration in Late Eighteenth-Century Ireland: The "Paper War" of 1786–88', *Eighteenth-Century Ireland*, 3 (1988), 39–67.

KELLY, JAMES, 'The Origins of the Act of Union: An Examination of Unionist Opinion in Britain and Ireland 1650–1800', *IHS* 25 (1987), 236–63.

KELLY, PATRICK, 'Berkeley and Ireland', *Etudes Irlandaises*, 2 (1986), 7–25.

—— 'Ireland and the Critique of Mercantilism in Berkeley's *Querist*', *Hermathena*, 139 (1985), 101–16.

—— 'The Irish Woollen Export Prohibition Act of 1699: Kearney Revisited', *Irish Economic & Social History*, 7 (1980), 22–44.

—— '"A Light to the Blind": The Voice of the Dispossessed Elite in the Generation after the Defeat at Limerick', *IHS* 24 (1985), 431–62.

—— 'Lord Galway and the Penal Laws', in Caldicott *et al.* (eds.), *The Huguenots and Ireland*, 239–54.

Kenmare, earls of, *The Kenmare Manuscripts*, ed. Edward MacLysaght (Dublin, 1942).

KENNEDY, R. T. C., 'The Administration of the Diocese of Dublin and Glendalough in the Eighteenth Century' (unpublished M.Litt. thesis, TCD, 1968).

KENNY, COLUM, 'The Exclusion of Catholics from the Legal Profession in Ireland 1537–1829', *IHS* 25 (1987), 337–58.

KENYON, JOHN, *The Popish Plot* (Harmondsworth, 1974).

KIERNAN, T. J., *History of the Financial Administration of Ireland to 1817* (London, 1930).

KIERNAN, V. G., *The Duel in European History: Honour and the Reign of Aristocracy* (Oxford, 1988).

KING, C. S., *A Great Archbishop of Dublin, William King D.D. 1650–1729* (London, 1906).

KING, PETER, 'Decision Makers and Decision Making in the English Criminal Law 1750–1800', *Historical Journal*, 27/1 (1984), 25–58.

KING, WILLIAM, *The State of the Protestants of Ireland under the Late King James's Government*, 4th edn. (London, 1692).

KIRKHAM, GRAEME, '"To Pay the Rent and Lay up Riches": Economic Opportunity in Eighteenth-Century North West Ulster', in Rosalind Mitchison and Peter Roebuck (eds.), *Economy and Society in Scotland and Ireland 1500–1939* (Edinburgh, 1988), 95–104.

KNIGHT, P., *Erris in the 'Irish Highlands' and the 'Atlantic Railway'* (Dublin, 1836).

LAMMEY, DAVID, 'The Free Trade Crisis: A Reappraisal', in O'Brien (ed.), *Parliament, Politics and People*, 69–92.

LANDA, L. A., *Swift and the Church of Ireland* (Oxford, 1954).

LANGBEIN, J. H., 'Albion's Fatal Flaws', *Past & Present*, 98 (1983), 96–120.

LARGE, DAVID, 'The Irish House of Commons in 1769', *IHS* 11 (1958), 18–45.

LARNER, CHRISTINA, *Enemies of God: The Witch-Hunt in Scotland* (Oxford, 1983).

LATOCNAYE, CHEVALIER DE, *A Frenchman's Walk through Ireland*, trans. John Stevenson (Belfast, 1917).

LEA, S. P., *The Present State of the Established Church or Ecclesiastical Registry of Ireland for the Year 1814* (Dublin, 1814).

LECKY, W. E. H., *A History of Ireland in the Eighteenth Century* (5 vols., London, 1892).

LEERSSEN, J. Th., 'Anglo-Irish Patriotism and its European Context: Notes towards a Reassessment', *Eighteenth-Century Ireland*, 3 (1988), 7–24.

—— *Mere Irish and Fíor-Ghael: Studies in the Idea of Irish Nationality, its Development and Literary Expression Prior to the Nineteenth Century* (Amsterdam and Philadelphia, 1986).

LEIN, C. D., 'Jonathan Swift and the Population of Ireland', *Eighteenth-Century Studies*, / 8/4 (1975), 431–53.

Leinster, Duchess of, *Correspondence of Emily, Duchess of Leinster 1731–1814*, ed. Brian Fitzgerald (3 vols., Dublin, 1949–57).

LENMAN, BRUCE, *The Jacobite Risings in Britain 1689–1746* (London, 1980).

—— and PARKER, GEOFFREY, 'The State, the Community and the Criminal Law in Early Modern Europe', in V. A. C. Gatrell, Bruce Lenman, and Geoffrey Parker (eds.), *Crime and the Law: The Social History of Crime in Western Europe since 1500* (London, 1980), 11–48.

A Letter Sent from Ireland, Dated at Dublin December 15 1659 Superscribed for the Right Honourable William Lenthall (London, 1659 [1660]).

LEWIN, LINDA, 'The Oligarchical Limitations of Social Banditry in Brazil: The Case of the "Good" Thief Antonio Silvino', *Past & Present*, 82 (1979), 116–46.

LEWIS, G. C., *On Local Disturbances in Ireland, and on the Irish Church Question* (London, 1836).

LIS, CATHARINA, and SOLY, HUGO, *Poverty and Capitalism in Pre-Industrial Europe* (London, 1982).

LODGE, Sir RICHARD, *Private Correspondence of Chesterfield and Newcastle 1744–6* (London, 1930).

LONERGAN, PATRICK, 'The Life and Death of Father Sheehy', *Irish Ecclesiastical Record*, ser. 3, 17 (1896), 600–32.

LOUPES, PHILIPPE, 'Bishop Dopping's Visitation of the Diocese of Meath 1693', *Studia Hibernica*, 24 (1984–8), 127–51.

LUDLOW, EDMUND, *The Memoirs of Edmund Ludlow*, ed. C. Firth (2 vols., Oxford, 1894).

LYNCH, KATHLEEN M., *Roger Boyle, First Earl of Orrery* (Knoxville, Tenn., 1965).

LYNE, G. J., 'Dr Dermot Lyne: An Irish Catholic Landholder in Cork and Kerry under the Penal Laws', *Kerry Archaeological & Historical Society Journal*, 8 (1975), 45–72.

MCANALLY, Sir HENRY, 'The Militia Array of 1756 in Ireland', *Irish Sword*, 1/2 (1950–1), 94–104.

MCCORMACK, W. J., *Ascendancy and Tradition in Anglo-Irish Literary History from 1789 to 1939* (Oxford, 1985).

—— 'Eighteenth-Century Ascendancy: Yeats and the Historians', *Eighteenth-Century Ireland*, 4 (1989), 159–81.

—— 'Vision and Revision in the Study of Eighteenth-Century Irish Parliamentary Rhetoric', *Eighteenth-Century Ireland*, 2 (1987), 7–35.

MCCRACKEN, EILEEN, *The Irish Woods since Tudor Times* (Newton Abbot, 1971).

MCCRACKEN, J. L., 'Central and Local Administration in Ireland under George II' (unpublished Ph.D. thesis, Queen's University, Belfast, 1948).

—— 'The Conflict between the Irish Administration and Parliament 1753–6', *IHS* 3 (1942), 159–79.

—— *The Irish Parliament in the Eighteenth Century* (Dundalk, 1971).

—— 'Irish Parliamentary Elections 1727–68', *IHS* 5 (1947), 209–30.

—— 'The Undertakers in Ireland and their Relations with the Lords Lieutenant 1724–71' (unpublished MA thesis, Queen's University, Belfast, 1941).

MACCURTAIN, MARGARET, *Tudor and Stuart Ireland* (Dublin, 1972).

MCDOWELL, R. B., *Ireland in the Age of Imperialism and Revolution* (Oxford, 1979).
—— and WEBB, D. A., *Trinity College, Dublin, 1592–1952: An Academic History* (Cambridge, 1982).
MCGRATH, KEVIN, 'John Garzia, a Noted Priest-Catcher and his Activities 1717–23', *Irish Ecclesiastical Record*, 72 (1949), 494–514.
MCGUIRE, J. I., 'The Church of Ireland and the "Glorious Revolution" of 1688', in Art Cosgrove and Donal McCartney (eds.), *Studies in Irish History* (Dublin, 1979), 137–49.
—— 'The Dublin Convention, the Protestant Community and the Emergence of an Ecclesiastical Settlement in 1660', in Art Cosgrove and J. I. McGuire (eds.), *Parliament and Community* (Belfast, 1983), 121–46.
—— 'The Irish Parliament of 1692', in Bartlett and Hayton (eds.), *Penal Era and Golden Age*, 1–31.
—— 'Why was Ormond Dismissed in 1669?', *IHS* 18 (1973), 295–312.
MCHUGH, ROGER (ed.), *Carlow in '98: The Autobiography of William Farrell of Carlow* (Dublin, 1949).
MCINNES, ANGUS, 'When was the English Revolution?', *History*, 67/221 (1982), 377–92.
MCLYNN, F. J., '"Good Behaviour": Irish Catholics and the Jacobite Rising of 1745', *Eire-Ireland*, 16/2 (1981), 43–58.
MACLYSAGHT, EDWARD, *Irish Life in the Seventeenth Century*, 3rd edn. (Shannon, 1969).
[MCSKIMMIN, SAMUEL (ed.)], *Narrative of Some Strange Events that Took Place in Island Magee and Neighbourhood in 1711* (Belfast, 1822).
MACAFEE, WILLIAM, 'The Population of Ulster 1630–1841: Evidence from Mid-Ulster' (unpublished D.Phil. thesis, University of Ulster, 1987).
—— and MORGAN, VALERIE, 'Population in Ulster 1660–1760', in Peter Roebuck (ed.), *Plantation to Partition* (Belfast, 1981), 46–63.
[MADDEN, SAMUEL], *Reflections and Resolutions Proper for the Gentlemen of Ireland* (Dublin, 1738).
MADDISON, R. E. W., 'Robert Boyle and the Irish Bible', *Bull. John Rylands Library*, 41/1 (1958), 81–101.
MALCOLM, ELIZABETH, *'Ireland Sober, Ireland Free': Drink and Temperance in Nineteenth-Century Ireland* (Dublin, 1986).
MALCOMSON, A. P. W., 'Absenteeism in Eighteenth-Century Ireland', *Irish Economic & Social History*, 1 (1974), 15–35.
—— *John Foster: The Politics of the Anglo-Irish Ascendancy* (Oxford, 1978).
—— '"The Parliamentary Traffic of this Country"', in Bartlett and Hayton (eds.), *Penal Era and Golden Age*, 137–61.
—— *The Pursuit of the Heiress: Aristocratic Marriage in Ireland 1750–1820* (Belfast, 1982).
MANT, RICHARD, *History of the Church of Ireland* (2 vols., London, 1840).
MELVIN, PATRICK, 'Letters of Lord Longford and Others on Irish Affairs', *Analecta Hibernica*, 32 (1985), 35–111.
—— 'Sir Paul Rycaut's Memoranda and Letters from Ireland 1686–1687', *Analecta Hibernica*, 27 (1972), 123–82.
'Memorandum on the Sarsfield-Vesey Papers', Public Record Office of Ireland, *Report of the Deputy Keeper*, 56 (1931), 344–82.

MILLER, D. W., 'The Armagh Troubles 1784–95', in Clark and Donnelly (eds.), *Irish Peasants*, 155–91.

—— 'Irish Catholicism and the Great Famine', *Journal of Social History*, 9/1 (1975), 81–98.

MILLER, JOHN, 'The Earl of Tyrconnell and James II's Irish Policy 1685–1688', *Historical Journal*, 20/4 (1977), 803–23.

—— *James II: A Study in Kingship* (Hove, 1978).

—— *Popery and Politics in England 1660–1688* (Cambridge, 1973).

MILLETT, BENIGNUS, *The Irish Franciscans 1651–1665* (Rome, 1964).

—— *Survival and Reorganisation 1650–95*, iii. 7, in P. J. Corish (ed.), *A History of Irish Catholicism* (Dublin, 1968).

MILNE, KENNETH, 'The Irish Charter Schools', *Irish Journal of Education*, 8/1 (1974), 3–29.

MOKYR, JOEL, *Why Ireland Starved: A Quantitative and Analytical History of the Irish Economy 1800–1850* (London, 1985).

[MOLESWORTH, Viscount ROBERT], *Some Considerations for the Promoting of Agriculture and Employing the Poor* (Dublin, 1723).

MOLYNEUX, THOMAS [recte Samuel], 'Journey to Connaught—April 1709', ed. A. Smith, *Miscellany of the Irish Archaeological Society*, 1 (1846), 161–78.

MOLYNEUX, WILLIAM, *The Case of Ireland Stated* (1698), ed. J. G. Simms (Dublin, 1977).

MONTER, WILLIAM, *Ritual, Myth and Magic in Early Modern Europe* (Brighton, 1983).

MONTGOMERY, WILLIAM, *The Montgomery Manuscripts 1603–1706*, ed. Revd George Hill (Belfast, 1869).

MOODY, T. W., 'Redmond O'Hanlon', *Belfast Natural Historical and Philosophical Society Proceedings*, ser. 2, 1 (1937), 17–33.

MORGAN, PRYS, 'From a Death to a View: The Hunt for the Welsh Past in the Romantic Period', in Eric Hobsbawm and Terence Ranger (eds.), *The Invention of Tradition* (Cambridge, 1983), 43–100.

MUCHEMBLED, ROBERT, *Popular Culture and Elite Culture in France 1400–1750* (Baton Rouge and London, 1985).

MUNTER, ROBERT, *The History of the Irish Newspaper 1685–1760* (Cambridge, 1967).

MURPHY, FRANK, *The Bog Irish* (Harmondsworth, 1987).

MURPHY, SEAN, 'The Dublin Anti-Union Riot of 3 December 1759', in O'Brien (ed.), *Parliament, Politics and People*, 49–68.

NARY, CORNELIUS, *The Case of the Roman Catholics of Ireland, Humbly Represented to Both Houses of Parliament, 1724, in Relation to a Bill now under Consideration*, printed in Hugh Reily, *The Impartial History of Ireland* (Limerick, n.d.), 122–43.

NEVILLE, J. D., 'Irish Presbyterians under the Restored Stuart Monarchy', *Eire-Ireland*, 16/2 (1981), 29–42.

New History of Ireland, vol. iii, T. W. Moody, F. X. Martin, and F. J. Byrne (eds.), *Early Modern Ireland 1534–1691* (Oxford, 1976); vol. iv, T. W. Moody and W. E. Vaughan (eds.), *Eighteenth-Century Ireland 1691–1800* (Oxford, 1986); vol. v, W. E. Vaughan (ed.), *Ireland under the Union 1800–1870* (Oxford, 1989).

NEWENHAM, THOMAS, *A View of the Natural, Political and Commercial Circumstances of Ireland* (London, 1809).

NICOLSON, WILLIAM, *Letters on Various Subjects, Literary, Political and Ecclesiastical, to and from William Nicolson, D.D.*, ed. John Nichols (2 vols., London, 1809).

NOKES, DAVID, *Jonathan Swift: A Hypocrite Reversed* (Oxford, 1987).

O'BRIEN, GEORGE, *The Economic History of Ireland in the Eighteenth Century* (1918) (Philadelphia, 1977).

O'BRIEN, GERARD (ed.), *Parliament, Politics and People: Essays in Eighteenth-Century Irish History* (Dublin, 1989).

Ó BRUADAIR, DAVID, *The Poems of David Ó Bruadair*, ed. J. C. McErlean (3 vols., London, 1910–16).

O'BYRNE, EILEEN (ed.), *The Convert Rolls* (Dublin, 1981).

Ó CAITHNIA, LIAM, *Scéal na hIomána: Ó Thosach Ama go 1884* (Dublin, 1980).

Ó CATHÁIN, DIARMAID, 'Dermot O'Connor, Translator of Keating', *Eighteenth-Century Ireland*, 2 (1987), 67–87.

O'CONNELL, PHILIP, 'The Plot against Father Nicholas Sheehy: The Historical Background', *Irish Ecclesiastical Record*, ser. 5, 108/6 (1967), 372–84.

O'DONOGHUE, F. M., 'Parliament in Ireland under Charles II' (unpublished MA thesis, University College, Dublin, 1970).

O'DONOVAN, DECLAN, 'The Money Bill Dispute of 1753', in Bartlett and Hayton (eds.), *Penal Era and Golden Age*, 55–87.

O'DONOVAN, JIM, 'The Militia in Munster 1715–78', in O'Brien (ed.), *Parliament, Politics and People*, 31–47.

O'DWYER, CHRISTOPHER, 'Archbishop Butler's Visitation Book', *Arch. Hib.* 33 (1975), 1–90; 34 (1976–7), 1–49.

Ó FIAICH, TOMÁS, 'Edmund O'Reilly, Archbishop of Armagh 1657–1669', in Franciscan Fathers (eds.), *Father Luke Wadding Commemorative Volume* (Dublin, 1957), 171–228.

—— 'The Registration of the Clergy in 1704', *Seanchas Ardmhacha*, 6 (1971), 46–69.

O'FLANAGAN, PATRICK; FERGUSON, PAUL; and WHELAN, KEVIN (eds.), *Rural Ireland 1600–1900: Modernisation and Change* (Cork, 1987).

O'LAVERTY, JAMES, *An Historical Account of the Diocese of Down and Connor, Ancient and Modern* (5 vols., Dublin, 1878–95).

Ó MAOLFABHAIL, ART, *Camán: Two Thousand Years of Hurling in Ireland* (Dundalk, 1973).

Orrery, Earl of, *The Orrery Papers*, ed. Countess of Cork and Orrery (2 vols., London, 1903).

O'SHEA, KEVIN, 'Bishop Moylan's Relatio Status, 1785', *Kerry Archaeological & Historical Society Journal*, 7 (1974), 21–6.

O'SULLIVAN, DONAL, *Carolan: The Life, Times and Music of an Irish Harper* (2 vols., London, 1958).

PALMER, S. H., *Police and Protest in England and Ireland 1780–1850* (Cambridge, 1988).

PETTY, WILLIAM, *The Political Anatomy of Ireland, with the Establishment for that Kingdom when the Late Duke of Ormond was Lord Lieutenant* (London, 1691).

PHILLIPS, W. A. (ed.), *History of the Church of Ireland from the Earliest Times to the Present Day* (3 vols., London, 1933).

PIERS, Sir HENRY, *A Chorographical Description of the County of Westmeath, Written A.D. 1682* (Naas, 1981).

PLUMB, J. H., *The Growth of Political Stability in England 1675–1725* (Harmondsworth, 1969).

PLUNKETT, OLIVER, *The Letters of Saint Oliver Plunkett 1625–1681*, ed. John Hanly (Dublin, 1979).

POCOCKE, RICHARD, *Pococke's Tour in Ireland in 1752*, ed. G. T. Stokes (Dublin, 1891).

POWER, PATRICK, *A Bishop of the Penal Times: Being Letters and Reports of John Brennan, Bishop of Waterford (1671–93) and Archbishop of Cashel (1677–93)* (Cork, 1932).

POWER, T. P., and WHELAN, KEVIN (eds.), *Endurance and Emergence; Catholics in Ireland in the Eighteenth Century* (Dublin, 1990).

PRIM, J. G. A., 'Documents Connected with the City of Kilkenny Militia in the Seventeenth and Eighteenth Centuries', *Journal of the Royal Society of Antiquaries of Ireland*, 3/2 (1855), 231–74.

Queries Humbly Proposed to the Consideration of the Public (Dublin, 1746).

QUINN, M. G., 'Religion and Landownership in County Louth 1641–*c*.1750' (unpublished MA thesis, New University of Ulster, 1984).

'Report on the State of Popery, Ireland 1731', *Arch. Hib.* 1 (1912)–4 (1915).

RICHARDSON, JOHN, *A Proposal for the Conversion of the Popish Natives of Ireland to the Established Religion* (Dublin, 1711).

——*A Short History of the Attempts that have been Made to Convert the Popish Natives of Ireland to the Established Religion*, 2nd edn. (London, 1713).

ROBINSON, NICHOLAS, 'Caricature and the Regency Crisis: An Irish Perspective', *Eighteenth-Century Ireland*, 1 (1986), 157–76.

ROBINSON, P. S., *The Plantation of Ulster: British Settlement in an Irish Landscape* (Dublin, 1984).

——'The Spread of Hedged Enclosure in Ulster', *Ulster Folklife*, 23 (1977), 57–69.

ROEBUCK, PETER, 'The Irish Registry of Deeds', *IHS* 18 (1972), 61–73.

——'Landlord Indebtedness in Ulster in the Seventeenth and Eighteenth Centuries', in J. M. Goldstrom and L. A. Clarkson (eds.), *Irish Population, Economy and Society* (Oxford, 1981), 135–54.

RUDE, GEORGE, *Paris and London in the Eighteenth Century* (London, 1974).

RULE, J. G., 'Wrecking and Coastal Plunder', in Hay *et al.* (eds.), *Albion's Fatal Tree*, 167–88.

RYAN, CONOR, 'Religion and State in Seventeenth-Century Ireland', *Arch. Hib.* 33 (1975), 122–32.

RYDER, MICHAEL, 'The Bank of Ireland 1721: Land, Credit and Dependency', *Historical Journal*, 25/3 (1982), 557–82.

SEARLE, C. E., 'Custom, Class Conflict and Agrarian Capitalism: The Cumbrian Customary Economy in the Eighteenth Century', *Past & Present*, 110 (1986), 106–33.

SEDGWICK, R. R. (ed.), *The History of Parliament: The House of Commons 1715–54* (2 vols., London, 1970).

SHARPE, J. A., *Crime in Early Modern England 1550–1750* (London, 1984).

SHAW, B. D., 'Bandits in the Roman Empire', *Past & Present*, 105 (1984), 3–52.

SHAW, J. S., *The Management of Scottish Society 1707–1764: Power, Nobles, Lawyers, Edinburgh Agents and English Influences* (Edinburgh, 1983).

SIDER, G. M., 'Christmas Mumming and the New Year in Outport Newfoundland', *Past & Present*, 71 (1976), 102–25.

SIMMS, J. G., 'The Bishops' Banishment Act of 1697', *IHS* 17 (1970–1), 185–99.

SIMMS, J. G., 'The Irish Parliament of 1713', in G. A. Hayes-McCoy (ed.), *Historical Studies*, iv (London, 1963), 82–92.

—— *Jacobite Ireland 1685–91* (London, 1969).

—— 'Lord Kilmallock's Letters to his Wife', *Journal of the Royal Society of Antiquaries of Ireland*, 87 (1957), 135–40.

—— 'The Making of a Penal Law (2 Anne, c. 6), 1703–4', *IHS* 12 (1960), 105–18.

—— *War and Politics in Ireland 1649–1730*, ed. D. W. Hayton and Gerard O'Brien (London, 1986).

—— *William Molyneux of Dublin: A Life of the Seventeenth-Century Political Writer and Scientist*, ed. P. H. Kelly (Dublin, 1982).

—— *The Williamite Confiscation in Ireland 1690–1703* (London, 1956).

SKELTON, PHILIP, *The Complete Works of the Late Rev. Philip Skelton*, ed. Robert Lynam (6 vols., London, 1824).

SMITH, CHARLES, *The Antient and Present State of the County and City of Cork* (1750), (Cork, 1815).

—— *The Antient and Present State of the County and City of Waterford* (Dublin, 1746).

SMOUT, T. C., *A History of the Scottish People 1560–1830* (London, 1972).

SMYTH, P. D. H., 'The Volunteer Movement in Ulster: Background and Development 1745–85' (unpublished Ph.D. thesis, Queen's University, Belfast, 1974).

SPECK, W. A., *The Butcher: The Duke of Cumberland and the Suppression of the 45* (Oxford, 1981).

—— *Stability and Strife: England 1714–1760* (London, 1977).

SPRING, DAVID (ed.), *European Landed Elites in the Nineteenth Century* (Baltimore and London, 1977).

STARR, J. P., 'The Enforcing of Law and Order in Eighteenth-Century Ireland: A Study of Irish Police and Prisons from 1665 to 1800' (unpublished Ph.D. thesis, TCD, 1968).

STEVENS, JOHN, *The Journal of John Stevens, Containing a Brief Account of the War in Ireland 1689–91*, ed. R. H. Murray (Oxford, 1912).

STEVENSON, JOHN, *Two Centuries of Life in Down 1600–1800* (Belfast, 1920).

STEWART, A. T. Q., '"The Harp New Strung": Nationalism, Culture and the United Irishmen', in Oliver MacDonagh and W. F. Mandle (eds.), *Ireland and Irish Australia* (London, 1986), 175–94.

—— *The Narrow Ground: Aspects of Ulster 1609–1969* (London, 1977).

STEWART, M. A., 'John Smith and the Molesworth Circle', *Eighteenth-Century Ireland*, 2 (1987), 89–102.

STOCK, JOSEPH, *A Narrative of what Passed at Killala*, ed. Grattan Freyer (Ballina, 1982).

STONE, LAWRENCE, 'Interpersonal Violence in English Society 1300–1980', *Past & Present*, 101 (1983), 22–33.

—— 'Social Mobility in England 1500–1700', *Past & Present*, 33 (1966), 16–55.

—— and STONE, J. C. FAWTIER, *An Open Elite? England 1540–1880* (Oxford, 1984).

SWIFT, JONATHAN, *Correspondence of Jonathan Swift*, ed. Harold Williams (5 vols., Oxford, 1963–5).

—— *Journal to Stella*, ed. Harold Williams (2 vols., Oxford, 1948).

—— *The Prose Works of Jonathan Swift*, ed. Herbert Davis (14 vols., Oxford, 1939–68).

SYNGE, EDWARD, *A Sermon against Persecution on Account of Religion* (Dublin, 1721).

SYNGE, EDWARD [jun.], *The Case of Toleration Considered in a Sermon Preached in St Andrew's, Dublin* (Dublin, 1725).

SZECHI, D., *Jacobitism and Tory Politics 1710–14* (Edinburgh, 1984).

TAYLOR, STEPHEN, 'Sir Robert Walpole, the Church of England and the Quakers' Tithe Bill of 1736', *Historical Journal*, 18/1 (1985), 51–77.

THOMAS, KEITH, *Religion and the Decline of Magic* (Harmondsworth, 1973).

THOMPSON, E. P., *Whigs and Hunters: The Origin of the Black Act* (Harmondsworth, 1977).

TILLY, CHARLES, 'Collective Violence in European Perspective', in H. D. Graham and T. R. Gurr (eds.), *Violence in America: Historical and Comparative Perspectives* (London, 1979), 83–118.

TROOST, WOUTER, 'Letters from Bartholomew van Homrigh to General Ginkel, Earl of Athlone, 1692–1700', *Analecta Hibernica*, 33 (1986), 59–128.

—— *William III and the Treaty of Limerick (1691–1697): A Study of his Irish Policy* (Leiden, 1983).

TWISS, RICHARD, *A Tour in Ireland in 1775*, 2nd edn. (Dublin, 1776).

VANCE, NORMAN, 'Celts, Carthaginians and Constitutions: Anglo-Irish Literary Relations 1780–1820', *IHS* 22 (1981), 216–38.

VAUGHAN, W. E., *Landlords and Tenants in Ireland 1848–1904* (Dundalk, 1984).

VICTORY, ISOLDE, 'Colonial Nationalism in Ireland 1692–1725: From Common Law to Natural Right' (unpublished Ph.D. thesis, TCD, 1984).

—— 'The Making of the 1720 Declaratory Act', in O'Brien (ed.), *Parliament, Politics and People*, 9–29.

WAKEFIELD, EDWARD, *An Account of Ireland, Statistical and Political* (2 vols., London, 1812).

WALKER, GEORGE, *The Siege of Londonderry in 1689, as Set Forth in the Literary Remains of Col. the Rev. George Walker D.D.*, ed. Philip Dwyer (London, 1893).

WALL, MAUREEN, *Catholic Ireland in the Eighteenth Century: Collected Essays of Maureen Wall*, ed. Gerard O'Brien (Dublin, 1989).

—— 'Catholic Loyalty to King and Pope in Eighteenth-Century Ireland', *Irish Catholic Historical Committee Proceedings* (1960), 17–24.

—— *The Penal Laws 1691–1760: Church and State from the Treaty of Limerick to the Accession of George III* (Dundalk, 1961).

WALPOLE, Sir ROBERT, *Memoirs of the Life and Administration of Sir Robert Walpole, Earl of Orford*, ed. Willian Coxe (3 vols., London, 1798).

WHELAN, KEVIN, 'The Catholic Church in County Tipperary 1700–1900', in William Nolan and T. G. McGrath (eds.), *Tipperary: History and Society* (Dublin, 1985), 217–55.

WHITEFIELD, GEORGE, *George Whitefield's Journals*, ed. Iain Murray (London, 1960).

WILLIAMS, N. J. A., 'Thomas Wilson, Francis Hutchinson agus Litriú na Gaeilge', *Eighteenth-Century Ireland*, 1 (1986), 204–7.

—— (ed.), *I bPrionta i Leabhar: Na Protastún agus Prós na Gaeilge 1567–1724* (Dublin, 1986).

—— (ed.), *Pairlement Chloinne Tomais* (Dublin, 1981).

WINNETT, A. R., 'An Irish Heretic Bishop: Robert Clayton of Clogher', in Derek Baker (ed.), *Schism, Heresy and Religious Protest* (Cambridge, 1972), 311–21.

—— *Peter Browne: Provost, Bishop, Metaphysician* (London, 1974).

WINSLOW, CAL, 'Sussex Smugglers', in Hay *et al.*, *Albion's Fatal Tree*, 119–66.

WITHERS, C. W. J., *Gaelic Scotland: The Transformation of a Cultural Region* (London, 1988).

WRIGHTSON, KEITH, *English Society 1580–1680* (London, 1982).

YOUNG, ARTHUR, *A Tour in Ireland 1776–1779*, ed. A. H. Hutton (2 vols., London, 1892).

Index

Dioceses and clergymen are of the Church of Ireland unless otherwise stated.

Abbreviations: abp. archbishop; bp. bishop; LD lord deputy; LL lord lieutenant; RC Catholic